West's

INDIANA

LAW ENCYCLOPEDIA

**Based on Indiana Statutes and Regulations,
and Case Law, State and Federal**

VOLUME 6

CONTEMPT—CORPORATIONS § 121

WEST GROUP

Bancroft-Whitney • Clark Boardman Callaghan
Lawyers Cooperative Publishing • WESTLAW® • West Publishing

For Customer Assistance Call 1-800-328-4880

Preface

WEST'S INDIANA LAW ENCYCLOPEDIA is designed to enable Indiana judges and lawyers to do their legal research with a minimum of time and effort. The law of Indiana has been developing for many years, and because of the growing bulk of the statutory and case law the Indiana lawyer's task of finding the law has become time-consuming and burdensome. The search is now shortened and the result made more certain.

Indiana Law Encyclopedia (cited **I.L.E.**) gives the Bench and Bar of Indiana quick access to the law in a narrative form more useful and satisfactory than anything heretofore presented.

Based on Indiana Statutes and Cases. I.L.E. sets forth the law of Indiana, as gathered from the reported cases and statutes of Indiana, as well as cases in the Supreme Court of the United States and other United States Courts arising in Indiana, insofar as the latter deal with Indiana law. It presents the rules of Indiana law and their exceptions, qualifications, limitations, and extensions in concise but completely comprehensive text, written so that Indiana lawyers and judges can with confidence buttress their arguments and opinions therewith.

Factual Applications of the Law. I.L.E. is not a mere statement of the fundamental rules. The work of judges and lawyers consists mainly of applying legal rules to the varying facts of litigated cases. The text of I.L.E. is supported by references to the decisions which make it the law, with illustrations of the application of legal rules to the fact of particular cases.

Often, the particular application or illustration set out will fit the facts in a case presented to a lawyer, and his or her argument of reason and logic under a general rule may be fortified by pointing out that in prior litigated cases, the rule has been applied in the manner contended for. This factual background of the law is presented in the text itself and in reading and parenthetical notes contained in the footnotes.

iii

Landmark Cases are discussed in the text. Important passages from the opinions of the Indiana courts may be briefly quoted, particularly where a doubtful question is clarified or a longstanding principle is overruled.

Local Terminology and Classification. Important fields of Indiana law are separately treated in titles devised and arranged according to local terminology and statutory classification.

A Concise Text Summary, set out in distinctive type, precedes the statement of the law in each section. These introductory summaries are of great convenience and value in legal research.

An Index is found in each volume for the titles contained therein, thus providing a convenient means of access to the law on a specific problem. A complete index for the entire set will be an additional convenience.

Section Analysis for Each Title. As an invaluable aid in finding the pertinent section of text desired, a complete section analysis is provided at the head of each title.

Cross References to related material are to be found throughout the work, assuring the user of the completeness of his or her search.

Supplemental Service. I.L.E. will be kept to date by means of annual cumulative pocket parts. This supplementation will conveniently, and with certainty, keep subscribers abreast of current cases and new developments in Indiana Law.

The Publisher.

PUBLISHER
Matthew J. Canavan, J.D.

PUBLICATION EDITOR
Thomas M. Fleming, J.D.

LEGAL EDITORS
William J. Finan, Jr., J.D.
Michael Rossman, J.D.
Alan Wasserstrom, J.D.

CONTRIBUTING AUTHORS
Lisa D. Horowitz, J.D.
Thomas Muskus, J.D.
Linda Odom, J.D.
David J. Rynkowski, J.D.
Elizabeth Williams, J.D.
Rosemary E. Williams, J.D.

LEGAL RESEARCH SPECIALIST
Scott M. Ratcliffe, J.D.

MANUSCRIPT EDITORS
Rhonda J. Caceci
Karen A. Grimm
Sarah N. Hooper
Michael J. Russo
Catherine J. Smith

Table of Abbreviations

A.L.R.	American Law Reports
A.L.R.2d	American Law Reports, Second Series
A.L.R.3d	American Law Reports, Third Series
A.L.R.4th	American Law Reports, Fourth Series
A.L.R.5th	American Law Reports, Fifth Series
A.L.R. Fed	American Law Reports, Federal
Am Jur 2d	American Jurisprudence, Second Edition
Am Jur Legal Forms 2d	American Jurisprudence Legal Forms 2d
Am Jur Pl & Pr Forms (Rev)	American Jurisprudence Pleading and Practice Forms, Revised Edition
Am Jur Proof of Facts	American Jurisprudence, Proof of Facts
Am Jur POF2d	American Jurisprudence, Proof of Facts, Second Series
Am Jur POF3d	American Jurisprudence, Proof of Facts, Third Series
Am Jur Trials	American Jurisprudence Trials
Black	Black's Reports, U.S.
Bland	Bland's Chancery Reports
B.R.	United States Bankruptcy Court
C.C.A.	United States Court of Appeals Reports
C.F.R	Code of Federal Regulations
C.J.S.	Corpus Juris Secundum
Cranch	Cranch's Reports, U.S.
Dall.	Dallas' Reports, U.S.
F.	Federal Reporter
F.2d	Federal Reporter, Second Series
F.3d	Federal Reporter, Third Series
Fed.Cas.No.	Federal Cases
Fed Proc Forms, L Ed	Federal Procedural Forms, Lawyers Edition
Fed Proc L Ed	Federal Procedure, Lawyers Edition
Fed R App P	Federal Rules of Appellate Procedure
Fed RCP	Federal Rules of Civil Procedure
Fed R Cr P	Federal Rules of Criminal Procedure
Fed R Evid	Federal Rules of Evidence
F.R.D.	Federal Rules Decisions
F.Supp.	Federal Supplement

F.Supp.2d	Federal Supplement, Second Series
Gill	Gill's Reports
Gill & J.	Gill and Johnson's Reports
Harr. & G.	Harris and Gill's Reports
Harr. & J.	Harris and Johnson's Reports
Harr. & McH.	Harris and McHenry's Reports
How.	Howard's Reports, U.S.
IC	West's Annotated Indiana Code
ILE	Indiana Law Encyclopedia
Ind.	Indiana Reports
Ind. Admin. Code	Indiana Administrative Code
Ind. App.	Indiana Appellate Court Reports
Ind. Const.	Indiana Constitution
Indiana Practice, Legal Business Forms	Indiana Practice, Legal Business Forms
Indiana Practice, Procedural Forms	Indiana Practice, Procedural Forms
Ind. Law J.	Indiana Law Journal
Ind. Leg. Forum	Indiana Legal Forum
N.E.	North Eastern Reporter
N.E.2d	North Eastern Reporter, Second Series
Notre Dame L.	Notre Dame Lawyer
Op. Att'y Gen.	Opinions of the Attorney General of Indiana
Pet.	Peter's Reports, U.S.
RAP	Rules of Appellate Procedure
Restatement	American Law Institute, Restatement of the Law
S. Ct.	United States Supreme Court Reporter
ULA	Uniform Laws Annotated
U.S.	United States Supreme Court Reports
U.S.C.A.	United States Code Annotated
US Const.	United States Constitution
Wall.	Wallace's Reports, U.S.
Wheat.	Wheaton's Reports, U.S.

CONTENTS OF THIS VOLUME

	Page
Table of Abbreviations	vii
Table of Parallel References	xv
Contempt	1
Continuance	53
Contracts	77
Contribution	329
Conversion	339
Coroners	385
Corporations	401

WESTLAW® ELECTRONIC RESEARCH GUIDE

WESTLAW, Computer-Assisted Legal Research

WESTLAW is part of the research system provided by West Group. With WESTLAW, you find the same quality and integrity that you have come to expect from West books. For the most current and comprehensive legal research, combine the strengths of West books and WESTLAW.

WESTLAW Adds to Your Library

Whether you wish to expand or update your research, WESTLAW can help. For instance, WESTLAW is the most current source for case law, including slip opinions and unreported decisions. In addition to case law, the online availability of statutes, statutory indexes, legislation, court rules and orders, administrative materials, looseleaf publications, texts, periodicals, news, and business information makes WESTLAW an important asset to any library. Check the online WESTLAW Directory or the print WESTLAW Database Directory for a list of available databases and services. Following is a brief description of some of the capabilities that WESTLAW offers.

Natural Language Searching

You can search most WESTLAW databases using WIN®, the revolutionary Natural Language search method. As an alternative to formulating a query using terms and connectors, WIN allows you to simply enter a description of your research issue in plain English:

What is the government's obligation to warn military personnel of the danger of past exposure to radiation?

WESTLAW then retrieves the set of documents that have the highest statistical likelihood of matching your description.

Retrieving a Specific Document

When you know the citation to a case or statute that is not in your library, use the Find service to retrieve the document on WESTLAW. Access Find and type a citation like the following:

700 NE2d 102

Databases

A database is a collection of documents with some features in common. It may contain statutes, court decisions, administrative materials, commentaries, news, or other information. Each database has a unique identifier, used in many WESTLAW commands to select a database of interest. For example, the database containing Indiana cases has the identifier IN-CS.

The WESTLAW Directory is a comprehensive list of databases with information about each database, including the types of documents each contains. The first page of a standard or customized WESTLAW Directory is displayed upon signing on to WESTLAW, except when prior, saved research is resumed. To access the WESTLAW Directory at any time, enter DB.

A special subdirectory, accessible from the main WESTLAW Directory, lists databases applicable to Taxation research.

Databases of potential interest in connection with your research include:

IN-CS	**Indiana Cases**
INPL-CS	**Indiana Products Liability Cases**
IN-RULES	**Indiana Court Rules**
IN-ST-ANN	**Indiana Statutes - Annotated**
IN-LEGIS	**Indiana Legislative Service**
IN-ADC	**Indiana Administrative Code**
IN-AG	**Indiana Attorney General Opinions**
IN-JLR	**Indiana Journals & Law Reviews**
WLD-IN	**West's Legal Directory - Indiana**

For information as to currentness and search tips regarding any WESTLAW database, enter the SCOPE command SC followed by the database identifier (e.g., SC IL-CS). It is not necessary to include the identifier to obtain scope information about the currently selected database.

Updating Your Research

You can use WESTLAW to update your research in many ways:

- Retrieve cases citing a particular statute.

- Update a state or federal statute by accessing the Update service from the displayed statute using the Jump marker.

- Retrieve newly enacted legislation by searching in the appropriate legislative service database.

- Retrieve cases not yet reported by searching in case-law databases.

- Read the latest U.S. Supreme Court opinions within an hour of their release.

- Update West digests by searching with topic and key numbers.

Determining Case History and Retrieving Citing Cases

KeyCite™, the new citation research service developed by West Group and made available through the WESTLAW computer-assisted legal research service, integrates all the case law on WESTLAW, giving you the power to

- trace the history of a case;

- retrieve a list of all cases on WESTLAW that cite a case; and

- track legal issues in a case.

Citing references from the extensive library of secondary sources on WESTLAW, such as ALR® annotations and law review articles, are covered by KeyCite as well. You can use these citing references to find case discussions by legal experts.

Now, in this one service on WESTLAW, you receive

- the case-verification functions of Insta-Cite®;

- the case-citing functions of Shepard's® and Shepard's PreView®; and

- the currentness of QuickCite®.

In addition, KeyCite is completely integrated with West's Key Number System so that it provides the tools for navigating the case-law databases on WESTLAW. Only KeyCite combines the up-to-the-minute case-verification functions of an online citator service with the case-finding tools needed to find relevant case law.

Additional Information

For more detailed information or assistance, contact your WESTLAW account representative or call 1-800-REF-ATTY (1-800-733-2889).

*

Table of Parallel References

This table shows where the subject matter of the various sections of articles in the Indiana Law Encyclopedia is treated in Indiana Law Encyclopedia revised volumes.

The reader should always consult the volume index for detail and for matters not appearing in the earlier edition.

CONTEMPT

I.L.E.	I.L.E.(Rev)	I.L.E.	I.L.E.(Rev)
1	1-3	8	21
1, 2, 4	7	21	14
1-4, 7	8, 9	22	16
2	4	23	17, 19
3	6	24	20
4, 7	5	25	15
5	13	26	18
6	10-12	27	22, 23

CONTINUANCE

I.L.E.	I.L.E.(Rev)	I.L.E.	I.L.E.(Rev)
1	1, 14	6	4
2	2, 11	7	5
3	10	8	15, 16
4	6-8	8-10	13
5	3		

CONTRACTS

I.L.E.	I.L.E.(Rev.)	I.L.E.	I.L.E.(Rev.)
1	1	6	5, 6
2, 112, 252	120	21	7
3	2	22	8
4	3	23	10
5	4	24	11

I.L.E.	I.L.E.(Rev.)	I.L.E.	I.L.E.(Rev.)
25	12	117	62
31	13	118	63
32	24	119	64
33	15	120-122	65
34	16	123	66
35	17	124	67
36	18	125	68
37	19	126	69
38	20	127	70
39	22	128	71
40	23	129	72
51	25-28	130	73
52	29	131	74
53	30, 80	132	75
61	31, 32	133, 269	136
62	33, 34	133, 136, 269	137
63	35	134	76
64	36	135	77
65	37	137	78
66	38	151	79
67	39, 40	152	81
68	41	153	82
69	42	154	83
81	43	161	85
82	44	162, 163, 229	84
83	45	164	86
84	46	171, 172	87
85	47, 48, 55	173	88
86	49	181	89
87	50	182	90
88	51	183	91
88-90	52	184	92
91	53	191	93
92	54	192	94
101, 102	56	193	95
103	57	194	96
104	Deleted	201, 202	98
111	58	201-204	100
113	59	203, 204	99
114	60	205	102
115, 195	97	206	101
116, 123	61	221	103

I.L.E.	I.L.E.(Rev.)	I.L.E.	I.L.E.(Rev.)
222	104	253	121
223	105	254	122
224	106	255	123
225	108	256	124
226	109	257, 259-261	125
227	Deleted	258	126
228	110	262	127
228, 236	117	263	128
228, 236	118	264, 265	Deleted
230	111, 112	266	130
231, 233	114	267, 271	131
232	113	268	132
234	116	270	138
234, 235	115	271	133, 134
237	Deleted	272	135
251	119		

CONTRIBUTION

I.L.E.	I.L.E.(Rev.)	I.L.E.	I.L.E.(Rev.)
1	1	4	4
2	2	5	5
3	3		

CONVERSION

I.L.E.	I.L.E.(Rev.)	I.L.E.	I.L.E.(Rev.)
1	1-3, 6-9	15	22
1, 2	4	16	29, 31
2	5	17	32
11	10	18	33
12	13, 14	19	34
13	15-21	20	35, 36
14	11	21	23-27

CORONERS

I.L.E.	I.L.E.(Rev.)	I.L.E.	I.L.E.(Rev.)
1	1-3	2	4-10

CORPORATIONS

I.L.E.	I.L.E.(Rev.)	I.L.E.	I.L.E.(Rev.)
1	1	106	41
2	2, 3	121, 124	65
3	4	122	69
4	5	123, 149	70
5	6	125	72
6	Deleted	126	73
7	17	127, 128	77
8	12	129	80-87
9	8	130	88-90
10	Deleted	131, 155	74-76
11	9	132	7, 78
12	10	134	79
13	11	141	96-101, 106
14	13-15	142	102
21	18-20	143	103-105, 107
22	22	145	108-114
23	Deleted	146	Deleted
24	23	147	117, 119
25	24	147, 148	115
26	26, 27	147, 152	118
26, 149	28	150, 151	Deleted
41, 42	36	153	Deleted
42	37	154	116
43	40, 43, 44	156	Deleted
44, 45	Deleted	157	120
46	45	171	122
61, 62, 64	38	172	123, 124
65	39	173	125
66-70	Deleted	174	126, 127
81, 83, 85, 86	46	175	128
82	47	176	129,130
84	55	177	131-133
87	57	178	134
88	50	191	135, 136, 138
89	51	192	137
90	49	193	139, 140
101, 102	58	194	141
103	62	195	142
104	63	196	143, 144
105	64	211	145-149

TABLE OF PARALLEL REFERENCES

I.L.E.	I.L.E.(Rev.)	I.L.E.	I.L.E.(Rev.)
212	150	264	190
213	151	265	191, 192
214	152	266	193
215	153-155	267	171
216	156	268	172
231	157	269	181
231	158	281	194-196
232	159	282, 283	197, 198
233	160	284	199, 200
234	161	291	202
235	162	291	203-205, 207
236	163-166	292	206
251	168, 169	293	208
252	170	301	209, 210
253	173, 174	302	211
254	175-177	303	212, 213
255	178	304	214
256	179	305	215
257	182	307	216
258	183, 184	308	217
259	185	309	218
260	186, 187	310	219, 220
261	188	311	221
262	189	312	222
263	180		

CONTEMPT

Rosemary E. Williams, J.D.

Scope of Topic

This article discusses acts or omissions, consequences, and punishment of disobedience to the process, rules, or orders of courts, and other acts or omissions made in disregard of judicial authority or dignity which are found to impede or frustrate the administration of law; the grounds and procedure for civil or criminal contempt; identification of those persons who may be found liable for contempt; and the assessment of punishment for civil or criminal contempt.

Treated Elsewhere

Administrative tribunals, contempt of, see I.L.E., Administrative Law & Procedure

Attorneys generally, see I.L.E., Attorney and Client

Habeas corpus relief from judgment of contempt, see I.L.E., Habeas Corpus

Labor relations cases, contempt of court arising in, see I.L.E., Labor Relations

Legislature, contempt of, see I.L.E., State

Support orders, contempt of court for violation of, generally, see I.L.E., Divorce

Tax Court, contempt of, see I.L.E., Taxation

Research References

Text References

17 Am Jur 2d, Contempt.
17 C.J.S., Contempt.

West's Digest References

West's Digest, Contempt.

Annotation References

ALR Digest: Contempt
ALR Index: Contempt

Forms References

7 Am Jur Pleading and Practice Forms, Annotated (rev. ed.), Contempt.

Trial Strategy References

Disqualification of Trial Judge for Cause, 50 Am Jur POF3d 449; Proof of Violation of Federal Rule of Civil Procedure 11 and of Sanctions Thereunder, 47 Am Jur POF3d 241; Civil Discovery Sanctions in the Federal Courts, 33 Am Jur POF3d 459; Intentional Spoliation of Evidence, 18 Am Jur POF3d 515.

Jury Misconduct Warranting New Trial, 24 Am Jur POF2d 633.

A Guide to the Federal Rules of Civil Procedure, 56 Am Jur Trials 293; Dealing With Judges and Court Personnel, 55 Am Jur Trials 443; Commonsense Principles of Civil Litigation, 52 Am Jur Trials 1.

Miscellaneous References

Indiana Practice, Rules of Procedure, Rule 4.1, 4.16, 37, 45, 70.

Indiana Practice, Appellate Procedure §§ 2.5, 9.3, 10.4, 13.19.

Indiana Practice, Civil Trial Practice §§ 7.21, 21.27, 23.06, 25.09, 27.06, 28.06, 29.01, 30.18, 30.50.

Indiana Practice, Procedural Forms With Practice Commentary §§ 79.10, 79.11.

Indiana Practice, Indiana Evidence §§ 101.201, 101.308.

Statutory References

Ind Const Art 1 § 22

Ind Const Art 4 § 15

IC 14-27-3-1; IC 15-2.1-24-24; IC 22-1-1-17; IC 29-1-7-3; IC 31-16-12-1; IC 31-16-12-6; IC 31-32-14-1; IC 33-2-1-4; IC 33-4-2-8; IC 33-4-11-24; IC 33-10.5-2-5; IC 33-21-1-9; IC 34-1-10-10; IC 34-12-2-6; IC 34-26-1-14 to IC 34-26-1-16; IC 34-35-3-3; IC 34-47-1-1; IC-34-47-2-5; IC 34-47-2-7; IC 34-47-4-1; IC 34-47-4-2; IC 34-47-2-1 to IC 34-47-2-5; IC 34-47-3-1 to IC 34-47-3-8; IC 35-34-2-5; IC 35-34-2-5.5; IC 35-37-3-3; IC 35-37-5-2

Court Rules

A.D.R. Rule 6.3

Trial R. 37, 45, 56, 65, 70

KeyCite®: Cases and other legal materials listed in KeyCite Scope can be researched through West Group's KeyCite service on Westlaw®. Use KeyCite to check citations for form, parallel references, prior and later history, and comprehensive citator information, including citations to other decisions and secondary materials.

Table of Parallel References:

To convert General Index references to section references in this volume, or to ascertain the disposition (or current equivalent) of articles in the prior edition of this publication, see the Table of Parallel References at the beginning of this volume.

I. IN GENERAL (§§ 1 TO 6)

II. PARTICULAR CONDUCT AS CONTEMPTUOUS (§§ 7 TO 13)

III. PROCEDURE, PUNISHMENT, AND APPEAL (§§ 14 TO 23)

I. IN GENERAL

§ 1 Definition of contempt; purpose and scope of contempt power
§ 2 Who has contempt power
§ 3 Legislative regulation of contempt power
§ 4 Direct and indirect contempt
§ 5 Civil and criminal contempt
§ 6 Intent; good faith or motive

II. PARTICULAR CONDUCT AS CONTEMPTUOUS

§ 7 Disruptive or disrespectful conduct or remarks
§ 8 Disobedience or hindrance of process or order, generally
§ 9 —Existence, validity, and specificity of order; impossibility of performance
§ 10 Failure to appear for hearing, trial, deposition, or jury service
§ 11 Refusal to be sworn or to testify; false testimony
§ 12 Influencing or intimidating witness, juror, or court officer
§ 13 Contemptuous publications

III. PROCEDURE, PUNISHMENT, AND APPEAL

§ 14 Contempt proceedings, generally
§ 15 Civil contempt
§ 16 Direct criminal contempt
§ 17 Indirect criminal contempt, generally
§ 18 Notice and process; rule, citation, attachment, and bail
§ 19 Special judge
§ 20 Answer and determination
§ 21 Punishment and other sanctions for contempt
§ 22 Appeal and review
§ 23 —Standard and scope of review

I. IN GENERAL

Research References

Ind Const Art 4 § 15

IC 14-27-3-1; IC 15-2.1-24-24; IC 22-1-1-17; IC 29-1-7-3; IC 31-32-14-1; IC 33-2-1-4; IC 33-4-2-8; IC 33-10.5-2-5; IC 34-1-10-10; IC 34-12-2-6; IC 34-26-1-14; IC 34-47-1-1; IC 34-47-2-1; IC 34-47-2-2; IC 34-47-2-7; IC 34-47-3-1; IC 34-47-3-8
A.D.R. Rule 6.3
Trial R. 37, 56

17 Am Jur 2d, Contempt §§ 1-66, 248-253, 266-273.
17 C.J.S., Contempt §§ 1-10, 35-62.
West's Digest, Contempt ⊚1-7, 30, 31.
ALR Digest: Contempt §§ 1-3, 55-65.7
ALR Index: Contempt
7 Am Jur Pleading and Practice Forms, Annotated (rev. ed.), Contempt §§ 113-143.

§ 1 Definition of contempt; purpose and scope of contempt power

Contempt of court is any act or refusal to act in disobedience to or disrespect of a court, and includes any act which pertains to a pending proceeding and tends to deter the court from the performance of its duties, or to otherwise obstruct the administration of justice.

West's Digest, Contempt ⊚1-6, 30-36.

Contempt of court is an act or refusal to act[1] in disobedience to or disrespect of a court, arising from opposition to its authority, justice, and dignity.[2] Contempt includes any act which pertains to a pending proceeding, and which tends to deter the court from the performance of its duties or to obstruct the administration of justice.[3]

The power to punish for contempt, which is inherent in all courts of record,[4] serves two purposes: (1) vindication of the courts' dignity, and (2) enforcement of litigants' rights pur-

---

[1]Fishback v. State, 131 Ind. 304, 30 N.E. 1088 (1892).

[2]In re Nasser, 644 N.E.2d 93 (Ind. 1994); Hopping v. State, 637 N.E.2d 1294 (Ind. 1994); Brumbaugh v. State, 491 N.E.2d 983 (Ind. 1986); Hancz v. City of South Bend, 691 N.E.2d 1322 (Ind. Ct. App. 1998); Ellis v. State, 634 N.E.2d 771 (Ind. Ct. App. 2d Dist. 1994).

Legal Periodicals: McGregor, Use of the Contempt Power, 35 Res Gestae 12 (July 1991).

[3]In re Nasser, 644 N.E.2d 93 (Ind. 1994); Hopping v. State, 637 N.E.2d 1294 (Ind. 1994); Seniours v. State, 634 N.E.2d 803 (Ind. Ct. App. 5th Dist. 1994) (delaying tactics); Ellis v. State, 634 N.E.2d 771 (Ind. Ct. App. 2d Dist. 1994) (gross violation of decorum).

[4]§ 2.

suant to court orders.[5] The contempt power does not lie to soothe the wounded sensibilities of a judge[6] or to correct trial court errors;[7] it may be invoked only when the offending act impedes or disturbs the administration of justice.[8] While the contempt power should be promptly exercised in proper cases, it should be kept within prudent limits.[9]

The General Assembly has provided for exercise of the contempt power with respect to a variety of actions which may affect the administration of justice.[10] Contempt proceedings may be brought for matters contained in written pleadings and affidavits,[11] as well as for actual behavior within a courtroom.[12] Conduct outside a courtroom may also be contemptuous, as where a person testifying in an oral deposition refuses to be sworn or to answer a question after being ordered to do so by the court.[13]

§ 2 Who has contempt power

All courts of record in Indiana have inherent power to

---

[5]Crowl v. Berryhill, 678 N.E.2d 828 (Ind. Ct. App. 1997).

[6]Grimm v. State, 240 Ind. 125, 162 N.E.2d 454 (1959) (power to punish for contempt not to be misused to protect personal or individual feelings of judge).

[7]Crowl v. Berryhill, 678 N.E.2d 828 (Ind. Ct. App. 1997).

[8]State ex rel. Allen v. Vermillion Circuit Court of Vermillion County, 248 Ind. 258, 226 N.E.2d 324 (1967); Crowl v. Berryhill, 678 N.E.2d 828 (Ind. Ct. App. 1997).

[9]Grimm v. State, 240 Ind. 125, 162 N.E.2d 454 (1959).

[10]IC 29-1-7-3 (noncompliance with order to produce a will); IC 34-12-2-6 (prohibited identification of participant in marital misconduct); IC 34-26-1-14 et seq. (violation of injunction); IC 34-47-1-1 et seq. (contempt of court generally).

As to legislative regulation of the contempt power, generally, see § 3.

[11]Trial R. 56(G) (permitting an award of sanctions for contempt for the presentation by a party of affidavits in bad faith in a summary judgment proceeding).

Jacobsen v. State, 179 Ind. App. 37, 384 N.E.2d 1041 (3d Dist. 1979) (false and scurrilous charges in affidavit); Matter of May, 171 Ind. App. 440, 358 N.E.2d 138 (1st Dist. 1976) (irrelevant and unnecessary statements in pleading).

[12]IC 34-47-2-1 (disturbing the business and proceedings of a court); IC 34-47-2-2 (refusal of witness to testify under oath).

[13]Trial R. 37(B)(1) , more fully discussed in § 11.

A person may refuse to submit to a physical or mental examination without penalties of contempt.—Trial R. 37(B)(2)(d).

punish for contempt, and by statute the General Assembly has specifically conferred such power on various courts and judges.

West's Digest, Contempt ☞30-36.

The power to punish for contempt is inherent in all courts of record,[14] and by statute, the General Assembly has specifically conferred such power on various courts and judges.[15]

◆ **Observation:** The General Assembly itself has power to punish disorderly or contemptuous behavior committed by a nonmember in its presence,[16] and, by a number of statutes, has authorized administrative agencies to apply to courts for the punishment of persons who act in contempt of the agencies in the exercise of their proper authority.[17] Beyond this, however, the power to punish for contempt is purely judicial,[18] and may not be exercised by the legislative or executive branches of government absent special act of the General Assembly.[19]

The contempt power may be exercised by the judges of those courts in which the power inheres, or upon which it has been conferred, without regard to their individual identity or status. A special judge may punish for contempt

---

[14]In re Contempt of Houston, 711 N.E.2d 33 (Ind. 1999), order supplemented, 717 N.E.2d 1208 (Ind. 1999); Adler v. Adler, 713 N.E.2d 348 (Ind. Ct. App. 1999); Meyer v. Wolvos, 707 N.E.2d 1029 (Ind. Ct. App. 1999), reh'g denied, (May 13, 1999) and transfer denied, (Sept. 20, 1999); Crowl v. Berryhill, 678 N.E.2d 828 (Ind. Ct. App. 1997); B.L. v. State, 688 N.E.2d 1311 (Ind. Ct. App. 1997).

[15]IC 34-47-3-8 (Supreme and appellate courts); IC 33-2-1-4 (Supreme Court); IC 33-4-2-8 (Circuit Courts); IC 33-10.5-2-5 (county courts); IC 31-32-14-1 (juvenile courts).

[16]Ind Const Art 4 § 15.

As to powers of the General Assembly generally, see I.L.E. State.

[17]IC 22-1-1-17 (investigations regarding labor and employment); IC 14-27-3-1 (interference with superintendent of construction for levees and flood control); IC 15-2.1-24-24 (investigation of processing plants for poultry and poultry products).

As to administrative law and procedure, generally, see I.L.E. Administrative Law and Procedure.

[18]§ 3.

[19]Langenberg v. Decker, 131 Ind. 471, 31 N.E. 190 (1892).

As to legislative regulation of the contempt power, generally, see § 3.

of the court of which he or she is temporarily an official,[20] and a private judge appointed under the Alternative Dispute Resolution Rules has, for each case heard, the same contempt powers as a Circuit Court.[21]

If the contempt is indirect,[22] or if the trial judge waits until the end of court proceedings to cite a person for contempt, the judge has a duty to disqualify him- or herself. In these cases, the determination of whether the conduct constituted contempt would be made by another, detached judge.[23]

Where authority exists, the fact that a judge is not currently presiding has no effect on his or her authority to exercise the contempt power.[24]

§ 3   Legislative regulation of contempt power

The General Assembly may regulate proceedings for contempt and may designate as contempt acts not formerly found as such, but it may not abridge the courts' inherent authority to punish for contempt.

West's Digest, Contempt ⟐31.

Where a court has inherent authority to punish for contempt,[25] that authority exists independently of any statutory provision, and cannot be abridged by legislative act.[26] A court's inherent contempt power is purely judicial, and is not a creature of legislation.[27] The General Assembly may regulate the exercise of judicial power to punish for contempt,

---

[20]IC 34-47-2-7.

[21]A.D.R. Rule 6.3(B).

[22]As to the distinction between direct and indirect contempt, generally, see § 4.

[23]Skolnick v. State, 180 Ind. App. 253, 388 N.E.2d 1156 (3d Dist. 1979).

[24]IC 34-1-10-10.

[25]Regarding the contempt power as inherent in certain courts, see § 2.

[26]State ex rel. Goldsmith v. Marion County Superior Court, Criminal Division No. 1, 275 Ind. 545, 419 N.E.2d 109 (1981); La Grange v. State, 238 Ind. 689, 153 N.E.2d 593, 69 ALR 2d 668 (1958) (power to punish for contempt inherent in every court of superior jurisdiction, and is essential to existence and functioning of the judicial system, and the Legislature has no power to take away or materially impair it).

[27]Crowl v. Berryhill, 678 N.E.2d 828 (Ind. Ct. App. 1997).

and prescribe rules of practice and procedure, but it may not go so far as to limit the courts' inherent power of contempt.[28]

Although the General Assembly has enacted statutes specifically conferring on various courts the power to punish for contempt,[29] these statutes confer no additional power on courts of superior or general jurisdiction.[30]

The General Assembly has statutorily defined several forms of conduct as contempt of court,[31] and may declare certain conduct to be contempt which has not theretofore been so regarded.[32] However, the courts are not limited by legislative definitions of contempt.[33] These statutes do not embrace all forms of conduct amounting to contempt, and are merely a legislative recognition of the courts' inherent power to cite and punish for such conduct.[34]

§ 4 Direct and indirect contempt

A direct contempt is conduct occurring in the presence and with the personal knowledge of the judge, related to a current or pending proceeding, while an indirect contempt arises from conduct outside the court's presence, but which nevertheless tends to interfere with the due administration of justice, such as failure or refusal of a party to obey a court order, injunction, or decree.

West's Digest, Contempt ☞2, 6, 7.

Indiana law recognizes two forms of contempt, direct and

---

[28]LaGrange v. State, 238 Ind. 689, 153 N.E.2d 593, 69 ALR 2d 668 (Ind. 1958); B.L. v. State, 688 N.E.2d 1311 (Ind. Ct. App. 1997); Worthington v. State, 181 Ind. App. 365, 391 N.E.2d 1164 (3d Dist. 1979).

[29]§ 2.

[30]Matter of Crumpacker, 431 N.E.2d 91 (Ind. 1982); State ex rel. Goldsmith v. Marion County Superior Court, Criminal Division No. 1, 275 Ind. 545, 419 N.E.2d 109 (1981); Adler v. Adler, 713 N.E.2d 348 (Ind. Ct. App. 1999); Crowl v. Berryhill, 678 N.E.2d 828 (Ind. Ct. App. 1997).

[31]IC 34-47-2-1 et seq. (direct contempt of court); IC 34-47-3-1 et seq. (indirect contempt of court).

Regarding particular conduct as contemptuous, see §§ 7 et seq.

[32]Cheadle v. State, 110 Ind. 301, 11 N.E. 426 (1887).

[33]Matter of Crumpacker, 431 N.E.2d 91 (Ind. 1982); State ex rel. Goldsmith v. Marion County Superior Court, Criminal Division No. 1, 275 Ind. 545, 419 N.E.2d 109 (1981); Adler v. Adler, 713 N.E.2d 348 (Ind. Ct. App. 1999).

[34]Skolnick v. State, 180 Ind. App. 253, 388 N.E.2d 1156 (3d Dist. 1979).

indirect,[35] which are separately provided for by statute.[36] The practical significance of the distinction lies in the summary manner in which the court may respond to a direct contempt, while an indirect contempt may be punished only upon notice or process and other procedural safeguards for the alleged contemnor.[37]

> ◆ **Observation:** Nothing in the statutes governing direct and indirect contempt may be construed or held to embrace, limit, or control any proceeding against any officer or party for contempt for the enforcement of civil rights and remedies.[38]

"Direct contempt" of court refers to any conduct occurring in the presence and with the personal knowledge of the judge, related to a current or pending proceeding, which interferes with court proceedings or business or tends to deter the court from the performance of its duties.[39] Behavior constituting direct contempt may include the creation of noise or confusion in the courtroom, disrespectful conduct, or refusing to take the witness stand in a trial.[40] The extraordinary power to punish for a direct contempt is limited to those situations in which the conduct at issue creates an open threat to the orderly procedure of the court, and exhibits such flagrant defiance of the person and presence of the

---

[35]In re Nasser, 644 N.E.2d 93 (Ind. 1994); Williams v. State ex rel. Harris, 690 N.E.2d 315 (Ind. Ct. App. 1997); Crowl v. Berryhill, 678 N.E.2d 828 (Ind. Ct. App. 1997); Jackson v. State, 644 N.E.2d 607 (Ind. Ct. App. 3d Dist. 1994), transfer denied, (Feb. 28, 1995).

[36]IC 34-47-2-1 et seq. (direct contempt); IC 34-47-3-1 et seq. (indirect contempt).

[37]In re Marriage of Neiswinger, 477 N.E.2d 257 (Ind. 1985); La Grange v. State, 238 Ind. 689, 153 N.E.2d 593, 69 ALR 2d 668 (1958); Mitchell v. Stevenson, 677 N.E.2d 551 (Ind. Ct. App. 1997), transfer denied, 683 N.E.2d 594 (Ind. 1997).

As to procedures and punishment for direct contempt, see § 16.

As to procedures and punishment for indirect contempt, generally, see § 17.

[38]IC 34-47-1-1(b).

[39]In re Nasser, 644 N.E.2d 93 (Ind. 1994); Hopping v. State, 637 N.E.2d 1294 (Ind. 1994).

Forms References: Direct Contempt. 7 Am Jur Pleading and Practice Forms, Annotated (rev. ed.), Contempt §§ 113-125.

[40]Russell v. State, 428 N.E.2d 1271 (Ind. Ct. App. 4th Dist. 1981).

Regarding particular conduct as contemptuous, see §§ 7 et seq.

judge, that demoralization of the court's authority would follow if the conduct is not instantly suppressed and punished.[41]

While an act of direct contempt commonly will occur during the course of a judicial proceeding, it need only be within the judge's personal knowledge, and does not have to occur inside the courtroom or during a formal proceeding.[42] Thus, charges of direct contempt can be supported by contemptuous statements made in papers filed with the court.[43] It is necessary only that the inappropriate behavior bear a close relationship to the court's judicial activities.[44]

> ◆ **Illustration:** The court could hold summary proceedings for direct criminal contempt, although the individual charged did not interrupt an actual hearing and his misconduct occurred in an office outside the judge's chambers when court was not in session, where the judge had firsthand and immediate knowledge of the individual's outburst to a secretary about the scheduling of hearings in his small claims cases as well as of a subsequent racial slur directed at the judge, and the individual's acts demonstrated clear disregard for the court's authority, which threatened to undermine the integrity of the judicial process and impede the performance of the court's work.[45]

An "indirect" contempt arises from conduct outside the court's presence, but which nevertheless tends to interfere with the due administration of justice.[46] Conduct amounting to an indirect contempt may include a party's failure or refusal to obey a court order, injunction, or decree; failure to

---

[41]Curtis v. State, 625 N.E.2d 496 (Ind. Ct. App. 2d Dist. 1993).

[42]Hopping v. State, 637 N.E.2d 1294 (Ind. 1994); Williams v. State ex rel. Harris, 690 N.E.2d 315 (Ind. Ct. App. 1997); Jackson v. State, 644 N.E.2d 607 (Ind. Ct. App. 3d Dist. 1994), transfer denied, (Feb. 28, 1995); Andrews v. State, 505 N.E.2d 815 (Ind. Ct. App. 1st Dist. 1987).

[43]La Grange v. State, 238 Ind. 689, 153 N.E.2d 593, 69 ALR 2d 668 (1958); Kerr v. State, 194 Ind. 147, 141 N.E. 308 (1923); Ex parte Fennig, 216 Ind. 298, 23 N.E.2d 678 (1939); Matter of May, 171 Ind. App. 440, 358 N.E.2d 138 (1st Dist. 1976).

[44]Hopping v. State, 637 N.E.2d 1294 (Ind. 1994).

[45]Hopping v. State, 637 N.E.2d 1294 (Ind. 1994).

[46]Matter of Hatfield, 607 N.E.2d 384 (Ind. 1993); Meyer v. Wolvos, 707 N.E.2d 1029 (Ind. Ct. App. 1999), reh'g denied, (May 13, 1999) and transfer denied, (Sept. 20, 1999); Williams v. State ex rel. Harris, 690 N.E.2d 315 (Ind. Ct. App. 1997); Skolnick v. State, 180 Ind. App. 253, 388 N.E.2d 1156 (3d Dist. 1979); Hegedus v. Hegedus, 178 Ind. App. 620, 383 N.E.2d 446 (1st Dist. 1978).

appear for trial; resisting process; influencing or intimidating a witness; or publishing contemptuous matter.[47]

§ 5   Civil and criminal contempt

A criminal contempt is an act showing disrespect for or defiance of the court, or one directed against the court's dignity and authority which tends to obstruct the administration of justice and bring the court into disrepute. A civil contempt is the violation of a mandate or order issued for the benefit of a party to an action before the court.

West's Digest, Contempt ⇔3, 4.

Contempt proceedings may be generally categorized as civil or criminal, according to the nature and purpose of the sanction imposed.[48]

Criminal contempt may be defined as any act, direct or indirect,[49] showing disrespect for and defiance of the court,[50] or as any act directed against the dignity and authority of the court, which obstructs the administration of justice and tends to bring the court into disrepute.[51] As an affront to the dignity of the sovereign as embodied in the court, criminal contempt is a "public" matter,[52] and proceedings therefor are essentially punitive in character, such conduct being punish-

---

Forms References: Indirect Contempt. 7 Am Jur Pleading and Practice Forms, Annotated (rev. ed.), Contempt §§ 126-143.

[47]§§ 8, 10, 12, 13.

[48]Mitchell v. Stevenson, 677 N.E.2d 551 (Ind. Ct. App. 1997), transfer denied, 683 N.E.2d 594 (Ind. 1997).

[49]Matter of Hatfield, 607 N.E.2d 384 (Ind. 1993); Matter of Crumpacker, 431 N.E.2d 91 (Ind. 1982); Hancz v. City of South Bend, 691 N.E.2d 1322 (Ind. Ct. App. 1998); Peterson v. State, 468 N.E.2d 556 (Ind. Ct. App. 4th Dist. 1984), reh'g denied, (Nov. 2, 1984) and transfer denied, (Mar. 21, 1985).

As to direct and indirect contempt, generally, see § 4.

[50]Matter of Crumpacker, 431 N.E.2d 91 (Ind. 1982); Matter of Lemond, 274 Ind. 505, 413 N.E.2d 228 (1980); Skolnick v. State, 180 Ind. App. 253, 388 N.E.2d 1156 (3d Dist. 1979).

[51]Cowart v. White, 711 N.E.2d 523 (Ind. 1999), on reh'g, 716 N.E.2d 401 (Ind. 1999) and reh'g granted on other grounds, (Sept. 22, 1999); Hancz v. City of South Bend, 691 N.E.2d 1322 (Ind. Ct. App. 1998); Skolnick v. State, 180 Ind. App. 253, 388 N.E.2d 1156 (3d Dist. 1979).

[52]Matter of Craig, 552 N.E.2d 53 (Ind. Ct. App. 2d Dist. 1990), appeal after remand, 571 N.E.2d 1326 (Ind. Ct. App. 5th Dist. 1991).

able by a determinate sentence or fine[53] for the vindication of public authority and order.[54]

A civil contempt is the violation of a mandate or order issued for the benefit of a party to an action before the court.[55] In contrast to proceedings for criminal contempt, a civil contempt proceeding is essentially one to enforce private rights and remedies, without the objective of punishing the contemnor,[56] and seeks to coerce compliance with a specific order of the court for the benefit of the aggrieved party,[57] or to compensate that party when the court's order is violated.[58]

While the same act may constitute a civil and a criminal contempt, they are distinguished in that a civil contempt does not depend on the existence of an intention to defy the authority of the court.[59]

---

[53]Matter of Contempt of Steelman, 648 N.E.2d 366 (Ind. Ct. App. 2d Dist. 1995); Matter of Craig, 552 N.E.2d 53 (Ind. Ct. App. 2d Dist. 1990), appeal after remand, 571 N.E.2d 1326 (Ind. Ct. App. 5th Dist. 1991).

As to punishment for contempt generally, see § 21.

[54]Matter of Craig, 552 N.E.2d 53 (Ind. Ct. App. 2d Dist. 1990), appeal after remand, 571 N.E.2d 1326 (Ind. Ct. App. 5th Dist. 1991); Matter of Crumpacker, 431 N.E.2d 91 (Ind. 1982).

[55]Cowart v. White, 711 N.E.2d 523 (Ind. 1999), on reh'g, 716 N.E.2d 401 (Ind. 1999) and reh'g granted on other grounds, (Sept. 22, 1999); Hancz v. City of South Bend, 691 N.E.2d 1322 (Ind. Ct. App. 1998); Mitchell v. Stevenson, 677 N.E.2d 551 (Ind. Ct. App. 1997), transfer denied, 683 N.E.2d 594 (Ind. 1997); National Educ. Association—South Bend v. South Bend Community School Corp., 655 N.E.2d 516, 103 Ed. Law Rep. 1199 (Ind. Ct. App. 1995).

Regarding disobedience of court order as contempt, generally, see § 8.

[56]Cowart v. White, 711 N.E.2d 523 (Ind. 1999), on reh'g, 716 N.E.2d 401 (Ind. 1999) and reh'g granted on other grounds, (Sept. 22, 1999); Hancz v. City of South Bend, 691 N.E.2d 1322 (Ind. Ct. App. 1998); Mitchell v. Stevenson, 677 N.E.2d 551 (Ind. Ct. App. 1997), transfer denied, 683 N.E.2d 594 (Ind. 1997).

[57]Hancz v. City of South Bend, 691 N.E.2d 1322 (Ind. Ct. App. 1998) (primary objective of civil contempt proceeding not punishment but coercion of action for benefit of aggrieved party); Cass County v. Gotshall, 681 N.E.2d 227 (Ind. Ct. App. 1997); Crowl v. Berryhill, 678 N.E.2d 828 (Ind. Ct. App. 1997).

[58]National Educ. Association—South Bend v. South Bend Community School Corp., 655 N.E.2d 516, 103 Ed. Law Rep. 1199 (Ind. Ct. App. 1995); Moody v. Moody, 565 N.E.2d 388 (Ind. Ct. App. 1st Dist. 1991); Clark v. Atkins, 489 N.E.2d 90 (Ind. Ct. App. 3d Dist. 1986), reh'g denied, (May 14, 1986) and transfer denied, (Oct. 10, 1986).

[59]State ex rel. McMinn v. Gentry, 229 Ind. 615, 100 N.E.2d 676 (1951);

§ 6 Intent; good faith or motive

Intent is a necessary element of indirect criminal contempt, but not of indirect civil contempt. The existence of direct criminal contempt does not depend on evidence as to the intention of the offending party, but on the nature of the act done.

West's Digest, Contempt ⊜1-4.

To constitute criminal contempt, the acts in question must be characterized by a deliberate, willful intention to defy or disobey a court order or decree, or to show disrespect for the authority of the court, while an actual intent to do an act which violates the terms of a court order is sufficient to constitute a civil contempt.[60] Courts have held that the existence of direct criminal contempt does not depend on evidence as to the intention of the offending party, but on the nature of the act done.[61]

Whether good faith is relevant to a contempt proceeding depends on whether the proceeding is direct or indirect, criminal or civil, but it may be asserted as a defense when the issue is intent.[62] Apart from this, evidence of a good motive or a lawful objective normally will not justify an action taken in contempt of a court.[63] Also, it is not ordinarily a defense that the person violating the order acted in good faith, or

---

Hancz v. City of South Bend, 691 N.E.2d 1322 (Ind. Ct. App. 1998); National Educ. Association—South Bend v. South Bend Community School Corp., 655 N.E.2d 516, 103 Ed. Law Rep. 1199 (Ind. Ct. App. 1995).

As to intent for criminal and civil contempt, generally, see § 6.

[60]Matter of Hatfield, 607 N.E.2d 384 (Ind. 1993); In re Perrello, 260 Ind. 26, 291 N.E.2d 698 (1973); Rendon v. Rendon, 692 N.E.2d 889 (Ind. Ct. App. 1998); In re Marriage of Glendenning, 684 N.E.2d 1175 (Ind. Ct. App. 1997), transfer denied, 698 N.E.2d 1186 (Ind. 1998); Glick v. Lawmaster, 648 N.E.2d 370, 99 Ed. Law Rep. 570 (Ind. Ct. App. 5th Dist. 1995).

As to direct and indirect contempt, generally, see § 4.

As to criminal and civil contempt, generally, see § 5.

Regarding disobedience of court orders as contempt, generally, see § 8.

[61]Matter of Hatfield, 607 N.E.2d 384 (Ind. 1993); Matter of Lemond, 274 Ind. 505, 413 N.E.2d 228 (1980); La Grange v. State, 238 Ind. 689, 153 N.E.2d 593, 69 ALR 2d 668 (1958).

[62]Matter of Miller, 580 N.E.2d 313 (Ind. Ct. App. 2d Dist. 1991) (no contempt on statement of attorney more in nature of conclusion of law than statement of fact, and made in apparent good faith).

[63]Andrews v. State, 505 N.E.2d 815 (Ind. Ct. App. 1st Dist. 1987).

13

upon the instruction of another.[64] However, in cases of civil contempt, the alleged contemnor's good faith in attempting to obey the court's order may be a defense in certain circumstances.[65]

II. PARTICULAR CONDUCT AS CONTEMPTUOUS

Research References

Ind Const Art 1 § 22

IC 29-1-7-3; IC 31-16-12-1; IC 31-16-12-6; IC 33-2-1-4; IC 33-4-11-24; IC 33-21-1-9; IC 34-47-1-1; IC 34-47-3-6; IC 34-47-2-1 to IC 34-47-2-3; IC 34-47-3-1 to IC 34-47-3-4; IC 35-34-2-5; IC 35-34-2-5.5; IC 35-37-3-3; IC 35-37-5-2

Trial R. 37, 45, 65, 70

17 Am Jur 2d, Contempt §§ 67-164.
17 C.J.S., Contempt §§ 11-34.
West's Digest, Contempt ☞1-29.
ALR Digest: Contempt §§ 4-39
ALR Index: Contempt
7 Am Jur Pleading and Practice Forms, Annotated (rev. ed.), Contempt §§ 12-70, 113-143.

§ 7 Disruptive or disrespectful conduct or remarks

> **Contempt of court may be committed by conduct or remarks which are disrespectful or which disturb its business or proceedings.**

West's Digest, Contempt ☞6, 7.

A statute provides that a direct contempt is committed where one disturbs the business and proceedings of a court (1) by creating any noise or confusion, (2) in a court of record, and (3) while the court is open for and engaged in the transaction of business.[66]

◆ **Caution:** Although the statute refers to conduct "in" a court and "while the court is open for and engaged in the transaction of business," it has been held that pursuant to the courts' inherent contempt power, the disruption of an

---

[64]Adler v. Adler, 713 N.E.2d 348 (Ind. Ct. App. 1999).

[65]Regarding disobedience of court orders as contempt, generally, see § 8.

[66]IC 34-47-2-1(a).

Forms References: Direct Contempt. 7 Am Jur Pleading and Practice Forms, Annotated (rev. ed.), Contempt §§ 113-125.

actual court proceeding is not necessary to a finding of direct contempt, and that the offense may occur away from the courtroom while court is not in session, as long as the inappropriate conduct was committed in the judge's presence and bears a close relationship to the court's judicial activities.[67]

For purposes of the aforementioned statute, a "disturbance" may be created (1) by the commission of a felony, misdemeanor, or other unlawful act; (2) by talking, moving about, signs or gestures; or (3) in any other manner.[68] Even such potentially disruptive conduct as bringing a firearm into a courtroom does not constitute direct contempt, if the weapon remains concealed and unknown to others in or near the courtroom, and there is no actual disturbance of court proceedings.[69]

◆ **Observation:** Statutes or court rules may impose particular standards of conduct on the participants in a proceeding, the violation of which may be punishable as contempt. For example, an attorney representing a target witness before a grand jury may be held in contempt if the attorney violates statutory requirements to refrain from addressing the grand jury or prosecutor, making objections or arguments, questioning any person, or otherwise participating in the grand jury proceeding, or if the attorney in any other way disrupts or unnecessarily delays the proceeding.[70]

A profane outburst directed at the judge in a proceeding will support punishment for direct contempt,[71] as will any conduct by one on the witness stand which is purposely so

---

[67]Hopping v. State, 637 N.E.2d 1294 (Ind. 1994).

As to direct contempt, generally, see § 4.

[68]IC 34-47-2-1(b).

[69]Macon v. State, 629 N.E.2d 883 (Ind. Ct. App. 3d Dist. 1994) (defendant who had loaded weapon in her purse throughout courtroom proceeding involving traffic violation was not guilty of direct contempt, as there was no disturbance in courtroom and no one was aware of gun until defendant was booked into jail after conclusion of the proceeding); Davis v. State, 608 N.E.2d 995 (Ind. Ct. App. 3d Dist. 1993) (defendant who tried to bring loaded pistol into a courtroom while court was in session, but who did not interfere directly with court proceedings and made no resistance once gun was detected, could not be found in direct contempt summarily).

[70]IC 35-34-2-5.5.

[71]Holly v. State, 681 N.E.2d 1176 (Ind. Ct. App. 1997).

demeaning as to retard or disturb the proceedings of the court.[72] The manner of expression may itself make a remark contemptuous,[73] and certain statements, not in themselves contemptuous, may become so if made in a rude, insolent, and disrespectful manner.[74] On the other hand, impolite or sarcastic remarks in the court's presence have been found not to constitute direct contempt, where there was nothing to indicate that the comments were loud, disruptive, or accompanied by unruly physical conduct.[75]

An attorney may be found guilty of contempt for failing to show due respect and consideration to opposing counsel or to the court,[76] although it is not contemptuous for an attorney to point out respects in which he or she believes that the court has erred.[77] So long as one confines criticism of the court to the facts and bases it on decisions of the court, he or she commits no contempt, no matter how severe the criticism may be; but when a person passes beyond that line and charges in open court that judicial conduct was influenced by improper, corrupt, or selfish motives, or that such conduct was affected by political prejudice or interest, there is a contempt, because the tendency of such conduct is to poison the foundation of justice and create distrust, and to destroy the confidence of the people in the courts.[78]

◆ **Illustrations:** A party's conduct in accusing the trial

---

[72]IC 34-47-2-2.

[73]Russell v. State, 428 N.E.2d 1271 (Ind. Ct. App. 4th Dist. 1981).

[74]State ex rel. Stanton v. Murray, 231 Ind. 223, 108 N.E.2d 251 (1952); Macon v. State, 629 N.E.2d 883 (Ind. Ct. App. 3d Dist. 1994); Peterson v. State, 468 N.E.2d 556 (Ind. Ct. App. 4th Dist. 1984), reh'g denied, (Nov. 2, 1984) and transfer denied, (Mar. 21, 1985).

[75]Macon v. State, 629 N.E.2d 883 (Ind. Ct. App. 3d Dist. 1994) (pro se traffic defendant's comment "I knew that" in response to trial court's entering judgment for the state and defendant's comment "fine" in response to trial court's statement, "you just bought yourself two days in jail").

[76]State ex rel. Stanton v. Murray, 231 Ind. 223, 108 N.E.2d 251 (1952); Gerking v. Johnson, 220 Ind. 501, 44 N.E.2d 90 (1942); Russell v. State, 428 N.E.2d 1271 (Ind. Ct. App. 4th Dist. 1981) (ill-advised and rude response).

[77]Blankenbaker v. State, 201 Ind. 142, 166 N.E. 265 (1929).

Annotation References: Conduct of attorney in connection with making objections or taking exceptions as contempt of court, 68 ALR3d 314.

[78]Grimm v. State, 240 Ind. 125, 162 N.E.2d 454 (1959).

judge in open court of having a prejudicial interest in the case was sufficient to warrant a determination that the party was in direct contempt.[79] A defendant's action in making scurrilous charges against the judge in papers filed with the court in a contempt proceeding constituted direct contempt, and the defendant was not privileged to make such statements on the ground that he was the defendant in the contempt proceeding.[80]

Provocatory language cannot be cited to justify or excuse a contemptuous action, even when the contempt was provoked[81] or invited[82] by the judge's language.

◆ **Illustration:** A witness who was found in direct criminal contempt, after he alleged that the trial judge called him as a witness in order to elicit testimony usable to charge the witness with unauthorized practice of the law and that the judge was corrupt and had breached judicial ethics, was not entitled to relief on a theory that he had been entrapped into committing the contempt when the judge asked, "are you sitting here in this Court and calling me corrupt? Is that what you're doing?"[83]

§ 8 Disobedience or hindrance of process or order, generally

One who willfully disobeys any lawful court process or order that has been served upon the person, or who willfully resists, hinders, or delays the execution of any lawful process or order, is guilty of an indirect contempt of court.

West's Digest, Contempt ⚿14, 17-29.

By statute, a person who is guilty of any willful disobedience of any process, or any order lawfully issued (1) by any court of record, or by the proper officer of the court, (2) under the authority of law, or the direction of the court, and (3) after the process or order has been served upon the person, is

Annotation References: Oral communications insulting to particular state judge, made to third party out of judge's physical presence, as criminal contempt, 30 ALR4th 155.

Attacks on judiciary as a whole as indirect contempt, 40 ALR3d 1204.

79 Skolnick v. State, 180 Ind. App. 253, 388 N.E.2d 1156 (3d Dist. 1979).

80 Jacobsen v. State, 179 Ind. App. 37, 384 N.E.2d 1041 (3d Dist. 1979).

81 Dodge v. State, 140 Ind. 284, 39 N.E. 745 (1895).

82 Skolnick v. State, 180 Ind. App. 253, 388 N.E.2d 1156 (3d Dist. 1979).

83 Skolnick v. State, 180 Ind. App. 253, 388 N.E.2d 1156 (3d Dist. 1979).

guilty of an indirect contempt of the court that issued the process or order.[84] A person who willfully resists, hinders, or delays the execution of any lawful process or order of any court of record is likewise guilty of an indirect contempt of court.[85]

Statutes and rules of procedure authorize the imposition of contempt sanctions for the violation of various particular court mandates and orders.[86] A person may be held in civil or criminal contempt for disobeying an injunction,[87] and an officer who fails to serve process as ordered may be held in contempt.[88] Jurors who violate the court's instructions are subject to punishment by the court,[89] and an attorney's failure to abide by a standing court rule may constitute contempt of the court's authority and process.[90]

◆ **Observation:** Money judgments are generally enforced by execution or by other collateral and auxiliary remedies,

---

[84]IC 34-47-3-1.

[85]IC 34-47-3-2.

Forms References: Abusing or Obstructing Process. 7 Am Jur Pleading and Practice Forms, Annotated (rev. ed.), Contempt §§ 25-40.

Violation of Court Order. 7 Am Jur Pleading and Practice Forms, Annotated (rev. ed.), Contempt § 41-66.

[86]IC 29-1-7-3 (order to produce a will); IC 31-16-12-1 (orders and awards contained in child support decree); IC 31-16-12-6 (intentional violation of order for support); IC 33-2-1-4 (process and orders of Supreme Court); IC 33-21-1-9 (order that attorney turn over funds or papers to client).

Trial R. 37(B)(2)(d) (order to provide or permit discovery); Trial R. 65(E)(3) (temporary restraining order in domestic relations case); Trial R. 70(A) (order that party execute a conveyance of land or other property).

[87]Gillie v. Fleming, 191 Ind. 444, 133 N.E. 737 (1922); Hancz v. City of South Bend, 691 N.E.2d 1322 (Ind. Ct. App. 1998).

Forms References: Violation of Court Orders—Injunctions or Restraining Orders. 7 Am Jur Pleading and Practice Forms, Annotated (rev. ed.), Contempt §§ 59-66.

[88]State ex rel. Wheatley v. Beck, 175 Ind. 312, 93 N.E. 664 (1911) (where officer fails or refuses to perform duty in regard to the execution of process, injured party may proceed against him for contempt of court).

Forms References: Failure to Perform Judicial Duties. 7 Am Jur Pleading and Practice Forms, Annotated (rev. ed.), Contempt §§ 16-24.

[89]Wilson v. State, 247 Ind. 454, 217 N.E.2d 147 (1966); Murphy v. Wilson, 46 Ind. 537, 1874 WL 5746 (1874) (jury found in contempt for escaping without returning a verdict).

[90]Matter of Contempt of Lustina, 683 N.E.2d 236 (Ind. 1997) (court rule directing attorney to file affidavit upon suspension).

but not through contempt.[91] The rationale is that to permit the use of contempt for the enforcement of money judgments would violate that provision of the Indiana Constitution[92] which prohibits imprisonment for debt.[93] However, because a decree for child support is different than a judgment for money or property, being a continuing obligation based on the moral as well as legal duty of a parent to support his or her children, contempt is available to assist in the enforcement of child support orders in respect of unemancipated children, including orders to pay accrued arrearages and money judgments against delinquent parents for past due amounts.[94]

The violation of a mandate or order issued for the benefit of a particular litigant generally constitutes a civil contempt,[95] but may be treated as an indirect criminal contempt where the contemnor is shown to have willfully disregarded or violated the order with intent to show disrespect or defiance to the court.[96] One charged with failing to abide by a court order has the burden to prove a lack of willfulness.[97]

Acquiescing in an act prohibited by an injunction, while at the same time reaping the benefits thereof, is tantamount to

---

[91]Bahre v. Bahre, 248 Ind. 656, 230 N.E.2d 411 (1967); DeMichieli v. DeMichieli, 585 N.E.2d 297 (Ind. Ct. App. 1st Dist. 1992) (disapproved of on other grounds by, Pettit v. Pettit, 626 N.E.2d 444 (Ind. 1993)); Allee v. State, 462 N.E.2d 1074 (Ind. Ct. App. 1st Dist. 1984).

[92]Ind Const Art 1 § 22.

[93]DeMichieli v. DeMichieli, 585 N.E.2d 297 (Ind. Ct. App. 1st Dist. 1992) (disapproved of on other grounds by, Pettit v. Pettit, 626 N.E.2d 444 (Ind. 1993)).

[94]Pettit v. Pettit, 626 N.E.2d 444 (Ind. 1993).

[95]Cowart v. White, 711 N.E.2d 523 (Ind. 1999), on reh'g, 716 N.E.2d 401 (Ind. 1999) and reh'g granted on other grounds, (Sept. 22, 1999); Hancz v. City of South Bend, 691 N.E.2d 1322 (Ind. Ct. App. 1998); Mitchell v. Stevenson, 677 N.E.2d 551 (Ind. Ct. App. 1997), transfer denied, 683 N.E.2d 594 (Ind. 1997).

[96]Matter of Hatfield, 607 N.E.2d 384 (Ind. 1993); Matter of Lemond, 274 Ind. 505, 413 N.E.2d 228 (1980); In re Perrello, 260 Ind. 26, 291 N.E.2d 698 (1973).

As to direct and indirect contempt, generally, see § 4.

As to civil and criminal contempt, generally, see § 5.

[97]Adler v. Adler, 713 N.E.2d 348 (Ind. Ct. App. 1999); Meyer v. Wolvos, 707 N.E.2d 1029 (Ind. Ct. App. 1999), reh'g denied, (May 13, 1999) and transfer denied, (Sept. 20, 1999); Shively v. Shively, 680 N.E.2d 877 (Ind. Ct. App. 1997); Meade v. Levett, 671 N.E.2d 1172 (Ind. Ct. App. 1996).

ratification of the act and thus subjects the person to a finding of contempt for committing the prohibited act.[98] A nonparty who has knowledge of a court order, but who nevertheless aids, conspires with, and abets a party to an action in violating a court order entered therein, may be punished for contempt.[99]

◆ **Caution:** The Indiana Supreme Court has stated that an accomplice theory of culpability is not a viable means of finding one guilty of contempt.[1]

Before a person may be found in contempt for disobeying a court order, it must be shown that he or she had actual or constructive notice of the order and of the act or omission which was required thereby.[2] There is no presumption that affected persons have actual knowledge of a court's order, and such knowledge must be established from the facts presented to the trial court.[3]

§ 9   —Existence, validity, and specificity of order; impossibility of performance

In order for violation of a court order to be punishable as contempt, there must be a clear and certain order or decree in force, which commands a person to do or refrain from doing something. A void order cannot be the basis of a citation for contempt, but one may be held in contempt for disobeying an order that is merely erroneous.

West's Digest, Contempt ☞20, 21, 22, 24, 28.

In order for violation of a court order to be punishable as contempt, there must be an order or decree commanding a

---

[98]Caito v. Indianapolis Produce Terminal, Inc., 162 Ind. App. 590, 320 N.E.2d 821 (2d Dist. 1974).

[99]Owen v. Vaughn, 479 N.E.2d 83 (Ind. Ct. App. 4th Dist. 1985), reh'g denied, (Aug. 5, 1985).

[1]State v. Heltzel, 552 N.E.2d 31 (Ind. 1990).

[2]Meyer v. Wolvos, 707 N.E.2d 1029 (Ind. Ct. App. 1999), reh'g denied, (May 13, 1999) and transfer denied, (Sept. 20, 1999); Shively v. Shively, 680 N.E.2d 877 (Ind. Ct. App. 1997); Crowl v. Berryhill, 678 N.E.2d 828 (Ind. Ct. App. 1997); Mitchell v. Stevenson, 677 N.E.2d 551 (Ind. Ct. App. 1997), transfer denied, 683 N.E.2d 594 (Ind. 1997); Jackson v. State, 644 N.E.2d 607 (Ind. Ct. App. 3d Dist. 1994), transfer denied, (Feb. 28, 1995).

[3]Bottoms v. B & M Coal Corp., 405 N.E.2d 82 (Ind. Ct. App. 4th Dist. 1980).

person either to do or to refrain from doing something.[4] An order or judgment which merely declares the rights of the parties, without any express command or prohibition, cannot provide a foundation for contempt proceedings.[5] To be contemptuous, the violation must occur while the order is in force,[6] and one may not be held in contempt for disobeying an order that has been stayed[7] or has expired.[8]

A void order cannot be the basis of a citation for contempt.[9] An order is void if the court lacks jurisdiction to make it.[10] On the other hand, one may be held in contempt for disobeying an order that is merely erroneous, that is, an order that is unenforceable on appeal based upon nonjurisdictional irregularities.[11] An order which the alleged contemnor believes was issued in error must be obeyed until and unless the order is set aside according to applicable law and procedure.[12]

For purposes of contempt, the court's orders must be clear and certain, so that there can be no question as to what the person must do or not do, and no question regarding when

---

[4]Adler v. Adler, 713 N.E.2d 348 (Ind. Ct. App. 1999); Meyer v. Wolvos, 707 N.E.2d 1029 (Ind. Ct. App. 1999), reh'g denied, (May 13, 1999) and transfer denied, (Sept. 20, 1999); Carson v. Ross, 509 N.E.2d 239 (Ind. Ct. App. 1st Dist. 1987), transfer denied, (Apr. 5, 1988).

[5]Nicholas v. Nicholas, 482 N.E.2d 770 (Ind. Ct. App. 1st Dist. 1985).

[6]Carson v. Ross, 509 N.E.2d 239 (Ind. Ct. App. 1st Dist. 1987), transfer denied, (Apr. 5, 1988).

[7]State ex rel. Prosser v. Indiana Waste Systems, Inc., 603 N.E.2d 181 (Ind. Ct. App. 4th Dist. 1992).

[8]Schultz v. State, 227 Ind. 33, 83 N.E.2d 784 (1949).

[9]State ex rel. Taylor v. Circuit Court of Marion County, 240 Ind. 94, 162 N.E.2d 90 (1959); Carson v. Ross, 509 N.E.2d 239 (Ind. Ct. App. 1st Dist. 1987), transfer denied, (Apr. 5, 1988); Smith v. Indiana State Bd. of Health, 158 Ind. App. 445, 303 N.E.2d 50 (1st Dist. 1973).

[10]State ex rel. Leffingwell v. Superior Court No. 2 of Grant County, 262 Ind. 574, 321 N.E.2d 568 (1974) (court had no jurisdiction to order act in violation of statute); Carson v. Ross, 509 N.E.2d 239 (Ind. Ct. App. 1st Dist. 1987), transfer denied, (Apr. 5, 1988).

Annotation References: Right to punish for contempt for failure to obey court order or decree either beyond power or jurisdiction of court or merely erroneous, 12 ALR2d 1059.

[11]Carson v. Ross, 509 N.E.2d 239 (Ind. Ct. App. 1st Dist. 1987), transfer denied, (Apr. 5, 1988).

[12]Crowl v. Berryhill, 678 N.E.2d 828 (Ind. Ct. App. 1997).

the order is violated.[13] All conditions necessary to the performance or injunction in an order or decree must be set forth. Where performance is required, but no date for its completion is set out in the decree or order, no contempt proceeding will lie for nonperformance.[14] Further, a party may not be held in contempt for failing to comply with an order that is too ambiguous or indefinite to be obeyed.[15] On the other hand, one charged with contempt for disobeying an injunction may not set up his or her opinion as to the meaning of the order against that of the court, and still less may defeat the contempt action by showing partial obedience to the order in issue, while at the same time violating it in other essential particulars.[16]

Generally, inability to comply with a court's mandate or order will excuse noncompliance therewith, unless this inability results from the subject's own wrongful act.[17] The party claiming impossibility of performance has the burden of proof on the issue.[18]

In rare cases, conditions in existence when an order or decree is entered may change so dramatically as to provide a defense to a contempt proceeding, or the court may make a ruling which obviates some or all of the burden of performance or restraint in the order or decree in issue. The defense of changed conditions is more likely to be asserted

---

[13]Vanderkooi v. Echelbarger, 250 Ind. 175, 235 N.E.2d 165 (1968); Meyer v. Wolvos, 707 N.E.2d 1029 (Ind. Ct. App. 1999), reh'g denied, (May 13, 1999) and transfer denied, (Sept. 20, 1999).

[14]Rielay v. Whitcher, 18 Ind. 458, 1862 WL 2172 (1862) (no attachment of party for failure to answer interrogatories under a rule prescribing no deadline for answers).

[15]Uservo, Inc. v. Selking, 217 Ind. 567, 28 N.E.2d 61 (1940) (decree calling for exchange of "standard" milk bottles not sufficiently specific absent definition of "standard"); Rendon v. Rendon, 692 N.E.2d 889 (Ind. Ct. App. 1998).

[16]United Farm Bureau Mut. Ins. Co. v. Ira, 577 N.E.2d 588 (Ind. Ct. App. 4th Dist. 1991), transfer denied, (Dec. 30, 1991).

[17]Thomas v. Woollen, 255 Ind. 612, 266 N.E.2d 20 (1971); Adler v. Adler, 713 N.E.2d 348 (Ind. Ct. App. 1999).

Annotation References: Pleading and burden of proof, in contempt proceedings, as to ability to comply with order for payment of alimony or child support, 53 ALR2d 591.

[18]Head v. Commissioner, Indiana Dept. of Environmental Management, 626 N.E.2d 518 (Ind. Ct. App. 3d Dist. 1993), reh'g denied, (Mar. 7, 1994) and transfer denied, (June 20, 1994).

as part of a defense of impossibility of performance, but subsequent rulings may provide a defense of new determination.[19]

§ 10 Failure to appear for hearing, trial, deposition, or jury service

Failure without adequate excuse to appear as ordered at a hearing or trial, to produce documentary evidence, or for the taking of a deposition may be deemed a contempt of court.

West's Digest, Contempt ⊸12-14, 20, 23.

Statutes and rules of procedure provide that a failure by any person without adequate excuse to obey a subpoena served upon him or her, for attendance or testimony at a hearing or trial, to produce documentary evidence, or for the taking of a deposition, may be deemed a contempt of (1) the court from which the subpoena is issued, or (2) the court of the county where the witness was required to appear or act.[20] If a witness subpoenaed to appear before a grand jury fails to appear at the time and place stated in the subpoena, the court may hold the witness in contempt of court, unless he or she had filed a motion to quash the subpoena and the motion has been granted or was pending at the time the witness was to have appeared.[21]

 ◆ **Observation:** The statutes pertaining generally to direct and indirect contempt[22] do not apply to any case where a person has been personally served with notice to appear and testify as a witness in any court in Indiana in any civil or criminal case. A court may proceed against a person who fails to appear as a witness for contempt of

---

[19]17 C.J.S., Contempt § 17.

Bowers v. State ex rel. Taylor, 127 Ind. 272, 26 N.E. 798 (1891) (child suspended from school for rule not violated could not be suspended for violation after rule changed).

[20]IC 35-37-5-2(g) (criminal and grand jury proceedings); Trial R. 45(F) (civil proceedings).

[21]IC 35-34-2-5(c).

Forms References: Motion—For order to show cause—Alleged contempt by witness for refusal to comply with order to appear before grand jury. 7 Am Jur Pleading and Practice Forms, Annotated (rev. ed.), Contempt § 39.

[22]IC 34-47-2-1 et seq.; IC 34-47-3-1 et seq.

court (1) by attachment, and (2) as though the statutes pertaining generally to direct and indirect contempt were not in force.[23]

The failure of an ordinary lay witness to appear for a hearing as ordered will generally constitute an indirect contempt, where the witness has not been given an opportunity to explain his or her absence and thereby purge the contempt; in such a case, the judge has not had personal knowledge of contemptuous conduct by the witness.[24] An attorney or other court officer stands in contempt upon failure to appear at a judicial proceeding that he or she is legally required to attend, and if the attorney or officer refuses to explain such absence, or offers an insulting, frivolous, or clearly inadequate explanation, both the absence and the lack of an adequate reason therefor occur in the presence of the court, and the attorney or officer may be cited summarily for direct contempt.[25] However, the matter should be treated as indirect contempt if the attorney or officer presents an adequate explanation for his or her absence from the courtroom, and the court's business has not been interfered with.[26]

A person summoned for jury service who fails to appear or complete jury service as directed must be ordered by the

---

[23]IC 34-47-1-1.

[24]Williams v. State ex rel. Harris, 690 N.E.2d 315 (Ind. Ct. App. 1997) (father's unexplained failure to appear at a hearing to determine child support was not direct contempt).

[25]In re Nasser, 644 N.E.2d 93 (Ind. 1994) (attorney failed to appear on trial date without verifying whether continuance granted); Howard v. Korte, 555 N.E.2d 166 (Ind. Ct. App. 3d Dist. 1990) (attorney claimed that he missed mailed notice because he was a sole practitioner involved in many other matters and his secretary was sick and he did not open mail).

Annotation References: Attorney's failure to attend court, or tardiness, as contempt, 13 ALR4th 122.

Forms References: Order of Direct Contempt—Oral form—Nonappearance or late appearance of attorney. 7 Am Jur Pleading and Practice Forms, Annotated (rev. ed.), Contempt § 122.

Order of Direct Contempt—Written order following oral order—Nonappearance or late appearance of attorney. 7 Am Jur Pleading and Practice Forms, Annotated (rev. ed.), Contempt § 123.

Affidavit of contempt—For failure of attorney to appear. 7 Am Jur Pleading and Practice Forms, Annotated (rev. ed.), Contempt §§ 18-19.1.

[26]Curtis v. State, 625 N.E.2d 496 (Ind. Ct. App. 2d Dist. 1993); Broderick v. Denbo, 413 N.E.2d 948 (Ind. Ct. App. 4th Dist. 1980), reh'g denied, 416 N.E.2d 175 (Ind. Ct. App. 4th Dist. 1981), opinion vacated on other grounds, 422 N.E.2d 1334 (Ind. Ct. App. 4th Dist. 1981) and opinion

court to immediately appear and show cause for the person's failure to comply with the summons. If the person fails to show good cause for noncompliance with the summons, the person is guilty of criminal contempt and upon conviction may be fined not more than $100 or imprisoned in the county jail for not more than three days, or both.[27]

§ 11 Refusal to be sworn or to testify; false testimony

A direct contempt of court is committed where one is sworn to testify as a witness in a trial or proceeding and he or she refuses to do so, or a person is required by the court to be sworn in a trial or proceeding and he or she refuses to take an oath or affirmation. A witness who knowingly gives false testimony after taking the oath is guilty of direct contempt.

West's Digest, Contempt ⊙13, 14, 20, 23.

One is guilty of direct contempt of court who (1) is sworn to testify as a witness, in any trial or proceeding, in any court of record, and refuses to testify in the trial or proceeding; or (2) is required by any court to be sworn in any trial or proceeding, and refuses to take an oath or affirmation.[28] Thus, a witness who is sworn but refuses to answer proper questions during a hearing commits a direct contempt.[29] If a witness refuses to give the evidence after he or she has been granted use immunity, the court may likewise find the witness in direct[30] contempt.[31]

---

vacated in part on other grounds, 422 N.E.2d 1334 (Ind. Ct. App. 4th Dist. 1981) supra.

Forms References: Indirect Contempt. 7 Am Jur Pleading and Practice Forms, Annotated (rev. ed.), Contempt §§ 126-143.

[27]IC 33-4-11-24.

[28]IC 34-47-2-2.

As to direct contempt, generally, see § 4.

As to contempt liability for influencing or intimidating a witness to abstain from giving testimony in any case, see § 12.

[29]Matter of Contempt of Lustina, 683 N.E.2d 236 (Ind. 1997); Jacobsen v. State, 179 Ind. App. 37, 384 N.E.2d 1041 (3d Dist. 1979).

[30]In re Caito, 459 N.E.2d 1179 (Ind. 1984).

[31]IC 35-37-3-3(c).

◆ **Observation:** The court may not find a witness guilty of a separate act of contempt for each time he or she refuses to answer a question.[32]

A finding that a witness is in direct contempt for refusing to answer proper questions is not precluded by the witness' unilateral determination that the testimony called for by the questions is immaterial or irrelevant to the issues in the case.[33] If the witness asserts an inability to answer questions as ordered by the court, the burden is on the witness to prove such inability.[34]

If the defendant in a proceeding for indirect contempt appears in court, but fails or refuses to answer concerning the alleged contempt, the court may proceed at once, and without any further delay, to attach and punish the defendant for contempt.[35]

If a deponent fails to be sworn or to answer a question after being directed to do so by the court in the county in which the deposition is being taken, the failure may be considered a contempt of that court.[36]

Giving false testimony under oath, the falsity of which cannot be known personally by the court but only inferred by reference to later testimony, and which causes no disturbance, disruption, or palpable offense to the proceedings, unlike a refusal to testify, does not warrant a summary conviction and, therefore, is not a direct contempt.[37]

§ 12 Influencing or intimidating witness, juror, or court officer

Influencing, intimidating, or attempting to influence a witness to give or abstain from giving testimony in a case, or to abstain from attending as a witness in a case, is a

---

[32]In re Contempt Findings Against Schultz, 428 N.E.2d 1284 (Ind. Ct. App. 1st Dist. 1981).

[33]Aguilar v. State, 416 N.E.2d 887 (Ind. Ct. App. 2d Dist. 1981) (expert opinion in criminal trial).

[34]Aguilar v. State, 416 N.E.2d 887 (Ind. Ct. App. 2d Dist. 1981).

[35]IC 34-47-3-6.

[36]Trial R. 37(B)(1).

[37]In re Marriage of Neiswinger, 477 N.E.2d 257 (Ind. 1985).

Forms References: Affidavit of Contempt—For perjury by witness. 7 Am Jur Pleading and Practice Forms, Annotated (rev. ed.), Contempt § 33.

contempt of court. Assaulting or attempting to influence a judge, juror, or other court officer in connection with his or her duties in a proceeding is likewise a contempt of court.

West's Digest, Contempt ☞3, 6, 7, 12, 13.

A person commits a direct contempt of court if, in the court's presence, the person (1) offers, gives, or promises any reward to a witness, (2) threatens to assault or injure a witness, (3) assaults or beats a witness, or (4) in any other manner influences, intimidates, or attempts to influence such witness to give or abstain from giving testimony in any case, or to abstain from attending as a witness in any case.[38] One also commits a direct contempt by doing any act in the court's presence to put a witness in fear, on account of any testimony that the witness may have given,[39] or, on account of any testimony, by injuring or threatening to injure a witness.[40] If the acts are done elsewhere, out of the presence of the court, such acts constitute indirect contempt.[41]

A person may be punished for contempt if he or she removes a witness, and by advice and direction causes the witness to avoid service of a subpoena as such,[42] but not if no subpoena has yet issued,[43] or if he or she merely aids and assists a person's departure, without persuasion or coercion.[44]

Assaulting a judge, juror, attorney, or officer of the court on account of the performance of his or her duties in connec-

---

[38]IC 34-47-2-3(1).

As to contempt liability for failure to appear as ordered or required in a proceeding, see § 10.

As to contempt liability for refusing to be sworn or to testify in a proceeding, or for giving false testimony, see § 11.

Forms References: Affidavit of Contempt—For dissuading witness under subpoena from attending court. 7 Am Jur Pleading and Practice Forms, Annotated (rev. ed.), Contempt § 32.

Affidavit of Contempt—For attempting to bribe juror. 7 Am Jur Pleading and Practice Forms, Annotated (rev. ed.), Contempt § 37.

[39]IC 34-47-2-3(2).

[40]IC 34-47-2-3(3).

[41]IC 34-47-3-3.

As to direct and indirect contempt, generally, see § 4.

[42]Haskett v. State, 51 Ind. 176, 1875 WL 6107 (1875).

[43]McConnell v. State, 46 Ind. 298, 1874 WL 6095 (1874).

[44]Whittem v. State, 36 Ind. 196, 1871 WL 5004 (1871) (absence of party).

tion with court proceedings, or to deter him or her from such performance in the future, is a contempt of court.[45]

Willful attempts to improperly influence jurors in the impartial discharge of their duties constitute criminal contempt,[46] as does a purported offer to bribe a juror.[47]

§ 13   Contemptuous publications

A false or grossly inaccurate report of a pending trial or proceeding, of a character tending or calculated to corrupt or embarrass the administration of justice or to reflect negatively on the court, parties, jurors, witnesses, or counsel, is an indirect contempt.

West's Digest, Contempt ☞8, 9.

A person who makes, utters, or publishes any false or grossly inaccurate report of any case, trial, or proceeding, or part of any case, trial, or proceeding, is considered guilty of an indirect contempt of the court in which the case, trial, or proceeding was instituted, held, or determined, if made at any time:

(1) after the proceeding commenced;

(2) while the proceeding is pending;

(3) while the court has jurisdiction; and

(4) before the proceeding is fully determined and ended.[48]

If a such a report is made pending the case, trial, or proceeding, and concerning any ruling or order of the court,

---

[45]Dossett v. State, 226 Ind. 142, 78 N.E.2d 435 (1948).

[46]17 C.J.S., Contempt § 24.

[47]Little v. State, 90 Ind. 338, 1883 WL 5624 (1883).

[48]IC 34-47-3-4(a).

As to direct and indirect contempt, generally, see § 4.

Annotation References: Publication or broadcast, during course of trial, of matter prejudicial to criminal defendant, as contempt, 53 ALR3d 591.

False or inaccurate report of judicial proceedings as contempt, 99 ALR2d 440.

Published article or broadcast as direct contempt of court, 69 ALR2d 676.

Forms References: Proceedings to Punish For Contempt—Particular Acts—Publication Critical of Court or Judicial Officer. 7 Am Jur Pleading and Practice Forms, Annotated (rev. ed.), Contempt §§ 67-70.

the person is considered guilty of an indirect contempt of the
court making the ruling or order.[49]

◆ **Observation:** Issues involving constitutional rights to
free speech and freedom of the press have arisen in actions to punish an allegedly contemptuous publication.
The Untied States Supreme Court has reversed several
decisions from other jurisdictions finding such contempt,
holding that the particular publications were within
constitutional protections guaranteeing freedom of the
press, and that they did not sufficiently endanger the
administration of justice to take them outside the cloak of
that protection.[50]

To be contemptuous, it is not enough that a report be false
or grossly inaccurate,[51] but it must be of a character tending
or calculated to corrupt or embarrass the administration of
justice, or to reflect negatively on the court or its proceedings,
or on the parties, jurors, witnesses, or counsel.[52] Moreover,
the publication generally must have reference to a matter
pending in court.[53] Publications regarding a matter that has
been finally adjudicated, so that carrying out of the court's
judgment cannot be obstructed by the publication, are not
contempt[54] and cannot be summarily punished, unless the

---

[49]IC 34-47-3-4(b).

[50]Craig v. Harney, 331 U.S. 367, 67 S. Ct. 1249, 91 L. Ed. 1546 (1947),
mandate conformed to, 150 Tex. Crim. 598, 204 S.W.2d 842 (1947); Pen-
nekamp v. State of Fla., 328 U.S. 331, 66 S. Ct. 1029, 90 L. Ed. 1295 (1946);
Bridges v. State of Cal., 314 U.S. 252, 62 S. Ct. 190, 86 L. Ed. 192, 159
ALR 1346 (1941).

[51]Cheadle v. State, 110 Ind. 301, 11 N.E. 426 (1887).

[52]Nixon v. State, 207 Ind. 426, 193 N.E. 591, 97 ALR 894 (1935); Dale
v. State, 198 Ind. 110, 150 N.E. 781, 49 ALR 647 (1926), error dismissed,
273 U.S. 776, 47 S. Ct. 332, 71 L. Ed. 886 (1927) and error dismissed, 274
U.S. 763, 47 S. Ct. 591, 71 L. Ed. 1322 (1927) and (disapproved of on other
grounds by, La Grange v. State, 238 Ind. 689, 153 N.E.2d 593, 69 ALR 2d
668 (1958)); Kilgallen v. State, 192 Ind. 531, 132 N.E. 682 (1921), reh'g
overruled, 192 Ind. 531, 137 N.E. 178 (1922); Ray v. State, 186 Ind. 396,
114 N.E. 866 (1917); Cheadle v. State, 110 Ind. 301, 11 N.E. 426 (1887).

[53]Nixon v. State, 207 Ind. 426, 193 N.E. 591, 97 ALR 894 (1935).

[54]Nixon v. State, 207 Ind. 426, 193 N.E. 591, 97 ALR 894 (1935); Zuver
v. State, 188 Ind. 60, 121 N.E. 828 (1919) (unjustifiable criticism of court's
conduct is not contempt where matter had been fully disposed of before
criticism was published); Cheadle v. State, 110 Ind. 301, 11 N.E. 426
(1887) (however stringent or libelous, newspaper comments relating to

publication may obstruct, impede, interfere with, or embarrass the court in future stages of the case.[55]

◆ **Illustrations:** Publications referring to the prior appointment of a receiver and to his character, qualifications, and the influence which brought about his appointment did not constitute contempt and could not be summarily punished, although the receivership proceeding was still pending, because the publications related to a past transaction and would not obstruct, impede, interfere with, or embarrass the court in the administration of justice in future stages of the case.[56] On the other hand, the publisher of an article reflecting on a grand jury during its session, tending to bring its members into disrepute and embarrass their investigation as to the commission of a crime, was liable for contempt even though the investigation had been suspended with no intention at the time to pursue it further, where the investigation might nevertheless have been resumed.[57]

The meaning and intent of an allegedly contemptuous publication are questions of law to be determined by the court,[58] upon a consideration of the whole document.[59] To constitute a criminal contempt, a publication must be characterized by a deliberate intention to defy the authority of the court.[60] Where the content of the publication is unambiguous and clearly contemptuous, the author's intent is conclusively established, but where the content is ambiguous, and the al-

---

proceedings which are past and ended are not in contempt of the authority of the court to which reference is made).

[55]Nixon v. State, 207 Ind. 426, 193 N.E. 591, 97 ALR 894 (1935).

[56]Nixon v. State, 207 Ind. 426, 193 N.E. 591, 97 ALR 894 (1935).

[57]Allen v. State, 131 Ind. 599, 30 N.E. 1093 (1892).

[58]Dale v. State, 198 Ind. 110, 150 N.E. 781, 49 ALR 647 (1926), error dismissed, 273 U.S. 776, 47 S. Ct. 332, 71 L. Ed. 886 (1927) and error dismissed, 274 U.S. 763, 47 S. Ct. 591, 71 L. Ed. 1322 (1927) and (disapproved of on other grounds by, La Grange v. State, 238 Ind. 689, 153 N.E.2d 593, 69 ALR 2d 668 (1958)).

[59]State v. Shumaker, 200 Ind. 623, 157 N.E. 769, 58 ALR 954 (1927), opinion supplemented on denial of reh'g, 200 Ind. 623, 162 N.E. 441, 58 ALR 954 (1928).

[60]State ex rel. Indianapolis Bar Ass'n v. Fletcher Trust Co., 211 Ind. 27, 5 N.E.2d 538 (1937) (overruled on other grounds by, In re Perrello, 260 Ind. 26, 291 N.E.2d 698 (1973)); Denny v. State, 203 Ind. 682, 182 N.E. 313 (1932).

As to criminal contempt, generally, see § 5.

leged contemnor swears to his or her lack of intent to be disrespectful to the court or to bring it into disrepute, the sworn statement may be considered in defense of the charge.[61] If the publication is considered an indirect contempt, lack of contemptuous intent is a defense.[62]

◆ **Observation:** Where the publication of a newspaper report or comment is charged as constituting contempt, such contempt must be treated as indirect or constructive.[63]

III. PROCEDURE, PUNISHMENT, AND APPEAL

Research References

IC 31-16-12-6; IC 34-26-1-14 to IC 34-26-1-16; IC 34-35-3-3; IC 34-47-2-4; IC 34-47-2-5; IC 34-47-3-5 to IC 34-47-3-8; IC 34-47-4-1; IC 34-47-4-2

17 Am Jur 2d, Contempt §§ 165-247, 254-265.
17 C.J.S., Contempt §§ 63-149.
West's Digest, Contempt ☞30-69.
ALR Digest: Contempt §§ 40-53, 66-73
ALR Index: Contempt
7 Am Jur Pleading and Practice Forms, Annotated (rev. ed.), Contempt §§ 1-189.

§ 14 Contempt proceedings, generally

A contempt proceeding is neither criminal nor civil, but is sui generis.

West's Digest, Contempt ☞37, 39, 40.

While it has been said that a prosecution for criminal contempt is in the nature of a criminal action, because the purpose of both is punishment for some sort of undesirable act or omission,[64] contempt proceedings are essentially sui

---

[61]La Grange v. State, 238 Ind. 689, 153 N.E.2d 593, 69 ALR 2d 668 (1958); State ex rel. Indianapolis Bar Ass'n v. Fletcher Trust Co., 211 Ind. 27, 5 N.E.2d 538 (1937) (overruled on other grounds by, In re Perrello, 260 Ind. 26, 291 N.E.2d 698 (1973)).

[62]Nixon v. State, 207 Ind. 426, 193 N.E. 591, 97 ALR 894 (1935).

[63]La Grange v. State, 238 Ind. 689, 153 N.E.2d 593, 69 ALR 2d 668 (1958) (radio newscast interview could only be considered indirect contempt).

[64]Allison v. State ex rel. Allison, 243 Ind. 489, 187 N.E.2d 565 (1963).

generis, being neither civil, criminal, nor equitable.[65] Both civil and criminal contempt can arise out of the same conduct.[66]

An allegation of willfulness is not decisive of whether a contempt proceeding is civil or criminal.[67] At least in the case of criminal contempt, the existence of another remedy does not preclude an adjudication of contempt, and the doctrine of election of remedies is therefore inapplicable.[68]

Whether a party is in contempt is a matter within the discretion of the trial court.[69]

§ 15 Civil contempt

Civil contempt may be instituted on a motion or petition in the civil action from which the alleged contempt arose.

West's Digest, Contempt ☞41-50, 54-61.

A proceeding for civil contempt should be filed in the original civil action out of which it grew,[70] and should bear the same caption.[71] Although a civil contempt proceeding may be

---

[65]Crowl v. Berryhill, 678 N.E.2d 828 (Ind. Ct. App. 1997); Mitchell v. Stevenson, 677 N.E.2d 551 (Ind. Ct. App. 1997), transfer denied, 683 N.E.2d 594 (Ind. 1997).

As to criminal and civil contempt, generally, see § 5.

[66]Mitchell v. Stevenson, 677 N.E.2d 551 (Ind. Ct. App. 1997), transfer denied, 683 N.E.2d 594 (Ind. 1997).

[67]Duemling v. Fort Wayne Community Concerts, Inc., 243 Ind. 521, 188 N.E.2d 274 (1963).

[68]Coons v. State, 191 Ind. 580, 134 N.E. 194, 20 ALR 900 (1922) (action for libel where defendant accused in grand jury report of conspiracy).

[69]Cowart v. White, 711 N.E.2d 523 (Ind. 1999), on reh'g, 716 N.E.2d 401 (Ind. 1999) and reh'g granted on other grounds, (Sept. 22, 1999); Meyer v. Wolvos, 707 N.E.2d 1029 (Ind. Ct. App. 1999), reh'g denied, (May 13, 1999) and transfer denied, (Sept. 20, 1999); Hancz v. City of South Bend, 691 N.E.2d 1322 (Ind. Ct. App. 1998); Williams v. State ex rel. Harris, 690 N.E.2d 315 (Ind. Ct. App. 1997); Mitchell v. Stevenson, 677 N.E.2d 551 (Ind. Ct. App. 1997), transfer denied, 683 N.E.2d 594 (Ind. 1997).

[70]State ex rel. Cook v. Superior Court of Allen County, No. 1, 247 Ind. 614, 220 N.E.2d 342 (1966); State ex rel. Brubaker v. Pritchard, 236 Ind. 222, 138 N.E.2d 233, 60 ALR 2d 1239 (1956).

As to civil contempt, generally, see § 5.

Forms References: Proceeding to Punish For Contempt. 7 Am Jur Pleading and Practice Forms, Annotated (rev. ed.), Contempt §§ 5-154.

[71]State ex rel. McMinn v. Gentry, 229 Ind. 615, 100 N.E.2d 676 (1951).

part of another action, an adjudication of contempt is not a judgment on the merits of the pre-existing cause of action, or on the rights of the litigants.[72]

A civil contempt proceeding may be instituted by a motion or petition,[73] which should either be verified or supported by the affidavit of someone having personal knowledge of the relevant facts.[74] The strictness in pleading required in cases of criminal contempt does not apply to civil proceedings,[75] and it is sufficient that the charge show the order of the court and facts evidencing its violation.[76] The defendant may interpose an unverified answer,[77] to which the accuser may make a reply.[78]

Contrary to the practice in cases of indirect criminal contempt,[79] the defendant's answer, even if verified, is not conclusive,[80] and the court may hear evidence[81] introduced by either party.[82] Generally, the burden of proving contempt in a civil proceeding is on the accuser,[83] but the defendant

---

[72]Smoot v. Smoot, 604 N.E.2d 618 (Ind. Ct. App. 1st Dist. 1992), transfer denied, (Mar. 26, 1993); Matter of May, 171 Ind. App. 440, 358 N.E.2d 138 (1st Dist. 1976).

[73]State ex rel. Brubaker v. Pritchard, 236 Ind. 222, 138 N.E.2d 233, 60 ALR 2d 1239 (1956); Lane v. Campbell, 214 Ind. 376, 14 N.E.2d 552 (1938); Denny v. State, 203 Ind. 682, 182 N.E. 313 (1932).

[74]In re Perrello, 260 Ind. 26, 291 N.E.2d 698 (1973); Allison v. State ex rel. Allison, 243 Ind. 489, 187 N.E.2d 565 (1963); Carey v. Carey, 132 Ind. App. 30, 171 N.E.2d 487 (Div. 1 1961).

[75]Hays v. Hays, 216 Ind. 62, 22 N.E.2d 971 (1939).

As to pleading in cases of indirect criminal contempt, generally, see § 17.

[76]Carey v. Carey, 132 Ind. App. 30, 171 N.E.2d 487 (Div. 1 1961); Hays v. Hays, 216 Ind. 62, 22 N.E.2d 971 (1939).

[77]Local Union No. 135, Affiliated with Intern. Broth. of Teamsters, Chauffeurs, Warehousemen and Helpers of America, A. F. L. v. Merchandise Warehouse Co., 240 Ind. 153, 159 N.E.2d 388 (1959).

[78]Denny v. State, 203 Ind. 682, 182 N.E. 313 (1932).

[79]§ 17.

[80]Duemling v. Fort Wayne Community Concerts, Inc., 243 Ind. 521, 188 N.E.2d 274 (1963) (verified answer in purgation is not sufficient).

[81]Duemling v. Fort Wayne Community Concerts, Inc., 243 Ind. 521, 188 N.E.2d 274 (1963); Hays v. Hays, 216 Ind. 62, 22 N.E.2d 971 (1939).

[82]Denny v. State, 203 Ind. 682, 182 N.E. 313 (1932).

[83]In re Savage, 213 Ind. 228, 12 N.E.2d 141 (1938).

has the burden of proof on any affirmative defenses.[84] If the alleged contemnor seeks to excuse him- or herself from obeying an order on account of inability, he or she has the burden of showing inability.[85]

The defendant in a civil contempt proceeding is not entitled to a change of venue under the statute providing for such a change in any matter of a civil, statutory, or equitable nature not triable by a jury[86] because contempt is none of these.[87] Nor is a change of venue in civil contempt proceedings authorized by the statute providing for special judges in cases of indirect contempt,[88] as this statute applies to criminal contempt only.[89]

§ 16 Direct criminal contempt

Direct criminal contempt may be punished summarily, without notice or evidence, but the judge must make a written statement detailing the conduct of the defendant that is alleged to constitute the contempt.

West's Digest, Contempt ☞51-53, 54(1), 57, 61(6), 62, 63.

Trial and punishment for direct contempt is summary.[90] A statute provides that when a person is arraigned for a direct contempt in any court of record in Indiana, no affidavit, written charge, or complaint is required to be filed against the contemnor.[91] The contemnor may be arrested and brought before the court without any initiatory accusation,[92] and he or she may be punished instantly, without proof or examina-

---

[84]Thomas v. Woollen, 255 Ind. 612, 266 N.E.2d 20 (1971).

[85]Carey v. Carey, 132 Ind. App. 30, 171 N.E.2d 487 (Div. 1 1961).

[86]IC 34-35-3-3.

[87]State ex rel. Trotcky v. Hutchinson, 224 Ind. 443, 68 N.E.2d 649 (1946).

[88]IC 34-47-3-7, discussed more fully in § 19.

[89]In re Savage, 213 Ind. 228, 12 N.E.2d 141 (1938).

[90]Williams v. State ex rel. Harris, 690 N.E.2d 315 (Ind. Ct. App. 1997); Johnson v. State, 426 N.E.2d 104 (Ind. Ct. App. 3d Dist. 1981).

As to direct contempt, generally, see § 4.

As to punishment for contempt, generally, see § 21.

[91]IC 34-47-2-4(a).

[92]Coons v. State, 191 Ind. 580, 134 N.E. 194, 20 ALR 900 (1922).

tion other than what is known to the senses of the trial judge.[93]

> ◆ **Observation:** While the statute refers to the offender as a person "arraigned," the word is not used in the same sense as it is used in criminal law,[94] and there is no separate privilege of arraignment.[95]

Although no formal written charge is required, the judge must distinctly state the act, words, signs, gestures, or other conduct of the defendant that is alleged to constitute the contempt, which statement must be reduced to writing either by the judge making the statement or by a reporter authorized by the judge to take down the statement when it is made.[96] The court may reduce the charge to writing on a date subsequent to the contempt proceeding.[97] To satisfy the statutory requirement that the trial court distinctly state the acts constituting a party's direct contempt, the court's finding must recite in detail the acts found to have been committed and which constitute contempt.[98] A determination that a party was guilty of contempt may be reversed if the court's finding merely recites conclusions that the defendant was contemptuous.[99] If the statement made by the trial court does not disclose contemptuous conduct, it may be presumed that there was none.[1]

The court's order on the contempt must substantially set forth the court's factual findings, together with any statement made in explanation, extenuation, or denial of the contempt, which the defendant may make in response to the judge's statement.[2] A verified denial does not entitle a defendant to a discharge.[3]

Because criminal contempt is disrespect or disobedience to

---

[93]Curtis v. State, 625 N.E.2d 496 (Ind.App. 2 Dist. 1993).

[94]Mahoney v. State, 33 Ind. App. 655, 72 N.E. 151 (Div. 1 1904).

[95]Coons v. State, 191 Ind. 580, 134 N.E. 194, 20 ALR 900 (1922).

[96]IC 34-47-2-4(b).

[97]Mahoney v. State, 33 Ind. App. 655, 72 N.E. 151 (Div. 1 1904).

[98]Matter of Contempt of Steelman, 648 N.E.2d 366 (Ind. Ct. App. 2d Dist. 1995).

[99]State ex rel. Stanton v. Murray, 231 Ind. 223, 108 N.E.2d 251 (1952); Carey v. Carey, 132 Ind. App. 30, 171 N.E.2d 487 (Ind. App. 1961).

[1]State ex rel. Stanton v. Murray, 231 Ind. 223, 108 N.E.2d 251 (1952).

[2]IC 34-47-2-4(b).

[3]Skolnick v. State, 180 Ind. App. 253, 388 N.E.2d 1156 (3d Dist. 1979)

the sovereign power as exercised by and residing in the court,[4] the state is a necessary and proper party to a criminal contempt proceeding;[5] however, the failure to bring a criminal contempt proceeding in the name of the state does not make the proceeding defective.[6]

The court is to pronounce judgment upon the judge's and defendant's statements as discussed above, either acquitting and discharging the defendant or inflicting such punishment upon the defendant as may be consistent with the applicable statutes.[7] In all cases where the defendant is adjudged to pay a fine of at least $50 or to be imprisoned for contempt, the defendant has the right, either before or after paying the fine or undergoing the imprisonment, to move the court to reconsider its opinion and judgment of the case upon the facts before the court, or the affidavits of any or all persons who were actually present and heard or saw the conduct that was alleged to have constituted the contempt.[8] If the defendant does not present affidavits, the court may, on its own motion, direct their procurement.[9]

The defendant may also move the court for a new trial and recision of the court's judgment against the defendant, based upon all affidavits and the original statements of the court and the defendant concerning the contempt.[10] If the court overrules such a motion, the defendant may appeal as in other criminal actions.[11]

§ 17   Indirect criminal contempt, generally

A proceeding to punish for indirect criminal contempt is

(denial of due process); La Grange v. State, 238 Ind. 689, 153 N.E.2d 593, 69 ALR 2d 668 (1958).

[4]§ 5.

[5]Brumbaugh v. State, 491 N.E.2d 983 (Ind. 1986); In re Perrello, 260 Ind. 26, 291 N.E.2d 698 (1973).

[6]Matter of May, 171 Ind. App. 440, 358 N.E.2d 138 (1st Dist. 1976).

[7]IC 34-47-2-4(d).

As to punishment and other sanctions for contempt, generally, see § 21.

[8]IC-34-47-2-5(b).

[9]IC 34-47-2-5(c).

[10]IC 34-47-2-5(d).

[11]IC 34-47-2-5(e).

As to appeal and review of contempt findings, generally, see § 22.

>commenced by the state through the filing of a verified
>charge.

West's Digest, Contempt ☞41-50, 54.

A proceeding to punish for indirect criminal contempt is
an action independent from any judicial matter already
pending before the court.[12] Such a proceeding should be prosecuted by the state[13] and entitled "State of Indiana versus
the defendant."[14] Although the better practice is to entitle
the proceedings as being brought by the state alone, the
joinder of an improper party as the "petitioner" or "plaintiff"
is not a defect which would obviate the standing of the proper
party.[15] The criminal contempt proceeding may be commenced by an "information" which must state the act or
refusal to act for which contempt punishment is sought.[16]
This is the procedure followed in an original indirect
contempt proceeding in the Supreme Court.[17]

Punishment for an indirect contempt may not be summary,
as in the case of a direct contempt,[18] and steps can be taken
only after the filing of a verified charge.[19]

The facts relating to an alleged indirect contempt are
determined from verified pleadings, and the affidavit should
charge that acts have been done or omitted with the intention to defy the authority of the state as vested in the court.[20]
The affidavit should be upon the informant's oath and upon

---

[12]Brumbaugh v. State, 491 N.E.2d 983 (Ind. 1986); Hancz v. City of
South Bend, 691 N.E.2d 1322 (Ind. Ct. App. 1998).

[13]Brumbaugh v. State, 491 N.E.2d 983 (Ind. 1986); In re Perrello, 260
Ind. 26, 291 N.E.2d 698 (1973); Allison v. State ex rel. Allison, 243 Ind.
489, 187 N.E.2d 565 (1963) (no private party as prosecutor in criminal
contempt); Hancz v. City of South Bend, 691 N.E.2d 1322 (Ind. Ct. App.
1998).

[14]Brumbaugh v. State, 491 N.E.2d 983 (Ind. 1986); In re Perrello, 260
Ind. 26, 291 N.E.2d 698 (1973).

[15]Allison v. State ex rel. Allison, 243 Ind. 489, 187 N.E.2d 565 (1963).

[16]Brumbaugh v. State, 491 N.E.2d 983 (Ind. 1986).

[17]Brumbaugh v. State, 491 N.E.2d 983 (Ind. 1986).

[18]La Grange v. State, 238 Ind. 689, 153 N.E.2d 593, 69 ALR 2d 668
(1958); State ex rel. Stanton v. Murray, 231 Ind. 223, 108 N.E.2d 251
(1952).

As to proceedings for direct contempt, generally, see § 16.

[19]In re Perrello, 260 Ind. 26, 291 N.E.2d 698 (1973); Allison v. State ex
rel. Allison, 243 Ind. 489, 187 N.E.2d 565 (1963).

[20]Carey v. Carey, 132 Ind. App. 30, 171 N.E.2d 487 (Ind.App. 1961).

the informant's personal responsibility, and a proceeding is defective if the affidavit is unverified, even though made by the judge on his or her personal knowledge.[21] The affidavit should clearly and distinctly charge the acts alleged, specifying their time and place with such reasonable certainty as to inform the defendant of the nature and circumstances of the charge.[22] The affidavit should state the necessary facts with the certainty required in a complaint or indictment,[23] and all ambiguities or uncertainties therein must be construed against the state.[24]

§ 18 Notice and process; rule, citation, attachment, and bail

> Indirect contempt of court may be punished only upon notice or process, in the form of a rule to show cause or citation served upon the alleged contemnor. To procure personal jurisdiction over the alleged contemnor, the court may issue a writ of attachment directing that such person be taken into custody and subject to release on bail or escrow.

West's Digest, Contempt ☞54-57.

A court may not punish for indirect contempt one who is not subject to the court's jurisdiction[25] or who has no notice of the entry of the order allegedly disobeyed or of the contempt proceeding.[26] A person guilty of a direct contempt may be arrested and brought before the court without any initiatory accusation,[27] but the rule is otherwise as to indirect contempt, which requires written notice or process and service thereof on the alleged contemnor.[28] A defendant may,

---

[21]In re Perrello, 260 Ind. 26, 291 N.E.2d 698 (1973); Allison v. State ex rel. Allison, 243 Ind. 489, 187 N.E.2d 565 (1963).

[22]In re Perrello, 260 Ind. 26, 291 N.E.2d 698 (1973); Kilgallen v. State, 192 Ind. 531, 132 N.E. 682 (1921), reh'g overruled, 192 Ind. 531, 137 N.E. 178 (1922); Hancz v. City of South Bend, 691 N.E.2d 1322 (Ind.App. 1998).

[23]In re Perrello, 260 Ind. 26, 291 N.E.2d 698 (1973); Davis v. Overman, 184 Ind. 647, 112 N.E. 243 (1916).

[24]Tusing v. State, 241 Ind. 650, 175 N.E.2d 17 (1961).

[25]Jacobsen v. State, 179 Ind. App. 37, 384 N.E.2d 1041 (3d Dist. 1979).

[26]Meade v. Levett, 671 N.E.2d 1172 (Ind. Ct. App. 1996).

[27]§ 16.

[28]Meade v. Levett, 671 N.E.2d 1172 (Ind. Ct. App. 1996); National Educ. Association—South Bend v. South Bend Community School Corp.,

however, waive lack of notice or process by appearing voluntarily.[29]

Before answering the charge or being punished for the contempt, a person charged with indirect contempt is entitled to be served with a rule of the court against which the contempt was alleged to have been committed.[30] The rule to show cause must:[31]

(1) clearly and distinctly set forth the facts that are alleged to constitute the contempt;

(2) specify the time and place of the facts with reasonable certainty, as to inform the defendant of the nature and circumstances of the charge against the defendant; and

(3) specify a time and place at which the defendant is required to show cause, in the court, why the defendant should not be attached and punished for such contempt.

The court shall, on a proper showing, extend the time provided in the rule for showing cause to give the defendant a reasonable and just opportunity to be purged of the contempt.[32] A rule to show cause may not issue until the facts alleged to constitute the contempt have been brought to the knowledge of the court by an information and duly verified by the oath of affirmation of some officer of the court or other responsible person.[33]

The court is also statutorily authorized to order a citation issued to the sheriff of any county for service upon a person alleged to be guilty of contempt, or in violation of any order of the court, to (1) appear before the court at the time fixed in the citation; and (2) show cause why the person should

---

655 N.E.2d 516, 103 Ed. Law Rep. 1199 (Ind. Ct. App. 1995); Showalter v. Brubaker, 650 N.E.2d 693 (Ind. Ct. App. 4th Dist. 1995).

[29]McCulloch v. State, 174 Ind. 525, 92 N.E. 543 (1910); Anderson v. Indianapolis Drop Forging Co., 34 Ind. App. 100, 72 N.E. 277 (Div. 2 1904).

[30]IC 34-47-3-5(a).

[31]IC 34-47-3-5(b).

Forms References: Orders To Show Cause Why Party Should Not Be Punished. 7 Am Jur Pleading and Practice Forms, Annotated (rev. ed.), Contempt §§ 71-86.

[32]IC 34-47-3-5(c).

[33]IC 34-47-3-5(d).

not be punished for contempt of court.[34] The citation shall be served by the sheriff to whom it is addressed in the same manner as summons is served in a civil proceeding, and due return shall be made to the court issuing the citation.[35] This statute applies to any proceeding in any court of record and of original jurisdiction authorized or empowered by law to punish for contempts of court, or to enforce its orders by contempt proceedings, whether the contempt proceedings are civil or criminal in nature.[36]

For the purpose of procuring personal jurisdiction over a person who has allegedly violated a court order or who is otherwise in contempt of court, the court may issue a writ of attachment of the body of the person.[37] Such a writ is to be directed to a sheriff or assisting sheriff and should fix an amount of bail, if the order that the person has allegedly violated does not concern a child support obligation, or escrow, if the order allegedly violated concerns a child support obligation.[38] A sheriff or assisting sheriff who receives an order of attachment shall immediately serve the writ and take the person into custody, which may be done in any county.[39]

    ◆ **Caution:** The issuance of a citation and arrest pursuant to an attachment is not a mandatory procedure;[40] thus, punishment for contempt may be imposed without the issue of an attachment where, on a rule to show cause, the defendant appears and answers.[41] Moreover, where a defendant was already properly a party to a pending action and the defendant's attorney had notice of a pending motion charge of civil contempt, personal service on the defendant was not necessary.[42]

If an assisting sheriff takes a person into custody under a

---

[34]IC 34-47-4-1(b).

[35]IC 34-47-4-1(c).

[36]IC 34-47-4-1(a).

[37]IC 34-47-4-2(a).

[38]IC 34-47-4-2(b).

[39]IC 34-47-4-2(c).

[40]State ex rel. Brubaker v. Pritchard, 236 Ind. 222, 138 N.E.2d 233, 60 ALR 2d 1239 (1956).

[41]Hawkins v. State, 125 Ind. 570, 25 N.E. 818 (1890).

[42]State ex rel. Brubaker v. Pritchard, 236 Ind. 222, 138 N.E.2d 233, 60 ALR 2d 1239 (1956).

writ of attachment, he or she is to notify the sheriff, who shall then immediately return the person to the county in which the writ was issued and take the person before the court that issued the writ; however, the sheriff may release the person on bail as in criminal matters, or after any person has deposited the amount of escrow provided with respect to an order concerning a child support obligation.[43] Such escrow must be deposited with the clerk of the court in an amount fixed by the court and not more than any delinquent child support allegedly owed by the person to another.[44]

◆ **Observation:** The injunction statutes also provide for the issuance of an attachment upon a showing that the injunction was willfully disobeyed[45] and authorize an arrest on the attachment[46] and release on surety[47] as in other cases of contempt.

§ 19 Special judge

In certain cases of indirect criminal contempt, the case is to be heard by a special judge chosen from a panel nominated by the court against which the alleged contempt has been committed.

West's Digest, Contempt ☞44, 45.

A statute provides that in cases of indirect contempt other than of the Supreme Court or appellate courts,[48] and except with respect to indirect contempt growing out of willfully resisting, hindering, delaying, or disobeying any lawful process or order,[49] the case is to be heard by a special judge chosen from a panel nominated by the court against which the alleged contempt has been committed. That court, at the

---

[43]IC 34-47-4-2(d).

[44]IC 34-47-4-2(e).

[45]IC 34-26-1-14.

[46]IC 34-26-1-15.

Forms References: Orders for and Warrants of Attachment. 7 Am Jur Pleading and Practice Forms, Annotated (rev. ed.), Contempt §§ 87-103.

[47]IC 34-26-1-16.

[48]IC 34-47-3-7(a).

As to indirect criminal contempt generally, see § 17.

[49]IC 34-47-3-7(b).

Regarding disobedience or hindrance of court order as contempt, generally, see § 8.

time a rule to show cause is issued, must nominate three competent and disinterested persons, each of whom must be an available judge or member of the Indiana bar, to be submitted to the parties in the action, from which the prosecuting attorney and the defendant are to immediately strike off one name each.[50] If the prosecuting attorney, the defendant, or the defendant's attorney refuse to strike off the names, then the clerk of the court shall strike for them.[51] The court must then appoint the person who remains unchallenged to preside in the cause as special judge,[52] and the appointed person may hear and determine the cause until the cause is disposed of.[53] These provisions apply only to cases of indirect criminal contempt.[54]

♦ **Observation:** Except as the statute discussed above provides, a defendant in an indirect criminal contempt proceeding is not entitled to a change of venue.[55]

A similar procedure applies in cases of indirect contempt of the Supreme Court or the Court of Appeals,[56] except with respect to contempt growing out of willfully resisting, hindering, delaying, or disobeying any lawful process or order of the court.[57] A special commissioner is appointed, after strike-offs by the parties from a three-person panel nominated by the court,[58] who is authorized to hear the evidence in the cause and report in writing to the court his or her findings as to the guilt or innocence of the cited person, and

---

[50]IC 34-47-3-7(c).

Annotation References: Disqualification of judge in state proceedings to punish contempt against or involving himself in open court and in his actual presence, 37 ALR4th 1004.

[51]IC 34-47-3-7(e).

[52]IC 34-47-3-7(d).

[53]IC 34-47-3-7(f).

[54]In re Savage, 213 Ind. 228, 12 N.E.2d 141 (1938); Bangs v. Northern Indiana Power Co., 211 Ind. 628, 6 N.E.2d 563 (1937).

[55]Allison v. State ex rel. Allison, 243 Ind. 489, 187 N.E.2d 565 (1963); La Grange v. State, 238 Ind. 689, 153 N.E.2d 593, 69 ALR 2d 668 (1958).

[56]IC 34-47-3-8(a).

[57]IC 34-47-3-8(b).

[58]IC 34-47-3-8(c).

recommendations for punishment of the cited person, if the person is found guilty of contempt as charged.[59]

§ 20 Answer and determination

In an indirect contempt proceeding, the affidavit supporting a rule to show cause may be met by an answer, or its sufficiency may be tested by a motion to discharge the rule. The defendant's verified answer to a charge of indirect criminal contempt is generally conclusive as to the facts stated.

West's Digest, Contempt ☜57, 58, 61.

In indirect contempt proceedings, the affidavit supporting a rule to show cause may be met by an answer,[60] or its sufficiency may be tested by a motion to discharge the order to show cause, as by a demurrer.[61] If the defendant (1) fails to appear in court at the time and place specified in the rule to show cause, to answer the rule, or (2) appears in court but fails or refuses to answer concerning the alleged contempt, the court may proceed at once, and without any further delay, to attach and punish the defendant for contempt.[62]

If one charged with indirect criminal contempt answers to the facts set forth in the rule to show cause by (1) showing that even if the facts set forth are all true, they do not constitute a contempt of the court, or (2) denying, explaining, or confessing and avoiding the facts, so as to show that no contempt was intended, the court must acquit and discharge the defendant.[63] If the defendant's answer to the rule does not sufficiently deny, explain, or avoid the facts set forth in the rule, so as to show that no contempt has been committed,

[59]IC 34-47-3-8(d).

[60]La Grange v. State, 238 Ind. 689, 153 N.E.2d 593, 69 ALR 2d 668 (1958).

As to the commencement of indirect contempt proceedings, see § 17.

As to the rule to show cause why the defendant should not be held in contempt, generally, see § 18.

[61]Tusing v. State, 241 Ind. 650, 175 N.E.2d 17 (1961); Locrasto v. State, 202 Ind. 277, 173 N.E. 456 (1930).

[62]IC 34-47-3-6(a).

As to punishment for contempt, generally, see § 21.

[63]IC 34-47-3-6(b).

the court may proceed to attach and punish the defendant for the contempt by fine, imprisonment, or both.[64]

In light of the statute, facts well pled in the defendant's verified answer must be taken as true.[65] If such facts, considered with the affidavit against the alleged contemnor,[66] refute the charge of contempt, a defendant is entitled to acquittal and discharge,[67] and the trial court has no right to determine the truth or falsity of the defendant's statement.[68] Evidence is heard neither when the answer purges nor when it fails to purge the defendant of contempt, and a prohibition will lie to restrain a court from taking any action other than determining the sufficiency of an answer.[69] This rule of "purgation by oath" applies in proceedings outside the statute and in proceedings before the Supreme Court.[70] There is no occasion for the filing of a reply to the answer.[71]

The doctrine that one charged with indirect criminal contempt may purge him- or herself by answer under oath does not apply where the charge is based on acts and statements that are clearly contemptuous.[72] In a case of indirect contempt by publication, if the alleged contemnor's verified answer denies any contemptuous intent, the contemnor must be discharged unless the language used, without aid of innuendoes, is clear and not susceptible to a construction

---

[64]IC 34-47-3-6(c).

[65]Tusing v. State, 241 Ind. 650, 175 N.E.2d 17 (1961); Nixon v. State, 207 Ind. 426, 193 N.E. 591, 97 ALR 894 (1935); Denny v. State, 203 Ind. 682, 182 N.E. 313 (1932).

[66]Denny v. State, 203 Ind. 682, 182 N.E. 313 (1932).

[67]Tusing v. State, 241 Ind. 650, 175 N.E.2d 17 (1961); La Grange v. State, 238 Ind. 689, 153 N.E.2d 593, 69 ALR 2d 668 (1958); Dossett v. State, 226 Ind. 142, 78 N.E.2d 435 (1948).

Forms References: Proceedings in Avoidance or to Obtain Release. 7 Am Jur Pleading and Practice Forms, Annotated (rev. ed.), Contempt §§ 155-189.

[68]State ex rel. Allison v. Marion Municipal Court Room 4, 222 Ind. 602, 56 N.E.2d 493 (1944); Denny v. State, 203 Ind. 682, 182 N.E. 313 (1932).

[69]Matter of Lemond, 274 Ind. 505, 413 N.E.2d 228 (1980); La Grange v. State, 238 Ind. 689, 153 N.E.2d 593, 69 ALR 2d 668 (1958).

[70]In re Perrello, 260 Ind. 26, 291 N.E.2d 698 (1973).

[71]Duemling v. Fort Wayne Community Concerts, Inc., 243 Ind. 521, 188 N.E.2d 274 (1963).

[72]Kilgallen v. State, 192 Ind. 531, 132 N.E. 682 (1921), reh'g overruled, 192 Ind. 531, 137 N.E. 178 (1922).

consistent with innocent intent.[73] Where violations of a court order are not denied, the alleged contemnor's denial of contemptuous intent will not prevent a conviction.[74]

§ 21 Punishment and other sanctions for contempt

In the case of criminal contempt, a punitive judgment, including imprisonment or fine, may be proper, but only a compensatory judgment is proper in a civil contempt proceeding.

West's Digest, Contempt ☞64, 68, 70 et seq.

The assessment of punishment for contempt is generally within the sound discretion of the trial court.[75] The power to punish for contempt should be exercised promptly in proper cases, but should be kept within prudent limits of reasonableness, particularly where the alleged contempt is indirect.[76]

Generally, criminal contempt may be punished by fine or imprisonment or both,[77] and the court may inflict such punishment for direct contempt as may be consistent with applicable law.[78] Imprisonment ordinarily must be for a certain and definite time,[79] although it may be made to

---

[73]La Grange v. State, 238 Ind. 689, 153 N.E.2d 593, 69 ALR 2d 668 (1958); State ex rel. Indianapolis Bar Ass'n v. Fletcher Trust Co., 211 Ind. 27, 5 N.E.2d 538 (1937) (overruled on other grounds by, In re Perrello, 260 Ind. 26, 291 N.E.2d 698 (1973)).

[74]State ex rel. Goldsmith v. Marion County Superior Court, Criminal Division No. 1, 275 Ind. 545, 419 N.E.2d 109 (1981); In re Perrello, 260 Ind. 26, 291 N.E.2d 698 (1973); Allison v. State ex rel. Allison, 243 Ind. 489, 187 N.E.2d 565 (1963).

[75]In re Gardner, 713 N.E.2d 346 (Ind. Ct. App. 1999); Kimbrell v. Secrist, 613 N.E.2d 451 (Ind. Ct. App. 3d Dist. 1993); Kimbrell v. Secrist, 613 N.E.2d 451 (Ind. Ct. App. 3d Dist. 1993); Davis v. Sponhauer, 574 N.E.2d 292 (Ind. Ct. App. 3d Dist. 1991), transfer dismissed, (Dec. 4, 1991); Indiana Stream Pollution Control Bd. v. Tippecanoe Sanitary Landfill, Inc., 511 N.E.2d 473 (Ind. Ct. App. 3d Dist. 1987), reh'g denied, (Oct. 15, 1987) and transfer denied, (Apr. 26, 1988).

[76]In re Gardner, 713 N.E.2d 346 (Ind. Ct. App. 1999); Clark v. Clark, 404 N.E.2d 23 (Ind. Ct. App. 1st Dist. 1980).

[77]IC 34-47-3-6(c) (indirect contempt).

McQueen v. State, 272 Ind. 229, 396 N.E.2d 903 (1979); State ex rel. Sedam v. Ripley Circuit Court, 262 Ind. 25, 302 N.E.2d 761 (1973).

[78]IC 34-47-2-4(d)(2).

[79]In re Perrello, 260 Ind. 26, 291 N.E.2d 698 (1973); Matter of Craig,

extend until the payment of a fine and costs.[80] A party who is found in contempt for intentionally violating an order for support may be ordered to perform community service without compensation in a manner specified by the court.[81] Suspending an attorney from the practice of law in a particular court is not, however, among the court's available punishments for contempt.[82]

Properly speaking, there is no "punishment" in a civil contempt proceeding because the judgment in such a proceeding should be for compensatory, rather than punitive, relief.[83] A person adjudged to be in civil contempt may be imprisoned[84] without violation of the constitutional prohibition against imprisonment for debt, provided that the judgment of commitment is merely coercive directing that the defendant be released upon his or her compliance with the court's order.[85] A civil contempt sentence does not become punitive merely because consecutive terms of imprisonment are imposed, and the only limit on the sentence is that it must give the contemnor an opportunity to purge him- or herself from contempt.[86]

A fine is proper in a civil contempt proceeding only so long as it is compensatory and based on the complainant's dam-

---

571 N.E.2d 1326 (Ind. Ct. App. 5th Dist. 1991) (single sentence for single contemptuous act); Matter of Craig, 552 N.E.2d 53 (Ind. Ct. App. 2d Dist. 1990), appeal after remand, 571 N.E.2d 1326 (Ind. Ct. App. 5th Dist. 1991).

[80]Ramer v. State, 190 Ind. 124, 128 N.E. 440 (1920).

[81]IC 31-16-12-6.

[82]McQueen v. State, 272 Ind. 229, 396 N.E.2d 903 (1979).

[83]Meyer v. Wolvos, 707 N.E.2d 1029 (Ind. Ct. App. 1999), reh'g denied, (May 13, 1999) and transfer denied, (Sept. 20, 1999); Clark v. Atkins, 489 N.E.2d 90 (Ind. Ct. App. 3d Dist. 1986), reh'g denied, (May 14, 1986) and transfer denied, (Oct. 10, 1986); Thrasher v. Van Buren Tp. of Monroe County, 182 Ind. App. 121, 394 N.E.2d 215 (1st Dist. 1979).

[84]Duemling v. Fort Wayne Community Concerts, Inc., 243 Ind. 521, 188 N.E.2d 274 (1963); Carey v. Carey, 132 Ind. App. 30, 171 N.E.2d 487 (Div. 1 1961).

[85]Duemling v. Fort Wayne Community Concerts, Inc., 243 Ind. 521, 188 N.E.2d 274 (1963); State ex rel. McMinn v. Gentry, 229 Ind. 615, 100 N.E.2d 676 (1951); Clark v. Clark, 404 N.E.2d 23 (Ind. Ct. App. 1st Dist. 1980) (power to arrest not punishment, but only means of obtaining compliance with order).

[86]Moore v. Ferguson, 680 N.E.2d 862 (Ind. Ct. App. 1997), transfer denied, 690 N.E.2d 1182 (Ind. 1997).

ages[87] and so long as it is directed to be paid to the injured person, rather than to the state.[88] The determination of damages in a contempt proceeding is within trial court's discretion.[89] As a general rule, the damage award or indemnity must be measured by the actual injury.[90] Where the alleged contemnor has violated an injunctive decree, the award of damages may be calculated by its deterrent effect,[91] but the court may not fix damages for the future violation of an order.[92]

Attorney fees incurred in a contempt proceeding arising from the violation of a domestic-support order may be awarded.[93]

When a conspiracy is alleged in a civil contempt action, each participant in the conspiracy may be held responsible for the consequences in the same manner as a joint tortfeasor and be found liable for damages caused by the wrongful or contemptuous acts regardless of the degree of relative participation among the conspirators.[94]

§ 22 Appeal and review

A final adjudication of contempt may be appealed to the Court of Appeals.

West's Digest, Contempt ⊂⊃66.

A defendant found guilty of direct contempt has the right

---

[87]Moore v. Polk Sanitary Milk Co., 209 Ind. 558, 200 N.E. 228 (1936); Denny v. State, 203 Ind. 682, 182 N.E. 313 (1932).

[88]Duemling v. Fort Wayne Community Concerts, Inc., 243 Ind. 521, 188 N.E.2d 274 (1963); Clark v. Atkins, 489 N.E.2d 90 (Ind. Ct. App. 3d Dist. 1986), reh'g denied, (May 14, 1986) and transfer denied, (Oct. 10, 1986); Bottoms v. B & M Coal Corp., 405 N.E.2d 82 (Ind. Ct. App. 4th Dist. 1980).

[89]Meade v. Levett, 671 N.E.2d 1172 (Ind. Ct. App. 1996).

[90]Thomas v. Woollen, 255 Ind. 612, 266 N.E.2d 20 (1971); New York, C. & St. L.R. Co. v. Meek, 210 Ind. 322, 1 N.E.2d 611 (1936).

[91]Chadwick v. Alleshouse, 250 Ind. 348, 233 N.E.2d 162 (1968); Thomas v. Woollen, 255 Ind. 612, 266 N.E.2d 20 (1971).

[92]Thomas v. Woollen, 255 Ind. 612, 266 N.E.2d 20 (1971); Green v. Maginn, 684 N.E.2d 553 (Ind. Ct. App. 1997).

[93]Haycraft v. Haycraft, 176 Ind. App. 211, 375 N.E.2d 252 (1st Dist. 1978); Marburger v. Marburger, 175 Ind. App. 612, 372 N.E.2d 1250 (1st Dist. 1978).

[94]Bottoms v. B & M Coal Corp., 405 N.E.2d 82 (Ind. Ct. App. 4th Dist. 1980).

to appeal the judgment of the court.[95] The appeal may be made as in other criminal actions, by a defendant who is fined at least $50 or is imprisoned, where the court overrules a motion for new trial or recision of its judgment.[96] In all such cases, the appeal lies to the Court of Appeals from a trial court judgment.[97] As to indirect criminal contempt, a defendant who appeared to respond to the rule to show cause may appeal to the Court of Appeals in the same manner as in cases of direct contempt.[98]

An appeal may be taken only from a final judgment in a contempt proceeding;[99] thus, a determination of contempt has been held not to be an appealable final judgment where the sentence imposed was suspended[1] and where the order reserved the right to remit the defendant's fine before final disposition of the cause.[2] Appeal has been permitted where

---

[95]IC 34-47-2-5(a).

As to direct contempt, generally, see § 4.

Annotation References: Appealability of contempt adjudication or conviction, 33 ALR3d 448.

Contempt adjudication or conviction as subject to review, other than by appeal or writ of error, 33 ALR3d 589.

[96]IC 34-47-2-5(e).

As to motions for new trial or rescission in cases of direct contempt, generally, see § 16.

As to punishment and other sanctions for contempt, generally, see § 21.

[97]IC 34-47-2-5(f).

State's rules of trial de novo did not apply to city court's direct criminal contempt citation of defendant, and thus superior court was without jurisdiction to review the citation; defendant should have instead appealed citation to Court of Appeals pursuant to statutory procedure.—Azhar v. State, 712 N.E.2d 1018 (Ind. Ct. App. 1999).

[98]IC 34-47-3-6(d).

As to the rule to show cause, generally, see § 18.

[99]State ex rel. Crumpacker v. Lake Superior Court, Room No. One, 270 Ind. 413, 386 N.E.2d 663 (1979); State ex rel. Neal v. Hamilton Circuit Court, 248 Ind. 130, 224 N.E.2d 55 (1967) (no final judgment for appeal unless trial court has attached and punished defendant by fine or imprisonment); Azhar v. State, 712 N.E.2d 1018 (Ind. Ct. App. 1999) (same).

[1]Montgomery v. State, 182 Ind. 276, 106 N.E. 370 (1914); Azhar v. State, 712 N.E.2d 1018 (Ind. Ct. App. 1999).

[2]Home Electric Light & Power Co. v. Globe Tissue Paper Co., 145 Ind. 174, 44 N.E. 191 (1896).

the defendants were ordered confined until such time as they should execute the court's order.[3]

An appeal from a judgment of contempt will not be considered where the matter is moot.[4]

◆ **Illustration:** Where the defendant was found guilty of civil contempt because of his violation of an order enjoining him from obstructing a certain right of way, an appeal from a judgment directing his commitment to the state farm until he removed the obstructions was moot and could not be considered, where the obstructions had been removed and the defendant had been discharged from custody.[5]

An appeal may be taken from a judgment convicting the defendant of indirect criminal contempt without a motion for new trial.[6] Appeals from the court's ruling on a motion to discharge a rule to show cause or on a motion to quash an answer should be presented by independent assignments of error, rather than by a motion for a new trial.[7] In a civil contempt proceeding, objections should be saved by a motion for new trial.[8]

◆ **Observation:** It has been held that because contempt proceedings are neither civil, criminal, nor equitable, a party appealing from a dismissal of a complaint for indirect contempt did not have to file a pre-appeal statement in accordance with appellate rules applicable to "civil" appeals.[9]

§ 23 —Standard and scope of review

On appeal from an adjudication of contempt, every presumption will be made in favor of the lower court's judgment; the appellate court will not weigh conflicting evidence presented below and will not interfere with the exercise of the trial court's sound discretion.

---

[3]McKinney v. Frankfort & State Line Co., 140 Ind. 95, 38 N.E. 170 (1894), reh'g denied, 140 Ind. 95, 39 N.E. 500 (1895).

[4]Wools v. Reberger, 209 Ind. 99, 198 N.E. 65 (1935).

[5]Wools v. Reberger, 209 Ind. 99, 198 N.E. 65 (1935).

[6]McSwane v. Foreman, 167 Ind. 171, 78 N.E. 630 (1906).

[7]Skolnick v. State, 180 Ind. App. 253, 388 N.E.2d 1156 (3d Dist. 1979); Stone v. Stone, 134 Ind. App. 396, 188 N.E.2d 833 (Div. 1 1963).

[8]Kilander v. Kilander, 249 Ind. 589, 233 N.E.2d 626 (1968).

[9]State v. Heltzel, 526 N.E.2d 1229 (Ind. Ct. App. 3d Dist. 1988).

West's Digest, Contempt ⏁66(2), 66(7).

Where the jurisdiction of the lower court sufficiently appears in a contempt proceeding, every presumption will be made in favor of its judgment on appeal.[10] The court will not weigh conflicting evidence on appeal[11] and will not interfere with the exercise of the trial court's sound discretion.[12] The trial court's determination as to whether a person is in contempt will be reversed only when such determination is against the logic and effect of the facts and circumstances before the court,[13] and any reasonable inferences arising therefrom,[14] or when the determination is otherwise contrary to law.[15] This is also true with respect to the trial court's determination regarding punishment or refusal to punish for contempt[16] and as to damages for contempt.[17]

---

[10]Crowl v. Berryhill, 678 N.E.2d 828 (Ind. Ct. App. 1997); Mitchell v. Stevenson, 677 N.E.2d 551 (Ind. Ct. App. 1997), transfer denied, 683 N.E.2d 594 (Ind. 1997); DeBoer v. DeBoer, 669 N.E.2d 415 (Ind. Ct. App. 1996), transfer denied, (Dec. 31, 1996) and (disapproved of on other grounds by, Merritt v. Merritt, 693 N.E.2d 1320 (Ind. Ct. App. 1998)).

[11]Hopping v. State, 637 N.E.2d 1294 (Ind. 1994); In re Marriage of Glendenning, 684 N.E.2d 1175 (Ind. Ct. App. 1997), transfer denied, 698 N.E.2d 1186 (Ind. 1998); Shively v. Shively, 680 N.E.2d 877 (Ind. Ct. App. 1997); Russell v. State, 428 N.E.2d 1271 (Ind. Ct. App. 4th Dist. 1981) (trial court's statement of record presumed true on appeal).

[12]Meyer v. Wolvos, 707 N.E.2d 1029 (Ind. Ct. App. 1999), reh'g denied, (May 13, 1999) and transfer denied, (Sept. 20, 1999); Hancz v. City of South Bend, 691 N.E.2d 1322 (Ind. Ct. App. 1998); Williams v. State ex rel. Harris, 690 N.E.2d 315 (Ind. Ct. App. 1997); DeBoer v. DeBoer, 669 N.E.2d 415 (Ind. Ct. App. 1996), transfer denied, (Dec. 31, 1996) and (disapproved of on other grounds by, Merritt v. Merritt, 693 N.E.2d 1320 (Ind. Ct. App. 1998)).

[13]Meyer v. Wolvos, 707 N.E.2d 1029 (Ind. Ct. App. 1999), reh'g denied, (May 13, 1999) and transfer denied, (Sept. 20, 1999); Hancz v. City of South Bend, 691 N.E.2d 1322 (Ind. Ct. App. 1998).

[14]State ex rel. Prosser v. Indiana Waste Systems, Inc., 603 N.E.2d 181 (Ind. Ct. App. 4th Dist. 1992).

[15]Williams v. State ex rel. Harris, 690 N.E.2d 315 (Ind. Ct. App. 1997).

[16]Davis v. Sponhauer, 574 N.E.2d 292 (Ind. Ct. App. 3d Dist. 1991), transfer dismissed, (Dec. 4, 1991); Indiana Stream Pollution Control Bd. v. Tippecanoe Sanitary Landfill, Inc., 511 N.E.2d 473 (Ind. Ct. App. 3d Dist. 1987), reh'g denied, (Oct. 15, 1987) and transfer denied, (Apr. 26, 1988).

As to punishment and other sanctions for contempt, generally, see § 21.

[17]Meade v. Levett, 671 N.E.2d 1172 (Ind. Ct. App. 1996).

When the trial judge in a direct contempt proceeding makes a written statement of the facts, this statement will be accepted on appeal as true[18] and is presumed to contain all the facts;[19] however, the appellate court will also examine the record to determine if the acts alleged constituted contempt.[20] If the record is silent on the subject, it is presumed that the trial judge made the written statement as required,[21] and even the judge's failure to make the statement is not available as error if the defendant, having an opportunity, failed to object.[22]

---

[18]In re Caito, 459 N.E.2d 1179 (Ind. 1984); Russell v. State, 428 N.E.2d 1271 (Ind. Ct. App. 4th Dist. 1981); Jacobsen v. State, 179 Ind. App. 37, 384 N.E.2d 1041 (3d Dist. 1979).

As to procedure in direct contempt proceedings, generally, see § 16.

[19]Adler v. Adler, 713 N.E.2d 348 (Ind. Ct. App. 1999); Williams v. State ex rel. Harris, 690 N.E.2d 315 (Ind. Ct. App. 1997); Funk v. Macaulay, 457 N.E.2d 223 (Ind. Ct. App. 2d Dist. 1983).

[20]Meyer v. Wolvos, 707 N.E.2d 1029 (Ind. Ct. App. 1999), reh'g denied, (May 13, 1999) and transfer denied, (Sept. 20, 1999); Hancz v. City of South Bend, 691 N.E.2d 1322 (Ind. Ct. App. 1998); Russell v. State, 428 N.E.2d 1271 (Ind. Ct. App. 4th Dist. 1981).

[21]National Educ. Association—South Bend v. South Bend Community School Corp., 655 N.E.2d 516, 103 Ed. Law Rep. 1199 (Ind. Ct. App. 1995).

[22]Young v. State, 198 Ind. 629, 154 N.E. 478 (1926); National Educ. Association—South Bend v. South Bend Community School Corp., 655 N.E.2d 516, 103 Ed. Law Rep. 1199 (Ind. Ct. App. 1995); United Farm Bureau Mut. Ins. Co. v. Ira, 577 N.E.2d 588 (Ind. Ct. App. 4th Dist. 1991), transfer denied, (Dec. 30, 1991).

CONTINUANCE

Linda Odom, J.D.

Scope of Topic

This article discusses the continuance or postponement of the trial or hearing of civil cases and proceedings generally, including the powers, duties, and discretion of the court in relation to a continuance, the grounds for a continuance, and the procedure involved in obtaining a continuance.

Treated Elsewhere

Abatement of action, see I.L.E., Abatement

Administrative proceedings, continuance of, see I.L.E., Administrative Law and Procedure

Appeal, continuance of hearings on, see I.L.E., Appeals

Court adjournments and vacations, see I.L.E., Courts

Criminal proceedings, continuance in, see I.L.E., Criminal Law

Dismissal, discontinuance, and nonsuit, see I.L.E., Dismissal

Divorce actions, continuance in, see I.L.E., Divorce

Juvenile proceedings, continuance in, see I.L.E., Minors

New trial, denial of request for continuance as ground for, see I.L.E., New Trial

Stay of actions or proceedings, see I.L.E., Actions

Research References

Text References

17 Am Jur 2d, Continuance.

17 C.J.S., Continuances.

West's Digest References

West's Digest, Pretrial Procedure.

Annotation References

ALR Digest: Appeal and Error; Continuance and Adjournment; New Trial

ALR Index: Continuance and Adjournment

Forms References

2 Am Jur Pleading and Practice Forms, Annotated (rev. ed.), Appeal and Error.

7 Am Jur Pleading and Practice Forms, Annotated (rev. ed.), Continuance.

Trial Strategy References

Intentional Spoliation of Evidence, 18 Am Jur POF3d 515; Civil Discovery Sanctions in the Federal Courts, 33 Am Jur POF3d 459; Entitlement to a Stay or Default Judgment Relief Under the Soldiers' and Sailors' Civil Relief Act, 35 Am Jur POF3d 323.

A Guide to the Federal Rules of Civil Procedure, 56 Am Jur Trials 293.

Miscellaneous References

Indiana Practice, Rules of Procedure Annotated, Rule 53.5.

Indiana Practice, Civil Trial Practice §§ 13.08, 16.02, 21.37, 28.23, 36.23.

Indiana Practice, Procedural Forms With Practice Commentary §§ 69.06, 86.01 et seq., 89.14, 98.09.

Statutory References

IC 2-3-5-1; IC 33-4-3-8; IC 33-5-2-5; IC 34-33-3-6

Court Rules

Small Claims R. 9
Trial R. 37, 53.5

KeyCite®: Cases and other legal materials listed in KeyCite Scope can be researched through West Group's KeyCite service on Westlaw®. Use KeyCite to check citations for form, parallel references, prior and later history, and comprehensive citator information, including citations to other decisions and secondary materials.

Table of Parallel References:

To convert General Index references to section references in this volume, or to ascertain the disposition (or current equivalent) of articles in the prior edition of this publication, see the Table of Parallel References at the beginning of this volume.

I. IN GENERAL; GROUNDS FOR CONTINUANCE (§§ 1 TO 12)

II. PROCEDURE; APPEAL AND REVIEW (§§ 13 TO 18)

I. IN GENERAL; GROUNDS FOR CONTINUANCE

§ 1   Generally; power and discretion of court

§ 2   Grounds for continuance, generally; good cause
§ 3   Absence of evidence or witness
§ 4   —Diligence in attempting to procure evidence or witness
§ 5   —Admissions to prevent continuance
§ 6   Absence of party
§ 7   —Illness of party or of member of party's family
§ 8   Absence of counsel
§ 9   Surprise, generally
§ 10   Amendment of pleadings; change of parties
§ 11   Lack of time to prepare
§ 12   Public sentiment or prejudice

II. PROCEDURE; APPEAL AND REVIEW

§ 13   Motion, generally; supporting affidavit or evidence
§ 14   Continuance on court's own motion; stipulation of parties
§ 15   Hearing and determination
§ 16   Costs
§ 17   Rescission of continuance
§ 18   Appeal and review

I. IN GENERAL; GROUNDS FOR CONTINUANCE

Research References
IC 2-3-5-1; IC 33-4-3-8; IC 33-5-2-5; IC 34-33-3-6
Small Claims R. 9
Trial R. 37, 53.5

17 Am Jur 2d, Continuance §§ 1-58.
17 C.J.S., Continuances §§ 1-93, 124-126.
West's Digest, Pretrial Procedure ☞711-726.
ALR Digest: Continuance and Adjournment §§ 1-8
ALR Index: Continuance and Adjournment
7 Am Jur Pleading and Practice Forms, Annotated (rev. ed.), Continuance §§ 1-65.

§ 1   Generally; power and discretion of court

A continuance is the adjournment of a cause to a future date. Subject to statutes and rules of procedure providing the grounds for and procedures relating to continuances, the courts have broad discretionary power in determining whether to grant or refuse continuances.

West's Digest, Pretrial Procedure ☞711, 713.

A continuance is the adjournment of a cause to a future

date[1] and is usually granted to permit a party to prosecute or defend adequately.[2] In Indiana, the grounds for and procedures relating to continuances are provided for by statute[3] and rules of procedure.[4]

Courts generally have inherent power to grant or refuse continuances, as an incident to their authority to hear and determine causes.[5] One limitation upon such power is that the court must have jurisdiction of the cause in question.[6]

The decision whether to grant or deny a continuance lies within the trial court's sound discretion,[7] and a cause will not be reversed based on such a decision unless it is clearly shown that the court's discretion has been abused.[8]

§ 2   Grounds for continuance, generally; good cause

A motion for continuance must be allowed upon a showing of good cause. The party moving for a continuance must be free from fault and demonstrate that a denial of the motion would prejudice such party's rights in maintaining his or her action or defense.

West's Digest, Pretrial Procedure ☞712, 714.

The Rules of Trial Procedure state that a motion for continuance shall be allowed upon a showing of good cause.[9] The applicable rule prescribes detailed requirements in connection with the granting of a continuance on the ground of

---

[1] 17 Am Jur 2d, Continuance § 1.

[2] 17 Am Jur 2d, Continuance § 3.

[3] IC 33-4-3-8(c) (small claims cases in Circuit Court); IC 33-5-2-5(c) (small claims cases in superior court); IC 34-33-3-6 (actions involving non-resident motor vehicle operators).

[4] Trial R. 53.5; Small Claims R. 9

[5] 17 Am Jur 2d, Continuance § 3.

[6] Cincinnati & C.R. Co. v. Rowe, 17 Ind. 568, 1861 WL 2887 (1861).

[7] Robertson v. Board of Zoning Appeals, Town of Chesterton, 699 N.E.2d 310 (Ind. Ct. App. 1998); Vanderbilt v. Vanderbilt, 679 N.E.2d 909 (Ind. Ct. App. 1997), transfer denied, 683 N.E.2d 596 (Ind. 1997); Hess v. Hess, 679 N.E.2d 153 (Ind. Ct. App. 1997); Homehealth, Inc. v. Heritage Mut. Ins. Co., 662 N.E.2d 195 (Ind. Ct. App. 1996), transfer denied, (Oct. 10, 1996); Matter of L.C., 659 N.E.2d 593 (Ind. Ct. App. 1995), reh'g denied, (Feb. 6, 1996) and transfer denied, 683 N.E.2d 582 (Ind. 1997) and cert. denied, 521 U.S. 1122, 117 S. Ct. 2515, 138 L. Ed. 2d 1017 (1997).

[8] § 18.

[9] Trial R. 53.5.

As to motions for continuance, generally, see § 13.

absent witnesses or evidence,[10] but otherwise the grounds for a continuance are very broad.

◆ **Observation:** If it is sought to delay a trial until the decision of an appeal in another action, the proper motion is for a stay rather than a continuance.[11]

The basis of a continuance rests upon the right of a party to have a reasonable opportunity to try the cause upon its merits, and relief, timely and appropriately sought in the form of a continuance, is properly granted where the applicant acts in good faith and with due diligence and where it clearly appears that the applicant will be deprived of a fair trial if forced to proceed at the appointed time or continue with a trial or hearing already in progress.[12]

In determining whether to grant a continuance, the trial court must decide whether the moving party has shown "good cause" for a continuance.[13] The burden is on the moving party to establish good cause.[14] While the grant or denial of a continuance are clearly matters within the trial court's discretion,[15] a motion for continuance should be granted when good cause is shown,[16] and if such a showing is made, a denial of the motion will be deemed an abuse of discre-

---

As to court discretion in the grant or refusal of continuances, generally, see § 1

Forms References: Grounds for Continuance. 7 Am Jur Pleading and Practice Forms, Annotated (rev. ed.), Continuance §§ 6-58.

[10]As to continuance on the ground of absent witnesses or evidence, generally, see § 3.

[11]Peters v. Banta, 120 Ind. 416, 22 N.E. 95 (1889), reh'g denied, 120 Ind. 416, 23 N.E. 84 (1889); Walker v. Heller, 73 Ind. 46, 1880 WL 6378 (1880).

Forms References: Prior Action Pending. 7 Am Jur Pleading and Practice Forms, Annotated (rev. ed.), Continuance §§ 49-52.

[12]17 Am Jur 2d, Continuance § 6.

[13]James v. Picou, 162 Ind. App. 134, 318 N.E.2d 377 (Ind. Ct. App. 1st Dist. 1974).

[14]Farm Burean Mut. Ins. Co. v. Dercach, 450 N.E.2d 537 (3 Dist. 1983); Clark v. Clark, 404 N.E.2d 23 (Ind. Ct. App. 1st Dist. 1980); Farley v. Farley, 172 Ind. App. 120, 359 N.E.2d 583 (1st Dist. 1977).

[15]§ 1.

[16]Indiana Alcoholic Beverage Commission v. State ex rel. Harmon, 269 Ind. 48, 379 N.E.2d 140 (1978); Homehealth, Inc. v. Heritage Mut. Ins. Co., 662 N.E.2d 195 (Ind. Ct. App. 1996), transfer denied, (Oct. 10, 1996); Hambey v. Hill, 148 Ind. App. 662, 269 N.E.2d 394 (Div. 1 1971).

tion.[17] A prompt disposal of cases should never be accomplished by stripping fundamental rights to a continuance from a party in any type of action.[18]

The party moving for a continuance must be free from fault[19] and demonstrate that a denial of the motion would prejudice such party's rights in maintaining his or her action or defense.[20] The denial of a continuance may be error when the moving party is free from fault and his or her rights are likely to be prejudiced by such denial.[21]

§ 3   Absence of evidence or witness

A continuance may be granted on proper motion to permit a party to procure absent evidence or an absent witness.

West's Digest, Pretrial Procedure ☞717, 717.1.

A continuance due to the absence of evidence or witnesses may be granted only upon an affidavit that shows the materiality of the anticipated evidence, the due diligence of the movant to obtain it, and the location of the evidence.[22] For an absent witness, the movant must further show the name and address of the witness, if available; the likelihood of obtaining the testimony within a reasonable amount of time; that the movant has not played a role in the witness's absence; the facts the movant believes to be true about the witness' testimony; and that the movant is unable to prove those facts as readily by any other witness or evidence.[23]

---

[17]Homehealth, Inc. v. Heritage Mut. Ins. Co., 662 N.E.2d 195 (Ind. Ct. App. 1996), transfer denied, (Oct. 10, 1996); Plan-Tec, Inc. v. Wiggins, 443 N.E.2d 1212 (Ind. Ct. App. 1st Dist. 1983).

[18]Kaiser Aluminum & Chemical Sales, Inc. v. Dickerhoff, 136 Ind. App. 258, 199 N.E.2d 719 (Div. 1 1964).

[19]Danner v. Danner, 573 N.E.2d 934 (Ind. Ct. App. 1st Dist. 1991), decision clarified on reh'g, (Aug. 20, 1991) and transfer denied, (Feb. 14, 1992).

[20]Ayr-Way Stores, Inc. v. Chitwood, 261 Ind. 86, 300 N.E.2d 335 (1973); Danner v. Danner, 573 N.E.2d 934 (Ind. Ct. App. 1st Dist. 1991), decision clarified on reh'g, (Aug. 20, 1991) and transfer denied, (Feb. 14, 1992).

[21]Hess v. Hess, 679 N.E.2d 153 (Ind. Ct. App. 1997).

[22]Trial R. 53.5.

As to the movant's diligence in procuring the evidence, see § 4.

[23]Trial R. 53.5.

Generally, the question of a continuance on account of absent witnesses or evidence is in the discretion of the trial court.[24]

> ◆ **Practice Guide:** Where the absence of evidence results from a party's failure to respond to interrogatories or other discovery, the court may, on a motion for sanctions, grant a stay until the discovery is produced.[25] If a party has been harmed by another party's failure to respond to proper discovery requests, the party should seek a continuance or will be found to have waived any objection to the lack of response.[26]

The movant for a continuance must show the necessity or materiality of the absent evidence,[27] and the motion should be refused if it appears that the evidence would be material only to a defective pleading,[28] or that the testimony would be privileged;[29] in the latter case, a party's opposition to a continuance constitutes a sufficient indication of his or her intention to object to the evidence.[30]

The movant for a continuance must also show that he or she is unable to prove the facts by any other witness whose testimony can be as readily procured.[31] A continuance for the absence of witnesses or evidence is properly denied where

---

Forms References: Absence of Witness. 7 Am Jur Pleading and Practice Forms, Annotated (rev. ed.), Continuance §§ 28-36.

[24]Indiana Tri-City Plaza Bowl, Inc. v. Glueck's Estate, 422 N.E.2d 670 (Ind. Ct. App. 3d Dist. 1981); Dilley v. Scott, 167 Ind. App. 177, 338 N.E.2d 296 (3d Dist. 1975).

As to court discretion in the grant or refusal of continuances, generally, see § 1.

[25]Trial R. 37(B)(2)

[26]Bay v. Barenie, 421 N.E.2d 6 (Ind. Ct. App. 3d Dist. 1981).

[27]Dilley v. Scott, 167 Ind. App. 177, 338 N.E.2d 296 (3d Dist. 1975); City of Shelbyville v. Morton, 138 Ind. App. 460, 208 N.E.2d 705 (Div. 2 1965).

[28]Prather v. Young, 67 Ind. 480, 1879 WL 5833 (1879); Swift v. Ellsworth, 10 Ind. 205, 1858 WL 4000 (1858).

[29]Carthage Turnpike Co. v. Andrews, 102 Ind. 138, 1 N.E. 364 (1885); Post v. State ex rel. Hill, 14 Ind. App. 452, 42 N.E. 1120 (1896).

[30]Post v. State ex rel. Hill, 14 Ind. App. 452, 42 N.E. 1120 (1896).

[31]Indiana Tri-City Plaza Bowl, Inc. v. Glueck's Estate, 422 N.E.2d 670 (Ind. Ct. App. 3d Dist. 1981) (illness of corporate officer not good cause for continuance unless it is shown that no other officer could assist in company's representation).

the movant fails to demonstrate any probability of obtaining the testimony or evidence within a reasonable time.[32]

§ 4 —Diligence in attempting to procure evidence or witness

The party seeking a continuance must show due diligence in attempting to procure the absent evidence or witness.

West's Digest, Pretrial Procedure ☞718.

A continuance on account of the absence of evidence or witnesses may be granted only upon a showing that the movant has been duly diligent in attempting to obtain the evidence or testimony in question.[33] It is not an abuse of discretion for the trial court to deny a continuance absent a showing of diligence by the movant in attempting to procure the attendance of an absent witness at trial, or in taking such witness' deposition.[34]

Generally, sufficient diligence is not shown if it appears that the moving party failed to issue a proper subpoena.[35] While it is no excuse that the movant expected the witness' appearance because the witness was summoned by the opposing party,[36] or is him- or herself an opposing party,[37] it has been held that where the defendant promised the plaintiff that certain of the defendant's employees would appear, the plaintiff was excused from taking steps to ensure their appearance and could obtain a continuance for this purpose.[38] It is no excuse that the witness in question has had insufficient time to inform him- or herself,[39] or that the movant has been sick, unless it is made to appear that the

---

[32]Dunnington v. Syfers, 157 Ind. 458, 62 N.E. 29 (1901).

[33]Trial R. 53.5.

[34]Hambey v. Hill, 148 Ind. App. 662, 269 N.E.2d 394 (Div. 1 1971); City of Shelbyville v. Morton, 138 Ind. App. 460, 208 N.E.2d 705 (Div. 2 1965).

[35]Dilley v. Scott, 167 Ind. App. 177, 338 N.E.2d 296 (3d Dist. 1975); Hambey v. Hill, 148 Ind. App. 662, 269 N.E.2d 394 (Div. 1 1971).

[36]Hutts v. Shoaf, 88 Ind. 395, 1882 WL 6628 (1882).

[37]Lane v. State ex rel. Harmon's Adm'r, 27 Ind. 108, 1866 WL 2531 (1866).

[38]Toledo, St. L. & K.C.R. Co. v. Stevenson, 131 Ind. 203, 30 N.E. 1082 (1892).

[39]Brown v. Shearon, 17 Ind. 239, 1861 WL 2956 (1861) (examination of accounts).

sickness disabled him or her from procuring an appearance.[40] The illness of the witness is not an excuse if the movant was otherwise guilty of laches.[41]

§ 5 —Admissions to prevent continuance

Generally, the absence of evidence or witnesses is not a ground for a continuance if the opposing party is willing to admit the truth of the evidence sought.

West's Digest, Pretrial Procedure ⬅722.

The continuance should not be granted if the party opposing a motion for a continuance will stipulate that the facts stated in the movant's supporting affidavit about the absent evidence shall be taken as true on trial, if such evidence is written or documentary, or that he or she will testify to said facts as true, in the case of an absent witness.[42] Such an admission permits the movant to use such facts in his or her affidavit as competent evidence,[43] excluding irrelevant matter,[44] but the movant's opponent is not bound to admit statements of conclusions contained in the affidavit.[45]

The nonmoving party will have the right to impeach the absent witness at trial as if the witness were present or his or her deposition were used.[46] As in other cases, however, a proper foundation must be laid, and the opposing party is not excused from laying a foundation by the witness's absence.[47]

§ 6   Absence of party

For good cause shown, a court may grant a continuance due to the absence of a party.

West's Digest, Pretrial Procedure ⬅715.

---

[40]Deming v. Ferry, 8 Ind. 418, 1856 WL 5494 (1856).

[41]Briggs v. Garner, 54 Ind. 572, 1876 WL 6729 (1876) (subpoena delayed).

[42]Trial R. 53.5.

Annotation References: Admissions to prevent continuance sought to secure testimony of absent witness in civil case, 15 ALR3d 1272.

[43]Downs v. Opp, 82 Ind. 166, 1882 WL 6164 (1882).

[44]Nave v. Horton, 9 Ind. 563, 1857 WL 3728 (1857).

[45]Indiana Ry. Co. v. Maurer, 160 Ind. 25, 66 N.E. 156 (1903).

[46]Trial R. 53.5.

[47]New York, C. & St. L. R. Co. v. Flynn, 41 Ind. App. 501, 81 N.E. 741 (Div. 1 1907), reh'g denied, 41 Ind. App. 501, 82 N.E. 1009 (Div. 1 1907).

It is an important privilege of a party to be present at the trial of his or her cause,[48] where the party may aid and assist counsel, and his or her unavoidable absence is good cause for a continuance.[49] This privilege should not be denied on a proper application made when the party is without fault.[50]

Applications for continuance by reason of the absence of a party need not contain all the allegations required when the absence is that of a witness.[51] A continuance by reason of an absent witness may be obviated by the opposing party's admission that the witness, if present, would testify to certain facts,[52] but such admissions as to what a party would testify to are not sufficient reason for refusing a continuance where the party is necessarily absent.[53]

The presumptions are in favor of the action of the court upon such an application, however, and such action will not be reversed unless shown affirmatively to have been wrong; thus, in the absence of a showing that the party might be able to attend at some reasonable future time, it is not error

---

[48]Pate v. Tait, 72 Ind. 450, 1880 WL 6355 (1880); Kline v. Kline, 455 N.E.2d 407 (Ind. Ct. App. 2d Dist. 1983); Flick v. Simpson, 145 Ind. App. 698, 252 N.E.2d 508 (Div. 2 1969), reh'g denied, 145 Ind. App. 698, 255 N.E.2d 118 (Div. 2 1970).

[49]Breezewood Management Co. v. Maltbie, 411 N.E.2d 670 (Ind. Ct. App. 1st Dist. 1980); Flick v. Simpson, 145 Ind. App. 698, 252 N.E.2d 508 (Div. 2 1969), reh'g denied, 145 Ind. App. 698, 255 N.E.2d 118 (Div. 2 1970).

Forms References: Absence of Party. 7 Am Jur Pleading and Practice Forms, Annotated (rev. ed.), Continuance §§ 17-27.

[50]Pate v. Tait, 72 Ind. 450, 1880 WL 6355 (1880); Kline v. Kline, 455 N.E.2d 407 (Ind. Ct. App. 2d Dist. 1983) (former husband was absent due to unavoidable military assignment and should have been granted continuance); Flick v. Simpson, 145 Ind. App. 698, 252 N.E.2d 508 (Div. 2 1969), reh'g denied, 145 Ind. App. 698, 255 N.E.2d 118 (Div. 2 1970) (except for "weighty reasons," a continuance should not be denied when application therefor is proper and shows good cause).

[51]Welcome v. Boswell, 54 Ind. 297, 1876 WL 6718 (1876); Schwartz v. Parsons, 22 Ind. App. 340, 53 N.E. 785 (1899).

As to the showing required to obtain a continuance on the ground of a witness' absence, generally, see § 3.

[52]§ 5.

[53]Breezewood Management Co. v. Maltbie, 411 N.E.2d 670 (Ind. Ct. App. 1st Dist. 1980).

to deny the continuance.[54] There should be no continuance if the party's absence appears to be the result of his or her own negligence or choice,[55] or if the parties reach an agreement regarding the absence of a party.[56] It is not error to deny a motion for continuance if a party shows insufficient reasons for his or her absence.[57]

A party does not have the same privilege with respect to the absence of a coparty. If the presence of a coparty is desired, he or she should be subpoenaed in the same manner as other witnesses.[58]

Upon motion for a continuance on the ground that a party is a member of the General Assembly, the court shall continue the case to a date not sooner than 30 days following the date of adjournment of the session of the General Assembly during which such cause of action has been set or rule has been made returnable.[59]

§ 7 —Illness of party or of member of party's family

A party may be entitled to a continuance upon a showing that he or she is too ill to attend the trial.

West's Digest, Pretrial Procedure ☞715.

---

[54]Pate v. Tait, 72 Ind. 450, 1880 WL 6355 (1880); Indiana Tri-City Plaza Bowl, Inc. v. Glueck's Estate, 422 N.E.2d 670 (3d Dist. 1981); Loudermilk v. Feld Truck Leasing Co. of Indiana, 171 Ind. App. 498, 358 N.E.2d 160 (2d Dist. 1976).

[55]Loudermilk v. Feld Truck Leasing Co. of Indiana, 171 Ind. App. 498, 358 N.E.2d 160 (2d Dist. 1976) (no continuance where party was absent to attend convention).

[56]Kroll v. Smith, 127 Ind. App. 178, 139 N.E.2d 573 (1957) (where defendant moved for postponement on ground that on day of trial, defendant was a witness in other litigation and that defendant's cocounsel was also engaged in such litigation, denial of continuance was proper because defendant agreed with plaintiffs that plaintiffs should put in their case and that defendant's counsel would have an opportunity to cross-examine plaintiffs' witnesses and then, if defendant was not available, case would be finished at some later date).

[57]Multivest Properties v. Hughes, 671 N.E.2d 199 (Ind. Ct. App. 1996) (continuance denied due to lack of showing of reasons for granting continuance); Breezewood Management Co. v. Maltbie, 411 N.E.2d 670 (Ind. Ct. App. 1st Dist. 1980); Loudermilk v. Feld Truck Leasing Co. of Indiana, 171 Ind. App. 498, 358 N.E.2d 160 (2d Dist. 1976) (no continuance where party was absent to attend convention).

[58]Chamberlain v. Reid, 49 Ind. 332, 1874 WL 6068 (1874); Lane v. State ex rel. Harmon's Adm'r, 27 Ind. 108, 1866 WL 2531 (1866).

[59]IC 2-3-5-1.

A party may be entitled to a continuance upon a showing that he or she is too ill to attend the trial,[60] or that there was illness in the party's family, so that the party is too materially harassed to assist counsel.[61]

A court is not bound to grant a continuance on its own motion due to the illness of a party during trial,[62] neither is a continuance required merely upon a general and indefinite statement that a party's absence is caused by the illness of a member of his or her family.[63] The illness of a corporate officer is not good cause for a continuance unless it is shown that no other officer could assist in the company's representation.[64]

§ 8 Absence of counsel

A continuance may be granted where the attorney who has been employed to conduct a trial is absent due to an illness or other cause.

West's Digest, Pretrial Procedure ☞716.

The absence of the attorney who has been employed to conduct a trial, due to an illness or other cause, may be a ground for a continuance[65] in the trial court's discretion.[66] If counsel cannot attend because of his or her duties as a

---

[60]Pierce v. Merchants' Heat & Light Co., 189 Ind. 571, 127 N.E. 765 (1920), reh'g denied, 189 Ind. 571, 128 N.E. 598 (1920); Welcome v. Boswell, 54 Ind. 297, 1876 WL 6718 (1876); Terry v. Terry, 160 Ind. App. 653, 313 N.E.2d 83 (1st Dist. 1974).

[61]Pierce v. Merchants' Heat & Light Co., 189 Ind. 571, 127 N.E. 765 (1920), reh'g denied, 189 Ind. 571, 128 N.E. 598 (1920) (defendant also ill).

Annotation References: Party's absence in civil case because of illness of relative as ground for continuance, 47 ALR2d 1058.

[62]Terry v. Terry, 160 Ind. App. 653, 313 N.E.2d 83 (1st Dist. 1974).

[63]McBride v. Stradley, 103 Ind. 465, 2 N.E. 358 (1885).

[64]Indiana Tri-City Plaza Bowl, Inc. v. Glueck's Estate, 422 N.E.2d 670 (Ind. Ct. App. 3d Dist. 1981).

[65]Bartel v. Tieman, 55 Ind. 438, 1876 WL 6651 (1876); Graves v. Rayle, 19 Ind. 83, 1862 WL 2178 (1862).

Annotation References: Continuance of civil case because of illness or death of attorney, 67 ALR2d 497.

Forms References: Absence of Counsel. 7 Am Jur Pleading and Practice Forms, Annotated (rev. ed.), Continuance §§ 37-48.

[66]Evansville & Indianapolis R. Co. v. Hawkins, 111 Ind. 549, 13 N.E. 63 (1887); Eslinger v. East, 100 Ind. 434, 1885 WL 4228 (1885); Belck v. Belck, 97 Ind. 73, 1884 WL 5394 (1884).

member of the General Assembly, the court shall grant a motion for a continuance to a date not sooner than 30 days following the date of adjournment of the session of the General Assembly.[67]

A continuance may be warranted if counsel withdraws or is terminated, and a party is entitled to a continuance if it is shown that new counsel is unable to prepare and conduct a proper case without one.[68] Where counsel has been required to withdraw, the court must determine whether denial of a continuance would deprive the party of counsel at a crucial point in the case.[69]

A motion for a continuance due to absence of counsel is properly denied if it appears that the movant did not employ diligence to insure his or her representation,[70] or that the party will not be prejudiced by the refusal.[71]

§ 9 Surprise, generally

If a party is surprised by the evidence or conduct of the other party during trial, a continuance may be granted upon good cause shown.

West's Digest, Pretrial Procedure ☞719.

During a trial or hearing, a party may be taken by surprise by the evidence or conduct of the other party, without any fault on its part. If the party would be prejudiced if forced to

---

[67]IC 2-3-5-1.

Annotation References: Counsel's absence because of attendance on legislature as ground for continuance, 49 ALR2d 10.

[68]Koors v. Great Southwest Fire Ins. Co., 530 N.E.2d 780 (Ind. Ct. App. 2d Dist. 1988), reh'g denied, 538 N.E.2d 259 (Ind. Ct. App. 2d Dist. 1989) and (abrogation on other grounds recognized by, Martin v. Amoco Oil Co., 679 N.E.2d 139 (Ind. Ct. App. 1997).

[69]Hess v. Hess, 679 N.E.2d 153 (Ind. Ct. App. 1997); Homehealth, Inc. v. Heritage Mut. Ins. Co., 662 N.E.2d 195 (Ind. Ct. App. 1996), transfer denied, (Oct. 10, 1996).

[70]Fetner v. Maury Boyd & Associates, Inc., 563 N.E.2d 1334 (Ind. Ct. App. 4th Dist. 1990), reh'g denied, (Jan. 25, 1991) and transfer denied, (July 10, 1991) (good cause not shown where pro se attorney lacked diligence in securing local counsel); Farley v. Farley, 172 Ind. App. 120, 359 N.E.2d 583 (1st Dist. 1977).

[71]Mann v. City of Terre Haute, 240 Ind. 245, 163 N.E.2d 577 (1960) (absent a showing of priority of District Court action, party whose counsel had trial on same day in Federal District Court not entitled to continuance).

proceed without being able to prepare for the new situation, a good ground for continuance arises.[72]

A continuance is not warranted on the ground of surprise where the movant should have anticipated the evidence, particularly where no harm is shown.[73] This would be true, for example, when the pleadings are broad enough to give adequate notice of the likelihood that the evidence in question would be used during trial.[74]

> ◆ **Illustration:** In a personal injury action brought by a subcontractor's employee against the construction manager, subcontractor, and others, the trial court did not abuse its discretion in denying the construction manager's motion for a continuance after modifying the manager's instruction concerning the existence of a valid indemnity agreement and agreeing to give the subcontractor's instruction on the subject, because the construction manager could not contend that the substance of the subcontractor's tendered instruction came as a complete surprise.[75]

§ 10   Amendment of pleadings; change of parties

> **The amendment of a pleading is a ground for a continuance upon a showing of good cause for the continuance and of prejudice if the continuance is not granted. Unless it effects a substantial change in the cause of action or defense, there is no occasion for a continuance upon an amendment correcting a party's name, or substituting or deleting parties.**

West's Digest, Pretrial Procedure ☜720.

The amendment of a pleading is a ground for a continuance, upon good cause shown, where the party moving for the continuance shows that he or she has been

---

[72]Plan-Tec, Inc. v. Wiggins, 443 N.E.2d 1212 (Ind. Ct. App. 1st Dist. 1983); Dilley v. Scott, 167 Ind. App. 177, 338 N.E.2d 296 (3d Dist. 1975); James v. Picou, 162 Ind. App. 134, 318 N.E.2d 377 (Ind. Ct. App. 1st Dist. 1974).

[73]Plan-Tec, Inc. v. Wiggins, 443 N.E.2d 1212 (Ind. Ct. App. 1st Dist. 1983).

[74]17 Am Jur 2d, Continuance § 44.

[75]Plan-Tec, Inc. v. Wiggins, 443 N.E.2d 1212 (Ind. Ct. App. 1st Dist. 1983).

prejudiced in preparing for trial by the amendment.[76] The matter is within the trial court's discretion, subject to review only for abuse.[77]

If the trial court allows the introduction of an issue not raised before trial, an objecting party may seek a reasonable continuance in order to prepare to litigate the new issue.[78] A continuance may be allowed, for example, when amendments to a plaintiffs' pleadings make substantial changes, as when they assert new causes of action or demands[79] or introduce a new theory as to the cause of action,[80] or where the defendant amends so as to change his or her ground of defense.[81]

An amendment should not be considered a ground for continuance if it does not appear that the other party is prejudiced thereby in preparing for trial,[82] as when adequate time for preparation remains before trial,[83] or when the amendment is unnecessary[84] or immaterial,[85] or raises no new issue.[86]

◆ **Illustration:** The seller of a lounge chair was fully informed prior to trial that the injured buyer was proceed-

---

[76]Ayr-Way Stores, Inc. v. Chitwood, 261 Ind. 86, 300 N.E.2d 335 (1973); SCM Corp. v. Letterer, 448 N.E.2d 686 (Ind. Ct. App. 4th Dist. 1983).

[77]Ayr-Way Stores, Inc. v. Chitwood, 261 Ind. 86, 300 N.E.2d 335 (1973); Jerry Alderman Ford Sales, Inc. v. Bailey, 154 Ind. App. 632, 291 N.E.2d 92, 12 U.C.C. Rep. Serv. (CBC) 47 (2d Dist. 1972), reh'g denied and opinion modified on other grounds, 154 Ind. App. 632, 294 N.E.2d 617, 12 U.C.C. Rep. Serv. (CBC) 442 (2d Dist. 1973).

As to appellate review of trial court decisions regarding continuances, generally, see § 18.

[78]Baker v. Midland-Ross Corp., 508 N.E.2d 32 (Ind. Ct. App. 1st Dist. 1987), reh'g denied, (July 10, 1987) and transfer denied, (Dec. 17, 1987).

[79]Farrington v. Hawkins, 24 Ind. 253, 1865 WL 1842 (1865); Meredith v. Lackey, 14 Ind. 529, 1860 WL 4169 (1860).

[80]Donley v. Scanlon, 116 Ind. 8, 17 N.E. 158 (1888) (new allegation as to cause of injury).

[81]Makepeace v. State ex rel. Quarles, 8 Ind. 41, 1856 WL 3642 (1856).

[82]Ayr-Way Stores, Inc. v. Chitwood, 261 Ind. 86, 300 N.E.2d 335 (1973); Farm Burean Mut. Ins. Co. v. Dercach, 450 N.E.2d 537 (3 Dist. 1983); SCM Corp. v. Letterer, 448 N.E.2d 686 (Ind. Ct. App. 4th Dist. 1983); Hancock v. York, 141 Ind. App. 212, 227 N.E.2d 187 (Div. 2 1967).

[83]Morris v. Graves, 2 Ind. 354, 1850 WL 3159 (1850).

[84]City of Richmond v. Land-Dilks Co., 80 Ind. App. 586, 141 N.E. 652 (Div. 1 1923).

[85]Epperly v. Little, 6 Ind. 344, 1855 WL 3575 (1855).

[86]Magnuson v. Billings, 152 Ind. 177, 52 N.E. 803 (1899).

ing under both negligence and strict liability theories and thus was not entitled to a continuance when, immediately before trial, the buyer was permitted to strike the words "of negligence" from the title of her contentions and proceed solely on a theory of strict liability.[87]

Unless there is effected a substantial change in the cause of action or defense, there is no occasion for a continuance upon an amendment correcting a party's name,[88] substituting parties,[89] or deleting parties.[90]

§ 11 Lack of time to prepare

Where its lack of preparation is not the fault of the moving party and good cause is otherwise shown, a continuance may be granted to a party on the ground that it has not had reasonable time to prepare for trial.

West's Digest, Pretrial Procedure ☞721.

A continuance may be granted to a party in a civil case on the ground that it has not had reasonable time to prepare for trial, if good cause is shown in support of the motion.[91] Where its lack of preparation is not the fault of the moving party and good cause is otherwise shown, refusing a continuance to a party that has not had adequate time to prepare for trial will be deemed a denial of due process.[92]

On the other hand, a motion for continuance based on lack of time to prepare will be denied where the lack of prepara-

---

Where complaint in passenger's action for injuries caused by derailment alleged that defect in cars causing injuries was unknown, amendment alleging specific defects did not bring in new charge of negligence, and continuance was properly denied.—Cleveland, C., C. & St. L. Ry. Co. v. Locke, 71 Ind. App. 35, 123 N.E. 814 (Div. 2 1919).

[87]Kroger Co. Sav-On Store v. Presnell, 515 N.E.2d 538 (Ind. Ct. App. 4th Dist. 1987), reh'g denied, (Jan. 5, 1988) and transfer denied, (June 23, 1988).

[88]Nimmon v. Worthington, 1 Ind. 376, 1849 WL 3089 (1849).

[89]Hubler v. Pullen, 9 Ind. 273, 1857 WL 3711 (1857).

[90]Taylor v. Jones, 1 Ind. 17, 1848 WL 2854 (1848).

Annotation References: Amendment of pleading with respect to parties or their capacity as grounds for continuance, 67 ALR2d 477.

[91]17 Am Jur 2d, Continuance § 53.

Forms References: Preparation for Trial. 7 Am Jur Pleading and Practice Forms, Annotated (rev. ed.), Continuance §§ 6-16.

[92]Kaiser Aluminum & Chemical Sales, Inc. v. Dickerhoff, 136 Ind. App. 258, 199 N.E.2d 719 (Div. 1 1964) (filing of counterclaim left plaintiff about

tion is due to the movant's own neglect or want of diligence,[93] or where the movant fails to show that its cause would be prejudiced by a denial of additional time.[94]

◆ **Illustration:** In an action for mandate to compel the Alcoholic Beverage Commission to issue a liquor permit, the trial court did not abuse its discretion in denying the Commission's request for a continuance although counsel in the Attorney General's office did not receive notice of the trial date until 3:30 p.m. on the day preceding trial, where the Attorney General's office had been directly involved in the matter for more than two months prior to trial and had several hours immediately prior to trial to make any last minute preparation, the Commission made no attempt to show how it was prejudiced by the denial of a continuance, and there was no allegation that any necessary witness was absent or that time was needed to procure additional evidence.[95]

§ 12 Public sentiment or prejudice

An action may be continued on the ground of public sentiment or prejudice against the party seeking relief, in order to allow the prejudice or excitement to dissipate.

West's Digest, Pretrial Procedure ☞714.

A court may continue an action on the ground of public sentiment or prejudice against the party seeking relief, in order to allow the prejudice or excitement to dissipate, but denial of a continuance on such grounds may be appropriate where the moving party has the benefit of a voir dire examination or an opportunity to challenge any juror, or where there is nothing to show that the prejudice complained of would lessen with the passage of time.[96]

In a case tried to the court, a motion for continuance on the ground of local prejudice resulting from biased news media coverage may be denied if the movant is unable to

three days in which to receive mailed counterclaim and to prepare answer and defense thereto).

[93] 17 Am Jur 2d, Continuance § 53.

[94] Indiana Alcoholic Beverage Commission v. State ex rel. Harmon, 269 Ind. 48, 379 N.E.2d 140 (1978).

[95] Indiana Alcoholic Beverage Commission v. State ex rel. Harmon, 269 Ind. 48, 379 N.E.2d 140 (1978).

[96] 17 Am Jur 2d, Continuance § 57.

show that the trial judge had been somehow contaminated by such coverage.[97]

II. PROCEDURE; APPEAL AND REVIEW

Research References

Trial R. 53.5

4 Am Jur 2d, Appellate Review § 145.
17 Am Jur 2d, Continuance §§ 117-132.
17 C.J.S., Continuances §§ 94-123, 127-133.
West's Digest, Pretrial Procedure ☞723-726.
ALR Digest: Appeal and Error §§ 368, 537, 538; Continuance and Adjournment §§ 8.5-10; New Trial § 13
ALR Index: Continuance and Adjournment
2 Am Jur Pleading and Practice Forms, Annotated (rev. ed.), Appeal and Error §§ 785-788.
7 Am Jur Pleading and Practice Forms, Annotated (rev. ed.), Continuance §§ 53-58, 78-101.

§ 13 Motion, generally; supporting affidavit or evidence

A continuance should be sought by a proper motion as soon as practicable after the movant learns of the need for a continuance and should be supported by an affidavit or other evidence showing good cause for the relief.

West's Digest, Pretrial Procedure ☞723.1, 724.

A party seeking a continuance should make a written and verified motion or application setting forth the basis for the applicant's right to a continuance.[98]

While a court may continue an action at any time, an application or motion for continuance should be made at the earliest practicable time after a party becomes aware of the need for a continuance. Where a party has not been diligent in seeking a continuance, its motion for continuance after a case has been called for trial, or after trial has begun, is not

---

[97]Hunter v. Milhous, 159 Ind. App. 105, 305 N.E.2d 448 (2d Dist. 1973).

[98]Indiana Tri-City Plaza Bowl, Inc. v. Glueck's Estate, 422 N.E.2d 670 (Ind. Ct. App. 3d. Dist. 1980); Breezewood Management Co. v. Maltbie, 411 N.E.2d 670 (Ind. Ct. App. 1st Dist. 1980).

As to continuance on the court's own motion or by stipulation of the parties, see § 14.

Forms References: Notice of Motion. 7 Am Jur Pleading and Practice Forms, Annotated (rev. ed.), Continuance §§ 78-85.

timely.[99] Failure to make a timely application is deemed a waiver of the right to a continuance.[1]

◆ **Illustration:** The trial court in a tort action acted within its discretion in denying a motion by the corporate defendant, acting through its president, for a continuance so that it could obtain counsel, despite the corporation's alleged ignorance of a prohibition against corporations proceeding pro se, where the motion for continuance was not made until the day of a summary judgment hearing.[2]

Under the Rules of Trial Procedure, an application for continuance must be supported by an affidavit or other evidence showing good cause for such relief. A motion to postpone a trial on account of the absence of evidence can be made only upon affidavit, showing the materiality of the evidence expected to be obtained, the location of the evidence, and that due diligence has been used to obtain it. For an absent witness, the affidavit must further show the name and address of the witness, if available; the likelihood of obtaining the testimony within a reasonable amount of time; that the movant has not played a role in the witness's absence; the facts the movant believes to be true about the witness' testimony; and that the movant is unable to prove those facts as readily by any other witness or evidence.[3]

§ 14 Continuance on court's own motion; stipulation of parties

A continuance may be granted on the court's own motion or upon the agreement or stipulation of the parties.

---

[99]Clodfelder v. Walker, 234 Ind. 219, 125 N.E.2d 799 (1955); Breezewood Management Co. v. Maltbie, 411 N.E.2d 670 (Ind. Ct. App. 1st Dist. 1980).

Forms References: After Commencement of Trial. 7 Am Jur Pleading and Practice Forms, Annotated (rev. ed.), Continuance §§ 53-58.

[1]Clodfelder v. Walker, 234 Ind. 219, 125 N.E.2d 799 (1955); Terre Haute Regional Hosp., Inc. v. El-Issa, 470 N.E.2d 1371 (Ind. App. 1 Dist. 1984), rehearing denied (Jan 04, 1985), and transfer denied (Mar 28, 1985); Bay v. Barenie, 421 N.E.2d 6 (Ind. Ct. App. 3d Dist. 1981); Breezewood Management Co. v. Maltbie, 411 N.E.2d 670 (Ind. Ct. App. 1st Dist. 1980).

[2]Royalty Vans, Inc. v. Hill Bros. Plumbing and Heating, Inc., 605 N.E.2d 1217 (Ind. Ct. App. 5th Dist. 1993), reh'g denied, (Mar. 8, 1993).

[3]Trial R. 53.5.

As to good cause for a continuance, generally, see § 2.

As to continuance based on the absence of evidence or witnesses, generally, see § 3.

West's Digest, Pretrial Procedure ☞711, 712, 723.1.

In a proper case and within its sound discretion, a court may grant a continuance on its own motion,[4] as well as upon the motion of a party to the action.[5]

A court may also, in its discretion, continue a case upon the agreement or stipulation of the parties.[6] A stipulation for a postponement requires the sanction of the court,[7] so that a party is not justified in assuming that a cause will be postponed simply because of an agreement reached with the opposing party.[8] An agreement for continuance between one of several plaintiffs and the defendants does not bind the other plaintiffs.[9]

§ 15 Hearing and determination

An application for a continuance must be heard and determined by the court.

West's Digest, Pretrial Procedure ☞725.

The determination of whether a continuance should be granted is a judicial act, and an application for a continuance must be heard by the court.[10] In making its decision, the court must weigh the prejudice to the moving party if a continuance is not granted against the prejudice to the nonmoving party if the continuance is granted.[11]

If the relief is granted, the order for continuance should

---

[4]Dorsey Mach. Co. v. McCaffrey, 139 Ind. 545, 38 N.E. 208 (1894); Terry v. Terry, 160 Ind. App. 653, 313 N.E.2d 83 (1st Dist. 1974).

[5]§ 13.

[6]17 C.J.S., Continuances § 12.

[7]Moulder v. Kempff, 115 Ind. 459, 17 N.E. 906 (1888).

[8]17 C.J.S., Continuances § 12.

[9]Midland R. Co. v. Island Coal Co., 126 Ind. 384, 26 N.E. 68 (1890).

[10]17 C.J.S., Continuances § 112.

A judge's secretary does not have authority to grant a continuance over the telephone.—In re Marriage of Robbins, 171 Ind. App. 509, 358 N.E.2d 153 (3d Dist. 1976) (overruled on other grounds by, Siebert Oxidermo, Inc. v. Shields, 446 N.E.2d 332 (Ind. 1983)) and (overruling on other grounds recognized by, Hawblitzel v. Hawblitzel, 447 N.E.2d 1156 (Ind. Ct. App. 3d Dist. 1983)).

[11]Homehealth, Inc. v. Heritage Mut. Ins. Co., 662 N.E.2d 195 (Ind. Ct. App. 1996), transfer denied, (Oct. 10, 1996); Koors v. Great Southwest Fire Ins. Co., 530 N.E.2d 780 (Ind. Ct. App. 2d Dist. 1988), reh'g denied, 538 N.E.2d 259 (Ind. Ct. App. 2d Dist. 1989) and (abrogation on other

indicate such definite period as is reasonably necessary to accomplish the purpose for which the continuance is requested.[12] A continuance for four hours only has been found equivalent to a denial of relief.[13]

Generally, a court that has once denied a continuance should not consider a new application on the same facts,[14] or on facts which could have been presented with the first application.[15] If the continuance has been granted, a further continuance may be allowed if adequate reason therefor remains,[16] but not if the reason has disappeared[17] or the party has failed to exercise diligence during the term of the continuance.[18]

§ 16 Costs

Costs and other expenses incurred by the nonmoving party in preparing for trial may be imposed by the court as a condition of granting a continuance.

West's Digest, Pretrial Procedure ☞725.

A court may impose costs and other expenses incurred in preparing for trial as a condition of granting a continuance of a civil case.[19] Under the Rules of Trial Procedure, the court may award such costs as will reimburse the other parties for

---

grounds recognized by, Martin v. Amoco Oil Co., 679 N.E.2d 139 (Ind. Ct. App. 1997); Ashbrook v. Ashbrook, 174 Ind. App. 134, 366 N.E.2d 667 (1st Dist. 1977).

[12]17 Am Jur 2d, Continuance § 130.

Forms References: Order for continuance. 7 Am Jur Pleading and Practice Forms, Annotated (rev. ed.), Continuance §§ 86-98.

[13]Burch v. Smock, 85 Ind. App. 536, 154 N.E. 675 (1927).

[14]Garrett v. Garrett, 12 Ind. 407, 1859 WL 4849 (1859).

[15]Shattuck v. Myers, 13 Ind. 46, 1859 WL 4737 (1859).

[16]Pierce v. Merchants' Heat & Light Co., 189 Ind. 571, 127 N.E. 765 (1920), reh'g denied, 189 Ind. 571, 128 N.E. 598 (1920) (where affidavits showed that defendant was too ill to attend trial and that there was sickness in his family, court abused its discretion in denying continuance, even though defendant had previously delayed trial and even though on former continuance his attorneys had promised not to ask for another).

[17]Dannhauer v. Kaylor, 74 Ind. App. 524, 126 N.E. 31 (Div. 2 1920).

[18]Sutherlin v. State, 108 Ind. 389, 9 N.E. 298 (1886); Rodgers v. McLeary, 5 Ind. 236, 1854 WL 3315 (1854).

[19]17 Am Jur 2d, Continuance § 132.

Forms References: Conditional Continuance. 7 Am Jur Pleading and Practice Forms, Annotated (rev. ed.), Continuance §§ 99-101.

their actual expenses incurred from the delay.[20] Such an award is made to overcome prejudice to the nonmoving party in the grant of a continuance[21] and rests within the sound discretion of the trial court.[22]

> ◆ **Observation:** The act of one's attorney is the act of the client, and expenses incurred from delay caused by the attorney may properly be taxed to the client.[23]

The court is not precluded from taking evidence as to the expenses incurred by a party resulting from the grant of a continuance, but an award of costs may be upheld although the court did not take evidence as to the basis for an award.[24] Costs awarded incident to a continuance may not include the attorney fees of the nonmovant.[25]

Although normally imposed as a condition of the relief, costs may be awarded even after the entry of a continuance.[26]

§ 17 Rescission of continuance

A court may rescind a continuance previously granted, upon motion of a party or upon its own motion.

West's Digest, Pretrial Procedure ☞725.

A court may set aside a continuance previously granted, on the motion of a party or on its own motion.[27]

---

[20]Trial R. 53.5.

Annotation References: Continuance of civil case as conditioned upon applicant's payment of costs or expenses incurred by other party, 9 ALR4th 1144.

[21]Kline v. Kline, 455 N.E.2d 407 (Ind. Ct. App. 2d Dist. 1983).

[22]Brutus v. Wright, 163 Ind. App. 366, 324 N.E.2d 165 (3d Dist. 1975).

[23]Brutus v. Wright, 163 Ind. App. 366, 324 N.E.2d 165 (3d Dist. 1975).

[24]Gentry v. Lakey, 150 Ind. App. 612, 276 N.E.2d 857 (Div. 1 1971).

[25]Maggio v. Lee, 511 N.E.2d 1084 (Ind. Ct. App. 3d Dist. 1987).

[26]Brutus v. Wright, 163 Ind. App. 366, 324 N.E.2d 165 (3d Dist. 1975).

[27]Town of Portage v. Clifford, 254 Ind. 443, 260 N.E.2d 566 (1970); Castillo v. Ruggiero, 562 N.E.2d 446 (Ind. Ct. App. 3d Dist. 1990), transfer denied, (Apr. 8, 1991).

A continuance should not be rescinded if either party will be harmed.[28] There is no prejudice where the original motion was not supported by affidavit or other evidence.[29]

§ 18 Appeal and review

A court's ruling regarding a continuance is subject to review only for an abuse of discretion.

West's Digest, Pretrial Procedure ☞713.

On appeal, the denial of a continuance may be raised as an issue by challenging the trial court's overruling of a motion for new trial based on such denial.[30]

The grant or denial of a motion for a continuance is a matter within the trial court's sound discretion[31] and will only be reviewed for an abuse of that discretion.[32]

A cause will not be reversed based on the denial of a continuance unless it is clearly shown that the court's discretion has been abused.[33] Where the denial of a continuance is clearly against the logic and effect of the evidence presented in favor of the motion, the denial will be reversed for an abuse of discretion.[34]

---

[28]Town of Portage v. Clifford, 254 Ind. 443, 260 N.E.2d 566 (1970).

[29]Castillo v. Ruggiero, 562 N.E.2d 446 (Ind. Ct. App. 3d Dist. 1990), transfer denied, (Apr. 8, 1991).

[30]Flick v. Simpson, 145 Ind. App. 698, 252 N.E.2d 508 (Div. 2 1969), reh'g denied, 145 Ind. App. 698, 255 N.E.2d 118 (Div. 2 1970); Grand Rapids Motor Exp. v. Crosbie, 117 Ind. App. 360, 69 N.E.2d 247 (1947).

Forms References: Bills of Exception Involving Continuances. 2 Am Jur Pleading and Practice Forms, Annotated (rev. ed.), Appeal and Error §§ 785-788.

[31]§ 1.

[32]Boles v. Weidner, 449 N.E.2d 288 (Ind. 1983); Robertson v. Board of Zoning Appeals, Town of Chesterton, 699 N.E.2d 310 (Ind. Ct. App. 1998); Royalty Vans, Inc. v. Hill Bros. Plumbing and Heating, Inc., 605 N.E.2d 1217 (Ind. Ct. App. 5th Dist. 1993), reh'g denied, (Mar. 8, 1993); Farm Burean Mut. Ins. Co. v. Dercach, 450 N.E.2d 537 (3 Dist. 1983).

[33]Chambers v. Public Service Co. of Indiana, Inc., 265 Ind. 336, 355 N.E.2d 781 (1976); Plan-Tec, Inc. v. Wiggins, 443 N.E.2d 1212 (Ind. Ct. App. 1st Dist. 1983); Spangler v. U. S. Rubber Co., 133 Ind. App. 468, 183 N.E.2d 212 (Div. 2 1962); Woodrow v. Woodrow, 131 Ind. App. 523, 172 N.E.2d 883 (Div. 1 1961).

[34]Boles v. Weidner, 449 N.E.2d 288 (Ind. 1983); Hess v. Hess, 679 N.E.2d 153 (Ind. Ct. App. 1997); Trojnar v. Trojnar, 676 N.E.2d 1094 (Ind. Ct. App. 1997), reh'g denied, (May 9, 1997) and transfer granted, opinion

The denial of a motion showing good cause for a continuance may be deemed an abuse of discretion;[35] however, a trial court's ruling will not be overturned unless the moving party can show that it was free from fault[36] and prejudiced by the denial.[37]

---

vacated on other grounds, 706 N.E.2d 168 (Ind. 1998) and opinion vacated on other grounds, 698 N.E.2d 301 (Ind. 1998).

[35]Robertson v. Board of Zoning Appeals, Town of Chesterton, 699 N.E.2d 310 (Ind. Ct. App. 1998); Homehealth, Inc. v. Heritage Mut. Ins. Co., 662 N.E.2d 195 (Ind. Ct. App. 1996), transfer denied, (Oct. 10, 1996); Danner v. Danner, 573 N.E.2d 934 (Ind. Ct. App. 1st Dist. 1991), decision clarified on reh'g, (Aug. 20, 1991) and transfer denied, (Feb. 14, 1992).

[36]Hess v. Hess, 679 N.E.2d 153 (Ind. Ct. App. 1997); Homehealth, Inc. v. Heritage Mut. Ins. Co., 662 N.E.2d 195 (Ind. Ct. App. 1996), transfer denied, (Oct. 10, 1996); Danner v. Danner, 573 N.E.2d 934 (Ind. Ct. App. 1st Dist. 1991), decision clarified on reh'g, (Aug. 20, 1991) and transfer denied, (Feb. 14, 1992).

[37]Robertson v. Board of Zoning Appeals, Town of Chesterton, 699 N.E.2d 310 (Ind. Ct. App. 1998); Matter of L.C., 659 N.E.2d 593 (Ind. Ct. App. 1995), reh'g denied, (Feb. 6, 1996) and transfer denied, 683 N.E.2d 582 (Ind. 1997) and cert. denied, 521 U.S. 1122, 117 S. Ct. 2515, 138 L. Ed. 2d 1017 (1997); Communications Workers of America, Locals 5800, 5714 v. Beckman, 540 N.E.2d 117 (Ind. Ct. App. 4th Dist. 1989); Koors v. Great Southwest Fire Ins. Co., 530 N.E.2d 780 (Ind. Ct. App. 2d Dist. 1988), reh'g denied, 538 N.E.2d 259 (Ind. Ct. App. 2d Dist. 1989) and (abrogation on other grounds recognized by, Martin v. Amoco Oil Co., 679 N.E.2d 139 (Ind. Ct. App. 1997); Farm Burean Mut. Ins. Co. v. Dercach, 450 N.E.2d 537 (3 Dist. 1983).

CONTRACTS

Elizabeth Williams, J.D.

Scope of Topic

This article discusses the law of contracts generally, including the principles governing the formation of contracts and the requisites therefor, such as assent, offer, acceptance, consideration, definiteness, and formalities; illegality arising from violation of constitution, statute, or public policy; construction of contracts; parties to contracts; time for performance, conditions, and compensation; modification, merger, and rescission of contracts; performance of breach of contracts; and practice and actions for breach of contracts.

Treated Elsewhere

Assignability of contracts, see I.L.E., Assignments

Businesses or occupations, contracts incident to particular kinds of, see I.L.E., Attorney and Client; Auctions and Auctioneers; Banks and Banking; Brokers; Carriers; Factors; Franchises; Hotels; Insurance; Mining; Oil and Gas; Pawnbrokers and Money Lenders; Physicians and Surgeons; Railroads; Shipping; Telecommunications; Warehouses

Cancellation or reformation of contracts by judicial decree, see I.L.E., Cancellation of Instruments; Reformation of Instruments

Corporations, contracts by private and public, see I.L.E., Corporations; Education; Municipal Corporations

Express contracts and instruments, particular kinds of, see I.L.E., Accord and Satisfaction; Arbitration; Bailment; Bonds; Chattel Mortgages; Compromise and Settlement; Deeds; Guaranty; Indemnity; Mortgages; Negotiable Instruments; Novation; Release; Rewards; Sales of Personalty; Sales of Realty; Subscriptions

Illegality, certain grounds of, see I.L.E., Champerty and Maintenance; Interest and Usury; Monopolies and Unfair Trade

Interference with contractual relations, see I.L.E., Torts

Persons, contracts by aggregation of, see I.L.E., Associations, Clubs, and Societies; Joint Venture; Partnership

Persons, contracts by particular classes of, see I.L.E., Executors and Administrators; Minors; Officers

Persons in special relation to each other, contracts by, see I.L.E., Agency; Employment; Guardian and Ward; Husband and Wife; Landlord and Tenant; Parent and Child

Property, contracts affecting particular kinds of, see I.L.E., Animals; Crops; Easements; Fixtures; Good Will

Remedial and procedural law in actions involving contracts, see I.L.E., Action; Damages; Declaratory Judgment; Evidence; Injunction; Parties; Pleading, Discovery and Pre-Trial Procedure; Set-off and Counterclaim; Specific Performance; Subrogation; Trial

Research References

Text References

17A Am Jur 2d, Contracts.
17 C.J.S., Contracts.
17A C.J.S., Contracts.
17B C.J.S., Contracts.

West's Digest References

West's Digest, Contracts.

Annotation References

ALR Digest: Contracts
ALR Index: Adhesion Contracts; Anticipatory Breach; Anticipatory Renunciation or Repudiation; Bids and Bidding; Cancellation of Rescission; Consideration; Contracts; Covenants; Covenants Not to Compete; Estoppel and Waiver; Executory Contracts; Implied Contracts; Offer and Acceptance; Parol Contracts and Agreements; Parol Evidence; Third-Party Beneficiaries; Unconscionability

Forms References

5A Am Jur Legal Forms 2d, Contracts.
7A Am Jur Pleading and Practice Forms, Annotated (rev. ed.), Contracts.

Trial Strategy References

Negligent Performance of Advertising Contract, 14 Am Jur POF3d 699; Tortious Interference by Parent Corporation With Subsidiary's Contract With Third Party, 17 Am Jur POF3d 685; Real Property Contracts—Specific Performance With Abatement of Purchase Price, 19 Am Jur POF3d 543; Insurer's Right to Rescind Insurance Contract Fort the Insured's False Statements, 21 Am Jur POF3d 565; Proving the Contractually Binding Effect of a Personnel Manual Provision as to Discharge Only for "Good Cause", 32 Am Jur POF3d 229; Validity and Applicability of Contractual Allocations of Environmental Risk, 34 Am Jur POF3d 465; Proof of Fraudulent Inducement of a Contract and Entitlement to Remedies, 48 Am Jur POF3d 329; Mutual Mistake Over Physical Condition of Real Estate as Basis for Rescission of Contract, 48 Am Jur POF3d 505.

Detrimental Reliance on Promise, 4 Am Jur POF2d 641; Promise Made With Intent Not to Perform, 5 Am Jur POF2d 727; Intent of Contracting Parties to Benefit Third Person, 16 Am Jur POF2d 55; Estoppel to Assert Statute of Limitations in Contract Action, 21 Am Jur POF2d 463; "Impossibility" of Performing Contract, 24 Am Jur POF2d 269; Meaning of Abbreviation, Word, or Phrase According to Usage of Trade, 26 Am Jur POF2d 299; Offeree's Acceptance of Contract Offer, 27 Am Jur POF2d 559; Acts Constituting Rejection of Contract Offer, 27 Am Jur POF2d 605; Terms of Oral Contract with Decedent, 39 Am Jur POF2d 91; Recovery for Part Performance of Contract, 43 Am Jur POF2d 523; Breach of Contract Resulting in Loss of Personal Publicity, 50 Am Jur POF2d 563.

Selecting the Remedy, 3 Am Jur Trials 637; Tactics and Strategy of Pleading, 3 Am Jur Trials 681; Jury or Non-Jury Trial—Defense Viewpoint, 5 Am Jur Trials 105; Interference With Attorney's Contingent Fee Contract, 13 Am Jur Trials 153; Actions for Interference with Contract Rights, 18 Am Jur Trials 57; Defense of a First-party Extra-Contract Claims Action Against a Life, Health, and Accident Insurer, 29 Am Jur Trials 481; Bad Faith Tort Remedy for Breach of Contract, 34 Am Jur Trials 343; Trial Report: Defending a Celebrity in a Breach of Employment Contract Case, 37 Am Jur Trials 597; Contractual Indemnifications and Releases From Environmental Liability, 59 Am Jur Trials 231; Trials Over Arbitration Clauses in Securities Broker Contracts, 61 Am Jur Trials 357.

Miscellaneous References

Corbin on Contracts (rev. ed.).

Statutory References

IC 2-7-1-1; IC 4-13.6-5-11; IC 8-1-2-106; IC 8-3-1-13; IC 8-21-4-7; IC 10-5-10-1; IC 20-1-19-19; IC 24-1-1-1; IC 24-1-2-1; IC 24-1-2-3; IC 24-1-2-7; IC 24-4-9-19; IC 24-5-7-10; IC 24-5-11.5-12 to IC 24-5-11.5-14; IC 24-5-13-15; IC 25-34.1-3-2; IC 26-1-1-1; IC 26-1-1-101 et seq.; IC 26-1-2-201; IC 26-1-2-204; IC 26-1-2-207; IC 26-1-2-306; IC 26-1-2-309; IC 26-1-2-508; IC 26-1-2-719; IC 26-1-3-408; IC 26-2-5-1; IC 27-1-12-15; IC 27-1-20-30; IC 29-1-11-3; IC 29-1-14-5; IC 29-3-1-10; IC 29-3-1-13; IC 29-3-4-2; IC 29-3-8-2; IC 29-3-8-5; IC 29-3-8-7; IC 31-1-11.5-1 et seq.; IC 31-1-11.5-12; IC 31-11-7-1; IC 32-2-1-1; IC 32-2-1.5-4; IC 32-8-3-1; IC 34-11-2-3; IC 34-11-2-7; IC 34-11-2-9; IC 34-11-2-11; IC 34-11-3-1; IC 34-37-1-1; IC 34-37-1-2; IC 35-15-1-2; IC 35-44-1-1

45 IAC 2.2-4-1

11 U.S.C.A. § 1129

29 U.S.C.A. § 185

Court Rules

Prof. Cond. R. 7.3

Trial R. 7-12, 17, 19, 41, 52

KeyCite®: Cases and other legal materials listed in KeyCite Scope can be researched through West Group's KeyCite service on Westlaw®. Use KeyCite to check citations for form, parallel references, prior and later history, and comprehensive citator information, including citations to other decisions and secondary materials.

Table of Parallel References:
To convert General Index references to section references in this volume, or to ascertain the disposition (or current equivalent) of articles in the prior edition of this publication, see the Table of Parallel References at the beginning of this volume.

I. IN GENERAL (§§ 1 TO 6)

II. OFFER AND ACCEPTANCE (§§ 7 TO 12)

III. CONSIDERATION (§§ 13 TO 24)
   A. IN GENERAL (§§ 13 TO 14)
   B. SUFFICIENCY OF CONSIDERATION (§§ 15 TO 22)
   C. FAILURE AND ADEQUACY OF CONSIDERATION (§§ 23 TO 24)

IV. FORMAL REQUISITES (§§ 25 TO 30)

V. VALIDITY OF ASSENT (§§ 31 TO 42)

VI. ILLEGALITY AND CONTRAVENTION OF PUBLIC POLICY (§§ 43 TO 57)
   A. IN GENERAL (§§ 43 TO 55)
   B. EFFECT OF ILLEGALITY (§§ 56 TO 57)

VII. GENERAL RULES OF CONSTRUCTION (§§ 58 TO 78)

VIII. PARTIES TO CONTRACTS (§§ 79 TO 83)

IX. TIME FOR PERFORMANCE (§§ 84 TO 86)

X.   CONDITIONS (§§ 87 TO 88)

XI.   COMPENSATION (§§ 89 TO 92)

XII.   MODIFICATION AND MERGER (§§ 93 TO 97)

XIII.   RESCISSION (§§ 98 TO 102)

XIV.   PERFORMANCE OR BREACH (§§ 103 TO 118)
A.   PERFORMANCE (§§ 103 TO 112)
B.   BREACH (§§ 113 TO 118)

XV.   ACTIONS FOR BREACH OF CONTRACT (§§ 119 TO 138)
A.   GENERALLY (§§ 119 TO 135)
B.   EVIDENCE (§§ 136 TO 138)

I.   IN GENERAL
§ 1   Generally
§ 2   Definiteness and certainty
§ 3   Parties
§ 4   Mutuality of obligation
§ 5   Express and implied contracts
§ 6   Constructive contracts

II.   OFFER AND ACCEPTANCE
§ 7   Generally
§ 8   Offer
§ 9   —Option contracts and rights of first refusal
§ 10   Acceptance
§ 11   —Acceptance at variance with offer
§ 12   Communication of acceptance

III.   CONSIDERATION
A.   IN GENERAL
§ 13   Generally

§ 14   Promissory estoppel

B.   SUFFICIENCY OF CONSIDERATION

§ 15   Generally
§ 16   Benefit or detriment
§ 17   Forbearance
§ 18   Past consideration
§ 19   Performance of legal obligation
§ 20   Personal rights, relations and services
§ 21   Employment
§ 22   Love and affection

C.   FAILURE AND ADEQUACY OF CONSIDERATION

§ 23   Failure of consideration
§ 24   Adequacy of consideration

IV.   FORMAL REQUISITES

§ 25   Generally
§ 26   Writing
§ 27   —Effect of parties' agreement
§ 28   —Effect of statute
§ 29   Execution and delivery
§ 30   —Signature

V.   VALIDITY OF ASSENT

§ 31   Mental condition or age of party
§ 32   —Contracts for necessaries
§ 33   Mutual mistake
§ 34   Unilateral mistake
§ 35   Fraud
§ 36   —Representations of opinion of law, or as to future events
§ 37   —Reliance on representation
§ 38   —Knowledge of falsity of representation; intent to deceive
§ 39   —Effect of fraud
§ 40   —Ratification and estoppel
§ 41   Undue influence and unconscionability
§ 42   Duress

VI. ILLEGALITY AND CONTRAVENTION OF PUBLIC POLICY

A. IN GENERAL

§ 43   Generally
§ 44   What law governs
§ 45   Violation of statute
§ 46   Public policy in absence of statute
§ 47   Exculpatory clauses
§ 48   —Adhesion contracts
§ 49   Agreements harmful to justice
§ 50   Contracts in restraint or derogation of marriage
§ 51   Contracts in restraint of trade
§ 52   —Covenants not to compete
§ 53   Agreements harmful to public service
§ 54   —Public offices and emoluments
§ 55   Particular contracts

B. EFFECT OF ILLEGALITY

§ 56   Generally
§ 57   Partial illegality

VII. GENERAL RULES OF CONSTRUCTION

§ 58   Generally
§ 59   Intent of parties
§ 60   —As determined by language of contract
§ 61   Construction as a whole
§ 62   Oral contracts, generally
§ 63   Written contracts, generally
§ 64   Meaning of words used
§ 65   —Particular words and phrases construed
§ 66   Construction favoring validity of contract
§ 67   Reasonable and equitable construction
§ 68   Construction against drafting party
§ 69   General and specific words
§ 70   Omissions or mistakes
§ 71   Recitals
§ 72   Conflicting clauses in general
§ 73   Construing instruments together
§ 74   Existing law as part of contract
§ 75   Implied terms

§ 76   Construction by parties
§ 77   Severability of contract
§ 78   Questions of law and fact

VIII.   PARTIES TO CONTRACTS

§ 79   In general
§ 80   Effect of signature by fewer than all parties
§ 81   Joint, several, or joint and several contracts
§ 82   Privity of contract
§ 83   Agreements for benefit of third persons

IX.   TIME FOR PERFORMANCE

§ 84   In general
§ 85   Stipulations as to time
§ 86   Duration and termination of contract

X.   CONDITIONS

§ 87   In general
§ 88   Waiver

XI.   COMPENSATION

§ 89   In general
§ 90   Building and construction contracts
§ 91   —Extra work
§ 92   Medium of payment

XII.   MODIFICATION AND MERGER

§ 93   Modification
§ 94   —Consideration for modification
§ 95   —Oral modification of written contract
§ 96   —Operation and effect
§ 97   Merger

XIII.   RESCISSION

§ 98   Rescission by agreement
§ 99   Rescission by one party
§ 100   Return to status quo
§ 101   Partial rescission
§ 102   Time for rescission

XIV. PERFORMANCE OR BREACH
A. PERFORMANCE

§ 103 Generally
§ 104 Demand for performance
§ 105 Performance of conditions
§ 106 Tender of performance
§ 107 Delegation of performance; assignment
§ 108 Sufficiency of performance as determined by party
§ 109 Sufficiency of performance as determined by third person
§ 110 Substantial performance
§ 111 Act of other party as excuse for nonperformance
§ 112 Other excuse for nonperformance

B. BREACH

§ 113 Acts constituting breach of contract
§ 114 Waiver of breach or defective performance
§ 115 Effect of breach, generally
§ 116 —Forfeiture
§ 117 Effect of substantial or partial performance
§ 118 —Altered performance; deviations

XV. ACTIONS FOR BREACH OF CONTRACT
A. GENERALLY

§ 119 Nature and form of action
§ 120 Conflict of Laws
§ 121 Conditions precedent to suit
§ 122 Defenses
§ 123 Time to sue and limitations
§ 124 Parties
§ 125 Complaint, generally
§ 126 —Inclusion of written contract
§ 127 —Damages
§ 128 Answer
§ 129 —Affirmative defenses
§ 130 Reply
§ 131 Issues, proof, and variance
§ 132 Presumptions and burden of proof
§ 133 Questions of law and fact
§ 134 Findings and judgment
§ 135 Instructions

B. EVIDENCE

§ 136　Admissibility of evidence, generally
§ 137　—Parol evidence
§ 138　Weight and sufficiency of evidence

I. IN GENERAL

Research References

IC 26-1-2-306; IC 31-11-7-1

17A Am Jur 2d, Contracts §§ 1-15.
17 C.J.S., Contracts §§ 1-38.
West's Digest, Contracts ☞1-10.
ALR Digest: Contracts §§ 1-5
ALR Index: Adhesion Contracts; Anticipatory Breach; Anticipatory Renunciation or Repudiation; Bids and Bidding; Cancellation of Rescission; Consideration; Contracts; Covenants; Covenants Not to Compete; Estoppel and Waiver; Executory Contracts; Implied Contracts; Offer and Acceptance; Parol Contracts and Agreements; Parol Evidence; Third-Party Beneficiaries; Unconscionability
Corbin on Contracts (rev. ed.), §§ 1.1-1.23.

§ 1　Generally

A contract is a promise directly or indirectly enforceable at law.

West's Digest, Contracts ☞1.

A contract is a promise that is directly or indirectly enforceable at law.[1] Indiana courts recognize that it is in the best interest of the public not to restrict unnecessarily the freedom to contract.[2] Thus, as a general rule, the law allows competent adults the utmost liberty in entering into contracts, and contracts entered into freely and voluntarily will generally be enforced by the courts.[3] The parties to a contract have the right to define their mutual rights and

---

[1] Corbin on Contracts (rev. ed.), § 3.

[2] Trimble v. Ameritech Pub., Inc., 700 N.E.2d 1128 (Ind. 1998); Fresh Cut, Inc. v. Fazli, 650 N.E.2d 1126 (Ind. 1995).

[3] Peoples Bank & Trust Co. v. Price, 714 N.E.2d 712 (Ind. Ct. App. 1999), transfer denied, (Nov. 19, 1999); Town and Country Ford, Inc. v. Busch, 709 N.E.2d 1030 (Ind. Ct. App. 1999); Indiana-American Water Co., Inc. v. Town of Seelyville, 698 N.E.2d 1255, 38 U.C.C. Rep. Serv. 2d (CBC) 1133 (Ind. Ct. App. 1998); Federal Kemper Ins. Co. v. Brown, 674

obligations as they see fit,[4] provided the agreement is not illegal and does not violate public policy.[5]

Contracts are sometimes spoken of as "void" or "voidable". While the expression "void contract" is in a sense a contradiction in terms, it is used to denote that the parties to the transaction have gone through the form of making a contract, but that no binding contract has been formed because of the lack of some essential element of a contract.[6] A void contract is an absolute nullity, incapable of ratification, while a voidable contract is one with respect to which a party has the privilege of electing it to be either valid or void at his pleasure.[7]

§ 2 Definiteness and certainty

The terms of a contract must be reasonably definite as to its essential elements.

West's Digest, Contracts ☜9(1)-9(3).

To be valid and enforceable, a contract must be reasonably definite and certain.[8]

If any essential element is omitted from a contract, or is left obscure or undefined, so as to leave the intention of the parties uncertain as to any substantial term of the contract,

---

N.E.2d 1030 (Ind. Ct. App. 1997), reh'g denied, (Mar. 6, 1997) and transfer denied, 690 N.E.2d 1190 (Ind. 1997).

[4]Southern, School Bldgs., Inc. v. Loew Elec., Inc., 407 N.E.2d 240 (Ind. Ct. App. 3d Dist. 1980).

[5]Indiana-American Water Co., Inc. v. Town of Seelyville, 698 N.E.2d 1255, 38 U.C.C. Rep. Serv. 2d (CBC) 1133 (Ind. Ct. App. 1998); Rumple v. Bloomington Hospital, 422 N.E.2d 1309 (Ind. Ct. App. 1st Dist. 1981), transfer denied, 429 N.E.2d 214 (Ind. 1981).

As to the effect of illegality and unconscionability on contract enforceability, see §§ 41, 56 et seq.

Legal Periodicals: Newly Identified Contract Unconscionability: Unconscionability of Remedy, 63 Notre Dame L.Rev. 247 (1988).

Unconscionability revisited in the Seventh Circuit, 36 Res Gestae 314 (1993).

[6]Griffin v. Smith, 101 F.2d 348 (C.C.A. 7th Cir. 1938) (applying Indiana law).

[7]Griffin v. Smith, 101 F.2d 348 (C.C.A. 7th Cir. 1938) (applying Indiana law).

[8]Dayhuff v. Canonie Const. Co., 152 Ind. App. 154, 283 N.E.2d 425 (1st Dist. 1972); International Shoe Co. v. Lacy, 114 Ind. App. 641, 53 N.E.2d 636 (1944), opinion supplemented, 116 Ind. App. 78, 61 N.E.2d 85 (1945).

the contract may not be specifically enforced.[9] For instance, amounts and prices must be fixed, or must be subject to some ascertainable formula or standard.[10]

Contracts have been held unenforceable as uncertain where they did not specify the price at which an article should be sold,[11] the character of services to be rendered[12] or the amount of compensation for services,[13] and where performance was left to the uncontrolled discretion of a party.[14]

An insufficiently definite contract may be validated if the terms are specified in a later agreement.[15]

However, absolute certainty in all of the contract's terms is not required,[16] as long as the contract is reasonably definite.[17] A court will not find that a contract is so uncertain as to preclude specific enforcement where a reasonable and logical interpretation will render the contract valid.[18] Moreover, if the parties do not expressly agree as to an essential term of the contract, the term may be supplied by applicable law in force at the time of the agreement, as the law impliedly

---

[9]Johnson v. Sprague, 614 N.E.2d 585 (Ind. Ct. App. 1st Dist. 1993).

[10]Inman's Inc. v. City of Greenfield, 412 N.E.2d 126 (Ind. Ct. App. 1st Dist. 1980); Marshall v. Ahrendt, 165 Ind. App. 359, 332 N.E.2d 223 (3d Dist. 1975).

[11]International Shoe Co. v. Lacy, 114 Ind. App. 641, 53 N.E.2d 636 (1944), opinion supplemented, 116 Ind. App. 78, 61 N.E.2d 85 (1945).

[12]Lost Creek School Tp., Vigo County v. York, 215 Ind. 636, 21 N.E.2d 58, 127 A.L.R. 1287 (1939); Lester v. Hinkle, 193 Ind. 605, 141 N.E. 463 (1923).

[13]Lost Creek School Tp., Vigo County v. York, 215 Ind. 636, 21 N.E.2d 58, 127 A.L.R. 1287 (1939); Fairplay School Tp. v. O'Neal, 127 Ind. 95, 26 N.E. 686 (1891) (contract between school trustee and teacher to pay "good wages" was too indefinite to found action upon).

[14]Keith v. Crump, 22 Ind. App. 364, 53 N.E. 839 (1899) (agreement by trustee to insure property "in such sums or amounts and manner as he may deem proper").

[15]Martin Bros. Box Co. v. Orem, 117 Ind. App. 110, 69 N.E.2d 605 (1946).

[16]Johnson v. Sprague, 614 N.E.2d 585 (Ind. Ct. App. 1st Dist. 1993).

[17]Donavan v. Ivy Knoll Apartments Partnership, 537 N.E.2d 47 (Ind. Ct. App. 4th Dist. 1989); Kokomo Veterans, Inc. v. Schick, 439 N.E.2d 639 (Ind. Ct. App. 3d Dist. 1982).

[18]Donavan v. Ivy Knoll Apartments Partnership, 537 N.E.2d 47 (Ind. Ct. App. 4th Dist. 1989); Dayhuff v. Canonie Const. Co., 152 Ind. App. 154, 283 N.E.2d 425 (1st Dist. 1972); International Shoe Co. v. Lacy, 114 Ind. App. 641, 53 N.E.2d 636 (1944), opinion supplemented, 116 Ind. App. 78, 61 N.E.2d 85 (1945).

forms part of the agreement without any express statement to that effect.[19]

Under the Indiana version of the Uniform Commercial Code, parties may enter into an "indefinite quantities" or "requirements" contract, in which one party agrees to purchase all of a commodity it requires from the other.[20]

A contract may be enforceable if the subject matter is not susceptible of an exact description,[21] or even if it is not yet in existence.[22]

§ 3 Parties

At least two competent persons are necessary to the formation of a contract.

West's Digest, Contracts ☜11-13.

There must be at least two parties to a contract,[23] as a person cannot contract with him- or herself.[24]

◆ **Observation:** Although officers of the state, such as judges, are in a sense the state itself, they may contract

---

[19]Johnson v. Sprague, 614 N.E.2d 585 (Ind. Ct. App. 1st Dist. 1993) (because statute provides that conveyance to fee simple title to real property is to be free from all encumbrances, parties' failure to agree expressly as to payment of real estate taxes did not render agreement for sale of property unenforceable).

[20]IC 26-1-2-306(1).

Indiana-American Water Co., Inc. v. Town of Seelyville, 698 N.E.2d 1255, 38 U.C.C. Rep. Serv. 2d (CBC) 1133 (Ind. Ct. App. 1998).

As to transactions governed by the Uniform Commercial Code, see I.L.E., Sales of Personalty.

[21]Martin Bros. Box Co. v. Orem, 117 Ind. App. 110, 69 N.E.2d 605 (1946) (contract to haul dirt not uncertain even though amount could only be approximated when contract was executed).

[22]Hight v. Carr, 185 Ind. 39, 112 N.E. 881 (1916) (expectancy under grandmother's will); Wolf v. Esteb, 7 Ind. 448, 1856 WL 3564 (1856) (unborn animal).

[23]Board of Trustees of Public Employees' Retirement Fund v. Hill, 472 N.E.2d 204 (Ind. 1985), reh'g denied, (Mar. 19, 1985); Henry School Tp. of Henry County, Ind. v. Meredith, 32 Ind. App. 607, 70 N.E. 393 (Div. 1 1904).

[24]Board of Trustees of Public Employees' Retirement Fund v. Hill, 472 N.E.2d 204 (Ind. 1985), reh'g denied, (Mar. 19, 1985); Groub v. Blish, 88 Ind. App. 309, 153 N.E. 895 (1926).

with the state as to such matters as pay and retirement benefits.[25]

The parties to a contract must be legally capable of contracting.[26] It is presumed that persons who enter into an agreement are adults and competent to contract.[27] Married women may contract on their own accounts.[28]

§ 4 Mutuality of obligation

Both parties to a contract must be bound by correlative obligations.

West's Digest, Contracts ⬤➙10(1)-10(7), 57.

An agreement will not be treated as a valid, enforceable contract unless both parties to the agreement are bound by some obligation.[29] This concept is known as mutuality.[30]

Although the parties' obligations must be correlative,[31] a contract does not become unenforceable merely because the obligations of the parties differ in quality or quantity.[32] Mutuality does not require that every duty within a contract be based upon a correlative obligation outlined in minute

---

[25]Board of Trustees of Public Employees' Retirement Fund v. Hill, 472 N.E.2d 204 (Ind. 1985), reh'g denied, (Mar. 19, 1985).

[26]Stropes v. Board of Com'rs of Greene County, 72 Ind. 42, 1880 WL 6301 (1880).

As to the validity of a contract as affected by certain conditions, such as a party's incompetency or minority, see §§ 31 et seq.

[27]Foltz v. Wert, 103 Ind. 404, 2 N.E. 950 (1885).

[28]IC 31-11-7-1.

Hamilton v. Hamilton's Estate, 26 Ind. App. 114, 59 N.E. 344 (1901).

[29]Davis v. Davis, 197 Ind. 386, 151 N.E. 134 (1926); Terre Haute Regional Hosp., Inc. v. El-Issa, 470 N.E.2d 1371 (Ind. Ct. App. 1st Dist. 1984), reh'g denied, (Jan. 4, 1985) and transfer denied, (Mar. 28, 1985).

As to consideration, see §§ 13 et seq.

[30]Security Bank & Trust Co. v. Bogard, 494 N.E.2d 965 (Ind. Ct. App. 4th Dist. 1986) (bank's alleged agreement to extend credit to farmer who was not legally bound to borrow money from bank lacked mutuality of obligation and was therefore unenforceable); Kokomo Veterans, Inc. v. Schick, 439 N.E.2d 639 (Ind. Ct. App. 3d Dist. 1982).

[31]Kokomo Veterans, Inc. v. Schick, 439 N.E.2d 639 (Ind. Ct. App. 3d Dist. 1982).

[32]Terre Haute Regional Hosp., Inc. v. El-Issa, 470 N.E.2d 1371 (Ind. Ct. App. 1st Dist. 1984), reh'g denied, (Jan. 4, 1985) and transfer denied, (Mar. 28, 1985).

detail, as long as the contract is reasonably definite as to its material terms.[33]

A promise which, by its terms, makes performance entirely optional with the promisor, is termed an "illusory promise," and is unenforceable for lack of mutuality.[34]

If the contract does not impose mutual obligations upon the parties, but one party to the agreement acts upon the promise of the other party and performs his or her part of the agreement, the contract is not unenforceable for lack of mutuality.[35] Thus, while an unsatisfied condition precedent may render a contract unenforceable, the contract is not void for lack of mutuality, as mutuality will exist as soon as the condition is performed.[36]

§ 5 Express and implied contracts

A contract may be express or implied from the acts of the parties.

West's Digest, Contracts ☞27.
West's Digest, Implied and Constructive Contracts ☞1 et seq.

There are three general types of contracts—express, implied and constructive.[37] Express and implied contracts differ only in that an express contract is evidenced by spoken

---

[33]Jordan v. Indianapolis Water Co., 159 Ind. 337, 64 N.E. 680 (1902); Kokomo Veterans, Inc. v. Schick, 439 N.E.2d 639 (Ind. Ct. App. 3d Dist. 1982).

[34]Pardieck v. Pardieck, 676 N.E.2d 359 (Ind. Ct. App. 1997), transfer denied, 683 N.E.2d 595 (Ind. 1997).

[35]Eichholtz v. Taylor, 88 Ind. 38, 1882 WL 7043 (1882); Marksill Specialties, Inc. v. Barger, 428 N.E.2d 65 (Ind. Ct. App. 3d Dist. 1981) (where defendant promised to compensate plaintiff for efforts in securing new accounts, defendant was obligated to compensate plaintiff after plaintiff made efforts to secure new accounts); Seco Chemicals, Inc., Division of Stan Sax Corp. v. Stewart, 169 Ind. App. 624, 349 N.E.2d 733 (1st Dist. 1976).

As to performance of contract obligations, see §§ 103 et seq.

[36]Indiana State Highway Com'n v. Curtis, 695 N.E.2d 143 (Ind. Ct. App. 1998), transfer granted, (Oct. 2, 1998) and aff'd, 704 N.E.2d 1015 (Ind. 1998); Donavan v. Ivy Knoll Apartments Partnership, 537 N.E.2d 47 (Ind. Ct. App. 4th Dist. 1989); Kokomo Veterans, Inc. v. Schick, 439 N.E.2d 639 (Ind. Ct. App. 3d Dist. 1982).

[37]Ahuja v. Lynco Ltd. Medical Research, 675 N.E.2d 704 (Ind. Ct. App. 1996), transfer denied, 683 N.E.2d 590 (Ind. 1997); Wagoner v. Joe Mater and Associates, Inc., 461 N.E.2d 706 (Ind. Ct. App. 3d Dist. 1984).

or written words, while an implied contract is evidenced by the conduct of the parties.[38] An implied contract is as binding as an express contract.[39]

Where there is no express contract, the right to recover may rest upon an implied contract or an implied promise to pay. Such a contract may be inferred from the conduct, situation, or material relations of the parties where equity, justice, and fair dealing require compensation, and may be enforced by law.[40]

A party seeking to recover on an implied contract theory must show that a benefit was rendered to the other party at that other party's express or implied request.[41] Any benefit for which pecuniary compensation is commonly made, which one person, without intending to make a gift, confers upon another, who accepts it, is an adequate foundation for a legally implied or created promise to render back its value.[42] Where one accepts valuable services from another, the law implies a promise to pay for them.[43]

◆ **Illustration:** Where potential purchasers of real property had, with the seller's knowledge and permission, made improvements to a house on the property before they had entered into a contract to purchase the property, their work conferred a benefit upon the seller even though the house was destroyed by fire before they had formed more than an agreement to agree. Even if both parties had

---

[38]Ahuja v. Lynco Ltd. Medical Research, 675 N.E.2d 704 (Ind. Ct. App. 1996), transfer denied, 683 N.E.2d 590 (Ind. 1997); Wagoner v. Joe Mater and Associates, Inc., 461 N.E.2d 706 (Ind. Ct. App. 3d Dist. 1984) (both express and implied contracts require meeting of minds of contracting parties).

[39]Retter v. Retter, 110 Ind. App. 659, 40 N.E.2d 385 (1942).

[40]Grose v. Bow Lanes, Inc., 661 N.E.2d 1220 (Ind. Ct. App. 1996); Cole v. Cole, 517 N.E.2d 1248 (Ind. Ct. App. 1st Dist. 1988).

[41]Lakes and Rivers Transfer, a Div. of Jack Gray Transport, Inc. v. Rudolph Robinson Steel Co., 691 N.E.2d 1294 (Ind. Ct. App. 1998); Galloway v. Methodist Hospitals, Inc., 658 N.E.2d 611 (Ind. Ct. App. 1995), reh'g denied, (Jan. 24, 1996) (husband and wife made implied request for medical services by going to hospital's emergency room for premature delivery of their child); Timothy F. Kelly and Associates v. Illinois Farmers Ins. Co., 640 N.E.2d 82 (Ind. Ct. App. 3d Dist. 1994).

[42]Grose v. Bow Lanes, Inc., 661 N.E.2d 1220 (Ind. Ct. App. 1996); Cole v. Cole, 517 N.E.2d 1248 (Ind. Ct. App. 1st Dist. 1988).

[43]Estate of Hann v. Hann, 614 N.E.2d 973 (Ind. Ct. App. 1st Dist. 1993); Silverthorne v. King, 179 Ind. App. 310, 385 N.E.2d 473 (3d Dist. 1979).

intended the work to be for the purchasers' benefit, the
seller was nevertheless the legal and equitable owner at
the time of the fire, and the value of the house had been
increased.[44]

However, a party's receipt of a benefit from a plaintiff's
action, with no express or implied request for the action, is
not enough to support recovery under an implied contract
theory.[45] Likewise, no payment will be required if the services were rendered without expectation of pay except for
hope of future reward through the generosity of the recipient.[46]

Similarly, when a person has received money from the
plaintiff or from a third person through a mistake of fact, or
without consideration, or upon failed consideration, the
plaintiff may recover in an action for money had and
received, which rests on an implied promise.[47]

Where services are performed by a non-family member, an
agreement to pay may be implied from the relationship of
the parties, the situation, the conduct of the parties, and the
nature and character of the services rendered.[48] However,
where the parties are family members living together, and
the services are rendered in the family context, no implication of a promise to pay by the recipient arises. Rather, there
is a rebuttable presumption that services are performed
gratuitously when there is evidence of a blood or family relationship between the decedent and the claimant.[49] Even in
the absence of blood or family relationship, a claimant has

---

[44]Olsson v. Moore, 590 N.E.2d 160 (Ind. Ct. App. 1st Dist. 1992), reh'g
denied, (July 13, 1992).

[45]Timothy F. Kelly and Associates v. Illinois Farmers Ins. Co., 640
N.E.2d 82 (Ind. Ct. App. 3d Dist. 1994).

[46]Briggs v. Clinton County Bank & Trust Co. of Frankfort, Ind., 452
N.E.2d 989 (Ind. Ct. App. 2d Dist. 1983).

[47]Shelby Engineering Co., Inc. v. Action Steel Supply, Inc., 707 N.E.2d
1026 (Ind. Ct. App. 1999); Chosnek v. Rolley, 688 N.E.2d 202 (Ind. Ct.
App. 1997); Duran v. Duran, 585 N.E.2d 1373 (Ind. Ct. App. 5th Dist.
1992), reh'g denied, (Apr. 7, 1992).

[48]Estate of Hann v. Hann, 614 N.E.2d 973 (Ind. Ct. App. 1st Dist. 1993);
Cole v. Cole, 517 N.E.2d 1248 (Ind. Ct. App. 1st Dist. 1988).

[49]Estate of Hann v. Hann, 614 N.E.2d 973 (Ind. Ct. App. 1st Dist. 1993);
Cole v. Cole, 517 N.E.2d 1248 (Ind. Ct. App. 1st Dist. 1988); Matter of
Estate of Gray, 505 N.E.2d 806 (Ind. Ct. App. 4th Dist. 1987), reh'g
denied, (Apr. 30, 1987) and transfer denied, (Sept. 2, 1987).

the burden of proving an implied contract for payment for services rendered.[50]

Implied contract theories are frequently used in actions involving principals and subcontractors, where the general contractor has defaulted on its obligation to the subcontractor.[51] Four criteria are applied in such cases to determine whether a contract should be implied:[52]

- whether the owner impliedly requested the subcontractor to do the work
- whether the owner reasonably expected to pay the subcontractor, or the subcontractor reasonably expected to be paid by the owner
- whether there was an actual wrong perpetrated by the owner
- whether the owner's conduct was so active and instrumental that the owner "stepped into the shoes" of the contractor

◆ **Illustration:** Where evidence showed that, after it became evident that no further payment would be forthcoming from the general contractor, a homeowner requested that the subcontractors complete the work they had agreed to do and that they make certain changes and additions, the trial court properly allowed the subcontractors to recover from the homeowner under a theory of unjust enrichment.[53]

When the rights of the parties are controlled by an express contract, recovery cannot be based upon a theory implied in law. Thus, the existence of a valid express contract for services precludes the implication of a contract covering the

---

[50]Briggs v. Clinton County Bank & Trust Co. of Frankfort, Ind., 452 N.E.2d 989 (Ind. Ct. App. 2d Dist. 1983).

[51]Stafford v. Barnard Lumber Co., Inc., 531 N.E.2d 202 (Ind. 1988); McCorry v. G. Cowser Const., Inc., 636 N.E.2d 1273 (Ind. Ct. App. 5th Dist. 1994), opinion adopted, 644 N.E.2d 550 (Ind. 1994); Kern v. City of Lawrenceburg, 625 N.E.2d 1326 (Ind. Ct. App. 1st Dist. 1993).

[52]Stafford v. Barnard Lumber Co., Inc., 531 N.E.2d 202 (Ind. 1988); McCorry v. G. Cowser Const., Inc., 636 N.E.2d 1273 (Ind. Ct. App. 5th Dist. 1994), opinion adopted, 644 N.E.2d 550 (Ind. 1994).

[53]McCorry v. G. Cowser Const., Inc., 636 N.E.2d 1273 (Ind. Ct. App. 5th Dist. 1994), opinion adopted, 644 N.E.2d 550 (Ind. 1994).

same subject matter.[54] An implied contract may exist, however, between parties who have an express contract with respect to different matters.[55]

If the parties have been operating under an express contract, and continue to conduct themselves after the expiration of that contract as if it were still in force, an implied contract with the same terms as the express contract exists between them.[56]

§ 6 Constructive contracts

A constructive contract arises where, although no contract actually exists, justice warrants a recovery as if a contract did exist.

West's Digest, Contracts ☞27.
West's Digest, Implied and Constructive Contracts ☞1 et seq.

Constructive contracts are also known as quasi-contracts or contracts implied at law.[57] Quasi-contractual remedies permit recovery where no contract in fact exists.[58] The constructive contract theory is used in situations where, even though no contract actually exists, justice nevertheless warrants a recovery under the circumstances as though there had been a promise.[59] Quantum meruit is a remedy for breach of contract under which an innocent party can recover damages for services rendered under a contract.

---

[54]Huff v. Biomet, Inc., 654 N.E.2d 830 (Ind. Ct. App. 1995); Kern v. City of Lawrenceburg, 625 N.E.2d 1326 (Ind. Ct. App. 1st Dist. 1993); Kincaid v. Lazar, 405 N.E.2d 615 (Ind. Ct. App. 1st Dist. 1980).

[55]Union Mut. Life Ins. Co. v. Buchanan, 100 Ind. 63, 1885 WL 4302 (1885).

[56]JKL Components Corp. v. Insul-Reps, Inc., 596 N.E.2d 945 (Ind. Ct. App. 2d Dist. 1992), transfer denied, (Nov. 20, 1992).

[57]Ahuja v. Lynco Ltd. Medical Research, 675 N.E.2d 704 (Ind. Ct. App. 1996), transfer denied, 683 N.E.2d 590 (Ind. 1997); Bailey v. Manors Group, 642 N.E.2d 249 (Ind. Ct. App. 5th Dist. 1994), reh'g denied, (Jan. 23, 1995) and transfer denied, (May 16, 1995).

[58]Bailey v. Manors Group, 642 N.E.2d 249 (Ind. Ct. App. 5th Dist. 1994), reh'g denied, (Jan. 23, 1995) and transfer denied, (May 16, 1995); Bayh v. Sonnenburg, 573 N.E.2d 398 (Ind. 1991), reh'g denied, (Sept. 17, 1991).

[59]Ahuja v. Lynco Ltd. Medical Research, 675 N.E.2d 704 (Ind. Ct. App. 1996), transfer denied, 683 N.E.2d 590 (Ind. 1997); Bailey v. Manors Group, 642 N.E.2d 249 (Ind. Ct. App. 5th Dist. 1994), reh'g denied, (Jan. 23, 1995) and transfer denied, (May 16, 1995).

However, courts have also used the term quantum meruit synonymously with the terms constructive contract and quasi-contract.[60] They are all legal fictions created by courts of law to provide remedies which promote justice and equity by providing the injured party with the fair value of the work and services rendered and thus preventing unjust enrichment to the person who benefited from the services.[61] A constructive contract, like an implied contract, cannot exist where an express contract as to the disputed subject matter exists.[62]

Recovery will usually be denied if a benefit has been officiously thrust upon the recipient.[63] However, principles of equity prohibit unjust enrichment in cases where a party accepts the unrequested benefits another provides despite having the opportunity to decline those benefits.[64] Thus, to prevail on a claim of unjust enrichment, a plaintiff must establish that it conferred a measurable benefit on the defen-

---

Annotation References: Building and construction contracts: Right of subcontractor who has dealt only with primary contractor to recover against property owner in quasi contract, 62 ALR3d 288.

[60]Ahuja v. Lynco Ltd. Medical Research, 675 N.E.2d 704 (Ind. Ct. App. 1996), transfer denied, 683 N.E.2d 590 (Ind. 1997); Wright v. Pennamped, 657 N.E.2d 1223 (Ind. Ct. App. 1995), decision clarified on denial of reh'g, 664 N.E.2d 394 (Ind. Ct. App. 1996) and transfer denied, (Nov. 13, 1996); City of Indianapolis v. Twin Lakes Enterprises, Inc., 568 N.E.2d 1073 (Ind. Ct. App. 1st Dist. 1991), reh'g denied, (May 16, 1991) and transfer denied, (Dec. 12, 1991).

[61]Wright v. Pennamped, 657 N.E.2d 1223 (Ind. Ct. App. 1995), decision clarified on denial of reh'g, 664 N.E.2d 394 (Ind. Ct. App. 1996) and transfer denied, (Nov. 13, 1996); Timothy F. Kelly and Associates v. Illinois Farmers Ins. Co., 640 N.E.2d 82 (Ind. Ct. App. 3d Dist. 1994); City of Indianapolis v. Twin Lakes Enterprises, Inc., 568 N.E.2d 1073 (Ind. Ct. App. 1st Dist. 1991), reh'g denied, (May 16, 1991) and transfer denied, (Dec. 12, 1991).

[62]Engelbrecht v. Property Developers, Inc., 156 Ind. App. 354, 296 N.E.2d 798 (1st Dist. 1973).

[63]Kody Engineering Co., Inc. v. Fox & Fox Ins. Agency, Inc., 158 Ind. App. 498, 303 N.E.2d 307 (2d Dist. 1973); Wagoner v. Joe Mater and Associates, Inc., 461 N.E.2d 706 (Ind. Ct. App. 3d Dist. 1984) (no constructive contract where father was willing to pay for son's therapy, but was not willing for son to have therapy from particular treatment center to which mother took him).

[64]Wright v. Pennamped, 657 N.E.2d 1223 (Ind. Ct. App. 1995), decision clarified on denial of reh'g, 664 N.E.2d 394 (Ind. Ct. App. 1996) and transfer denied, (Nov. 13, 1996); Olsson v. Moore, 590 N.E.2d 160 (Ind. Ct. App. 1st Dist. 1992), reh'g denied, (July 13, 1992).

dant under circumstances in which the defendant's retention of the benefit without payment would be unjust.[65]

◆ **Illustration:** A husband and wife were liable under quasi-contract theory for medical services rendered to the wife and their child in the premature delivery of the child, where the husband and not the wife made an implied request for medical service by going to the hospital's emergency room, and a benefit in the form of medical services was rendered to the husband and wife at their implied request and under circumstances which equity demanded they pay the hospital in order to prevent unjust enrichment.[66]

A person who performs work for another without any expectation of payment cannot recover in quasi-contract.[67]

◆ **Illustration:** A sheriff was required on the basis of quasi-contract to pay for medical services rendered to prisoners by a municipal hospital corporation. Medical services are commonly subject to monetary compensation, and the sheriff received a benefit from the medical treatment because he was required by statute to provide necessary medical services to inmates. Moreover, the record clearly reflected that the sheriff accepted the services, and gave no indication that the hospital intended to render the services gratuitously.[68]

A person may be prevented from obtaining compensation on a theory of quasi-contract if, in connection with the trans-

---

[65]Wright v. Pennamped, 657 N.E.2d 1223 (Ind. Ct. App. 1995), decision clarified on denial of reh'g, 664 N.E.2d 394 (Ind. Ct. App. 1996) and transfer denied, (Nov. 13, 1996); Bayh v. Sonnenburg, 573 N.E.2d 398 (Ind. 1991), reh'g denied, (Sept. 17, 1991).

[66]Galloway v. Methodist Hospitals, Inc., 658 N.E.2d 611 (Ind. Ct. App. 1995), reh'g denied, (Jan. 24, 1996).

[67]Bayh v. Sonnenburg, 573 N.E.2d 398 (Ind. 1991), reh'g denied, (Sept. 17, 1991) (mental patients committed to state facilities were not entitled to recover back pay for services they performed on quasi-contract theory, as evidence was uncontroverted that many patients were told by hospital officials that they would not be paid for their work, and there was no evidence that patients performed services with any expectation of payment).

[68]Health and Hosp. Corp. of Marion County v. Marion County, 470 N.E.2d 1348 (Ind. Ct. App. 2d Dist. 1984), reh'g denied, 476 N.E.2d 887 (Ind. Ct. App. 2d Dist. 1985), reh'g denied, (May 23, 1985) and transfer denied, (July 3, 1985).

action upon which the claim is based, his or her conduct has been wrongful.[69]

II. OFFER AND ACCEPTANCE

Research References

IC 26-1-2-201 et seq.

17A Am Jur 2d, Contracts §§ 26-112.
17 C.J.S., Contracts §§ 39-65.
West's Digest, Contracts ☞15-29.
ALR Digest: Contracts §§ 93-106.5
ALR Index: Adhesion Contracts; Anticipatory Breach; Anticipatory Renunciation or Repudiation; Bids and Bidding; Cancellation of Rescission; Consideration; Contracts; Covenants; Covenants Not to Compete; Estoppel and Waiver; Executory Contracts; Implied Contracts; Offer and Acceptance; Parol Contracts and Agreements; Parol Evidence; Third-Party Beneficiaries; Unconscionability
5A Am Jur Legal Forms 2d, Contracts §§ 68:81, 68:85, 68:87, 68:91, 68:92.
Corbin on Contracts (rev. ed.), §§ 2.1-3.41.

§ 7 Generally

A contract is formed when an offer is made, the offer is accepted and the acceptance communicated to the offeror, and consideration is provided.

West's Digest, Contracts ☞16.

A contract is based upon an offer, acceptance, and consideration. An offer must be extended and the offeree must accept it and communicate his or her acceptance to the offeror.[70]

◆ **Illustration:** An interoffice document created for the

---

[69]Briggs v. Clinton County Bank & Trust Co. of Frankfort, Ind., 452 N.E.2d 989 (Ind. Ct. App. 2d Dist. 1983).

[70]I.C.C. Protective Coatings, Inc. v. A.E. Staley Mfg. Co., 695 N.E.2d 1030 (Ind. Ct. App. 1998), transfer denied, 706 N.E.2d 174 (Ind. 1998); Straub v. B.M.T. by Todd, 645 N.E.2d 597 (Ind. 1994), reh'g denied, (Apr. 12, 1995); Bain v. Board of Trustees of Starke Memorial Hosp., 550 N.E.2d 106 (Ind. Ct. App. 3d Dist. 1990), reh'g denied, (Mar. 30, 1990).

Forms References: Offer specifying mode of communication of acceptance. 5A Am Jur Legal Forms 2d, Contracts § 68:81.

Offer by newspaper, circular, or advertisement. 5A Am Jur Legal Forms 2d, Contracts § 68:85.

benefit of a plaintiff's employer's accounting department was not communicated to the plaintiff, who never saw it until after he had filed his lawsuit. The document, therefore, was not a contract fixing the amount of the plaintiff's compensation.[71]

If these components are present, the parties' bargaining gives rise to a legal obligation expressed in the language of the agreement or implied from other circumstances, as affected by various rules of law such as the Uniform Commercial Code.[72]

A mere inquiry about the price of a product or service, without more, does not create a binding contract which obliges the inquiring party to purchase the product or service.[73]

If one party makes an offer or promise which invites performance by another, performance constitutes both acceptance of the offer and consideration. A contract formed in this manner is called a unilateral contract. In such a contract, there is ordinarily no bargaining process or exchange of promises by the parties as in a bilateral contract.[74]

The formation of an enforceable contract also depends on a meeting of the minds of the contracting parties.[75] Thus, the parties must have the same intent.[76] Apparently, even an unconscionable contract may be enforceable if the party seeking to enforce the contract shows that the provisions were explained to the other party and the parties reached a real and voluntary meeting of the minds on the matter.[77]

---

[71]Rosi v. Business Furniture Corp., 615 N.E.2d 431 (Ind. 1993).

[72]Straub v. B.M.T. by Todd, 645 N.E.2d 597 (Ind. 1994), reh'g denied, (Apr. 12, 1995).

[73]Lakes and Rivers Transfer, a Div. of Jack Gray Transport, Inc. v. Rudolph Robinson Steel Co., 691 N.E.2d 1294 (Ind. Ct. App. 1998).

[74]Orr v. Westminster Village North, Inc., 689 N.E.2d 712 (Ind. 1997).

[75]Ochoa v. Ford, 641 N.E.2d 1042 (Ind. Ct. App. 1994); Bain v. Board of Trustees of Starke Memorial Hosp., 550 N.E.2d 106 (Ind. Ct. App. 3d Dist. 1990), reh'g denied, (Mar. 30, 1990).

[76]Bain v. Board of Trustees of Starke Memorial Hosp., 550 N.E.2d 106 (Ind. Ct. App. 3d Dist. 1990), reh'g denied, (Mar. 30, 1990); Wagoner v. Joe Mater and Associates, Inc., 461 N.E.2d 706 (Ind. Ct. App. 3d Dist. 1984).

[77]Weaver v. American Oil Co., 257 Ind. 458, 276 N.E.2d 144, 49 A.L.R.3d 306 (1971).

♦ **Observation:** A party seeking to enforce an unconscionable contract has the burden of showing that provisions were explained to other party and came to his knowledge and that there was in fact a real and voluntary
meeting of minds and not merely an objective meeting.[78]

The formation of a contract depends upon overt acts alone,
and an intention to make a legal obligation is not necessary,[79]
although a contract is not made if there is an expressed
intention that there should be no legal obligation.[80]

§ 8   Offer

**An offer is a manifestation of willingness to enter into a
bargain.**

West's Digest, Contracts ⚷18-20.

An offer is the manifestation of willingness to enter into a
bargain, so made as to justify another person in understanding that his or her consent to that bargain is invited and
that consent will conclude the bargain.[81] An offer may take
the form of a proposition.[82] As a general principle, an offer
must be sufficiently certain to allow a court to determine
what duties will be imposed and what consideration will
mature the obligation.[83]

As to unconscionable contracts, generally, see § 41.

[78]Weaver v. American Oil Co., 257 Ind. 458, 276 N.E.2d 144, 49
A.L.R.3d 306 (1971).

[79]State ex rel. Appleman v. Lake Circuit Court, 231 Ind. 378, 108
N.E.2d 898 (1952); Michael v. Holland, 111 Ind. App. 34, 40 N.E.2d 362
(1942).

[80]State ex rel. Appleman v. Lake Circuit Court, 231 Ind. 378, 108
N.E.2d 898 (1952).

[81]Barnum v. Review Bd. of Indiana Employment Sec. Div., 478 N.E.2d
1243 (Ind. Ct. App. 3d Dist. 1985).

[82]Olcott v. McClure, 50 Ind. App. 79, 98 N.E. 82 (1912) (defendant's letter stating that he would pay broker's commission to agent whose buyer
purchased defendant's real property constituted offer, not merely invita-
tion for offer).

[83]Barnum v. Review Bd. of Indiana Employment Sec. Div., 478 N.E.2d
1243 (Ind. Ct. App. 3d Dist. 1985); Suyemasa v. Myers, 420 N.E.2d 1334
(Ind. Ct. App. 1st Dist. 1981); Oedekerk v. Muncie Gear Works, 179 F.2d
821 (7th Cir. 1950) (applying Indiana law).

Bids are often used as a means to gather information from competitors for the best price possible.[84] A submission of bids or quotation of prices is generally not an offer, as it leaves unexpressed many terms that are necessary to the making of a contract, although it may constitute an offer if it is sufficiently detailed.[85] Similarly, an advertisement for bids or a request for an offer is not an offer, but is at best a request for offers or a request for a reply that will further negotiation in the direction of an offer.[86] The submission of a purchase order by a buyer in response to a bid or price quotation usually constitutes an offer.[87]

Generally, an offeree cannot accept an offer until its terms have been communicated to him by the offeror.[88] When an offer does not specify a time for termination, acceptance may be made during a reasonable time. What constitutes a reasonable time depends largely on the nature of the offer and the circumstances surrounding the transaction, and is a question to be determined by the trier of fact.[89]

An offeror may, however, limit the time within which the offeree may accept.[90] Further, the offeror is generally empowered to revoke the offer at any time before it has been

---

[84]Longmire v. Indiana Dept. of State Revenue, 638 N.E.2d 894 (Ind. Tax Ct. 1994).

[85]I.C.C. Protective Coatings, Inc. v. A.E. Staley Mfg. Co., 695 N.E.2d 1030 (Ind. Ct. App. 1998), transfer denied, 706 N.E.2d 174 (Ind. 1998); Longmire v. Indiana Dept. of State Revenue, 638 N.E.2d 894 (Ind. Tax Ct. 1994).

[86]Rice v. Scott County School Dist., 526 N.E.2d 1193, 48 Ed. Law Rep. 643 (Ind. Ct. App. 1st Dist. 1988).

[87]I.C.C. Protective Coatings, Inc. v. A.E. Staley Mfg. Co., 695 N.E.2d 1030 (Ind. Ct. App. 1998), transfer denied, 706 N.E.2d 174 (Ind. 1998); Longmire v. Indiana Dept. of State Revenue, 638 N.E.2d 894 (Ind. Tax Ct. 1994).

[88]Alfaro v. Stauffer Chemical Co., 173 Ind. App. 89, 362 N.E.2d 500 (3d Dist. 1977).

[89]Speiser v. Addis, 411 N.E.2d 439 (Ind. Ct. App. 3d Dist. 1980) (where landlord sent letter on September 5, 1975, proposing new lease when current lease expired on August 1, 1976, and asking for prompt reply, and there was no further communication until telephone conversation on April 12, 1976, at which time landlord informed tenant that rent would be higher than indicated in letter, trial court did not err in determining that tenant's acceptance on July 22, 1976, of proposal in September 5 letter was too late, as offer had lapsed).

[90]Glencoe Cotton Mills v. Capital Paper Co., 74 Ind. App. 239, 128 N.E. 699 (Div. 2 1920).

accepted,[91] even if the offeror has stated that the offer is irrevocable.[92]

§ 9 —Option contracts and rights of first refusal

An option is a continuing offer which is irrevocable for a specified period of time; a right of first refusal creates a power to preempt another from accepting an offer.

West's Digest, Contracts ☞25, 59.
West's Digest, Vendor and Purchaser ☞18(.5).

Generally, an offer is revocable at any time before it has been accepted.[93] However, an offer can be made irrevocable by contract or by statute.[94] An offer is contractually irrevocable only when the offeror has promised not to revoke it, or has promised the offered exchange of performances on condition of acceptance within a period of time, and that promise is binding by reason of a seal, consideration given in exchange, or subsequent action in reliance upon it.[95]

An option is a continuing offer whose duration and method of exercise is strictly controlled by the agreement that created it.[96] For instance, an option to purchase real estate is a contract by which the owner of realty agrees with another person that the latter is to have the power to purchase the

---

[91]Stanish v. Polish Roman Catholic Union of America, 484 F.2d 713 (7th Cir. 1973) (under Indiana law, where offer to lend money contained in corporation's letter of commitment was not withdrawn before it was accepted by prospective borrower, corporation was not entitled to withdraw offer or vary terms); Vigo Agricultural Soc. v. Brumfield, 102 Ind. 146, 1 N.E. 382 (1885); Davis v. Calloway, 30 Ind. 112, 1868 WL 3066 (1868).

As to irrevocable offers, also known as option contracts, see § 9.

[92]Stanish v. Polish Roman Catholic Union of America, 484 F.2d 713 (7th Cir. 1973) (applying Indiana law).

[93]§ 8.

[94]Stanish v. Polish Roman Catholic Union of America, 484 F.2d 713 (7th Cir. 1973) (applying Indiana law).

[95]Stanish v. Polish Roman Catholic Union of America, 484 F.2d 713 (7th Cir. 1973) (applying Indiana law).

Forms References: Continuing offer (option). 5A Am Jur Legal Forms 2d, Contracts § 68:87.

Acceptance of option. 5A Am Jur Legal Forms 2d, Contracts § 68:92.

[96]Beiger Heritage Corp. v. Estate of Kilbey, 667 N.E.2d 184 (Ind. Ct. App. 1996), reh'g denied, (Aug. 27, 1996) and transfer denied, 683 N.E.2d 582 (Ind. 1997).

property at a fixed price within a certain period of time.[97] Option contracts are most commonly used in the sale of property, especially where the potential purchaser is interested in the ownership of land, but at the time the option contract is formed may not have the money to pay for it, or may not be sufficiently sure of his or her interest to buy the land immediately.[98] Instead of an immediate purchase, the potential purchaser pays a much smaller amount in order to convert the offer to sell into an irrevocable offer for a limited amount of time. The potential purchaser then has the specified length of time to decide whether to exercise the option.[99] Option contracts commonly provide for a date when, or a time period within which, the option must be exercised. Some option contracts also contain a provision requiring notice of intent to exercise the option within a specified period prior to the expiration of the option.[1] Upon timely exercise of the option, an option agreement becomes an enforceable contract.[2]

To exercise an option to purchase, the decision to purchase must be made by the optionee under the terms of the option and the decision must be communicated within the life of the option.[3] Generally, the exercise of an option is effective only if it strictly adheres to the terms stipulated in the contract.[4] The optionee will be excused from strict compliance only where his or her failure to comply was not due to

---

[97]Lafayette Expo Center, Inc. v. Owens, 531 N.E.2d 508 (Ind. Ct. App. 3d Dist. 1988), reh'g denied, (Jan. 17, 1989) and transfer denied, (July 27, 1989); Romain v. A. Howard Wholesale Co., 506 N.E.2d 1124 (Ind. Ct. App. 1st Dist. 1987), reh'g denied, (June 8, 1987) and transfer denied, (Dec. 10, 1987).

[98]Wolvos v. Meyer, 668 N.E.2d 671 (Ind. 1996).

[99]Wolvos v. Meyer, 668 N.E.2d 671 (Ind. 1996).

[1]Hutchcraft v. Eastern Indiana Production Credit Ass'n, 486 N.E.2d 644 (Ind. Ct. App. 2d Dist. 1985), reh'g denied, (Mar. 13, 1986).

Annotation References: Lessee's first privilege option to purchase or terms of similar import as requiring existence of prior offer from third party, 76 ALR3d 1139.

[2]Wolvos v. Meyer, 668 N.E.2d 671 (Ind. 1996).

[3]Salin Bank and Trust Co. v. Violet U. Peden Trust, 715 N.E.2d 1003 (Ind. Ct. App. 1999); Lafayette Expo Center, Inc. v. Owens, 531 N.E.2d 508 (Ind. Ct. App. 3d Dist. 1988), reh'g denied, (Jan. 17, 1989) and transfer denied, (July 27, 1989); Theobald v. Chumley, 408 N.E.2d 603 (Ind. Ct. App. 1st Dist. 1980).

[4]Beiger Heritage Corp. v. Estate of Kilbey, 667 N.E.2d 184 (Ind. Ct.

willful or gross negligence on his or her part, but was the result of an honest and justifiable mistake.[5] The option holder's failure to comply with the option's terms deprives him or her of the right to demand the enforcement of the contract.[6]

Option contracts are to be distinguished from agreements to agree. An agreement to agree at some future time is unenforceable.[7] To be an option contract, the parties' agreement must contain all essential terms that are to be incorporated in the actual sale agreement. The option contract is only a memorial of the agreement already reached. If the document or contract that the parties agree to make is to contain any material term that is not already agreed on, no contract has been made.[8] Thus, to be an enforceable option contract, the parties must intend to be bound by the agreement, and the terms of the agreement must be definite. While minor matters may be left to the option of one of the parties or to what is customary or reasonable, the more important the uncertainty in the agreement, the stronger the indication that the parties do not intend to be bound by it.[9]

App. 1996), reh'g denied, (Aug. 27, 1996) and transfer denied, 683 N.E.2d 582 (Ind. 1997); Rowland v. Amoco Oil Co., 432 N.E.2d 414 (Ind. Ct. App. 3d Dist. 1982).

[5]Rowland v. Amoco Oil Co., 432 N.E.2d 414 (Ind. Ct. App. 3d Dist. 1982) (optionee entitled to relief where it stated wrong amount for purchase of gas station in letter announcing intention to exercise option by accident rather than design).

[6]Lafayette Expo Center, Inc. v. Owens, 531 N.E.2d 508 (Ind. Ct. App. 3d Dist. 1988), reh'g denied, (Jan. 17, 1989) and transfer denied, (July 27, 1989); Romain v. A. Howard Wholesale Co., 506 N.E.2d 1124 (Ind. Ct. App. 1st Dist. 1987), reh'g denied, (June 8, 1987) and transfer denied, (Dec. 10, 1987).

[7]Wolvos v. Meyer, 668 N.E.2d 671 (Ind. 1996).

[8]Wolvos v. Meyer, 668 N.E.2d 671 (Ind. 1996).

[9]Wolvos v. Meyer, 668 N.E.2d 671 (Ind. 1996), related reference, 707 N.E.2d 1029 (Ind. Ct. App. 1999), reh'g denied, (May 13, 1999) and transfer denied, (Sept. 20, 1999) (quoting Restatement (Second) of Contracts § 33, comment f).

As to the requirement that a contract be definite, see § 2.

◆ **Observation:** An option contract need not fix the
purchase price of the property to be sold if it describes the
method to be used for fixing the price.[10]

A right of first refusal, although its purposes are closely
related to those of an option contract, is not an offer and creates no power of acceptance, but instead creates a contractual
right to preempt another from accepting an offer.[11] Thus, a
right of first refusal, when initially granted, is a dormant set
of rights that does not entitle the holder to take any action
until he or she receives a bona fide offer.[12] Once the right
holder receives notice of a third party's offer, the right of
first refusal is transmuted into an option.[13]

As with option contracts, rights of first refusal are typically granted in real property transactions, but the subject
matter may be anything that may be made the subject of a
contract.[14] Rights of first refusal typically grant the holder
the right to purchase property on the same terms that the

[10]Salin Bank and Trust Co. v. Violet U. Peden Trust, 715 N.E.2d 1003
(Ind. Ct. App. 1999); Fetz v. Phillips, 591 N.E.2d 644 (Ind. Ct. App. 1st
Dist. 1992).

[11]Hyperbaric Oxygen Therapy Systems, Inc. v. St. Joseph Medical
Center of Ft. Wayne, Inc., 683 N.E.2d 243 (Ind. Ct. App. 1997), transfer
denied, 690 N.E.2d 1189 (Ind. 1997).

[12]Hyperbaric Oxygen Therapy Systems, Inc. v. St. Joseph Medical
Center of Ft. Wayne, Inc., 683 N.E.2d 243 (Ind. Ct. App. 1997), transfer
denied, 690 N.E.2d 1189 (Ind. 1997); Beiger Heritage Corp. v. Estate of
Kilbey, 667 N.E.2d 184 (Ind. Ct. App. 1996), reh'g denied, (Aug. 27, 1996)
and transfer denied, 683 N.E.2d 582 (Ind. 1997).

[13]Hyperbaric Oxygen Therapy Systems, Inc. v. St. Joseph Medical
Center of Ft. Wayne, Inc., 683 N.E.2d 243 (Ind. Ct. App. 1997), transfer
denied, 690 N.E.2d 1189 (Ind. 1997); Beiger Heritage Corp. v. Estate of
Kilbey, 667 N.E.2d 184 (Ind. Ct. App. 1996), reh'g denied, (Aug. 27, 1996)
and transfer denied, 683 N.E.2d 582 (Ind. 1997).

[14]Hyperbaric Oxygen Therapy Systems, Inc. v. St. Joseph Medical
Center of Ft. Wayne, Inc., 683 N.E.2d 243 (Ind. Ct. App. 1997), transfer
denied, 690 N.E.2d 1189 (Ind. 1997) (hospital equipment).

seller is willing to accept from a third party,[15] but a potential purchaser may also involve a right of first refusal to sell.[16]

§ 10   Acceptance

Acceptance of an offer must be made by an overt act, and the acceptance must meet the terms of the offer in every respect.

West's Digest, Contracts ☞22(1), (2), 23, 26.

Once an offer is accepted, a contract is formed.[17] In order for a contract to exist, there must be an acceptance of an offer which meets the terms of the offer in every respect.[18]

◆ **Illustration:** Where two parties negotiated the terms of an employment agreement for two months, and the offeree, though stating that he thought the agreement was substantially workable, declined to sign it because he disagreed with the termination clause, and suggested that they let their attorneys work it out while he came to work for the offeror, no oral contract existed between the two, as they had not agreed to all of the contract's terms.[19]

An acceptance must be evidenced by some overt act and must be communicated to the offeror.[20] Generally, a party making an offer may describe the mode in which acceptance

---

[15]See, for instance, Beiger Heritage Corp. v. Kilbey, 676 N.E.2d 784 (Ind. Ct. App. 1997); Arlington State Bank v. Colvin, 545 N.E.2d 572 (Ind. Ct. App. 1st Dist. 1989), reh'g denied, (Nov. 22, 1989) and transfer denied, (Apr. 12, 1990); Urban Hotel Management Corp. v. Main and Washington Joint Venture, 494 N.E.2d 334 (Ind. Ct. App. 3d Dist. 1986), reh'g denied, (Sept. 5, 1986) and transfer denied, (Mar. 10, 1987).

[16]Hyperbaric Oxygen Therapy Systems, Inc. v. St. Joseph Medical Center of Ft. Wayne, Inc., 683 N.E.2d 243 (Ind. Ct. App. 1997), transfer denied, 690 N.E.2d 1189 (Ind. 1997).

[17]Bain v. Board of Trustees of Starke Memorial Hosp., 550 N.E.2d 106 (Ind. Ct. App. 3d Dist. 1990), reh'g denied, (Mar. 30, 1990).

[18]Keating v. Burton, 617 N.E.2d 588 (Ind. Ct. App. 4th Dist. 1993), reh'g denied, (Sept. 14, 1993) and transfer denied, (Dec. 29, 1993); Gregory and Appel, Inc. v. Duck, 459 N.E.2d 46 (Ind. Ct. App. 2d Dist. 1984).

Forms References: Acceptance—General form. 5A Am Jur Legal Forms 2d, Contracts § 68:91.

Trial Strategy References: Offeree's Acceptance of Contract Offer, 27 Am Jur POF2d 559.

[19]Keating v. Burton, 617 N.E.2d 588 (Ind. Ct. App. 4th Dist. 1993), reh'g denied, (Sept. 14, 1993) and transfer denied, (Dec. 29, 1993).

[20]Herald Telephone v. Fatouros, 431 N.E.2d 171 (Ind. Ct. App. 4th Dist.

must be made.[21] If the offeror does not do so, assent to the terms of a contract may be expressed by acts which manifest acceptance.[22] The act of signing a written contract, for instance, constitutes assent to its terms and thus acceptance of the offer.[23] When an offer is communicated by mail, and no more specific provisions for acceptance are made, it may be accepted by a communication placed in the mail within a reasonable time.[24]

Contracts for the sale of goods between merchants may be made in any manner sufficient to show agreement, including conduct of the parties.[25] If, for instance, one party makes an offer, specifying certain terms, and the other does not expressly accept the terms, but performs in accordance with them, he or she has accepted the offer.[26]

1982); Young v. Bryan, 178 Ind. App. 702, 368 N.E.2d 1 (1st Dist. 1977), appeal after remand, 178 Ind. App. 702, 368 N.E.2d 3 (1st Dist. 1977).

As to communication of an acceptance, see § 11.

[21]Foltz v. Evans, 113 Ind. App. 596, 49 N.E.2d 358 (1943).

[22]Pinnacle Computer Services, Inc. v. Ameritech Pub., Inc., 642 N.E.2d 1011 (Ind. Ct. App. 1st Dist. 1994), reh'g denied, (Feb. 23, 1995); State v. Daily Exp., Inc., 465 N.E.2d 764 (Ind. Ct. App. 1st Dist. 1984); Herald Telephone v. Fatouros, 431 N.E.2d 171 (Ind. Ct. App. 4th Dist. 1982).

[23]Pinnacle Computer Services, Inc. v. Ameritech Pub., Inc., 642 N.E.2d 1011 (Ind. Ct. App. 1st Dist. 1994), reh'g denied, (Feb. 23, 1995) (offeree's agent's signature on line under clause stating that he had read terms and conditions of contract constituted assent to its terms); Eickmier v. Geddes, 73 Ind. App. 167, 126 N.E. 859 (Div. 2 1920).

[24]New v. Germania Fire Ins. Co., 171 Ind. 33, 85 N.E. 703 (1908); Warner v. Marshall, 166 Ind. 88, 75 N.E. 582 (1905); Swing v. Marion Pulp Co., 47 Ind. App. 199, 93 N.E. 1004 (Div. 1 1911).

[25]IC 26-1-2-204.

Radio Picture Show Partnership v. Exclusive Intern. Pictures, Inc., 482 N.E.2d 1159 (Ind. Ct. App. 1st Dist. 1985), reh'g denied, (Oct. 25, 1985) and transfer denied, (Feb. 11, 1986); Uniroyal, Inc. v. Chambers Gasket & Mfg. Co., 177 Ind. App. 508, 380 N.E.2d 571, 24 U.C.C. Rep. Serv. (CBC) 1109 (2d Dist. 1978).

[26]Radio Picture Show Partnership v. Exclusive Intern. Pictures, Inc., 482 N.E.2d 1159 (Ind. Ct. App. 1st Dist. 1985), reh'g denied, (Oct. 25, 1985) and transfer denied, (Feb. 11, 1986); Uniroyal, Inc. v. Chambers Gasket & Mfg. Co., 177 Ind. App. 508, 380 N.E.2d 571, 24 U.C.C. Rep. Serv. (CBC) 1109 (2d Dist. 1978).

Silence, or total inaction, may be a legally effective expression of acceptance, depending on the antecedent conduct of the parties and the surrounding circumstances.[27]

◆ **Illustration:** Where a political candidate submitted an advertisement for publishing in the defendant's newspaper, the newspaper accepted the ad when its apparent agent reviewed the copy and told the candidate she could see the proof the next day, even though the newspaper later claimed that its policy on advertisement content prevented it from printing the ad. The candidate was never shown the newspaper's policy on ad content, acceptance of the ad was not conditioned on compliance with the policy, and the agent, after having failed to reject the copy, failed to reserve any right to future review of the ad. The trial court could reasonably have found that the newspaper accepted the ad when the candidate left the office after submitting the ad.[28]

Acceptance may be shown through the course of the parties' dealings with each other.[29]

An offer can be accepted only by the offeree.[30]

§ 11   —Acceptance at variance with offer

Under common law, a purported acceptance which does not conform to the terms of the offer is not effective as an acceptance, but may be a counter offer.

West's Digest, Contracts ☞23, 24.
West's Digest, Sales ☞22(4), 23(4).

Under common law, in order for an offer and an acceptance to constitute a contract, the acceptance must meet and

---

[27]Herald Telephone v. Fatouros, 431 N.E.2d 171 (Ind. Ct. App. 4th Dist. 1982).

[28]Herald Telephone v. Fatouros, 431 N.E.2d 171 (Ind. Ct. App. 4th Dist. 1982).

[29]Freeman v. Mayer, 95 F.3d 569 (7th Cir. 1996), reh'g and suggestion for reh'g en banc denied, (Oct. 2, 1996) (applying Indiana law) (attorney's fee-splitting agreement was enforceable; letters between attorneys outlined agreement and described case to be referred, and defendant attorney worked on case for two years, meanwhile billing plaintiff attorney for his share of expenses as agreed in letters).

[30]Gates v. Petri, 127 Ind. App. 670, 143 N.E.2d 293 (1957) (offer to purchase land owned by husband and wife could not be accepted by husband alone, where there was no evidence that husband was agent of, or otherwise authorized to act for, wife).

correspond with the offer in every respect,[31] and must not go beyond it.[32] This rule is called the "mirror image rule."[33] An acceptance which varies the terms of the offer is considered a rejection and operates as a counteroffer,[34] which may be then accepted by the original offeror,[35] either expressly or by performing under the terms contained in the counteroffer.[36]

> ◆ **Illustration:** A bid provided that the offeror was to correct any nonconforming work, and that this was the only remedy available to the offeree. The offeree, in its purchase order sent in response, reserved the right to reject, refuse, or revoke any nonconforming goods or cancel any nonconforming performance, and stated that these remedies were not exclusive of any other remedy allowed by law. The purchase order, because it varied the terms of the bid, became a counteroffer, and the original offeror accepted the counteroffer by signing and returning the purchase order.[37]

A conditional acceptance or counter offer terminates the offeree's power to accept the original offer.[38]

An offeree need not necessarily know all of the terms in

---

[31]I.C.C. Protective Coatings, Inc. v. A.E. Staley Mfg. Co., 695 N.E.2d 1030 (Ind. Ct. App. 1998), transfer denied, 706 N.E.2d 174 (Ind. 1998); Gates v. Petri, 127 Ind. App. 670, 143 N.E.2d 293 (1957).

[32]Uniroyal, Inc. v. Chambers Gasket & Mfg. Co., 177 Ind. App. 508, 380 N.E.2d 571, 24 U.C.C. Rep. Serv. (CBC) 1109 (2d Dist. 1978); Gerardot v. Emenhiser, 173 Ind. App. 353, 363 N.E.2d 1072 (3d Dist. 1977).

[33]Radio Picture Show Partnership v. Exclusive Intern. Pictures, Inc., 482 N.E.2d 1159 (Ind. Ct. App. 1st Dist. 1985), reh'g denied, (Oct. 25, 1985) and transfer denied, (Feb. 11, 1986).

[34]Kokomo Veterans, Inc. v. Schick, 439 N.E.2d 639 (Ind. Ct. App. 3d Dist. 1982).

Trial Strategy References: Acts Constituting Rejection of Contract Offer, 27 Am Jur POF2d 605.

[35]I.C.C. Protective Coatings, Inc. v. A.E. Staley Mfg. Co., 695 N.E.2d 1030 (Ind. Ct. App. 1998), transfer denied, 706 N.E.2d 174 (Ind. 1998); Uniroyal, Inc. v. Chambers Gasket & Mfg. Co., 177 Ind. App. 508, 380 N.E.2d 571, 24 U.C.C. Rep. Serv. (CBC) 1109 (2d Dist. 1978).

[36]Radio Picture Show Partnership v. Exclusive Intern. Pictures, Inc., 482 N.E.2d 1159 (Ind. Ct. App. 1st Dist. 1985), reh'g denied, (Oct. 25, 1985) and transfer denied, (Feb. 11, 1986); Uniroyal, Inc. v. Chambers Gasket & Mfg. Co., 177 Ind. App. 508, 380 N.E.2d 571, 24 U.C.C. Rep. Serv. (CBC) 1109 (2d Dist. 1978).

[37]I.C.C. Protective Coatings, Inc. v. A.E. Staley Mfg. Co., 695 N.E.2d 1030 (Ind. Ct. App. 1998), transfer denied, 706 N.E.2d 174 (Ind. 1998).

[38]Kritz v. Moon, 88 Ind. App. 5, 163 N.E. 112 (1928).

the offer; as long as he or she is aware that an offer has been made to him or her, the offeree may accept whatever terms the offer contains.[39]

Contracts between merchants for the sale of goods, however, are governed not by common law, but by Chapter 2 of the Indiana version of the Uniform Commercial Code ("UCC").[40] Under the UCC, a definite acceptance or written confirmation sent within a reasonable time operates as an acceptance even if it states terms additional to or different from those in the offer, unless the acceptance is expressly conditioned on the original offeror's assent to the additional or different terms.[41] Thus, enforcement of a contract is permitted despite discrepancies between the offer and the acceptance if enforcement could be required without either party being bound to omit a material term to which he has not agreed.[42] If an acceptance is expressly conditioned on the offeror's assent to the new terms, and the offeror does not assent, the entire transaction fails, and there is no contract.[43]

§ 12   Communication of acceptance

An acceptance must be communicated to the offeror verbally, in writing, or by acts manifesting the acceptance.

West's Digest, Contracts ⟐22(3).

The communication of acceptance to the offeror is crucial to the formation of an enforceable contract,[44] The acceptance may be expressed verbally, in writing, or by acts which manifest the acceptance, so that a contract may be created

---

[39]Alfaro v. Stauffer Chemical Co., 173 Ind. App. 89, 362 N.E.2d 500 (3d Dist. 1977).

[40]IC 26-1-2-201 et seq.

[41]IC 26-1-2-207(1).

[42]Continental Grain Co. v. Followell, 475 N.E.2d 318, 40 U.C.C. Rep. Serv. (CBC) 1232 (Ind. Ct. App. 1st Dist. 1985), reh'g denied, (Apr. 25, 1985) and transfer denied, (July 3, 1985).

[43]Uniroyal, Inc. v. Chambers Gasket & Mfg. Co., 177 Ind. App. 508, 380 N.E.2d 571, 24 U.C.C. Rep. Serv. (CBC) 1109 (2d Dist. 1978).

For discussion of acceptance varying from offer under the UCC, see I.L.E., Sales of Personalty.

[44]Bain v. Board of Trustees of Starke Memorial Hosp., 550 N.E.2d 106 (Ind. Ct. App. 3d Dist. 1990), reh'g denied, (Mar. 30, 1990); Herald Telephone v. Fatouros, 431 N.E.2d 171 (Ind. Ct. App. 4th Dist. 1982).

even if the acceptance is not filed or delivered to the offeree.[45] A contract can arise by correspondence between the parties,[46] and may consist of several documents.[47]

Generally, a party making an offer may prescribe the mode in which an acceptance must be made, and an acceptance made otherwise will not bind the offeror unless the offeror expressly or impliedly modifies the requirements in that respect or waives them.[48]

III. CONSIDERATION

A. IN GENERAL

Research References

17A Am Jur 2d, Contracts §§ 113-180.
17 C.J.S., Contracts §§ 83-135.
West's Digest, Contracts ☞47-91.
ALR Digest: Contracts §§ 22-32.5
ALR Index: Adhesion Contracts; Anticipatory Breach; Anticipatory Renunciation or Repudiation; Bids and Bidding; Cancellation of Rescission; Consideration; Contracts; Covenants; Covenants Not to Compete; Estoppel and Waiver; Executory Contracts; Implied Contracts; Offer and Acceptance; Parol Contracts and Agreements; Parol Evidence; Third-Party Beneficiaries; Unconscionability
5A Am Jur Legal Forms 2d, Contracts § 68:121.
Corbin on Contracts (rev. ed.), §§ 5.1-9.30.

§ 13 Generally

To be enforceable, a promise must be supported by consideration.

West's Digest, Contracts ☞47-52, 85.

A mere promise does not, in and of itself, automatically

---

[45]Young v. Bryan, 178 Ind. App. 702, 368 N.E.2d 1 (1st Dist. 1977), appeal after remand, 178 Ind. App. 702, 368 N.E.2d 3 (1st Dist. 1977); Equitable Life Assur. Soc. of the U.S. v. Perkins, 41 Ind. App. 183, 80 N.E. 682 (1907).

[46]Freeman v. Mayer, 95 F.3d 569 (7th Cir. 1996), reh'g and suggestion for reh'g en banc denied, (Oct. 2, 1996) (applying Indiana law); Suyemasa v. Myers, 420 N.E.2d 1334 (Ind. Ct. App. 1st Dist. 1981) (letter and response constituted a valid contract, even though they did not specify time and place of performance).

[47]Wood v. Ridgeville College, 114 Ind. 320, 16 N.E. 619 (1888).

[48]Foltz v. Evans, 113 Ind. App. 596, 49 N.E.2d 358 (1943).

entitle the promisee to relief.[49] A promise is not enforceable unless it is supported by consideration.[50] Consideration, which consists of a bargained-for exchange,[51] is essential to every contract.[52]

When writings are construed together in determining the existence and terms of a contract, consideration for one instrument may be found in a contemporaneously executed instrument.[53] For instance, a guaranty executed contemporaneously with an extension of credit as an inducement for the guaranty is supported by consideration.[54]

If one party intends that the consideration will actually be provided by a third party, consideration may still be adequate to support a contract between the offeror and offeree.[55] Similarly, if a guaranty is executed by a third party at the time of the contract to which it relates, and induces the

---

[49]Burdsall v. City of Elwood, 454 N.E.2d 434 (Ind. Ct. App. 1st Dist. 1983); Jenkins v. Hatcher, 163 Ind. App. 95, 322 N.E.2d 117 (3d Dist. 1975).

[50]Puetz v. Cozmas, 237 Ind. 500, 147 N.E.2d 227 (1958); Herald Telephone v. Fatouros, 431 N.E.2d 171 (Ind. Ct. App. 4th Dist. 1982).

Forms References: Recital of consideration—General form. 5A Am Jur Legal Forms 2d, Contracts § 68:121.

[51]B-Dry Owners Ass'n v. B-Dry System, Inc., 636 N.E.2d 161 (Ind. Ct. App. 2d Dist. 1994), reh'g denied, (Aug. 17, 1994) and transfer denied, (Dec. 30, 1994); Hamlin v. Steward, 622 N.E.2d 535 (Ind. Ct. App. 1st Dist. 1993); In re Estate of Von Wendesse, 618 N.E.2d 1332 (Ind. Ct. App. 1st Dist. 1993), transfer denied, (Oct. 22, 1993); Wavetek Indiana, Inc. v. K.H. Gatewood Steel Co., Inc., 458 N.E.2d 265 (Ind. Ct. App. 3d Dist. 1984).

[52]Puetz v. Cozmas, 237 Ind. 500, 147 N.E.2d 227 (1958); Alber v. Standard Heating and Air Conditioning, Inc., 476 N.E.2d 507 (Ind. Ct. App. 3d Dist. 1985).

[53]Leatherman v. Management Advisors, Inc., 448 N.E.2d 1048 (Ind. 1983); Goeke v. Merchants Nat. Bank and Trust Co. of Indianapolis, 467 N.E.2d 760 (Ind. Ct. App. 1st Dist. 1984), reh'g denied, (Sept. 27, 1984) and transfer denied, (Jan. 14, 1985); Huntingburg Production Credit Ass'n v. Griese, 456 N.E.2d 448 (Ind. Ct. App. 1st Dist. 1983); Torres v. Meyer Paving Co., 423 N.E.2d 692 (Ind. Ct. App. 1st Dist. 1981).

As to the construction together of separate instruments, see § 73.

[54]Goeke v. Merchants Nat. Bank and Trust Co. of Indianapolis, 467 N.E.2d 760 (Ind. Ct. App. 1st Dist. 1984), reh'g denied, (Sept. 27, 1984) and transfer denied, (Jan. 14, 1985).

[55]Monarch Beverage Co., Inc. v. Indiana Dept. of State Revenue, 589 N.E.2d 1209 (Ind. Tax Ct. 1992) (where principal remained ultimately liable for payment); Huntingburg Production Credit Ass'n v. Griese, 456 N.E.2d 448 (Ind. Ct. App. 1st Dist. 1983).

promisee to execute the main contract with the principal so as to constitute part of the consideration for the contract, sufficient consideration exists.[56] The guarantor need not derive any benefit from the principal contract or from the guaranty.[57] The third party's consideration is the primary obligor's receipt of what was bargained for.[58]

A contract is presumed to be made upon consideration,[59] and a party raising the defense of want of consideration has the burden of proving it.[60]

If any part of an entire consideration for a promise, or of any part of an entire promise, is illegal, whether at common law or by statute, the whole contract is void, as the illegal part of the consideration vitiates the entire contract and renders it unenforceable. However, if several promises, some of which are legal and some illegal, are all based upon one entire consideration which is legal, the law will enforce the legal promise while denying relief in proceeding to enforce the illegal promises.[61]

§ 14 Promissory estoppel

Where one person makes a promise which could reasonably be expected to, and does, induce action or forbearance, and injustice can be avoided only by enforcing the promise, consideration is not necessary.

West's Digest, Contracts.

---

[56]Singer Mfg. Co. v. Forsythe, 108 Ind. 334, 9 N.E. 372 (1886); Loudermilk v. Casey, 441 N.E.2d 1379 (Ind. Ct. App. 1st Dist. 1982); Davis v. B. C. L. Enterprises, Inc., 406 N.E.2d 1204 (Ind. Ct. App. 1st Dist. 1980).

[57]Loudermilk v. Casey, 441 N.E.2d 1379 (Ind. Ct. App. 1st Dist. 1982).

[58]Harrison-Floyd Farm Bureau Co-op. Ass'n, Inc. v. Reed, 546 N.E.2d 855 (Ind. Ct. App. 1st Dist. 1989).

[59]Nelson v. White, 61 Ind. 139, 1878 WL 6289 (1878); Baker v. Board of Com'rs of Washington County, 53 Ind. 497, 1876 WL 6521 (1876); Beeson v. Howard, 44 Ind. 413, 1873 WL 5368 (1873); Brown v. Addington, 114 Ind. App. 404, 52 N.E.2d 640 (1944); Woodworth v. Veitch, 29 Ind. App. 589, 64 N.E. 932 (Div. 2 1902).

[60]Nelson v. White, 61 Ind. 139, 1878 WL 6289 (1878); Bright Nat. Bank of Flora v. Hartman, 61 Ind. App. 440, 109 N.E. 846 (Div. 1 1915).

For further discussion of presumptions and burden of proof in actions of breach of contract, see § 132.

[61]Hynds v. Hays, 25 Ind. 31, 1865 WL 1860 (1865); McClain's Estate v. McClain, 133 Ind. App. 645, 183 N.E.2d 842 (Div. 1 1962), reh'g dismissed, 133 Ind. App. 645, 184 N.E.2d 281 (Div. 1 1962); Simpson v. Fuller, 114 Ind. App. 583, 51 N.E.2d 870 (1943).

The doctrine of promissory estoppel can act as a substitute for lack of consideration.[62] Promissory estoppel applies where there is a promise upon which the promisor could reasonably expect to induce action or forbearance of a definite and substantial character which does in fact induce such action or forbearance, and injustice can only be avoided by enforcement of the promise.[63] The mere expression of an intention[64] or a prediction, opinion, or prophecy[65] is not a promise that will support enforcement of a contract under the doctrine of promissory estoppel.[66]

B.　SUFFICIENCY OF CONSIDERATION

Research References

IC 26-1-1-101; IC 26-1-2-106; IC 26-1-3-408
45 IAC 2.2-4-1

17A Am Jur 2d, Contracts §§ 126-180.
17 C.J.S., Contracts §§ 87-130.
West's Digest, Contracts ☞47-91.
ALR Digest: Contracts §§ 33-75.5
ALR Index: Adhesion Contracts; Anticipatory Breach; Anticipatory Renunciation or Repudiation; Bids and Bidding; Cancellation of Rescission; Consideration; Contracts; Covenants; Covenants Not to Compete; Estoppel and Waiver; Executory Contracts; Implied Contracts; Offer and Acceptance; Parol Contracts and Agree-

---

[62]Hamlin v. Steward, 622 N.E.2d 535 (Ind. Ct. App. 1st Dist. 1993); First Nat. Bank of Logansport v. Logan Mfg. Co., Inc., 577 N.E.2d 949, 18 A.L.R.5th 999 (Ind. 1991).

[63]Hamlin v. Steward, 622 N.E.2d 535 (Ind. Ct. App. 1st Dist. 1993) (when lenders agreed to forbear from collecting note until debtors had sold property, debtors changed their plans in reliance upon promise by not making annual payments on note, and lenders were estopped from claiming that oral modification was unenforceable); Medtech Corp. v. Indiana Ins. Co., 555 N.E.2d 844 (Ind. Ct. App. 1st Dist. 1990), transfer denied, (Oct. 18, 1990); Security Bank & Trust Co. v. Bogard, 494 N.E.2d 965 (Ind. Ct. App. 4th Dist. 1986).

[64]Security Bank & Trust Co. v. Bogard, 494 N.E.2d 965 (Ind. Ct. App. 4th Dist. 1986).

[65]Security Bank & Trust Co. v. Bogard, 494 N.E.2d 965 (Ind. Ct. App. 4th Dist. 1986).

[66]Security Bank & Trust Co. v. Bogard, 494 N.E.2d 965 (Ind. Ct. App. 4th Dist. 1986) (bank employee's statement to loan applicant that "within two or three days, we ought to have something here, ready for you to go with" was merely prediction that loan would be approved, and would not support application of promissory estoppel).

ments; Parol Evidence; Third-Party Beneficiaries; Unconscionability
5A Am Jur Legal Forms 2d, Contracts §§ 68:126, 68:127, 68:138.
Corbin on Contracts (rev. ed.), §§ 5.1-9.30.

§ 15 Generally

Consideration may, but need not be, a price in money.

West's Digest, Contracts ☞54.

In the context of a sale of goods, the term "consideration"
has been defined or construed to mean simply a price
estimated in money.[67] The Indiana Uniform Commercial
Code[68] defines a "sale" as "the passing of title from the seller
to the buyer for a price."[69] Under regulations of the Indiana
Department of Revenue, consideration subject to tax includes:[70]

> (1) the price arrived at between purchaser and seller;
> and
>
> (2) any additional bona fide charges added to or included
> in such price for preparation, fabrication, alteration,
> modification, finishing, completion, delivery, or other
> services performed in respect to or labor charges for
> work done with respect to such property prior to
> transfer.

However, consideration need not be in the form of money
to support a binding contract.[71] It is not necessary that the
obligee actually give anything of value to the obligor, and
sufficient consideration will be found if it is shown that the
obligee suffered any damage, inconvenience, detriment or

---

[67]Wayne Pump Co. v. Department of Treasury, Gross Income Tax
Division, 232 Ind. 147, 110 N.E.2d 284 (1953); Monarch Beverage Co., Inc.
v. Indiana Dept. of State Revenue, 589 N.E.2d 1209 (Ind. Tax Ct. 1992).

[68]IC 26-1-1-101 et seq.

[69]IC 26-1-2-106(1).

For general discussion of contracts between merchants for the sale of
goods, see I.L.E., Sales of Personalty.

[70]45 IAC 2.2-4-1(b).

[71]Kelley, Glover & Vale v. Heitman, 220 Ind. 625, 44 N.E.2d 981 (1942);
Tri-States Double Cola Bottling Co. v. Department of State Revenue, 706
N.E.2d 282 (Ind. Tax Ct. 1999).

loss, or that he or she extended any forbearance in reliance upon the mortgage.[72]

A promise may be sufficient consideration for another promise[73] if it is the result of a bargained-for exchange,[74] even if the promise serving as consideration is unenforceable.[75] Thus, a promise to pay a price is sufficient as consideration,[76] and a distributor's promise to carry only the promisee's products and to use its best efforts to sell those products may be consideration for a distributorship contract.[77] A promise may be consideration even though it is conditional.[78] Unless each promise is supported by a separate promise on the other side, and the promises are specifically identified to one another, one promise may support any number of counterpromises.[79]

§ 16 Benefit or detriment

A benefit accruing to the promisor or to a third person, or a detriment suffered by the promisee or by a third person, constitutes consideration.

West's Digest, Contracts ☞51, 52.

---

[72]Huntingburg Production Credit Ass'n v. Griese, 456 N.E.2d 448 (Ind. Ct. App. 1st Dist. 1983).

As to detriment to the obligee as consideration, see § 16.

As to forbearance as consideration, see § 17.

[73]Leatherman v. Management Advisors, Inc., 448 N.E.2d 1048 (Ind. 1983); Davis v. Calloway, 30 Ind. 112, 1868 WL 3066 (1868); Hamlin v. Steward, 622 N.E.2d 535 (Ind. Ct. App. 1st Dist. 1993) (consideration, rather than gratuitous promise, supported modified contract, where lender agreed to forbear from demanding payment and borrower made new promise to pay note in full after sale of real property); In re Estate of Von Wendesse, 618 N.E.2d 1332 (Ind. Ct. App. 1st Dist. 1993), transfer denied, (Oct. 22, 1993).

[74]Tolliver v. Mathas, 538 N.E.2d 971 (Ind. Ct. App. 4th Dist. 1989), reh'g denied, (July 10, 1989) and transfer denied, (Jan. 10, 1990); Burdsall v. City of Elwood, 454 N.E.2d 434 (Ind. Ct. App. 1st Dist. 1983).

[75]In re Marriage of Arvin, 689 N.E.2d 1270 (Ind. Ct. App. 1997), transfer denied, 698 N.E.2d 1187 (Ind. 1998).

[76]Monarch Beverage Co., Inc. v. Indiana Dept. of State Revenue, 589 N.E.2d 1209 (Ind. Tax Ct. 1992).

[77]Moridge Mfg. Co. v. Butler, 451 N.E.2d 677, 36 U.C.C. Rep. Serv. (CBC) 1548 (Ind. Ct. App. 3d Dist. 1983).

[78]Eichholtz v. Taylor, 88 Ind. 38, 1882 WL 7043 (1882).

[79]Leatherman v. Management Advisors, Inc., 448 N.E.2d 1048 (Ind. 1983).

To constitute consideration, there must be a benefit accruing to the promisor or a detriment to the promisee.[80] A benefit is a legal right given to the promisor to which the promisor would not otherwise be entitled. A detriment is a legal right the promisee has forborne.[81] One person's act performed at the request of another which may be a detrimental inconvenience, however slight, to the party doing it or may be a benefit, however slight, to the party at whose request it is performed, is legal consideration for a promise by the party at whose request the act was performed.[82] Detriment alone may be sufficient consideration.[83]

Performance in reliance on the parties' agreement is a detriment to the performing party, and thus may constitute consideration.[84] In a unilateral contract, performance in response to an offer may constitute both acceptance of the offer and consideration for the contract.[85]

Consideration need not be of benefit to the party making

---

[80]B-Dry Owners Ass'n v. B-Dry System, Inc., 636 N.E.2d 161 (Ind. Ct. App. 2d Dist. 1994), reh'g denied, (Aug. 17, 1994) and transfer denied, (Dec. 30, 1994); Hamlin v. Steward, 622 N.E.2d 535 (Ind. Ct. App. 1st Dist. 1993); In re Estate of Von Wendesse, 618 N.E.2d 1332 (Ind. Ct. App. 1st Dist. 1993), transfer denied, (Oct. 22, 1993); A & S Corp. v. Midwest Commerce Banking Co., 525 N.E.2d 1290 (Ind. Ct. App. 3d Dist. 1988); Urbanational Developers, Inc. v. Shamrock Engineering, Inc., 175 Ind. App. 416, 372 N.E.2d 742 (3d Dist. 1978).

[81]OVRS Acquisition Corp. v. Community Health Services, Inc., 657 N.E.2d 117 (Ind. Ct. App. 1995), reh'g denied, (Jan. 4, 1996) and transfer denied (Ind. May 17, 1996).

[82]Tolliver v. Mathas, 538 N.E.2d 971 (Ind. Ct. App. 4th Dist. 1989), reh'g denied, (July 10, 1989) and transfer denied, (Jan. 10, 1990); Harrison-Floyd Farm Bureau Co-op. Ass'n, Inc. v. Reed, 546 N.E.2d 855 (Ind. Ct. App. 1st Dist. 1989); Herrera v. Collection Service, Inc., 441 N.E.2d 981 (Ind. Ct. App. 2d Dist. 1982).

[83]Tolliver v. Mathas, 538 N.E.2d 971 (Ind. Ct. App. 4th Dist. 1989), reh'g denied, (July 10, 1989) and transfer denied, (Jan. 10, 1990); Goeke v. Merchants Nat. Bank and Trust Co. of Indianapolis, 467 N.E.2d 760 (Ind. Ct. App. 1st Dist. 1984), reh'g denied, (Sept. 27, 1984) and transfer denied, (Jan. 14, 1985).

[84]See, for instance, Monarch Beverage Co., Inc. v. Indiana Dept. of State Revenue, 589 N.E.2d 1209 (Ind. Tax Ct. 1992) (promisee's delivery of goods at promisor's request was consideration, especially where promisor used and benefited from goods).

[85]Orr v. Westminster Village North, Inc., 689 N.E.2d 712 (Ind. 1997) (declining, however, to rule that employee handbook can constitute valid unilateral contract in absence of adequate independent consideration).

the promise.[86] A benefit or detriment sufficient to constitute consideration may accrue to or be suffered by a third person.[87] For instance, a seller's extension of credit to a purchaser may be sufficient consideration to bind the surety.[88] Consideration may also be sufficient if the benefit accrues to the promissor to a lesser degree than to the direct beneficiary. For instance, a loan to a corporation can be valid consideration for a promissory note signed by shareholders of the corporation who have a vital interest in the corporation.[89]

The assumption of a liability at the request of the promisor, such as a promise to indemnify another against a prospective loss or damage, is a valuable consideration.[90]

§ 17 Forbearance

Forbearance from exercising a legal right may constitute consideration.

West's Digest, Contracts ☞70-73.

Consideration may consist of forbearance from exercising a legal right.[91] The forbearance must be expressly or impliedly bargained for.[92] Forbearance may be found in:

- the release of a lien[93]

---

[86]Timberlake v. J. R. Watkins Co., 138 Ind. App. 554, 209 N.E.2d 909 (Div. 1 1965), reh'g denied, 138 Ind. App. 554, 211 N.E.2d 193 (Div. 1 1965).

[87]Huntingburg Production Credit Ass'n v. Griese, 456 N.E.2d 448 (Ind. Ct. App. 1st Dist. 1983).

[88]Timberlake v. J. R. Watkins Co., 138 Ind. App. 554, 209 N.E.2d 909 (Div. 1 1965), reh'g denied, 138 Ind. App. 554, 211 N.E.2d 193 (Div. 1 1965).

[89]Parrish v. Terre Haute Sav. Bank, 431 N.E.2d 132 (Ind. Ct. App. 4th Dist. 1982), reh'g denied, 438 N.E.2d 1 (Ind. Ct. App. 4th Dist. 1982) and transfer denied, (Feb. 4, 1985); U.S. Rubber Co. v. Moon, 93 Ind. App. 571, 179 N.E. 26 (1931).

[90]Kincaid v. Lazar, 405 N.E.2d 615 (Ind. Ct. App. 1st Dist. 1980) (agreement to hold plaintiff harmless from any liability he may have incurred as shareholder or officer of corporation was consideration for his relinquishment of his interest in corporation).

[91]Farmers & Merchants Bank of Hanna v. Peoples Trust & Sav. Bank of La Porte, 101 Ind. App. 474, 199 N.E. 892 (1936).

[92]Blumenthal v. Tibbits, 160 Ind. 70, 66 N.E. 159 (1903).

[93]Piper v. Fosher, 121 Ind. 407, 23 N.E. 269 (1890); McOuat v. Cathcart, 84 Ind. 567, 1882 WL 6354 (1882).

- an agreement not to bring a meritorious action[94]
- the dismissal of an action[95]
- the abandonment of the right to appeal[96]
- an agreement to extend the time for payment of a debt[97]

◆ **Illustration:** A lender's agreement to forbear any activity to collect an overdue account from a farmer was sufficient consideration for a promissory note to which the unpaid balance was reduced, signed by not only the farmer, but also by the farmer's wife, his partner, and the partner's wife.[98]

§ 18 Past consideration

Past consideration does not support a later promise.

West's Digest, Contracts ⊂67, 76, 79.

As a general rule, past consideration which imposed no obligation when it was furnished will not support a subsequent promise.[99] A distinction must be made between consideration and motive. A mere moral obligation, without more, is not consideration,[1] and although a person has benefited in the past by some act or forbearance for which he or she incurred no legal liability, his or her later promise, whether made from good feeling or interested motives, to the person by whose act or forbearance the promisor has benefited is not enforceable.[2]

In a number of cases, however, past consideration is considered sufficient. Thus, if services were rendered at the

---

[94]Gregory v. Arms, 48 Ind. App. 562, 96 N.E. 196 (Div. 1 1911).

[95]Smith v. Smith, 106 Ind. 43, 5 N.E. 411 (1886); Jones v. Rittenhouse, 87 Ind. 348, 1882 WL 6539 (1882).

[96]Wray v. Chandler, 64 Ind. 146, 1878 WL 6195 (1878).

[97]Kester v. Hulman, 65 Ind. 100, 1878 WL 6404 (1878); Gilchrist v. Gough, 63 Ind. 576, 1878 WL 6172 (1878).

[98]Harrison-Floyd Farm Bureau Co-op. Ass'n, Inc. v. Reed, 546 N.E.2d 855 (Ind. Ct. App. 1st Dist. 1989).

[99]Wolford v. Powers, 85 Ind. 294, 1882 WL 6386 (1882); Brown v. Addington, 114 Ind. App. 404, 52 N.E.2d 640 (1944); Field v. Alexander & Alexander of Indiana, Inc., 503 N.E.2d 627 (Ind. Ct. App. 2d Dist. 1987), reh'g denied, (Aug. 10, 1987) and transfer denied, (Apr. 5, 1988).

[1]Wills v. Ross, 77 Ind. 1, 1881 WL 6622 (1881).

[2]Brown v. Addington, 114 Ind. App. 404, 52 N.E.2d 640 (1944).

promisor's request, a subsequent promise to pay for them is considered to be supported by consideration,[3] even if part of the services were rendered before the request.[4]

No consideration is necessary for an instrument or obligation given in payment of or as security for an antecedent obligation of any kind.[5] For instance, a pre-existing debt or liability is sufficient consideration to support a mortgage given as security, and there need not be a new consideration at the time of making the mortgage.[6] However, the existing debt of a third person will not support a promisor's promise to pay it.[7]

§ 19 Performance of legal obligation

A person's promise to perform an act he or she is already legally obligated to perform is not consideration.

West's Digest, Contracts ⊕75(1)-75(3).

A promise to do what one is already under a legal obligation to do is not sufficient consideration for another's promise.[8] A party to a contract is not bound to pay more for the

---

[3]Goldsby v. Robertson, 1 Blackf. 247, 1823 WL 1056 (Ind. 1823).

[4]Wolford v. Powers, 85 Ind. 294, 1882 WL 6386 (1882).

[5]IC 26-1-3-408.

Harrison-Floyd Farm Bureau Co-op. Ass'n, Inc. v. Reed, 546 N.E.2d 855 (Ind. Ct. App. 1st Dist. 1989); Stockwell v. Bloomfield State Bank, 174 Ind. App. 307, 367 N.E.2d 42, 22 U.C.C. Rep. Serv. (CBC) 726 (1st Dist. 1977) (overruled on other grounds by, Farner v. Farner, 480 N.E.2d 251 (Ind. Ct. App. 1st Dist. 1985)) and (overruling on other grounds recognized by, Harrison-Floyd Farm Bureau Co-op. Ass'n, Inc. v. Reed, 546 N.E.2d 855 (Ind. Ct. App. 1st Dist. 1989)) and (overruling on other grounds recognized by, Farmers Loan & Trust Co. v. Letsinger, 635 N.E.2d 194 (Ind. Ct. App. 3d Dist. 1994)) and (overruling on other grounds recognized by, Yin v. Society Nat. Bank Indiana, 665 N.E.2d 58, 31 U.C.C. Rep. Serv. 2d (CBC) 168 (Ind. Ct. App. 1996)); Gemmer v. Anthony Wayne Bank, 181 Ind. App. 379, 391 N.E.2d 1185, 27 U.C.C. Rep. Serv. (CBC) 168 (4th Dist. 1979), reh'g denied, 181 Ind. App. 379, 393 N.E.2d 784 (2d Dist. 1979).

[6]Huntingburg Production Credit Ass'n v. Griese, 456 N.E.2d 448 (Ind. Ct. App. 1st Dist. 1983).

[7]Schnell v. Nell, 17 Ind. 29, 1861 WL 2779 (1861); Southern Indiana Loan & Sav. Inst. v. Roberts, 42 Ind. App. 653, 86 N.E. 490 (Div. 2 1908); Sponhaur v. Malloy, 21 Ind. App. 287, 52 N.E. 245 (1898); Vogel v. O'Toole, 2 Ind. App. 196, 28 N.E. 209 (1891).

[8]Ritenour v. Mathews, 42 Ind. 7, 1873 WL 5451 (1873); Shanks v.

other party's performance of his or her contractual duty,[9] nor is a party bound by a promise, given without other consideration, to accept less than is due under an existing contract.[10] A principal debtor's performance or promised performance of his or her obligation is not considered consideration for a surety's new promise.[11]

> ◆ **Illustration:** Where a bank on the verge of failure agreed to consider a borrower's $3,797.50 mortgage satisfied in full if the borrower would pay it a lump sum of $2,719.85, and the borrower did so, there was no consideration for a new note signed by the borrower in the amount of $800, which represented the difference, or part of the difference, between the original indebtedness and the amount for which the debt had been discharged.[12]

This rule, too, is not without its limitations. If a person has a right to discontinue performance of a contract, his or her promise to fulfill the contract is consideration for a new promise.[13] Moreover, some earlier cases appear to adopt the theory that if a party to a contract announces his or her unwillingness to perform on the contract terms, and the other party is willing to alter the terms rather than seek a remedy for breach of the contract, a new promise of performance is consideration for the new terms.[14]

A promise to pay a debt for which the promisor is liable is not consideration for another's promise,[15] nor is payment of a part of a debt sufficient to support a promise to discharge

---

Fisher, 126 Ind. App. 402, 130 N.E.2d 231 (1956); Bowers v. Alexandria Bank, 75 Ind. App. 345, 130 N.E. 808 (Div. 1 1921).

[9]Shanks v. Fisher, 126 Ind. App. 402, 130 N.E.2d 231 (1956).

[10]Wendling v. Snyder, 30 Ind. App. 330, 65 N.E. 1041 (Div. 1 1903).

[11]Ritenour v. Mathews, 42 Ind. 7, 1873 WL 5451 (1873); Ford v. Garner, 15 Ind. 298, 1860 WL 4470 (1860); Cameron v. Warbritton, 9 Ind. 351, 1857 WL 3623 (1857); Peelman v. Peelman, 4 Ind. 612, 1853 WL 3507 (1853).

[12]Gramar Inv. Co. v. Cumberworth, 120 Ind. App. 379, 92 N.E.2d 736 (1950).

[13]Brownlee v. Lowe, 117 Ind. 420, 20 N.E. 301 (1889).

[14]Pierce v. Walton, 20 Ind. App. 66, 50 N.E. 309 (1898); Sargent v. Robertson, 17 Ind. App. 411, 46 N.E. 925 (1897).

[15]Harris v. Cassaday, 107 Ind. 158, 8 N.E. 29 (1886); Holmes v. Boyd, 90 Ind. 332, 1883 WL 5877 (1883); Hume v. Mazelin, 84 Ind. 574, 1882 WL 6754 (1882).

the whole liability,[16] even if the debtor is insolvent.[17] This rule does not, however, apply to payments made by a third party, so that a third party's payment of a part of a debtor's debt may be consideration for the debtor's discharge.[18] Also, the payment of a barred obligation may be consideration.[19]

While neither an agreement to continue the payment of interest at the same rate as that borne by the original debt nor an agreement to pay interest at a reduced rate constitutes consideration for the extension of the time for payment,[20] a promise to pay compound interest supports an agreement to forbear collection of an obligation bearing simple interest.[21]

§ 20 Personal rights, relations and services

Marriage constitutes consideration for an antenuptial agreement.

West's Digest, Contracts ☞60.

Although an agreement to marry may not be specifically enforced,[22] marriage constitutes consideration for a contract[23] such as an antenuptial agreement.[24] However, marriage is

---

[16]American Cent. Ins. Co. v. Sweetser, 116 Ind. 370, 19 N.E. 159 (1888); Smith v. Tyler, 51 Ind. 512, 1875 WL 6126 (1875); Fensler v. Prather, 43 Ind. 119, 1873 WL 5271 (1873); Swope v. Bier, 10 Ind. App. 613, 38 N.E. 340 (1894).

But see Scott v. Scott, 105 Ind. 584, 5 N.E. 397 (1886) (consideration for creditor's release of bankrupt debtor existed where debtor agreed to pay other creditors certain percentage of debts to them).

[17]Beaver v. Fulp, 136 Ind. 595, 36 N.E. 418 (1894).

[18]Laboyteaux v. Swigart, 103 Ind. 596, 3 N.E. 373 (1885).

Forms References: Recital of Consideration—Consideration moving from third party. 5A Am Jur Legal Forms 2d, Contracts § 68:138.

[19]Hill v. Kerstetter, 43 Ind. App. 1, 86 N.E. 858 (Div. 2 1909).

[20]Dare v. Hall, 70 Ind. 545, 1880 WL 6431 (1880).

[21]Bugh v. Crum, 26 Ind. App. 465, 59 N.E. 1076 (1901).

[22]Matter of Estate of Palamara, 513 N.E.2d 1223 (Ind. Ct. App. 1st Dist. 1987), reh'g denied, (Nov. 6, 1987).

[23]Marmon v. White, 151 Ind. 445, 51 N.E. 930 (1898).

[24]Matter of Estate of Palamara, 513 N.E.2d 1223 (Ind. Ct. App. 1st Dist. 1987), reh'g denied, (Nov. 6, 1987); Russell v. Walz, 458 N.E.2d 1172 (Ind. Ct. App. 3d Dist. 1984); Gillilan's Estate v. Gillilan's Estate, 406 N.E.2d 981 (Ind. Ct. App. 4th Dist. 1980) (marriage may be most valuable and highly respected consideration).

not consideration for a post-nuptial contract.[25] A promise to name a child after a person is sufficient consideration for that person's note, payable to the child.[26]

One person's promise to support another supports a conveyance of the second person's property.[27]

§ 21 Employment

A promise of employment, even if it is only continued employment at will, is consideration for a covenant not to compete.

West's Digest, Contracts ☞54(2).

A promise of employment[28] or continued employment[29] will support an employee's agreement not to compete with his or her employer after the employment relationship is terminated. Likewise, an agreement to rehire an employee if he or she signs a covenant not to compete serves as valid consideration for the covenant,[30] and a contract to employ a person in a capacity in which he or she will receive a percentage of the employer's profits in addition to his or her regular salary

---

Forms References: Recital of Consideration—Marriage. 5A Am Jur Legal Forms 2d, Contracts § 68:127.

[25]Unger v. Mellinger, 37 Ind. App. 639, 77 N.E. 814 (Div. 1 1906)

As to past consideration, see § 18.

[26]Diffenderfer v. Scott, 5 Ind. App. 243, 32 N.E. 87 (1892)

[27]Leedy v. Crumbaker, 13 Ind. 523, 1859 WL 5020 (1859).

[28]Licocci v. Cardinal Associates, Inc., 445 N.E.2d 556 (Ind. 1983), appeal after remand, 492 N.E.2d 48 (Ind. Ct. App. 1st Dist. 1986), reh'g denied, (June 3, 1986) and transfer denied, (Oct. 21, 1986).

[29]Leatherman v. Management Advisors, Inc., 448 N.E.2d 1048 (Ind. 1983); Ackerman v. Kimball Intern., Inc., 634 N.E.2d 778 (Ind. Ct. App. 1st Dist. 1994), vacated in part on other grounds, adopted in part, 652 N.E.2d 507 (Ind. 1995); Rollins v. American State Bank, 487 N.E.2d 842 (Ind. Ct. App. 3d Dist. 1986), reh'g denied, (Mar. 31, 1986) and transfer denied, (Nov. 13, 1986).

Annotation References: Sufficiency of consideration for employee's covenant not to compete, entered into after inception of employment, 51 ALR3d 825.

[30]4408, Inc. v. Losure, 175 Ind. App. 658, 373 N.E.2d 899 (3d Dist. 1978).

Annotation References: Enforceability of agreement restricting right of attorney to compete with former law firm, 28 ALR5th 420.

Enforceability, by purchaser or successor of business, of covenant not to compete entered into by predecessor and its employees, 12 ALR5th 847.

Enforceability of covenant against competition in accountant's employment contract, 15 ALR4th 559.

constitutes valid consideration for the employee's covenant not to compete.[31] Even an agreement of continued employment at will, in which the employer provides no additional benefits and reserves the right to terminate the employment at any time, may be sufficient consideration to support a covenant not to compete.[32] In a contract to refrain from competition the parties are presumed, as in case of any other contract, in the absence of fraud, to have determined the question of consideration for themselves, and the court will not determine the adequacy of the consideration.[33]

Similarly, an employee's appointment to a new position was consideration for his agreement to release his grievances against his employer, even though the position was eliminated a few years later, where there was no job security provision in the agreement.[34]

§ 22 Love and affection

Natural love and affection is sufficient consideration for an executed contract, but not an executory one.

West's Digest, Contracts ☞77.

While natural love and affection is sufficient consideration for a deed or any executed contract,[35] it is not sufficient

---

[31]Buanno v. Weinraub, 226 Ind. 557, 81 N.E.2d 600 (1948).

[32]Leatherman v. Management Advisors, Inc., 448 N.E.2d 1048 (Ind. 1983); Ackerman v. Kimball Intern., Inc., 634 N.E.2d 778 (Ind. Ct. App. 1st Dist. 1994), vacated in part on other grounds, adopted in part, 652 N.E.2d 507 (Ind. 1995); Rollins v. American State Bank, 487 N.E.2d 842 (Ind. Ct. App. 3d Dist. 1986), reh'g denied, (Mar. 31, 1986) and transfer denied, (Nov. 13, 1986).

Trial Strategy References: Proving the Contractually Binding Effect of a Personnel Manual Provision as to Discharge Only for "Good Cause", 32 Am Jur POF3d 229.

[33]Eisel v. Hayes, 141 Ind. 41, 40 N.E. 119 (1895); Ackerman v. Kimball Intern., Inc., 634 N.E.2d 778 (Ind. Ct. App. 1st Dist. 1994), vacated in part on other grounds, adopted in part, 652 N.E.2d 507 (Ind. 1995).

[34]Orem v. Ivy Tech State College, 711 N.E.2d 864, 135 Ed. Law Rep. 628 (Ind. Ct. App. 1999), reh'g denied, (Sept. 16, 1999).

[35]West v. Cavins, 74 Ind. 265, 1881 WL 6434 (1881); Brown v. Addington, 114 Ind. App. 404, 52 N.E.2d 640 (1944); Galbraith v. Galbraith, 99 Ind. App. 563, 193 N.E. 707 (1935).

Forms References: Recital of consideration—Love and affection. 5A Am Jur Legal Forms 2d, Contracts § 68:126.

consideration for an executory promise,[36] whether the sentiment be toward the promisee[37] or another.[38]

However, the fact that affection forms an element of the consideration does not impair the force of a contract.[39]

◆ **Illustration:** An agreement between a man and the woman he lived with that they would establish a home together, and that the man's personal property would be the woman's during her lifetime, in exchange for her promise to make a will leaving the house, which was in her name, and all of the personalty in it to the man's children was supported by adequate consideration. The man obtained a benefit both during his lifetime, the woman's kindness and companionship, and after his demise, his children's receipt of that part of his estate the woman had not exhausted during her lifetime. The woman, in exchange, gave up the right to determine the disposition of the property upon her own death, and obtained the benefit of a home and the man's property during her lifetime.[40]

C. FAILURE AND ADEQUACY OF CONSIDERATION

Research References

17A Am Jur 2d, Contracts §§ 113-180.
17 C.J.S., Contracts §§ 131-135.
West's Digest, Contracts ☞47-91.
ALR Digest: Contracts §§ 22, 32.5, 33, 75.5
ALR Index: Adhesion Contracts; Anticipatory Breach; Anticipatory Renunciation or Repudiation; Bids and Bidding; Cancellation of

---

[36]West v. Cavins, 74 Ind. 265, 1881 WL 6434 (1881); Brown v. Addington, 114 Ind. App. 404, 52 N.E.2d 640 (1944); Galbraith v. Galbraith, 99 Ind. App. 563, 193 N.E. 707 (1935).

[37]Denman v. McMahin, 37 Ind. 241, 1871 WL 5058 (1871).

[38]Schnell v. Nell, 17 Ind. 29, 1861 WL 2779 (1861) (where decedent bequeathed certain sum to each plaintiff, but left no property, her husband's agreement to pay legacies in consideration of one cent, his love and affection for his deceased wife, fact that she had done her part in acquisition of his property, and her desire, expressed in her will, that plaintiffs should have money, considerations were insufficient to support contract).

[39]Puterbaugh v. Puterbaugh, 131 Ind. 288, 30 N.E. 519 (1892).

Annotation References: Moral obligation as consideration for contract—modern trend, 8 ALR2d 787.

[40]In re Estate of Von Wendesse, 618 N.E.2d 1332 (Ind. Ct. App. 1st Dist. 1993), transfer denied, (Oct. 22, 1993).

Rescission; Consideration; Contracts; Covenants; Covenants Not
to Compete; Estoppel and Waiver; Executory Contracts; Implied
Contracts; Offer and Acceptance; Parol Contracts and Agreements; Parol Evidence; Third-Party Beneficiaries; Unconscionability

5A Am Jur Legal Forms 2d, Contracts § 68:128.
Corbin on Contracts (rev. ed.), §§ 5.1-9.30.

§ 23 Failure of consideration

**Failure of consideration occurs when one party to a
contract fails to perform the acts promised.**

West's Digest, Contracts ☞83-90.

There is a failure of consideration when a party to a
contract fails to perform the acts promised.[41] Lack of
consideration may be distinguished from a failure of
consideration in that where consideration is lacking, there
was never an enforceable contract, while where consideration
fails, there was once an enforceable promise which has been
rendered unenforceable by the other party's failure to render
the performance bargained for.[42]

There may be a partial failure of consideration if part of
the promised performance is not delivered. If the undelivered
consideration is allocable to an independent covenant by the
other party, the contract may be avoided on a pro tanto
basis.[43]

Generally, if a party receives all he or she has bargained
for, there is no lack or failure of consideration,[44] even though

---

[41]Jessup v. Trout, 77 Ind. 194, 1881 WL 7268 (1881); Alber v. Standard
Heating and Air Conditioning, Inc., 476 N.E.2d 507 (Ind. Ct. App. 3d Dist.
1985).

[42]Corbin on Contracts (rev. ed.), § 5.20.

[43]Beal v. Beal, 79 Ind. 280, 1881 WL 6811 (1881); Gamble v. Grimes, 2
Ind. 392, 1850 WL 3244 (1850); In re Marriage of Arvin, 689 N.E.2d 1270
(Ind. Ct. App. 1997), transfer denied, 698 N.E.2d 1187 (Ind. 1998)
(mother's immediate repudiation of her covenant that parties intended
their children, of whom mother had physical custody, to remain in the
Kokomo area constituted partial failure of consideration for settlement
agreement, as covenant regarding child custody was independent of rest
of agreement); Alber v. Standard Heating and Air Conditioning, Inc., 476
N.E.2d 507 (Ind. Ct. App. 3d Dist. 1985).

[44]Mullen v. Hawkins, 141 Ind. 363, 40 N.E. 797 (1895); McFadden v.
Fritz, 110 Ind. 1, 10 N.E. 120 (1887); Wolford v. Powers, 85 Ind. 294, 1882
WL 6386 (1882); Cagney v. Cuson, 77 Ind. 494, 1881 WL 6689 (1881).

what the party receives is not as valuable as he or she had supposed it to be.[45]

◆ **Illustration:** There was no failure of consideration for a contract whereby a decedent had agreed to leave most of her property to a home for the aged in exchange for lifetime care in an apartment which had been prepared for her, even though the decedent was physically unable to occupy the apartment and was confined to bed in the home's hospital wing for the 42 days she lived after entering the home.[46]

◆ **Caution:** Some older cases have held that there is a failure of consideration if a deed bargained for conveys nothing,[47] or if the benefits received are not in accordance with the other party's binding representations.[48]

If the failure is insignificant, it does not avoid the contract.[49]

§ 24 Adequacy of consideration

Where consideration agreed upon by the parties is of indeterminate value, the court will not inquire into its adequacy.

West's Digest, Contracts ☞53.

Where consideration of an indeterminate value is agreed upon by the parties, the judgment of the parties as to its sufficiency will not be disturbed by the court,[50] and the court

---

[45]White v. Butler University, 78 Ind. 585, 1881 WL 6775 (1881).

[46]Wilson v. Dexter, 135 Ind. App. 247, 192 N.E.2d 469 (Div. 2 1963).

Annotation References: Validity and construction of contract under which applicant for admission to home for aged or infirm turns over his property to institution in return for lifetime care, 44 ALR3d 1174.

Forms References: Recital of consideration—Support, care, and maintenance. 5A Am Jur Legal Forms 2d, Contracts § 68:128.

[47]Murphy v. Jones, 7 Ind. 529, 1856 WL 3762 (1856).

[48]Jones v. Hathaway, 77 Ind. 14, 1881 WL 6623 (1881); McFadden v. Blair, 72 Ind. 365, 1880 WL 6558 (1880).

[49]Clark v. Continental Imp. Co., 57 Ind. 135, 1877 WL 6432 (1877) (one dollar was too insignificant to serve as consideration for agreement to purchase railroad stock).

[50]First Nat. Bank of Peoria v. Farmers' & Merchants' Nat. Bank of Wabash, 171 Ind. 323, 86 N.E. 417 (1908); Tanton v. Grochow, 707 N.E.2d 1010 (Ind. Ct. App. 1999) (agreement creating joint easement for access

may not inquire into the adequacy of the consideration,[51] at least where there is no fraud or deception.[52] The consideration agreed upon may indefinitely exceed the value of the thing for which it is promised, and still support the contract,[53] unless the consideration is so inadequate as to shock the conscience.[54]

This is not the case, however, where the contract is one for an exchange of fixed sums of money.[55]

IV. FORMAL REQUISITES

Research References

IC 32-2-1-1; IC 32-2-1.5-4; IC 32-8-3-1; IC 34-37-1-1; IC 34-37-1-2 Trial R. 9.2

17A Am Jur 2d, Contracts §§ 181-191.
17 C.J.S., Contracts §§ 66-82.
West's Digest, Contracts ⇔30-46.
ALR Digest: Contracts §§ 107-195
ALR Index: Adhesion Contracts; Anticipatory Breach; Anticipatory Renunciation or Repudiation; Bids and Bidding; Cancellation of Rescission; Consideration; Contracts; Covenants; Covenants Not

---

over driveway which straddled property line was supported by consideration); Hamlin v. Steward, 622 N.E.2d 535 (Ind. Ct. App. 1st Dist. 1993); Harrison-Floyd Farm Bureau Co-op. Ass'n, Inc. v. Reed, 546 N.E.2d 855 (Ind. Ct. App. 1st Dist. 1989).

[51]Orem v. Ivy Tech State College, 711 N.E.2d 864, 135 Ed. Law Rep. 628 (Ind. Ct. App. 1999), reh'g denied, (Sept. 16, 1999); Tanton v. Grochow, 707 N.E.2d 1010 (Ind. Ct. App. 1999); Ackerman v. Kimball Intern., Inc., 634 N.E.2d 778 (Ind. Ct. App. 1st Dist. 1994), vacated in part on other grounds, adopted in part, 652 N.E.2d 507 (Ind. 1995).

[52]Huntingburg Production Credit Ass'n v. Griese, 456 N.E.2d 448 (Ind. Ct. App. 1st Dist. 1983).

[53]Mullen v. Hawkins, 141 Ind. 363, 40 N.E. 797 (1895); Wavetek Indiana, Inc. v. K.H. Gatewood Steel Co., Inc., 458 N.E.2d 265 (Ind. Ct. App. 3d Dist. 1984); Herrera v. Collection Service, Inc., 441 N.E.2d 981 (Ind. Ct. App. 2d Dist. 1982) (used water heater was consideration for note, even though it stopped working correctly and had to be replaced within short time after purchase).

[54]Abel v. Burgett, 3 Blackf. 502, 1834 WL 1942 (Ind. 1834); Franklin Fire Ins. Co. v. Noll, 115 Ind. App. 289, 58 N.E.2d 947 (1945).

[55]Chicago & A.R. Co. v. Derkes, 103 Ind. 520, 3 N.E. 239 (1885); Smock v. Pierson, 68 Ind. 405, 1879 WL 5856 (1879); Schnell v. Nell, 17 Ind. 29, 1861 WL 2779 (1861) (consideration of one cent would not support promise to pay $600, although it might have if the one cent had been an old or otherwise remarkable coin with indeterminate value extrinsic to its simple money value); Hall v. Allfree, 51 Ind. App. 387, 99 N.E. 813 (Div. 2 1912).

to Compete; Estoppel and Waiver; Executory Contracts; Implied Contracts; Offer and Acceptance; Parol Contracts and Agreements; Parol Evidence; Third-Party Beneficiaries; Unconscionability

Corbin on Contracts (rev. ed.), §§ 23.1-23.11.

§ 25 Generally

A contract need not be in any particular form, and generally need not be sealed or recorded.

West's Digest, Contracts ⊶30-44.

Because its interpretation is governed by substance,[56] a contract need not be in any particular form.[57]

Generally, contracts need not be recorded. Some particular types of contracts, however, are required by statute to be recorded.[58]

§ 26 Writing

A contract need not be written unless a writing is required by statute or by the parties' agreement.

West's Digest, Contracts ⊶31.

An express contract generally need not be in writing to be valid,[59] but may be oral, or partly written and partly oral.[60] However, a writing is necessary if the parties have agreed to be bound only by a written contract,[61] or if a writing is required by statute for the particular kind of contract in question.[62]

---

[56]Zenor v. Pryor, 57 Ind. App. 222, 106 N.E. 746 (Div. 1 1914).

[57]Keller v. Orr, 106 Ind. 406, 7 N.E. 195 (1886).

[58]IC 32-8-3-1(c), requiring filing and recording of contract containing provision that mechanic's lien shall attach to real property upon which specified persons have performed labor or for which they have provided materials or machinery.

[59]Haggerty v. Johnston, 48 Ind. 41, 1874 WL 5839 (1874).

[60]Wilson v. Montgomery Ward & Co., Inc., 610 F. Supp. 1035 (N.D. Ind. 1985) (applying Indiana law); Sand Creek Country Club, Ltd. v. CSO Architects, Inc., 582 N.E.2d 872 (Ind. Ct. App. 3d Dist. 1991); Citizens Progress Co., Inc. v. James O. Held & Co., Inc., 438 N.E.2d 1016 (Ind. Ct. App. 1st Dist. 1982).

For discussion of combined oral and written contracts, see § 62.

[61]See § 27.

[62]See § 28.

If the parties' agreement does not require the execution of a written contract,[63] and if no statute requires that the contract be written,[64] a written contract may be modified by the parties' oral agreement, provided the new contract is supported by consideration.[65] Similarly, a counteroffer need not be in writing unless the offeror expressly states that it must.[66]

Where the terms of a contract are definitely agreed upon and the parties' understanding is that a written contract embodying the terms agreed upon shall be executed, the contract will date from the making of the oral agreement.[67]

§ 27 —Effect of parties' agreement

A contract must be written if the parties agree that they will be bound only after the execution of a written contract.

West's Digest, Contracts ⊕32.

When a person enters into an agreement with the understanding that neither party is bound until a subsequent formal written document is executed, no enforceable contract exists until the subsequent document is executed.[68] However, the mere fact that parties who orally assent to all terms of a contract refer to a future written contract does not negate the existence of an existing oral contract.[69] If the parties agree orally on all essential terms of a contract, and later prepare and execute a final written agreement, the oral

---

[63]Gordon v. Gordon, 96 Ind. 134, 1884 WL 5333 (1884).

[64]Radio Picture Show Partnership v. Exclusive Intern. Pictures, Inc., 482 N.E.2d 1159 (Ind. Ct. App. 1st Dist. 1985), reh'g denied, (Oct. 25, 1985) and transfer denied, (Feb. 11, 1986).

[65]Wilson v. Montgomery Ward & Co., Inc., 610 F. Supp. 1035 (N.D. Ind. 1985) (applying Indiana law).

[66]Radio Picture Show Partnership v. Exclusive Intern. Pictures, Inc., 482 N.E.2d 1159 (Ind. Ct. App. 1st Dist. 1985), reh'g denied, (Oct. 25, 1985) and transfer denied, (Feb. 11, 1986).

[67]Avery v. Citizens' Loan & Trust Co., 94 Ind. App. 161, 180 N.E. 23 (1932).

[68]Wolvos v. Meyer, 668 N.E.2d 671 (Ind. 1996); Foster v. United Home Imp. Co., Inc., 428 N.E.2d 1351 (Ind. Ct. App. 4th Dist. 1981); International Shoe Co. v. Lacy, 114 Ind. App. 641, 53 N.E.2d 636 (1944), opinion supplemented, 116 Ind. App. 78, 61 N.E.2d 85 (1945).

[69]Foster v. United Home Imp. Co., Inc., 428 N.E.2d 1351 (Ind. Ct. App. 4th Dist. 1981).

contract is valid, and the written agreement is considered to be a memorial of the agreement already reached.[70] The parties in such a case are bound as if a written contract had been executed.[71] The parties' anticipation that they will execute a formal written contract does not constitute an agreement that they will not be bound until such a contract is executed.[72]

> ◆ **Illustration:** Even though a general contractor, which informed a corporation that its bid for providing athletic lockers for a school construction project was the low bid, and that it would be sent a formal contract in June, failed to provide the corporation with a contract until September, the corporation was not relieved of its obligation to provide the lockers in accordance with its bid.[73]

In determining whether the parties intended to be bound only by a formal written contract, courts typically consider not only the parties' communications but also the circumstances of the transaction itself. Whether it is reasonable to expect an agreement to be reduced to writing depends, in part, on the sophistication of the parties and the kind of bargain that is negotiated.[74]

§ 28 —Effect of statute

A contract must be written if a statute requires that contracts of the type involved must be in writing to be enforceable.

---

[70]Wolvos v. Meyer, 668 N.E.2d 671 (Ind. 1996).

[71]Clark Realty, Inc. v. Clarke, 171 Ind. App. 46, 354 N.E.2d 779 (3d Dist. 1976).

[72]Foster v. United Home Imp. Co., Inc., 428 N.E.2d 1351 (Ind. Ct. App. 4th Dist. 1981) (where contractor testified that he had not anticipated beginning work without a written contract, and homeowner testified only that the parties had generally agreed and anticipated that they would sign written contract before contractor would commence work, written a contract was not required).

[73]Lyon Metal Products, Inc. v. Hagerman Const. Corp., 181 Ind. App. 336, 391 N.E.2d 1152 (3d Dist. 1979) (where corporation made no attempt to find out why it had not received contract, which had been sent to wrong address).

[74]Kinko's Graphics Corp. v. Townsend, 803 F. Supp. 1450 (S.D. Ind. 1992) (applying Indiana law) (where contract was for lease of prime real estate and was negotiated at length between lawyer and professional real estate agent, fax transmission with sketchy details of purported agreement was agreement to agree rather than explicit agreement sufficient to induce one party's detrimental reliance).

West's Digest, Contracts ⌐30.
West's Digest, Frauds, Statute of ⌐1 et seq.

The Indiana statute of frauds requires that certain types of contracts, such as a contract for the sale of land or an agreement that is not to be performed within one year from the time it is made, be in writing.[75] Credit agreements must also be in writing, must set forth all the material terms and conditions of the agreement, including the loan amount, rate of interest, duration, and security, and must be signed by the creditor and the debtor.[76]

A written memorandum is sufficient to remove a transaction from the operation of the statute of frauds, and thus supports an enforceable contract, if it:[77]

- is signed by the party to be charged, or by his or her actual or apparent agent
- states with reasonable certainty each party to the contract either by his or her own name, or by such a description as will serve to identify him or her, or by the name or description of his or her agent
- states with reasonable certainty the land, goods or other subject matter to which the contract relates
- states with reasonable certainty the terms and conditions of all the promises constituting the contract and by whom and to whom the promises are made

Sufficient partial performance under an agreement may also remove the transaction from the operation of the statute of frauds, so that no writing is required. The degree of performance required varies with each case.[78] Possession, payment, or partial payment alone is not sufficient to constitute partial performance and removal from within the statute of frauds.[79]

◆ **Illustration:** A highway construction contractor

---

[75]IC 32-2-1-1.

For discussion of the statute of frauds, see I.L.E., Statute of Frauds.

[76]IC 32-2-1.5-4.

[77]McMahan Const. Co. v. Wegehoft Bros., Inc., 170 Ind. App. 558, 354 N.E.2d 278 (1st Dist. 1976); Block v. Sherman, 109 Ind. App. 330, 34 N.E.2d 951 (1941).

[78]McMahan Const. Co. v. Wegehoft Bros., Inc., 170 Ind. App. 558, 354 N.E.2d 278 (1st Dist. 1976); Sourbier v. Claman, 101 Ind. App. 679, 200 N.E. 721 (1936).

[79]McMahan Const. Co. v. Wegehoft Bros., Inc., 170 Ind. App. 558, 354

agreed with a landowner that the contractor could remove fill dirt from the landowner's land in exchange for $.25 per cubic yard, to be applied toward the purchase price of the contractor's land which adjoined the landowner's, and an option to purchase the land. Part performance of the agreement removed it from within the statute of frauds where the landowner paid a substantial amount of the purchase price of the contractor's land, continually questioned when it would receive the deed to the contractor's property and was stalled by the contractor's agents, and allowed the removal of dirt from its property in reliance on the contract and its future right to receive the property in question, and where the contractor made internal accounting notations indicating the accounts payable to the landowner but forwarded no funds in payment for the fill dirt. The court pointed out that taken individually, these acts and circumstances might not be sufficient to remove the transaction from the operation of the statute of frauds, but that collectively they were sufficient.[80]

§ 29 Execution and delivery

Execution of a contract consists of its subscription and delivery.

West's Digest, Contracts ☞34, 36, 42.

The execution of an instrument is the subscribing and delivering of the instrument with or without affixing a seal.[81] A written instrument is executed when the following requirements are fulfilled:[82]

- a signature was made with express, implied or apparent authority and was not forged
- the instrument was properly delivered, including any requisite intent that it be effective
- the written terms of the instrument have not been materially altered without the express, implied or apparent authority of the person bound thereon

---

N.E.2d 278 (1st Dist. 1976); Genda v. Hall, 129 Ind. App. 643, 154 N.E.2d 527 (1958); Jackson v. First Nat. Bank & Trust Co. of La Porte, 115 Ind. App. 313, 57 N.E.2d 946 (1944).

[80]McMahan Const. Co. v. Wegehoft Bros., Inc., 170 Ind. App. 558, 354 N.E.2d 278 (1st Dist. 1976).

[81]IC 34-37-1-2.

[82]Trial R. 9.2(H).

- the person seeking its enforcement is in possession of the instrument when required
- the names or identity of the persons named in the instrument are correct

Indiana has eliminated the necessity of sealing a written instrument to give it greater credibility,[83] and an unsealed writing has the same force and effect it would have if it were sealed.[84] Except where a writing conveys an interest in real property, a sealed writing may be changed or discharged by an unsealed writing.[85]

It is not necessary, to entitle a written instrument to be read in evidence, that its execution be proved by direct evidence, but it will be sufficient if that fact is fairly inferable from the facts and circumstances proved.[86]

Delivery of a contract is the final act of its execution,[87] and determines the time[88] and place[89] of execution. While delivery is necessary, it may be actual or constructive.[90] If a contract is for the benefit of a third party, delivery to the third party is not necessary.[91]

Defects in, or want of, execution of a written instrument evidencing a contract may generally be ratified,[92] and are considered ratified if the contract is fully recognized and acted upon by both parties.[93]

---

[83]Lewis v. Burke, 248 Ind. 297, 226 N.E.2d 332 (1967).

[84]IC 34-37-1-1(a).

[85]IC 34-37-1-1(b).

[86]Forgerson v. Smith, 104 Ind. 246, 3 N.E. 866 (1885); Ferris Realty, Inc. v. Abco Signs, Inc., 135 Ind. App. 679, 182 N.E.2d 456 (Div. 2 1962), transfer denied, 245 Ind. 163, 196 N.E.2d 893 (1964) (where defendant did not deny execution of contract, contract could be read in evidence without proving its execution).

[87]Prather v. Zulauf, 38 Ind. 155, 1871 WL 5325 (1871).

[88]Merritt v. Temple, 155 Ind. 497, 58 N.E. 699 (1900).

[89]Butler v. Myer, 17 Ind. 77, 1861 WL 2938 (1861).

[90]Hockett v. Jones, 70 Ind. 227, 1880 WL 6189 (1880).

[91]Copeland v. Summers, 138 Ind. 219, 35 N.E. 514 (1893), reh'g denied, 138 Ind. 219, 37 N.E. 971 (1894); Waltz v. Waltz, 84 Ind. 403, 1882 WL 6336 (1882).

[92]Seymour Imp. Co. v. Viking Sprinkler Co., 87 Ind. App. 179, 161 N.E. 389 (1928).

[93]Indianapolis Natural Gas Co. v. Kibby, 135 Ind. 357, 35 N.E. 392 (1893); Cincinnati, U. & Ft. W. R. Co. v. Pearce, 28 Ind. 502, 1867 WL

§ 30 —Signature

An unsigned contract may be valid, unless a party's signature is made a condition of the agreement.

West's Digest, Contracts ☞35.

Although some form of assent to the terms of a contract is necessary before the contract is enforceable,[94] the validity of a contract is not dependent upon the signature of the parties, unless their signature is made a condition of the agreement.[95]

If a person's signature on a contract is obtained by trick or artifice, the contract may be invalidated.[96]

A signing may be in a number of different fashions.[97] For instance, under certain circumstances, initials may constitute a legal signature.[98] However, the appearance of a party's name in the body of a document, rather than on a signature line at the end, is not considered his or her signature in the absence of satisfactory evidence that it was intended to operate as an indication of his or her assent.[99]

3004 (1867); McCauley v. Schatzley, 44 Ind. App. 262, 88 N.E. 972 (Div. 1 1909); American Quarries Co. v. Lay, 37 Ind. App. 386, 73 N.E. 608 (Div. 2 1905), reh'g denied, 166 Ind. 234, 76 N.E. 517 (1906).

[94]As to acceptance of an offer, see §§ 7 et seq.

[95]International Creative Management, Inc. v. D & R Entertainment Co., Inc., 670 N.E.2d 1305 (Ind. Ct. App. 1996), reh'g denied, (Oct. 29, 1996) and transfer denied, 683 N.E.2d 589 (Ind. 1997); State v. Daily Exp., Inc., 465 N.E.2d 764 (Ind. Ct. App. 1st Dist. 1984); Parrish v. Terre Haute Sav. Bank, 431 N.E.2d 132 (Ind. Ct. App. 4th Dist. 1982), reh'g denied, 438 N.E.2d 1 (Ind. Ct. App. 4th Dist. 1982) and transfer denied, (Feb. 4, 1985); Seco Chemicals, Inc., Division of Stan Sax Corp. v. Stewart, 169 Ind. App. 624, 349 N.E.2d 733 (1st Dist. 1976).

For discussion of the effect of fewer than all parties' signature of a written contract, see § 80.

[96]Hogan Transfer and Storage Corp. v. Waymire, 399 N.E.2d 779 (Ind. Ct. App. 4th Dist. 1980).

[97]State v. Schell, 248 Ind. 183, 224 N.E.2d 49 (1967).

[98]Brown v. Grzeskowiak, 230 Ind. 110, 102 N.E.2d 372 (1951) (clerk's initials in absentee ballots sufficient, where authenticity of ballots was not questioned).

[99]McMillen v. Terrell, 23 Ind. 163, 1864 WL 1995 (1864); Ellison v. Towne, 34 Ind. App. 22, 72 N.E. 270 (Div. 1 1904).

Assent may also be expressed by acts which manifest acceptance.[1]

♦ **Illustration:** A trucking company applied by telephone for a permit to transport an overheight load through Indiana by a specified route. Upon entering the state, the company's driver picked up a short form permit, which specified that it was granted subject to provisions on the state's written application form for overheight permits. One of the provisions on the written form was an indemnity clause stating that the company would hold the state harmless for any loss it incurred resulting from the issuance of the permit. The trucking company had not signed a written application, and the driver did not have the form with him when his load was knocked off by a low bridge on the route the state had approved. However, because the company acted in accordance with the permit and had transported oversize loads through Indiana before with state permits, so that it could not claim that it was unaware of the indemnity provision, the company could not recover its damages resulting from the accident from the state.[2]

♦ **Practice Guide:** Where the president of a corporation signs a contract in the name of the corporation, execution of the contract is presumed to be on behalf of the corporation.[3]

V. VALIDITY OF ASSENT

Research References

IC 10-5-10-1; IC 27-1-12-15; IC 29-3-1-10; IC 29-3-1-13; IC 29-3-4-2; IC 29-3-8-2; IC 29-3-8-5; IC 29-3-8-7

17A Am Jur 2d, Contracts §§ 213-237.
17A C.J.S., Contracts §§ 136-194.
West's Digest, Contracts ☞92-100.
ALR Digest: Contracts §§ 78-85
ALR Index: Adhesion Contracts; Anticipatory Breach; Anticipatory Renunciation or Repudiation; Bids and Bidding; Cancellation of Rescission; Consideration; Contracts; Covenants; Covenants Not to Compete; Estoppel and Waiver; Executory Contracts; Implied

---

[1]Herald Telephone v. Fatouros, 431 N.E.2d 171 (Ind. Ct. App. 4th Dist. 1982).

[2]State v. Daily Exp., Inc., 465 N.E.2d 764 (Ind. Ct. App. 1st Dist. 1984).

[3]Ferris Realty, Inc. v. Abco Signs, Inc., 135 Ind. App. 679, 182 N.E.2d 456 (Div. 2 1962), transfer denied, 245 Ind. 163, 196 N.E.2d 893 (1964).

Contracts; Offer and Acceptance; Parol Contracts and Agreements; Parol Evidence; Third-Party Beneficiaries; Unconscionability

5A Am Jur Legal Forms 2d, Contracts § 68:162.

Proof of Fraudulent Inducement of a Contract and Entitlement to Remedies, 48 Am Jur POF3d 329.

§ 31 Mental condition or age of party

A contract into which a minor has entered is voidable at the minor's option; contracts undertaken by persons adjudged to be incompetent are void.

West's Digest, Contracts ⚍92.
West's Digest, Infants ⚍59(1).
West's Digest, Mental Health ⚍372.

Contracts executed by protected persons, except those who are protected persons solely on account of their minority, are void.[4] For this purpose, a "protected person" is an individual for whom a guardian has been appointed, or with respect to whom a protective order has been issued.[5] A "minor" is an unemancipated individual under 18 years of age.[6]

On the other hand, a contract of an insane person, whose disability has not been judicially determined, is only voidable[7] and subject to disaffirmance,[8] and will not generally be enforced against the disabled person.[9] Thus, incapacity may provide a defense to a contract.[10] The test for determining a person's mental capacity to contract is whether the person was able to understand in a reasonable manner the nature and effect of his or her act. In order to avoid a contract, the party must not only have been of unsound mind, but also

---

[4]IC 29-3-8-5(b).

Annotation References: Commitment of grantor to institution for insane as ground for setting aside conveyance in consideration of support, 18 ALR2d 906.

[5]IC 29-3-1-13.

[6]IC 29-3-1-10.

[7]Fay v. Burditt, 81 Ind. 433, 1882 WL 6121 (1882); McClain v. Davis, 77 Ind. 419, 1881 WL 6678 (1881); Wilder v. Weakley's Estate, 34 Ind. 181, 1870 WL 3727 (1870); Haskell & Barker Car Co. v. Logermann, 71 Ind. App. 69, 123 N.E. 818 (Div. 1 1919).

[8]McClain v. Davis, 77 Ind. 419, 1881 WL 6678 (1881).

[9]Musselman v. Cravens, 47 Ind. 1, 1874 WL 5754 (1874).

[10]Scherer v. Scherer, 405 N.E.2d 40 (Ind. Ct. App. 4th Dist. 1980); Mahin v. Soshnick, 128 Ind. App. 342, 148 N.E.2d 852 (1958).

must have had no reasonable understanding of the contract's terms due to his or her instability.[11] A party is presumed to have known and understood the effect of entering into a contract.[12]

> ◆ **Observation:** Some cases before the enactment of the current statute pertaining to incapacitated persons stated that intoxication may be considered an incapacity sufficient to constitute a defense to a contract.[13] Under the current statutes making void or voidable contracts entered into by minors and protected persons, an "incapacitated person" is defined to include one who is incapacitated by habitual drunkenness or excessive use of drugs, but not by occasional intoxication.[14] As the definitions of "minor" and "protected person" in the same statutory section[15] are used to determine whether contracts entered into by persons of those classes are void or voidable,[16] it may be that intoxication no longer provides a defense to a contract.

Even if a party's mental deficiencies are insufficient, in themselves, to avoid a contract, they may be considered in connection with the alleged exercise of fraud or undue influence.[17]

Although an executory contract will generally not be enforced against an insane person, if a person has entered into a contract with an insane person in good faith, without

---

[11]Gallagher v. Central Indiana Bank, N.A., 448 N.E.2d 304 (Ind. Ct. App. 1st Dist. 1983) (evidence that allegedly incapacitated elderly man participated in business transactions after his stroke supported inference that he understood those transactions and disputed mortgage); Mahin v. Soshnick, 128 Ind. App. 342, 148 N.E.2d 852 (1958); Daugherty v. Daugherty, 115 Ind. App. 253, 57 N.E.2d 599 (1944).

[12]Hill v. Jessup, 139 Ind. App. 467, 220 N.E.2d 662 (Div. 2 1966) (woman who had undergone physical and mental therapy after she was deserted by prospective spouse did not sustain burden of proving mental incapacity to contract).

[13]Devin v. Scott, 34 Ind. 67, 1870 WL 3713 (1870); Gates v. Meredith, 7 Ind. 440, 1856 WL 3561 (1856); Marshall v. Billingsly, 7 Ind. 250, 1855 WL 3663 (1855); Scherer v. Scherer, 405 N.E.2d 40 (Ind. Ct. App. 4th Dist. 1980).

[14]IC 29-3-1-10(2).

[15]IC 29-3-1-10(1), (3).

[16]IC 29-3-8-5(b).

[17]Brannon v. Hayes, 190 Ind. 420, 130 N.E. 803 (1921); In re Haas' Will, 115 Ind. App. 1, 54 N.E.2d 119 (1944).

fraud or imposition, for a fair consideration, and without notice of the insanity, before an adjudication of insanity, and the contract has been executed in whole or in part, the contract will not be set aside unless the parties can be restored to their original positions.[18] If an incapacitated person who is also a protected person entered into a valid written contract before he or she became incapacitated, and the obligations of the contract have not been fully carried out, the court is to authorize the protected person's guardian to perform the contract.[19]

Contracts to which a minor is a party are voidable at the minor's option.[20] If the minor retains the consideration he or she received under the contract, he or she is required to return the consideration to the other party;[21] however, return of the consideration has been held not to be a condition precedent to the power to void the contract.[22]

♦ **Practice Guide:** Specific classes of minors are authorized by statute to enter into valid contracts.[23]

The guardian of a minor or protected person may generally enter into contracts on behalf of the minor or incapacitated person.[24] Moreover, a court may ratify a contract relating to a minor or protected person's property and financial or business affairs without appointing a guardian if the court determined that the transaction is in the minor or protected person's best interest.[25] Old age[26] or serious illness[27] does not

---

[18]Wells v. Wells, 197 Ind. 236, 150 N.E. 361 (1926).

[19]IC 29-3-8-7.

[20]IC 29-3-8-5(b).

Clark v. Van Court, 100 Ind. 113, 1884 WL 5774 (1884); Mullen v. Tucker, 510 N.E.2d 711 (Ind. Ct. App. 4th Dist. 1987).

[21]Story & Clark Piano Co. v. Davy, 68 Ind. App. 150, 119 N.E. 177 (Div. 1 1918).

[22]Bowling v. Sperry, 133 Ind. App. 692, 184 N.E.2d 901 (Div. 1 1962).

[23]IC 10-5-10-1, authorizing minors to enter into contracts necessary to receive veterans' benefits; IC 27-1-12-15, allowing 16-year-olds to contract for life, accident and sickness insurance for the benefit of the minor or certain specified relatives.

[24]IC 29-3-8-2.

[25]IC 29-3-4-2.

[26]Daugherty v. Daugherty, 115 Ind. App. 253, 57 N.E.2d 599 (1944).

[27]Wallace v. McVey, 6 Ind. 300, 1855 WL 3565 (1855).

render a party incapable of contracting, unless the party's mental faculties are affected.

§ 32   —Contracts for necessaries

A contract for necessary goods or services may be enforced against a minor or against the estate of an incapacitated person.

West's Digest, Contracts ☞92.
West's Digest, Infants ☞59(1).
West's Digest, Mental Health ☞372.

Although the law will not enforce an express contract against a person who is shown to have been incapacitated at the time he or she entered into the contract,[28] the law will allow a recovery against the incapacitated person's estate for the reasonable value of necessary services rendered at the request of the incapacitated person.[29]

A minor may also be held liable on a contract for necessaries, such as medical services provided to the minor.[30] The person seeking to enforce the contract must show that the subject matter of the contract was a necessity for the minor.[31] If the minor is living at home or being supported by his or her parents, a creditor who can prove that the goods or services contracted for were necessary may recover from either the parents or the child.[32] This exception exists to prevent a minor being denied credit for necessary goods and services.[33]

"Necessaries" are such things as are necessary to the minor or incapacitated person's support, use, or comfort, including such personal comforts as comport with his or her

---

[28]§ 31.

[29]Wyneken v. Long, 400 N.E.2d 1147 (Ind. Ct. App. 3d Dist. 1980); Rautenkranz v. Plummer, 75 Ind. App. 269, 130 N.E. 435 (Div. 2 1921).

[30]Scott County School Dist. 1 v. Asher, 263 Ind. 47, 324 N.E.2d 496 (1975); Hagerman v. Mutual Hospital Ins., Inc., 175 Ind. App. 293, 371 N.E.2d 394 (1st Dist. 1978).

[31]Bowling v. Sperry, 133 Ind. App. 692, 184 N.E.2d 901 (Div. 1 1962) (minor could disaffirm his purchase of automobile because creditor could not show that it was necessary for minor).

[32]Scott County School Dist. 1 v. Asher, 263 Ind. 47, 324 N.E.2d 496 (1975).

[33]Scott County School Dist. 1 v. Asher, 263 Ind. 47, 324 N.E.2d 496 (1975).

condition and circumstances in life, provided he or she is in actual need of such things at the time and is obliged to procure them for him- or herself.[34]

§ 33 Mutual mistake

A contract may be avoided if each party to it independently makes a mistake of material fact upon which the contract is based.

West's Digest, Contracts ☞93(1), 93(4), 93(5).

Equitable relief may be granted if a contract is based upon a mutual mistake of material fact.[35] This is true whether the contract is executed or executory.[36]

Mutual mistake involves a mistake independently made by each party to the contract.[37] Because mutual assent is a prerequisite to the creation of a contract,[38] where both parties share a common assumption about a vital fact upon which they based their bargain, and that assumption is false, the transaction may be avoided if, because of the mistake, the exchange of values accomplished is quite different from that contemplated by the parties.[39] There is no contract in such a case, because the minds of the parties have in fact never met, and one has realized an unexpected, unbargained-

---

[34]Bowling v. Sperry, 133 Ind. App. 692, 184 N.E.2d 901 (Div. 1 1962).

[35]Franklin v. White, 493 N.E.2d 161 (Ind. 1986); Hancock v. Kentucky Cent. Life Ins. Co., 527 N.E.2d 720 (Ind. Ct. App. 1st Dist. 1988), transfer denied, (Feb. 14, 1989).

[36]Solinger v. Jewett, 25 Ind. 479, 1865 WL 1933 (1865).

[37]Tri-Professional Realty, Inc. v. Hillenburg, 669 N.E.2d 1064 (Ind. Ct. App. 1996), transfer denied, 683 N.E.2d 583 (Ind. 1997); Fultz v. Cox, 574 N.E.2d 956 (Ind. Ct. App. 1st Dist. 1991).

[38]§ 10.

[39]Showalter, Inc. v. Smith, 629 N.E.2d 272 (Ind. Ct. App. 3d Dist. 1994), transfer denied, (June 22, 1994) and (abrogated on other grounds by, Mitchell v. Mitchell, 695 N.E.2d 920 (Ind. 1998)); Jackson v. Blanchard, 601 N.E.2d 411 (Ind. Ct. App. 4th Dist. 1992); Wilkin v. 1st Source Bank, 548 N.E.2d 170 (Ind. Ct. App. 3d Dist. 1990).

Annotation References: Vendor and purchaser: Mutual mistake as to physical condition of realty as ground for rescission, 50 ALR3d 1188.

Trial Strategy References: Mutual Mistake Over Physical Condition of Real Estate as Basis for Rescission of Contract, 48 Am Jur POF3d 505.

for gain while the other has suffered an unexpected, unbargained-for loss.[40]

> ◆ **Illustration:** A couple purchased a house from a bank handling the estate of a recently deceased woman, who had been the widow of an internationally known sculptor and artist. The couple discovered after the purchase that the house was quite cluttered and would require a substantial cleaning effort. The bank and the couple agreed that the couple would clean the house themselves, and that they could retain any items of personal property they wanted. Neither was aware at the time of the agreement that several of the artist's sketches and a sculpture remained in the house. Because of the mutual mistake, the couple was not permitted to retain the works of art. The court noted that the couple and the bank shared a common assumption that the personal property in the house was junk, and neither suspected that any of the artist's works remained on the premises.[41]

It is not enough that both parties are mistaken about any fact; rather, the mistaken fact complained of must be one that is of the essence of the agreement, and must be such that it animates and controls the conduct of the parties.[42] For instance, a gross mistake as to the quantity of real property involved in an agreement[43] or the parties' misapprehension as to the subject matter of the contract[44] may entitle a party to relief from the legal effect of the contract.

A mistake of law rather than fact will not allow a party to avoid a contract.[45] Generally, a party may not successfully claim that there was a mistake as to the legal effect of words

---

[40]Wilkin v. 1st Source Bank, 548 N.E.2d 170 (Ind. Ct. App. 3d Dist. 1990).

[41]Wilkin v. 1st Source Bank, 548 N.E.2d 170 (Ind. Ct. App. 3d Dist. 1990).

[42]Jackson v. Blanchard, 601 N.E.2d 411 (Ind. Ct. App. 4th Dist. 1992).

[43]Solinger v. Jewett, 25 Ind. 479, 1865 WL 1933 (1865); Hellyer Communications, Inc. v. WRC Properties, Inc., 969 F. Supp. 1150 (S.D. Ind. 1997) (applying Indiana law).

[44]Martin Bros. Box Co. v. Orem, 117 Ind. App. 110, 69 N.E.2d 605 (1946).

[45]Zenor v. Johnson, 107 Ind. 69, 7 N.E. 751 (1886); Oiler v. Gard, 23 Ind. 212, 1864 WL 2166 (1864); American Mut. Life Ins. Co. v. Mead, 39 Ind. App. 215, 79 N.E. 526 (Div. 1 1906).

used in a contract,[46] or that a contract was made because of a mistake as to a person's liability,[47] although it has been held that a party to a contract could not be permitted to benefit by a mistake of law which he had induced or encouraged by his own misrepresentation.[48] Nor does the doctrine of mutual mistake apply to erroneous predictions or judgments as to future occurrences.[49]

§ 34 Unilateral mistake

Unless it is induced by the other party's misrepresentation, a unilateral mistake does not entitle the mistaken party to relief from a contract.

West's Digest, Contracts ⏤93(2), 93(3).

Generally, a contract may not be avoided for one party's unilateral mistake,[50] if the mistake could have been avoided by due diligence.[51] A person is bound to know and understand the contents of the contract he or she signs,[52] and one who signs a contract in the absence of fraud or deceit generally cannot avoid the contract on the grounds that he or she did

---

[46]Heavenridge v. Mondy, 49 Ind. 434, 1875 WL 5738 (1875); Nelson v. Davis, 40 Ind. 366, 1872 WL 5402 (1872).

[47]Bennett v. Ford, 47 Ind. 264, 1874 WL 5800 (1874); Bond v. Coats, 16 Ind. 202, 1861 WL 2900 (1861).

[48]Johnson v. Fox, 110 Ind. App. 698, 38 N.E.2d 865 (1942) (attorney misrepresented effect of instrument to ignorant, elderly and inexperienced woman); American Mut. Life Ins. Co. v. Mead, 39 Ind. App. 215, 79 N.E. 526 (Div. 1 1906).

[49]Jay County Rural Elec. Membership Corp. v. Wabash Valley Power Ass'n, Inc., 692 N.E.2d 905 (Ind. Ct. App. 1998), transfer denied, 706 N.E.2d 167 (Ind. 1998).

[50]Hancock v. Kentucky Cent. Life Ins. Co., 527 N.E.2d 720 (Ind. Ct. App. 1st Dist. 1988), transfer denied, (Feb. 14, 1989); Eastman v. U. S., 257 F. Supp. 315 (S.D. Ind. 1966) (applying Indiana law).

[51]Robinson v. Glass, 94 Ind. 211, 1884 WL 5217 (1884); Williamson v. Hitner, 79 Ind. 233, 1881 WL 6804 (1881).

[52]NationsCredit Commercial Corp. v. Grauel Enterprises, Inc., 703 N.E.2d 1072 (Ind. Ct. App. 1998), reh'g denied, (Mar. 15, 1999) and transfer denied, (Aug. 12, 1999) (especially where plaintiff was represented by counsel and accountant when negotiating contract); Clanton v. United Skates of America, 686 N.E.2d 896 (Ind. Ct. App. 1997); Pinnacle Computer Services, Inc. v. Ameritech Pub., Inc., 642 N.E.2d 1011 (Ind. Ct. App. 1st Dist. 1994), reh'g denied, (Feb. 23, 1995); Fultz v. Cox, 574 N.E.2d 956 (Ind. Ct. App. 1st Dist. 1991).

not read it or took someone else's word as to what it contained.[53]

A party may not avoid a written agreement on the ground that he or she does not speak English well,[54] unless it is established that the party's failure to read the contract can be excused because of a fiduciary relationship between the parties[55] or that some trick or artifice was employed to induce the party to sign.[56] Equity will provide relief from the consequences of a mistake induced by the misrepresentation of the opposite party,[57] such as a mistake as to the identity of the paper he or she signed.[58]

   ◆ **Caution:** At least one court has permitted a party to rescind a contract based on his or her unilateral mistake.[59]

---

[53]Mayflower Transit, Inc. v. Davenport, 714 N.E.2d 794 (Ind. Ct. App. 1999); Clanton v. United Skates of America, 686 N.E.2d 896 (Ind. Ct. App. 1997); Fultz v. Cox, 574 N.E.2d 956 (Ind. Ct. App. 1st Dist. 1991).

[54]Keller v. Orr, 106 Ind. 406, 7 N.E. 195 (1886) (where plaintiff said that agreement was not as it had been explained to him); Paper Exp., Ltd. v. Pfankuch Maschinen GmbH, 972 F.2d 753 (7th Cir. 1992) (applying Indiana law) (fact that forum selection clause was in fine print and in German did not entitled plaintiff to relief from contract which incorporated two-page document containing clause).

[55]Givan v. Masterson, 152 Ind. 127, 51 N.E. 237 (1898); Williamson v. Hitner, 79 Ind. 233, 1881 WL 6804 (1881); Cox v. Aetna Ins. Co., 29 Ind. 586, 1868 WL 2880 (1868) (party illiterate); Hoerger v. Citizens' Street R. Co., 36 Ind. App. 662, 76 N.E. 328 (Div. 2 1905); Wood v. Wack, 31 Ind. App. 252, 67 N.E. 562 (1903).

[56]Fidelity & Cas. Co. of N.Y. v. Teter, 136 Ind. 672, 36 N.E. 283 (1894); New v. Wambach, 42 Ind. 456, 1873 WL 5235 (1873) (contract defeated where plaintiff wrote contract different from agreement, and read it to defendant as though it contained terms agreed upon).

[57]Hancock v. Kentucky Cent. Life Ins. Co., 527 N.E.2d 720 (Ind. Ct. App. 1st Dist. 1988), transfer denied, (Feb. 14, 1989).

   As to fraud in the inducement of a contract, see §§ 35 et seq.

[58]Cline v. Guthrie, 42 Ind. 227, 1873 WL 5584 (1873); Byers v. Daugherty, 40 Ind. 198, 1872 WL 5603 (1872).

[59]Board of School Com'rs of City of Indianapolis v. Bender, 36 Ind. App. 164, 72 N.E. 154 (Div. 2 1904) (contractor who erred in computing bid, which was subsequently accepted, allowed to withdraw bid).

Annotation References: Right of bidder for state or municipal contract to rescind bid on ground that bid was based upon his own mistake or that of his employee, 2 ALR4th 991.

On the other hand, a contractor has no duty to determine whether a bid will enable the bidder to maintain a favorable cash flow.[60]

§ 35 Fraud

A party may avoid a contract where his or her obligation has been induced by actual or constructive fraud.

West's Digest, Contracts ☞94(1)-94(8).

Generally, parties are obligated to know the terms of the agreement they are signing, and cannot avoid their obligations under the agreement due to a failure to read it. However, where one employs fraud or misrepresentation to induce a party's obligation under a contract, the party cannot be bound to the terms of the agreement.[61]

Fraud as a contract defense may be actual or constructive.[62] In order to establish actual fraud, the plaintiff must prove (1) a material misrepresentation of past or existing fact by the party to be charged, which (2) was false, (3) was made with knowledge or in reckless ignorance of the falsity, (4) was relied upon by the complaining party, and (5) proximately caused the complaining party injury.[63]

The presence of fraud is a question for the trial court to

---

[60]Cummings v. Hoosier Marine Properties, Inc., 173 Ind. App. 372, 363 N.E.2d 1266 (3d Dist. 1977).

[61]Park 100 Investors, Inc. v. Kartes, 650 N.E.2d 347 (Ind. Ct. App. 1995).

Annotation References: Fraud in connection with franchise of distributorship relationship, 64 ALR3d 6.

Trial Strategy References: Proof of Fraudulent Inducement of a Contract and Entitlement to Remedies, 48 Am Jur POF3d 329.

Promise Made With Intent Not to Perform, 5 Am Jur POF2d 727.

[62]Abbott v. Bates, 670 N.E.2d 916 (Ind. Ct. App. 1996), reh'g denied, (Oct. 31, 1996).

[63]Hart v. Steel Products, Inc., 666 N.E.2d 1270 (Ind. Ct. App. 1996), reh'g denied, (Aug. 22, 1996) and transfer denied, 683 N.E.2d 582 (Ind. 1997); Park 100 Investors, Inc. v. Kartes, 650 N.E.2d 347 (Ind. Ct. App. 1995); Showalter, Inc. v. Smith, 629 N.E.2d 272 (Ind. Ct. App. 3d Dist. 1994), transfer denied, (June 22, 1994) and (abrogated on other grounds by, Mitchell v. Mitchell, 695 N.E.2d 920 (Ind. 1998)); Biberstine v. New York Blower Co., 625 N.E.2d 1308 (Ind. Ct. App. 5th Dist. 1993), reh'g denied, (Jan. 24, 1994) and transfer dismissed, (Apr. 12, 1994).

Annotation References: Necessity of showing damage to establish fraud as defense to action on contract, 91 ALR2d 346.

determine from the surrounding facts and circumstances.[64]
Fraud will not be presumed, but must be proved by the party
alleging it. It is not necessary, however, that fraud be proved
by direct or positive evidence; it may be established by
circumstantial evidence.[65] A fraudulent purpose may be
inferred from an unqualified assertion that a fact exists when
such a statement is false and induces reliance.[66]

Ordinarily, a party's mere failure to disclose facts does not
constitute fraud invalidating a contract,[67] although active
concealment of facts may be fraudulent.[68]

Constructive fraud is fraud that arises by operation of law
from conduct which, if sanctioned by law, would secure an
unconscionable advantage.[69] The elements of constructive
fraud are:

1. a duty existing by virtue of the relationship between
   the parties;

2. representations or omissions made in violation of that
   duty;

3. justifiable reliance by the complaining party which
   proximately resulted in injury; and

Contracting party's right of redress for fraud as affected by his own
breach of the contract before discovering the fraud, 13 ALR2d 1248.

[64]Property Owners, Inc. v. City of Anderson, 231 Ind. 78, 107 N.E.2d 3
(1952); Park 100 Investors, Inc. v. Kartes, 650 N.E.2d 347 (Ind. Ct. App.
1995); A.G. Edwards and Sons, Inc. v. Hilligoss, 597 N.E.2d 1 (Ind. Ct.
App. 4th Dist. 1991); Holtzclaw v. Bankers Mut. Ins. Co., 448 N.E.2d 55
(Ind. Ct. App. 3d Dist. 1983).

[65]Shuee v. Gedert, 182 Ind. App. 432, 395 N.E.2d 804 (1st Dist. 1979);
Grissom v. Moran, 154 Ind. App. 419, 290 N.E.2d 119 (2d Dist. 1972),
reh'g denied, 154 Ind. App. 419, 292 N.E.2d 627 (2d Dist. 1973); Middelkamp v. Hanewich, 147 Ind. App. 561, 263 N.E.2d 189 (Div. 2 1970).

[66]Shuee v. Gedert, 182 Ind. App. 432, 395 N.E.2d 804 (1st Dist. 1979);
Grissom v. Moran, 154 Ind. App. 419, 290 N.E.2d 119 (2d Dist. 1972),
reh'g denied, 154 Ind. App. 419, 292 N.E.2d 627 (2d Dist. 1973).

[67]Gregory v. Schoenell, 55 Ind. 101, 1876 WL 6615 (1876) (where seller
sold personal property on credit based on his confidence in buyer acquired
in prior dealings between parties, rather than on false representations
made to him by buyer, sale could not be rescinded for fraud).

[68]C.J.S., Contracts § 165.

[69]Dominion Investments v. Yasechko, 767 F. Supp. 1460 (N.D. Ind.
1991).

    4. the gaining of an advantage by the party to be charged at the expense of the complaining party.[70]

Thus, intent to deceive is not an element of constructive fraud, as it is of actual fraud; instead, the law infers fraud from the relationship between the parties and the surrounding circumstances.[71]

Where a fiduciary relationship exists and the fiduciary purposely and materially misstates a contract's contents, the contract is vitiated for fraud.[72] However, a confidential relationship between the parties is not essential to a finding of constructive fraud in the inducement of a contract.[73] Constructive fraud may be based on positive affirmations made by a seller to a potential purchaser even if no other relationship exists between the parties.[74]

◆ **Practice Guide·** A contract clause stating that no oral representations were made does not bind the plaintiff when the question of fraud is present.[75]

§ 36 —Representations of opinion of law, or as to future events

    A misrepresentation of a person's opinion, or a misrep-

---

[70]Abbott v. Bates, 670 N.E.2d 916 (Ind. Ct. App. 1996), reh'g denied, (Oct. 31, 1996); McDaniel v. Shepherd, 577 N.E.2d 239 (Ind. Ct. App. 4th Dist. 1991).

    Annotation References: Necessity of showing damage to establish fraud as defense to action on contract, 91 ALR2d 346.

[71]O.K. Sand and Gravel, Inc. v. Martin Marietta Corp., 786 F. Supp. 1442 (S.D. Ind. 1992); W & W Equipment Co., Inc. v. Mink, 568 N.E.2d 564 (Ind. Ct. App. 1st Dist. 1991), reh'g denied, (May 10, 1991) and transfer denied, (Dec. 12, 1991); Dotlich v. Dotlich, 475 N.E.2d 331 (Ind. Ct. App. 1st Dist. 1985), reh'g denied, (Apr. 23, 1985) and transfer denied, (July 3, 1985).

[72]O.K. Sand and Gravel, Inc. v. Martin Marietta Corp., 786 F. Supp. 1442 (S.D. Ind. 1992); A.G. Edwards and Sons, Inc. v. Hilligoss, 597 N.E.2d 1 (Ind. Ct. App. 4th Dist. 1991).

[73]Abbott v. Bates, 670 N.E.2d 916 (Ind. Ct. App. 1996), reh'g denied, (Oct. 31, 1996); Scott v. Bodor, Inc., 571 N.E.2d 313 (Ind. Ct. App. 5th Dist. 1991).

[74]Abbott v. Bates, 670 N.E.2d 916 (Ind. Ct. App. 1996), reh'g denied, (Oct. 31, 1996); Plohg v. NN Investors Life Ins. Co., Inc., 583 N.E.2d 1233 (Ind. Ct. App. 3d Dist. 1992), transfer denied, (May 19, 1992); Scott v. Bodor, Inc., 571 N.E.2d 313 (Ind. Ct. App. 5th Dist. 1991).

[75]Jenkins v. Nebo Properties, Inc., 439 N.E.2d 686 (Ind. Ct. App. 1st Dist. 1982).

resentation of a matter of law or as to future events does
not generally constitute fraud.

West's Digest, Contracts ☞94(6), 94(7).

Honest expressions of opinion do not constitute actionable
fraud that will invalidate a contract,[76] even if the opinion is
erroneous,[77] and a party may not be held guilty of fraud
merely for exaggerating.[78] Mere puffing,[79] or representations
as to value,[80] may not be relied upon to avoid a contract, although it is considered fraudulent if a party states falsely a
fact which contributes to the item's value,[81] or if an expert
makes a willful misstatement of opinion.[82]

However, what might be a statement of opinion from a
person with no special knowledge of the matter may be a
statement of fact from a person who does have such knowledge.[83]

[76]Vernon Fire & Cas. Ins. Co. v. Thatcher, 152 Ind. App. 692, 285
N.E.2d 660 (2d Dist. 1972), reh'g denied, 152 Ind. App. 692, 287 N.E.2d
776 (2d Dist. 1972), transfer denied, 260 Ind. 55, 292 N.E.2d 606 (1973);
Mahin v. Soshnick, 128 Ind. App. 342, 148 N.E.2d 852 (1958).

[77]Sieveking v. Litzler, 31 Ind. 13, 1869 WL 3180 (1869); Gatling v.
Newell, 9 Ind. 572, 1857 WL 3671 (1857).

[78]Gatling v. Newell, 9 Ind. 572, 1857 WL 3671 (1857).

[79]Gatling v. Newell, 9 Ind. 572, 1857 WL 3671 (1857).

[80]Sieveking v. Litzler, 31 Ind. 13, 1869 WL 3180 (1869); Kluge v. Ries,
66 Ind. App. 610, 117 N.E. 262 (Div. 1 1917).

[81]Sieveking v. Litzler, 31 Ind. 13, 1869 WL 3180 (1869).

[82]Coulter v. Clark, 160 Ind. 311, 66 N.E. 739 (1903) (businessman's
representations that valueless patent rights were worth $25,000 but could
be secured for $12,500; that stock in corporation to be organized to
purchase such rights would be more valuable than bank stock; and that
dividends therefrom would soon pay for stock); Louisville, N. A. & C. R.
Co. v. Bodenschatz-Bedford Stone Co., 141 Ind. 251, 39 N.E. 703 (1895)
(civil engineer's false statement to quarry company that, because of
character of land, it could not build railroad switch to connect to any
railroad but plaintiff's).

[83]See, for instance, Vernon Fire & Cas. Ins. Co. v. Thatcher, 152 Ind.
App. 692, 285 N.E.2d 660 (2d Dist. 1972), reh'g denied, 152 Ind. App. 692,
287 N.E.2d 776 (2d Dist. 1972), transfer denied, 260 Ind. 55, 292 N.E.2d
606 (1973) (insurance agent's statement that certain property was covered
by policy); Bailey v. London Guarantee & Acc. Co., 72 Ind. App. 84, 121
N.E. 128 (1918) (doctor's statement that broken bones were doing nicely).

Similarly, a party is generally not held responsible for his misrepresentation of the legal effect of a contract,[84] although it has been said that where a mistake of law is induced or encouraged by the misrepresentation of a party, and through this mistake the other party assumes obligations or gives up rights, he or she may be entitled to relief.[85]

Actual fraud may not be predicated upon broken promises or representations as to future conduct.[86] A fraudulent representation must be of past or existing fact, rather than of acts to be performed in the future,[87] even if the promisor had no intention of fulfilling the promise when it was made.[88] However, fraud may be found in an insolvent buyer's representation, actual or implied,[89] that he or she intends to pay for goods, when in fact he or she has neither the ability nor the intention to pay for them.[90]

Unlike actual fraud, constructive fraud may be based upon

---

[84]New Albany and Salem Railroad Co. v. Slaughter, 10 Ind. 218, 1858 WL 5044 (1858); New Albany & S.R. Co. v. Fields, 10 Ind. 187, 1858 WL 4257 (1858); Clem v. Newcastle & D.R. Co., 9 Ind. 488, 1857 WL 3721 (1857); Russell v. Branham, 8 Blackf. 277, 1846 WL 2725 (Ind. 1846); Gipe v. Pittsburgh, C., C. & St. L. Ry. Co., 41 Ind. App. 156, 82 N.E. 471 (1907).

[85]Bales v. Hunt, 77 Ind. 355, 1881 WL 7270 (1881); Vernon Fire & Cas. Ins. Co. v. Thatcher, 152 Ind. App. 692, 285 N.E.2d 660 (2d Dist. 1972), reh'g denied, 152 Ind. App. 692, 287 N.E.2d 776 (2d Dist. 1972), transfer denied, 260 Ind. 55, 292 N.E.2d 606 (1973) (insured entitled to relief where insurance agent had represented to him that policy would cover certain personal property that was not actually covered); Johnson v. Fox, 110 Ind. App. 698, 38 N.E.2d 865 (1942) (ignorant, inexperienced, elderly woman entitled to have deed and contract set aside where attorney falsely represented to her that instruments preserved life estate in real property for her).

[86]Maynard v. 84 Lumber Co., 657 N.E.2d 406 (Ind. Ct. App. 1995), transfer denied, (Mar. 20, 1996); Nestor v. Kapetanovic, 573 N.E.2d 457 (Ind. Ct. App. 3d Dist. 1991); Wisconics Engineering, Inc. v. Fisher, 466 N.E.2d 745, 39 U.C.C. Rep. Serv. (CBC) 1151 (Ind. Ct. App. 2d Dist. 1984), reh'g denied, (Sept. 27, 1984) and transfer denied, (Jan. 28, 1985).

[87]Smith v. Parker, 148 Ind. 127, 45 N.E. 770 (1897); Middelkamp v. Hanewich, 147 Ind. App. 561, 263 N.E.2d 189 (Div. 2 1970); Johnson-Johnson, Inc. v. Farah, 123 Ind. App. 87, 108 N.E.2d 638 (1952).

[88]Balue v. Taylor, 136 Ind. 368, 36 N.E. 269 (1894); Ayres v. Blevins, 28 Ind. App. 101, 62 N.E. 305 (Div. 2 1901).

[89]Scandinavian-American Trading Co. v. Skinner, 56 Ind. App. 520, 105 N.E. 784 (Div. 2 1914).

[90]Brower v. Goodyer, 88 Ind. 572, 1883 WL 5501 (1883); Scandinavian-

---

promissory misrepresentations.[91] A claim of constructive fraud can be based on promissory misrepresentations if the misrepresentations are false, cause a reliance upon such representation to the detriment of the promisee, and create an advantage for the promisor.[92]

§ 37 —Reliance on representation

The party seeking to avoid a contract on the basis of the other party's fraud must show that he or she reasonably relied on the other party's misrepresentation.

West's Digest, Contracts ☞94(5).

A party seeking to avoid a contract on the basis of the other party's fraud must establish that he or she relied on the other party's misrepresentation.[93]

Whether one has the right to rely on another's representation depends largely on the facts of the case.[94] Generally, a person may rely on an unqualified assertion of fact where reliance is reasonable under all the circumstances.[95] However, a party to a contract may not rescind the contract

---

American Trading Co. v. Skinner, 56 Ind. App. 520, 105 N.E. 784 (Div. 2 1914); Peninsular Stove Co. v. Ellis, 20 Ind. App. 491, 51 N.E. 105 (1898).

[91]Dominion Investments v. Yasechko, 767 F. Supp. 1460 (N.D. Ind. 1991); Nestor v. Kapetanovic, 573 N.E.2d 457 (Ind. Ct. App. 3d Dist. 1991).

[92]Dominion Investments v. Yasechko, 767 F. Supp. 1460 (N.D. Ind. 1991)(applying Indiana law); Eby v. York-Division, Borg-Warner, 455 N.E.2d 623 (Ind. Ct. App. 4th Dist. 1983); Blaising v. Mills, 176 Ind. App. 141, 374 N.E.2d 1166, 99 A.L.R.3d 1238 (3d Dist. 1978); Lawshe v. Glen Park Lumber Co., Inc., 176 Ind. App. 344, 375 N.E.2d 275 (3d Dist. 1978).

[93]Hart v. Steel Products, Inc., 666 N.E.2d 1270 (Ind. Ct. App. 1996), reh'g denied, (Aug. 22, 1996) and transfer denied, 683 N.E.2d 582 (Ind. 1997); Park 100 Investors, Inc. v. Kartes, 650 N.E.2d 347 (Ind. Ct. App. 1995); Showalter, Inc. v. Smith, 629 N.E.2d 272 (Ind. Ct. App. 3d Dist. 1994), transfer denied, (June 22, 1994) and (abrogated on other grounds by, Mitchell v. Mitchell, 695 N.E.2d 920 (Ind. 1998)); Biberstine v. New York Blower Co., 625 N.E.2d 1308 (Ind. Ct. App. 5th Dist. 1993), reh'g denied, (Jan. 24, 1994) and transfer dismissed, (Apr. 12, 1994).

[94]Park 100 Investors, Inc. v. Kartes, 650 N.E.2d 347 (Ind. Ct. App. 1995) (lessee exercised reasonable care before signing purported lease agreement, which was actually personal guaranty, by asking vice-president who had negotiated lease if attorney had approved lease agreement); Fire Ins. Exchange v. Bell by Bell, 634 N.E.2d 517 (Ind. Ct. App. 2d Dist. 1994), aff'd in part, vacated in part on other grounds, 643 N.E.2d 310 (Ind. 1994).

[95]Shuee v. Gedert, 182 Ind. App. 432, 395 N.E.2d 804 (1st Dist. 1979);

based on a misrepresentation where the party had information which would cause a reasonably prudent person to inquire further. Where a party had knowledge which would be sufficient to lead a prudent person to inquire about the matter, and where the truth could have been ascertained conveniently, such knowledge constitutes notice of whatever the inquiry would have discovered and will be regarded as knowledge of the facts.[96] A person is not justified in relying upon another's statement when, before entering into the contract, he or she has actually employed the proper means of verifying the statement, or when the representation concerns generalities equally within both parties' knowledge or means of acquiring knowledge. When the person has had the opportunity to verify the other's statement, he or she is charged with the knowledge which he or she necessarily would have obtained if he or she had been diligent in the attempt. However, when the representation concerns facts of which the party making it has, or is supposed to have, knowledge, and the other party has no such knowledge or means of acquiring it, the party to whom the representation is made is justified in relying on it.[97]

This rule is applied more leniently in cases of intentional fraud.[98] In the case of an intentional fraud, where the party has no reason to doubt the validity of the statement, he or she may rely on the statement without undertaking an investigation or further inquiry,[99] as a person who has perpetrated an intentional fraud should not be permitted to escape the legal consequences of his or her conduct by saying that the other party to the contract could have discovered it through the exercise of reasonable diligence and care.[1] If the party does have some reason to doubt the statement, however, or has actual knowledge of its falsity, he or she

Grissom v. Moran, 154 Ind. App. 419, 290 N.E.2d 119 (2d Dist. 1972), reh'g denied, 154 Ind. App. 419, 292 N.E.2d 627 (2d Dist. 1973).

[96]State Farm Mut. Auto. Ins. Co. v. Price, 181 Ind. App. 258, 396 N.E.2d 134 (3d Dist. 1979).

[97]Welsh v. Kelly-Springfield Tire Co., 213 Ind. 188, 12 N.E.2d 254 (1938).

[98]Fleetwood Corp. v. Mirich, 404 N.E.2d 38 (Ind. Ct. App. 3d Dist. 1980).

[99]State Farm Mut. Auto. Ins. Co. v. Price, 181 Ind. App. 258, 396 N.E.2d 134 (3d Dist. 1979).

[1]Rushville Nat. Bank of Rushville v. State Life Ins. Co., 210 Ind. 492, 1 N.E.2d 445 (1936); Fleetwood Corp. v. Mirich, 404 N.E.2d 38 (Ind. Ct. App. 3d Dist. 1980).

may not rely on it and later attempt to avoid the contract on that basis.[2]

♦ **Illustrations:** Experienced hog farmers who testified that disease is ubiquitous in livestock breeding and that they had had cases of rhinitis in previous herds could not persuasively argue that they acted reasonably in relying on a salesperson's statements that hogs sold to the farmers were free of rhinitis, and in signing contracts that expressly disclaimed any warranty that the hogs were rhinitis-free without reading them.[3]

A used car salesman did not reasonably rely on a 16-year-old's representation that he was a married college student as an indication that he was at least 21 years old and a licensed driver, as required by the car dealership for an unaccompanied test drive, where the minor, although he was large and wore a suit and carried a briefcase, nonetheless looked very young, and where the salesman did not ask to see the minor's driver's license.[4]

Otherwise unjustified reliance may be excused if there exists a confidential relation between the parties.[5]

§ 38 —Knowledge of falsity of representation; intent to deceive

If the party making a misrepresentation is not aware of its falsity, and does not make it for a fraudulent purpose, there is no fraud.

West's Digest, Contracts ☞94(3).

If a false statement is made for a fraudulent purpose, which is in fact accomplished, the contract can be avoided even if the person who made the statement believed it to be

---

[2]Stanish v. Polish Roman Catholic Union of America, 484 F.2d 713 (7th Cir. 1973) (applying Indiana law).

[3]Urschel Farms, Inc. v. Dekalb Swine Breeders, Inc., 858 F. Supp. 831 (N.D. Ind. 1994) (applying Indiana law).

[4]Auto Owners (Mut.) Ins. Co. v. Stanley, 262 F. Supp. 1 (N.D. Ind. 1967) (applying Indiana law).

[5]Givan v. Masterson, 152 Ind. 127, 51 N.E. 237 (1898) (stepfather and stepchild); Peter v. Wright, 6 Ind. 183, 1855 WL 3551 (1855); A.G. Edwards and Sons, Inc. v. Hilligoss, 597 N.E.2d 1 (Ind. Ct. App. 4th Dist. 1991) (broker and client).

true.[6] Fraud may not, however, be found where there is an honest purpose, and neither recklessness nor carelessness, on the part of the party making the representation.[7]

Even in the absence of fraud, an innocent misrepresentation respecting material matters may be a ground for the invalidation of a contract induced by the misrepresentation.[8] The injured party may rescind the contract for an innocent misrepresentation if the parties can be placed in status quo.[9]

§ 39 —Effect of fraud

A contract obtained by fraud is voidable, but not void; the complaining party may seek either rescission or damages.

West's Digest, Contracts ☞94(1).

A contract obtained by fraud is not void, but voidable[10] at the election of the defrauded party[11] when the fraud is the natural and proximate cause of damage sustained by the injured party.[12] Generally, only a party to the contract may take advantage of another party's fraud to avoid the contract.[13]

A person who has been induced to enter a contract by fraud may either rescind the contract, restore any benefits he or she received from it, and be returned to the status quo; or affirm it, retain the benefits, and recover the damages caused by the fraud.[14]

---

[6]Woodruff v. Garner, 27 Ind. 4, 1866 WL 2506 (1866); Baker v. Meenach, 119 Ind. App. 154, 84 N.E.2d 719 (1949).

[7]Furnas v. Friday, 102 Ind. 129, 1 N.E. 296 (1885).

[8]Reed v. Diven, 7 Ind. 189, 1855 WL 3780 (1855); Shaeffer v. Sleade, 7 Blackf. 178, 1844 WL 2923 (Ind. 1844); McCormick v. Malin, 5 Blackf. 509, 1841 WL 2505 (Ind. 1841).

[9]Gardner v. Mann, 36 Ind. App. 694, 76 N.E. 417 (Div. 1 1905).

[10]Raymundo v. Hammond Clinic Ass'n, 449 N.E.2d 276 (Ind. 1983); Brotherhood of R.R. Trainmen v. Virden, 216 Ind. 324, 24 N.E.2d 934 (1940); Thompson v. Peck, 115 Ind. 512, 18 N.E. 16 (1888); Norwood v. Erie R. Co., 114 Ind. App. 526, 53 N.E.2d 189 (1944).

[11]Brumbaugh v. Mellinger, 68 Ind. App. 410, 120 N.E. 676 (1918).

[12]Wolcott v. Wise, 75 Ind. App. 301, 130 N.E. 544 (Div. 1 1921).

[13]Doe ex dem. Cooper v. Harter, 2 Ind. 252, 1850 WL 3144 (1850).

[14]Grissom v. Moran, 154 Ind. App. 419, 292 N.E.2d 627 (2d Dist. 1973); Ohlwine v. Pfaffman, 52 Ind. App. 357, 100 N.E. 777 (1913); Wulschner-Stewart Music Co. v. Hubbard, 44 Ind. App. 526, 89 N.E. 794 (Div. 2 1909).

Fraud in the inducement of a contract is a basis for rescission of the contract.[15] but only if the injured party returns or tenders back the benefits he or she has received,[16] or shows that he or she received no benefit of value.[17] Retention of property received under a contract, after acquiring knowledge of the fraud, constitutes ratification.[18]

If a party elects to rescind a contract on the basis of fraud, he or she may not recover general damages. He or she may, however, recover any money he or she paid under the contract plus interest, as well as monetary reimbursement for any reasonable repairs, expenditures and improvements made on the property by the plaintiff.[19]

§ 40 —Ratification and estoppel

A party may ratify a contract induced by fraud.

West's Digest, Contracts ☞97(1), 97(2).

Where a party has full knowledge of alleged fraud in the inducement of a contract, but acts in a manner which shows his or her intent to confirm the contract, he or she waives any claim for damages relating to the alleged fraud.[20] This

---

[15]Bales v. Weddle, 14 Ind. 349, 1860 WL 4111 (1860); A.G. Edwards and Sons, Inc. v. Hilligoss, 597 N.E.2d 1 (Ind. Ct. App. 4th Dist. 1991); Indiana & Michigan Elec. Co. v. Harlan, 504 N.E.2d 301 (Ind. Ct. App. 1st Dist. 1987), reh'g denied, (Apr. 7, 1987) and transfer denied, (Sept. 22, 1987); Hogan Transfer and Storage Corp. v. Waymire, 399 N.E.2d 779 (Ind. Ct. App. 4th Dist. 1980); Shuee v. Gedert, 182 Ind. App. 432, 395 N.E.2d 804 (1st Dist. 1979).

[16]Brotherhood of R.R. Trainmen v. Virden, 216 Ind. 324, 24 N.E.2d 934 (1940); Ohlwine v. Pfaffman, 52 Ind. App. 357, 100 N.E. 777 (1913); Aetna Life Ins. Co. v. Bockting, 39 Ind. App. 586, 79 N.E. 524 (Div. 2 1906).

[17]Wulschner-Stewart Music Co. v. Hubbard, 44 Ind. App. 526, 89 N.E. 794 (Div. 2 1909).

[18]Himes v. Langley, 85 Ind. 77, 1882 WL 6968 (1882); Gatling v. Newell, 9 Ind. 572, 1857 WL 3671 (1857).

As to ratification of a voidable contract, see § 40.

[19]Grissom v. Moran, 154 Ind. App. 419, 292 N.E.2d 627 (2d Dist. 1973).

[20]Lawlis v. Kightlinger & Gray, 562 N.E.2d 435 (Ind. Ct. App. 4th Dist. 1990), reh'g denied, (Dec. 13, 1990) and transfer denied, (Apr. 23, 1991).

Annotation References: Proceeding under executory contract after discovering fraud as waiver of right to recover damages for the fraud, 13 ALR2d 807.

doctrine, known as waiver or ratification, depends on an intentional relinquishment of a known right.[21]

Although one may ratify another's unauthorized acts through silence and acceptance of the benefits attaching to such acts,[22] mere silence, acquiescence, or inactivity does not constitute ratification unless the ratifying party had a duty to speak or act.[23]

Ratification is a question of fact.[24]

> ◆ **Caution:** Recall that a party who has been fraudulently induced to enter into a contract may elect between rescission of the contract and damages.[25] A ratification implies a release from the consequences of fraud only when it is inconsistent with a claim for damages arising from the fraud.[26]

Estoppel is related to ratification, but it focuses on the effect of the party's conduct, rather than on the party's intent.[27] Estoppel arises when a party's conduct, as opposed to his or her manifested intent, misleads another to believe that the first party will not seek to enforce a right, and causes the second party to act to his or her own detriment.[28] Estoppel may be applied where a party who has a duty to speak or act remains silent or acquiesces without objection in the treatment of property in a manner inconsistent with his or her

---

[21]Ogle v. Wright, 172 Ind. App. 309, 360 N.E.2d 240 (1st Dist. 1977); O.K. Sand and Gravel, Inc. v. Martin Marietta Corp., 786 F. Supp. 1442 (S.D. Ind. 1992) (applying Indiana law).

[22]Wright v. State, 266 Ind. 327, 363 N.E.2d 1221 (1977).

[23]O.K. Sand and Gravel, Inc. v. Martin Marietta Corp., 786 F. Supp. 1442 (S.D. Ind. 1992) (applying Indiana law).

[24]Dominion Investments v. Yasechko, 767 F. Supp. 1460 (N.D. Ind. 1991) (applying Indiana law).

[25]$\S$ 39.

[26]Vernon Fire & Cas. Ins. Co. v. Thatcher, 152 Ind. App. 692, 285 N.E.2d 660 (2d Dist. 1972), reh'g denied, 152 Ind. App. 692, 287 N.E.2d 776 (2d Dist. 1972), transfer denied, 260 Ind. 55, 292 N.E.2d 606 (1973).

[27]Saverslak v. Davis-Cleaver Produce Co., 606 F.2d 208 (7th Cir. 1979) (applying Indiana law).

[28]O.K. Sand and Gravel, Inc. v. Martin Marietta Corp., 786 F. Supp. 1442 (S.D. Ind. 1992) (applying Indiana law).

Forms References: Waiver of statute of limitations. 5A Am Jur Legal Forms 2d, Contracts $\S$ 68:162.

rights.[29] For the application of estoppel by acquiescence to be proper, the person estopped must have had knowledge of the fraud or other facts entitling him or her to rescind the contract.[30]

§ 41 Undue influence and unconscionability

A contract executed as the result of one person's advantage over another which prevents the complaining party from exercising free will and unbiased judgment may be avoided.

West's Digest, Contracts ☞96.

Undue influence is the exercise of control over a person sufficient to destroy his or her free agency and constraint regarding something he or she would not have done without such control.[31] Undue influence exists when one person obtains an ascendancy over another through the other's weakness, ignorance, dependence or implicit reliance on the first person's good faith, and thus prevents the other from exercising an unbiased judgment.[32]

A contract procured from a person in a situation of distress and necessity by another person who stands in a relation of confidence to, or who has an advantage over, the first person, may be avoided.[33] An inference that a contract was executed under undue influence, requiring the party who has procured the benefit of the contract to show that no such influence was used, has been found to arise from one party's sickness,

---

[29]O.K. Sand and Gravel, Inc. v. Martin Marietta Corp., 786 F. Supp. 1442 (S.D. Ind. 1992) (applying Indiana law); Board of Com'rs of Cass County v. Plotner, 149 Ind. 116, 48 N.E. 635 (1897); Warner v. Riddell Nat. Bank, 482 N.E.2d 772 (Ind. Ct. App. 1st Dist. 1985), reh'g denied, (Oct. 18, 1985) and transfer denied, (Feb. 17, 1986); Erie-Haven, Inc. v. First Church of Christ, 155 Ind. App. 283, 292 N.E.2d 837 (3d Dist. 1973).

[30]O.K. Sand and Gravel, Inc. v. Martin Marietta Corp., 786 F. Supp. 1442 (S.D. Ind. 1992) (applying Indiana law); City of Hammond v. Welsh, 224 Ind. 349, 67 N.E.2d 390 (1946).

[31]Day v. Bicknell Minerals, Inc., 480 N.E.2d 567 (Ind. Ct. App. 4th Dist. 1985), reh'g denied, (Aug. 28, 1985); Hunter v. Milhous, 159 Ind. App. 105, 305 N.E.2d 448 (2d Dist. 1973).

[32]Hill v. Jessup, 139 Ind. App. 467, 220 N.E.2d 662 (Div. 2 1966).

[33]Day v. Bicknell Minerals, Inc., 480 N.E.2d 567 (Ind. Ct. App. 4th Dist. 1985), reh'g denied, (Aug. 28, 1985); McClamroch v. McClamroch, 476 N.E.2d 514 (Ind. Ct. App. 4th Dist. 1985), reh'g denied, (May 16, 1985) and transfer denied, (Aug. 12, 1985); Lucas v. Frazee, 471 N.E.2d 1163 (Ind. Ct. App. 4th Dist. 1984).

age, depression, and dependence on the other party.[34] Undue influence has also been found to arise from a family relationship, especially when one of the parties is elderly or feeble,[35] but not from an arms'-length business relationship[36] or even a close and long-term friendship.[37] The relationship need not be a fiduciary one, however,[38] as long as there is a relationship of trust and confidence between the parties justifying one of them in relying on that relationship, and where the party occupying the superior position has abused the relationship and used it to gain an unfair advantage over the other party.[39]

What constitutes undue influence depends upon the particular circumstances of the case.[40] It may arise from the mental weakness of one of the parties[41] or from the victim's financially embarrassed circumstances, which place him or her at the mercy of the stronger party.[42]

♦ **Illustrations:** A father whose sons had been charged with murder under many circumstances indicating their guilt retained attorneys who insisted on the execution of a note and mortgage for their fee of $3,000, an enormous sum at the time. The grand jury did not indict the sons. The court presiding over a subsequent breach of contract action brought by the attorneys held that the note was invalid, except as to the reasonable value of the attorneys' services, since it had been made when the father was

---

[34]Ikerd v. Beavers, 106 Ind. 483, 7 N.E. 326 (1886).

[35]Ashmead v. Reynolds, 134 Ind. 139, 33 N.E. 763 (1893).

[36]Day v. Bicknell Minerals, Inc., 480 N.E.2d 567 (Ind. Ct. App. 4th Dist. 1985), reh'g denied, (Aug. 28, 1985).

[37]Middelkamp v. Hanewich, 147 Ind. App. 561, 263 N.E.2d 189 (Div. 2 1970).

[38]Middelkamp v. Hanewich, 147 Ind. App. 561, 263 N.E.2d 189 (Div. 2 1970); Firebaugh v. Trough, 57 Ind. App. 421, 107 N.E. 301 (Div. 1 1914).

[39]Firebaugh v. Trough, 57 Ind. App. 421, 107 N.E. 301 (Div. 1 1914).

[40]Daugherty v. Daugherty, 115 Ind. App. 253, 57 N.E.2d 599 (1944).

[41]Yount v. Yount, 144 Ind. 133, 43 N.E. 136 (1896); Tucker v. Roach, 139 Ind. 275, 38 N.E. 822 (1894); Wray v. Wray, 32 Ind. 126, 1869 WL 3255 (1869); Marshall v. Billingsly, 7 Ind. 250, 1855 WL 3663 (1855); McCormick v. Malin, 5 Blackf. 509, 1841 WL 2505 (Ind. 1841); Curtis v. Corya, 117 Ind. App. 244, 69 N.E.2d 742 (1946).

[42]Stiefler v. McCullough, 97 Ind. App. 123, 174 N.E. 823 (1931).

under such stress as to have no adequate power against the unjust exaction.[43]

However, even though the owners of a mining business were faced with a choice between selling the business and facing legal action by a creditor, their contract of sale with the purchaser was not executed as a result of undue influence, as the owner could have dealt with another purchaser.[44]

The concepts of undue influence and unconscionability are very similar. As a general rule, a contract is unconscionable if there was a gross disparity in bargaining power which led the party with the lesser bargaining power to sign a contract unwillingly or unaware of its terms, and the contract is one that no sensible person who was not under delusion, duress or distress would accept.[45] The doctrine of unconscionability necessarily looks to the time of execution of the contract,[46] and requires a comparison of the parties' situations.[47]

§ 42 Duress

A transaction is voidable where a party was induced to enter into it by a threat.

West's Digest, Contracts ☞95(1)-95(5).

A contract induced by duress is voidable.[48] Duress has traditionally been defined as an actual or threatened physical violence or restraint, contrary to law, to compel a person

---

[43]Shirk v. Neible, 156 Ind. 66, 59 N.E. 281 (1901).

[44]Day v. Bicknell Minerals, Inc., 480 N.E.2d 567 (Ind. Ct. App. 4th Dist. 1985), reh'g denied, (Aug. 28, 1985).

[45]Justus v. Justus, 581 N.E.2d 1265 (Ind. Ct. App. 5th Dist. 1991), reh'g denied, (Jan. 29, 1992) and transfer denied, (May 29, 1992); Stech v. Panel Mart, Inc., 434 N.E.2d 97 (Ind. Ct. App. 3d Dist. 1982).

Annotation References: Doctrine or unconscionability as applied to insurance contracts, 86 ALR3d 862.

Legal Periodicals: Hunter, Unconscionability Revisited in the Seventh Circuit, 36 Res Gestae 314(4) (Jan. 1993).

[46]Justus v. Justus, 581 N.E.2d 1265 (Ind. Ct. App. 5th Dist. 1991), reh'g denied, (Jan. 29, 1992) and transfer denied, (May 29, 1992).

[47]Pardieck v. Pardieck, 676 N.E.2d 359 (Ind. Ct. App. 1997), transfer denied, 683 N.E.2d 595 (Ind. 1997).

[48]Raymundo v. Hammond Clinic Ass'n, 449 N.E.2d 276 (Ind. 1983).

to enter into a contract.[49] Under this definition, a purported threat to withhold an employee's salary until he or she signed a covenant not to compete,[50] a threat to attempt to remove a corporate officer for cause,[51] the threat of a lawful strike,[52] or a threat to breach an employment contract[53] does not constitute duress.

◆ **Observation:** Some early cases, however, found duress in the absence of physical violence or restraint.[54]

More recently, courts have demonstrated their willingness to regard a transaction as voidable where the party seeking to avoid it was not bound to enter into the contract but was coerced by fear of a wrongful act by the other party to the transaction.[55] The basic concept of duress, however, remains the same, and the ultimate fact to be determined is whether the purported victim was deprived of the free exercise of his or her own will.[56]

Duress may be found in the act of the promisee or his agent,[57] and, generally, may be taken advantage of only by the person coerced,[58] although it may also consist of coercion

---

[49]Williamson v. Bendix Corp., 289 F.2d 389 (7th Cir. 1961) (applying Indiana law); Adams v. Stringer, 78 Ind. 175, 1881 WL 6718 (1881); Bush v. Brown, 49 Ind. 573, 1875 WL 5758 (1875); Rutter v. Excel Industries, Inc., 438 N.E.2d 1030 (Ind. Ct. App. 3d Dist. 1982).

[50]Raymundo v. Hammond Clinic Ass'n, 449 N.E.2d 276 (Ind. 1983).

[51]Rutter v. Excel Industries, Inc., 438 N.E.2d 1030 (Ind. Ct. App. 3d Dist. 1982).

[52]Lewis v. Kerns, 175 F. Supp. 115 (S.D. Ind. 1959) (applying Indiana law).

[53]Williamson v. Bendix Corp., 289 F.2d 389 (7th Cir. 1961) (applying Indiana law).

[54]Tucker v. Roach, 139 Ind. 275, 38 N.E. 822 (1894); Rose v. Owen, 42 Ind. App. 137, 85 N.E. 129 (Div. 1 1908) (actual or threatened institution of unjustified and embarrassing civil action may be considered duress).

[55]Raymundo v. Hammond Clinic Ass'n, 449 N.E.2d 276 (Ind. 1983) (recognizing that there may be such a thing as economic duress).

[56]Raymundo v. Hammond Clinic Ass'n, 449 N.E.2d 276 (Ind. 1983); Day v. Bicknell Minerals, Inc., 480 N.E.2d 567 (Ind. Ct. App. 4th Dist. 1985), reh'g denied, (Aug. 28, 1985).

[57]Bush v. Brown, 49 Ind. 573, 1875 WL 5758 (1875).

[58]Barnes v. Stevens, 62 Ind. 226, 1878 WL 6046 (1878) (threat to institute bankruptcy proceedings against debtor of plaintiff did not constitute duress to plaintiff).

of a party's near relative.[59] In determining the existence of duress, the court may consider the age, sex, capacity, situation, and relation of the parties, and all attending circumstances.[60]

A threat to perform an act or to do an injury which may be redressed by legal process is not considered duress.[61] Thus, duress may not be found in a threat to perform a legal action,[62] or, generally, in a threat to sue on a legal demand.[63]

A well-grounded fear of illegal imprisonment constitutes duress,[64] although the mere threat of a criminal prosecution does not constitute duress.[65] However, the threat to imprison the husband constituted duress against the wife.[66]

VI. ILLEGALITY AND CONTRAVENTION OF PUBLIC POLICY

A. IN GENERAL

Research References

IC 2-7-1-1 et seq.; IC 4-13.6-5-11; IC 8-1-2-106; IC 8-3-1-13; IC 20-1-19-19; IC 24-1-1-1; IC 24-1-2-3; IC 24-1-2-7; IC 24-4-9-19; IC 25-34.1-3-2; IC 26-1-2-719; IC 26-2-5-1; IC 27-1-20-30; IC 31-1-11.5-1; IC 31-1-11.5-12; IC 35-44-1-1
Prof. Cond. R. 7.3

17A Am Jur 2d, Contracts §§ 238-303.
17A C.J.S., Contracts §§ 195-301.
West's Digest, Contracts ⬤=101-134.
ALR Digest: Contracts §§ 269-441.5

---

[59]Denney v. Reber, 63 Ind. App. 192, 114 N.E. 424 (1916) (threat to husband was duress as to wife).

[60]Denney v. Reber, 63 Ind. App. 192, 114 N.E. 424 (1916).

[61]Tucker v. State, 72 Ind. 242, 1880 WL 6325 (1880).

[62]Lewis v. Kerns, 175 F. Supp. 115 (S.D. Ind. 1959) (applying Indiana law); Board of School Com'rs of City of Indianapolis v. State ex rel. Bever, 211 Ind. 257, 5 N.E.2d 307 (1936), reh'g denied, 211 Ind. 257, 6 N.E.2d 702 (1937) (cancellation of contract for good cause).

[63]In re Liquidation of Bourbon Banking Co., Bourbon, 218 Ind. 96, 31 N.E.2d 52 (1941); Wilson S. M. Co. v. Curry, 126 Ind. 161, 25 N.E. 896 (1890).

[64]Bush v. Brown, 49 Ind. 573, 1875 WL 5758 (1875).

[65]Harrison Tp. v. Addison, 176 Ind. 389, 96 N.E. 146 (1911); Legg v. Leyman, 8 Blackf. 148, 1846 WL 2681 (Ind. 1846); U.S. Rubber Co. v. Moon, 93 Ind. App. 571, 179 N.E. 26 (1931).

[66]Denney v. Reber, 63 Ind. App. 192, 114 N.E. 424 (1916).

ALR Index: Adhesion Contracts; Anticipatory Breach; Anticipatory Renunciation or Repudiation; Bids and Bidding; Cancellation of Rescission; Consideration; Contracts; Covenants; Covenants Not to Compete; Estoppel and Waiver; Executory Contracts; Implied Contracts; Offer and Acceptance; Parol Contracts and Agreements; Parol Evidence; Third-Party Beneficiaries; Unconscionability

5A Am Jur Legal Forms 2d, Contracts §§ 68:161, 68:192, 68:194, 68:195, 68:198.

§43 Generally

Courts will not enforce a contract that contravenes the state's public policy, regardless of whether the policy is declared in a statute.

West's Digest, Contracts ☜100.

Generally, contracting parties may enter into any agreement they desire so long as it is not illegal or contrary to public policy.[67] Contracts are against public policy when they create incentives to commit acts that society has made illegal or, at least, disapproves of.[68] Illegality is in a sense a subset of public policy, as the public policy of the state is expressed in the state's constitution, legislative enactments, and judicial pronouncements; a violation of public policy may be found, however, even when no such declaration addresses the matter in question.[69] Thus, courts will generally refuse to enforce an agreement on public policy grounds if any of the following apply:

- the agreement contravenes a statute
- the agreement clearly tends to injure the public in some way

---

[67]Indiana-American Water Co., Inc. v. Town of Seelyville, 698 N.E.2d 1255, 38 U.C.C. Rep. Serv. 2d (CBC) 1133 (Ind. Ct. App. 1998); Barrington Management Co., Inc. v. Paul E. Draper Family Ltd. Partnership, 695 N.E.2d 135 (Ind. Ct. App. 1998); Robinson v. Century Personnel, Inc., 678 N.E.2d 1268 (Ind. Ct. App. 1997), transfer denied, 690 N.E.2d 1179 (Ind. 1997); Valparaiso Technical Institute, Inc. v. Porter County Treasurer, 676 N.E.2d 416 (Ind. Ct. App. 1997), reh'g denied, 682 N.E.2d 819 (Ind. Ct. App. 1997).

[68]Truck Ins. Exchange v. Ashland Oil, Inc., 951 F.2d 787 (7th Cir. 1992) (applying Indiana law).

[69]Trotter v. Nelson, 684 N.E.2d 1150 (Ind. 1997).

- the agreement is otherwise contrary to the declared public policy of Indiana[70]

A contract founded on illegal consideration is also unenforceable.[71]

Courts have traditionally stated that agreements which contravene public policy are void and unenforceable,[72] It may be more exact, however, to say that no contract is created when an agreement violates public policy, because the agreement imposes no legal obligation on the promisor.[73]

A court considering whether a contract is against public policy will consider that it is in the public's best interest that persons should not be unnecessarily restricted in their freedom of contract.[74]

An otherwise valid contract is not rendered illegal because improper means or agencies might be[75] or are[76] employed in its performance, nor is it defeated by a party's intention to perform it in an illegal manner;[77] on the other hand, an illegal contract is not saved by the fact that no corruption or bad faith was intended.[78]

---

[70]Trotter v. Nelson, 684 N.E.2d 1150 (Ind. 1997); Continental Basketball Ass'n, Inc. v. Ellenstein Enterprises, Inc., 669 N.E.2d 134 (Ind. 1996); Fresh Cut, Inc. v. Fazli, 650 N.E.2d 1126 (Ind. 1995).

[71]Wilson v. Ensworth, 85 Ind. 399, 1882 WL 6396 (1882) (unlawful sexual intercourse); Blont v. Proctor, 5 Blackf. 265, 1840 WL 2349 (Ind. 1840) (counterfeit bank notes); Van Orman Fort Wayne Corp. v. Edwards Motor Co., 148 Ind. App. 66, 263 N.E.2d 746 (Div. 1 1970) (percentage of proceeds of illegal alcohol sales).

[72]Trotter v. Nelson, 684 N.E.2d 1150 (Ind. 1997); Kahn v. Gumberts, 9 Ind. 430, 1857 WL 3638 (1857).

[73]Straub v. B.M.T. by Todd, 645 N.E.2d 597 (Ind. 1994), reh'g denied, (Apr. 12, 1995).

[74]Allstate Ins. Co. v. Boles, 481 N.E.2d 1096 (Ind. 1985); Medical Specialists, Inc. v. Sleweon, 652 N.E.2d 517 (Ind. Ct. App. 1995), transfer denied, (Sept. 28, 1995); Lexington Ins. Co. v. American Healthcare Providers, 621 N.E.2d 332 (Ind. Ct. App. 2d Dist. 1993), transfer denied, (Mar. 3, 1994).

[75]Hogston v. Bell, 185 Ind. 536, 112 N.E. 883 (1916).

[76]Phend v. Midwest Engineering & Equipment Co., 93 Ind. App. 165, 177 N.E. 879 (1931).

[77]Hogston v. Bell, 185 Ind. 536, 112 N.E. 883 (1916); Jackson v. City Nat. Bank of Goshen, 125 Ind. 347, 25 N.E. 430 (1890).

[78]Brown v. First Nat. Bank, 137 Ind. 655, 37 N.E. 158 (1894).

A contract which is void as against public policy cannot be ratified,[79] although a party maybe estopped to plead that the contract is illegal.[80]

An illegal public contract may not be ratified by public officials.[81]

> ◆ **Observation:** Contracts void as in violation of public policy are distinguished from contracts voidable because of grounds such as fraud or undue influence according to the identities of the people harmed by the violation. The public policy defense applies when the contract harms others, or the general public; fraud, undue influence, and similar principles apply when one party to a contract exploits the other.[82] Note, however, that the line between the two becomes fuzzy in some cases;[83] for instance, where an uneducated gas station lessee was more or less force fed a lease containing a clause stating that the lessee would indemnify the lessor oil company for damages arising from occurrences on the leased premises, the Indiana Supreme Court, in determining the validity of a clause, treated the concepts of unconscionability and violation of public policy as interchangeable.[84]

§ 44 What law governs

The legality of a contract's performance is determined by the law of the place of performance.

West's Digest, Contracts ☞101(1), 101(2).

The legality of a contract's performance is determined by

---

[79]Jessup v. Hinchman, 77 Ind. App. 460, 133 N.E. 853 (Div. 1 1922); Millett v. Aetna Trust & Savings Co., 70 Ind. App. 451, 122 N.E. 344 (Div. 1 1919); Wilson v. Fahnestock, 44 Ind. App. 35, 86 N.E. 1037 (Div. 2 1909); Robison v. Wolf, 27 Ind. App. 683, 62 N.E. 74 (1901).

[80]Pritchett v. Ahrens, 26 Ind. App. 56, 59 N.E. 42 (1901).

As to ratification of a contract or estoppel to seek its rescission, see § 39.

[81]State ex rel. Blair v. Gettinger, 230 Ind. 588, 105 N.E.2d 161 (1952); Indiana Ins. Co. v. Noble, 148 Ind. App. 297, 265 N.E.2d 419 (Div. 2 1970).

[82]Truck Ins. Exchange v. Ashland Oil, Inc., 951 F.2d 787 (7th Cir. 1992) (applying Indiana law).

[83]Truck Ins. Exchange v. Ashland Oil, Inc., 951 F.2d 787 (7th Cir. 1992) (applying Indiana law).

[84]Weaver v. American Oil Co., 257 Ind. 458, 276 N.E.2d 144, 49 A.L.R.3d 306 (1971), discussed in § 47.

For a discussion of unconscionability and undue influence, see § 41.

the law of the place where it has been or is to be rendered.[85]
If performance is illegal in a state in which a contract is
made, the contract may validly provide for performance
instead in a state where it would be permissible.[86]

If a contract is valid under the applicable law of a foreign
state, it may be enforceable in Indiana even though Indiana
law may forbid the making of such a contract.[87] However,
comity does not require the enforcement of a contract, even
though valid under the applicable law of a foreign state, if
the contract contravenes Indiana's public policy.[88]

♦ **Illustration:** An agreement between two Indiana
residents to purchase an Illinois lottery ticket was
enforceable, notwithstanding the fact that the contract
violated Indiana's law at the time against gambling, as
the basic activity was legal where the contract was to be
performed.[89]

The law in effect at the time an agreement is made
determines its validity.[90]

♦ **Practice Guide:** Parties to a contract may generally
choose what law will govern the agreement.[91]

§ 45 Violation of statute

**An agreement in direct contravention of a statute is void
and unenforceable.**

West's Digest, Contracts ☞104-107.

Generally, an agreement in direct contravention of a statute is void,[92] and its terms are unenforceable.[93] Thus, the

---

[85]Thompson v. Edwards, 85 Ind. 414, 1882 WL 6397 (1882).

[86]Smith v. Muncie Nat. Bank, 29 Ind. 158, 1867 WL 3034 (1867).

[87]American Furniture Mart Bldg. Corp. v. W.C. Redmon, Sons & Co.,
210 Ind. 112, 1 N.E.2d 606 (1936).

[88]Vandalia R. Co. v. Kelly, 187 Ind. 323, 119 N.E. 257 (1918); Carl
Hagenbeck & Great Wallace Show Co. v. Randall, 75 Ind. App. 417, 126
N.E. 501 (Div. 1 1920).

[89]Kaszuba v. Zientara, 506 N.E.2d 1 (Ind. 1987), reh'g denied, (June 23,
1987).

[90]Bell v. Rush, 98 Ind. App. 303, 189 N.E. 181 (1934).

[91]For a discussion of choice of law clauses, see § 49.

[92]Trotter v. Nelson, 684 N.E.2d 1150 (Ind. 1997); Continental
Basketball Ass'n, Inc. v. Ellenstein Enterprises, Inc., 669 N.E.2d 134 (Ind.

rules of contract law must yield to statutory provisions.[94] Such a contract may be considered illegal even though the statute merely prohibits it without providing a penalty.[95]

However, because courts place such a high value on the freedom to contract freely, they will not find that a contract contravenes a statute unless the language of the implicated statute clearly and unambiguously indicates that the legislature intended agreements made in violation of the statute to be unenforceable.[96] In some instances, the legislature has clearly and unambiguously shown its intent that certain types of contracts not be enforced by expressly declaring them void or unenforceable.[97] These provisions appear infrequently, however,[98] and when a statute does not include such a provision, courts are hesitant to assume that the legislature intended every contract that does not comply with the statute to be void and unenforceable.[99] When presented with a contract violating such a statute, courts bal-

---

1996); Stampco Const. Co., Inc. v. Guffey, 572 N.E.2d 510 (Ind. Ct. App. 1st Dist. 1991).

[93]Meehan v. Meehan, 425 N.E.2d 157 (Ind. 1981).

Forms References: Compliance with law. 5A Am Jur Legal Forms 2d, Contracts § 68:161.

[94]Meehan v. Meehan, 425 N.E.2d 157 (Ind. 1981) (Dissolution of Marriage Act, IC 31-1-11.5-1 et seq., limits the parties' contractual capacity to determine their child support obligations so that they are not subject to judicial modification).

[95]Skelton v. Bliss, 7 Ind. 77, 1855 WL 3629 (1855); State Bank v. Coquillard, 6 Ind. 232, 1855 WL 3758 (1855).

[96]Continental Basketball Ass'n, Inc. v. Ellenstein Enterprises, Inc., 669 N.E.2d 134 (Ind. 1996); Tolliver v. Mathas, 538 N.E.2d 971 (Ind. Ct. App. 4th Dist. 1989), reh'g denied, (July 10, 1989) and transfer denied, (Jan. 10, 1990); Noble v. Alis, 474 N.E.2d 109 (Ind. Ct. App. 1st Dist. 1985), reh'g denied, (Mar. 25, 1985) and transfer denied, (June 27, 1985).

[97]Continental Basketball Ass'n, Inc. v. Ellenstein Enterprises, Inc., 669 N.E.2d 134 (Ind. 1996) (citing IC 4-13.6-5-11, all bids let that do not conform with statute void; IC 20-1-19-19, regarding payment obligations to nonaccredited postsecondary educational institutions; IC 26-2-5-1, regarding indemnity clauses in most construction and design contracts); Harbour v. Arelco, Inc., 678 N.E.2d 381 (Ind. 1997) (citing IC 24-4-9-19, regarding contracts for vehicle rental nonconforming with statute void).

[98]Noble v. Alis, 474 N.E.2d 109 (Ind. Ct. App. 1st Dist. 1985), reh'g denied, (Mar. 25, 1985) and transfer denied, (June 27, 1985).

[99]Continental Basketball Ass'n, Inc. v. Ellenstein Enterprises, Inc., 669 N.E.2d 134 (Ind. 1996).

ance the following considerations in determining whether to enforce the contract:[1]

- the nature of the contract's subject matter
- the strength of the public policy underlying the statute
- the likelihood that refusal to enforce the bargain or term will further that policy
- how serious or deserved would be the forfeiture suffered by the party attempting to enforce the bargain
- the parties' relative bargaining power and freedom to contract

Courts are less likely to enforce an agreement in contravention of a statute designed for the protection of the public health, safety, and welfare than an agreement in contravention of a revenue statute.[2]

◆ **Illustration:** A sports franchise agreement which violated the Indiana Franchise Act would be enforced, as the parties to it were highly sophisticated and had relatively equal bargaining power, and as the transaction was so different from the typical franchise transaction which the Act was designed to regulate that enforcement of the agreement would not undermine the purposes of the Act.[3]

◆ **Caution:** This balancing approach may call into question several earlier decisions holding that when a statute fixes certain requirements as conditions precedent to the right to carry on a particular business, noncompliance with the statute renders void any contracts made in carrying on the business, even if the statute contains no provision to that effect.[4]

---

[1]Trimble v. Ameritech Pub., Inc., 700 N.E.2d 1128 (Ind. 1998); Continental Basketball Ass'n, Inc. v. Ellenstein Enterprises, Inc., 669 N.E.2d 134 (Ind. 1996); Fresh Cut, Inc. v. Fazli, 650 N.E.2d 1126 (Ind. 1995).

[2]Trimble v. Ameritech Pub., Inc., 700 N.E.2d 1128 (Ind. 1998); Continental Basketball Ass'n, Inc. v. Ellenstein Enterprises, Inc., 669 N.E.2d 134 (Ind. 1996); Fresh Cut, Inc. v. Fazli, 650 N.E.2d 1126 (Ind. 1995); Noble v. Alis, 474 N.E.2d 109 (Ind. Ct. App. 1st Dist. 1985), reh'g denied, (Mar. 25, 1985) and transfer denied, (June 27, 1985).

[3]Continental Basketball Ass'n, Inc. v. Ellenstein Enterprises, Inc., 669 N.E.2d 134 (Ind. 1996).

[4]Faust v. Design Consultants, Inc., 542 N.E.2d 1383 (Ind. Ct. App. 3d

§ 46 Public policy in absence of statute

A contract that does not violate a statute may be void as against public policy if it tends to injure the public, is against the public good, or is inconsistent with sound policy and good morals.

West's Digest, Contracts ☞108(1), 108(2).

Where public policy is not explicit, courts look to the overall implications of constitutional and statutory enactments, practices of officials and judicial decisions to disclose the public policy of the state.[5] In the absence of clear manifestation of public policy in some vehicle such as a statute, constitutional provision, or judicial pronouncement, courts faced with a claim that a contract violates public policy consider whether it can be clearly shown that the agreement "has a tendency to injure the public, or is against the public good, or is inconsistent with sound policy and good morals as to the consideration or as to the thing to be done or not to be done."[6] Where public policy is not explicit, courts look for guidance to the overall implications of constitutional and statutory enactments, practices of officials, judicial decisions,[7] legislative history of statutes,[8] and regulatory provisions such as those in the Rules of Professional Conduct.[9]

Dist. 1989); Bright Nat. Bank of Flora v. Hartman, 61 Ind. App. 440, 109 N.E. 846 (Div. 1 1915); Beecher v. Peru Trust Co., 49 Ind. App. 184, 97 N.E. 23 (Div. 1 1912).

[5]Straub v. B.M.T. by Todd, 645 N.E.2d 597 (Ind. 1994), reh'g denied, (Apr. 12, 1995); Hogston v. Bell, 185 Ind. 536, 112 N.E. 883 (1916).

[6]Trotter v. Nelson, 684 N.E.2d 1150 (Ind. 1997); Straub v. B.M.T. by Todd, 645 N.E.2d 597 (Ind. 1994), reh'g denied, (Apr. 12, 1995); Raymundo v. Hammond Clinic Ass'n, 449 N.E.2d 276 (Ind. 1983).

[7]Schornick v. Butler, 205 Ind. 304, 185 N.E. 111 (1933), reh'g denied, 205 Ind. 304, 186 N.E. 326 (1933); Parker v. Camp, 656 N.E.2d 882 (Ind. Ct. App. 1995); Franklin Fire Ins. Co. v. Noll, 115 Ind. App. 289, 58 N.E.2d 947 (1945).

[8]American Underwriters, Inc. v. Turpin, 149 Ind. App. 473, 273 N.E.2d 761 (Div. 2 1971).

[9]Trotter v. Nelson, 684 N.E.2d 1150 (Ind. 1997); Straub v. B.M.T. by Todd, 645 N.E.2d 597 (Ind. 1994), reh'g denied, (Apr. 12, 1995).

Whether a contract is against public policy is a question of law to be determined from the circumstances of the particular case.[10]

§ 47 Exculpatory clauses

Exculpatory clauses are generally not against public policy, as long as they are not obtained through fraud, misrepresentation, or unequal bargaining power.

West's Digest, Contracts ⊙114.

Exculpatory agreements are not against public policy.[11] Where there is no legislation to the contrary,[12] parties are permitted to agree in advance that a party owes no obligation of care for the benefit of another, and will not be held liable for the consequences of his or her own negligence.[13]

◆ **Practice Guide:** Although an exculpatory clause not referring specifically to the released party's negligence may act to bar liability for damages incurred which are inherent in the nature of the activity,[14] an exculpatory clause will not act to absolve the party who drafted it from

---

[10]Trotter v. Nelson, 684 N.E.2d 1150 (Ind. 1997); Straub v. B.M.T. by Todd, 645 N.E.2d 597 (Ind. 1994), reh'g denied, (Apr. 12, 1995).

[11]Marsh v. Dixon, 707 N.E.2d 998 (Ind. Ct. App. 1999), transfer denied, (Aug. 27, 1999); Powell v. American Health Fitness Center of Fort Wayne, Inc., 694 N.E.2d 757 (Ind. Ct. App. 1998).

[12]Terry v. Indiana State University, 666 N.E.2d 87, 110 Ed. Law Rep. 390 (Ind. Ct. App. 1996); LaFrenz v. Lake County Fair Bd., 172 Ind. App. 389, 360 N.E.2d 605 (3d Dist. 1977).

For instance, certain indemnification clauses in construction contracts are prohibited by IC 26-2-5-1.

[13]Indianapolis Power & Light Co. v. Brad Snodgrass, Inc., 578 N.E.2d 669 (Ind. 1991); Marsh v. Dixon, 707 N.E.2d 998 (Ind. Ct. App. 1999), transfer denied, (Aug. 27, 1999); Powell v. American Health Fitness Center of Fort Wayne, Inc., 694 N.E.2d 757 (Ind. Ct. App. 1998); Clanton v. United Skates of America, 686 N.E.2d 896 (Ind. Ct. App. 1997).

Annotation References: Construction and effect of provision in contract for sale of realty by which purchaser agrees to take property "as is" or in its existing condition, 8 ALR5th 312.

Trial Strategy References: Contractual Indemnifications and Releases From Environmental Liability, 59 Am Jur Trials 231.

[14]Marsh v. Dixon, 707 N.E.2d 998 (Ind. Ct. App. 1999), transfer denied, (Aug. 27, 1999).

liability unless it specifically and explicitly refers to the negligence of the party seeking release from liability.[15]

The signer's failure to read the release before he or she signs it does not render the release unenforceable where there is no evidence of fraud or misrepresentation by the released party.[16] However, a contractual release of liability is not valid if there is unequal bargaining power between the parties such that the party against whom the release is to be enforced did not knowingly and willingly execute the release.[17] The party seeking to enforce a contract alleged to be unenforceable because of unequal bargaining power has the burden of showing that the provisions were explained to the other party and that there was in fact a real and voluntary meeting of the parties' minds.[18] To sign a release knowingly, the party must understand it, and to sign it willingly, he or she must not sign it under economic or other duress.[19]

◆ **Illustration:** A gas station operator with a 10th-grade education who had previously worked only as a skilled and unskilled laborer entered into a gas station lease with an oil company. The lease contained a clause in fine print and with no heading, providing in substance that the operator would hold harmless and indemnify the oil

---

[15]Powell v. American Health Fitness Center of Fort Wayne, Inc., 694 N.E.2d 757 (Ind. Ct. App. 1998) (clause purporting to release defendant "from any damages" and placing on plaintiff responsibility for "any injuries, damages, or losses" did not release defendant from liability for injuries allegedly caused by its negligence).

[16]Shumate v. Lycan, 675 N.E.2d 749 (Ind. Ct. App. 1997), transfer denied, 683 N.E.2d 595 (Ind. 1997).

[17]Weaver v. American Oil Co., 257 Ind. 458, 276 N.E.2d 144, 49 A.L.R.3d 306 (1971); Shumate v. Lycan, 675 N.E.2d 749 (Ind. Ct. App. 1997), transfer denied, 683 N.E.2d 595 (Ind. 1997); Dawson v. Hummer, 649 N.E.2d 653 (Ind. Ct. App. 4th Dist. 1995); Marshall v. Blue Springs Corp., 641 N.E.2d 92, 95 Ed. Law Rep. 641 (Ind. Ct. App. 5th Dist. 1994) (scuba diving student willingly signed release exculpating diving school and owner of dive site from liability, despite his claim that he was under economic duress because he had already paid for diving course and rented scuba equipment before entering into releases; student chose to be certified as scuba diver for his own personal enjoyment and was under no compulsion by outside source to do so).

For discussion of undue influence and unconscionability, see § 41.

[18]Weaver v. American Oil Co., 257 Ind. 458, 276 N.E.2d 144, 49 A.L.R.3d 306 (1971).

[19]Clanton v. United Skates of America, 686 N.E.2d 896 (Ind. Ct. App. 1997).

company for any negligence of the oil company occurring on the leased premises. The oil company sought to enforce the clause against the operator after the oil company's employee negligently sprayed gasoline on the operator and his assistant on the leased premises, causing them to be burned. Nothing in the record indicated that the lessee had read the lease, or that the lessor's agent had asked him to read it, or explained or attempted to call his attention to the indemnification clause. Because of the oil company's vastly superior bargaining power, the clause was held unenforceable on public policy grounds.[20]

A party may disclaim or limit liability arising not only from his or her actions, but from products or services he or she sells.[21] However, a party may not disclaim liability where a statute imposes strict liability on the party.[22] Under the Uniform Commercial Code as adopted in Indiana, a contractual limitation of consequential damages for injury to the person in the case of consumer goods is prima facie unconscionable, but limitation of damages where the loss is commercial is not.[23]

Public policy also prohibits exculpatory clauses where the transaction affects the public interest, such as those involving public utilities, common carriers, innkeepers and public warehousemen and situations where the indispensable need of one party for the services of another deprives the customer of all real equal bargaining power.[24] One involved in transactions affecting the public interest may not contract for indemnity against its own tort liability when it is perform-

---

[20]Weaver v. American Oil Co., 257 Ind. 458, 276 N.E.2d 144, 49 A.L.R.3d 306 (1971).

[21]Trimble v. Ameritech Pub., Inc., 700 N.E.2d 1128 (Ind. 1998) (liability for failure to publish advertisement in yellow pages limited to less of contract price or amount actually paid to further contract); Town and Country Ford, Inc. v. Busch, 709 N.E.2d 1030 (Ind. Ct. App. 1999) (citing IC 26-1-2-316); General Bargain Center v. American Alarm Co., Inc., 430 N.E.2d 407 (Ind. Ct. App. 1st Dist. 1982) (liability for failure of alarm system limited to $250).

[22]McGraw-Edison Co. v. Northeastern Rural Elec. Membership Corp., 678 N.E.2d 1120 (Ind. 1997) (under Indiana Product Liability Act).

[23]IC 26-1-2-719.

[24]Pinnacle Computer Services, Inc. v. Ameritech Pub., Inc., 642 N.E.2d 1011 (Ind. Ct. App. 1st Dist. 1994), reh'g denied, (Feb. 23, 1995); General Bargain Center v. American Alarm Co., Inc., 430 N.E.2d 407 (Ind. Ct. App. 1st Dist. 1982).

ing either a public or a quasi-public duty.[25] Moreover, although a party may contractually relieve him- or herself of
liability to the other party to the contract, a party cannot
contract out of his or her duty to exercise reasonable care
with respect to third parties.[26]

A private agreement or contract cannot release a party
from a statutorily imposed obligation.[27] A party may not
contractually disavow a legal responsibility properly imposed
by a legislative body.[28] For instance, a parent cannot
contractually relieve him- or herself of the legal obligation to
support his or her minor children.[29]

§ 48 —Adhesion contracts

**Contracts presented to a party on a take-it-or-leave-it
basis are not per se void as against public policy.**

West's Digest, Contracts ☞108(1).

An adhesion contract is defined as "a standardized
contract, which, imposed and drafted by the party of superior
bargaining strength, relegates to the subscribing party only
the opportunity to adhere to the contract or reject it."[30] It is
generally a standardized form offered to a consumer on a
take-it-or-leave-it basis.[31] Contracts of adhesion appear in
many circumstances and are not necessarily unconsciona-

---

[25]Center Tp. of Porter County v. City of Valparaiso, 420 N.E.2d 1272
(Ind. Ct. App. 3d Dist. 1981).

[26]CSX Transp., Inc. v. Kirby, 687 N.E.2d 611 (Ind. Ct. App. 1997),
transfer denied, 698 N.E.2d 1193 (Ind. 1998); Morris v. McDonald's Corp.,
650 N.E.2d 1219 (Ind. Ct. App. 1995).

[27]Stevens v. Thompson, 525 N.E.2d 353 (Ind. Ct. App. 1st Dist. 1988).

[28]Connolly v. Pension Ben. Guar. Corp., 475 U.S. 211, 106 S. Ct. 1018,
89 L. Ed. 2d 166 (1986); Davon, Inc. v. Shalala, 75 F.3d 1114 (7th Cir.
1996) (applying Indiana law); Hatfield v. La Charmant Home Owners
Ass'n, Inc., 469 N.E.2d 1218 (Ind. Ct. App. 1st Dist. 1984), reh'g denied,
(Dec. 11, 1984) and transfer denied, (Mar. 6, 1985).

[29]Brokaw v. Brokaw, 398 N.E.2d 1385 (Ind. Ct. App. 3d Dist. 1980).

This obligation is imposed by IC 31-1-11.5-12(d), as discussed in I.L.E.,
Parent and Child.

[30]C.J.S., Contracts § 12.

[31]Pigman v. Ameritech Pub., Inc., 641 N.E.2d 1026 (Ind. Ct. App. 1st
Dist. 1994), reh'g denied, 650 N.E.2d 67 (Ind. Ct. App. 1st Dist. 1995) and
(disapproved of on other grounds by, Trimble v. Ameritech Pub., Inc., 700
N.E.2d 1128 (Ind. 1998)).

ble.[32] For instance, insurance contracts are typically contracts of adhesion.[33] Any ambiguities in an adhesion contract, however, will be construed against the drafter.[34]

§ 49 Agreements harmful to justice

Contracts tending to impede the regular administration of justice are void as against public policy.

West's Digest, Contracts ☞127(1)-127(4), 129(1)-129(5).

Express or implied agreements tending to impede the regular administration of justice are void as against public policy, regardless of the means used, the natural results, or the motives of the parties.[35]

A contract provision limiting a person's access to the courts and opportunity to obtain remedy for an injury is against public policy.[36] However, forum selection clauses are enforceable, if they are freely negotiated and not unreasonable or unjust,[37] and if there is no evidence of fraud or over-reaching such that the agreeing party would effectively be deprived of a day in court.[38] A contractual provision which would allow a court to exercise personal jurisdiction over a

---

[32]Pigman v. Ameritech Pub., Inc., 641 N.E.2d 1026 (Ind. Ct. App. 1st Dist. 1994), reh'g denied, 650 N.E.2d 67 (Ind. Ct. App. 1st Dist. 1995) and (disapproved of on other grounds by, Trimble v. Ameritech Pub., Inc., 700 N.E.2d 1128 (Ind. 1998)).

[33]Evans v. National Life Acc. Ins. Co., 467 N.E.2d 1216 (Ind. Ct. App. 2d Dist. 1984).

[34]Evans v. National Life Acc. Ins. Co., 467 N.E.2d 1216 (Ind. Ct. App. 2d Dist. 1984).

[35]Franklin v. White, 493 N.E.2d 161 (Ind. 1986); Brown v. First Nat. Bank, 137 Ind. 655, 37 N.E. 158 (1894).

[36]George S. May Intern. Co. v. King, 629 N.E.2d 257 (Ind. Ct. App. 1st Dist. 1994), reh'g denied, (May 11, 1994) and transfer denied, (Sept. 2, 1994).

[37]Pollas v. Hardware Wholesalers, Inc., 663 N.E.2d 1188 (Ind. Ct. App. 1996), reh'g denied, (June 12, 1996); Horner v. Tilton, 650 N.E.2d 759 (Ind. Ct. App. 1995), reh'g denied, (July 7, 1995) and transfer denied, (Nov. 15, 1995).

Annotation References: Validity of contractual provision limiting place or court in which action may be brought, 31 ALR4th 404.

Forms References: Place of suit. 5A Am Jur Legal Forms 2d, Contracts § 68:192.

[38]Mechanics Laundry & Supply, Inc. v. Wilder Oil Co., Inc., 596 N.E.2d 248 (Ind. Ct. App. 5th Dist. 1992), reh'g denied, (Aug. 27, 1992) and transfer denied, (Dec. 17, 1992).

nonresident party is not necessarily invalid.[39] Generally, parties to a contract may also choose what law will govern the contract,[40] unless the application of another state's law is forbidden by Indiana statute and Indiana has a materially greater interest in the litigation that the state chosen in the contract.[41] If, however, a choice of forum or choice of law clause in a contract operates as a prospective waiver of the party's right to pursue a remedy, the clause is void as against public policy.[42]

A contract clause shortening the time within which a plaintiff must bring suit, although not favored,[43] is valid and enforceable in Indiana if the parties mutually consented and agreed to the provision.[44]

Annotation References: Validity and effect of stipulation in contract to effect that it shall be governed by law of particular state which is neither place where contract is made not place where it is to be performed, 16 ALR4th 967.

[39]Tandy Computer Leasing v. Milam, 555 N.E.2d 174 (Ind. Ct. App. 2d Dist. 1990).

[40]Hoehn v. Hoehn, 716 N.E.2d 479 (Ind. Ct. App. 1999).

Forms References: Law governing. 5A Am Jur Legal Forms 2d, Contracts §§ 68:194, 68:195.

[41]Wright-Moore Corp. v. Ricoh Corp., 908 F.2d 128 (7th Cir. 1990), reh'g denied, (Aug. 28, 1990) and on remand to, 794 F. Supp. 844 (N.D. Ind. 1991), judgment aff'd, 980 F.2d 432 (7th Cir. 1992), reh'g denied, (Dec. 10, 1992) (Indiana law applied to franchise dispute, despite New York choice of law cause, because Indiana had materially greater interest in litigation than New York and because Indiana Franchise Law makes it unlawful to enter into franchise agreement "requiring the franchisee to prospectively assent to a release . . . [or] waiver . . . which purports to relieve any person from liability to be imposed by this chapter" or to enter into an agreement "limiting litigation brought for breach of the agreement in any manner whatsoever.").

Annotation References: Choice of law as to applicable statute of limitations in contract actions, 78 ALR3d 639.

[42]Vimar Seguros y Reaseguros, S.A. v. M/V Sky Reefer, 515 U.S. 528, 115 S. Ct. 2322, 132 L. Ed. 2d 462 (1995).

[43]Huff v. Travelers Indem. Co., 266 Ind. 414, 363 N.E.2d 985 (1977).

[44]Huff v. Travelers Indem. Co., 266 Ind. 414, 363 N.E.2d 985 (1977); Meridian Mut. Ins. Co. v. Caveletto, 553 N.E.2d 1269 (Ind. Ct. App. 1st Dist. 1990); State v. Lidster, 467 N.E.2d 47 (Ind. Ct. App. 1st Dist. 1984).

Modification of warranties and limitations of remedy are not per se unconscionable.[45]

Although at common law agreements to arbitrate future disputes were unenforceable because public policy considerations were said to disfavor contracts ousting courts of jurisdiction, more recently arbitration agreements have become favored by the law as a speedy, efficient, and economical dispute settlement mechanism relieving congestion in the court system.[46] Now, public policy strongly favors the enforcement of arbitration agreements.[47]

A contract provision which states that in an action on the contract, the defendant's liability can be proved only by means of certain specified evidence,[48] or otherwise unduly influences the production or suppression of evidence,[49] is contrary to public policy and void. An integration clause in a contract, stating that the written agreement reflects the parties' entire agreement and supersedes any previously made oral agreements, cannot prevent a court from hearing relevant parol evidence.[50]

A bargain whose purpose is the stifling of a criminal prosecution is contrary to public policy and illegal,[51] even if the

---

[45]Hahn v. Ford Motor Co., Inc., 434 N.E.2d 943, 33 U.C.C. Rep. Serv. (CBC) 1277 (Ind. Ct. App. 2d Dist. 1982).

Trial Strategy References: Validity and Applicability of Contractual Allocations of Environmental Risk, 34 Am Jur POF3d 465.

[46]Kendrick Memorial Hospital, Inc. v. Totten, 408 N.E.2d 130 (Ind. Ct. App. 1st Dist. 1980); Pathman Const. Co. v. Knox County Hospital Ass'n, 164 Ind. App. 121, 326 N.E.2d 844 (1st Dist. 1975).

Annotation References: Contractual jury trial waivers in state civil cases, 42 ALR5th 53.

Trial Strategy References: Trials Over Arbitration Clauses in Securities Broker Contracts, 61 Am Jur Trials 357.

[47]Homes By Pate, Inc. v. DeHaan, 713 N.E.2d 303 (Ind. Ct. App. 1999); Northwestern Mut. Life Ins. Co. v. Stinnett, 698 N.E.2d 339 (Ind. Ct. App. 1998).

[48]American Ben. Life Ass'n v. Hall, 96 Ind. App. 498, 185 N.E. 344 (1933).

[49]Franklin v. White, 493 N.E.2d 161 (Ind. 1986).

[50]Franklin v. White, 493 N.E.2d 161 (Ind. 1986).

For discussion of integration clauses, see § 97.

For discussion of parol evidence, see § 137.

[51]Ricketts v. Harvey, 106 Ind. 564, 6 N.E. 325 (1886); Stout v. Turner,

person charged is innocent.[52] A contract under which a prosecution is to be stifled upon the payment of compensation to the victim of the crime is void,[53] although there is no objection to a contract for the payment of compensation in return for a promise that the injured person will inform the court in the hope of mitigating punishment,[54] or to the giving of compensation merely in hope that a criminal prosecution may be avoided.[55]

> ◆ **Illustration:** A contract entered into between a father and two neighbors, whereby the neighbors agreed not to prosecute the father's son for vandalizing the neighbors' cars in return for the father's agreement to pay for the damages caused by his son, was unenforceable. The contract was contrary to public policy because it sought to interfere with the fair and efficient operation of the criminal justice system.[56]

§ 50 Contracts in restraint or derogation of marriage

Antenuptial contracts are not per se void as against public policy.

West's Digest, Contracts ⊖111.

Antenuptial agreements are legal contracts by which parties entering into a marriage relationship attempt to settle the interest of each in the property of the other during the course of the marriage and upon its termination by death or other means.[57] Although antenuptial contracts providing for support in the event of a couple's separation[58] and contracts between a husband and wife concerning the disposal of prop-

---

102 Ind. 418, 26 N.E. 85 (1885); Crowder v. Reed, 80 Ind. 1, 1881 WL 6853 (1881); Collier v. Waugh, 64 Ind. 456, 1878 WL 6485 (1878).

[52]Crowder v. Reed, 80 Ind. 1, 1881 WL 6853 (1881).

[53]Harrison Tp. v. Addison, 176 Ind. 389, 96 N.E. 146 (1911) (contract with prosecuting attorney); Budd v. Rutherford, 4 Ind. App. 386, 30 N.E. 1111 (1892).

[54]Kosiba v. Gary Wholesale Grocery Co., 91 Ind. App. 71, 170 N.E. 105 (1930).

[55]Wells v. Sutton, 85 Ind. 70, 1882 WL 6758 (1882).

[56]Hyman v. Davies, 453 N.E.2d 336 (Ind. Ct. App. 3d Dist. 1983).

[57]In re Marriage of Boren, 475 N.E.2d 690 (Ind. 1985); Russell v. Walz, 458 N.E.2d 1172 (Ind. Ct. App. 3d Dist. 1984).

[58]Watson v. Watson, 37 Ind. App. 548, 77 N.E. 355 (Div. 1 1906) (abrogation recognized by, Rider v. Rider, 669 N.E.2d 160 (Ind. 1996)).

erty subsequent to a divorce[59] were held in early cases to be void as being in derogation of marriage and thus contrary to public policy, today antenuptial agreements settling the property rights of the parties upon dissolution of marriage are not per se void as against public policy. Such agreements are valid and binding if they were entered into freely and without fraud, duress, or misrepresentation, and are not unconscionable under the particular circumstances of the case.[60] Antenuptial agreements, especially between spouses who have been married previously, facilitate marital stability by settling the parties' expectations and responsibilities.[61]

Generally, a promise to remain unmarried is considered to be against public policy and will not be enforced.[62]

§ 51 Contracts in restraint of trade

Contracts in general restraint of trade are void as against public policy.

West's Digest, Contracts ☞115-118.

A covenant in general restraint of trade is void as against public policy.[63] Contracts between persons who control the output of any article of merchandise which are intended to control the output or price of merchandise or to lessen full and free competition in the importation or sale of articles imported into the state are unlawful and void as against public policy.[64]

It is, however, permissible for a manufacturer or distribu-

---

[59]Muckenburg v. Holler, 29 Ind. 139, 1867 WL 3167 (1867); Wilson v. Fahnestock, 44 Ind. App. 35, 86 N.E. 1037 (Div. 2 1909); Frederick v. Sault, 19 Ind. App. 604, 49 N.E. 909 (1898).

[60]In re Marriage of Boren, 475 N.E.2d 690 (Ind. 1985); Justus v. Justus, 581 N.E.2d 1265 (Ind. Ct. App. 5th Dist. 1991), reh'g denied, (Jan. 29, 1992) and transfer denied, (May 29, 1992).

[61]In re Marriage of Boren, 475 N.E.2d 690 (Ind. 1985).

For further discussion of marital and premarital agreements, see I.L.E., Husband and Wife.

[62]Chalfant v. Payton, 91 Ind. 202, 1883 WL 6000 (1883); Stauffer v. Kessler, 81 Ind. App. 436, 130 N.E. 651 (Div. 1 1921).

[63]Fumo v. Medical Group of Michigan City, Inc., 590 N.E.2d 1103 (Ind. Ct. App. 3d Dist. 1992), reh'g denied, (June 23, 1992) and transfer denied, (Oct. 8, 1992); McCart v. H & R Block, Inc., 470 N.E.2d 756 (Ind. Ct. App. 3d Dist. 1984), reh'g denied, (Jan. 22, 1985) and transfer denied, (Apr. 24, 1985).

[64]IC 24-1-1-1, discussed in I.L.E., Monopolies and Unfair Trade.

tor to grant an exclusive agency in a specific area,[65] or for co-operative marketing associations to contract for the exclusive right to buy their members' products.[66]

A promise to pay a rebate is not in itself contrary to public policy,[67] although such promises are often prohibited by statute.[68]

§ 52 —Covenants not to compete

Covenants not to compete are disfavored, but will be enforced if they are reasonable.

West's Digest, Contracts ☞115-118.

Covenants not to compete are in restraint of trade and are not favored by law.[69] They are to be narrowly construed against the covenantee.[70] Nonetheless, if the restriction is reasonable as to the parties and the general public, it is en-

---

[65]Johnston v. Franklin Kirk Co., 83 Ind. App. 519, 148 N.E. 177 (Div. 1 1925) (contracts requiring automobile dealers selling in other dealers' territories to pay latter percentage of list price were not against public policy nor in restraint of trade).

[66]Burley Tobacco Growers' Co-op. Ass'n v. Rogers, 88 Ind. App. 469, 150 N.E. 384 (1926); Dark Tobacco Growers' Co-op. Ass'n v. Robertson, 84 Ind. App. 51, 150 N.E. 106 (1926); Burley Tobacco Soc. v. Gillaspy, 51 Ind. App. 583, 100 N.E. 89 (Div. 2 1912).

[67]Cleveland, C., C. & I. Ry. Co. v. Closser, 126 Ind. 348, 26 N.E. 159 (1890); Bessire & Co. v. Corn Products Mfg. Co., 47 Ind. App. 298, 94 N.E. 353 (Div. 1 1911).

[68]IC 8-1-2-106 (public utilities); IC 8-3-1-13 (common carriers); IC 27-1-20-30 (insurance premiums).

[69]Ackerman v. Kimball Intern., Inc., 652 N.E.2d 507 (Ind. 1995); Licocci v. Cardinal Associates, Inc., 445 N.E.2d 556 (Ind. 1983), appeal after remand, 492 N.E.2d 48 (Ind. Ct. App. 1st Dist. 1986), reh'g denied, (June 3, 1986) and transfer denied, (Oct. 21, 1986); McGlothen v. Heritage Environmental Services, L.L.C., 705 N.E.2d 1069 (Ind. Ct. App. 1999).

[70]Harvest Ins. Agency, Inc. v. Inter-Ocean Ins. Co., 492 N.E.2d 686 (Ind. 1986); Raymundo v. Hammond Clinic Ass'n, 449 N.E.2d 276 (Ind. 1983); Norlund v. Faust, 675 N.E.2d 1142 (Ind. Ct. App. 1997), decision clarified on denial of reh'g, 678 N.E.2d 421 (Ind. Ct. App. 1997) and transfer denied, 690 N.E.2d 1180 (Ind. 1997); Fogle v. Shah, 539 N.E.2d 500 (Ind. Ct. App. 4th Dist. 1989).

Annotation References: Enforceability of agreement restricting right of attorney to compete with former law firm, 28 ALR5th 420.

Enforceability, by purchaser or successor of business, of covenant not to compete entered into by predecessor and its employees, 12 ALR5th 847.

Enforceability of covenant against competition in accountant's employment contract, 15 ALR4th 559.

forceable and not void as against public policy.[71] Noncompetition agreements will be enforced where they meet the following test:[72]

- the restraint is reasonably necessary to protect the employer's interests

- it is not unreasonably restrictive of the employee

- the covenant is not antagonistic to the general public

The question of reasonableness is one of law for the court,[73] and it is to be determined by looking at all the facts and circumstances surrounding each case,[74] keeping in mind that persons should not be unnecessarily restricted in their freedom to contract.[75]

Indiana courts will not hesitate to strike down a restrictive covenant which is the least bit overly broad with respect to the protectible interest at stake. Where the underlying protectible interest is minimal, courts will closely scrutinize

---

Forms References: Noncompetition with former employer. 5A Am Jur Legal Forms, Contracts § 99:198.

[71]Ackerman v. Kimball Intern., Inc., 652 N.E.2d 507 (Ind. 1995); Norlund v. Faust, 675 N.E.2d 1142 (Ind. Ct. App. 1997), decision clarified on denial of reh'g, 678 N.E.2d 421 (Ind. Ct. App. 1997) and transfer denied, 690 N.E.2d 1180 (Ind. 1997); Fumo v. Medical Group of Michigan City, Inc., 590 N.E.2d 1103 (Ind. Ct. App. 3d Dist. 1992), reh'g denied, (June 23, 1992) and transfer denied, (Oct. 8, 1992).

[72]Ackerman v. Kimball Intern., Inc., 652 N.E.2d 507 (Ind. 1995); Donahue v. Permacel Tape Corp., 234 Ind. 398, 127 N.E.2d 235 (1955); McGlothen v. Heritage Environmental Services, L.L.C., 705 N.E.2d 1069 (Ind. Ct. App. 1999).

[73]Raymundo v. Hammond Clinic Ass'n, 449 N.E.2d 276 (Ind. 1983); Fumo v. Medical Group of Michigan City, Inc., 590 N.E.2d 1103 (Ind. Ct. App. 3d Dist. 1992), reh'g denied, (June 23, 1992) and transfer denied, (Oct. 8, 1992); Brunner v. Hand Industries, Inc., 603 N.E.2d 157 (Ind. Ct. App. 3d Dist. 1992).

[74]Raymundo v. Hammond Clinic Ass'n, 449 N.E.2d 276 (Ind. 1983); Fumo v. Medical Group of Michigan City, Inc., 590 N.E.2d 1103 (Ind. Ct. App. 3d Dist. 1992), reh'g denied, (June 23, 1992) and transfer denied, (Oct. 8, 1992) (totality of circumstances involves interrelationship of protectible interest, time, space, and proscribed activity); Frederick v. Professional Bldg. Maintenance Industries, Inc., 168 Ind. App. 647, 344 N.E.2d 299 (3d Dist. 1976).

[75]Fumo v. Medical Group of Michigan City, Inc., 590 N.E.2d 1103 (Ind. Ct. App. 3d Dist. 1992), reh'g denied, (June 23, 1992) and transfer denied, (Oct. 8, 1992).

the terms of the restraint.[76] The party seeking to enforce the covenant through the imposition of an injunction has the burden of demonstrating that the injunction is necessary to protect a legitimate business interest.[77]

A party to a covenant not to compete is generally either an employer and employee who agrees that the employee's competitive activities will be restricted after he or she leaves the employer, or the buyer and seller of a business who agree that the seller's competitive activities will be restricted after the sale.[78] The law looks with somewhat less disfavor on covenants involved in the sale of a business than it does employee covenants,[79] as parties involved in the sale and purchase of a business are more likely to have equal bargaining power and, where the sale involves the purchase of the business's good will, a broad noncompetition agreement may be necessary to assure that the buyer receives what he or she purchased.[80] However, while covenants involved in the sale of a business are not as ill-favored at law as are employee covenants, they are also subject to the test of reasonableness and will not be enforced where they are found to be unreasonable.[81] If the restraint is found to be greater

---

[76]Wagler Excavating Corp. v. McKibben Const., Inc., 679 N.E.2d 155 (Ind. Ct. App. 1997), transfer denied, 690 N.E.2d 1181 (Ind. 1997); Slisz v. Munzenreider Corp., 411 N.E.2d 700 (Ind. Ct. App. 4th Dist. 1980).

[77]Wagler Excavating Corp. v. McKibben Const., Inc., 679 N.E.2d 155 (Ind. Ct. App. 1997), transfer denied, 690 N.E.2d 1181 (Ind. 1997); Smart Corp. v. Grider, 650 N.E.2d 80 (Ind. Ct. App. 1st Dist. 1995), reh'g denied, (July 27, 1995) and transfer denied, (Apr. 17, 1996).

[78]Brunner v. Hand Industries, Inc., 603 N.E.2d 157 (Ind. Ct. App. 3d Dist. 1992); Seach v. Richards, Dieterle & Co., 439 N.E.2d 208 (Ind. Ct. App. 2d Dist. 1982).

Annotation References: Validity and construction of contractual restrictions on right of medical practitioner to practice, incident to sale of practice, 62 ALR3d 918.

Conflict of laws as to validity, enforceability, and effect of ancillary restrictive covenant not to compete, on contract of employment or for sale of business, 70 ALR2d 1292.

[79]Brunner v. Hand Industries, Inc., 603 N.E.2d 157 (Ind. Ct. App. 3d Dist. 1992); Seach v. Richards, Dieterle & Co., 439 N.E.2d 208 (Ind. Ct. App. 2d Dist. 1982).

[80]Fogle v. Shah, 539 N.E.2d 500 (Ind. Ct. App. 4th Dist. 1989).

[81]Young v. Van Zandt, 449 N.E.2d 300 (Ind. Ct. App. 1st Dist. 1983).

than necessary to protect the good will of the business, the contract is invalid.[82]

Employer-employee covenants not to compete are reviewed with stricter scrutiny than covenants not to compete ancillary to the sale of a business.[83] The determination of the reasonableness of the restraint focuses on the legitimate interests of the employer which might be protected and the protection granted by the covenant in terms of time, space and types of activity proscribed.[84] An employer seeking to enforce a restrictive covenant against a former employee must demonstrate special facts giving the former employee a unique competitive advantage, such as trade secrets or confidential information known to the employee, the employee's unique services, or the existence of a confidential relationship. An employer is not entitled to protection from the employee's use of knowledge, skill, or general information acquired during his or her employment with the employer.[85] Although the balance may be more likely to tip in favor of the employer where trade secrets are involved, the court must still determine whether the provisions of the covenant are reasonably necessary to protect the employer, not unreasonably restrictive of the employee, and not against public policy.[86]

Some employment cases have also discussed the requirement that a covenant not to compete be "ancillary to the main thrust of the contract."[87] "Ancillary," when used in this context, connotes an auxiliary, secondary, or supplemental,

---

[82]Young v. Van Zandt, 449 N.E.2d 300 (Ind. Ct. App. 1st Dist. 1983).

[83]Harvest Ins. Agency, Inc. v. Inter-Ocean Ins. Co., 492 N.E.2d 686 (Ind. 1986); Fogle v. Shah, 539 N.E.2d 500 (Ind. Ct. App. 4th Dist. 1989).

[84]Ackerman v. Kimball Intern., Inc., 652 N.E.2d 507 (Ind. 1995); 4408, Inc. v. Losure, 175 Ind. App. 658, 373 N.E.2d 899 (3d Dist. 1978).

[85]Licocci v. Cardinal Associates, Inc., 445 N.E.2d 556 (Ind. 1983), appeal after remand, 492 N.E.2d 48 (Ind. Ct. App. 1st Dist. 1986), reh'g denied, (June 3, 1986) and transfer denied, (Oct. 21, 1986); McGlothen v. Heritage Environmental Services, L.L.C., 705 N.E.2d 1069 (Ind. Ct. App. 1999).

[86]Ackerman v. Kimball Intern., Inc., 652 N.E.2d 507 (Ind. 1995).

[87]Woodward Ins., Inc. v. White, 437 N.E.2d 59 (Ind. 1982); Milgram v. Milgram, 105 Ind. App. 57, 12 N.E.2d 394 (1938).

as compared to the primary, purpose of the contract.[88] The Seventh Circuit has speculated that this requirement exists because a covenant which is merely part of a larger employment agreement is less likely to be abused than one which simply eliminates a competitor.[89]

Assuming that the terms of a covenant not to compete between an employer and employee are reasonable, the covenant is enforceable where the employee voluntarily leaves the employment and where the employee is discharged for cause.[90] When the employee is discharged in bad faith, equitable defenses such as clean hands will apply to bar enforcement of the covenant.[91]

A third type of covenant not to compete, which appears less frequently than covenants by employees and sellers of businesses, is that between the lessor and lessee of real property. Although, as with the other types of noncompetition agreements, a lessee's covenant not to engage in certain commercial activities in which the lessor is already engaged creates a limited monopoly and, as such, is a restraint of trade,[92] such a covenant will be enforced and injunctive relief will be extended to prevent the breach if the restraint is reasonable with respect to the parties involved and the public interest.[93]

Covenants not to compete which restrict medical services in a particular area are not void, per se, as against public policy,[94] although some Indiana judges have expressed the belief that physicians, like firefighters and police officers,

---

[88]JAK Productions, Inc. v. Wiza, 986 F.2d 1080 (7th Cir. 1993) (applying Indiana law).

[89]JAK Productions, Inc. v. Wiza, 986 F.2d 1080 (7th Cir. 1993) (applying Indiana law).

[90]Gomez v. Chua Medical Corp., 510 N.E.2d 191 (Ind. Ct. App. 3d Dist. 1987), reh'g denied, (Oct. 15, 1987).

[91]Gomez v. Chua Medical Corp., 510 N.E.2d 191 (Ind. Ct. App. 3d Dist. 1987), reh'g denied, (Oct. 15, 1987).

[92]Howard D. Johnson Co. v. Parkside Development Corp., 169 Ind. App. 379, 348 N.E.2d 656 (1st Dist. 1976).

[93]Grand Union Tea Co. v. Walker, 208 Ind. 245, 195 N.E. 277, 98 A.L.R. 958 (1935); Unishops, Inc. v. May's Family Centers, Inc., 399 N.E.2d 760 (Ind. Ct. App. 3d Dist. 1980).

[94]Raymundo v. Hammond Clinic Ass'n, 449 N.E.2d 276 (Ind. 1983); Medical Specialists, Inc. v. Sleweon, 652 N.E.2d 517 (Ind. Ct. App. 1995), transfer denied, (Sept. 28, 1995); Fumo v. Medical Group of Michigan City, Inc., 590 N.E.2d 1103 (Ind. Ct. App. 3d Dist. 1992), reh'g denied, (June 23, 1992) and transfer denied, (Oct. 8, 1992).

provide necessary services of which the public should not be deprived through a covenant not to compete.[95] Because of the importance of upholding individuals' freedom to contract, a physician's agreement not to compete is to be treated no differently than that of any other business or professional person.[96]

> ◆ **Illustration:** An anticompetition covenant in a physician's contract was not against public policy insofar as its 25-mile radius encompassed hospitals other than those at which the medical group members practiced and the prohibition extended to a medical specialty not practiced by any group member.[97]

§ 53 Agreements harmful to public service

A contract made to influence a public official's exercise of his or her duties is void as against public policy.

West's Digest, Contracts ☞123.

An agreement or contract made by an individual with a public official for the purpose of influencing the official's exercise of his or her discretion as to matters in connection with his or her public duties,[98] or which has a tendency to

---

[95]Gomez v. Chua Medical Corp., 510 N.E.2d 191 (Ind. Ct. App. 3d Dist. 1987), reh'g denied, (Oct. 15, 1987).

Annotation References: Validity and construction of contractual restrictions on right of medical practitioner to practice, incident to partnership agreement, 62 ALR3d 970.

[96]Raymundo v. Hammond Clinic Ass'n, 449 N.E.2d 276 (Ind. 1983); Norlund v. Faust, 675 N.E.2d 1142 (Ind. Ct. App. 1997), decision clarified on denial of reh'g, 678 N.E.2d 421 (Ind. Ct. App. 1997) and transfer denied, 690 N.E.2d 1180 (Ind. 1997); Medical Specialists, Inc. v. Sleweon, 652 N.E.2d 517 (Ind. Ct. App. 1995), transfer denied, (Sept. 28, 1995) (covenant which barred physician from competing with medical group for two years within 10 miles of 10 hospitals at which group rendered services was reasonable and enforceable, as group's continued success was worthy of protection, practice had been damaged by physician's competition, and there was no shortage of doctors specializing in defendant's field).

[97]Fumo v. Medical Group of Michigan City, Inc., 590 N.E.2d 1103 (Ind. Ct. App. 3d Dist. 1992), reh'g denied, (June 23, 1992) and transfer denied, (Oct. 8, 1992).

[98]Pippenger v. City of Mishawaka, 119 Ind. App. 397, 88 N.E.2d 168 (1949).

lessen the officer's performance of a public duty,[99] is void as against public policy. There is, however, no objection to a public officer's acquiring a valid claim against the public treasury, if this does not tend to affect his or her official conduct.[1]

Although an unsuccessful bidder on a nongovernmental project for which competitive bids are sought has no common-law cause of action against the party soliciting the bids if another bidder is chosen,[2] an unsuccessful bidder on a private project does have a cause of action if fraud or collusion is alleged.[3] Moreover, a public official's agreement to accept a bribe is a felony offense,[4] and a private citizen who offers a bribe to a public official may be prosecuted for conspiracy to commit bribery.[5] A contract tending to influence an officer's discretion may be held illegal even though the consideration inures to the benefit of the public, rather than to that of the officer.[6]

It is illegal for a public service corporation to enter into a contract which interferes with, or tends to interfere with, the performance of its duties to the public.[7] Such a corporation is, of course, free to contract with respect to matters which affect only the contracting parties,[8] and may enter a contract for the life-long employment of a person, so long as

---

[99]Cheney v. Unroe, 166 Ind. 550, 77 N.E. 1041 (1906).

[1]Watkins v. State ex rel. Van Auken, 151 Ind. 123, 49 N.E. 169 (1898), reh'g denied, 151 Ind. 123, 51 N.E. 79 (1898); Smiley v. State, 60 Ind. App. 507, 110 N.E. 222 (Div. 2 1915).

[2]Shook Heavy and Environmental Const. Group, a Div. of Shook, Inc. v. City of Kokomo, 632 N.E.2d 355 (Ind. 1994).

[3]IC 24-1-2-7.

Shook Heavy and Environmental Const. Group, a Div. of Shook, Inc. v. City of Kokomo, 632 N.E.2d 355 (Ind. 1994).

[4]IC 35-44-1-1(a)(2).

[5]Sawyer v. State, 583 N.E.2d 795 (Ind. Ct. App. 2d Dist. 1991).

For discussion of contracts made in violation of statute, see § 45.

For discussion of bribery as a criminal offense, see I.L.E., Bribery.

[6]Pippenger v. City of Mishawaka, 119 Ind. App. 397, 88 N.E.2d 168 (1949).

[7]Niederhaus v. Jackson, 79 Ind. App. 551, 137 N.E. 623 (Div. 2 1922).

[8]Niederhaus v. Jackson, 79 Ind. App. 551, 137 N.E. 623 (Div. 2 1922).

his or her employment does not impair the corporation's efficiency.[9]

Lobbying is not illegal, although it is closely regulated.[10] A contract providing for the payment of a fee contingent upon a lobbyist's obtaining of favorable legislative action, through improper means, is void.[11] Contracts providing for a fee contingent upon a person's procuring for another a government contract are also void.[12]

A contract to restrain or restrict bidding for the award of a contract for public or private work, or restricting free competition in such bidding, constitutes a Class A misdemeanor.[13]

§ 54 —Public offices and emoluments

A contract for the sale of public office is unenforceable.

West's Digest, Contracts ⟜124, 125.

The sale of public offices is against public policy and illegal.[14] A contract for the sale of a public office is unenforceable whether it is made by the occupant of the office,[15] an officer with the power of appointment,[16] or a candidate for an office which carries the power of appointment.[17]

The courts will not enforce an agreement to assign the salary of a public officer before it is earned,[18] and have refused to enforce a contract whereby a constable was to contribute a portion of his fee toward the maintenance of a justice's court.[19] On the other hand, no objection has been found to a contract whereby a person appointed as postmaster agreed to pay half of his salary in this office to another, who was

---

[9]Cox v. Baltimore & O.S.W.R. Co., 180 Ind. 495, 103 N.E. 337 (1913); Pennsylvania Co. v. Dolan, 6 Ind. App. 109, 32 N.E. 802 (1892).

[10]IC 2-7-1-1 et seq.

[11]Coquillard's Adm'r v. Bearss, 21 Ind. 479, 1863 WL 2086 (1863).

[12]Hardesty v. Dodge Mfg. Co., 89 Ind. App. 184, 154 N.E. 697 (1927).

[13]IC 24-1-2-3.

[14]Hall v. Gavitt, 18 Ind. 390, 1862 WL 2252 (1862).

[15]Hall v. Gavitt, 18 Ind. 390, 1862 WL 2252 (1862) (sheriff).

[16]Board of Com'rs of Johnson County v. Mullikin, 7 Blackf. 301, 1844 WL 3020 (Ind. 1844).

[17]Conner v. Canter, 15 Ind. App. 690, 44 N.E. 656 (1896).

[18]Moynihan v. Rockhill, 62 Ind. App. 685, 113 N.E. 734 (Div. 1 1916).

[19]American Surety Co. v. State ex rel. Taber, 102 Ind. App. 378, 1 N.E.2d 295 (1936).

jointly interested with him in a corporation and who agreed to perform the duties of both with respect to the corporation, since in this case the postmaster's salary was merely the measure, not the source, of the payment.[20]

A public officer may contract to accept additional part-time work beyond his or her public duties for additional compensation,[21] but such a contract is void if it would tend to influence the official's judgment in the performance of his or her official duties.[22]

§ 55 Particular contracts

Various contract provisions have been held unenforceable as against public policy; others have been upheld.

West's Digest, Contracts ⊙108(2).

Courts have held the following types of contracts void or voidable as against public policy:

- a lease for an apartment with no occupancy permit, in violation of a municipal ordinance, where the tenants never entered into possession of the apartment and thus did not benefit from the lease[23]
- a life insurance policy issued on a life in which the beneficiary has no insurable interest, without the insured's knowledge[24]
- a contract for a real estate commission, because one of the partners of the real estate company acting as broker was not a licensed real estate broker, as statutorily required for the partnership to have a valid real estate license[25]
- a lease for an apartment with no occupancy permit, in violation of a municipal ordinance, where the tenants

---

[20]Moynihan v. Rockhill, 62 Ind. App. 685, 113 N.E. 734 (Div. 1 1916).

[21]Wurster v. State, 708 N.E.2d 587 (Ind. Ct. App. 1999), transfer granted, (July 28, 1999), and opinion aff'd, 715 N.E.2d 341 (Ind. 1999), reh'g denied, (Sept. 28, 1999).

[22]Williams v. Segur, 106 Ind. 368, 1 N.E. 707 (1885).

[23]Noble v. Alis, 474 N.E.2d 109 (Ind. Ct. App. 1st Dist. 1985), reh'g denied, (Mar. 25, 1985) and transfer denied, (June 27, 1985).

[24]American Mut. Life Ins. Co. v. Bertram, 163 Ind. 51, 70 N.E. 258 (1904).

[25]Hoffman v. Dunn, 496 N.E.2d 818 (Ind. Ct. App. 4th Dist. 1986) (under IC 25-34.1-3-2, requiring persons buying, selling, or performing other acts with regard to Indiana real estate to be licensed brokers; contract void).

never entered into possession of the apartment and thus did not benefit from the lease[26]

- an agreement under which a man agreed to impregnate a woman in return for her promise not to seek child support from him[27]

- an agreement to accept less than the statutorily mandated hourly wage for work on a public works project[28]

- a referral fee agreement between an attorney and a non-attorney employee[29]

- a forfeiture provision in a contract for the conditional sale of real property, which allowed the seller to seek forfeiture of the property, rather than foreclosure, if the buyer defaulted before paying 75% of the purchase price[30]

The following types of contracts have been held not to violate public policy:

- an exculpatory clause limiting a yellow pages publisher's liability to the lesser of the amount paid for the advertising or the contract price[31]

- an antenuptial agreement between a couple in their fifties which provided that, in the event of their divorce, the husband would make no claim to the wife's estate and the wife would seek no more than $5,000 from the husband, even though the husband refused to set a date for the wedding until the agreement was signed[32]

- a clause in a liability insurance policy issued to a health maintenance organization (HMO) which ex-

---

[26]Noble v. Alis, 474 N.E.2d 109 (Ind. Ct. App. 1st Dist. 1985), reh'g denied, (Mar. 25, 1985) and transfer denied, (June 27, 1985)

[27]Straub v. B.M.T. by Todd, 645 N.E.2d 597 (Ind. 1994), reh'g denied, (Apr. 12, 1995) (holding that right to support lies exclusively with child).

[28]Stampco Const. Co., Inc. v. Guffey, 572 N.E.2d 510 (Ind. Ct. App. 1st Dist. 1991).

[29]Prof. Cond. R. 7.3(f).

Trotter v. Nelson, 684 N.E.2d 1150 (Ind. 1997).

[30]Parker v. Camp, 656 N.E.2d 882 (Ind. Ct. App. 1995).

[31]Trimble v. Ameritech Pub., Inc., 700 N.E.2d 1128 (Ind. 1998); Pinnacle Computer Services, Inc. v. Ameritech Pub., Inc., 642 N.E.2d 1011 (Ind. Ct. App. 1st Dist. 1994), reh'g denied, (Feb. 23, 1995).

[32]In re Marriage of Boren, 475 N.E.2d 690 (Ind. 1985).

cluded claims involving the insolvency or liquidation of the HMO[33]

- a financial institution bond issued to an insurance company which terminated immediately upon the company's takeover by a receiver or other liquidator or by state or federal officials did not violate public policy[34]

- a "household exclusion" clause in an automobile liability policy, excluding coverage for any injury to a person related to the insured by blood, marriage, or adoption[35]

- a contract for the construction of a building, despite the contractors' failure to obtain a building permit[36]

A building owner and a tenant may contract to shift the owner's responsibility, imposed by municipal ordinance, to maintain the building's safety features to the tenant.[37] An agreement between an architect and his or her employer to produce building plans that do not conform to a municipal ordinance is not necessarily violative of public policy, as long as the public is not endangered by the nonconformity.[38]

B.   EFFECT OF ILLEGALITY

Research References
IC 24-1-2-1; IC 24-1-2-3
11 U.S.C.A. § 1129

17A Am Jur 2d, Contracts §§ 304-335.
17A C.J.S., Contracts §§ 280-301.
West's Digest, Contracts ☞135-140.
ALR Digest: Contracts §§ 269-441.5

---

[33]Lexington Ins. Co. v. American Healthcare Providers, 621 N.E.2d 332 (Ind. Ct. App. 2d Dist. 1993), transfer denied, (Mar. 3, 1994).

[34]Mutual Sec. Life Ins. Co. by Bennett v. Fidelity and Deposit Co. of Maryland, 659 N.E.2d 1096 (Ind. Ct. App. 1995), transfer denied (Ind. May 17, 1996).

[35]Allstate Ins. Co. v. Boles, 481 N.E.2d 1096 (Ind. 1985).

[36]Drost v. Professional Bldg. Service Corp., 153 Ind. App. 273, 286 N.E.2d 846 (3d Dist. 1972).

[37]Fresh Cut, Inc. v. Fazli, 650 N.E.2d 1126 (Ind. 1995).

[38]Greenhaven Corp. v. Hutchcraft & Associates, Inc., 463 N.E.2d 283 (Ind. Ct. App. 2d Dist. 1984) (agreement to have only one remote fire exit, rather than two as required by fire code, was not against public policy, as fire marshall would have to find building safe for public use before it could be lawfully occupied).

ALR Index: Adhesion Contracts; Anticipatory Breach; Anticipatory Renunciation or Repudiation; Bids and Bidding; Cancellation of Rescission; Consideration; Contracts; Covenants; Covenants Not to Compete; Estoppel and Waiver; Executory Contracts; Implied Contracts; Offer and Acceptance; Parol Contracts and Agreements; Parol Evidence; Third-Party Beneficiaries; Unconscionability

§ 56   Generally

Although a court will generally not enforce an illegal contract, it may do so when it would be unconscionable not to, where the illegality does not involve moral turpitude, or where the rule of law making the contract illegal is intended for the protection of the plaintiff.

West's Digest, Contracts ⬅136.

Generally, a court will leave the parties to an illegal contract where it finds them,[39] and will not help one party recover benefits the other has realized from the contract.[40] That is, a court will not enforce an illegal contract, so that such a contract may not be sued upon[41] or illegality employed as a defense to it,[42] at least if the parties are equally guilty.[43] Under the doctrine of in pari delicto, a plaintiff who has cooperated with a defendant in violating a statute will be denied relief.[44]

---

[39]Harrison Tp. v. Addison, 176 Ind. 389, 96 N.E. 146 (1911); Michener v. Watts, 176 Ind. 376, 96 N.E. 127 (1911); Van Orman Fort Wayne Corp. v. Edwards Motor Co., 148 Ind. App. 66, 263 N.E.2d 746 (Div. 1 1970).

[40]Harrison Tp. v. Addison, 176 Ind. 389, 96 N.E. 146 (1911); Michener v. Watts, 176 Ind. 376, 96 N.E. 127 (1911).

[41]Harbour v. Arelco, Inc., 678 N.E.2d 381 (Ind. 1997); Noble v. Davison, 177 Ind. 19, 96 N.E. 325 (1911).

[42]Hancock v. Yaden, 121 Ind. 366, 23 N.E. 253 (1890).

[43]Dumont v. Dufore, 27 Ind. 263, 1866 WL 2553 (1866); Swain v. Bussell, 10 Ind. 438, 1858 WL 4058 (1858); American Mut. Life Ins. Co. v. Mead, 39 Ind. App. 215, 79 N.E. 526 (Div. 1 1906).

[44]Gilchrist v. Hatch, 183 Ind. 371, 106 N.E. 694 (1914); Dan Purvis Drugs, Inc. v. Aetna Life Ins. Co., 412 N.E.2d 129 (Ind. Ct. App. 3d Dist. 1980) (plaintiff and defendant entered into contract in restraint of trade); Bizik v. Bizik, 124 Ind. App. 146, 111 N.E.2d 823 (1953), reh'g denied, 124 Ind. App. 146, 112 N.E.2d 760 (1953) and transfer denied, 232 Ind. 617, 115 N.E.2d 503 (1953).

However, a contract may be enforced even if it violates a statute, and even if both parties participated in the violation, where it would be unconscionable not to do so.[45]

◆ **Illustration:** A solvent business instructed an individual party to buy stock in a bankrupt business it was interested in purchasing, and agreed to reimburse the individual for his funds spent on that purchase. It later instructed him to use his own money to keep the bankrupt business operating while the purchase of the bankrupt business was being negotiated, and agreed to reimburse him for that expenditure. The bankruptcy court approved the sale of the business, but was not informed of the arrangement between the solvent business and the third party, in violation of the Bankruptcy Code.[46] Under these circumstances, it would be unconscionable to allow the solvent business to avoid its obligations to the individual.[47]

An illegal contract may also be enforced where the violation of a statute making the contract illegal did not involve moral turpitude. Under such circumstances, a party who has parted with money or property under the contract may recover the money or property.[48]

If the rule rendering a certain contract is illegal is intended to protect of one of the parties against an undue advantage supposedly enjoyed by the other party, the protected party may choose to enforce the contract.[49] Thus,

---

[45]Tolliver v. Mathas, 538 N.E.2d 971 (Ind. Ct. App. 4th Dist. 1989), reh'g denied, (July 10, 1989) and transfer denied, (Jan. 10, 1990); Bizik v. Bizik, 124 Ind. App. 146, 111 N.E.2d 823 (1953), reh'g denied, 124 Ind. App. 146, 112 N.E.2d 760 (1953) and transfer denied, 232 Ind. 617, 115 N.E.2d 503 (1953).

For a discussion of the enforceability of a contract which violates a statute, see § 45.

[46]11 U.S.C.A. § 1129(a)(4).

[47]Tolliver v. Mathas, 538 N.E.2d 971 (Ind. Ct. App. 4th Dist. 1989), reh'g denied, (July 10, 1989) and transfer denied, (Jan. 10, 1990).

[48]Zorich v. Zorich, 119 Ind. App. 547, 88 N.E.2d 694 (1949) (although postal savings law permitted individual to have only one account not to exceed $2500, children's oral agreement to hold postal savings certificates in trust for father, who purchased them, did not involve moral turpitude, and father would be allowed to recover money from children).

[49]Scotten v. State, 51 Ind. 52, 1875 WL 5859 (1875); Deming v. State ex rel. Miller, 23 Ind. 416, 1864 WL 2024 (1864).

an employee who contracts to work for less than a statutory minimum wage may recover for his or her work.[50]

Only the parties to a contract may question its legality.[51]

A valid contract is not destroyed or affected by an attempt to execute an invalid contract in its stead.[52]

> ◆ **Observation:** Criminal penalties are available for certain illegal contracts. For instance, a contract to create or carry out restrictions in trade or commerce,[53] or a contract to restrict bidding for the award of a public or private contract[54] is a Class A misdemeanor.

§ 57 Partial illegality

> **If the legal and illegal portions of a contract are severable, a court will enforce the legal portion of the contract.**

West's Digest, Contracts ☜137(1)-137(4).

Generally, a contract made in violation of a statute is void. However, if a contract contains an illegal provision which can be eliminated without frustrating the basic purpose of the contract, the court will enforce the remainder of the contract.[55] If the contract is clearly separated into parts, some of which are enforceable and others of which are not, the contract may be held to be divisible. The proper provi-

---

[50]Stampco Const. Co., Inc. v. Guffey, 572 N.E.2d 510 (Ind. Ct. App. 1st Dist. 1991); City School Corporation of Evansville v. Hickman, 47 Ind. App. 500, 94 N.E. 828 (Div. 2 1911).

[51]Stolz-Wicks, Inc. v. Commercial Television Service Co., 271 F.2d 586 (7th Cir. 1959) (applying Indiana law); Woodruff v. Board of Com'rs of Noble County, 10 Ind. App. 179, 37 N.E. 732 (1894).

[52]Walter v. Balogh, 619 N.E.2d 566 (Ind. 1993) (1984 agreement reinstated where agreement contracted in 1985, which was intended to supersede 1984 agreement, was illegal and unenforceable); Foster v. United Home Imp. Co., Inc., 428 N.E.2d 1351 (Ind. Ct. App. 4th Dist. 1981).

[53]IC 24-1-2-1.

[54]IC 24-1-2-3.

[55]Harbour v. Arelco, Inc., 678 N.E.2d 381 (Ind. 1997) (inclusion of attorney fee provision in car rental agreement, although contrary to statute, did not by itself render entire contract invalid); Corner v. Mills, 650 N.E.2d 712 (Ind. Ct. App. 1995); Brokaw v. Brokaw, 398 N.E.2d 1385 (Ind. Ct. App. 3d Dist. 1980); Crescent City Aviation, Inc. v. Beverly Bank, 139 Ind. App. 669, 219 N.E.2d 446 (Div. 1 1966).

sions may be enforced, and the improper ones stricken.[56] This is known as the "blue pencil" doctrine.[57]

If the contract cannot be separated into enforceable and unenforceable parts, the entire contract will be unenforceable.[58]

> ◆ **Illustration:** Although a prohibition in a covenant not to compete against a former employee's contacting, soliciting or working for past and prospective clients who may have dealt with the employer at any time in the past was too broad and too vague to be enforceable, a prohibition in the same covenant applicable to present clients of the employer was reasonable and would be enforced.[59]

Although a court will not enforce a provision which violates public policy, it will not rewrite the provision so as to make it legal. If a covenant not to compete as written is not reasonable, for instance, a court may not create and enforce a reasonable restriction, since doing so would subject the parties to agreement they have not made. Thus, a court blue penciling a contract is restricted to applying terms which already clearly exist in the contract.[60] The court may not, under

---

[56]Licocci v. Cardinal Associates, Inc., 445 N.E.2d 556 (Ind. 1983), appeal after remand, 492 N.E.2d 48 (Ind. Ct. App. 1st Dist. 1986), reh'g denied, (June 3, 1986) and transfer denied, (Oct. 21, 1986); Smart Corp. v. Grider, 650 N.E.2d 80 (Ind. Ct. App. 1st Dist. 1995), reh'g denied, (July 27, 1995) and transfer denied, (Apr. 17, 1996) (overbroad geographic restriction redacted from covenant not to compete); Hahn v. Drees, Perugini & Co., 581 N.E.2d 457 (Ind. Ct. App. 2d Dist. 1991).

[57]Smart Corp. v. Grider, 650 N.E.2d 80 (Ind. Ct. App. 1st Dist. 1995), reh'g denied, (July 27, 1995) and transfer denied, (Apr. 17, 1996); JAK Productions, Inc. v. Wiza, 986 F.2d 1080 (7th Cir. 1993) (applying Indiana law).

[58]Young v. Van Zandt, 449 N.E.2d 300 (Ind. Ct. App. 1st Dist. 1983) (covenant which prohibited seller of business from engaging "in any activity or enterprise" in competition with business did not contain any language which could be stricken in order to make it enforceable); Seach v. Richards, Dieterle & Co., 439 N.E.2d 208 (Ind. Ct. App. 2d Dist. 1982); Bridgestone/Firestone, Inc. v. Lockhart, 5 F. Supp. 2d 667 (S.D. Ind. 1998) (applying Indiana law).

[59]Seach v. Richards, Dieterle & Co., 439 N.E.2d 208 (Ind. Ct. App. 2d Dist. 1982).

[60]Smart Corp. v. Grider, 650 N.E.2d 80 (Ind. Ct. App. 1st Dist. 1995), reh'g denied, (July 27, 1995) and transfer denied, (Apr. 17, 1996).

the guise of interpreting the contract, add terms that were not originally part of the contract.[61]

If an entire contract is based on several considerations, one of which is illegal, the contract is unenforceable.[62] The illegal part of the consideration vitiates the entire contract and renders it unenforceable.[63]

VII. GENERAL RULES OF CONSTRUCTION

Research References

17A Am Jur 2d, Contracts §§ 336-413.
17A C.J.S., Contracts §§ 302-345.
West's Digest, Contracts ☞143-176.
ALR Digest: Contracts §§ 201-268
ALR Index: Adhesion Contracts; Anticipatory Breach; Anticipatory Renunciation or Repudiation; Bids and Bidding; Cancellation of Rescission; Consideration; Contracts; Covenants; Covenants Not to Compete; Estoppel and Waiver; Executory Contracts; Implied Contracts; Offer and Acceptance; Parol Contracts and Agreements; Parol Evidence; Third-Party Beneficiaries; Unconscionability
5A Am Jur Legal Forms 2d, Contracts § 68:241.

§ 58 Generally

A court will not construe an unambiguous contract, but will merely apply it as written.

West's Digest, Contracts ☞143(1)-143(4).

The interpretation of a contract is controlled by the intention of the parties as expressed by the clear language of the contract,[64] as long as that intent is consistent with law and

---

[61]Licocci v. Cardinal Associates, Inc., 445 N.E.2d 556 (Ind. 1983), appeal after remand, 492 N.E.2d 48 (Ind. Ct. App. 1st Dist. 1986), reh'g denied, (June 3, 1986) and transfer denied, (Oct. 21, 1986); Hahn v. Drees, Perugini & Co., 581 N.E.2d 457 (Ind. Ct. App. 2d Dist. 1991); Young v. Van Zandt, 449 N.E.2d 300 (Ind. Ct. App. 1st Dist. 1983).

[62]Baltimore & O.S.W.R. Co. v. Hagan, 183 Ind. 522, 109 N.E. 194 (1915); Ricketts v. Harvey, 106 Ind. 564, 6 N.E. 325 (1886); McClain's Estate v. McClain, 133 Ind. App. 645, 183 N.E.2d 842 (Div. 1 1962), reh'g dismissed, 133 Ind. App. 645, 184 N.E.2d 281 (Div. 1 1962).

[63]McClain's Estate v. McClain, 133 Ind. App. 645, 183 N.E.2d 842 (Div. 1 1962), reh'g dismissed, 133 Ind. App. 645, 184 N.E.2d 281 (Div. 1 1962).

[64]First Federal Sav. Bank of Indiana v. Key Markets, Inc., 559 N.E.2d

public policy.[65] Where no defect is alleged to have occurred in
the formation of the contract,[66] such as fraud, mistake,
illegality, duress, or undue influence,[67] clear, plain, and
unambiguous terms used in the contract are conclusive of
the parties' intent,[68] and a court will not construe the
contract or consider extrinsic evidence, but will merely apply
the contractual provisions as they are written.[69]

Ambiguity in a contract can be either patent or latent. A
patent ambiguity is one apparent on the face of the contract.
It arises from the inconsistency or inherent uncertainty of
the language used so that it conveys either no definite meaning or a confused meaning. A latent ambiguity is one which
does not become apparent until one attempts to implement

600 (Ind. 1990); Hyperbaric Oxygen Therapy Systems, Inc. v. St. Joseph
Modical Center of Ft. Wayne, Inc., 683 N.E.2d 243 (Ind. Ct. App. 1997),
transfer denied, 690 N.E.2d 1189 (Ind. 1997); City of Evansville v. Braun,
619 N.E.2d 956 (Ind. Ct. App. 1st Dist. 1993), appeal after remand, 677
N.E.2d 597 (Ind. Ct. App. 1997), transfer denied, 690 N.E.2d 1180 (Ind.
1997).

[65]George S. May Intern. Co. v. King, 629 N.E.2d 257 (Ind. Ct. App. 1st
Dist. 1994), reh'g denied, (May 11, 1994) and transfer denied, (Sept. 2,
1994).

For discussion of contracts which are illegal or contravene public
policy, see §§ 43 et seq.

[66]Whiteco Industries, Inc. v. Nickolick, 571 N.E.2d 1337 (Ind. Ct. App.
1st Dist. 1991), transfer denied, (Dec. 12, 1991); Slutsky-Peltz Plumbing &
Heating Co., Inc. v. Vincennes Community School Corp., 556 N.E.2d 344,
61 Ed. Law Rep. 263 (Ind. Ct. App. 1st Dist. 1990); THQ Venture v. SW,
Inc., 444 N.E.2d 335 (Ind. Ct. App. 1st Dist. 1983); Piskorowski v. Shell
Oil Co., 403 N.E.2d 838 (Ind. Ct. App. 3d Dist. 1980).

[67]Ethyl Corp. v. Forcum-Lannom Associates, Inc., 433 N.E.2d 1214
(Ind. Ct. App. 4th Dist. 1982); Lippeatt v. Comet Coal and Clay Co., Inc.,
419 N.E.2d 1332 (Ind. Ct. App. 1st Dist. 1981).

As to matters such as fraud, mistake, and duress, see §§ 31 et seq.

As to illegal contracts, see §§ 43 et seq.

[68]Kiltz v. Kiltz, 708 N.E.2d 600 (Ind. Ct. App. 1999), transfer denied,
(Aug. 27, 1999); Dvorak v. Christ, 692 N.E.2d 920 (Ind. Ct. App. 1998),
reh'g denied, (May 27, 1998) and transfer denied, 706 N.E.2d 171 (Ind.
1998); Hyperbaric Oxygen Therapy Systems, Inc. v. St. Joseph Medical
Center of Ft. Wayne, Inc., 683 N.E.2d 243 (Ind. Ct. App. 1997), transfer
denied, 690 N.E.2d 1189 (Ind. 1997).

[69]Kiltz v. Kiltz, 708 N.E.2d 600 (Ind. Ct. App. 1999), transfer denied,
(Aug. 27, 1999); Indiana Port Com'n v. Consolidated Grain and Barge Co.,
701 N.E.2d 882 (Ind. Ct. App. 1998), transfer denied, 714 N.E.2d 172 (Ind.
1999); Grand Trunk Western R. Co. v. Kapitan, 698 N.E.2d 363 (Ind. Ct.
App. 1998), transfer denied, 714 N.E.2d 163 (Ind. 1999).

the language as directed in the contract.[70] Extrinsic evidence is admissible to explain a latent ambiguity, but not a patent one.[71]

If the meaning of contract terms cannot be sufficiently discerned because language necessary to determine the contract's meaning has not been presented to the court, the contract may be deemed ambiguous, which would require the submission of extrinsic evidence.[72]

The meaning of a contract is clear if a reasonable interpretation of the language used expresses an intention,[73] even if another possible intention could be gathered from the language, if the other intention must be discerned through forced construction, circuitous reasoning, or speculation.[74] The terms of a contract are not ambiguous merely because the parties disagree concerning the proper interpretation of the terms.[75] A contract is ambiguous only if it is susceptible to more than one interpretation,[76] so that reasonably intelligent people could come to different conclusions as to its

---

[70]Eckart v. Davis, 631 N.E.2d 494 (Ind. Ct. App. 1st Dist. 1994).

[71]First Federal Sav. Bank of Indiana v. Key Markets, Inc., 559 N.E.2d 600 (Ind. 1990); Eckart v. Davis, 631 N.E.2d 494 (Ind. Ct. App. 1st Dist. 1994).

[72]Collins v. J.A. House, Inc., 705 N.E.2d 568 (Ind. Ct. App. 1999), reh'g denied, (Mar. 26, 1999) and transfer denied, (Aug. 26, 1999).

[73]Bressler v. Bressler, 601 N.E.2d 392 (Ind. Ct. App. 3d Dist. 1992).

[74]DeBoer v. DeBoer, 669 N.E.2d 415 (Ind. Ct. App. 1996), transfer denied, (Dec. 31, 1996) and (disapproved of on other grounds by, Merritt v. Merritt, 693 N.E.2d 1320 (Ind. Ct. App. 1998)) (where couple's separation agreement specified that payments to wife were to be alimony, and could not be altered by court, court would not accept husband's contention that payments were characterized as alimony only for tax purposes); Bressler v. Bressler, 601 N.E.2d 392 (Ind. Ct. App. 3d Dist. 1992).

[75]Kiltz v. Kiltz, 708 N.E.2d 600 (Ind. Ct. App. 1999), transfer denied, (Aug. 27, 1999); Tanton v. Grochow, 707 N.E.2d 1010 (Ind. Ct. App. 1999); Wright v. State, 700 N.E.2d 1153 (Ind. Ct. App. 1998); Jones v. Western Reserve Group/Lightning Rod Mut. Ins. Co., 699 N.E.2d 711 (Ind. Ct. App. 1998), reh'g denied, (Oct. 16, 1998) and transfer denied, 714 N.E.2d 169 (Ind. 1999).

[76]Jones v. Western Reserve Group/Lightning Rod Mut. Ins. Co., 699 N.E.2d 711 (Ind. Ct. App. 1998), reh'g denied, (Oct. 16, 1998) and transfer denied, 714 N.E.2d 169 (Ind. 1999); Bastin v. First Indiana Bank, 694 N.E.2d 740 (Ind. Ct. App. 1998), reh'g denied, (June 30, 1998) and transfer denied, 706 N.E.2d 178 (Ind. 1998).

meaning.[77] A contract term is not ambiguous simply because it is not defined in the contract.[78]

If a contract is ambiguous and its meaning may be determined by extrinsic evidence, the finder of fact may employ the rules of contract construction and extrinsic evidence in giving effect to the parties' reasonable expectations.[79] A court should construe a contract liberally to effectuate the intent of parties at the time the agreement was signed.[80] A contract should not be so narrowly interpreted as to frustrate the parties' obvious intent, but neither should it be so loosely interpreted as to relieve a party of a liability fairly within the scope of the contract terms.[81]

The parties to a contract have the right to define their mutual rights and obligations themselves.[82] A court may not add contract provisions that are not agreed upon by the parties,[83] nor can it change the terms of a contract[84] under

---

[77]Wright v. State, 700 N.E.2d 1153 (Ind. Ct. App. 1998); Ruff v. Charter Behavioral Health System of Northwest Indiana, Inc., 699 N.E.2d 1171 (Ind. Ct. App. 1998), reh'g denied, (Nov. 6, 1998) and transfer denied, 714 N.E.2d 170 (Ind. 1999); Stout v. Kokomo Manor Apartments, 677 N.E.2d 1060, 22 A.D.D. 244 (Ind. Ct. App. 1997).

[78]Bastin v. First Indiana Bank, 694 N.E.2d 740 (Ind. Ct. App. 1998), reh'g denied, (June 30, 1998) and transfer denied, 706 N.E.2d 178 (Ind. 1998).

[79]First Federal Sav. Bank of Indiana v. Key Markets, Inc., 559 N.E.2d 600 (Ind. 1990).

[80]Ryan v. Ryan, 659 N.E.2d 1088 (Ind. Ct. App. 1995), transfer denied (Ind. May 17, 1996).

[81]Anderson v. Horizon Homes, Inc., 644 N.E.2d 1281 (Ind. Ct. App. 5th Dist. 1995), transfer denied, (Apr. 21, 1995); Chicago Southshore & South Bend R.R. v. Itel Rail Corp., 658 N.E.2d 624 (Ind. Ct. App. 1995).

[82]Bethlehem Steel Corp. v. Sercon Corp., 654 N.E.2d 1163 (Ind. Ct. App. 1995), reh'g denied, (Oct. 27, 1995) and transfer denied, (Apr. 11, 1996); Ochoa v. Ford, 641 N.E.2d 1042 (Ind. Ct. App. 1994); Johnson v. Sprague, 614 N.E.2d 585 (Ind. Ct. App. 1st Dist. 1993).

[83]Kaghann's Korner, Inc. v. Brown & Sons Fuel Co., Inc., 706 N.E.2d 556 (Ind. Ct. App. 1999), decision clarified on reh'g, 711 N.E.2d 1286 (Ind. Ct. App. 1999); Western Ohio Pizza, Inc. v. Clark Oil & Refining Corp., 704 N.E.2d 1086 (Ind. Ct. App. 1999), transfer denied, 714 N.E.2d 176 (Ind. 1999); Biberstine v. New York Blower Co., 625 N.E.2d 1308 (Ind. Ct. App. 5th Dist. 1993), reh'g denied, (Jan. 24, 1994) and transfer dismissed, (Apr. 12, 1994); Fetz v. Phillips, 591 N.E.2d 644 (Ind. Ct. App. 1st Dist. 1992).

[84]Colonial Penn Ins. Co. v. Guzorek, 690 N.E.2d 664 (Ind. 1997); Eck &

the guise of construing it,[85] since to do so would be to subject the parties to an agreement they have not made.[86]

> ◆ **Illustration:** Where a shopping center lease agreement unambiguously required consent to an assignment, but was silent as to whether any refusal of such consent was required to be reasonable, the lessor was not required to be reasonable in its withholding of consent to the requested assignment.[87]

The court may neither make a new contract for the parties, nor ignore or eliminate and provisions in the existing contract.[88] When the parties have failed to include an important term in their contract, the court may not do what it feels the parties should have done in the first place.[89] Rather than rewriting the contract to suit one party, the court must apply the plain and obvious meaning of the language.[90]

§ 59 Intent of parties

The primary purpose of contract law is to ascertain and give effect to the intent of the parties.

West's Digest, Contracts ☞147(1).

Because a court, in interpreting a contract, must read the contract in a manner which gives effect to the parties' expressed intent,[91] the court's first task when confronted with a case requiring the interpretation of a contract is to

---

Associates, Inc. v. Alusuisse Flexible Packaging, Inc., 700 N.E.2d 1163 (Ind. Ct. App. 1998), transfer denied, 714 N.E.2d 167 (Ind. 1999).

[85]Orem v. Ivy Tech State College, 711 N.E.2d 864, 135 Ed. Law Rep. 628 (Ind. Ct. App. 1999), reh'g denied, (Sept. 16, 1999); Smart Corp. v. Grider, 650 N.E.2d 80 (Ind. Ct. App. 1st Dist. 1995), reh'g denied, (July 27, 1995) and transfer denied, (Apr. 17, 1996).

[86]Smart Corp. v. Grider, 650 N.E.2d 80 (Ind. Ct. App. 1st Dist. 1995), reh'g denied, (July 27, 1995) and transfer denied, (Apr. 17, 1996).

[87]First Federal Sav. Bank of Indiana v. Key Markets, Inc., 559 N.E.2d 600 (Ind. 1990).

[88]Huntington Mortg. Co. v. DeBrota, 703 N.E.2d 160 (Ind. Ct. App. 1998).

[89]Wright Motors, Inc. v. Marathon Oil Co., 631 N.E.2d 923 (Ind. Ct. App. 1st Dist. 1994).

[90]George S. May Intern. Co. v. King, 629 N.E.2d 257 (Ind. Ct. App. 1st Dist. 1994), reh'g denied, (May 11, 1994) and transfer denied, (Sept. 2, 1994).

[91]For discussion of contract interpretation generally, see § 58.

ascertain the parties' intent.[92] Ascertaining and giving effect to the parties' intentions is the primary and overriding purpose of contract law.[93] Therefore, it is the trial court's duty to interpret a contract so as to ascertain the intent of the parties[94] at the time they formed the contract.[95]

The intention of the parties to a contract is a factual matter to be determined from all the circumstances which existed at the time the contract was made,[96] including the nature of the agreement, all facts and circumstances leading up to the execution of the contract, the relation of the parties, the nature and situation of the subject matter, and the apparent purpose of making the contract.[97] Generally, where

---

[92]INB Banking Co. v. Opportunity Options, Inc., 598 N.E.2d 580 (Ind. Ct. App. 1st Dist. 1992), reh'g denied, (Oct. 29, 1992) and transfer denied, (Dec. 31, 1992).

[93]Hutchinson, Shockey, Erley & Co. v. Evansville-Vanderburgh County Bldg. Authority, 644 N.E.2d 1228 (Ind. 1994), reh'g denied, (May 17, 1995); Eck & Associates, Inc. v. Alusuisse Flexible Packaging, Inc., 700 N.E.2d 1163 (Ind. Ct. App. 1998), transfer denied, 714 N.E.2d 167 (Ind. 1999); Indiana-American Water Co., Inc. v. Town of Seelyville, 698 N.E.2d 1255, 38 U.C.C. Rep. Serv. 2d (CBC) 1133 (Ind. Ct. App. 1998); Engelking v. Estate of Engelking, 686 N.E.2d 932 (Ind. Ct. App. 1997).

[94]Ruff v. Charter Behavioral Health System of Northwest Indiana, Inc., 699 N.E.2d 1171 (Ind. Ct. App. 1998), reh'g denied, (Nov. 6, 1998) and transfer denied, 714 N.E.2d 170 (Ind. 1999); I.C.C. Protective Coatings, Inc. v. A.E. Staley Mfg. Co., 695 N.E.2d 1030 (Ind. Ct. App. 1998), transfer denied, 706 N.E.2d 174 (Ind. 1998).

[95]Wior v. Anchor Industries, Inc., 669 N.E.2d 172 (Ind. 1996), reh'g denied, (Nov. 27, 1996); Mortgage Consultants, Inc. v. Mahaney, 655 N.E.2d 493 (Ind. 1995); Kelly v. Smith, 611 N.E.2d 118 (Ind. 1993); Ryan v. Ryan, 659 N.E.2d 1088 (Ind. Ct. App. 1995), transfer denied (Ind. May 17, 1996); George S. May Intern. Co. v. King, 629 N.E.2d 257 (Ind. Ct. App. 1st Dist. 1994), reh'g denied, (May 11, 1994) and transfer denied, (Sept. 2, 1994).

[96]Real Estate Support Services, Inc. v. Nauman, 644 N.E.2d 907 (Ind. Ct. App. 1st Dist. 1994), reh'g denied, (Mar. 6, 1995) and transfer denied, (July 17, 1995); Sho-Pro of Indiana, Inc. v. Brown, 585 N.E.2d 1357, 17 U.C.C. Rep. Serv. 2d (CBC) 56 (Ind. Ct. App. 3d Dist. 1992); Wallace v. Rogier, 182 Ind. App. 303, 395 N.E.2d 297 (1st Dist. 1979).

[97]Ruff v. Charter Behavioral Health System of Northwest Indiana, Inc., 699 N.E.2d 1171 (Ind. Ct. App. 1998), reh'g denied, (Nov. 6, 1998) and transfer denied, 714 N.E.2d 170 (Ind. 1999); Shahan v. Brinegar, 181 Ind. App. 39, 390 N.E.2d 1036 (1st Dist. 1979); Coleman v. Chapman, 220 N.E.2d 285 (Ind. App. 1966).

the parties' intent can be clearly ascertained, the court will recognize and enforce their agreement.[98]

Indiana takes an objective view of "intent" in contract disputes.[99] The intent relevant in contract matters is not the parties' subjective intent, but their outward manifestation of it.[1] The intention of the parties in an express contract is evidenced by words, while their intention in an implied contract is evidenced by actions, circumstances, and implications.[2]

§ 60 —As determined by language of contract

If the parties' intent can be ascertained from the four corners of their written contract, the court will not look beyond that document.

West's Digest, Contracts ⊶147(2).

In interpreting a written contract, the court will attempt to determine the intent of the parties at the time the contract was made as disclosed by the language used to express their rights and duties.[3] When there is an unambiguous written contract, the court looks only to that document to ascertain the parties' intent.[4] Clear, plain, and unambiguous contract

---

[98]Wior v. Anchor Industries, Inc., 669 N.E.2d 172 (Ind. 1996), reh'g denied, (Nov. 27, 1996).

[99]Kinko's Graphics Corp. v. Townsend, 803 F. Supp. 1450 (S.D. Ind. 1992) (applying Indiana law).

[1]Real Estate Support Services, Inc. v. Nauman, 644 N.E.2d 907 (Ind. Ct. App. 1st Dist. 1994), reh'g denied, (Mar. 6, 1995) and transfer denied, (July 17, 1995); Holloway v. Giganti, Inc., 540 N.E.2d 97 (Ind. Ct. App. 1st Dist. 1989), reh'g denied, (Aug. 1, 1989).

[2]Indianapolis Real Estate Board v. Willson, 98 Ind. App. 72, 187 N.E. 400 (1933).

[3]First Federal Sav. Bank of Indiana v. Key Markets, Inc., 559 N.E.2d 600 (Ind. 1990); I.C.C. Protective Coatings, Inc. v. A.E. Staley Mfg. Co., 695 N.E.2d 1030 (Ind. Ct. App. 1998), transfer denied, 706 N.E.2d 174 (Ind. 1998); Barrington Management Co., Inc. v. Paul E. Draper Family Ltd. Partnership, 695 N.E.2d 135 (Ind. Ct. App. 1998); Schoemer v. Hanes & Associates, Inc., 693 N.E.2d 1333 (Ind. Ct. App. 1998); Robinson v. Century Personnel, Inc., 678 N.E.2d 1268 (Ind. Ct. App. 1997), transfer denied, 690 N.E.2d 1179 (Ind. 1997).

[4]OEC-Diasonics, Inc. v. Major, 674 N.E.2d 1312 (Ind. 1996); Francis v. Yates, 700 N.E.2d 504 (Ind. Ct. App. 1998); Prall v. Indiana Nat. Bank, 627 N.E.2d 1374 (Ind. Ct. App. 4th Dist. 1994); McCae Management Corp. v. Merchants Nat. Bank and Trust Co. of Indianapolis, 553 N.E.2d 884 (Ind. Ct. App. 4th Dist. 1990), transfer denied, (Oct. 2, 1990).

terms are conclusive of the parties' intent,[5] and if there is no ambiguity in the contract, the court will not look outside the written instrument to ascertain the parties' intent.[6] Where the parties' intent can be clearly ascertained from the contract's language, courts will generally recognize and enforce the parties' agreement.[7]

Although the parties' intent is ordinarily determined by examining the four corners of their written contract,[8] the court may also consider the rules of contract construction and extrinsic evidence[9] if the contractual language is ambiguous, inconsistent, or uncertain.[10]

◆ **Caution:** A few courts have stated that the intent of parties to a contract should be gathered not only from the terms of the contract, but should be considered against

---

[5]Kaghann's Korner, Inc. v. Brown & Sons Fuel Co., Inc., 706 N.E.2d 556 (Ind. Ct. App. 1999), decision clarified on reh'g, 711 N.E.2d 1286 (Ind. Ct. App. 1999); Biberstine v. New York Blower Co., 625 N.E.2d 1308 (Ind. Ct. App. 5th Dist. 1993), reh'g denied, (Jan. 24, 1994) and transfer dismissed, (Apr. 12, 1994); City of Evansville v. Braun, 619 N.E.2d 956 (Ind. Ct. App. 1st Dist. 1993), appeal after remand, 677 N.E.2d 597 (Ind. Ct. App. 1997), transfer denied, 690 N.E.2d 1180 (Ind. 1997).

[6]Citizens Nat. Bank of Tipton v. Indianapolis Auto Auction, 592 N.E.2d 1256 (Ind. Ct. App. 1st Dist. 1992); Peter C. Reilly Trust v. Anthony Wayne Oil Corp., 574 N.E.2d 318 (Ind. Ct. App. 2d Dist. 1991), reh'g denied, (Aug. 16, 1991); Wright v. State, 700 N.E.2d 1153 (Ind. Ct. App. 1998).

[7]Mortgage Consultants, Inc. v. Mahaney, 655 N.E.2d 493 (Ind. 1995).

[8]Ruff v. Charter Behavioral Health System of Northwest Indiana, Inc., 699 N.E.2d 1171 (Ind. Ct. App. 1998), reh'g denied, (Nov. 6, 1998) and transfer denied, 714 N.E.2d 170 (Ind. 1999); Dvorak v. Christ, 692 N.E.2d 920 (Ind. Ct. App. 1998), reh'g denied, (May 27, 1998) and transfer denied, 706 N.E.2d 171 (Ind. 1998); Kutche Chevrolet-Oldsmobile-Pontiac-Buick, Inc. v. Anderson Banking Co., 597 N.E.2d 1307 (Ind. Ct. App. 5th Dist. 1992)

[9]Kutche Chevrolet-Oldsmobile-Pontiac-Buick, Inc. v. Anderson Banking Co., 597 N.E.2d 1307 (Ind. Ct. App. 5th Dist. 1992); Bicknell Minerals, Inc. v. Tilly, 570 N.E.2d 1307 (Ind. Ct. App. 4th Dist. 1991), reh'g denied, (July 10, 1991) and transfer denied, (Feb. 26, 1992).

[10]INB Banking Co. v. Opportunity Options, Inc., 598 N.E.2d 580 (Ind. Ct. App. 1st Dist. 1992), reh'g denied, (Oct. 29, 1992) and transfer denied, (Dec. 31, 1992).

For discussion of the use of extrinsic evidence in contract interpretation, see § 137.

the background of circumstances which existed at the time
of its execution.[11]

§ 61 Construction as a whole

**A court interpreting a contract must consider the
contract as a whole, rather than reading individual
phrases or clauses in isolation.**

West's Digest, Contracts ☞147(3).

The intentions of the parties to a contract must be
determined from the contract read in its entirety.[12] Even
when an ambiguity in the contract is apparent, the instrument will not be considered ambiguous until the entire document has been searched to determine if the parties' intent
can be ascertained from it.[13]

The meaning of a contract is to be determined from an examination of all of the provisions of the entire contract,[14] and
not from a consideration of individual words, phrases or even
paragraphs read alone.[15] All words in a contract must be
considered in determining its meaning.[16] Particular words or

---

[11]Haxton v. McClure Oil Corp., 697 N.E.2d 1277 (Ind. Ct. App. 1998);
Real Estate Support Services, Inc. v. Nauman, 644 N.E.2d 907 (Ind. Ct.
App. 1st Dist. 1994), reh'g denied, (Mar. 6, 1995) and transfer denied,
(July 17, 1995).

[12]Francis v. Yates, 700 N.E.2d 504 (Ind. Ct. App. 1998); Wendy's of Ft.
Wayne, Inc. v. Fagan, 644 N.E.2d 159 (Ind. Ct. App. 1st Dist. 1994); INB
Banking Co. v. Opportunity Options, Inc., 598 N.E.2d 580 (Ind. Ct. App.
1st Dist. 1992), reh'g denied, (Oct. 29, 1992) and transfer denied, (Dec. 31,
1992).

[13]Pennington v. American Family Ins. Group, 626 N.E.2d 461 (Ind. Ct.
App. 1st Dist. 1993).

[14]Huntington Mortg. Co. v. DeBrota, 703 N.E.2d 160 (Ind. Ct. App.
1998); Eck & Associates, Inc. v. Alusuisse Flexible Packaging, Inc., 700
N.E.2d 1163 (Ind. Ct. App. 1998), transfer denied, 714 N.E.2d 167 (Ind.
1999); Francis v. Yates, 700 N.E.2d 504 (Ind. Ct. App. 1998); Indiana-
American Water Co., Inc. v. Town of Seelyville, 698 N.E.2d 1255, 38
U.C.C. Rep. Serv. 2d (CBC) 1133 (Ind. Ct. App. 1998).

[15]Eck & Associates, Inc. v. Alusuisse Flexible Packaging, Inc., 700
N.E.2d 1163 (Ind. Ct. App. 1998), transfer denied, 714 N.E.2d 167 (Ind.
1999); Francis v. Yates, 700 N.E.2d 504 (Ind. Ct. App. 1998); Indiana-
American Water Co., Inc. v. Town of Seelyville, 698 N.E.2d 1255, 38
U.C.C. Rep. Serv. 2d (CBC) 1133 (Ind. Ct. App. 1998).

[16]Modern Photo Offset Supply v. Woodfield Group, 663 N.E.2d 547 (Ind.
Ct. App. 1996), reh'g denied, (June 7, 1996) and transfer denied, (Nov. 19,
1996).

paragraphs cannot be isolated from the remainder of the agreement,[17] which must be read as a whole.[18]

A court construing a contract presumes that all provisions were included for a purpose, and, if possible, reconciles seemingly conflicting provisions to give effect to all provisions.[19] A court must accept an interpretation of a contract which harmonizes all of the contract's provisions,[20] so that no provision is deemed conflicting with, repugnant to, or neutralizing of any other provision.[21] Moreover, the interpretation accepted must not render words, phrases or terms ineffective or meaningless,[22] and must not place undue emphasis upon

---

[17]Huntington Mortg. Co. v. DeBrota, 703 N.E.2d 160 (Ind. Ct. App. 1998); Grand Trunk Western R. Co. v. Kapitan, 698 N.E.2d 363 (Ind. Ct. App. 1998), transfer denied, 714 N.E.2d 163 (Ind. 1999); Hyperbaric Oxygen Therapy Systems, Inc. v. St. Joseph Medical Center of Ft. Wayne, Inc., 683 N.E.2d 243 (Ind. Ct. App. 1997), transfer denied, 690 N.E.2d 1189 (Ind. 1997); Wright Motors, Inc. v. Marathon Oil Co., 631 N.E.2d 923 (Ind. Ct. App. 1st Dist. 1994).

[18]Huntington Mortg. Co. v. DeBrota, 703 N.E.2d 160 (Ind. Ct. App. 1998); Grand Trunk Western R. Co. v. Kapitan, 698 N.E.2d 363 (Ind. Ct. App. 1998), transfer denied, 714 N.E.2d 163 (Ind. 1999); Hyperbaric Oxygen Therapy Systems, Inc. v. St. Joseph Medical Center of Ft. Wayne, Inc., 683 N.E.2d 243 (Ind. Ct. App. 1997), transfer denied, 690 N.E.2d 1189 (Ind. 1997).

[19]Salcedo v. Toepp, 696 N.E.2d 426 (Ind. Ct. App. 1998).

[20]OEC-Diasonics, Inc. v. Major, 674 N.E.2d 1312 (Ind. 1996); Kelly v. Smith, 611 N.E.2d 118 (Ind. 1993); Ryan v. Ryan, 659 N.E.2d 1088 (Ind. Ct. App. 1995), transfer denied (Ind. May 17, 1996); Norwest Bank Indiana, N.A. v. Friedline, 591 N.E.2d 599 (Ind. Ct. App. 3d Dist. 1992); DeHaan v. DeHaan, 572 N.E.2d 1315 (Ind. Ct. App. 1st Dist. 1991), reh'g denied, (July 31, 1991) and transfer denied, (Feb. 14, 1992).

[21]Salcedo v. Toepp, 696 N.E.2d 426 (Ind. Ct. App. 1998); Barrington Management Co., Inc. v. Paul E. Draper Family Ltd. Partnership, 695 N.E.2d 135 (Ind. Ct. App. 1998); Schoemer v. Hanes & Associates, Inc., 693 N.E.2d 1333 (Ind. Ct. App. 1998); Robinson v. Century Personnel, Inc., 678 N.E.2d 1268 (Ind. Ct. App. 1997), transfer denied, 690 N.E.2d 1179 (Ind. 1997).

[22]Kiltz v. Kiltz, 708 N.E.2d 600 (Ind. Ct. App. 1999), transfer denied, (Aug. 27, 1999); American Family Life Assur. Co. v. Russell, 700 N.E.2d 1174 (Ind. Ct. App. 1998), transfer denied, 714 N.E.2d 168 (Ind. 1999); Barrington Management Co., Inc. v. Paul E. Draper Family Ltd. Partnership, 695 N.E.2d 135 (Ind. Ct. App. 1998); Indiana-American Water Co., Inc. v. Town of Seelyville, 698 N.E.2d 1255, 38 U.C.C. Rep. Serv. 2d (CBC) 1133 (Ind. Ct. App. 1998); Schoemer v. Hanes & Associates, Inc., 693 N.E.2d 1333 (Ind. Ct. App. 1998).

a particular clause or take language in the contract out of context.[23]

§ 62 Oral contracts, generally

An express contract may be oral; an agreement with both oral and written terms is considered to be an oral contract.

West's Digest, Contracts ☞149.

In an express contract, the intent of parties may be evidenced either by spoken words or by a written instrument.[24]

An agreement containing both oral and written terms is considered an oral contract;[25] where parol evidence must be presented to establish the terms of the contract, the whole contract is oral.[26] If a writing constitutes a complete contract, however, it will be considered a written contract for statute of limitations purposes, even if one party claims that the contract was amended by the parties' oral agreement.[27] A contract is not rendered partly oral merely because it was not accepted in writing, or because its acceptance will have to be proved by parol evidence.[28]

§ 63 Written contracts, generally

The character of a written contract is determined by the nature of the transaction.

West's Digest, Contracts ☞150, 163.

The character of an instrument must be determined from

---

[23]Wright Motors, Inc. v. Marathon Oil Co., 631 N.E.2d 923 (Ind. Ct. App. 1st Dist. 1994).

[24]Bain v. Board of Trustees of Starke Memorial Hosp., 550 N.E.2d 106 (Ind. Ct. App. 3d Dist. 1990), reh'g denied, (Mar. 30, 1990).

[25]Michael v. Rainier, 246 Ind. 293, 205 N.E.2d 543 (1965); Majd Pour v. Basic American Medical, Inc., 555 N.E.2d 155 (Ind. Ct. App. 2d Dist. 1990), reh'g denied, (July 24, 1990); Citizens Progress Co., Inc. v. James O. Held & Co., Inc., 438 N.E.2d 1016 (Ind. Ct. App. 1st Dist. 1982).

[26]Citizens Progress Co., Inc. v. James O. Held & Co., Inc., 438 N.E.2d 1016 (Ind. Ct. App. 1st Dist. 1982) (contract where oral where written documents clearly reflected oral agreements).

[27]De Vay v. Dunlap, 7 Ind. App. 690, 35 N.E. 195 (1893).

As to statutes of limitations for oral and written contracts, see § 122.

[28]Majd Pour v. Basic American Medical, Inc., 555 N.E.2d 155 (Ind. Ct. App. 2d Dist. 1990), reh'g denied, (July 24, 1990).

For a discussion of parol evidence offered to prove the terms of a contract, see § 137.

the real nature of the transaction, rather than the designation given it by the parties.[29] A written instrument is assumed to reflect the type of transaction described by the parties, unless a contrary construction is required because of the legal effect of the transaction as treated by the parties.[30]

The physical possession of a written contract cannot give or take away any rights a person may have by virtue of the contract, and court-mandated delivery of a document cannot add or take away anything from the agreement.[31]

Where the contract is on a printed form and there is an apparent conflict between terms written by different methods, writing prevails over printing, handwriting over typewriting, and typewriting over printing.[32]

§ 64 Meaning of words used

Terms used in a written contract are to be given their plain and usual meaning.

West's Digest, Contracts ⬦152.

The language of a written contract is to be given its plain and usual meaning[33] as understood by the community and the ordinary reader,[34] unless they are ambiguous,[35] unless

---

[29]Thompson v Arnold, 238 Ind. 177, 147 N.E.2d 903 (1958); Mendenhall v. First New Church Society of Indianapolis, 177 Ind. 336, 98 N.E. 57 (1912).

[30]Thompson v. Arnold, 238 Ind. 177, 147 N.E.2d 903 (1958) (character of transaction showed that it was loan and mortgage, rather than sale).

[31]Bradfield v. Hendrickson, 128 Ind. App. 598, 151 N.E.2d 300 (1958).

[32]Scott v. Anderson Newspapers, Inc., 477 N.E.2d 553 (Ind. Ct. App. 4th Dist. 1985), reh'g denied, (June 19, 1985) and transfer denied, (Nov. 4, 1985); State v. Scott Const. Co., 97 Ind. App. 652, 174 N.E. 429 (1931).

[33]Orem v. Ivy Tech State College, 711 N.E.2d 864, 135 Ed. Law Rep. 628 (Ind. Ct. App. 1999), reh'g denied, (Sept. 16, 1999); Eckart v. Davis, 631 N.E.2d 494 (Ind. Ct. App. 1st Dist. 1994); Battershell v. Prestwick Sales, Inc., 585 N.E.2d 1 (Ind. Ct. App. 1st Dist. 1992), transfer denied, (June 24, 1992); Christensen v. Sears, Roebuck and Co., 565 N.E.2d 1103 (Ind. Ct. App. 1st Dist. 1991), reh'g denied, (Mar. 18, 1991) and transfer denied, (Dec. 13, 1991).

[34]P.C. Management, Inc. v. Page Two, Inc., 573 N.E.2d 434 (Ind. Ct. App. 1st Dist. 1991), reh'g denied, (July 18, 1991).

[35]Orem v. Ivy Tech State College, 711 N.E.2d 864, 135 Ed. Law Rep. 628 (Ind. Ct. App. 1999), reh'g denied, (Sept. 16, 1999); Kiltz v. Kiltz, 708 N.E.2d 600 (Ind. Ct. App. 1999), transfer denied, (Aug. 27, 1999); Tanton v. Grochow, 707 N.E.2d 1010 (Ind. Ct. App. 1999).

there is some indication that a word or phrase has been used in a technical sense or should be afforded a special meaning in light of parties' relationship,[36] or unless it is clear from the entire contract and its subject matter that the parties intended some other meaning.[37] Thus, a written instrument should ordinarily be interpreted to mean on its face what it purports to mean, unless some good reason can be assigned to show that the words used in the instrument can be understood in a different sense.[38] A party is held to the natural legal consequences of words consciously chosen and used in a contract,[39] even if one of the parties thought a word meant something different than it actually does.[40]

Technical words and terms of art are given their technical meanings,[41] unless they are clearly used in a different sense.[42]

Contract terms which affect public policy are strictly construed, even if neither party urges a strict construction.[43]

§ 65 —Particular words and phrases construed

Various contract terms have been judicially interpreted.

---

[36]Nimet Industries, Inc. v. Joy Mfg. Co., 419 N.E.2d 779 (Ind. Ct. App. 4th Dist. 1981).

[37]Buck v. Banks, 668 N.E.2d 1259 (Ind. Ct. App. 1996); George S. May Intern. Co. v. King, 629 N.E.2d 257 (Ind. Ct. App. 1st Dist. 1994), reh'g denied, (May 11, 1994) and transfer denied, (Sept. 2, 1994); City of Evansville v. Braun, 619 N.E.2d 956 (Ind. Ct. App. 1st Dist. 1993), appeal after remand, 677 N.E.2d 597 (Ind. Ct. App. 1997), transfer denied, 690 N.E.2d 1180 (Ind. 1997); Whiteco Industries, Inc. v. Nickolick, 571 N.E.2d 1337 (Ind. Ct. App. 1st Dist. 1991), transfer denied, (Dec. 12, 1991).

   Forms References: Definition of words or phrases. 5A Am Jur Legal Forms 2d, Contracts § 68:241.

[38]Dayhuff v. Canonie Const. Co., 152 Ind. App. 154, 283 N.E.2d 425 (1st Dist. 1972).

[39]Robison v. Fickle, 167 Ind. App. 651, 340 N.E.2d 824, 18 U.C.C. Rep. Serv. (CBC) 1044 (2d Dist. 1976).

[40]Miller v. Frankfort Bottle Gas, Inc., 136 Ind. App. 456, 202 N.E.2d 395 (Div. 1 1964).

[41]George S. May Intern. Co. v. King, 629 N.E.2d 257 (Ind. Ct. App. 1st Dist. 1994), reh'g denied, (May 11, 1994) and transfer denied, (Sept. 2, 1994).

   Trial Strategy References: Meaning of Abbreviation, Word, or Phrase According to Usage of Trade, 26 Am Jur POF2d 299.

[42]Thompson v. Arnold, 238 Ind. 177, 147 N.E.2d 903 (1958).

[43]George S. May Intern. Co. v. King, 629 N.E.2d 257 (Ind. Ct. App. 1st Dist. 1994), reh'g denied, (May 11, 1994) and transfer denied, (Sept. 2, 1994).

West's Digest, Contracts ☞159.

The expression "and/or" is taken to mean whatever will best effect the purpose of the parties as gathered from the contract taken as a whole.[44]

In the context of insurance coverage, an "accident" is an unexpected happening without an intention or design.[45]

The phrase "at any time," as used in a contract in connection with time of performance, is a relative and flexible term not susceptible of precise definition, and its meaning in a particular case depends on the facts and circumstances.[46] The term "immediate", when used in a contract, means that the act referred to is to be accomplished within such convenient time as is reasonably necessary.[47] The words "first day of the year," as used in a contract or lease, usually refer to the first day of January.[48]

A contract to provide a home for the promisee so long as she lives cannot be satisfied by merely furnishing shelter and substance, but the performance of such a contract does not require perfection; a reasonably strict and substantial compliance is sufficient.[49] A "home" furnished the grantor as part consideration for a deed has been held to include care, rather than simply shelter.[50]

The phrase "personal property" in a divorce settlement agreement requiring the ex-wife to release her rights, interest, and title in any of the couple's "household furniture and personal property" not expressly awarded to her

---

[44]Jones v. Servel, Inc., 135 Ind. App. 171, 186 N.E.2d 689 (Div. 2 1962) (where contract provided that party would be paid for "obligations assumed and/or services rendered," term was meant in conjunctive, as parties did not intend that party be able to default on one obligation and receive full payment for performing other).

[45]Erie Ins. Co. v. American Painting Co., 678 N.E.2d 844 (Ind. Ct. App. 1997), transfer dismissed, 690 N.E.2d 1178 (Ind. 1997); Wayne Tp. Bd. of School Com'rs v. Indiana Ins. Co., 650 N.E.2d 1205, 100 Ed. Law Rep. 1123 (Ind. Ct. App. 5th Dist. 1995), reh'g denied, (July 24, 1995) and transfer denied (Ind. Jan. 31, 1996).

[46]Haworth v. Hubbard, 220 Ind. 611, 44 N.E.2d 967, 144 A.L.R. 887 (1942).

[47]Gross Income Tax Dept. of Treasury v. Harbison-Walker Refractories Co., 113 Ind. App. 695, 48 N.E.2d 834 (1943).

[48]Bojarski v. Ballard, 113 Ind. App. 6, 44 N.E.2d 200 (1942).

[49]McConnell v. Fulmer, 230 Ind. 576, 105 N.E.2d 817 (1952).

[50]Gwinn v. Hobbs, 83 Ind. App. 263, 144 N.E. 648 (1924).

included United States savings bonds found in the husband's safe deposit box after his death.[51]

"School," as used in an agreement between photographers not to compete for school business, has been defined as an institution of learning of a lower grade, below a college or a university; a place of primary instruction.[52]

A requirement that an employee provide two weeks' notice before leaving her employment includes a requirement that the employee work the entire two weeks.[53]

Damage other than that caused by ordinary wear and tear, referred to in a lease agreement, is damage other than the gradual deterioration of the condition of the leased premises which results from their appropriate use over time. Where the tenants are required to clean the premises but have failed to do so, the premises are damaged if they require cleaning.[54]

§ 66   Construction favoring validity of contract

Where possible, courts will construe contracts as being valid.

West's Digest, Contracts ⚭153.

Where possible, courts will construe contracts as being valid, rather than void.[55] When construing a contract, a court will not find that it is invalid for lack of mutuality or uncertainty where a reasonable and logical interpretation will render the contract valid and enforceable.[56]

---

[51]Wolf v. Wolf, 147 Ind. App. 251, 259 N.E.2d 89 (Div. 2 1970).

[52]Lawrence v. Cain, 144 Ind. App. 210, 245 N.E.2d 663 (Div. 1 1969).

[53]Haxton v. McClure Oil Corp., 697 N.E.2d 1277 (Ind. Ct. App. 1998).

[54]Miller v. Geels, 643 N.E.2d 922 (Ind. Ct. App. 1st Dist. 1994), transfer denied, (Mar. 22, 1995).

[55]Indiana-American Water Co., Inc. v. Town of Seelyville, 698 N.E.2d 1255, 38 U.C.C. Rep. Serv. 2d (CBC) 1133 (Ind. Ct. App. 1998); Smart Corp. v. Grider, 650 N.E.2d 80 (Ind. Ct. App. 1st Dist. 1995), reh'g denied, (July 27, 1995) and transfer denied, (Apr. 17, 1996); Glasgo v. Glasgo, 410 N.E.2d 1325 (Ind. Ct. App. 1st Dist. 1980); Prell v. Trustees of Baird and Warner Mortg. and Realty Investors, 179 Ind. App. 642, 386 N.E.2d 1221 (1st Dist. 1979).

[56]Kokomo Veterans, Inc. v. Schick, 439 N.E.2d 639 (Ind. Ct. App. 3d Dist. 1982).

§ 67 Reasonable and equitable construction

A court will avoid an unreasonable or inequitable construction of a contract.

West's Digest, Contracts ☞154.

Courts will avoid an inequitable construction of a contract,[57] as well as a construction which gives an unfair or unreasonable advantage to one of the parties.[58] Thus, where one construction of the contract would make it unusual and extraordinary, or another, equally consistent with the language, would make it reasonable, just, and fair, the latter will prevail.[59]

§ 68 Construction against drafting party

Contract terms are construed against the drafter of the contract.

West's Digest, Contracts ☞155.

An ambiguous contract, that is, one which requires construction,[60] will be strictly construed against the party who prepared the document, or was otherwise responsible for the wording.[61] If the contract is oral, it will be construed against the party who used the ambiguous language.[62] If the contract is on a printed form prepared by one of the parties,

---

[57]Komisarow v. Lansky, 139 Ind. App. 351, 219 N.E.2d 913 (Div. 1 1966).

[58]Western & Southern Life Ins. Co. v. Vale, 213 Ind. 601, 12 N.E.2d 350 (1938); Komisarow v. Lansky, 139 Ind. App. 351, 219 N.E.2d 913 (Div. 1 1966).

[59]Thomas v. Hennes, 78 Ind. App. 275, 135 N.E. 392 (Div. 1 1922).

[60]For discussion of the necessity of construing an ambiguous contract, see § 58.

[61]Fresh Cut, Inc. v. Fazli, 650 N.E.2d 1126 (Ind. 1995); Vertucci v. NHP Management Co., 701 N.E.2d 604 (Ind. Ct. App. 1998); Ruff v. Charter Behavioral Health System of Northwest Indiana, Inc., 699 N.E.2d 1171 (Ind. Ct. App. 1998), reh'g denied, (Nov. 6, 1998) and transfer denied, 714 N.E.2d 170 (Ind. 1999); INB Banking Co. v. Opportunity Options, Inc., 598 N.E.2d 580 (Ind. Ct. App. 1st Dist. 1992), reh'g denied, (Oct. 29, 1992) and transfer denied, (Dec. 31, 1992); Indiana Comprehensive Health Ins. Ass'n v. Dye, 531 N.E.2d 505 (Ind. Ct. App. 3d Dist. 1988) (insurance contracts and other contracts of adhesion).

[62]Rahn v. School City of Gary, 216 Ind. 542, 25 N.E.2d 441 (1940).

the words used in the contract will be construed most strongly against the party who prepared the form.[63]

This is the case, however, only if the court cannot ascertain the parties' intent by other rules of construction.[64]

§ 69 General and specific words

Specific terms in a contract control over more general terms.

West's Digest, Contracts ☞156.

When a contract contains general and specific provisions relating to the same subject, the specific provision controls over an apparently inconsistent general statement.[65] For instance, if a general recital of consideration is inconsistent with subsequent provisions regarding the terms of payment for property, the latter provisions will control.[66]

§ 70 Omissions or mistakes

If a contract contains a clerical error or omission which would change the parties' intention if not corrected, the court will interpret the contract according to the parties' intention.

West's Digest, Contracts ☞157.

A contract must be read according to the intent of the parties in spite of clerical errors and omissions which if followed would change that intention. Thus, when the contract and the terms of the entire instrument taken together show conclusively that the wrong word has been used through inadvertence, it is the duty of the court to interpret the

---

[63]Colonial Discount Corp. v. Berkhardt, 435 N.E.2d 65 (Ind. Ct. App. 1st Dist. 1982); Western & Southern Life Ins. Co. v. Vale, 213 Ind. 601, 12 N.E.2d 350 (1938).

[64]George S. May Intern. Co. v. King, 629 N.E.2d 257 (Ind. Ct. App. 1st Dist. 1994), reh'g denied, (May 11, 1994) and transfer denied, (Sept. 2, 1994); Bishop v. Sanders, 624 N.E.2d 64 (Ind. Ct. App. 1st Dist. 1993), reh'g denied, (Jan. 28, 1994) and transfer denied, (June 2, 1994); Indiana-Kentucky Elec. Corp. v. Green, 476 N.E.2d 141 (Ind. Ct. App. 1st Dist. 1985), reh'g denied, (May 8, 1985) and transfer denied, (Aug. 30, 1985).

[65]Arnold v. Burton, 651 N.E.2d 1202 (Ind. Ct. App. 1995), transfer denied, (Nov. 15, 1995); Salcedo v. Toepp, 696 N.E.2d 426 (Ind. Ct. App. 1998); Arnold v. Burton, 651 N.E.2d 1202 (Ind. Ct. App. 1995), transfer denied, (Nov. 15, 1995).

[66]Wiltse v. Cornell, 146 Ind. App. 447, 256 N.E.2d 572 (Div. 2 1970).

contract according to the manifest intention of the parties, and to instruct the jury accordingly.[67] Likewise, a term improperly employed in a written agreement will not control its construction, where the meaning of the parties is palpable.[68]

Similarly, a word plainly omitted from a contract by inadvertence will always be supplied to accomplish justice by enforcing the intention of the parties.[69] If a form contract contains blank spaces, the contract will be enforced if there is sufficient testimony from which the court can ascertain the terms of the parties' agreement.[70]

§ 71   Recitals

While recitals may be persuasive in determining the parties' intention, when the language expressing their contractual relations is ambiguous, they cannot control the clearly expressed stipulations of the parties.

West's Digest, Contracts ☞160.

Recitals, or "whereas" clauses, may be referred to in determining the intent of the parties when their intent is not clear from the operative part of the contract.[71] If the recitals are clear and the operative part of the contract is ambiguous, the recitals govern the construction. If the recitals are ambiguous and the operative part is clear, the operative part governs. If both the recitals and the operative part are clear, but they are inconsistent with each other, the operative part controls.[72]

§ 72   Conflicting clauses in general

If possible, the court must reconcile apparently conflicting contract provisions so as to give effect to all of the contract provisions.

West's Digest, Contracts ☞162.

---

[67]Russell v. Merrifield, 131 Ind. 148, 30 N.E. 957 (1892).

[68]Cones v. Vanosdol, 4 Ind. 248, 1853 WL 3319 (1853).

[69]Dodd v. Mitchell, 77 Ind. 388, 1881 WL 6673 (1881).

[70]Marksill Specialties, Inc. v. Barger, 428 N.E.2d 65 (Ind. Ct. App. 3d Dist. 1981).

[71]Ohio Valley Gas, Inc. v. Blackburn, 445 N.E.2d 1378 (Ind. Ct. App. 4th Dist. 1983); Stech v. Panel Mart, Inc., 434 N.E.2d 97 (Ind. Ct. App. 3d Dist. 1982).

[72]Stech v. Panel Mart, Inc., 434 N.E.2d 97 (Ind. Ct. App. 3d Dist. 1982).

When construing a contract, the court presumes that all of the provisions in the contract were included for a purpose, and if possible it reconciles the seemingly conflicting provisions to give effect to all of the contract provisions.[73] Thus, the court must accept an interpretation of the contract which harmonizes its provisions, as opposed to one which causes the provisions to be conflicting.[74]

> ◆ **Illustration:** A covenant not to compete contained a forum selection clause providing that "any legal suit, action, or proceeding" was to be brought in the courts of Illinois. The same covenant contained another clause stating that the plaintiff could seek relief "in any court of competent jurisdiction." The court reconciled the two provisions by ruling that the plaintiff could bring an action for injunction, an equitable rather than legal remedy, in any court of competent jurisdiction, but would be limited to the Illinois courts if he sought a legal rather than equitable remedy.[75]

§ 73   Construing instruments together

Instruments between the same parties, signed at the same time, and dealing with the same transaction will generally be construed together.

West's Digest, Contracts ☞164.

In the absence of anything to indicate a contrary intention, writings executed at the same time and relating to the same transaction will be construed together in determining the contract.[76] The application of this rule, known as the

---

[73]George S. May Intern. Co. v. King, 629 N.E.2d 257 (Ind. Ct. App. 1st Dist. 1994), reh'g denied, (May 11, 1994) and transfer denied, (Sept. 2, 1994); Rosenbaum Bros. v. Nowak Milling Corp., 222 Ind. 108, 51 N.E.2d 623 (1943); Prudential Ins. Co. of America v. Citizens Trust & Sav. Bank of Evansville, 101 Ind. App. 168, 198 N.E. 116 (1935).

[74]Evansville-Vanderburgh School Corp. v. Moll, 264 Ind. 356, 344 N.E.2d 831 (1976); R. R. Donnelley & Sons, Co. v. Henry-Williams, Inc., 422 N.E.2d 353 (Ind. Ct. App. 3d Dist. 1981).

[75]George S. May Intern. Co. v. King, 629 N.E.2d 257 (Ind. Ct. App. 1st Dist. 1994), reh'g denied, (May 11, 1994) and transfer denied, (Sept. 2, 1994).

[76]GEICO Ins. Co. v. Rowell, 705 N.E.2d 476 (Ind. Ct. App. 1999), reh'g denied, (Feb. 18, 1999); Salcedo v. Toepp, 696 N.E.2d 426 (Ind. Ct. App. 1998); Beradi v. Hardware Wholesalers, Inc., 625 N.E.2d 1259 (Ind. Ct.

contemporaneous documents rule, depends on the facts of each particular case.[77]

◆ **Illustration:** On the same day, a borrower signed a loan adjustment agreement, which provided that the borrower would make monthly payments on a loan that would have otherwise fallen due in its entirety two months later, and a loan settlement agreement, increasing the annual interest rate payable on the debt. Because the documents were executed on the same day and pertained to the same transaction, the preexisting debt, the court was required to construe them together, so that the new interest rate would apply to the monthly payments.[78]

Even if the documents are not executed at the same time, they may still be construed together as long as they are part of the same transaction.[79]

◆ **Illustration:** A release agreement purported to release "all other persons" from liability in connection with an automobile accident. However, a stipulation for dismissal executed subsequently provided that only the other driver and his insurance carrier, and not the plaintiff's uninsured/underinsured insurance carrier, were being released. Because both of the documents related to the same transaction, and they and the settlement offer were sent together to the plaintiff's attorney, the two documents were considered together, and the uninsured/underinsured carrier was not released.[80]

App. 3d Dist. 1993), reh'g denied, (Feb. 16, 1994) and transfer denied, (May 24, 1994); Ruth v. First Federal Sav. and Loan Ass'n of LaPorte County, 492 N.E.2d 1105 (Ind. Ct. App. 3d Dist. 1986).

[77]GEICO Ins. Co. v. Rowell, 705 N.E.2d 476 (Ind. Ct. App. 1999), reh'g denied, (Feb. 18, 1999); Beradi v. Hardware Wholesalers, Inc., 625 N.E.2d 1259 (Ind. Ct. App. 3d Dist. 1993), reh'g denied, (Feb. 16, 1994) and transfer denied, (May 24, 1994); Ruth v. First Federal Sav. and Loan Ass'n of LaPorte County, 492 N.E.2d 1105 (Ind. Ct. App. 3d Dist. 1986).

[78]Ruth v. First Federal Sav. and Loan Ass'n of LaPorte County, 492 N.E.2d 1105 (Ind. Ct. App. 3d Dist. 1986).

[79]GEICO Ins. Co. v. Rowell, 705 N.E.2d 476 (Ind. Ct. App. 1999), reh'g denied, (Feb. 18, 1999); McCae Management Corp. v. Merchants Nat. Bank and Trust Co. of Indianapolis, 553 N.E.2d 884 (Ind. Ct. App. 4th Dist. 1990), transfer denied, (Oct. 2, 1990).

[80]GEICO Ins. Co. v. Rowell, 705 N.E.2d 476 (Ind. Ct. App. 1999), reh'g denied, (Feb. 18, 1999).

Consideration for one instrument may be found in a contemporaneously executed instrument.[81]

However, contemporaneously executed contracts are construed together only when they relate to the same transaction or subject matter.[82] Likewise, where the parties to two contracts are not the same, even if they have a party in common, the court need not construe the contracts together.[83]

If one writing is not executed contemporaneously with another, it may nonetheless be incorporated into the other by reference. Other writings, or matters contained in them, which are referred to in a written contract may be regarded as incorporated by the reference as a part of the contract and, therefore, may properly be considered in the construction of the contract. Where a written contract refers to another instrument and makes the terms and conditions of such other instrument a part of it, the two will be construed together as the agreement of the parties.[84] However, if, in a written contract, a reference is made to another writing for a particularly designated purpose, the other writing becomes a part of the contract only for the purpose specified, and is foreign to the contract for all purposes other than the one specified.[85]

[81]Leatherman v. Management Advisors, Inc., 448 N.E.2d 1048 (Ind. 1983); Goeke v. Merchants Nat. Bank and Trust Co. of Indianapolis, 467 N.E.2d 760 (Ind. Ct. App. 1st Dist. 1984), reh'g denied, (Sept. 27, 1984) and transfer denied, (Jan. 14, 1985) (guaranty executed contemporaneously with extension of credit as inducement for guaranty is supported by consideration); Torres v. Meyer Paving Co., 423 N.E.2d 692 (Ind. Ct. App. 1st Dist. 1981) (consideration for agreement not to impose mechanic's lien could be found in contemporaneously executed construction contract).

[82]Leatherman v. Management Advisors, Inc., 448 N.E.2d 1048 (Ind. 1983) (insurance company's purchase of two accounts from new employee did not provide consideration for noncompetition agreement, as transactions were unrelated); McGann & Marsh Co., Inc. v. K & F Mfg. Co., Inc., 179 Ind. App. 411, 385 N.E.2d 1183 (3d Dist. 1979).

[83]Nash Engineering Co. v. Marcy Realty Corporation, 222 Ind. 396, 54 N.E.2d 263 (1944); Utopia Coach Corp. v. Weatherwax, 177 Ind. App. 321, 379 N.E.2d 518 (3d Dist. 1978).

[84]I.C.C. Protective Coatings, Inc. v. A.E. Staley Mfg. Co., 695 N.E.2d 1030 (Ind. Ct. App. 1998), transfer denied, 706 N.E.2d 174 (Ind. 1998).

[85]I.C.C. Protective Coatings, Inc. v. A.E. Staley Mfg. Co., 695 N.E.2d 1030 (Ind. Ct. App. 1998), transfer denied, 706 N.E.2d 174 (Ind. 1998) (where purchase order referred to application process and rates and time

§ 74 Existing law as part of contract

Unless the contract provides otherwise, the law existing at the time and place of the making of a contract forms a part of the contract without any statement to that effect.

West's Digest, Contracts ⬤167.

Unless the contract provides otherwise, all applicable law in force at the time the agreement is made implicitly forms a part of the agreement without any express statement to that effect.[86] Thus, existing law must be read into contracts to which it is applicable.[87] For instance, when a statute prescribes a duty, and a contract is made involving a performance of that duty, the statute becomes a part of the contract.[88] Thus, the law may provide terms missing from the parties' agreement.[89] This rule includes not only statutes, but city ordinances,[90] as well as law declared by the courts.[91]

Unless the contract clearly provides that the parties intended to incorporate changes in the law becoming effective after the date of their agreement, such laws are not part

---

specifications contained in seller's bid, right to cure for which bid provided was not incorporated into agreement).

[86]Miller v. Geels, 643 N.E.2d 922 (Ind. Ct. App. 1st Dist. 1994), transfer denied, (Mar. 22, 1995); Johnson v. Sprague, 614 N.E.2d 585 (Ind. Ct. App. 1st Dist. 1993); Essex Group, Inc. v. Nill, 594 N.E.2d 503 (Ind. Ct. App. 3d Dist. 1992).

[87]Bishop v. Sanders, 624 N.E.2d 64 (Ind. Ct. App. 1st Dist. 1993), reh'g denied, (Jan. 28, 1994) and transfer denied, (June 2, 1994).

[88]Kirmse v. City of Gary, 114 Ind. App. 558, 51 N.E.2d 883 (1944).

[89]Johnson v. Sprague, 614 N.E.2d 585 (Ind. Ct. App. 1st Dist. 1993) (because statute provided that conveyance of fee simple title through general warranty deed is to be "free from all encumbrances" seller was responsible for real estate taxes and maintenance fees which at time of closing were or could give rise to lien on property, even though parties did not negotiate and agree as to payment of taxes).

[90]Dollman v. Pauley, 202 Ind. 387, 174 N.E. 729 (1931); Miller v. Geels, 643 N.E.2d 922 (Ind. Ct. App. 1st Dist. 1994), transfer denied, (Mar. 22, 1995) (landlord had duty to comply with provisions of local housing code, which were incorporated into lease); Ethyl Corp. v. Forcum-Lannom Associates, Inc., 433 N.E.2d 1214 (Ind. Ct. App. 4th Dist. 1982) (builder who agrees to design and construct building or addition impliedly agrees to comply with all applicable building codes and regulations).

[91]U.S. Saving Fund & Investment Co. v. Harris, 142 Ind. 226, 40 N.E. 1072 (1895), reh'g denied, 142 Ind. 226, 41 N.E. 451 (1895); Free v. Haworth, 19 Ind. 404, 1862 WL 2104 (1862).

of the contract.[92] Thus, a structure on which construction has begun at the time a zoning ordinance is enacted or becomes effective is exempt from the operation of the ordinance.[93] However, parties to a contract may bind themselves to be governed by the provisions of a specific pending amendment to the law existing at the time the contract is executed, where the contract will not be performed until after the amendment becomes effective.[94]

The meaning of terms used in a contract and defined by statute becomes fixed at the time the contract is executed.[95]

§ 75 Implied terms

Implied terms of a contract are as much a part of it as if expressly written, but there can be no implication as against the express terms of the contract.

West's Digest, Contracts ☞168.

Although implied covenants are not favored in Indiana, especially where they restrict freedom to enter into contracts,[96] several are recognized. For instance, in any contract for work or services, the law implies a duty to work skillfully, carefully, diligently, and in a workmanlike manner;[97] where a person, at the request of the owner of real property, performs labor on the property without an express agree-

---

[92]Essex Group, Inc. v. Nill, 594 N.E.2d 503 (Ind. Ct. App. 3d Dist. 1992).

[93]Lutz v. New Albany City Plan Com'n, 230 Ind. 74, 101 N.E.2d 187 (1951).

[94]Evansville-Vanderburgh School Corp. v. Moll, 264 Ind. 356, 344 N.E.2d 831 (1976); Mouch v. Indiana Rolling Mill Co., 93 Ind. App. 540, 151 N.E. 137 (1926).

[95]Adult Group Properties, Ltd. v. Imler, 505 N.E.2d 459 (Ind. Ct. App. 4th Dist. 1987), reh'g denied, (Apr. 29, 1987) and transfer denied, (Oct. 15, 1987) (meaning of "family" as used in statute affecting contract to establish home for developmentally disabled adults became fixed in 1960, when contract was formed).

[96]Keystone Carbon Co. v. Black, 599 N.E.2d 213 (Ind. Ct. App. 1st Dist. 1992), transfer denied, (Dec. 2, 1992); First Federal Sav. Bank of Indiana v. Key Markets, Inc., 559 N.E.2d 600 (Ind. 1990) (where lease agreement required lessor's consent to any assignment of lease, but did not indicate whether refusal of such consent was required to be reasonable, court refused to imply reasonableness requirement).

[97]Mullis v. Brennan, 716 N.E.2d 58 (Ind. Ct. App. 1999); Hagerman Const., Inc. v. Copeland, 697 N.E.2d 948 (Ind. Ct. App. 1998), opinion amended on reh'g, (Oct. 6, 1998) and transfer denied, 714 N.E.2d 171 (Ind. 1999).

ment concerning the amount of compensation to be paid, the law implies a promise on the part of the owner to pay a reasonable compensation for the labor;[98] a warranty of habitability may be implied in a residential construction contract.[99]

Unlike many states, Indiana does not require that a general duty of good faith and reasonableness be implied in every contract.[1] In Indiana, the duty of good faith is generally applied in contract law only under limited circumstances such as those involving insurance contracts.[2] When the parties are in a fiduciary relationship, courts require the party with a fiduciary duty to act with utmost good faith.[3] A duty of good faith may also apply to a contract where the terms of the contract are ambiguous or where the terms expressly apply such a duty.[4]

The existence of express terms in a valid contract precludes any implication of terms regarding the subject matter covered by the express terms.[5] That is, where parties form a valid contract specifying under what circumstances an obligation may arise with reference to certain subject matter,

---

[98]Coleman v. Chapman, 139 Ind. App. 385, 220 N.E.2d 285 (Div. 2 1966).

[99]Rogers v. Lewton, 570 N.E.2d 133 (Ind. Ct. App. 4th Dist. 1991).

Annotation References: Breach of Warranty in Sale, Installation, Repair, Design or Inspection of Septic or Sewage Disposal Systems, 50 ALR5th 417.

[1]Pardieck v. Pardieck, 676 N.E.2d 359 (Ind. Ct. App. 1997), transfer denied, 683 N.E.2d 595 (Ind. 1997).

As to the implied warranty of good faith and fair dealing imposed under the Uniform Commercial Code, see I.L.E., Sales of Personalty.

[2]First Federal Sav. Bank of Indiana v. Key Markets, Inc., 559 N.E.2d 600 (Ind. 1990).

[3]Sanders v. Townsend, 582 N.E.2d 355 (Ind. 1991); W & W Equipment Co., Inc. v. Mink, 568 N.E.2d 564 (Ind. Ct. App. 1st Dist. 1991), reh'g denied, (May 10, 1991) and transfer denied, (Dec. 12, 1991); O.K. Sand and Gravel, Inc. v. Martin Marietta Corp., 786 F. Supp. 1442 (S.D. Ind. 1992).

[4]First Federal Sav. Bank of Indiana v. Key Markets, Inc., 559 N.E.2d 600 (Ind. 1990) (when parties' intentions are not clear because of ambiguity in contract, court may be required to presume that parties were acting in good faith when entering into contract); Lake County Trust Co. v. Wine, 704 N.E.2d 1035 (Ind. Ct. App. 1998).

[5]Peoples Bank & Trust Co. v. Price, 714 N.E.2d 712 (Ind. Ct. App. 1999), transfer denied, (Nov. 19, 1999); Keystone Carbon Co. v. Black, 599 N.E.2d 213 (Ind. Ct. App. 1st Dist. 1992), transfer denied, (Dec. 2, 1992); Murray v. Monroe-Gregg School Dist., 585 N.E.2d 687, 72 Ed. Law Rep. 337 (Ind. Ct. App. 4th Dist. 1992).

it excludes the possibility of an implied covenant of a contra-
dictory or different nature.[6]

> ◆ **Illustrations:** Where a contract unambiguously
> provided that a woman was hired as a school principal,
> the court would not imply a contract provision allowing
> the school board to remove her from that position and
> employ her as a teacher, even at the same salary she
> would have received as a principal.[7]

The sole shareholder of a landfill sold his interest in the
operation for about $750,000. The parties agreed that if the
purchaser's permit to expend the landfill was granted by a
certain date, the purchaser would pay the seller an additional $4.5 million. The purchaser's permit application was
approved over a year after the cutoff date. Because the parties' contract expressly covered the matter, the court refused
to imply a contract for the payment of the additional sum
based on a theory of unjust enrichment.[8]

§ 76 Construction by parties

**A court interpreting an ambiguous contract may apply
the construction the parties have given the contract.**

West's Digest, Contracts ⇔170(1), 170(2).

The best criterion for judging the meaning of a contract is
the construction which the parties themselves place on it,[9]
and, ordinarily, the court will look to their interpretation in
determining the meaning of the contract.[10] as evidenced by
such things as acts in partial performance of the contract[11]

---

[6]Murray v. Monroe-Gregg School Dist., 585 N.E.2d 687, 72 Ed. Law
Rep. 337 (Ind. Ct. App. 4th Dist. 1992).

[7]Murray v. Monroe-Gregg School Dist., 585 N.E.2d 687, 72 Ed. Law
Rep. 337 (Ind. Ct. App. 4th Dist. 1992).

[8]Brown v. Mid-American Waste Systems, Inc., 924 F. Supp. 92 (S.D.
Ind. 1996) (applying Indiana law).

[9]Clark Mut. Life Ins. Co. v. Lewis, 139 Ind. App. 230, 217 N.E.2d 853
(Div. 2 1966).

[10]DeHaan v. DeHaan, 572 N.E.2d 1315 (Ind. Ct. App. 1st Dist. 1991),
reh'g denied, (July 31, 1991) and transfer denied, (Feb. 14, 1992); Clark
Mut. Life Ins. Co. v. Lewis, 139 Ind. App. 230, 217 N.E.2d 853 (Div. 2
1966).

[11]Brumfield v. State ex rel. Wallace, 206 Ind. 647, 190 N.E. 863 (1934);

and their present and past business dealings.[12] For instance, the time of performance of a contract and the time that the parties thereto intended to be bound by the contract may be made determined according to their conduct.[13] The construction placed upon a contract by the parties to it will be adopted by the court unless it is at variance with the correct legal interpretation of the contract.[14]

However, the rule permitting a consideration of the practical construction of a contract by the conduct of the parties may only be applied when the language of the contract is ambiguous, uncertain, indefinite, obscure, or not clear, so that there is doubt as to the meaning and proper construction thereof.[15] If the meaning of the contract is clear and unambiguous on its face, the court will not rely on, and is not bound by, an erroneous construction placed upon the contract by the parties.[16]

§ 77 Severability of contract

A contract is entire when the parties intend that each and all of its parts and consideration be common to each other and interdependent.

West's Digest, Contracts ☞171(1)-171(3).

A contract embraced in one instrument and executed by the same parties is not necessarily indivisible.[17] A single

---

Ketcham v. Brazil Block Coal Co., 88 Ind. 515, 1883 WL 5497 (1883); Cunningham v. New York Cent. R. Co., 114 Ind. App. 90, 48 N.E.2d 176 (1943).

[12]Bain v. Board of Trustees of Starke Memorial Hosp., 550 N.E.2d 106 (Ind. Ct. App. 3d Dist. 1990), reh'g denied, (Mar. 30, 1990).

[13]Albright v. Hughes, 107 Ind. App. 651, 26 N.E.2d 576 (1940).

[14]Albright v. Hughes, 107 Ind. App. 651, 26 N.E.2d 576 (1940).

[15]Vinton v. Baldwin, 95 Ind. 433, 1884 WL 5302 (1884); Johnson v. Gibson, 78 Ind. 282, 1881 WL 7099 (1881); Smith v. Mercer, 118 Ind. App. 575, 79 N.E.2d 772 (1948); Graham v. Mercereau Hawkins Tie Co., 81 Ind. App. 371, 139 N.E. 374 (Div. 1 1923).

[16]Heredia v. Sandler, 605 N.E.2d 1212 (Ind. Ct. App. 5th Dist. 1993); City of Evansville v. Old State Utility Corp., 550 N.E.2d 1339 (Ind. Ct. App. 1st Dist. 1990), appeal after remand, 576 N.E.2d 1311 (Ind. Ct. App. 1st Dist. 1991), reh'g denied, (Sept. 18, 1991).

[17]Beiger Heritage Corp. v. Montandon, 691 N.E.2d 1334 (Ind. Ct. App. 1998); Stoneburner v. Fletcher, 408 N.E.2d 545 (Ind. Ct. App. 2d Dist. 1980).

instrument may contain two distinct contracts, each of which may be enforced independently of the other.[18]

Whether a contract can be severed into separate parts, or must be treated as entire, is controlled by the intention of the parties.[19] The parties to a contract intend that the contract be entire and indivisible when by its terms, nature and purposes it contemplates and intends that each and all of its parts, material provisions, and consideration are common each to the other and interdependent.[20] If the contract could be completed in part only, it is more likely to be severable.[21]

> ◆ **Illustrations:** A contract contained both lease provisions and an option to purchase the real property subject to the lease. It also contained an attorney fee provision for actions arising "out of the possession of the premises." The lessor, against whom the lessee brought an action purportedly based on a dispute over the option contract, claimed that the attorney fee provision applied only to the lease, and that the lessee therefore could not recover attorney fees. The court, however, determined that all of the contract's material provisions were interdependent, that the contract was thus not divisible, and that the attorney fee provision pertained to the entire instrument.[22]

An individual purchased a lot, and in the same instrument was given a preemptive right to purchase the adjoining lot "at any time in the future." Because the main purpose of the contract was the purchase of the first lot, and because the use of the phrase "at any time in the future" could be reasonably interpreted as an expression of the parties' intent that the preemptive right survive the conveyance of the

---

[18]Crowell v. Himes, 117 Ind. App. 56, 69 N.E.2d 135 (1946).

For discussion of partial enforcement of partially illegal contracts, see § 57.

[19]Beiger Heritage Corp. v. Montandon, 691 N.E.2d 1334 (Ind. Ct. App. 1998).

[20]Samper v. Indiana Dept. of State Revenue, 231 Ind. 26, 106 N.E.2d 797 (1952); Beiger Heritage Corp. v. Montandon, 691 N.E.2d 1334 (Ind. Ct. App. 1998); Stoneburner v. Fletcher, 408 N.E.2d 545 (Ind. Ct. App. 2d Dist. 1980).

[21]Samper v. Indiana Dept. of State Revenue, 231 Ind. 26, 106 N.E.2d 797 (1952).

[22]Beiger Heritage Corp. v. Montandon, 691 N.E.2d 1334 (Ind. Ct. App. 1998).

principal property, the preemptive right was divisible from the main sale contract, and survived after the deed to the principal lot was delivered, even though the contract could have been completed in part only.[23]

A contract which was to be completed as an entirety and is not actually severable must be completed in its entirety before there can be recovery thereon. This rule, however, is inapplicable to contracts which have been partially performed, where benefits have accrued and have been accepted so as to imply an agreement to sever and divide the contract.[24]

§ 78 Questions of law and fact

The interpretation of an unambiguous contract, or one whose ambiguity arises from the language used, is a question for the court.

West's Digest, Contracts ⊕176(1)-176(11).

Generally, the interpretation and construction of contract provisions is a question of law to be determined by the courts.[25] If the language of a written contract is not ambiguous, its meaning is a question of law to be determined by the court,[26] and summary judgment is particularly appropriate.[27] When there is no conflicting evidence relating to the construction of a written instrument, the trial court may also direct a verdict according to the legal effect of the instru-

---

[23]Stoneburner v. Fletcher, 408 N.E.2d 545 (Ind. Ct. App. 2d Dist. 1980).

[24]Western Wheeled Scraper Co. v. Scott Const. Co., 217 Ind. 408, 27 N.E.2d 879 (1940).

[25]Kiltz v. Kiltz, 708 N.E.2d 600 (Ind. Ct. App. 1999), transfer denied, (Aug. 27, 1999); Tanton v. Grochow, 707 N.E.2d 1010 (Ind. Ct. App. 1999); Wildman v. National Fire and Marine Ins. Co., 703 N.E.2d 683 (Ind. Ct. App. 1998), transfer denied, 714 N.E.2d 173 (Ind. 1999); Eck & Associates, Inc. v. Alusuisse Flexible Packaging, Inc., 700 N.E.2d 1163 (Ind. Ct. App. 1998), transfer denied, 714 N.E.2d 167 (Ind. 1999).

[26]Eckart v. Davis, 631 N.E.2d 494 (Ind. Ct. App. 1st Dist. 1994).

[27]GEICO Ins. Co. v. Rowell, 705 N.E.2d 476 (Ind. Ct. App. 1999), reh'g denied, (Feb. 18, 1999); Sample v. Kinser Ins. Agency, Inc., 700 N.E.2d 802 (Ind. Ct. App. 1998); Hyperbaric Oxygen Therapy Systems, Inc. v. St. Joseph Medical Center of Ft. Wayne, Inc., 683 N.E.2d 243 (Ind. Ct. App. 1997), transfer denied, 690 N.E.2d 1189 (Ind. 1997); Plumlee v. Monroe Guar. Ins. Co., 655 N.E.2d 350 (Ind. Ct. App. 1995), reh'g denied, (Jan. 10, 1996) and transfer denied (Ind. June 4, 1996); Wright Motors, Inc. v. Marathon Oil Co., 631 N.E.2d 923 (Ind. Ct. App. 1st Dist. 1994).

ment.[28] Even if there is an ambiguity in the contract, if the ambiguity arises solely because of the language used in the contract and not because of extrinsic facts, then its construction is purely a question of law to be determined by the trial court.[29]

> ◆ **Illustration:** Ambiguity in a coal mining lease arose from the language employed in the lease, where the same lease paragraph contemplated two entirely different types of payment, both designated as "advanced royalties," and one of the types of advanced royalties, requiring minimum payments to the owner of the land, was actually a form of rent, although the term "rent" was not used in the contract.[30]

However, where the parties' paper trail leaves conflicting inferences which may be drawn from the facts, it is for the trier of fact to resolve any doubts, even slight ones.[31] Any ambiguity found to exist in a contract arising from extrinsic facts is to be resolved by the trier of fact.[32] so as to give effect to the parties' reasonable expectations.[33] Only where the contract is ambiguous and its interpretation requires extrinsic evidence must the fact finder determine the facts upon which the contract rests.[34]

---

[28]Noblesville Redevelopment Com'n v. Noblesville Associates Ltd. Partnership, 674 N.E.2d 558 (Ind. 1996).

[29]Fresh Cut, Inc. v. Fazli, 650 N.E.2d 1126 (Ind. 1995); First Federal Sav. Bank of Indiana v. Key Markets, Inc., 559 N.E.2d 600 (Ind. 1990); Francis v. Yates, 700 N.E.2d 504 (Ind. Ct. App. 1998).

[30]Bicknell Minerals, Inc. v. Tilly, 570 N.E.2d 1307 (Ind. Ct. App. 4th Dist. 1991), reh'g denied, (July 10, 1991) and transfer denied, (Feb. 26, 1992).

[31]JWP Zack, Inc. v. Hoosier Energy Rural Elec. Co-op., Inc., 709 N.E.2d 336 (Ind. Ct. App. 1999).

[32]Salin Bank and Trust Co. v. Review Bd. of Indiana Dept. of Workforce Development, 698 N.E.2d 1 (Ind. Ct. App. 1998); Hyperbaric Oxygen Therapy Systems, Inc. v. St. Joseph Medical Center of Ft. Wayne, Inc., 683 N.E.2d 243 (Ind. Ct. App. 1997), transfer denied, 690 N.E.2d 1189 (Ind. 1997); Ahuja v. Lynco Ltd. Medical Research, 675 N.E.2d 704 (Ind. Ct. App. 1996), transfer denied, 683 N.E.2d 590 (Ind. 1997); Anderson v. Horizon Homes, Inc., 644 N.E.2d 1281 (Ind. Ct. App. 5th Dist. 1995), transfer denied, (Apr. 21, 1995); Fetz v. Phillips, 591 N.E.2d 644 (Ind. Ct. App. 1st Dist. 1992).

[33]Campbell v. Spade, 617 N.E.2d 580 (Ind. Ct. App. 5th Dist. 1993).

[34]Noblesville Redevelopment Com'n v. Noblesville Associates Ltd.

The existence of an oral contract, and its terms, are matters to be determined by the trier of fact.[35]

Whether a contract is ambiguous to begin with is a question of law for the court.[36]

The legal effect of a written document is a question of law for the court to decide, whether the document is ambiguous or unambiguous.[37]

VIII. PARTIES TO CONTRACTS

Research References

IC 29-1-11-3; IC 29-1-14-5

17A Am Jur 2d, Contracts §§ 421-464.
17 C.J.S., Contracts §§ 30-33.
17A C.J.S., Contracts §§ 363-371.
West's Digest, Contracts ☞177-188.5.
ALR Digest: Contracts §§ 4, 4.5, 165
ALR Index: Adhesion Contracts; Anticipatory Breach; Anticipatory Renunciation or Repudiation; Bids and Bidding; Cancellation of Rescission; Consideration; Contracts; Covenants; Covenants Not to Compete; Estoppel and Waiver; Executory Contracts; Implied Contracts; Offer and Acceptance; Parol Contracts and Agreements; Parol Evidence; Third-Party Beneficiaries; Unconscionability
5A Am Jur Legal Forms 2d, Contracts §§ 68:61-68:63.

Partnership, 674 N.E.2d 558 (Ind. 1996); Fresh Cut, Inc. v. Fazli, 650 N.E.2d 1126 (Ind. 1995); Tate v. Secura Ins., 587 N.E.2d 665 (Ind. 1992); Barrington Management Co., Inc. v. Paul E. Draper Family Ltd. Partnership, 695 N.E.2d 135 (Ind. Ct. App. 1998); Schoemer v. Hanes & Associates, Inc., 693 N.E.2d 1333 (Ind. Ct. App. 1998).

For discussion of the admissibility of extrinsic evidence, see § 137.

[35]Annadall v. Union Cement & Lime Co., 165 Ind. 110, 74 N.E. 893 (1905); Ballew v. Town of Clarksville, 683 N.E.2d 636 (Ind. Ct. App. 1997), transfer denied, 698 N.E.2d 1182 (Ind. 1998); Tuthill Corp., Fill-Rite Div. v. Wolfe, 451 N.E.2d 72 (Ind. Ct. App. 3d Dist. 1983).

[36]Western Ohio Pizza, Inc. v. Clark Oil & Refining Corp., 704 N.E.2d 1086 (Ind. Ct. App. 1999), transfer denied, 714 N.E.2d 176 (Ind. 1999); Stevenson v. Hamilton Mut. Ins. Co., 672 N.E.2d 467 (Ind. Ct. App. 1996), reh'g denied, (Jan. 8, 1997); Harden v. Monroe Guar. Ins. Co., 626 N.E.2d 814 (Ind. Ct. App. 1st Dist. 1993), transfer denied, (June 22, 1994).

[37]Duchon v. Ross, 599 N.E.2d 621 (Ind. Ct. App. 2d Dist. 1992); Battershell v. Prestwick Sales, Inc., 585 N.E.2d 1 (Ind. Ct. App. 1st Dist. 1992), transfer denied, (June 24, 1992).

§ 79 In general

The parties to a contract may normally be identified from the terms of the contract.

West's Digest, Contracts ☜177-180.

The parties to a particular contract normally may be identified as a matter of law from the terms of the contract, unless there is some sort of ambiguity.[38]

♦ **Illustration:** Three individuals who were both school trustees and officers of a school building corporation signed a contract in their capacities as officers of the corporation, where two of them qualified their signatures by indicating their capacities as officers of the corporation and where the contract clearly designated the building corporation, rather than the school townships, as a party.[39]

A public officer is presumed to sign a contract dealing with his or her official duties in his or her official capacity.[40]

§ 80 Effect of signature by fewer than all parties

Parties to a contract who do not actually sign the document may be liable under the contract if that is the parties' intent.

West's Digest, Contracts ☜35, 177.

Where fewer than all of the proposed parties to a contract sign the document, the intent of the parties determines whether the signers are liable on the contract.[41] It can be assumed that the parties signing an agreement are bound by

---

[38]Implement Service, Inc. v. Tecumseh Products Co., 726 F. Supp. 1171 (S.D. Ind. 1989) (applying Indiana law); Broadhurst v. Moenning, 633 N.E.2d 326 (Ind. Ct. App. 5th Dist. 1994); Sunman-Dearborn Community School Corp. v. Kral-Zepf-Freitag and Associates, 167 Ind. App. 339, 338 N.E.2d 707 (1st Dist. 1975).

[39]Sunman-Dearborn Community School Corp. v. Kral-Zepf-Freitag and Associates, 167 Ind. App. 339, 338 N.E.2d 707 (1st Dist. 1975).

[40]Sparta School Tp. in Dearborn County v. Mendell, 138 Ind. 188, 37 N.E. 604 (1894).

[41]Anderson v. Indianapolis Indiana AAMCO Dealers Advertising Pool, 678 N.E.2d 832 (Ind. Ct. App. 1997), transfer denied, 690 N.E.2d 1183 (Ind. 1997); International Creative Management, Inc. v. D & R Entertainment Co., Inc., 670 N.E.2d 1305 (Ind. Ct. App. 1996), reh'g denied, (Oct. 29, 1996) and transfer denied, 683 N.E.2d 589 (Ind. 1997); Kruse Classic Auction Co., Inc. v. Aetna Cas. & Sur. Co., 511 N.E.2d 326 (Ind. Ct. App.

the agreement, unless it affirmatively appears that they did not intend to be bound unless others also signed.[42]

◆ **Illustration:** Where 10 of a corporation's shareholders signed a promissory note in exchange for a loan to the corporation, but two did not sign because they were out of the country at the time the loan was made, the signing shareholders were liable on the note, as none of them told the lender they would not be liable unless all shareholders' signatures were obtained and as both the corporation and the individual shareholders benefited from the loan.[43]

Even if the signature of all the parties might otherwise be considered necessary, the contract may be considered binding on the signatories if the nonsignatories accept the contract and perform affirmative acts thereunder.[44]

◆ **Observation:** In at least one case, the court has imposed the requirements of a contract on a nonsignatory where failing to do so would have permitted the signatory to circumvent the contract. Two employees of the same company signed slightly different covenants not to compete, one specifying that the employee, for one year after his employment ended, was to refrain from performing certain services for anyone who was a customer at the time the employee's employment ended, and the other specifying that the employee was not to perform these services for anyone who was a current customer or a potential customer who had received an offer from the employer or

---

3d Dist. 1987), reh'g denied, (Oct. 28, 1987) and transfer denied, (May 31, 1988); Curtis v. Hannah, 414 N.E.2d 962 (Ind. Ct. App. 1st Dist. 1981).

[42]Anderson v. Indianapolis Indiana AAMCO Dealers Advertising Pool, 678 N.E.2d 832 (Ind. Ct. App. 1997), transfer denied, 690 N.E.2d 1183 (Ind. 1997); International Creative Management, Inc. v. D & R Entertainment Co., Inc., 670 N.E.2d 1305 (Ind. Ct. App. 1996), reh'g denied, (Oct. 29, 1996) and transfer denied, 683 N.E.2d 589 (Ind. 1997); Kruse Classic Auction Co., Inc. v. Aetna Cas. & Sur. Co., 511 N.E.2d 326 (Ind. Ct. App. 3d Dist. 1987), reh'g denied, (Oct. 28, 1987) and transfer denied, (May 31, 1988); Curtis v. Hannah, 414 N.E.2d 962 (Ind. Ct. App. 1st Dist. 1981).

[43]Parrish v. Terre Haute Sav. Bank, 431 N.E.2d 132 (Ind. Ct. App. 4th Dist. 1982), reh'g denied, 438 N.E.2d 1 (Ind. Ct. App. 4th Dist. 1982) and transfer denied, (Feb. 4, 1985).

[44]Fairbanks v. Meyers, 98 Ind. 92, 1884 WL 5866 (1884); Street v. Chapman, 29 Ind. 142, 1867 WL 3032 (1867); Cincinnati, U. & Ft. W. R. Co. v. Pearce, 28 Ind. 502, 1867 WL 3004 (1867); Seymour Imp. Co. v. Viking Sprinkler Co., 87 Ind. App. 179, 161 N.E. 389 (1928); McCauley v. Schatzley, 44 Ind. App. 262, 88 N.E. 972 (Div. 1 1909).

for whom an offer was being prepared at the time his employment ended. The two subsequently left and formed their own company, of which they were the officers and sole employees. The first ex-employee, as a coincorporator and officer of the company, was bound by the broader covenant signed by the second ex-employee.[45]

§ 81 Joint, several, or joint and several contracts

Liability on a contract may be joint and several.

West's Digest, Contracts ☞181.

A creditor may enforce a joint and several contract obligation against either obligor or against both obligors.[46] If one of the parties to a joint contract dies, the whole interest vests in the survivors.[47]

Between obligors who are jointly and severally bound on a contract, each is ordinarily liable for one half of the debt or liability.[48]

An obligation entered into by two or more persons and a third person is presumed to be joint.[49] A mortgage executed by a partner on behalf of the partnership imposes joint liability for the mortgage on all of the partners.[50]

Joint and several contractual liability may be imposed by statute. For instance, contracts executed jointly by a decedent with any other person or persons are deemed to be

---

[45]Franke v. Honeywell, Inc., 516 N.E.2d 1090 (Ind. Ct. App. 3d Dist. 1987), transfer denied, (Aug. 31, 1988).

[46]McLochlin v. Miller, 139 Ind. App. 443, 217 N.E.2d 50, 3 U.C.C. Rep. Serv. (CBC) 526 (Div. 1 1966) (executor of deceased wife was liable to surviving husband, where husband and wife had been joint principals on note and husband had paid note).

[47]McIntosh v. Zaring, 150 Ind. 301, 49 N.E. 164 (1898); Brower v. Nellis, 6 Ind. App. 323, 33 N.E. 672 (1893).

[48]McLochlin v. Miller, 139 Ind. App. 443, 217 N.E.2d 50, 3 U.C.C. Rep. Serv. (CBC) 526 (Div. 1 1966).

[49]Cline v. Rodabaugh, 97 Ind. App. 258, 179 N.E. 6 (1931).

Forms References: Obligation as joint. 5A Am Jur Legal Forms 2d, Contracts § 68:61.

Obligation as several. 5A Am Jur Legal Forms 2d, Contracts § 68:62.

Obligation as joint and several. 5A Am Jur Legal Forms 2d, Contracts § 68:63.

[50]Crosby v. Jeroloman, 37 Ind. 264, 1871 WL 5061 (1871).

joint and several,[51] and sureties on a personal representative's bond are jointly and severally liable with the personal representative and with each other.[52] However, a contract with multiple signatories, in which the signatories specify that each is liable only for a certain amount or percentage of the obligation, is several.[53]

An obligation which purports to be that of one person, as by stating the obligation in the first person singular, and which is executed by more than one person may be treated as the several obligation of each person who signs it or as the joint obligation of all.[54]

§ 82 Privity of contract

Generally, only parties to a contract or those in privity with a party may enforce a contract.

West's Digest, Contracts ⚮100(1)-100(4).

Generally, only the parties to a contract or those in privity with the parties have rights under a contract.[55] For instance, an agent acting within the scope of his or her authority may bind his or her principal to a contract with a third party,[56] and a successor in interest may enforce or sue on a contract entered into by his or her predecessor in interest.[57] Two major exceptions to this rule exist. A third party intended by the parties to the contract to benefit from the contract may

---

[51]IC 29-1-14-5.

[52]IC 29-1-11-3.

[53]Davis & Rankin Bldg. & Mfg. Co. v. McKinney, 11 Ind. App. 696, 38 N.E. 1093 (1894); Davis & Rankin Bldg. & Mfg. Co. v. Booth, 10 Ind. App. 364, 37 N.E. 818 (1894); Davis & Rankin Bldg. & Mfg. Co. v. Hillsboro Creamery Co., 10 Ind. App. 42, 37 N.E. 549 (1894).

[54]Scheid v. Leibshultz, 51 Ind. 38, 1875 WL 6007 (1875).

[55]OEC-Diasonics, Inc. v. Major, 674 N.E.2d 1312 (Ind. 1996); Angell Enterprises, Inc. v. Abram & Hawkins Excavating Co., Inc., 643 N.E.2d 362 (Ind. Ct. App. 1st Dist. 1994), on reh'g, (Jan. 31, 1995); Gonzales v. Kil Nam Chun, 465 N.E.2d 727 (Ind. Ct. App. 4th Dist. 1984).

[56]Dominion Investments v. Yasechko, 767 F. Supp. 1460 (N.D. Ind. 1991) (applying Indiana law); Gonzales v. Kil Nam Chun, 465 N.E.2d 727 (Ind. Ct. App. 4th Dist. 1984).

[57]Tanton v. Grochow, 707 N.E.2d 1010 (Ind. Ct. App. 1999) (successors in interest to original parties who agreed to grant easements for joint driveway between their properties could sue on contract by which easement was formed).

enforce the contract,[58] and a subsequent purchaser of defective real[59] or personal[60] property may enforce the implied warranty of habitability or merchantability[61] against the original builder or manufacturer of the property. In the case of real property, the breach of warranty claim must be based on latent defects caused by the original builder-seller which become manifest after the purchase and which are not discoverable by the subsequent purchaser's reasonable inspection.[62]

A party who receives a benefit he or she has not expressly or impliedly agreed to is under no obligation to pay for that benefit, as he or she is not a party to a contract requiring such payment.[63]

§ 83 Agreements for benefit of third persons

A person who is not a party to a contract may enforce it if the contract was intended for his or her benefit.

West's Digest, Contracts ☞187(1)-188.

A person who is not a party to an agreement or in privity with a party may nonetheless directly enforce it[64] by demonstrating that he or she is a third-party beneficiary of the contract;[65] that is, that the parties to the contract intended

---

[58]For discussion of third-party beneficiaries, see § 83.

[59]Barnes v. Mac Brown & Co., Inc., 264 Ind. 227, 342 N.E.2d 619 (1976); Wagner Const. Co., Inc. v. Noonan, 403 N.E.2d 1144 (Ind. Ct. App. 1st Dist. 1980).

[60]J. I. Case Co. v. Sandefur, 245 Ind. 213, 197 N.E.2d 519 (1964).

[61]For discussion of implied warranties, see § 75.

For further discussion of the implied warranty of merchantability, see I.L.E., Sales of Personalty.

For further discussion of the implied warranty of habitability, see I.L.E., Sales of Realty.

[62]Barnes v. Mac Brown & Co., Inc., 264 Ind. 227, 342 N.E.2d 619 (1976); Wagner Const. Co., Inc. v. Noonan, 403 N.E.2d 1144 (Ind. Ct. App. 1st Dist. 1980).

[63]Olsson v. Moore, 590 N.E.2d 160 (Ind. Ct. App. 1st Dist. 1992), reh'g denied, (July 13, 1992).

[64]St. Paul Fire & Marine Ins. Co. v. Pearson Const. Co., 547 N.E.2d 853 (Ind. Ct. App. 4th Dist. 1989), transfer denied, (Dec. 5, 1990).

[65]National Bd. of Examiners for Osteopathic Physicians and Surgeons, Inc. v. American Osteopathic Ass'n, 645 N.E.2d 608 (Ind. Ct. App. 4th

to protect him or her under the agreement by imposition of a duty in his or her favor.[66]

◆ **Illustration:** A party granted a right of survivorship in a certificate of deposit may be a third-party beneficiary of the contract between the bank and the depositor,[67] and employees of a public contractor may sue as third-party beneficiaries for wages on a contract between the contractor and the public.[68]

A third-party beneficiary contract is one in which the promisor has a legal interest in performance in favor of a third party and in which performance of the terms of the contract will necessarily result in a direct benefit to the third party that was intended by the parties;[69] thus, a third-party beneficiary contract exists when:

- the parties intend to benefit the third party
- the contract imposes a duty on one of the parties in favor of the third party
- the performance of the terms of the contract renders a direct benefit to the third party intended by the parties to the contract[70]

The intent of the contracting parties to benefit the third party is the controlling factor in this analysis.[71] The parties'

Dist. 1994); Barth Elec. Co. v. Traylor Bros., Inc., 553 N.E.2d 504 (Ind. Ct. App. 1st Dist. 1990).

[66]OEC-Diasonics, Inc. v. Major, 674 N.E.2d 1312 (Ind. 1996).

[67]Parke State Bank v. Akers, 659 N.E.2d 1031 (Ind. 1995), reh'g denied, (May 22, 1996) (per Selby, J., with one judge concurring and one judge concurring in the result).

[68]Indiana State Bldg. and Const. Trades Council v. Warsaw Community School Corp., 493 N.E.2d 800 (Ind. Ct. App. 2d Dist. 1986).

[69]In re Estate of Von Wendesse, 618 N.E.2d 1332 (Ind. Ct. App. 1st Dist. 1993), transfer denied, (Oct. 22, 1993).

[70]Gilliana v. Paniaguas, 708 N.E.2d 895 (Ind. Ct. App. 1999), reh'g denied, (June 8, 1999) and transfer denied, (Oct. 13, 1999); Kiltz v. Kiltz, 708 N.E.2d 600 (Ind. Ct. App. 1999), transfer denied, (Aug. 27, 1999); Holloway v. Bob Evans Farms, Inc., 695 N.E.2d 991 (Ind. Ct. App. 1998); Rollins Burdick Hunter of Utah, Inc. v. Board of Trustees of Ball State University, 665 N.E.2d 914, 110 Ed. Law Rep. 373 (Ind. Ct. App. 1996).

[71]National Bd. of Examiners for Osteopathic Physicians and Surgeons, Inc. v. American Osteopathic Ass'n, 645 N.E.2d 608 (Ind. Ct. App. 4th Dist. 1994).

intent must be distinguished from their motives.[72] A third
party does not gain the right to sue under a contract merely
because he or she derives an incidental benefit from the
promisor's performance.[73] The parties must intend that they,
or one of them, shall assume a direct obligation to the third
party; it is not enough that they intend merely to benefit the
third party or promote his or her welfare.[74] This intention
must clearly appear from the terms of the contract itself,[75]
considered in its entirety against the background of the circumstances known to and shown to surround the contracting
parties at the time of its execution,[76] although it need not be
demonstrated any more clearly than the parties' intent
regarding any other terms of contract.[77] The parties' intent
to benefit the third party may be demonstrated by naming a
specific third party or class of third parties,[78] or by other
evidence,[79] and may be inferred.[80]

Trial Strategy References: Intent of Contracting Parties to Benefit Third Person, 16 Am Jur POF2d 55.

[72]St. Paul Fire & Marine Ins. Co. v. Pearson Const. Co., 547 N.E.2d 853
(Ind. Ct. App. 4th Dist. 1989), transfer denied, (Dec. 5, 1990).

[73]Harvey v. Lowry, 204 Ind. 93, 183 N.E. 309 (1932).

[74]National Bd. of Examiners for Osteopathic Physicians and Surgeons,
Inc. v. American Osteopathic Ass'n, 645 N.E.2d 608 (Ind. Ct. App. 4th
Dist. 1994).

[75]OEC-Diasonics, Inc. v. Major, 674 N.E.2d 1312 (Ind. 1996); St. Paul
Fire & Marine Ins. Co. v. Pearson Const. Co., 547 N.E.2d 853 (Ind. Ct.
App. 4th Dist. 1989), transfer denied, (Dec. 5, 1990); E.I. Dupont De
Nemours & Co. v. Ferguson, 86 Ind. App. 429, 158 N.E. 488 (1927).

[76]St. Paul Fire & Marine Ins. Co. v. Pearson Const. Co., 547 N.E.2d 853
(Ind. Ct. App. 4th Dist. 1989), transfer denied, (Dec. 5, 1990).

[77]OEC-Diasonics, Inc. v. Major, 674 N.E.2d 1312 (Ind. 1996).

[78]Tonn & Blank, Inc. v. Board of Com'rs of LaPorte County, 554 N.E.2d
827 (Ind. Ct. App. 3d Dist. 1990), transfer denied, (Oct. 2, 1990); St. Paul
Fire & Marine Ins. Co. v. Pearson Const. Co., 547 N.E.2d 853 (Ind. Ct.
App. 4th Dist. 1989), transfer denied, (Dec. 5, 1990); Russell v. Posey
County Dept. of Public Welfare, 471 N.E.2d 1209 (Ind. Ct. App. 1st Dist.
1984), reh'g denied, (Jan. 23, 1985) and transfer denied, (Apr. 24, 1985).

[79]National Bd. of Examiners for Osteopathic Physicians and Surgeons,
Inc. v. American Osteopathic Ass'n, 645 N.E.2d 608 (Ind. Ct. App. 4th
Dist. 1994); Gonzales v. Kil Nam Chun, 465 N.E.2d 727 (Ind. Ct. App. 4th
Dist. 1984).

[80]Gonzales v. Kil Nam Chun, 465 N.E.2d 727 (Ind. Ct. App. 4th Dist.
1984).

◆ **Illustration:** The general conditions in co-contractors' construction contracts required that each party pay for damages caused by the other contractors on the project. It was reasonable to conclude from this requirement that the contracting parties intended each contractor involved in the project to benefit from the timely, competent work of the other contractors or to be able to seek compensation from those contractors who failed to complete their work in an appropriate manner; therefore, the project's electric contractor was a third-party beneficiary to contracts entered into by the general contractor and the mechanical contractor and was entitled to compensation for any damages it suffered due to their delays.[81]

Individual members of the general public generally do not qualify as third-party beneficiaries.[82]

A contract for the benefit of a third person does not create a liability in the third person's favor until he or she has accepted the contract by some overt act. The commencement of an action to enforce the contract is a sufficient acceptance.[83] The acceptance of a contract made by a third person for the benefit of a minor is presumed from its beneficial character.[84] By acquiescing in and accepting the benefits of a contract as third-party beneficiaries, such parties, by so doing, must also be deemed to have accepted the contract's burdens and conditions.[85]

Third-party beneficiaries have no contractual obligations,

---

[81]Barth Elec. Co. v. Traylor Bros., Inc., 553 N.E.2d 504 (Ind. Ct. App. 1st Dist. 1990).

[82]Ayres v. Indian Heights Volunteer Fire Dept., Inc., 493 N.E.2d 1229 (Ind. 1986) (contract between township trustee and fire department was for benefit of residents of township as whole, and not of any single resident of township, so that individual residents were not third-party beneficiaries of contract); Holloway v. Bob Evans Farms, Inc., 695 N.E.2d 991 (Ind. Ct. App. 1998) (restaurant customer who consumed food in which worm had been cooked failed to show that she was third-party beneficiary of supplier's contract to provide restaurant with frozen food).

[83]Johnson v. Central Trust Co., 159 Ind. 605, 65 N.E. 1028 (1903); Copeland v. Summers, 138 Ind. 219, 37 N.E. 971 (1894); McCoy v. McCoy, 32 Ind. App. 38, 69 N.E. 193 (Div. 2 1903).

For discussion of modification of third party contracts which have not yet been accepted, see § 93.

[84]Copeland v. Summers, 138 Ind. 219, 35 N.E. 514 (1893), reh'g denied, 138 Ind. 219, 37 N.E. 971 (1894); Johnson v. Staley, 32 Ind. App. 628, 70 N.E. 541 (Div. 2 1904).

[85]Long v. Van Osdale, 218 Ind. 483, 29 N.E.2d 953 (1940).

only benefits;[86] thus, a third-party beneficiary may not be sued on contract.[87]

IX. TIME FOR PERFORMANCE

Research References

IC 26-1-2-309

17A Am Jur 2d, Contracts §§ 478-480, 483-499.
17A C.J.S., Contracts §§ 374-376.
West's Digest, Contracts ☞210-217.
ALR Digest: Contracts §§ 265-268
ALR Index: Adhesion Contracts; Anticipatory Breach; Anticipatory Renunciation or Repudiation; Bids and Bidding; Cancellation of Rescission; Consideration; Contracts; Covenants; Covenants Not to Compete; Estoppel and Waiver; Executory Contracts; Implied Contracts; Offer and Acceptance; Parol Contracts and Agreements; Parol Evidence; Third-Party Beneficiaries; Unconscionability
5A Am Jur Legal Forms 2d, Contracts §§ 68:224, 68:293, 68:295, 68:296.
Corbin on Contracts (rev. ed.), §§ 6.10-6.19.

§ 84 In general

If a contract does not prescribe a specific time for performance, it is presumed that the parties intended it to be performed within a reasonable time.

West's Digest, Contracts ☞212(1) - 213.

Payment or performance under a contract is to be made at the time prescribed by the contract;[88] however, a contract's failure to specify a definite time for performance does not, of itself, render the contract invalid.[89]

Where no time for performance is specified in a contract,

---

[86]Implement Service, Inc. v. Tecumseh Products Co., 726 F. Supp. 1171 (S.D. Ind. 1989) (applying Indiana law); Evansville & S. I. Traction Co. v. Evansville Belt Ry. Co., 44 Ind. App. 155, 87 N.E. 21 (Div. 2 1909).

[87]Implement Service, Inc. v. Tecumseh Products Co., 726 F. Supp. 1171 (S.D. Ind. 1989) (applying Indiana law).

[88]Cleveland, C., C. & St. L. Ry. Co. v. Scott, 39 Ind. App. 420, 79 N.E. 226 (Div. 2 1906).

Forms References: Time for payment. 5A Am Jur Legal Forms 2d, Contracts § 68:224.

[89]Indiana Bell Telephone Co. v. Ice Service, Inc., 142 Ind. App. 23, 231 N.E.2d 820 (Div. 2 1967).

the law will imply that it must be performed within a reasonable time.[90] Similarly, if payment of an existing debt is postponed until the occurrence of some contingency and the contingency does not happen, the debt is required to be paid within a reasonable time.[91] A performance not made within a reasonable time may allow the other party to the contract to avoid the contract on the basis of failure of consideration.[92]

◆ **Caution:** The Indiana Supreme Court has held that money not made payable at any fixed or certain time is payable only on demand, and the person to whom the money is owed cannot sue for it until he or she has demanded payment.[93]

What constitutes a reasonable time within which an act is to be performed is a question of fact[94] and depends on the subject matter of the contract, the situation of the parties, and the circumstances attending the performance.[95]

◆ **Illustrations:** A two-and-a-half month delay in grading a roadbed on land on which the owner had built apartments was not reasonable under the circumstances. The apartments, which the owner intended to open in May,

---

[90]In re Estate of Moore, 714 N.E.2d 675 (Ind. Ct. App. 1999); Lightle v. Harcourt Management Co., Inc., 634 N.E.2d 858 (Ind. Ct. App. 5th Dist. 1994), transfer denied, (Nov. 3, 1994); Community State Bank Royal Center v. O'Neill, 553 N.E.2d 174 (Ind. Ct. App. 2d Dist. 1990); Jay Clutter Custom Digging v. English, 181 Ind. App. 603, 393 N.E.2d 230 (3d Dist. 1979).

[91]Prell v. Trustees of Baird and Warner Mortg. and Realty Investors, 179 Ind. App. 642, 386 N.E.2d 1221 (1st Dist. 1979); Stolkin v. Abrams, 104 Ind. App. 587, 12 N.E.2d 377 (1938).

[92]McCartin McAuliffe Mechanical Contractor, Inc. v. Midwest Gas Storage, Inc., 685 N.E.2d 165 (Ind. Ct. App. 1997), reh'g denied, (Nov. 24, 1997) and transfer denied, 706 N.E.2d 166 (Ind. 1998).

For discussion of consideration, see §§ 13 et seq.

[93]Cole v. Wright, 70 Ind. 179, 1880 WL 6185 (1880).

[94]In re Estate of Moore, 714 N.E.2d 675 (Ind. Ct. App. 1999); Hamlin v. Steward, 622 N.E.2d 535 (Ind. Ct. App. 1st Dist. 1993); Albright v. Hughes, 107 Ind. App. 651, 26 N.E.2d 576 (1940).

[95]Indiana Farmers Mut. Ins. Co. v. Walters, 221 Ind. 642, 50 N.E.2d 868 (1943); Fraternal Order of Police Lodge No. 52 v. Civil City of Elkhart, Ind., 551 N.E.2d 469 (Ind. Ct. App. 3d Dist. 1990), reh'g denied, (May 9, 1990) and transfer granted, opinion vacated on other grounds, (Sept. 10, 1990) and transfer dismissed, (Sept. 19, 1990); Jay Clutter Custom Digging v. English, 181 Ind. App. 603, 393 N.E.2d 230 (3d Dist. 1979); Albright v. Hughes, 107 Ind. App. 651, 26 N.E.2d 576 (1940).

could not be occupied until the grading was done because the roadway was impassable when it rained. Although the grading company was delayed by rain for about two weeks in mid- and late March, it did not come back to finish the work on the three occasions the owner called in April and May to inform the company that the ground was dry and the work could be resumed, even though the company informed the owner on each occasion that it would resume work within a few days. The company returned on June 1, by which time the owner had hired another contractor to make the road passable.[96]

An agreed order between two beneficiaries of a will to sell the testator's home and divide the net estate was performed within a reasonable time where the complaining beneficiary received her share of the proceeds less than four months after the order was entered. The testator's original personal representative had died after the agreed order was entered, requiring the appointment of a successor before the estate could be administered and the value of the net estate determined.[97]

When both parties to a contract acquiesce in a delay, neither side can suddenly declare the contract rescinded and simply walk away. Notice must be given to the other party along with an opportunity to perform within a reasonable time.[98]

§ 85 Stipulations as to time

The parties must intend that time will be of the essence of their contract before a court from which equitable relief is sought will consider it so.

West's Digest, Contracts ☞210, 211.

Courts presiding over actions for equitable relief do not generally view time as being of the essence of a contract unless the terms of the contract or the conduct of the parties indicate that the parties intended to make it so.[99] A party to a contract can prove time to be of the essence by either the

---

[96]Jay Clutter Custom Digging v. English, 181 Ind. App. 603, 393 N.E.2d 230 (3d Dist. 1979).

[97]In re Estate of Moore, 714 N.E.2d 675 (Ind. Ct. App. 1999).

[98]Scott-Reitz Ltd. v. Rein Warsaw Associates, 658 N.E.2d 98 (Ind. Ct. App. 1995); Keliher v. Cure, 534 N.E.2d 1133 (Ind. Ct. App. 2d Dist. 1989).

[99]Keller v. Fisher, 7 Ind. 718, 1856 WL 3635 (1856); Smith v. Potter,

terms of the instrument or evidence of circumstances establishing that the parties intended time to be the controlling element of the contract.[1] A time limit placed in the contract at the request of one of the parties makes time of the essence even if the contract does not specifically so state, where the party later seeks legal, as opposed to equitable, relief.[2]

Where time is of the essence of the contract and a time for performance is specified, strict performance at that time is necessary unless the requirement is waived.[3] When a written agreement to convey real property makes time of the essence and fixes a termination date, and there is no conduct giving rise to estoppel or waiver, the agreement becomes legally defunct upon the stated termination date if performance is not tendered.[4]

Time cannot be made essential to a contract if doing so would be unconscionable.[5]

---

652 N.E.2d 538 (Ind. Ct. App. 1995), transfer denied, (Nov. 22, 1995); Hollars v. Randall, 554 N.E.2d 1177 (Ind. Ct. App. 2d Dist. 1990); Donavan v. Ivy Knoll Apartments Partnership, 537 N.E.2d 47 (Ind. Ct. App. 4th Dist. 1989).

[1]McClellan v. Coffin, 93 Ind. 456, 1884 WL 5627 (1884); Smith v. Potter, 652 N.E.2d 538 (Ind. Ct. App. 1995), transfer denied, (Nov. 22, 1995); Donavan v. Ivy Knoll Apartments Partnership, 537 N.E.2d 47 (Ind. Ct. App. 4th Dist. 1989).

[2]Ohio Valley Buggy Co. v. Anderson Forging Co., 168 Ind. 593, 81 N.E. 574 (1907); Orto v. Jackson, 413 N.E.2d 273 (Ind. Ct. App. 4th Dist. 1980).

Where a contract consisting of an offer letter and a purchase-order acceptance showed no fixed time for performance, but only estimates of the time required to complete the project, time was not of the essence of the contract.—Kokomo Tube Co. v. Dayton Equipment Services Co., 123 F.3d 616 (7th Cir. 1997) (applying Indiana law).

[3]Barrington Management Co., Inc. v. Paul E. Draper Family Ltd. Partnership, 695 N.E.2d 135 (Ind. Ct. App. 1998).

[4]Barrington Management Co., Inc. v. Paul E. Draper Family Ltd. Partnership, 695 N.E.2d 135 (Ind. Ct. App. 1998); Smith v. Potter, 652 N.E.2d 538 (Ind. Ct. App. 1995), transfer denied, (Nov. 22, 1995) (trial court did not commit clear error in determining that plaintiff's failure to close real estate transaction within time specified by contract extinguished defendants' obligation to convey property).

[5]Spath v. Hankins, 55 Ind. 155, 1876 WL 6855 (1876).

For discussion of unconscionability, see § 41.

Where the duration of an option is specified, time is of the essence in an option contract.[6]

§ 86   Duration and termination of contract

A continuing contract may terminate at a time specified in the contract, at the will of either party, or after a reasonable time.

West's Digest, Contracts ☞215(1)-217.

A contract which calls for some continuing action by both parties may terminate at a time[7] or upon an occurrence[8] specified in the contract. A continuing contract which contains no specific time for termination or provides that it is to last indefinitely may be terminated by either party at will.[9]

An agreement imposing a duty on one party, in which the time of performance is not otherwise limited, is presumed to

---

[6]Calwell v. Bankers Trust Co., 113 Ind. App. 345, 47 N.E.2d 170 (1943).

[7]THQ Venture v. SW, Inc., 444 N.E.2d 335 (Ind. Ct. App. 1st Dist. 1983) (where cattle purchase contract specified that it was to last five years, guarantor was not obligated to guarantee contracts in sixth and seventh years, even though calves born in fourth and fifth years of contract would be ready for market in those years).

Forms References: Fixed duration with future right of cancellation. 5A Am Jur Legal Forms 2d, Contracts § 68:293.

[8]Hacienda Mexican Restaurant of Kalamazoo Corp. v. Hacienda Franchise Group, Inc., 569 N.E.2d 661 (Ind. Ct. App. 5th Dist. 1991), transfer denied, (May 30, 1991) and transfer denied, (Dec. 6, 1991) and appeal after remand, 641 N.E.2d 1036 (Ind. Ct. App. 4th Dist. 1994) (franchisor properly terminated franchise agreement after franchisees were late with royalty payments three times, where agreement specified that franchisor could terminate agreement any time franchisees were late with payment three times within 18-month period); Marksill Specialties, Inc. v. Barger, 428 N.E.2d 65 (Ind. Ct. App. 3d Dist. 1981).

Forms References: Breach as terminating contract. 5A Am Jur Legal Forms 2d, Contracts § 68:295.

Future event as terminating contract. 5A Am Jur Legal Forms 2d, Contracts § 68:296.

[9]Bell v. Speed Queen, 407 F.2d 1022 (7th Cir. 1969) (applying Indiana law); Best Distributing Co., Inc. v. Seyfert Foods, Inc., 714 N.E.2d 1196 (Ind. Ct. App. 1999); House of Crane Inc. v. H. Fendrich, Inc., 146 Ind. App. 478, 256 N.E.2d 578 (Div. 1 1970); Monon R. R. v. New York Cent. R. Co., 141 Ind. App. 277, 227 N.E.2d 450 (Div. 1 1967).

For discussion of the employment-at-will doctrine, see I.L.E., Employment.

continue in force for a reasonable time.[10] For instance, the implied warranty of habitability is deemed to last for a reasonable period of time;[11] nevertheless, absent some indication that the original covenantors intended to limit its duration, a covenant which runs with real property generally survives as long as the estate with which it runs.[12]

Ordinarily, the death of either party to a contract does not discharge it, if it may be performed by the party's personal representative;[13] however, a contract for personal services terminates upon the death of the person for whose services are contracted.[14]

◆ **Caution:** In an action governed by the Uniform Commercial Code, the party terminating a contract terminable at will must give reasonable notification of the termination.[15]

X. CONDITIONS

Research References

17A Am Jur 2d, Contracts §§ 465-477.
17A C.J.S., Contracts §§ 355-360.
West's Digest, Contracts ☞218-227.

---

[10]Grand Lodge Hall Ass'n, I. O. O. F. v. Moore, 224 Ind. 575, 70 N.E.2d 19, 173 A.L.R. 6 (1945), judgment aff'd, 330 U.S. 808, 67 S. Ct. 1088, 91 L. Ed. 1265 (1947); Albright v. Hughes, 107 Ind. App. 651, 26 N.E.2d 576 (1940).

[11]Wagner Const. Co., Inc. v. Noonan, 403 N.E.2d 1144 (Ind. Ct. App. 1st Dist. 1980).

[12]Moseley v. Bishop, 470 N.E.2d 773 (Ind. Ct. App. 4th Dist. 1984) (where defendant agreed to maintain tile in drainage ditch on plaintiff's land and ditch was vital to keep plaintiff's land tillable, parties intended agreement to last beyond useful life of original tile); Chicago, I. & L. Ry. Co. v. Beisel, 122 Ind. App. 448, 106 N.E.2d 117 (1952).

[13]Miller v. Ready, 59 Ind. App. 195, 108 N.E. 605 (Div. 2 1915).

Annotation References: Death of lessee as terminating lease, 42 ALR4th 963.

Validity and effect of agreement that debt or legal obligation contemporaneously or subsequently incurred shall be canceled by death of creditor or obligee, 11 ALR3d 1427.

[14]Jones v. Servel, Inc., 135 Ind. App. 171, 186 N.E.2d 689 (Div. 2 1962).

[15]IC 26-1-2-309(3).

Monarch Beverage Co., Inc. v. Tyfield Importers, Inc., 823 F.2d 1187, 4 U.C.C. Rep. Serv. 2d (CBC) 388 (7th Cir. 1987) (applying Indiana law).

ALR Digest: Contracts §§ 28, 29, 102, 162, 299-302, 482-490.5, 527-530

ALR Index: Adhesion Contracts; Anticipatory Breach; Anticipatory Renunciation or Repudiation; Bids and Bidding; Cancellation of Rescission; Consideration; Contracts; Covenants; Covenants Not to Compete; Estoppel and Waiver; Executory Contracts; Implied Contracts; Offer and Acceptance; Parol Contracts and Agreements; Parol Evidence; Third-Party Beneficiaries; Unconscionability

Corbin on Contracts (rev. ed.), §§ 5.31-5.34.

§ 87　In general

A condition precedent must be performed before a contract becomes binding; a condition subsequent may defeat a contract.

West's Digest, Contracts ☞218-221.

A condition is an event which qualifies a duty under an existing contract.[16] Generally, an express condition must be fulfilled or no liability can arise on the promise that the condition qualifies.[17] A condition precedent does not destroy mutuality, because once a condition is fulfilled, mutuality of obligation exists.[18]

Although a condition may be excused if the requirement will involve extreme forfeiture or penalty and if its existence or occurrence forms no essential part of the exchange for the promisor's performance, the mere harshness or unfairness of a condition in its operation will not excuse performance.[19] Performance of the condition may also be excused by waiver.[20]

A condition may be either a condition precedent or a condition subsequent. A condition precedent is a condition that must be performed before the agreement of the parties becomes a binding contract or that must be fulfilled before

---

[16]Hamlin v. Steward, 622 N.E.2d 535 (Ind. Ct. App. 1st Dist. 1993).

For more specific discussion of conditions, see specific topics, including I.L.E., Arbitration; Chattel Mortgages; Landlord and Tenant; Sales of Personalty; Sales of Realty.

[17]Indiana State Highway Com'n v. Curtis, 704 N.E.2d 1015 (Ind. 1998).

[18]Kokomo Veterans, Inc. v. Schick, 439 N.E.2d 639 (Ind. Ct. App. 3d Dist. 1982).

For discussion of mutuality, see § 4.

[19]Indiana State Highway Com'n v. Curtis, 704 N.E.2d 1015 (Ind. 1998).

[20]For discussion of waiver of conditions, see § 88.

the duty to perform a specific obligation arises,[21] such as the requirement that a purchaser obtain financing.[22] A condition subsequent is a condition which, if performed or violated (as the case may be), defeats the contract.[23] An expiration date, for instance, is a condition subsequent.[24]

The parties to a contract containing a condition have an implied obligation to make a reasonable and good-faith effort to satisfy the condition.[25] A party may not rely on a failure of a condition precedent where that party's inaction caused the failure.[26] Where a condition in a contract is the approval by another component of one of the parties, the component from which approval is sought is required only to consider ap-

---

[21]Indiana State Highway Com'n v. Curtis, 704 N.E.2d 1015 (Ind. 1998) (state Department of Transportation's approval of easement granted in settlement agreement was condition precedent to settlement); Dvorak v. Christ, 692 N.E.2d 920 (Ind. Ct. App. 1998), reh'g denied, (May 27, 1998) and transfer denied, 706 N.E.2d 171 (Ind. 1998); Worrell v. WLT Corp., 653 N.E.2d 1054 (Ind. Ct. App. 1995), transfer denied, (Dec. 5, 1995) (exercise of option to purchase golf course was condition precedent to purchasers' sale of part interest in golf course).

[22]Barrington Management Co., Inc. v. Paul E. Draper Family Ltd. Partnership, 695 N.E.2d 135 (Ind. Ct. App. 1998); Dvorak v. Christ, 692 N.E.2d 920 (Ind. Ct. App. 1998), reh'g denied, (May 27, 1998) and transfer denied, 706 N.E.2d 171 (Ind. 1998); Sand Creek Country Club, Ltd. v. CSO Architects, Inc., 582 N.E.2d 872 (Ind. Ct. App. 3d Dist. 1991).

[23]Barrington Management Co., Inc. v. Paul E. Draper Family Ltd. Partnership, 695 N.E.2d 135 (Ind. Ct. App. 1998); Dvorak v. Christ, 692 N.E.2d 920 (Ind. Ct. App. 1998), reh'g denied, (May 27, 1998) and transfer denied, 706 N.E.2d 171 (Ind. 1998); Knauf Fiber Glass, GmbH v. Stein, 615 N.E.2d 115 (Ind. Ct. App. 5th Dist. 1993), aff'd in part, vacated in part on other grounds, 622 N.E.2d 163 (Ind. 1993), reh'g denied, (Aug. 16, 1994).

[24]Barrington Management Co., Inc. v. Paul E. Draper Family Ltd. Partnership, 695 N.E.2d 135 (Ind. Ct. App. 1998); Dvorak v. Christ, 692 N.E.2d 920 (Ind. Ct. App. 1998), reh'g denied, (May 27, 1998) and transfer denied, 706 N.E.2d 171 (Ind. 1998).

[25]Indiana State Highway Com'n v. Curtis, 704 N.E.2d 1015 (Ind. 1998); Hamlin v. Steward, 622 N.E.2d 535 (Ind. Ct. App. 1st Dist. 1993);

Billman v. Hensel, 181 Ind. App. 272, 391 N.E.2d 671 (3d Dist. 1979) (clause stating that contract for sale of property is subject to purchaser's obtaining financing imposes on purchaser implied obligation to make reasonable and good-faith effort to obtain financing).

[26]Indiana State Highway Com'n v. Curtis, 704 N.E.2d 1015 (Ind. 1998); Hamlin v. Steward, 622 N.E.2d 535 (Ind. Ct. App. 1st Dist. 1993); Billman v. Hensel, 181 Ind. App. 272, 391 N.E.2d 671 (3d Dist. 1979).

proval in good faith.[27] This issue arises when one governmental agency must approve action by another or when some organization such as a corporation's board of directors must approve action by the corporation.[28]

Conditions are disfavored and must be stated explicitly within the contract.[29] An existing contract may, however, be modified by the addition of a condition.[30]

§ 88 Waiver

Performance of a condition to a contract may be excused by waiver.

West's Digest, Contracts ☞218-220.

Ordinarily, a party can waive any contractual right provided for his or her benefit.[31] Waiver is the voluntary and intentional relinquishment of a known right;[32] thus, a party for whose benefit a condition has been inserted in a contract may voluntarily waive the condition[33] if the party wishes to proceed with the contract despite the failure of the condition.[34] A party may waive either a condition precedent to

---

[27]Indiana State Highway Com'n v. Curtis, 704 N.E.2d 1015 (Ind. 1998).

[28]Indiana State Highway Com'n v. Curtis, 704 N.E.2d 1015 (Ind. 1998).

[29]Scott-Reitz Ltd. v. Rein Warsaw Associates, 658 N.E.2d 98 (Ind. Ct. App. 1995); Knauf Fiber Glass, GmbH v. Stein, 615 N.E.2d 115 (Ind. Ct. App. 5th Dist. 1993), aff'd in part, vacated in part on other grounds, 622 N.E.2d 163 (Ind. 1993), reh'g denied, (Aug. 16, 1994); Sand Creek Country Club, Ltd. v. CSO Architects, Inc., 582 N.E.2d 872 (Ind. Ct. App. 3d Dist. 1991); Krukemeier v. Krukemeier Mach. & Tool Co., Inc., 551 N.E.2d 885 (Ind. Ct. App. 1st Dist. 1990).

[30]Hamlin v. Steward, 622 N.E.2d 535 (Ind. Ct. App. 1st Dist. 1993).

For discussion of modification of contracts, see §§ 93 et seq.

[31]Salcedo v. Toepp, 696 N.E.2d 426 (Ind. Ct. App. 1998).

[32]Indiana State Highway Com'n v. Curtis, 704 N.E.2d 1015 (Ind. 1998); Northern Indiana Commuter Transp. Dist. v. Chicago SouthShore, 685 N.E.2d 680 (Ind. 1997).

[33]Indiana State Highway Com'n v. Curtis, 704 N.E.2d 1015 (Ind. 1998).

[34]Crum v. AVCO Financial Services of Indianapolis, Inc., 552 N.E.2d 823 (Ind. Ct. App. 1st Dist. 1990), transfer denied, (Aug. 31, 1990);

Kokomo Veterans, Inc. v. Schick, 439 N.E.2d 639 (Ind. Ct. App. 3d Dist. 1982).

performance under a contract[35] or a condition subsequent, such as a contractual limitation of action.[36]

The existence of waiver may be implied from the acts, omissions, or conduct of one of the parties to the contract.[37] Silence can amount to a waiver of a contractual condition where the waiving party has a duty to speak.[38]

Once a condition has been waived and the waiver has been acted upon, the failure to perform the condition cannot be asserted as a breach of contract.[39] A party may not waive a condition after the contract has terminated because of failure of the condition.[40]

XI. COMPENSATION

Research References

17A Am Jur 2d, Contracts §§ 500-512.
17A C.J.S., Contracts §§ 377-406.
West's Digest, Contracts ☞228-235.
ALR Digest: Contracts §§ 257, 263, 394
ALR Index: Adhesion Contracts; Anticipatory Breach; Anticipatory Renunciation or Repudiation; Bids and Bidding; Cancellation of Rescission; Consideration; Contracts; Covenants; Covenants Not to Compete; Estoppel and Waiver; Executory Contracts; Implied Contracts; Offer and Acceptance; Parol Contracts and Agreements; Parol Evidence; Third-Party Beneficiaries; Unconscionability

[35]Indiana State Highway Com'n v. Curtis, 695 N.E.2d 143 (Ind. Ct. App. 1998), transfer granted, (Oct. 2, 1998) and aff'd, 704 N.E.2d 1015 (Ind. 1998); Powers v. City of Lafayette, 622 N.E.2d 1311 (Ind. Ct. App. 4th Dist. 1993), transfer denied, (Feb. 18, 1994).

[36]Lumpkins v. Grange Mut. Companies, 553 N.E.2d 871 (Ind. Ct. App. 2d Dist. 1990).

[37]Salcedo v. Toepp, 696 N.E.2d 426 (Ind. Ct. App. 1998); Hamlin v. Steward, 622 N.E.2d 535 (Ind. Ct. App. 1st Dist. 1993); Integrity Ins. Co. v. Lindsey, 444 N.E.2d 345 (Ind. Ct. App. 1st Dist. 1983).

[38]Stewart v. Walker, 597 N.E.2d 368 (Ind. Ct. App. 5th Dist. 1992), reh'g denied, (Oct. 16, 1992).

[39]Salcedo v. Toepp, 696 N.E.2d 426 (Ind. Ct. App. 1998); Integrity Ins. Co. v. Lindsey, 444 N.E.2d 345 (Ind. Ct. App. 1st Dist. 1983).

[40]Barrington Management Co., Inc. v. Paul E. Draper Family Ltd. Partnership, 695 N.E.2d 135 (Ind. Ct. App. 1998); Dvorak v. Christ, 692 N.E.2d 920 (Ind. Ct. App. 1998), reh'g denied, (May 27, 1998) and transfer denied, 706 N.E.2d 171 (Ind. 1998).

§ 89 In general

If no compensation is specified in a contract, the party furnishing services and materials is entitled to their reasonable value.

West's Digest, Contracts ⊜228-230, 233, 234.

Generally, the terms of compensation to be made under a contract are spelled out in the contract.

> ◆ **Illustrations:** A contract between a mobile home manufacturer and a dealer provided that the dealer was to be eligible for a competitive discount calculated as of the last day of the first four years in which the parties performed under the agreement, and it specifically stated that if the agreement was terminated for any reason before that date, all credits earned toward the discount were to be canceled. The agreement was terminated after two years. The dealer was not entitled to the discount.[41]

Where a credit application form provided that its terms were not binding on the applicant or the financing company until final legal documentation in connection with the extension of credit was executed, the financing company could not retain the applicant's deposit after the applicant terminated the negotiations before loan documents were executed.[42]

The failure to specify the amount of compensation to be made, however, does not invalidate the agreement.[43] When the parties to a contract have agreed that compensation is to be paid but have not fixed a price, a party furnishing services and materials in performance of the contract is entitled to the reasonable value of the services and materials.[44]

If a contract calls for a certain amount of payment or for payment to be calculated by a certain method, the court may

---

[41]Champion Home Builders Co. v. Potts, 538 N.E.2d 280 (Ind. Ct. App. 3d Dist. 1989).

[42]Excel Industries, Inc. v. Signal Capital Corp., 574 N.E.2d 946 (Ind. Ct. App. 3d Dist. 1991), transfer denied, (Jan. 23, 1992).

[43]Indiana Bell Telephone Co. v. Ice Service, Inc., 142 Ind. App. 23, 231 N.E.2d 820 (Div. 2 1967).

[44]Kokomo Tube Co. v. Dayton Equipment Services Co., 123 F.3d 616 (7th Cir. 1997) (applying Indiana law); Botts v. Fultz, 70 Ind. 396, 1880 WL 6426 (1880); Indiana Bell Telephone Co. v. Ice Service, Inc., 142 Ind. App. 23, 231 N.E.2d 820 (Div. 2 1967).

not change the amount or method on one party's request.[45] If a contract provides a guaranteed maximum price for services and materials, for instance, the provider of the services and materials will not be entitled to recover payment in excess of that amount. The party seeking recovery in excess of that amount will be required to show that the services or materials for which he or she seeks extra compensation were not included in the original contract.[46]

A party to a contract may lose his or her right to compensation if he or she does not perform in accordance with the contract.[47] Where a party performs some, but not all, of the services agreed upon, he or she is not entitled to full compensation as provided in the contract, but only for compensation for the work actually performed.[48]

Where parties contract for certain services and then rescind the contract, the party who was to provide the services is not entitled to compensation at the rate provided by the contract.[49]

§ 90   Building and construction contracts

Parties to a construction contract are bound to the contract price unless there have been so many substantial changes to the original contract that it can no longer be used to determine the value of the work done.

West's Digest, Contracts ☞231(1), 231(2).

The parties to a construction contract are generally bound

---

[45]Indiana Gas & Water Co. v. Williams, 132 Ind. App. 8, 175 N.E.2d 31 (Div. 2 1961) (contract for payment based in part on estimated total revenue from individual utility customers prevented party to whom payments were to be made from receiving amounts calculated on actual revenue received from customers, even though actual revenue was considerably more than estimates).

[46]TRW, Inc. v. Fox Development Corp., 604 N.E.2d 626 (Ind. Ct. App. 4th Dist. 1992), reh'g denied, (Feb. 19, 1993) and transfer denied, (May 21, 1993).

[47]Malo v. Gilman, 177 Ind. App. 365, 379 N.E.2d 554 (3d Dist. 1978) (architect lost right to compensation for designing building where contract called for building whose cost would not exceed $78,000 and lowest bid owner received from builders was $105,000).

[48]Greenhaven Corp. v. Hutchcraft & Associates, Inc., 463 N.E.2d 283 (Ind. Ct. App. 2d Dist. 1984) (where architect performed 95 to 97% of work contracted for before project was canceled, he was not entitled to recover all of the compensation agreed upon).

[49]Mills v. Riley, 7 Ind. 137, 1855 WL 3775 (1855).

by the price agreed upon in the contract.[50] Where the rights of the parties as to compensation are governed by an express contract, a party may not recover for his or her work based on quantum meruit.[51] Ordinarily, a mere cost estimate is not binding.[52]

Most construction contracts are either fixed price contracts, in which the parties agree on a specific price for the entire job, or time and materials contracts, in which the parties agree that the builder will be paid according to the time and materials used in the job. Under a time and materials contract, the owner must pay the builder the reasonable value of the labor and materials provided.[53] If the contract is for a fixed price or a guaranteed maximum price, the owner will not be liable for extra charges based on labor and material costs or management fees in excess of the price agreed upon.[54]

Where parties to a construction contract have originally agreed on a price for the work to be done, the party who is to perform the work may nonetheless recover for the reasonable value of the work done if there have been so many substantial changes to the original contract that it can no longer be used to determine the value of the work done.[55] In determining whether this rule should apply, courts consider the following circumstances:

---

[50]Prewitt v. Londeree, 141 Ind. App. 291, 216 N.E.2d 724 (Div. 2 1966).

[51]Kern v. City of Lawrenceburg, 625 N.E.2d 1326 (Ind. Ct. App. 1st Dist. 1993); Kincaid v. Lazar, 405 N.E.2d 615 (Ind. Ct. App. 1st Dist. 1980); Myers v. Maris, 164 Ind. App. 34, 326 N.E.2d 577 (1st Dist. 1975).

[52]McCoy v. Able, 131 Ind. 417, 30 N.E. 528 (1892), reh'g denied, 131 Ind. 417, 31 N.E. 453 (1892).

[53]Kokomo Tube Co. v. Dayton Equipment Services Co., 123 F.3d 616 (7th Cir. 1997) (applying Indiana law) (contract which gave estimated labor costs based on number of workers owner provided to work on project, along with suggestions on how to keep costs from escalating, and wherein the parties agreed to use and install used materials whenever possible, was time and materials contract).

[54]TRW, Inc. v. Fox Development Corp., 604 N.E.2d 626 (Ind. Ct. App. 4th Dist. 1992), reh'g denied, (Feb. 19, 1993) and transfer denied, (May 21, 1993).

[55]Cleveland, C., C. & St. L. Ry. Co. v. Moore, 170 Ind. 328, 82 N.E. 52 (1907), reh'g denied, 170 Ind. 328, 84 N.E. 540 (1908); Rudd v. Anderson, 153 Ind. App. 11, 285 N.E.2d 836 (3d Dist. 1972); Prewitt v. Londeree, 141 Ind. App. 291, 216 N.E.2d 724 (Div. 2 1966).

- whether there have been substantial changes, alterations, and modifications to the original contract
- whether cumulative changes and modifications have remained an appendage of the original contract
- whether the property owner has consented, either expressly or impliedly, to the changes
- whether the parties agreed upon any fixed price for the cost of the changes or modifications
- whether the contractor had informed the owner that the changes would cost more or whether the owner should have known that the changes would cost more[56]

◆ **Illustration:** The owner's price for remodeling work done to a building was calculated as the reasonable value of the work, where the owner requested 29 changes, of which at least 15 were substantial; the labor and materials involved for the changes exceeded the costs of the original contract; almost all of the work was done with the owner's consent; the parties did not agree on a price for the changes; and the owner was informed several times that the changes would cost extra.[57]

Where the contractor agrees with the property owner to furnish building materials, the contractor is primarily and personally liable therefor to a supplier, and if the contractor fails to pay and a lien is taken and paid by the property owner, the owner may deduct such amount from any sum due the contractor or may sue the contractor for that amount if necessary.[58]

§ 91 —Extra work

A builder may recover additional compensation for extra work necessitated by the owner of the property or her or her agent.

West's Digest, Contracts ☞232(1)-232(7).

Where extra work on a construction project is necessitated by acts, errors, or mistakes of the owner of the property, or of an architect or engineer employed by the owner to supervise the work, the loss should fall on the owner, and

---

[56]Rudd v. Anderson, 153 Ind. App. 11, 285 N.E.2d 836 (3d Dist. 1972).

[57]Rudd v. Anderson, 153 Ind. App. 11, 285 N.E.2d 836 (3d Dist. 1972).

[58]Midland Bldg. Industries v. Oldenkamp, 122 Ind. App. 347, 103 N.E.2d 451 (1952).

the builder may recover additional compensation.[59] This rule applies even if the original contract provides that the contractor will not charge for extra labor.[60] The builder may recover additional compensation for extra work which becomes necessary because a building cannot be constructed according to the plans and specifications furnished, or for additional work or expense which is rendered necessary by the owner's negligence or refusal to make timely suggested changes to the plans, or by the owner's failure to perform his or her part of the contract.[61]

An owner, however, is not obligated to reimburse a contractor for additional labor costs in the absence of a finding that the owner was responsible for the additional labor costs.[62] Work properly included in the contract cannot, of course, be charged for as extras.[63]

A subcontractor may not recover from a general contractor for extra work necessitated by the owner. The subcontractor's recovery, if any, is to come from the owner.[64]

The parties can provide contractually for additional costs necessitated by changed specifications or unforeseen conditions, as such eventualities occur frequently in construction work. Delays caused by the parties, however, are generally not contemplated, and in the absence of express language in the construction contract treating claims for

---

[59]Gorbett v. Claycamp, 553 N.E.2d 475 (Ind. 1990) (property owner who was having pond dug on property was liable for extra charges where he doubled size of pond after parties had agreed to price); Connersville Country Club v. F. N. Bunzendahl, Inc., 140 Ind. App. 215, 222 N.E.2d 417 (Div. 2 1966).

Annotation References: Enforceability of voluntary promise of additional compensation because of unforeseen difficulties in performance of existing contract, 85 ALR3d 259.

[60]Connersville Country Club v. F. N. Bunzendahl, Inc., 140 Ind. App. 215, 222 N.E.2d 417 (Div. 2 1966).

[61]Connersville Country Club v. F. N. Bunzendahl, Inc., 140 Ind. App. 215, 222 N.E.2d 417 (Div. 2 1966).

[62]Lesh v. Trustees of Purdue University, 124 Ind. App. 422, 116 N.E.2d 117 (1953).

[63]Urbanational Developers, Inc. v. Shamrock Engineering, Inc., 175 Ind. App. 416, 372 N.E.2d 742 (3d Dist. 1978); Rebekah Assembly I.O.O.F. of Indiana v. Pulse, 47 Ind. App. 466, 92 N.E. 1045 (Div. 2 1910), reh'g denied, 47 Ind. App. 466, 94 N.E. 779 (1911).

[64]Thatcher Engineering Corp. v. Bihlman, 473 N.E.2d 1022 (Ind. Ct. App. 3d Dist. 1985).

delay damages and claims for additional costs alike, delay damages will not be treated as additional costs.[65]

Many construction contracts require that any change in the work be authorized by a written change order.[66] Change orders are generally considered valid and binding upon the parties.[67] Where a contract calls for a written change order before work not contemplated by the original contract may be done, a party generally may not recover for extra work unless a written change order has been made.[68]

§ 92 Medium of payment

Compensation is payable in legal tender unless the parties agree otherwise.

West's Digest, Contracts ⊘235.

Compensation to the contractor is generally payable in legal tender,[69] unless the parties stipulate for payment in some other medium, in which case the medium and manner of payment are controlled by the terms of the contract.[70] If a party to the contract agrees to accept specified property as compensation for his or her performance under the contract, he or she is bound by the agreement, even if the property is worth less than he or she supposed;[71] however, if one party does not make payment when due in the special medium

---

[65]Osolo School Buildings, Inc. v. Thorleif Larsen & Son of Indiana, Inc., 473 N.E.2d 643, 22 Ed. Law Rep. 891 (Ind. Ct. App. 3d Dist. 1985), reh'g denied, (Mar. 14, 1985) and transfer denied, (May 17, 1985).

[66]Kern v. City of Lawrenceburg, 625 N.E.2d 1326 (Ind. Ct. App. 1st Dist. 1993); Urbanational Developers, Inc. v. Shamrock Engineering, Inc., 175 Ind. App. 416, 372 N.E.2d 742 (3d Dist. 1978); Rebekah Assembly I.O. O.F. of Indiana v. Pulse, 47 Ind. App. 466, 92 N.E. 1045 (Div. 2 1910), reh'g denied, 47 Ind. App. 466, 94 N.E. 779 (1911).

[67]Urbanational Developers, Inc. v. Shamrock Engineering, Inc., 175 Ind. App. 416, 372 N.E.2d 742 (3d Dist. 1978); Rebekah Assembly I.O.O.F. of Indiana v. Pulse, 47 Ind. App. 466, 92 N.E. 1045 (Div. 2 1910), reh'g denied, 47 Ind. App. 466, 94 N.E. 779 (1911).

[68]Kern v. City of Lawrenceburg, 625 N.E.2d 1326 (Ind. Ct. App. 1st Dist. 1993).

[69]C.J.S., Contracts § 383.

[70]Farmers' Loan & Trust Co. v. Canada & St. L. Ry. Co., 127 Ind. 250, 26 N.E. 784 (1891).

[71]State v. Beard, 1 Ind. 460, 1849 WL 3050 (1849).

provided for by the contract, the other may then demand payment in legal tender.[72]

XII. MODIFICATION AND MERGER

Research References

IC 26-1-2-207

17A Am Jur 2d, Contracts §§ 520-535.
17A C.J.S., Contracts §§ 407-420.
West's Digest, Contracts ☞236-248.
ALR Digest: Contracts §§ 28, 29, 56, 95, 197-200, 503-509
ALR Index: Adhesion Contracts; Anticipatory Breach; Anticipatory Renunciation or Repudiation; Bids and Bidding; Cancellation of Rescission; Consideration; Contracts; Covenants; Covenants Not to Compete; Estoppel and Waiver; Executory Contracts; Implied Contracts; Offer and Acceptance; Parol Contracts and Agreements; Parol Evidence; Third-Party Beneficiaries; Unconscionability
5A Am Jur Legal Forms 2d, Contracts §§ 68:332, 68:421, 68:422.

§ 93   Modification

The parties to a contract may modify their duties to each other under the contract.

West's Digest, Contracts ☞236, 238(1), 239-244.

Just as parties are free to impose new duties upon each other by agreement, they are also generally free to modify their duties to each other under an existing contract.[73] A written contract may be changed, modified, or waived in whole or in part by a subsequent contract, which may be express, written, oral, or implied.[74] For instance, a settle-

---

[72]Farmers' Loan & Trust Co. v. Canada & St. L. Ry. Co., 127 Ind. 250, 26 N.E. 784 (1891); Mason v. Toner, 6 Ind. 328, 1855 WL 3709 (1855).

[73]Miller v. Geels, 643 N.E.2d 922 (Ind. Ct. App. 1st Dist. 1994), transfer denied, (Mar. 22, 1995) (citing Restatement (Second) of Contracts § 92); Hamlin v. Steward, 622 N.E.2d 535 (Ind. Ct. App. 1st Dist. 1993) (motel seller's agreement that purchasers would not be required to pay note until after purchasers sold motel modified original agreement, which had called for immediate payment).

[74]Terry v. International Dairy Queen, Inc., 554 F. Supp. 1088 (N.D. Ind. 1983).

Forms References: Substituted agreement. 5A Am Jur Legal Forms 2d, Contracts § 68:421.

ment agreement reached in a breach-of-contract action,[75] or a change in the time or method of payment to be made under a contract,[76] may be a modification of the original contract.

> ◆ **Illustration:** Where a construction manager and an owner agreed that the manager would build the walls of a building itself and that the owner would pay the manager, as opposed to a third-party contractor, for the material and labor costs associated with the walls, the agreement was a modification of the original agreement rather than a separate agreement.[77]

Because the modification of contract is itself a contract, it must satisfy all of the requisite elements of a contract.[78] The modification of a contract requires the assent of both parties to the original contract.[79] A disagreement about a contract term and suggestions for modifications are not sufficient to constitute a modification of the term if the parties do not agree to conform to the suggestions.[80] If one party seeks to

---

Clause canceling prior agreement. 5A Am Jur Legal Forms 2d, Contracts § 68:422.

[75]Fort Wayne Bank Bldg., Inc. v. Bank Bldg. & Equipment Corp. of America, 160 Ind. App. 26, 309 N.E.2d 464 (3d Dist. 1974).

[76]Burras v. Canal Const. and Design Co., 470 N.E.2d 1362 (Ind. Ct. App. 1st Dist. 1984).

[77]TRW, Inc. v. Fox Development Corp., 604 N.E.2d 626 (Ind. Ct. App. 4th Dist. 1992), reh'g denied, (Feb. 19, 1993) and transfer denied, (May 21, 1993).

[78]Hamlin v. Steward, 622 N.E.2d 535 (Ind. Ct. App. 1st Dist. 1993); TRW, Inc. v. Fox Development Corp., 604 N.E.2d 626 (Ind. Ct. App. 4th Dist. 1992), reh'g denied, (Feb. 19, 1993) and transfer denied, (May 21, 1993); City of Indianapolis v. Twin Lakes Enterprises, Inc., 568 N.E.2d 1073 (Ind. Ct. App. 1st Dist. 1991), reh'g denied, (May 16, 1991) and transfer denied, (Dec. 12, 1991).

For discussion of offer and acceptance, see §§ 7 et seq.

For discussion of consideration for the modification of a contract, see § 94.

For discussion of consideration generally, see §§ 13 et seq.

[79]TRW, Inc. v. Fox Development Corp., 604 N.E.2d 626 (Ind. Ct. App. 4th Dist. 1992), reh'g denied, (Feb. 19, 1993) and transfer denied, (May 21, 1993); Burras v. Canal Const. and Design Co., 470 N.E.2d 1362 (Ind. Ct. App. 1st Dist. 1984).

[80]Willig v. Dowell, 625 N.E.2d 476 (Ind. Ct. App. 1st Dist. 1993), opinion vacated in part on other grounds on reh'g, 627 N.E.2d 1365 (Ind. Ct. App. 1st Dist. 1994), transfer denied, (May 24, 1994).

modify the contract unilaterally, the other may choose to treat the contract as terminated and sue for damages.[81]

Modification of a contract can be implied from the conduct of the parties.[82]

◆ **Caution:** If an attempted modification of a contract governed by the Uniform Commercial Code materially alters the original bargain, the other party must expressly agree to the modification.[83]

The parties to a contract entered into for the benefit of a third person may rescind, vary, or abrogate the contract as they see fit, without the assent of the third person, at any time before the contract is accepted, adopted, or acted upon by the third person.[84] The parties may not, however, modify a third-party beneficiary contract to the detriment of the third party without the third party's assent after he or she has accepted the contract,[85] such as by changing his or her position in reliance on it.[86]

To show that there has been a modification of a contract, evidence must be clear and convincing.[87] Questions regarding the modification of a contract are ones of fact and are to

---

[81]Burras v. Canal Const. and Design Co., 470 N.E.2d 1362 (Ind. Ct. App. 1st Dist. 1984).

[82]Gilliana v. Paniaguas, 708 N.E.2d 895 (Ind. Ct. App. 1999), reh'g denied, (June 8, 1999) and transfer denied, (Oct. 13, 1999); Skweres v. Diamond Craft Co., 512 N.E.2d 217 (Ind. Ct. App. 1st Dist. 1987), reh'g denied, (Oct. 19, 1987); Gorbett v. Estelle, 438 N.E.2d 766 (Ind. Ct. App. 1st Dist. 1982).

[83]IC 26-1-2-207, Official Comment 3.

[84]In re Estate of Fanning, 263 Ind. 414, 333 N.E.2d 80 (1975).

For discussion of third-party beneficiary contracts, see § 83.

[85]Russell v. Posey County Dept. of Public Welfare, 471 N.E.2d 1209 (Ind. Ct. App. 1st Dist. 1984), reh'g denied, (Jan. 23, 1985) and transfer denied, (Apr. 24, 1985); Matter of Bannon's Estate, 171 Ind. App. 610, 358 N.E.2d 215 (1st Dist. 1976).

Annotation References: What constitutes reservation of right to terminate, rescind, or modify contract, as against third-party beneficiary, 44 ALR2d 1270.

[86]Detroit Bank and Trust Co. v. Chicago Flame Hardening Co., Inc., 541 F. Supp. 1278 (N.D. Ind. 1982).

[87]Shanks v. Fisher, 126 Ind. App. 402, 130 N.E.2d 231 (1956) (evidence insufficient to support builder's claim that owners agreed to pay increased expenses for labor and materials); Arbaugh v. Shockney, 34 Ind. App. 268, 72 N.E. 668 (Div. 2 1904) (evidence sufficient to authorize a finding that provision for written notice to terminate contract was waived).

be determined by the trier of fact upon the evidence of the case.[88]

§94 —Consideration for modification

A modification to a contract must satisfy all requirements of a contract, including consideration.

West's Digest, Contracts ⊙237(1), 237(2).

Because it is itself a contract, a modification of a contract must meet all the requirements of a contract, including consideration.[89] If a contract is to be modified, a new and distinct consideration is necessary to support the new agreement;[90] of course, such consideration must be sufficient, and it will be sufficient where, for example, the parties agree to an additional payment for the additional goods supplied[91] or a payment of interest in advance in return for an extension of the time of payment of the amount owed.[92]

One party's action in accordance with a proposed modification may provide a substitute for consideration.[93]

§95 —Oral modification of written contract

A contract providing that it may be modified only in writing may nonetheless be modified orally.

West's Digest, Contracts ⊙238(2), 238(3).

A contract providing that any modification thereof must be

---

[88]Coyner v. Lynde, 10 Ind. 282, 1858 WL 4265 (1858); Gilliana v. Paniaguas, 708 N.E.2d 895 (Ind. Ct. App. 1999), reh'g denied, (June 8, 1999) and transfer denied, (Oct. 13, 1999); Zemco Mfg., Inc. v. Pecoraro, 703 N.E.2d 1064 (Ind. Ct. App. 1998), transfer denied, 714 N.E.2d 172 (Ind. 1999).

[89]Hamlin v. Steward, 622 N.E.2d 535 (Ind. Ct. App. 1st Dist. 1993); Myers v. Maris, 164 Ind. App. 34, 326 N.E.2d 577 (1st Dist. 1975).

For discussion of consideration generally, see §§ 13 et seq.

[90]Hyler v. Humble, 100 Ind. 38, 1885 WL 4209 (1885); Seastrom, Inc. v. Amick Const. Co., Inc., 161 Ind. App. 309, 315 N.E.2d 431 (1st Dist. 1974); Anderson v. Miller, 76 Ind. App. 681, 133 N.E. 29 (Div. 1 1921).

[91]Shanks v. Fisher, 126 Ind. App. 402, 130 N.E.2d 231 (1956).

[92]Williams v. Scott, 83 Ind. 405, 1882 WL 6712 (1882); Dickerson v. Board of Com'rs of Ripley County, 6 Ind. 128, 1855 WL 3546 (1855).

[93]Pierce v. Walton, 20 Ind. App. 66, 50 N.E. 309 (1898); Sargent v. Robertson, 17 Ind. App. 411, 46 N.E. 925 (1897) (modification calling for payment of reduced royalty binding where one party paid the reduced amount for several years).

in writing may nevertheless be modified orally, as long as all the requirements for a valid contract are met.[94] An oral modification may vary any of the terms of the written contract or rescind or discharge it altogether;[95] however, a contract that is required by law to be in writing can only be modified by a written agreement.[96] As a contract, however, modification can be implied from the parties' conduct;[97] it is not always necessary to prove the oral modification of a contract.[98]

§ 96   —Operation and effect

A modified contract consists of the new terms and as much of the original contract as has not been abandoned.

West's Digest, Contracts ☞246.

A contract that is modified by the mutual consent of the parties to it becomes a new agreement[99] and consists of the new terms and as much of the old agreement that has not been abandoned and still exists.[1]

   ◆ **Illustration:** An alleged modification to a farm

---

[94]van de Leuv v. Methodist Hosp. of Indiana, Inc., 642 N.E.2d 531 (Ind. Ct. App. 3d Dist. 1994), reh'g denied, (Feb. 23, 1995); Hamlin v. Steward, 622 N.E.2d 535 (Ind. Ct. App. 1st Dist. 1993); TRW, Inc. v. Fox Development Corp., 604 N.E.2d 626 (Ind. Ct. App. 4th Dist. 1992), reh'g denied, (Feb. 19, 1993) and transfer denied, (May 21, 1993); City of Indianapolis v. Twin Lakes Enterprises, Inc., 568 N.E.2d 1073 (Ind. Ct. App. 1st Dist. 1991), reh'g denied, (May 16, 1991) and transfer denied, (Dec. 12, 1991).

[95]Toledo, St. L. & K. C. R. Co. v. Levy, 127 Ind. 168, 26 N.E. 773 (1891); Ward v. Walton, 4 Ind. 75, 1853 WL 3461 (1853); Purity Maid Products Co. v. American Bank & Trust Co., 105 Ind. App. 541, 14 N.E.2d 755 (1938).

[96]Maglaris v. Claude Neon Federal Co., 101 Ind. App. 156, 198 N.E. 462 (1935).

As to contracts required to be in writing, see I.L.E., Statute of Frauds.

[97]See § 93.

[98]Gilliana v. Paniaguas, 708 N.E.2d 895 (Ind. Ct. App. 1999), reh'g denied, (June 8, 1999) and transfer denied, (Oct. 13, 1999).

[99]Hendrickson v. Reed, 126 Ind. 519, 26 N.E. 205 (1891); Francis v. Warren, 12 Ind. 563, 1859 WL 4968 (1859); Coyner v. Lynde, 10 Ind. 282, 1858 WL 4265 (1858); Rebekah Assembly I.O.O.F. of Indiana v. Pulse, 47 Ind. App. 466, 92 N.E. 1045 (Div. 2 1910), reh'g denied, 47 Ind. App. 466, 94 N.E. 779 (1911).

[1]Foltz v. Evans, 113 Ind. App. 596, 49 N.E.2d 358 (1943); College Inn Food Products Co. v. Loudon Packing Co., 65 F.2d 883 (C.C.A. 7th Cir. 1933) (applying Indiana law) (modification of contract for sale of product

machinery dealership contract, based on the manufacturer's acceptance of the return of its predecessor manufacturer's repair parts under the annual parts return program contained in the dealership contract, did not require the manufacturer to accept its predecessor's repair parts under the termination clause of the contract, as the modification of the parts return program did not modify the contract's termination provisions.[2]

If parties to an existing oral contract attempt but fail to agree on a written one to replace it, the verbal contract is not destroyed or affected by the attempt. A written instrument cannot supersede an oral contract until the parties have mutually adopted the written instrument as embodying the terms of their agreement.[3]

The outcome of any controversy as to the meaning of a contract modification is determined by the law of contract construction.[4]

§97 Merger

Preliminary negotiations and earlier agreements are generally treated as being embodied in the final written contract.

West's Digest, Contracts ☞148, 245(1)-245(3).

When a contract is reduced to writing, there is a presumption that the writing embraces the entire contract.[5] Where preliminary negotiations are consummated by a written agreement, the negotiations, any resulting agreements, and

---

to one company only, by granting seller restricted right to sell to others during period for which parties failed to agree on price, did not affect binding force of provision in original contract for seller's release from its obligations in such case).

[2]Farm Equipment Store, Inc. v. White Farm Equipment Co., a Div. of Allied Products Corp., 596 N.E.2d 274, 18 U.C.C. Rep. Serv. 2d (CBC) 1053 (Ind. Ct. App. 3d Dist. 1992).

[3]Foster v. United Home Imp. Co., Inc., 428 N.E.2d 1351 (Ind. Ct. App. 4th Dist. 1981).

[4]Fort Wayne Bank Bldg., Inc. v. Bank Bldg. & Equipment Corp. of America, 160 Ind. App. 26, 309 N.E.2d 464 (3d Dist. 1974).

For discussion of contract construction, see §§ 58 et seq.

[5]Swanson-Nunn Realty Co. v. Gentry, 134 Ind. App. 580, 186 N.E.2d 574 (Div. 2 1962) (in absence of special plea of fraud, mistake, illegality, etc., writing is to be treated as exclusive medium of ascertaining contract).

any prior contracts concerning the same subject matter are treated as embodied in the written contract.[6]

Where a contract embraces the entire substance of a former contract, with some variations, the first contract is merged into the second.[7]

◆ **Illustration:** Proof of a written contract containing no provision requiring the defendant to procure insurance for the plaintiff precluded the plaintiff from recovering on the basis of a prior oral agreement between the same parties and concerning the same subject matter, which allegedly did contain such a provision.[8]

While a written contract merges into itself all prior parol negotiations with reference to that contract, it need not necessarily merge all other contracts actually entered into between the parties, although they may deal with the same property,[9] especially if the first contract is breached before the second is executed.[10]

Many contracts contain integration clauses stating that all previous agreements or negotiations between the parties are withdrawn, annulled, or merged into the written contract.[11] An integration clause may, in fact, reflect the parties' mutual

---

[6]W.T. Rawleigh Co. v. Snider, 207 Ind. 686, 194 N.E. 356 (1935); Baldwin v. Burrows, 95 Ind. 81, 1884 WL 5262 (1884); McDonough v. Kane, 75 Ind. 181, 1881 WL 6498 (1881); McCae Management Corp. v. Merchants Nat. Bank and Trust Co. of Indianapolis, 553 N.E.2d 884 (Ind. Ct. App. 4th Dist. 1990), transfer denied, (Oct. 2, 1990).

[7]Skaggs v. Merchants Retail Credit Ass'n, Inc., 519 N.E.2d 202 (Ind. Ct. App. 3d Dist. 1988).

Annotation References: Deed as superseding or merging provisions of antecedent contract imposing obligations upon the vendor, 38 ALR2d 1310.

[8]Swanson-Nunn Realty Co. v. Gentry, 134 Ind. App. 580, 186 N.E.2d 574 (Div. 2 1962).

[9]Mitchelltree School Tp. of Martin County v. Carnahan, 42 Ind. App. 473, 84 N.E. 520 (Div. 2 1908) (school township warrant for goods sold and delivered to township did not merge oral contract by which goods were sold); Louisville, N.A. & C. Ry. Co. v. Craycraft, 12 Ind. App. 203, 39 N.E. 523 (1895) (shipper's right to recover damages for animals injured during shipping under oral contract was not affected by later written contract of carriage, in absence of express provision so stating).

[10]Louisville, N.A. & C. Ry. Co. v. Craycraft, 12 Ind. App. 203, 39 N.E. 523 (1895).

[11]Franklin v. White, 493 N.E.2d 161 (Ind. 1986); Barrington Management Co., Inc. v. Paul E. Draper Family Ltd. Partnership, 695 N.E.2d 135

intention to abandon preliminary negotiations in favor of a complete and final statement of the terms of their agreement.[12] and such clauses have been upheld against public policy arguments.[13]

> ◆ **Caution:** Integration clauses are not conclusive on the question of whether a writing was intended to be a completely integrated agreement, and parol evidence may be available under some circumstances to vary the terms of a written contract even if the contract contains an integration clause.[14]

The rule that all parol negotiations are conclusively presumed to be merged in the written contract has no application to contracts made after the execution of the writing,[15] nor does the rule apply where the contract was induced by fraud.[16]

Because the merger of two or more contracts is not a new or additional contract, consideration is not necessary to make it effective.[17]

XIII.   RESCISSION

Research References

17A Am Jur 2d, Contracts §§ 539-605.

(Ind. Ct. App. 1998); Lawlis v. Kightlinger & Gray, 562 N.E.2d 435 (Ind. Ct. App. 4th Dist. 1990), reh'g denied, (Dec. 13, 1990) and transfer denied, (Apr. 23, 1991).

   Forms References: Contract as including entire agreement. 5A Am Jur Legal Forms 2d, Contracts § 68:332.

   [12]I.C.C. Protective Coatings, Inc. v. A.E. Staley Mfg. Co., 695 N.E.2d 1030 (Ind. Ct. App. 1998), transfer denied, 706 N.E.2d 174 (Ind. 1998); Prall v. Indiana Nat. Bank, 627 N.E.2d 1374 (Ind. Ct. App. 4th Dist. 1994); OEC-Diasonics, Inc. v. Major, 622 N.E.2d 1025 (Ind. Ct. App. 3d Dist. 1993), reh'g denied, (Jan. 28, 1994) and opinion vacated on other grounds, 674 N.E.2d 1312 (Ind. 1996).

   [13]See § 49.

   [14]Franklin v. White, 493 N.E.2d 161 (Ind. 1986); I.C.C. Protective Coatings, Inc. v. A.E. Staley Mfg. Co., 695 N.E.2d 1030 (Ind. Ct. App. 1998), transfer denied, 706 N.E.2d 174 (Ind. 1998).

   For a discussion of parol evidence, see § 137.

   [15]Toledo, St. L. & K. C. R. Co. v. Levy, 127 Ind. 168, 26 N.E. 773 (1891).

   [16]Marker v. Outcault Advertising Co., 69 Ind. App. 344, 122 N.E. 32 (Div. 1 1919).

   [17]Burk v. Brown, 58 Ind. App. 410, 108 N.E. 252 (1915).

17B C.J.S., Contracts §§ 421-499.
West's Digest, Contracts ☞249-274.
ALR Digest: Contracts §§ 152.7, 157.5, 522-545.5
ALR Index: Adhesion Contracts; Anticipatory Breach; Anticipatory
   Renunciation or Repudiation; Bids and Bidding; Cancellation of
   Rescission; Consideration; Contracts; Covenants; Covenants Not
   to Compete; Estoppel and Waiver; Executory Contracts; Implied
   Contracts; Offer and Acceptance; Parol Contracts and Agree-
   ments; Parol Evidence; Third-Party Beneficiaries; Unconsciona-
   bility
5A Am Jur Legal Forms 2d, Contracts §§ 68:462, 68:471, 68:473.
7A Am Jur Pleading and Practice Forms, Contracts § 117.

§ 98   Rescission by agreement

**The parties to a contract may agree to terminate their
rights and duties under the contract.**

West's Digest, Contracts ☞249-256.

A contract may be rescinded by the parties' mutual agreement to discharge and terminate their rights and duties
under the contract.[18] All of the parties to the contract must
agree to the rescission. If the contract has three parties, it is
not enough if two agree to rescind.[19] Generally, where a
contract for the benefit of a third person has been accepted
or acted upon, it cannot be rescinded by the parties without
the consent of the third person.[20] Rescission of a contract by
mutual agreement terminates the parties' rights and duties
under the contract.[21]

Formal written notice is unnecessary in order to effect a
rescission of a contract. Any positive act which shows an
intention to rescind is sufficient.[22]

The agreed rescission of a contract can occur only by the

---

[18]Lindenborg v. M & L Builders & Brokers, Inc., 158 Ind. App. 311, 302
N.E.2d 816 (3d Dist. 1973).

   Forms References: Right to rescind. 5A Am Jur Legal Forms 2d,
Contracts § 68:462.

   General rescission agreement. 5A Am Jur Legal Forms 2d, Contracts
§ 68:471.

   [19]Vawter v. Griffin, 40 Ind. 593, 1872 WL 5427 (1872).

   [20]Blackard v. Monarch's Mfrs. & Distributors, Inc., 131 Ind. App. 514,
169 N.E.2d 735, 97 A.L.R.2d 1255 (Div. 1 1960).

   [21]Economy Leasing Co., Ltd. v. Wood, 427 N.E.2d 483 (Ind. Ct. App. 2d
Dist. 1981).

   [22]Brown v. Young, 62 Ind. App. 364, 110 N.E. 562 (Div. 1 1915).

mutual consent of the parties to the contract.[23] A party cannot force the rescission of a contractual agreement by his or
her unilateral breach.[24] The trial court looks to the course of
conduct of the parties to determine if rescission occurred in
fact.[25] Mutual consent to the rescission of a contract may be
evidenced by the parties' actions, as well as by their express
agreement.[26]

> ◆ **Illustrations:** The author of a cookbook and a publish-
> ing company had agreed that the company would publish
> the book when the manuscript was complete. After sev-
> eral lengthy deadline extensions, the author sent a large
> portion of the manuscript to the publisher, but in a
> subsequent letter to the publisher stated that if the
> publisher did not have a firm plan to publish the book,
> she would like the manuscript returned so that she could
> present it to another publisher. The publisher acknowl-
> edged the request and a little over two months later
> returned the manuscript, which the author then submit-
> ted to other publishers. The author and publisher had
> mutually rescinded their agreement, and the author could
> not recover from the publisher for breach of contract.[27]

A contractor of a newly constructed home wrongfully
ejected from it the persons who had contracted for its
construction, after they moved into the home without attending the closing. The contractor's sale of the home to a

---

[23]Bowyer v. Vollmar, 505 N.E.2d 162 (Ind. Ct. App. 4th Dist. 1987),
reh'g denied, (May 11, 1987) and transfer denied, (Sept. 22, 1987); Linden-
borg v. M & L Builders & Brokers, Inc., 158 Ind. App. 311, 302 N.E.2d
816 (3d Dist. 1973).

[24]Marshall v. State, 590 N.E.2d 627 (Ind. Ct. App. 2d Dist. 1992),
transfer denied, (June 4, 1992).

[25]Horine v. Greencastle Production Credit Ass'n, 505 N.E.2d 802 (Ind.
Ct. App. 4th Dist. 1987), reh'g denied, (Apr. 29, 1987) and transfer denied,
(Nov. 10, 1987).

[26]Horine v. Greencastle Production Credit Ass'n, 505 N.E.2d 802 (Ind.
Ct. App. 4th Dist. 1987), reh'g denied, (Apr. 29, 1987) and transfer denied,
(Nov. 10, 1987) (parties mutually agreed to rescind contract for sale of
land where purchasers failed to make payments required by contract, sellers received quitclaim and warranty deeds from escrow agent and took
possession of land, and contract did not contain forfeiture clause); Bowyer
v. Vollmar, 505 N.E.2d 162 (Ind. Ct. App. 4th Dist. 1987), reh'g denied,
(May 11, 1987) and transfer denied, (Sept. 22, 1987); Economy Leasing
Co., Ltd. v. Wood, 427 N.E.2d 483 (Ind. Ct. App. 2d Dist. 1981).

[27]Church v. Bobbs-Merrill Co., 272 F.2d 212 (7th Cir. 1959) (applying
Indiana law).

third party constituted acquiescence to the owners' rescission of the contract and resulted in mutual rescission.[28]

A party may rescind a contract if the other party fails to object and permits the rescission to occur. In either event, the rescission is deemed to take place by mutual consent.[29]

> ◆ **Illustration:** A property owner had a falling out with a contractor working on his property and told the contractor that he should consider himself a "volunteer" if he continued working. The contractor had a duty to respond in some fashion, and his failure to respond, either by objecting or seeking modification or termination of the contract, constituted his permission for rescission of the contract by mutual consent.[30]

Rescission of the contract is a proper remedy for mutual mistake;[31] however, where the parties cancel their contract under a misapprehension as to the rights or remedies which the law may afford them, the law will not reinstate the contract when the misapprehension is discovered.[32]

§ 99 Rescission by one party

One party to a contract may seek rescission where the other party is in default, where there has been a complete failure of consideration, or where the contract was fraudulently induced.

West's Digest, Contracts ☞257-161(7).

A court may render a decree of rescission where (1) the party seeking rescission is not in default, (2) the party

---

[28]Lindenborg v. M & L Builders & Brokers, Inc., 158 Ind. App. 311, 302 N.E.2d 816 (3d Dist. 1973).

[29]Bowyer v. Vollmar, 505 N.E.2d 162 (Ind. Ct. App. 4th Dist. 1987), reh'g denied, (May 11, 1987) and transfer denied, (Sept. 22, 1987); Detroit Bank and Trust Co. v. Chicago Flame Hardening Co., Inc., 541 F. Supp. 1278 (N.D. Ind. 1982).

[30]Glen Gilbert Const. Co., Inc. v. Garvish, 432 N.E.2d 455 (Ind. Ct. App. 1st Dist. 1982).

[31]Berry-Jefferson Corp. v. Gross, 171 Ind. App. 653, 358 N.E.2d 757 (3d Dist. 1977).

Annotation References: Vendor and purchaser: Mutual mistake as to physical condition of realty as ground for rescission, 50 ALR3d 1188.

[32]Board of School Com'rs of City of Indianapolis v. State ex rel. Bever, 211 Ind. 257, 5 N.E.2d 307 (1936), reh'g denied, 211 Ind. 257, 6 N.E.2d 702 (1937).

against whom rescission is sought is in default, (3) each party can be restored to the same condition he or she occupied before the making of the contract, and (4) the party seeking rescission has returned or offered to return any consideration or benefits he or she has received under the contract.[33]

A party to an agreement is bound by the position which he or she first adopts unless he or she annuls that election by restoring the benefits received under the agreement; that is, by returning the parties to the status quo.[34] Thus, an offer to return any consideration paid by the party against whom rescission is sought is a condition precedent to the rescission of an agreement.[35] If, for example, property sold pursuant to a contract has since been resold to a third party, the property cannot be restored to the original seller, and rescission is unavailable.[36] The party seeking to rescind the contract bears the burden of proving his or her right to rescission and his or her ability to return any property he or she received under the contract.[37] Once a party establishes the right to rescind a contract and the ability to return the property in specie, the burden shifts to the other party to prove the monetary specifics necessary to return both parties to the status quo.[38]

A court may not order rescission if neither party to the

---

[33]Watson Coal & Mining Co. v. Casteel, 68 Ind. 476, 1879 WL 5692 (1879); Hanna v. Shields, 34 Ind. 84, 1870 WL 3815 (1870); Barrington Management Co., Inc. v. Paul E. Draper Family Ltd. Partnership, 695 N.E.2d 135 (Ind. Ct. App. 1998); Kruse, Kruse & Miklosko, Inc. v. Beedy, 170 Ind. App. 373, 353 N.E.2d 514, 20 U.C.C. Rep. Serv. (CBC) 217 (3d Dist. 1976).

Forms References: Notice of rescission and offer of restoration. 5A Am Jur Legal Forms 2d, Contracts § 68:473.

7A Am Jur Pleading and Practice Forms, Annotated (rev. ed.), Contracts § 117.

[34]In re Marriage of Arvin, 689 N.E.2d 1270 (Ind. Ct. App. 1997), transfer denied, 698 N.E.2d 1187 (Ind. 1998).

[35]Peoples Marketing Corp. v. Hackman, 347 F.2d 398 (7th Cir. 1965) (applying Indiana law).

[36]Berry-Jefferson Corp. v. Gross, 171 Ind. App. 653, 358 N.E.2d 757 (3d Dist. 1977).

[37]Barrington Management Co., Inc. v. Paul E. Draper Family Ltd. Partnership, 695 N.E.2d 135 (Ind. Ct. App. 1998); Hart v. Steel Products, Inc., 666 N.E.2d 1270 (Ind. Ct. App. 1996), reh'g denied, (Aug. 22, 1996) and transfer denied, 683 N.E.2d 582 (Ind. 1997).

[38]Stephenson v. Frazier, 399 N.E.2d 794, 28 U.C.C. Rep. Serv. (CBC) 12 (Ind. Ct. App. 4th Dist. 1980), transfer denied, 425 N.E.2d 73 (Ind. 1981).

contract has requested such a remedy.[39] An application for rescission is addressed to the sound discretion of the trial court.[40]

A contract may be rescinded when a party has performed a substantial part of his or her obligation under the contract and the other party has refused to perform any of his or her obligations.[41] Rescission is available upon proof of substantial nonperformance by the other party so fundamental as to defeat the object of the contract.[42]

Courts are reluctant to order rescission of a contract where legal remedies will suffice;[43] thus, even when the contract has been breached, rescission of a contract is not automatically available.[44] However, if a breach of the contract is a material one which goes to the heart of the contract, rescission may be the proper remedy.[45]

A complete failure of consideration, such as a seller's

---

[39]New Life Community Church of God v. Adomatis, 672 N.E.2d 433 (Ind. Ct. App. 1996), reh'g denied, (Jan. 7, 1997).

[40]Barrington Management Co., Inc. v. Paul E. Draper Family Ltd. Partnership, 695 N.E.2d 135 (Ind. Ct. App. 1998); Hart v. Steel Products, Inc., 666 N.E.2d 1270 (Ind. Ct. App. 1996), reh'g denied, (Aug. 22, 1996) and transfer denied, 683 N.E.2d 582 (Ind. 1997); Kruse, Kruse & Miklosko, Inc. v. Beedy, 170 Ind. App. 373, 353 N.E.2d 514, 20 U.C.C. Rep. Serv. (CBC) 217 (3d Dist. 1976).

[41]Huff v. Biomet, Inc., 654 N.E.2d 830 (Ind. Ct. App. 1995).

[42]Bixwood, Inc. v. Becker, 181 Ind. App. 223, 391 N.E.2d 646 (3d Dist. 1979).

[43]Drudge v. Brandt, 698 N.E.2d 1245 (Ind. Ct. App. 1998) (trial court did not err in refusing to order that agreement between mother and daughter, in which mother purchased annuity and placed it in daughter's name, be rescinded for daughter's payment of interest to wrong party; property transferred was money rather than land and neither property conveyed nor property promised in exchange was unique, so that mother could be made whole by payment of damages); Stephenson v. Frazier, 399 N.E.2d 794, 28 U.C.C. Rep. Serv. (CBC) 12 (Ind. Ct. App. 4th Dist. 1980), transfer denied, 425 N.E.2d 73 (Ind. 1981).

[44]Barrington Management Co., Inc. v. Paul E. Draper Family Ltd. Partnership, 695 N.E.2d 135 (Ind. Ct. App. 1998); New Life Community Church of God v. Adomatis, 672 N.E.2d 433 (Ind. Ct. App. 1996), reh'g denied, (Jan. 7, 1997).

[45]Barrington Management Co., Inc. v. Paul E. Draper Family Ltd. Partnership, 695 N.E.2d 135 (Ind. Ct. App. 1998) (seller of real property was entitled to rescind purchase agreement upon failure of condition subsequent, expiration of time allotted for buyer to satisfy or waive condition regarding procurement of necessary approvals for proposed use of land); Stephenson v. Frazier, 399 N.E.2d 794, 28 U.C.C. Rep. Serv. (CBC)

wrongful withholding of property sold from the buyer, is grounds for rescission by a nondefaulting party.[46] A partial failure of consideration is usually not a ground for rescission, but if both parties can be placed in statu quo, a party not in default, who has returned or tendered what he or she has received under the contract, may sometimes rescind the contract.[47] A mere inadequacy of consideration is not a sufficient cause to justify a rescission of a contract.[48] In the absence of fraud, a party may not rescind a contract on the ground of failure of consideration when he or she has received all the consideration for which he or she contracted.[49]

A contract may also be rescinded on such bases as fraud, illegality, or mutual mistake, or where a contract provision provides for rescission upon the occurrence of a condition.[50] If the ground for rescission is fraud, the rescinding party must return the parties to the status quo as nearly as the fraud permits.[51]

Where either party has surrendered any rights or acquired any benefits under the contract, a contract made in good faith with an insane person without any notice of his or her mental incapacity may be rescinded if both parties are returned to the status quo;[52] however, if the party against whom rescission is sought had knowledge of the other party's mental incapacity when the contract was made, restoration

---

12 (Ind. Ct. App. 4th Dist. 1980), transfer denied, 425 N.E.2d 73 (Ind. 1981) (evidence that foundation of modular home was so inadequately constructed that it presented serious possibility of damage to home established prima facie case for rescission of contract); Bixwood, Inc. v. Becker, 181 Ind. App. 223, 391 N.E.2d 646 (3d Dist. 1979).

[46]Smeekens v. Bertrand, 262 Ind. 50, 311 N.E.2d 431 (1974).

[47]Williams v. Butler, 58 Ind. App. 47, 105 N.E. 387 (1914), reh'g denied, 58 Ind. App. 47, 107 N.E. 300 (Div. 1 1914).

[48]Brown v. Budd, 2 Ind. 442, 1850 WL 3177 (1850).

[49]Wolford v. Powers, 85 Ind. 294, 1882 WL 6386 (1882).

[50]Johnson v. Culver, 116 Ind. 278, 19 N.E. 129 (1888) (fraud); New Life Community Church of God v. Adomatis, 672 N.E.2d 433 (Ind. Ct. App. 1996), reh'g denied, (Jan. 7, 1997); Grissom v. Moran, 154 Ind. App. 419, 292 N.E.2d 627 (2d Dist. 1973) (fraud).

Trial Strategy References: Insurer's Right to Rescind Insurance Contract for the Insured's False Statements, 21 Am Jur POF3d 565.

[51]Higham v. Harris, 108 Ind. 246, 8 N.E. 255 (1886); De Ford v. Urbain, Wils. Super. 67 (Ind. Super. Ct. 1871).

[52]Wells v. Wells, 197 Ind. 236, 150 N.E. 361 (1926); Fulwider v. Ingels,

of the status quo is unnecessary.[53] It is also necessary for a party to place the other parties in statu quo if he or she wishes to rescind the contract on the ground that he or she was intoxicated at the time the contract was made.[54]

Inadequacy of the contract terms is an invalid reason for rescission.[55]

§ 100   Return to status quo

The function of rescission is to return the parties to their precontract positions.

West's Digest, Contracts ☞263-266(2).

The function of rescission is to restore the parties to the status quo; that is, to their precontract positions.[56] A return to the status quo usually necessitates the return of money or other things received or paid under contract, plus reimbursement for any reasonable expenditures incurred as proximate result of the other party's fraudulent conduct;[57] therefore, a party seeking rescission must return all consideration or benefits he or she received under the contract.[58] For example, when an insurance company seeks to rescind a policy on the

---

87 Ind. 414, 1882 WL 6548 (1882); Gwinn v. Hobbs, 83 Ind. App. 263, 141 N.E. 812 (Div. 2 1923).

[53]Brannon v. Hayes, 190 Ind. 420, 130 N.E. 803 (1921).

[54]Joest v. Williams, 42 Ind. 565, 1873 WL 5605 (1873).

[55]New Life Community Church of God v. Adomatis, 672 N.E.2d 433 (Ind. Ct. App. 1996), reh'g denied, (Jan. 7, 1997).

[56]Yates-Cobb v. Hays, 681 N.E.2d 729 (Ind. Ct. App. 1997); Bowyer v. Vollmar, 505 N.E.2d 162 (Ind. Ct. App. 4th Dist. 1987), reh'g denied, (May 11, 1987) and transfer denied, (Sept. 22, 1987); Glen Gilbert Const. Co., Inc. v. Garvish, 432 N.E.2d 455 (Ind. Ct. App. 1st Dist. 1982); American Standard Ins. Co. v. Durham, 403 N.E.2d 879 (Ind. Ct. App. 2d Dist. 1980); Gary Nat. Bank v. Crown Life Ins. Co., 181 Ind. App. 610, 392 N.E.2d 1180 (3d Dist. 1979).

[57]Hart v. Steel Products, Inc., 666 N.E.2d 1270 (Ind. Ct. App. 1996), reh'g denied, (Aug. 22, 1996) and transfer denied, 683 N.E.2d 582 (Ind. 1997).

[58]Smeekens v. Bertrand, 262 Ind. 50, 311 N.E.2d 431 (1974); Prall v. Indiana Nat. Bank, 627 N.E.2d 1374 (Ind. Ct. App. 4th Dist. 1994) (releasor who had executed and delivered release in return for releasee's agreement not to require him to repay balance of loan was precluded from having release set aside, by failing to offer to reassume loan obligation); Bowyer v. Vollmar, 505 N.E.2d 162 (Ind. Ct. App. 4th Dist. 1987), reh'g denied, (May 11, 1987) and transfer denied, (Sept. 22, 1987); American Standard Ins. Co. v. Durham, 403 N.E.2d 879 (Ind. Ct. App. 2d Dist. 1980).

grounds of a material misrepresentation in an application, generally it must first make a tender of the full amount of premiums paid under the policy.[59]

When a contract is rescinded, no action can be maintained for breach of contract,[60] and the parties may not seek general damages.[61]

§ 101 Partial rescission

Parties to a contract may agree to a partial rescission, and a separable contract may be rescinded in part.

West's Digest, Contracts ⚷273.

Generally, a party rescinding a contract must repudiate the part of the contract which is beneficial to him or her as well as the part which is not. He or she must affirm or avoid the contract in whole and cannot treat it as good in part and void in part.[62]

However, when a contract is clearly divisible or separable into two or more independent agreements and good cause exists for the rescission of one agreement, that agreement may be rescinded.[63]

It is also possible for the parties, by agreement, to rescind

---

[59]Prudential Ins. Co. of America v. Smith, 231 Ind. 403, 108 N.E.2d 61 (1952); American Standard Ins. Co. v. Durham, 403 N.E.2d 879 (Ind. Ct. App. 2d Dist. 1980) (noting that tender is not necessary where insurer has paid claim on policy which is larger than premiums paid); Great Eastern Cas. Co. v. Collins, 73 Ind. App. 207, 126 N.E. 86 (Div. 2 1920).

[60]Glen Gilbert Const. Co., Inc. v. Garvish, 432 N.E.2d 455 (Ind. Ct. App. 1st Dist. 1982); Church v. Bobbs-Merrill Co., 272 F.2d 212 (7th Cir. 1959) (applying Indiana law).

[61]Hart v. Steel Products, Inc., 666 N.E.2d 1270 (Ind. Ct. App. 1996), reh'g denied, (Aug. 22, 1996) and transfer denied, 683 N.E.2d 582 (Ind. 1997).

Annotation References: Necessity of real estate purchaser's election between remedy of rescission and remedy of damages for fraud, 40 ALR4th 627.

Trial Strategy References: Selecting the Remedy, 3 Am Jur Trials 627.

[62]Leake v. Ball, 116 Ind. 214, 17 N.E. 918 (1888); Barrington Management Co., Inc. v. Paul E. Draper Family Ltd. Partnership, 695 N.E.2d 135 (Ind. Ct. App. 1998); Prall v. Indiana Nat. Bank, 627 N.E.2d 1374 (Ind. Ct. App. 4th Dist. 1994); Peoples Marketing Corp. v. Hackman, 347 F.2d 398 (7th Cir. 1965) (applying Indiana law).

[63]Higham v. Harris, 108 Ind. 246, 8 N.E. 255 (1886); Smith v. Felton,

261

a contract in part, but if nothing is shown other than that there was a rescission, the inference is that the whole contract was annulled and that the parties were restored to the status quo.[64]

§ 102 Time for rescission

The right to rescind must be exercised within a reasonable time.

West's Digest, Contracts ☞270(1)-270(3).

A party who seeks the aid of the court to compel the rescission of a contract must show that he or she has exercised reasonable diligence in ascertaining the facts and has been prompt in seeking the remedy within a reasonable time after the facts have been discovered.[65] Whether a delay in bringing an action for rescission results in waiver depends on whether the delay has been long enough to result in prejudice to the other party.[66] Whether the party seeking rescission has acted within a reasonable time is ordinarily a question of fact, but where the facts have been ascertained or are undisputed, it becomes a question of law.[67]

The rescission of a contract based on fraud or mistake requires affirmative action immediately upon the discovery of the fraud or mistake.[68] If a party seeking rescission alleges that he or she did not know of fraud in the inducement

---

85 Ind. 223, 1882 WL 6768 (1882); Thompson v. Fesler, 74 Ind. App. 80, 123 N.E. 188 (1919).

[64]Prudential Ins. Co. of America v. Smith, 231 Ind. 403, 108 N.E.2d 61 (1952).

[65]Patten v. Stewart, 24 Ind. 332, 1865 WL 1728 (1865); INB Nat. Bank v. Moran Elec. Service, Inc., 608 N.E.2d 702 (Ind. Ct. App. 1st Dist. 1993), transfer denied, (Apr. 14, 1993); Griffin v. Axsom, 525 N.E.2d 346 (Ind. Ct. App. 1st Dist. 1988); Lewis v. Kerns, 175 F. Supp. 115 (S.D. Ind. 1959).

[66]INB Nat. Bank v. Moran Elec. Service, Inc., 608 N.E.2d 702 (Ind. Ct. App. 1st Dist. 1993), transfer denied, (Apr. 14, 1993); Brown v. Young, 62 Ind. App. 364, 110 N.E. 562 (Div. 1 1915).

Annotation References: Circumstances justifying delay in rescinding land contract after learning of ground of rescission, 1 ALR3d 542.

[67]Grand Lodge of Broth. of R.R. Trainmen v. Clark, 189 Ind. 373, 127 N.E. 280, 18 A.L.R. 1190 (1920); INB Nat. Bank v. Moran Elec. Service, Inc., 608 N.E.2d 702 (Ind. Ct. App. 1st Dist. 1993), transfer denied, (Apr. 14, 1993); Griffin v. Axsom, 525 N.E.2d 346 (Ind. Ct. App. 1st Dist. 1988).

[68]INB Nat. Bank v. Moran Elec. Service, Inc., 608 N.E.2d 702 (Ind. Ct. App. 1st Dist. 1993), transfer denied, (Apr. 14, 1993); Griffin v. Axsom,

of a contract until he or she brought suit, the action is not untimely.[69]

> ◆ **Illustration:** Where a bank was aware of an alleged fraud by no later than 1984 but waited until 1991, after the death of a defendant, before it filed suit to rescind a contract which had allegedly been induced by the fraud, the bank waived its remedy of rescission by unreasonable delay.[70]

Courts have denied rescission based on lapse of time where 17 months elapsed between the time the plaintiff discovered a fraud and the time it filed suit;[71] where six years elapsed between a sale of land and an action to rescind the sale;[72] where five months elapsed after a deed was executed before rescission was sought;[73] where the plaintiff possessed the land at issue for eight years, during which he collected rents and made improvements, so that he could not have placed the defendant in his precontract position;[74] where the buyers of property did not seek rescission until after the resale of the property was concluded;[75] and where a purchaser of land who learned of a defect in the legal description in 1979 waited until 1984 to seek rescission of the sale, during which time he benefited from the occupation and use of the property, made improvements, and lost a substantial portion of the property to a neighbor's adverse possession.[76]

The parties may rescind a contract by mutual consent at any stage before the contract has been fully performed on both sides.[77]

---

525 N.E.2d 346 (Ind. Ct. App. 1st Dist. 1988); Admire v. Brewer, 112 Ind. App. 92, 41 N.E.2d 662 (1942).

[69]Worley v. Moore, 77 Ind. 567, 1881 WL 6698 (1881).

[70]INB Nat. Bank v. Moran Elec. Service, Inc., 608 N.E.2d 702 (Ind. Ct. App. 1st Dist. 1993), transfer denied, (Apr. 14, 1993).

[71]Grand Lodge of Broth. of R.R. Trainmen v. Clark, 189 Ind. 373, 127 N.E. 280, 18 A.L.R. 1190 (1920).

[72]Matlock v. Todd, 25 Ind. 128, 1865 WL 1768 (1865).

[73]Hunt v. Blanton, 89 Ind. 38, 1883 WL 5508 (1883).

[74]Patten v. Stewart, 24 Ind. 332, 1865 WL 1728 (1865).

[75]Berry-Jefferson Corp. v. Gross, 171 Ind. App. 653, 358 N.E.2d 757 (3d Dist. 1977).

[76]Griffin v. Axsom, 525 N.E.2d 346 (Ind. Ct. App. 1st Dist. 1988).

[77]Lindsay v. Glass, 119 Ind. 301, 21 N.E. 897 (1889); Economy Leasing

XIV. PERFORMANCE OR BREACH

A. PERFORMANCE

Research References

IC 26-1-1-1; IC 26-1-2-508

17A Am Jur 2d, Contracts §§ 606-715.
17B C.J.S., Contracts §§ 502-599.
West's Digest, Contracts ☞275-313.
ALR Digest: Contracts §§ 442-490.5
ALR Index: Adhesion Contracts; Anticipatory Breach; Anticipatory Renunciation or Repudiation; Bids and Bidding; Cancellation of Rescission; Consideration; Contracts; Covenants; Covenants Not to Compete; Estoppel and Waiver; Executory Contracts; Implied Contracts; Offer and Acceptance; Parol Contracts and Agreements; Parol Evidence; Third-Party Beneficiaries; Unconscionability
5A Am Jur Legal Forms 2d, Contracts §§ 68:93, 68:373-68:375.

§ 103 Generally

If there has been no fraud, misrepresentation, or undue influence, a party is required to perform consistently with his or her bargain.

West's Digest, Contracts ☞275.

When a court finds a contract to be clear in its terms and finds the intentions of the parties apparent, the court will require the parties to perform consistently with the bargain they made,[78] unless some equitable consideration, such as fraud, misrepresentation, or undue influence, exists.[79]

However, one party's material breach of the contract will

Co., Ltd. v. Wood, 427 N.E.2d 483 (Ind. Ct. App. 2d Dist. 1981); Tibbetts v. Krall, 128 Ind. App. 215, 145 N.E.2d 577 (1957); Puller Mortg. Associates, Inc. v. Keegan, 829 F. Supp. 1507 (S.D. Ind. 1993).

[78]I.C.C. Protective Coatings, Inc. v. A.E. Staley Mfg. Co., 695 N.E.2d 1030 (Ind. Ct. App. 1998), transfer denied, 706 N.E.2d 174 (Ind. 1998); R. R. Donnelley & Sons, Co. v. Henry-Williams, Inc., 422 N.E.2d 353 (Ind. Ct. App. 3d Dist. 1981).

[79]First Federal Sav. Bank of Indiana v. Key Markets, Inc., 559 N.E.2d 600 (Ind. 1990); Bethlehem Steel Corp. v. Sercon Corp., 654 N.E.2d 1163 (Ind. Ct. App. 1995), reh'g denied, (Oct. 27, 1995) and transfer denied, (Apr. 11, 1996) (enforcing valid indemnity clause); INB Banking Co. v. Opportunity Options, Inc., 598 N.E.2d 580 (Ind. Ct. App. 1st Dist. 1992), reh'g denied, (Oct. 29, 1992) and transfer denied, (Dec. 31, 1992).

excuse the other party's nonperformance;[80] therefore, a party who him- or herself is in default usually cannot enforce performance.[81]

If a party fails to perform his or her part of a contract and if the amount spent by the other party in completing the contract, together with the damage suffered from noncompletion, exceeds the amount owed to the first party, then the first party may not recover the full amount due him or her at the time he or she abandoned the contract.[82] A party who suffers damage due to the refusal of the other party to complete the contract may recover damages, or the party may recover his or her expenses if he or she completes the contract at his or her own expense.[83]

§ 104   Demand for performance

Demand for performance under a contract is not necessary unless the terms of the contract are not definite or unless the contract requires demand.

West's Digest, Contracts ☞277(1), 277(2).

A demand for performance, unless required by the terms of the contract, is not required where an agreement is absolute and unconditional,[84] such as a contract for payment of money where the terms are fixed.[85] Ordinarily, when time of payment is of the essence of contract and the party from whom payment is due was not paid at the time named in the

---

[80]Licocci v. Cardinal Associates, Inc., 492 N.E.2d 48 (Ind. Ct. App. 1st Dist. 1986), reh'g denied, (June 3, 1986) and transfer denied, (Oct. 21, 1986); Lawrence v. Cain, 144 Ind. App. 210, 245 N.E.2d 663 (Div. 1 1969); Records v. Smith, 72 Ind. App. 618, 126 N.E. 335 (Div. 2 1920).

For discussion of what constitutes a material breach of contract, see § 113.

[81]Harshman v. Heavilon, 95 Ind. 147, 1884 WL 10362 (1884); McClellan v. Coffin, 93 Ind. 456, 1884 WL 5627 (1884).

[82]Louisville, N.A. & C. Ry. Co. v. Pope, 80 F. 745 (C.C.A. 7th Cir. 1897); School Town of Winamac v. Hess, 151 Ind. 229, 50 N.E. 81 (1898).

[83]Shank v. Trustees of McCordsville Lodge No. 338, I.O.O.F., 47 Ind. App. 331, 88 N.E. 85 (Div. 1 1909), reh'g denied, 47 Ind. App. 331, 93 N.E. 452 (Div. 1 1910).

[84]Ferguson v. State ex rel. Hagans, 90 Ind. 38, 1883 WL 5587 (1883); Frazee v. McChord, 1 Ind. 224, 1848 WL 2916 (1848); Licocci v. Cardinal Associates, Inc., 492 N.E.2d 48 (Ind. Ct. App. 1st Dist. 1986), reh'g denied, (June 3, 1986) and transfer denied, (Oct. 21, 1986).

[85]Licocci v. Cardinal Associates, Inc., 492 N.E.2d 48 (Ind. Ct. App. 1st

contract, and the payment provision has not been waived, the purchaser's obligation to pay is not conditioned on demand by the seller.[86]

Demand is necessary when the place of payment is fixed by the contract, but the time is left undetermined; when the time and place are both left undetermined; or when the contract is for payment on demand.[87] Where the terms are not fixed, the plaintiff must have made a demand for payment or have performed some act which is sufficient to constitute a demand.[88] Filing a complaint with the court may constitute a demand for performance.[89]

A demand is not necessary before an action is commenced where the other party repudiates or refuses to perform the contract,[90] where a demand would be unavailing,[91] where the other party denies the agreement[92] or is unable to perform the contract,[93] or where both parties know the duties imposed by the contract.[94]

Dist. 1986), reh'g denied, (June 3, 1986) and transfer denied, (Oct. 21, 1986).

[86]Conner v. Fisher, 136 Ind. App. 511, 202 N.E.2d 572 (Div. 2 1964).

[87]Ferguson v. State ex rel. Hagans, 90 Ind. 38, 1883 WL 5587 (1883); Sebrell v. Couch, 55 Ind. 122, 1876 WL 6738 (1876); Frazee v. McChord, 1 Ind. 224, 1848 WL 2916 (1848).

[88]Marsteller v. Crapp, 62 Ind. 359, 1878 WL 6334 (1878); Indiana Tel. Corp. v. Indiana Bell Tel. Co., Inc., 171 Ind. App. 616, 358 N.E.2d 218 (2d Dist. 1976), opinion modified on other grounds, 171 Ind. App. 616, 360 N.E.2d 610 (2d Dist. 1977) (where contract did not refer to compensation for late payment, demand was required before plaintiff could bring suit to recover such compensation).

[89]Indiana Tel. Corp. v. Indiana Bell Tel. Co., Inc., 171 Ind. App. 616, 358 N.E.2d 218 (2d Dist. 1976), opinion modified on other grounds, 171 Ind. App. 616, 360 N.E.2d 610 (2d Dist. 1977).

[90]Burns v. Fox, 113 Ind. 205, 14 N.E. 541 (1887); Holderbaugh v. Turpin, 75 Ind. 84, 1881 WL 6484 (1881); National Life & Acc. Ins. Co. v. Riley, 110 Ind. App. 226, 38 N.E.2d 855 (1942); American Income Ins. Co. v. Kindlesparker, 110 Ind. App. 517, 37 N.E.2d 304 (1941).

[91]Booth v. Fitzer, 82 Ind. 66, 1882 WL 6886 (1882); Wilstach v. Hawkins, 14 Ind. 541, 1860 WL 4319 (1860); Timmonds v. Taylor, 48 Ind. App. 531, 96 N.E. 331 (Div. 2 1911).

[92]Timmonds v. Taylor, 48 Ind. App. 531, 96 N.E. 331 (Div. 2 1911).

[93]Boyle v. Guysinger, 12 Ind. 273, 1859 WL 4940 (1859).

[94]Cree v. Sherfy, 138 Ind. 354, 37 N.E. 787 (1894).

A demand for money is not authorized, in the absence of proof of a breach of contract, where the purchase price is to be paid in specific articles.[95]

◆ **Caution:** If one party to a contract, either willfully or by mistake, demands of the other a performance to which he or she has no right under the contract and states definitely that unless the demand is complied with, he or she will not perform as promised, then an anticipatory breach has been committed.[96]

§ 105 Performance of conditions

A party to a contract must perform conditions imposed by the contract before he or she may sue the other party for breach of the contract.

West's Digest, Contracts ≍278(1), 278(2).

A party who seeks to enforce a contract must show that he or she has performed all conditions required of him or her,[97] or that he or she has done everything in his or her power to perform them.[98] A party who refuses or fails to perform the conditions imposed on him or her by the terms of a contract, and gives no valid excuse for the refusal or failure, cannot recover for a breach of the contract by the other party.[99] A condition imposed by a contract must be fulfilled before the other party's duty to perform an existing contract arises.[1] If an express condition of a contract is not fulfilled, no liability

---

[95]Indianapolis Conservatory of Music v. McConnell, 70 Ind. App. 597, 123 N.E. 652 (Div. 2 1919).

[96]Eden United, Inc. v. Short, 573 N.E.2d 920 (Ind. Ct. App. 1st Dist. 1991), reh'g denied, (Aug. 7, 1991) and transfer denied, (Mar. 19, 1992) and appeal after remand, 653 N.E.2d 126 (Ind. Ct. App. 1995), reh'g denied, (Sept. 5, 1995) and transfer denied, (Mar. 12, 1996).

For discussion of anticipatory breach, see § 113.

[97]Hooser v. Baltimore & O. R. Co., 177 F. Supp. 186 (S.D. Ind. 1959), judgment aff'd, 279 F.2d 197 (7th Cir. 1960) (applying Indiana law); Potomac Ins. Co. v. Stanley, 281 F.2d 775 (7th Cir. 1960) (applying Indiana law).

[98]Kroeger v. Kastner, 212 Ind. 649, 10 N.E.2d 902 (1937); Skehan v. Rummel, 124 Ind. 347, 24 N.E. 1089 (1890); Gibson Co. v. Morton, 88 Ind. App. 685, 148 N.E. 430 (1925).

[99]Morton v. Kane, 18 Ind. 191, 1862 WL 2234 (1862).

[1]Krukemeier v. Krukemeier Mach. & Tool Co., Inc., 551 N.E.2d 885 (Ind. Ct. App. 1st Dist. 1990); THQ Venture v. SW, Inc., 444 N.E.2d 335 (Ind. Ct. App. 1st Dist. 1983).

can arise on the promise the condition qualifies.[2] Nonperformance or defective performance of a condition relieves the other party of his or her duty to perform under the contract, even if the other party is unaware of the failure.[3]

A party, however, is not required to perform conditions precedent to the contract where the other party repudiates and denies any liability under it.[4] Furthermore, where a plaintiff's agreement constitutes only a part of the consideration for the defendant's agreement, the defendant has actually received the partial benefit, and the plaintiff's breach may be compensated in damages; the plaintiff may maintain an action on the contract without showing his or her own strict performance.[5]

Waiver of a condition prevents the waiving party from pleading the other party's failure to perform the condition as an excuse for nonperformance.[6] Similarly, a party may not rely on failure of a condition precedent to excuse performance where that party's action or inaction caused the condition to be unfulfilled.[7]

§ 106   Tender of performance

A party's tender of performance under the contract is a prerequisite to that party's maintenance of a breach-of-contract action.

---

[2]Indiana State Highway Com'n v. Curtis, 704 N.E.2d 1015 (Ind. 1998); Blakley v. Currence, 172 Ind. App. 668, 361 N.E.2d 921 (1977) (agreement containing clause "subject to loan approval" did not become binding contract because approval was not obtained); Wetzel v. Andrews, 136 Ind. App. 117, 198 N.E.2d 19 (Div. 2 1964) (lease was not valid where condition precedent of statutorily required approval by governmental entity was not met).

[3]Salin Bank and Trust Co. v. Violet U. Peden Trust, 715 N.E.2d 1003 (Ind. Ct. App. 1999).

[4]National Life & Acc. Ins. Co. v. Riley, 110 Ind. App. 226, 38 N.E.2d 855 (1942).

[5]Morton v. Kane, 18 Ind. 191, 1862 WL 2234 (1862); Gibson Co. v. Morton, 88 Ind. App. 685, 148 N.E. 430 (1925); Deep Vein Coal Co. v. Jones, 49 Ind. App. 314, 97 N.E. 341 (Div. 1 1912); Romel v. Alexander, 17 Ind. App. 257, 46 N.E. 595 (1897).

[6]Crum v. AVCO Financial Services of Indianapolis, Inc., 552 N.E.2d 823 (Ind. Ct. App. 1st Dist. 1990), transfer denied, (Aug. 31, 1990).

For discussion of waiver of conditions, see § 88.

[7]Kokomo Veterans, Inc. v. Schick, 439 N.E.2d 639 (Ind. Ct. App. 3d Dist. 1982).

West's Digest, Contracts ☞279(1), 279(2).

Where a contract contains mutual and dependent obligations, neither party may sue for breach of the contract without an offer to perform his or her obligations within a reasonable time.[8] A tender of performance must be complete and perfect,[9] unless the acts of the parties need not be performed concurrently, in which case such a tender need not be absolute. For instance, the tender of a deed may be conditioned on the buyer's subsequent execution of a mortgage and note.[10]

A tender will be insufficient if performance is not tendered exactly as outlined in the contract.[11]

A tender of performance by a party is excusable and not necessary where at the time of performance the other party refuses to perform his or her obligations,[12] repudiates, or has already repudiated, the contract,[13] or, by some act, prevents the contract from being performed.[14] A party who is induced by fraud to execute a contract is under no obligation to tender performance.[15]

Where a tender is made to a party who refuses to accept it or who repudiates the contract, a subsequent tender is

---

[8]Barbee v. Willard, 2 F. Cas. 768, No. 969 (C.C.D. Ind. 1848); Melton v. Coffelt, 59 Ind. 310, 1877 WL 6622 (1877).

[9]Schrader v. Wolflin, 21 Ind. 238, 1863 WL 2050 (1863).

[10]Huff v. Lawlor, 45 Ind. 80, 1873 WL 5644 (1873).

[11]Sharp v. Jones, 18 Ind. 314, 1862 WL 1995 (1862); Henly v. Streeter, 5 Ind. 207, 1854 WL 3185 (1854); Streeter v. Henley, 1 Ind. 401, 1849 WL 3131 (1849); Lane v. Ziemer, 54 Ind. App. 278, 98 N.E. 741 (Div. 1 1912).

[12]Turner v. Parry, 27 Ind. 163, 1866 WL 2543 (1866); American Income Ins. Co. v. Kindlesparker, 110 Ind. App. 517, 37 N.E.2d 304 (1941).

[13]Eden United, Inc. v. Short, 573 N.E.2d 920 (Ind. Ct. App. 1st Dist. 1991), reh'g denied, (Aug. 7, 1991) and transfer denied, (Mar. 19, 1992) and appeal after remand, 653 N.E.2d 126 (Ind. Ct. App. 1995), reh'g denied, (Sept. 5, 1995) and transfer denied, (Mar. 12, 1996); National Life & Acc. Ins. Co. v. Riley, 110 Ind. App. 226, 38 N.E.2d 855 (1942); American Income Ins. Co. v. Kindlesparker, 110 Ind. App. 517, 37 N.E.2d 304 (1941).

[14]Nesbit v. Miller, 125 Ind. 106, 25 N.E. 148 (1890) (tender of performance by intended purchaser of land not necessary where seller has conveyed land to third person); Willcuts v. Northwestern Mut. Life Ins. Co., 81 Ind. 300, 1882 WL 6643 (1882).

[15]Citizens' Bank v. Leonhart, 126 Ind. 206, 25 N.E. 1099 (1890).

unnecessary,[16] especially if the party's explanation for the rejection shows that a further tender would be useless.[17]

Where a contract states that payment may be made on or before a certain date, the tender may be made at any time after the date of the contract.[18]

§ 107   Delegation of performance; assignment

A party may delegate his or her duties under a contract unless the contract provides otherwise.

West's Digest, Contracts ☞280(2).

Generally, a party may delegate his or her duties under a contract, unless the contract provides otherwise or unless the duty imposed on the party by the contract is of a personal nature and performance by an assignee would vary materially from performance by the party.[19] The test is whether performance by the original obligor has been bargained for and is of the essence of the contract.[20]

A party's liability under the contract is not extinguished by the assignment of his or her duties under it. The assignor/assignee relationship, although it controls rights and liabilities as between those two parties, does not affect the assignor's obligations to the other party to the contract.[21]

§ 108   Sufficiency of performance as determined by party

Where a party to a contract is to determine whether the

---

[16]Mathis v. Thomas, 101 Ind. 119, 1885 WL 4245 (1885); Mitchell v. Merrill, 2 Blackf. 87, 1827 WL 1271 (Ind. 1827).

[17]House v. Alexander, 105 Ind. 109, 4 N.E. 891 (1886).

[18]Barbee v. Inman, 4 Blackf. 420, 1837 WL 2287 (Ind. 1837).

[19]Buckeye Ag-Center, Inc. v. Babchuk, 533 N.E.2d 179, 9 U.C.C. Rep. Serv. 2d (CBC) 76 (Ind. Ct. App. 3d Dist. 1989), transfer denied, (Mar. 22, 1989) and transfer denied, (Oct. 2, 1989) (contract for sale of corn, which involved no personal relationship, unique skill, or discretion, could be assigned); Boswell v. Lyon, 401 N.E.2d 735 (Ind. Ct. App. 2d Dist. 1980).

[20]Buckeye Ag-Center, Inc. v. Babchuk, 533 N.E.2d 179, 9 U.C.C. Rep. Serv. 2d (CBC) 76 (Ind. Ct. App. 3d Dist. 1989), transfer denied, (Mar. 22, 1989) and transfer denied, (Oct. 2, 1989).

[21]Buckeye Ag-Center, Inc. v. Babchuk, 533 N.E.2d 179, 9 U.C.C. Rep. Serv. 2d (CBC) 76 (Ind. Ct. App. 3d Dist. 1989), transfer denied, (Mar. 22, 1989) and transfer denied, (Oct. 2, 1989); Boswell v. Lyon, 401 N.E.2d 735 (Ind. Ct. App. 2d Dist. 1980).

other party's performance is sufficient, a reasonable-person standard is applied to commercial contracts, and a good-faith standard is applied to contracts involving aesthetics or personal taste.

West's Digest, Contracts ⚭282.

When sufficiency of performance under a contract is to be determined by the satisfaction of one of the parties, Indiana applies a reasonable-person standard or a good-faith standard depending upon the specific circumstances.[22] The reasonable-person standard is used to review performance of contracts involving commercial quality, operative fitness, or mechanical utility which other knowledgeable persons can judge.[23] Dissatisfaction under this standard cannot be claimed arbitrarily, capriciously, or unreasonably; the standard is met if a reasonable person in exactly the same circumstances would be satisfied.[24] The good-faith standard is used when performance requires the party's subjective satisfaction, such as in a contract involving personal taste or aesthetics.[25] When the good faith standard is used, the recipient of the work performed must be subjectively satisfied. However, the mere statement by the recipient that he or she is dissatisfied is not conclusive; he or she must be honestly,

---

[22]Willig v. Dowell, 625 N.E.2d 476 (Ind. Ct. App. 1st Dist. 1993), opinion vacated in part on other grounds on reh'g, 627 N.E.2d 1365 (Ind. Ct. App. 1st Dist. 1994), transfer denied, (May 24, 1994); Indiana Tri-City Plaza Bowl, Inc. v. Glueck's Estate, 422 N.E.2d 670 (Ind. Ct. App. 3d Dist. 1981).

Forms References: Approval of performance by party to contract. 5A Am Jur Legal Forms 2d, Contracts §§ 68:373, 68:374.

[23]Morin Bldg. Products Co., Inc. v. Baystone Const., Inc., 717 F.2d 413 (7th Cir. 1983) (applying Indiana law); Willig v. Dowell, 625 N.E.2d 476 (Ind. Ct. App. 1st Dist. 1993), opinion vacated in part on other grounds on reh'g, 627 N.E.2d 1365 (Ind. Ct. App. 1st Dist. 1994), transfer denied, (May 24, 1994) (adequacy of builder's performance in constructing house for plaintiffs judged by reasonable-person standard, as plaintiffs intended to sell house); Indiana Tri-City Plaza Bowl, Inc. v. Glueck's Estate, 422 N.E.2d 670 (Ind. Ct. App. 3d Dist. 1981).

[24]Willig v. Dowell, 625 N.E.2d 476 (Ind. Ct. App. 1st Dist. 1993), opinion vacated in part on other grounds on reh'g, 627 N.E.2d 1365 (Ind. Ct. App. 1st Dist. 1994), transfer denied, (May 24, 1994).

[25]Morin Bldg. Products Co., Inc. v. Baystone Const., Inc., 717 F.2d 413 (7th Cir. 1983) (applying Indiana law); Indiana Tri-City Plaza Bowl, Inc. v. Glueck's Estate, 422 N.E.2d 670 (Ind. Ct. App. 3d Dist. 1981).

even if unreasonably, dissatisfied before the other party's performance will be considered insufficient.[26]

A party's use of property does not necessarily indicate his or her satisfaction with it.[27]

§ 109 Sufficiency of performance as determined by third person

Sufficiency of performance under a contract may be conditioned on the satisfaction of a third party, such as an engineer or architect.

West's Digest, Contracts ☞283-292.

The parties to a contract may provide that work is to be done to the satisfaction of a specified architect or engineer.[28] Such a provision becomes part of the consideration for the contract.[29] If a contract contains such a provision, the architect or engineer is the sole judge of the work, and the parties are bound by his or her decision in the absence of fraud or so egregious a mistake as to imply bad faith or a failure to exercise honest judgment.[30] The third party's judgment is prima facie correct, and a party whose performance has been found inadequate has the burden of showing fraud

---

[26]Indiana Tri-City Plaza Bowl, Inc. v. Glueck's Estate, 422 N.E.2d 670 (Ind. Ct. App. 3d Dist. 1981).

[27]Gough Const. Co., Inc. v. Tri-State Supply Co., Inc., 493 N.E.2d 1283 (Ind. Ct. App. 3d Dist. 1986) (building constructed as showroom for carpet company was unfit for its intended use where carpet company president testified that carpet had to be placed on pallets to prevent water damage, that building could not be used in winter until employees removed ice inside building, and that poor quality of workmanship ruined aesthetics of building).

[28]James I. Barnes Const. Co. v. Washington Tp. of Starke County, 134 Ind. App. 461, 184 N.E.2d 763 (Div. 1 1962).

For discussion of arbitration, see I.L.E., Arbitration.

Forms References: Acceptance—Approval of specified party as condition. 5A Am Jur Legal Forms 2d, Contracts § 68:93.

Approval of performance by third person. 5A Am Jur Legal Forms 2d, Contracts § 68:375.

[29]Lake Michigan Water Co. v. U.S. Fidelity & Guaranty Co., 70 Ind. App. 537, 123 N.E. 703 (Div. 1 1919).

[30]Louisville, E. & St. L. Ry. Co. v. Donnegan, 111 Ind. 179, 12 N.E. 153 (1887); James I. Barnes Const. Co. v. Washington Tp. of Starke County, 134 Ind. App. 461, 184 N.E.2d 763 (Div. 1 1962); Lake Michigan Water Co. v. U.S. Fidelity & Guaranty Co., 70 Ind. App. 537, 123 N.E. 703 (Div. 1 1919).

or mistake.[31] Similarly, the estimates of an engineer hired to estimate the cost of work are merely prima facie correct.[32] If an engineer mistakenly or negligently fails to estimate or underestimates the value of such work, the builder may recover the correct amount.[33]

If a contract provides that the approval of a third person is a condition precedent, such a condition must be complied with before an action may be brought on the contract,[34] unless the third person arbitrarily or fraudulently refuses or fails to give his or her approval;[35] however, an action may be brought in quantum meruit for the value of services rendered and materials supplied although an architect's certificate is not procured.[36]

A contract may also make a third person's satisfaction one factor in determining whether the contract has been satisfactorily performed.[37]

An architect or engineer has no power to modify or alter the terms of the contract,[38] unless he or she is authorized to do so by the contract.[39]

---

[31]James I. Barnes Const. Co. v. Washington Tp. of Starke County, 134 Ind. App. 461, 184 N.E.2d 763 (Div. 1 1962).

[32]McCoy v. Able, 131 Ind. 417, 30 N.E. 528 (1892), reh'g denied, 131 Ind. 417, 31 N.E. 453 (1892).

[33]Kistler v. Indianapolis & St. L.R. Co., 88 Ind. 460, 1882 WL 6635 (1882).

[34]Cosby v. Adams, Wils. Super. 342 (Ind. Super. Ct. 1873).

[35]Wm. P. Jungclaus Co. v. Ratti, 67 Ind. App. 84, 118 N.E. 966 (Div. 1 1918).

[36]Everroad v. Schwartzkopf, 123 Ind. 35, 23 N.E. 969 (1890); Adams v. Cosby, 48 Ind. 153, 1874 WL 5858 (1874); Cosby v. Adams, Wils. Super. 342 (Ind. Super. Ct. 1873).

[37]Southern, School Bldgs., Inc. v. Loew Elec., Inc., 407 N.E.2d 240 (Ind. Ct. App. 3d Dist. 1980) (acceptance conditioned on completion of work, delivery of guarantee, architect's certificate, conformity to specifications as certified by independent engineering firm, and submission of application for final payment).

[38]Wm. P. Jungclaus Co. v. Ratti, 67 Ind. App. 84, 118 N.E. 966 (Div. 1 1918).

[39]Guthrie v. Carpenter, 162 Ind. 417, 70 N.E. 486 (1904); Cosby v. Adams, Wils. Super. 342 (Ind. Super. Ct. 1873).

§ 110   Substantial performance

"Substantial performance" is something less than full strict performance, but only in some nonessential way and is practically as good as strict performance.

West's Digest, Contracts ☞293-295(3).

"Substantial performance" is something less than full strict performance, but only in some nonessential way and is practically as good as strict performance.[40] If a party to a contract, acting in good faith, performs substantially all that is required of him or her by the contract, he or she may recover from the other party under the contract, less any damage sustained by the other party for minor defects in performance.[41] The amount of benefit realized by the party to whom performance was to be rendered is an important factor in determining whether the other party has substantially performed.[42]

§ 111   Act of other party as excuse for nonperformance

A party's performance under a contract may be excused where he or she has been prevented from performing by the other party.

West's Digest, Contracts ☞303(4).

One party's performance under a contract may be excused where the other party wrongfully prevents that performance.[43] For instance, one party may not rely on the failure of a condition precedent as grounds for a lawsuit where that

---

[40]Puller Mortg. Associates, Inc. v. Keegan, 829 F. Supp. 1507 (S.D. Ind. 1993).

[41]Puller Mortg. Associates, Inc. v. Keegan, 829 F. Supp. 1507 (S.D. Ind. 1993) (applying Indiana law).

[42]Drost v. Professional Bldg. Service Corp., 153 Ind. App. 273, 286 N.E.2d 846 (3d Dist. 1972).

[43]IC 26-1-2-508. Stephenson v. Frazier, 399 N.E.2d 794, 28 U.C.C. Rep. Serv. (CBC) 12 (Ind. Ct. App. 4th Dist. 1980), transfer denied, 425 N.E.2d 73 (Ind. 1981) (owners did not wrongfully prevent contractor's performance under construction contract by ordering him off construction site upon his insistence that foundation was sound and that they could take him to court over it).

For discussion of the Indiana version of the Uniform Commercial Code, IC 26-1-1-1 et seq., see I.L.E., Sales of Personalty.

party's inaction caused the failure.[44] "Causing" the failure of a condition means more than the mere rejection of the contract for a sound reason, such as newly discovered information, if the right to such rejection is preserved in the contract; the rule prevents a party from acting in bad faith to cause the failure of a condition.[45] The principle that no one is to be permitted to benefit from his or her own wrongful act forbids a party to a contract to take an unjustified step to prevent the other party from performing his or her contractual undertaking and thus to precipitate that party into a breach.[46] One party to a contract is not permitted to deprive the other of his or her remedy for breach of the contract by preventing the other from completing his or her agreed upon performance.[47]

§ 112   Other excuse for nonperformance

A party's performance under a contract may be excused where it has become impossible.

West's Digest, Contracts ☞303(1)-303(5), 309-311.

Where the performance of a contract becomes impossible, nonperformance is excused, and no damages can be recovered.[48] Generally, impossibility of performance is a defense to an action for damages. Upon failing to perform his or her part of the contract, a plaintiff cannot sue his or her adversary for damages alleging that his or her own nonperformance was caused by impossibility.[49] Performance of the contract must not be merely difficult, but absolutely impos-

---

[44]Indiana State Highway Com'n v. Curtis, 704 N.E.2d 1015 (Ind. 1998); Indiana State Highway Com'n v. Curtis, 695 N.E.2d 143 (Ind. Ct. App. 1998), transfer granted, (Oct. 2, 1998) and aff'd, 704 N.E.2d 1015 (Ind. 1998).

For discussion of conditions precedent, see §§ 87 et seq.

[45]Indiana State Highway Com'n v. Curtis, 704 N.E.2d 1015 (Ind. 1998).

[46]Scott-Reitz Ltd. v. Rein Warsaw Associates, 658 N.E.2d 98 (Ind. Ct. App. 1995); Maddox v. Wright, 489 N.E.2d 133 (Ind. Ct. App. 3d Dist. 1986), reh'g denied, (Apr. 18, 1986).

[47]Harold Wright Co., Inc. v. E.I. DuPont De Nemours & Co., Inc., 49 F.3d 308 (7th Cir. 1995), reh'g and suggestion for reh'g en banc denied, (Mar. 30, 1995).

[48]Gregg School Tp., Morgan County v. Hinshaw, 76 Ind. App. 503, 132 N.E. 586, 17 A.L.R. 1222 (1921).

[49]Dove v. Rose Acre Farms, Inc., 434 N.E.2d 931 (Ind. Ct. App. 1st Dist. 1982).

sible because of an act of God, an act of the law, or the loss or destruction of the subject matter of the contract.[50]

It has been stated, however, that whether Indiana courts will excuse a party's performance when performance is merely impractical remains unsettled.[51] A contractor is not relieved from his or her obligations under the contract by unexpected difficulties in performance, by his or her mere inability to perform, or by the fact that the contract is burdensome or unprofitable or causes hardship.[52]

Impossibility may be based on a change in the law.[53]

A defendant's failure to fulfill his or her own plans does not excuse his or her nonperformance.[54]

---

[50]Krause v. Board of Trustees of School Town of Crothersville, 162 Ind. 278, 70 N.E. 264 (1904); Ross Clinic, Inc. v. Tabion, 419 N.E.2d 219 (Ind. Ct. App. 3d Dist. 1981); Marcovich Land Co. v. J. J. Newberry Co., 413 N.E.2d 935 (Ind. Ct. App. 4th Dist. 1980) (landlord was not relieved of contractual duty to rebuild leased structure destroyed by fire by claiming to be unable to obtain financing, where it failed to show that financing was essential and evidence suggested that landlord did not attempt to obtain financing); Kruse, Kruse & Miklosko, Inc. v. Beedy, 170 Ind. App. 373, 353 N.E.2d 514, 20 U.C.C. Rep. Serv. (CBC) 217 (3d Dist. 1976).

[51]Brown v. Mid-American Waste Systems, Inc., 924 F. Supp. 92 (S.D. Ind. 1996) (applying Indiana law), citing Marcovich Land Co. v. J. J. Newberry Co., 413 N.E.2d 935 (Ind. Ct. App. 4th Dist. 1980).

[52]Marcovich Land Co. v. J. J. Newberry Co., 413 N.E.2d 935 (Ind. Ct. App. 4th Dist. 1980).

Trial Strategy References: "Impossibility" of Performing Contract, 24 Am Jur POF2d 269.

Legal Periodicals: Walt, Expectations, Loss Distributions, and Commercial Impracticability. 24 Ind. L. Rev. 65 (Winter 1991).

[53]Guenin v. Sendra Corp., 700 F. Supp. 973 (N.D. Ind. 1988) (legal impossibility excused firearms manufacturer's nonperformance of contract to sell machine guns to dealer where, at time dealer submitted its order, manufacturer could not have known that, one year later, Bureau of Alcohol, Tobacco and Firearms would disapprove transfer); Lutz v. New Albany City Plan Com'n, 230 Ind. 74, 101 N.E.2d 187 (1951); Poledor v. Mayerfield, 94 Ind. App. 601, 176 N.E. 32 (1931); Burgett v. Loeb, 43 Ind. App. 657, 88 N.E. 346 (Div. 2 1909).

[54]Sandock v. Taylor Const. Corp., 416 N.E.2d 882 (Ind. Ct. App. 3d Dist. 1981) (under contract in which corporation agreed to prepare and deliver to individual site-use plan and final construction drawings and specifications, and individual agreed to pay $1,000 when drawings were completed unless construction work was abandoned or suspended, or contract to construct or supply awarded to others, individual was not excused from payment upon receipt of drawings, even though construction never began on project).

A corporation will not be excused from its breach by its officers' ignorance of the misconduct.[55]

If an employer supplies an employee with materials of poor quality and the employee uses them in his or her work at the employer's direction, the employer cannot object that the product of the employee's work is of an inferior quality.[56] Similarly, a contractor cannot be held liable if he or she performed in accordance with the specifications in a construction contract and the specifications were provided by the property owner.[57]

A party who is notified by the other party that such other party will not perform his or her part of the contract need not perform.[58]

A party who creates an absolute obligation, the performance of which rests on him- or herself, is generally bound to make it good.[59] If the party who creates the obligation knows at that time that it will be impossible for him or her to perform it, such party is liable if the impossibility of the performance is unknown to the other party.[60]

◆ **Caution:** The doctrine of frustration of purpose, under which performance of a contract may be excused if the purpose of the contract can no longer be realized, has not been specifically recognized in Indiana.[61]

B. BREACH

Research References
IC 24-5-13-15; IC 24-5-7-10; IC 26-1-2-508

17A Am Jur 2d, Contracts §§ 716-745.
17B C.J.S., Contracts §§ 502-599.
West's Digest, Contracts ☞296, 313-323.
West's Digest, Damages ☞121.
ALR Digest: Contracts §§ 491-502
ALR Index: Adhesion Contracts; Anticipatory Breach; Anticipatory Renunciation or Repudiation; Bids and Bidding; Cancellation of

---

[55]BeerMart, Inc. v. Stroh Brewery Co., 804 F.2d 409 (7th Cir. 1986).

[56]Manville v. McCoy, 3 Ind. 148, 1851 WL 2930 (1851).

[57]Millner v. Mumby, 599 N.E.2d 627 (Ind. Ct. App. 5th Dist. 1992).

[58]Vinton v. Baldwin, 95 Ind. 433, 1884 WL 5302 (1884).

[59]Prather v. Latshaw, 188 Ind. 204, 122 N.E. 721 (1919).

[60]Ludlow v. Free, 222 Ind. 568, 55 N.E.2d 318 (1944).

[61]Ross Clinic, Inc. v. Tabion, 419 N.E.2d 219 (Ind. Ct. App. 3d Dist. 1981).

Rescission; Consideration; Contracts; Covenants; Covenants Not to Compete; Estoppel and Waiver; Executory Contracts; Implied Contracts; Offer and Acceptance; Parol Contracts and Agreements; Parol Evidence; Third-Party Beneficiaries; Unconscionability

5A Am Jur Legal Forms 2d, Contracts § 68:378.

§ 113   Acts constituting breach of contract

A party breaches a contract by placing him- or herself in such a position that he or she is unable to perform his or her obligations, or by failing to perform all of his or her contractual obligations.

West's Digest, Contracts ⚭321(1)-315.

A party breaches a contract either by placing him- or herself in a position where he or she is unable to perform his or her contractual obligations,[62] or by failing to perform all of his or her contractual obligations.[63]

◆ **Illustration:** A contractor breached a contract to build a pool by failing to construct the pool in accordance with the location and angle specified by a site survey, a site plan, the owners' stakes and markings, and a building permit.[64]

Failure to perform in a workmanlike manner may constitute a breach of contract for work or services.[65] A breach of contract may also be found in a breach of the implied war-

---

[62]Strodtman v. Integrity Builders, Inc., 668 N.E.2d 279 (Ind. Ct. App. 1996), on reh'g, (Sept. 18, 1996) and transfer denied, 683 N.E.2d 585 (Ind. 1997) (developer breached provision of contract with adjacent landowners, requiring developer to provide landscaping along common border, by transferring land to another owner and thereby voluntarily placing itself in position where it could not perform its contractual obligation; contract did not contain any provision that would release developer from landscaping obligation if it sold land to different developer); Indiana Gas & Water Co. v. Williams, 132 Ind. App. 8, 175 N.E.2d 31 (Div. 2 1961).

[63]Strodtman v. Integrity Builders, Inc., 668 N.E.2d 279 (Ind. Ct. App. 1996), on reh'g, (Sept. 18, 1996) and transfer denied, 683 N.E.2d 585 (Ind. 1997); Worrell v. WLT Corp., 653 N.E.2d 1054 (Ind. Ct. App. 1995), transfer denied, (Dec. 5, 1995); Indiana Gas & Water Co. v. Williams, 132 Ind. App. 8, 175 N.E.2d 31 (Div. 2 1961).

[64]Gilliana v. Paniaguas, 708 N.E.2d 895 (Ind. Ct. App. 1999), reh'g denied, (June 8, 1999) and transfer denied, (Oct. 13, 1999).

[65]Mullis v. Brennan, 716 N.E.2d 58 (Ind. Ct. App. 1999) (finding that contractor hired to build addition to home failed to perform in workmanlike manner, refused to correct defective work upon homeowners' request,

ranty of fitness for habitation. It is not necessary that the dwelling be rendered totally uninhabitable before there is a breach of the warranty; rather, breach of the warranty is established by proof of a defect of a nature which substantially impairs the owner's use and enjoyment of the residence.[66]

A repudiation of the contract before time for performance may be an anticipatory breach. Repudiation of the contract must be positive, absolute, and unconditional before it will be treated as an anticipatory breach.[67] This requirement is

and thus breached contract, supported by evidence that after several months of observing poor quality work which had been done, and after paying significant portion of contract price, homeowners made numerous demands that contractor correct problems and contractor refused to do any more work until he was paid further draws under contract); Bee Window, Inc. v. Stough Enterprises, Inc., 698 N.E.2d 328 (Ind. Ct. App. 1998), reh'g denied, (Oct. 1, 1998) and transfer denied, 714 N.E.2d 167 (Ind. 1999) (finding that contractor breached contract with building owner to furnish and install 23 windows was not clearly erroneous, where owner specified only that windows retain aesthetic vertical and horizontal pattern and where there was evidence that windows leaked rain, deflected inward and outward with changes in air pressure, failed to meet building code regulations, and created serious threat to life because they could explode or implode); Nelson v. Marchand, 691 N.E.2d 1264 (Ind. Ct. App. 1998) (contractor breached warranty to perform construction of home in good and workmanlike manner where homeowners and second contractor hired to remedy leaks testified to witnessing water in basement and where defendant failed to establish that leaks were result of act of God or negligence of landscapers).

[66]Callander v. Sheridan, 546 N.E.2d 850 (Ind. Ct. App. 3d Dist. 1989), reh'g denied, (Jan. 31, 1990) (faulty construction of porch); Wagner Const. Co., Inc. v. Noonan, 403 N.E.2d 1144 (Ind. Ct. App. 1st Dist. 1980) (depositing of raw sewage in basement of residence as result of improper functioning of admittedly defective septic tank system).

[67]Mullis v. Brennan, 716 N.E.2d 58 (Ind. Ct. App. 1999) (homeowners' request that contractor hired to build addition to home correct serious problems that had arisen due to his substandard work before they would make further payments under contract was neither absolute nor unconditional repudiation of contract and thus did not act as anticipatory breach of contract); Jay County Rural Elec. Membership Corp. v. Wabash Valley Power Ass'n, Inc., 692 N.E.2d 905 (Ind. Ct. App. 1998), transfer denied, 706 N.E.2d 167 (Ind. 1998); Eden United, Inc. v. Short, 573 N.E.2d 920 (Ind. Ct. App. 1st Dist. 1991), reh'g denied, (Aug. 7, 1991) and transfer denied, (Mar. 19, 1992) and appeal after remand, 653 N.E.2d 126 (Ind. Ct. App. 1995), reh'g denied, (Sept. 5, 1995) and transfer denied, (Mar. 12, 1996).

applied strictly.[68] A mere request to be released from a contract cannot act as an anticipatory breach;[69] however, demanding of the other party a performance to which the party making the demand has no right under the contract constitutes an anticipatory breach.[70]

Where a contract is terminable at the will of either party, one party's exercise of its power to terminate the contract does not render that party liable in damages for breach of contract.[71]

Partial satisfaction of the contract requirements may be a breach of the contract.[72]

Merely seeking to enforce a contractual clause does not constitute a breach of the contract even if the party seeking enforcement is later held to be incorrect in its interpretation of the clause.[73]

The breach of a condition of the contract, as opposed to the breach of a covenant, does not constitute breach of contract.[74]

---

[68]Jay County Rural Elec. Membership Corp. v. Wabash Valley Power Ass'n, Inc., 692 N.E.2d 905 (Ind. Ct. App. 1998), transfer denied, 706 N.E.2d 167 (Ind. 1998).

[69]Mullis v. Brennan, 716 N.E.2d 58 (Ind. Ct. App. 1999).

[70]Eden United, Inc. v. Short, 573 N.E.2d 920 (Ind. Ct. App. 1st Dist. 1991), reh'g denied, (Aug. 7, 1991) and transfer denied, (Mar. 19, 1992) and appeal after remand, 653 N.E.2d 126 (Ind. Ct. App. 1995), reh'g denied, (Sept. 5, 1995) and transfer denied, (Mar. 12, 1996).

[71]Knauf Fiber Glass, GmbH v. Stein, 615 N.E.2d 115 (Ind. Ct. App. 5th Dist. 1993), aff'd in part, vacated in part on other grounds, 622 N.E.2d 163 (Ind. 1993), reh'g denied, (Aug. 16, 1994).

[72]Fowler v. Campbell, 612 N.E.2d 596 (Ind. Ct. App. 1st Dist. 1993) (home builder breached contract provision calling for installation of septic system according to health department and homeowners' association plans; although department and association approved septic system as it was installed, system installed had smaller capacity than called for in plans).

For discussion of partial payment for partial performance, see § 117.

[73]Willsey v. Peoples Federal Sav. and Loan Ass'n of East Chicago, 529 N.E.2d 1199 (Ind. Ct. App. 4th Dist. 1988), transfer denied, (Mar. 31, 1989).

[74]Woodbridge Place Apartments v. Washington Square Capital, Inc., 965 F.2d 1429 (7th Cir. 1992) (applying Indiana law).

For discussion of conditions, see §§ 87 et seq.

An action or inaction for which the contract does not provide is not a breach of the contract.[75]

§114 Waiver of breach or defective performance

One party may waive the other's performance of contract terms.

West's Digest, Contracts ☞316(1)-316(6).

Waiver is a voluntary relinquishment of a known and existing right.[76] Ordinarily, a party may waive any provision included in the contract for his or her benefit.[77] Waiver in this context includes giving up the right to treat the contract as discharged because of the other party's breach.[78] A party who waives performance of a contract cannot rely on the other party's failure to perform it, either as a defense or as a cause of action.[79] A party who accepts defective performance of a contract is liable for the contract price.[80]

One party may waive the other's strict performance of the terms of a contract by acts showing relinquishment of one or

---

[75]Montgomery v. Amoco Oil Co., 804 F.2d 1000 (7th Cir. 1986) (oil company did not breach credit card agreement by imposing fee on gasoline dealers and jobbers for credit sales, as there was no express provision in agreement governing which party would bear cost of credit system and as it could be concluded that parties had not intended to limit oil company's ability to recover those costs).

[76]Kentucky Natural Gas Corporation v. Indiana Gas & Chemical Corporation, 129 F.2d 17, 143 A.L.R. 484 (C.C.A. 7th Cir. 1942); American Nat. Bank & Trust Co. v. St. Joseph Valley Bank, 180 Ind. App. 546, 391 N.E.2d 685 (4th Dist. 1979); Ogle v. Wright, 172 Ind. App. 309, 360 N.E.2d 240 (1st Dist. 1977).

[77]Terre Haute Regional Hosp., Inc. v. El-Issa, 470 N.E.2d 1371 (Ind. Ct. App. 1st Dist. 1984), reh'g denied, (Jan. 4, 1985) and transfer denied, (Mar. 28, 1985); Brown v. State, 219 Ind. 251, 37 N.E.2d 73, 137 A.L.R. 679 (1941); Cook & Bernheimer Co. v. Hagedorn, 82 Ind. App. 444, 131 N.E. 788 (Div. 1 1921).

[78]Waxman Industries, Inc. v. Trustco Development Co., 455 N.E.2d 376 (Ind. Ct. App. 1st Dist. 1983); Ogle v. Wright, 172 Ind. App. 309, 360 N.E.2d 240 (1st Dist. 1977).

[79]Mortgage Underwriters v. Stuckey, 108 Ind. App. 83, 27 N.E.2d 111 (1940).

[80]Waxman Industries, Inc. v. Trustco Development Co., 455 N.E.2d 376 (Ind. Ct. App. 1st Dist. 1983) (lessee waived any default in lease arising from slight difference in square footage of premises as represented in lease and as actually existing by execution of document stating that no default by either party or grounds for cancellation existed); Everroad v. Schwartzkopf, 123 Ind. 35, 23 N.E. 969 (1890).

more terms of the contract.[81] For example, the time fixed for the performance of a contract may be waived by either party.[82] Mere silence, acquiescence, or inactivity is not waiver unless the party against whom waiver is claimed had a duty to speak or act.[83]

A waiver of one part of a contract does not automatically result in a wholesale waiver of other provisions in the contract.[84] Similarly, accepting one defective performance under a contract does not constitute a continuing acceptance of defective performance, which would operate as a waiver of the breach of the entire contract;[85] however, where there has been a pattern of late payments, where the payee has not attempted to exercise any remedial provision of the contract, and where the payee has not been injured by the late payments, the payee has waived its objections to the lateness.[86]

A party who repudiates a contract and denies any liability

---

[81]Moffatt v. Green, 9 Ind. 198, 1857 WL 3584 (1857); Anderson v. Horizon Homes, Inc., 644 N.E.2d 1281 (Ind. Ct. App. 5th Dist. 1995), transfer denied, (Apr. 21, 1995) (homebuyers waived contract requirement that home be substantially completed within 120 days of mortgage commitment where they participated in builder's efforts to resolve problem causing delay and accepted continued performance from builder); White River Conservancy Dist. v. Commonwealth Engineers, Inc., 575 N.E.2d 1011, 16 U.C.C. Rep. Serv. 2d (CBC) 592 (Ind. Ct. App. 1st Dist. 1991), reh'g denied, (Oct. 9, 1991) and transfer denied, (Mar. 19, 1992) (although engineering company may not have complied strictly with contract terms in submitting its claims for payment to conservancy district, district waived compliance by accepting and approving claims); Clark Mut. Life Ins. Co. v. Lewis, 139 Ind. App. 230, 217 N.E.2d 853 (Div. 2 1966).

Annotation References: Antenuptial contracts: Parties' behavior during marriage as abandonment, estoppel, or waiver regarding contractual rights, 56 ALR4th 998.

[82]Mortgage Underwriters v. Stuckey, 108 Ind. App. 83, 27 N.E.2d 111 (1940).

[83]American Nat. Bank & Trust Co. v. St. Joseph Valley Bank, 180 Ind. App. 546, 391 N.E.2d 685 (4th Dist. 1979); Grenchik v. State ex rel. Pavlo, 175 Ind. App. 604, 373 N.E.2d 189 (3d Dist. 1978).

[84]Farm Equipment Store, Inc. v. White Farm Equipment Co., a Div. of Allied Products Corp., 596 N.E.2d 274, 18 U.C.C. Rep. Serv. 2d (CBC) 1053 (Ind. Ct. App. 3d Dist. 1992).

[85]Jackson v. DeFabis, 553 N.E.2d 1212 (Ind. Ct. App. 1st Dist. 1990) (acceptance of one late payment did not waive payee's right to insist on timely payment).

[86]Unishops, Inc. v. May's Family Centers, Inc., 399 N.E.2d 760 (Ind. Ct. App. 3d Dist. 1980).

under it waives the performance of any conditions precedent, such as notice, demand, or tender of performance, to which he or she may have been entitled.[87]

A payment on account for defective work does not amount to a waiver of any defects when at the time of payment the recipient of such payment is notified of such defects.[88] An acceptance of a payment does not constitute a waiver of any breach of contract, particularly where the payment was accepted after the payment was due.[89]

A contractor's failure to place the other party in default for repeated defective performances may not amount to a waiver if defaulting the other party is not a commercially reasonable alternative.[90]

§ 115   Effect of breach, generally

A party who is in breach of a contract may not maintain an action for the other party's subsequent breach of the contract.

West's Digest, Contracts ☞317.

One party's failure to perform under a contract discharges the other party from the obligation to perform his or her part of the contract;[91] thus, neither party can enforce the other's promise without performing his or her own.[92] For instance, an employer who breaches an employment contract

---

[87]Ohio Farmers' Ins. Co. v. Vogel, 166 Ind. 239, 76 N.E. 977 (1906).

[88]Tribune Co. v. Red Ball Transit Co., 84 Ind. App. 666, 151 N.E. 338 (1926), reh'g denied, 84 Ind. App. 666, 151 N.E. 836 (1926).

[89]Kokomo Steel & Wire Co. v. Macomber & Whyte Rope Co., 73 Ind. App. 619, 128 N.E. 362 (Div. 2 1920).

[90]Bowmar Instrument Corp. v. Allied Research Associates, Inc., 181 Ind. App. 514, 392 N.E.2d 825 (3d Dist. 1979) (where defaulting subcontractor would have made government contractor over a year late in meeting its production schedule, contractor's failure to default subcontractor did not waive subcontractor's breach).

[91]Kroeger v. Kastner, 212 Ind. 649, 10 N.E.2d 902 (1937); Abbey Villas Development Corp. v. Site Contractors, Inc., 716 N.E.2d 91 (Ind. Ct. App. 1999), reh'g denied, (Nov. 17, 1999); Bowmar Instrument Corp. v. Allied Research Associates, Inc., 181 Ind. App. 514, 392 N.E.2d 825 (3d Dist. 1979); American Nat. Bank & Trust Co. v. St. Joseph Valley Bank, 180 Ind. App. 546, 391 N.E.2d 685 (4th Dist. 1979).

[92]American Nat. Bank & Trust Co. v. St. Joseph Valley Bank, 180 Ind. App. 546, 391 N.E.2d 685 (4th Dist. 1979).

may not later enforce a covenant not to compete for which the employment was consideration.[93]

A party who breaks his or her contract is usually liable to the injured party for the resulting loss or damage.[94] Generally, a party who suffers a breach of contract is entitled to recover the benefit of his or her bargain;[95] however, merely showing that the other party has breached the contract does not necessarily entitle the plaintiff to damages. The plaintiff must also show that he or she has been harmed by the breach.[96]

When one party repudiates the contract before it is fully performed, the injured party may do any of the following:

- treat the contract as rescinded and recover upon quantum meruit
- keep the contract alive for the benefit of both parties, being at all times ready and able to perform, and at end of the time specified in the contract for performance, sue to recover under the contract
- treat the repudiation as putting an end to the contract and sue to recover damages[97]

When the injured party elects to treat the other's repudiation as putting an end to the contract for all purposes of performance, the injured party need not give further notice

---

[93]Sallee v. Mason, 714 N.E.2d 757 (Ind. Ct. App. 1999), reh'g denied, (Sept. 28, 1999); Licocci v. Cardinal Associates, Inc., 492 N.E.2d 48 (Ind. Ct. App. 1st Dist. 1986), reh'g denied, (June 3, 1986) and transfer denied, (Oct. 21, 1986) (employer's breach of employment contract by failure to pay salesman's year-end settlement of commissions or biannual draws of commissions and cut in weekly draws of commissions barred employer's claim against salesman for his subsequent alleged breach of covenant not to compete).

[94]Huffmond v. Bence, 128 Ind. 131, 27 N.E. 347 (1891); Logansport, C. & S.W. Ry. Co. v. Wray, 52 Ind. 578, 1876 WL 6666 (1876).

[95]National Advertising Co. v. Wilson Auto Parts, Inc., 569 N.E.2d 997 (Ind. Ct. App. 5th Dist. 1991); Indiana Tri-City Plaza Bowl, Inc. v. Glueck's Estate, 422 N.E.2d 670 (Ind. Ct. App. 3d Dist. 1981).

As to contract remedies, see I.L.E., Damages; Injunction; Specific Performance.

[96]Lincoln Nat. Life Ins. Co. v. NCR Corp., 772 F.2d 315 (7th Cir. 1985) (applying Indiana law).

[97]Scott-Reitz Ltd. v. Rein Warsaw Associates, 658 N.E.2d 98 (Ind. Ct. App. 1995); Page Two, Inc. v. P.C. Management, Inc., 517 N.E.2d 103 (Ind. Ct. App. 2d Dist. 1987).

For discussion of anticipatory repudiation, see § 113.

of this election to the defaulting party before bringing suit.[98] Moreover, the injured party need not allege or prove that he or she performed his or her part of the contract after the defendant has repudiated the contract[99] and is not bound to show that he or she has, at all times since the repudiation, been ready, willing, and able to perform his or her part of the contract.[1]

Although a party who has breached a contract cannot take advantage of his or her breach and cannot use it to relieve him or her of his or her contractual obligations, a breaching party may recover the value of what he or she has provided in quantum meruit; thus, where, despite a breach, performance of a building contract is completed and the value of the property is enhanced, the recipient of the improvement is liable for the value of the improvement.[2]

A party in breach of a contract will not necessarily be permitted to cure the breach,[3] although an opportunity for cure is a condition precedent to bringing a breach-of-contract action in some contexts.[4]

No action can be maintained for breach of a void contract.[5]

§ 116 —Forfeiture

Although forfeitures are disfavored, a forfeiture clause in a land sale contract may be enforced where the buyer has absconded or where the buyer has paid only a minimal

---

[98]City of Indianapolis v. Twin Lakes Enterprises, Inc., 568 N.E.2d 1073 (Ind. Ct. App. 1st Dist. 1991), reh'g denied, (May 16, 1991) and transfer denied, (Dec. 12, 1991).

[99]Foster v. Leininger, 33 Ind. App. 669, 72 N.E. 164 (Div. 2 1904).

[1]City of Indianapolis v. Twin Lakes Enterprises, Inc., 568 N.E.2d 1073 (Ind. Ct. App. 1st Dist. 1991), reh'g denied, (May 16, 1991) and transfer denied, (Dec. 12, 1991).

[2]American Nat. Bank & Trust Co. v. St. Joseph Valley Bank, 180 Ind. App. 546, 391 N.E.2d 685 (4th Dist. 1979).

[3]I.C.C. Protective Coatings, Inc. v. A.E. Staley Mfg. Co., 695 N.E.2d 1030 (Ind. Ct. App. 1998), transfer denied, 706 N.E.2d 174 (Ind. 1998).

[4]IC 26-1-2-508 (sale of goods governed by Uniform Commercial Code); IC 24-5-13-15 (sale of automobiles); IC 24-5-7-10 (sale of health spa).

Wagner Const. Co., Inc. v. Noonan, 403 N.E.2d 1144 (Ind. Ct. App. 1st Dist. 1980) (breach of implied warranty of habitability).

Forms References: Correction of defects. 5A Am Jur Legal Forms 2d, Contracts § 68:378.

[5]Rhoads v. Jones, 95 Ind. 341, 1884 WL 5287 (1884).

amount of the purchase price and the seller's interest is at risk.

West's Digest, Contracts ☞318.

The remedy of forfeiture for breach of a land contract is generally disfavored in Indiana[6] because of the possibility of inequitable dispossession of property and exorbitant monetary loss.[7] A forfeiture provision will be enforced where the contract clearly so requires, but if there is doubt, a construction avoiding a forfeiture is favored.[8] Generally, the proper remedy for a buyer's material breach of a contract for the sale of land is compensation,[9] rather than forfeiture.

To support a forfeiture, the forfeiting party's breach of the contract must be material. Factors to be considered in determining whether a breach was sufficiently material to support a forfeiture include:

- the extent to which the injured party will obtain the substantial benefit which he or she could have reasonably anticipated
- the extent to which the injured party may be adequately compensated in damages for lack of complete performance
- the extent to which the party failing to perform has already partly performed or made preparations for performance
- the greater or lesser hardship on the party failing to perform in terminating the contract
- the willful, negligent, or innocent behavior of the party failing to perform

---

[6]Skendzel v. Marshall, 261 Ind. 226, 301 N.E.2d 641 (1973), appeal after remand, 264 Ind. 77, 339 N.E.2d 57 (1975); Nelson v. Gurley, 673 N.E.2d 497 (Ind. Ct. App. 1996).

As to forfeitures of insurance contracts, see I.L.E., Insurance.

[7]Skendzel v. Marshall, 261 Ind. 226, 301 N.E.2d 641 (1973), appeal after remand, 264 Ind. 77, 339 N.E.2d 57 (1975).

[8]Colonial Mortg. Co. of Indiana, Inc. v. Windmiller, 176 Ind. App. 535, 376 N.E.2d 529 (3d Dist. 1978).

[9]Tidd v. Stauffer, 159 Ind. App. 570, 308 N.E.2d 415 (1st Dist. 1974); Rembold Motors, Inc. v. Bonfield, 155 Ind. App. 422, 293 N.E.2d 210 (3d Dist. 1973).

- the greater or lesser uncertainty that the party failing to perform will perform the remainder of the contract[10]

Even if the contract contains a forfeiture clause and the buyer has committed a material breach of the contract, forfeiture is appropriate only (1) in the case of an abandoning or absconding purchaser, or (2) where the purchaser has only paid a minimal amount of the contract price and the seller's interest is at risk.[11] Whether a particular sum paid toward a contract price is minimal depends upon the totality of the circumstances.[12]

When a party temporarily suspends his or her right under a contract to declare a forfeiture, such right can be resumed only by giving a specific and definite notice to that effect.[13]

§117 Effect of substantial or partial performance

A party who has rendered partial performance under a contract may recover for the value of the benefit accepted by the other party.

---

[10]Page Two, Inc. v. P.C. Management, Inc., 517 N.E.2d 103 (Ind. Ct. App. 2d Dist. 1987) (sublessee's breach of its contractual obligation to maintain fire, casualty, and personal-injury insurance on subleased premises was not sufficiently material to justify termination of lease, where sublessor was not harmed by omitted coverage; sublessee did not use premises for any business after coverage was terminated; premises were locked, secured, and serviced by 24-hour alarm; and sublessor never concerned itself with question of insurance, even after sublessee offered to reinstate omitted coverage); Goff v. Graham, 159 Ind. App. 324, 306 N.E.2d 758 (2d Dist. 1974).

[11]Skendzel v. Marshall, 261 Ind. 226, 301 N.E.2d 641 (1973), appeal after remand, 264 Ind. 77, 339 N.E.2d 57 (1975); Nelson v. Gurley, 673 N.E.2d 497 (Ind. Ct. App. 1996); Johnson v. Rutoskey, 472 N.E.2d 620 (Ind. Ct. App. 2d Dist. 1984).

[12]Morris v. Weigle, 270 Ind. 121, 383 N.E.2d 341 (1978) ($24,722.97 of $57,000 purchase price was substantial); Nelson v. Gurley, 673 N.E.2d 497 (Ind. Ct. App. 1996) (44.4% of purchase price was substantial); Johnson v. Rutoskey, 472 N.E.2d 620 (Ind. Ct. App. 2d Dist. 1984) ($11,200 of a purchase price of $52,000 was substantial, despite contract provision establishing $12,000 as "minimum equity threshold"); Goff v. Graham, 159 Ind. App. 324, 306 N.E.2d 758 (2d Dist. 1974) (forfeiture proper where purchaser of apartment units had paid only $562.62 of $61,750 and failed to make insurance premium payments as required by contract, removed furniture from apartments, knowingly allowed bootlegging operation to operate in one apartment, and permitted 'poker parlor' to operate all night long on weekends).

[13]Baird v. Aluminum Seal Co., 122 Ind. App. 572, 105 N.E.2d 825 (1952); Hill v. Rogers, 121 Ind. App. 708, 99 N.E.2d 270 (1951).

West's Digest, Contracts ☞296, 319(.5)-319(2).
West's Digest, Damages ☞121.

The rule that a party seeking enforcement of a contract
ordinarily must show that such party has done everything
the contract requires of it, or that the party against whom
relief is sought received that to which the contract entitled
it, is modified by the doctrine of substantial performance,
which applies where the performance of nonessential condition is lacking, so that benefits received by a party are far
greater than the injury done to such party by the other
party's breach.[14]

Where a party partially performs his or her obligations
under a contract, he or she is entitled to recover the value of
the benefits accepted by the other party under the theory of
quantum meruit.[15]

◆ **Illustration:** The estate of a decedent who had died
four months into an employment contract that was to last
a year could recover in quantum meruit for the value of
the decedent's services actually rendered during the four
months.[16]

To ascertain that value, the amount necessary to complete
the work contracted for must be deducted from the original
contract price agreed upon by the parties.[17]

The amount of the value of labor and material used in a
substantially completed job is the contract price less deduc-
tions for errors or omissions in doing the work and less pay-

---

[14]Dove v. Rose Acre Farms, Inc., 434 N.E.2d 931 (Ind. Ct. App. 1st Dist.
1982).

[15]Abbey Villas Development Corp. v. Site Contractors, Inc., 716 N.E.2d
91 (Ind. Ct. App. 1999), reh'g denied, (Nov. 17, 1999) (where contractor
had finished 70% of work when owner breached, contractor would be paid
70% of contract price); City of Indianapolis v. Twin Lakes Enterprises,
Inc., 568 N.E.2d 1073 (Ind. Ct. App. 1st Dist. 1991), reh'g denied, (May 16,
1991) and transfer denied, (Dec. 12, 1991); Charles F. Broughton, D.M.D.,
P.C. v. Riehle, 512 N.E.2d 1133 (Ind. Ct. App. 1st Dist. 1987).

Trial Strategy References: Recovery for Part Performance of
Contract, 43 Am Jur POF2d 523.

[16]Jones v. Servel, Inc., 135 Ind. App. 171, 186 N.E.2d 689 (Div. 2 1962).

[17]Pierce v. Drees, 607 N.E.2d 726 (Ind. Ct. App. 3d Dist. 1993); Charles
F. Broughton, D.M.D., P.C. v. Riehle, 512 N.E.2d 1133 (Ind. Ct. App. 1st
Dist. 1987); Blade Corp. v. American Drywall, Inc., 400 N.E.2d 1183 (Ind.
Ct. App. 1st Dist. 1980).

ment received.[18] The amount necessary to complete the work may be either the reasonable cost or the actual cost to the owner of completion.[19]

A lessor in breach of a lease may recover restitution for the lessee's continued occupancy of the lease premises if:

(1) the lessor has rendered a part performance under the contract that was a net benefit to the lessee;

(2) the lessee, with knowledge of the breach, has accepted the benefit of the lessor's part performance;

(3) the compensation sought is not merely a payment of earnest money; and

(4) the contract does not provide that the lessee could retain the rent in event of a breach by the lessor.[20]

If performance of a contract to repair a building has become impossible because the building has been destroyed, and neither party is at fault for the destruction, the contractor may not recover for the amount of the work he or she has already done.[21]

§ 118 —Altered performance; deviations

If one party deviates from the strict terms of a contract, the other cannot declare a default unless he or she has informed the first party that strict compliance with the contract is required in the future.

West's Digest, Contracts ⚯296.
West's Digest, Damages ⚯121.

When a party deviates from strict performance as called for by the contract, the other party cannot immediately de-

---

[18]Johnson v. Taylor Bldg. Corp., 171 Ind. App. 674, 371 N.E.2d 404 (1st Dist. 1978).

[19]Blade Corp. v. American Drywall, Inc., 400 N.E.2d 1183 (Ind. Ct. App. 1st Dist. 1980).

[20]Morrison's Southern Plaza Corp. v. Southern Plaza, Inc., 252 Ind. 109, 246 N.E.2d 191 (1969).

See also Welborn v. Society for Propagation of Faith, 411 N.E.2d 1267 (Ind. Ct. App. 2d Dist. 1980) (even though landlord was not performing all of its duties under lease, tenants owed restitution as long as they remained in possession of leased premises).

[21]Hipskind Heating & Plumbing Co. v. General Industries, Inc., 246 Ind. 215, 204 N.E.2d 339 (1965).

For discussion of impossibility as an excuse for nonperformance, see § 112.

clare the deviation a breach of contract,[22] but must give notice to the other party that strict performance will be
required in the future. If the other party then continues to
deviate, a default can be declared.[23] If any additions or
alterations are made to an original contract, the original
contract is binding on the parties and still exists unless it is
so abandoned that it is impossible to follow.[24] Thus, a party
who under a special contract does work different from that
agreed upon in the contract may recover from the latter the
value of such work, where such work is accepted by the other
party.[25]

XV. ACTIONS FOR BREACH OF CONTRACT

A. GENERALLY

Research References

IC 8-21-4-7; IC 24-5-11.5-12 to IC 24-5-11.5-14; IC 26-1-3-408; IC
    34-11-2-3; IC 34-11-2-7; IC 34-11-2-9; IC 34-11-2-11; IC 34-11-
    3-1; IC 35-15-1-2
29 U.S.C.A. § 185
Trial R. 7, 8, 9, 9.1, 9.2, 10, 11, 12, 17, 19, 41, 52

17A Am Jur 2d, Contracts §§ 746-748.
17B C.J.S., Contracts §§ 600-804.
West's Digest, Contracts ☞324-346, 351-355.
ALR Digest: Contracts §§ 546-552
ALR Index: Adhesion Contracts; Anticipatory Breach; Anticipatory
    Renunciation or Repudiation; Bids and Bidding; Cancellation of
    Rescission; Consideration; Contracts; Covenants; Covenants Not
    to Compete; Estoppel and Waiver; Executory Contracts; Implied
    Contracts; Offer and Acceptance; Parol Contracts and Agree-
    ments; Parol Evidence; Third-Party Beneficiaries; Unconsciona-
    bility
7A Am Jur Pleading and Practice Forms, Contracts §§ 10-26, 50,
    69-71, 110-114.

---

[22]Scott-Reitz Ltd. v. Rein Warsaw Associates, 658 N.E.2d 98 (Ind. Ct.
App. 1995); Pierce v. Yochum, 164 Ind. App. 443, 330 N.E.2d 102 (1st
Dist. 1975).

[23]Scott-Reitz Ltd. v. Rein Warsaw Associates, 658 N.E.2d 98 (Ind. Ct.
App. 1995); Pierce v. Yochum, 164 Ind. App. 443, 330 N.E.2d 102 (1st
Dist. 1975).

[24]McKinney v. Springer, 3 Ind. 59, 1851 WL 2916 (1851).

[25]Louisville, E. & St. L. Ry. Co. v. Donnegan, 111 Ind. 179, 12 N.E. 153
(1887); Branham v. Johnson, 62 Ind. 259, 1878 WL 6330 (1878).

§ 119 Nature and form of action

Any breach of a contract may be the basis of an action.

West's Digest, Contracts ☜324(1), 324(2).

The basic elements of a breach-of-contract action are:

- existence of a contract
- defendant's breach of the contract
- damages[26]

A party suing as the third-party beneficiary of a contract must show that:

- the contract was intended to benefit him or her directly
- the contract must necessarily benefit him or her
- the defendant has breached its contract[27]

A contract action which alleges breach of warranty requires proof of:

- the existence of the warranty
- a breach of that warranty
- causation
- resulting damages[28]

An action for breach of contract can be founded only upon the defendant's failure to perform in accordance with the obligation he or she assumed under the agreement,[29] and no action sounding in contract may be predicated upon the defendant's exercise of a right conferred by a valid contract,

---

[26]J.S. Sweet Co., Inc. v. White County Bridge Com'n, 714 N.E.2d 219 (Ind. Ct. App. 1999); White v. State Farm Mut. Auto. Ins. Co., 709 N.E.2d 1079 (Ind. Ct. App. 1999); Shumate v. Lycan, 675 N.E.2d 749 (Ind. Ct. App. 1997), transfer denied, 683 N.E.2d 595 (Ind. 1997); Peterson v. Culver Educational Foundation, 402 N.E.2d 448 (Ind. Ct. App. 1st Dist. 1980).

For discussion of remedies available for breach of contract, see I.L.E., Damages; Injunction; Specific Performance.

[27]Wilson v. Palmer, 452 N.E.2d 426 (Ind. Ct. App. 4th Dist. 1983); Fiat Distributors, Inc. v. Hidbrader, 178 Ind. App. 200, 381 N.E.2d 1069 (1st Dist. 1978).

[28]Peltz Const. Co. v. Dunham, 436 N.E.2d 892, 34 U.C.C. Rep. Serv. (CBC) 14 (Ind. Ct. App. 4th Dist. 1982).

[29]Reynolds v. Louisville, N.A. & C.R. Co., 143 Ind. 579, 40 N.E. 410 (1895).

regardless of his or her motives in exercising the right and regardless of the damage resulting to the plaintiff.[30]

The parties to a contract may provide for their own liability and remedies, such as by contractually modifying the usual implied warranties and limiting available remedies.[31]

A breach-of-contract action must be distinguished from an breach of warranty action, as the two are closely related but not identical. A warranty is usually, though not necessarily, collateral to the principal contract.[32] A defendant may be found liable for breach of warranty, but not for breach of contract.[33]

◆ **Caution:** Note that a breach-of-contract action may be preempted by federal law. Contract disputes between employers and labor organizations, for instance, are governed exclusively by the Labor Management Relations Act.[34]

Where an express contract has been fully performed by one of the parties, so that nothing remains unexecuted but the other party's obligation to pay the performing party, the performing party may either maintain an action on the contract or bring an action in quantum meruit to recover the value of the performance rendered.[35] While it has been held that recovery in excess of the contract price may not be had

---

[30]Jones v. Lathrop-Moyer Co., 99 Ind. App. 127, 190 N.E. 883 (1934); Dowagiac Mfg. Co. v. Thurston, 24 Ind. App. 264, 56 N.E. 684 (1900).

[31]Hahn v. Ford Motor Co., Inc., 434 N.E.2d 943, 33 U.C.C. Rep. Serv. (CBC) 1277 (Ind. Ct. App. 2d Dist. 1982).

[32]Nelson v. Marchand, 691 N.E.2d 1264 (Ind. Ct. App. 1998) (contract consisted of promise to build home; warranty was promise that home would be built in workmanlike manner); Modern Woodmen of America v. Vincent, 40 Ind. App. 711, 82 N.E. 475 (Div. 2 1907).

[33]Burras v. Canal Const. and Design Co., 470 N.E.2d 1362 (Ind. Ct. App. 1st Dist. 1984) (where homebuilder was notified of defects and expressed willingness to remedy them, but before it could do so, owner refused to continue payments as required by contract, justifying builder's suspension of performance, owner breached express warranty that work would be performed in workmanlike manner, but did not breach contract).

[34]29 U.S.C.A. § 185.

McCarty v. Reynolds Metals Co., 883 F. Supp. 356 (S.D. Ind. 1995).

[35]Scott v. Congdon, 106 Ind. 268, 6 N.E. 625 (1886); Shilling v. Templeton, 66 Ind. 585, 1879 WL 5552 (1879); Esarey v. Buhner Fertilizer Co., 117 Ind. App. 291, 69 N.E.2d 755 (1946).

in an action in quantum meruit,[36] it has also been held that if the defendant denies the existence of the contract, its provisions do not limit the plaintiff's recovery.[37]

◆ **Practice Guide:** Persons who are not parties to contracts may be civilly liable for their tortious interference with others' contract rights, as where they maliciously procure a breach of contract.[38]

Indiana does not recognize a separate cause of action for tortious breach of contract.[39]

A professional developer who improves land for the express purpose of residential homebuilding with knowledge but without disclosure of a latent defect in the land can be liable for the breach of an implied warranty of habitability to the purchasers of the land from the builder who actually built the home.[40] A subsequent purchaser of a home cannot seek damages from a builder for an alleged breach of implied warranty if the builder is not given an opportunity to repair the alleged defect.[41]

In performing home improvements and in contracting to perform home improvements, the remodeler may warrant certain things to the owner, including, during the 2-year period beginning on the warranty date, that the home improvement must be free from defects in workmanship and material.[42] The remodeler may only disclaim all implied warranties

---

[36]Cleveland, C., C. & St. L. Ry. Co. v. Moore, 170 Ind. 328, 82 N.E. 52 (1907), reh'g denied, 170 Ind. 328, 84 N.E. 540 (1908); Esarey v. Buhner Fertilizer Co., 117 Ind. App. 291, 69 N.E.2d 755 (1946).

[37]Gastlin v. Weeks, 2 Ind. App. 222, 28 N.E. 331 (1891).

[38]Wade v. Culp, 107 Ind. App. 503, 23 N.E.2d 615 (1939).

[39]Broadhurst v. Moenning, 633 N.E.2d 326 (Ind. Ct. App. 5th Dist. 1994); Comfax Corp. v. North American Van Lines, Inc., 587 N.E.2d 118 (Ind. Ct. App. 1st Dist. 1992), appeal after remand, 638 N.E.2d 476 (Ind. Ct. App. 5th Dist. 1994).

Trial Strategy References: Bad Faith Tort Remedy for Breach of Contract, 34 Am Jur Trials 343.

[40]Jordan v. Talaga, 532 N.E.2d 1174 (Ind. Ct. App. 4th Dist. 1989), reh'g denied, (Mar. 13, 1989) and transfer denied, (Oct. 3, 1989) (evidence permitted conclusion that the lot should never have been developed for homebuilding).

[41]Deckard v. Ratcliff, 553 N.E.2d 523 (Ind. Ct. App. 1st Dist. 1990).

[42]IC 24-5-11.5-12.

if certain conditions are met.[43] If a remodeler breaches a warranty, the owner may bring an action against the remodeler either for damages arising from the breach or for specific performance.[44]

§ 120 Conflict of Laws

In contract matters, the law of the forum with the most-intimate contacts to the facts governs.

West's Digest, Contracts ☞144, 325.

Indiana applies the "most intimate contacts" rule formulated by the Restatement (Second) Of Conflict of Laws to determine what forum's law governs in contract matters.[45] The law to be applied is that of the forum with the most-intimate contacts to the facts.[46]

Courts applying the most-intimate contacts test will consider all acts of the parties touching the transaction in relation to the various states involved.[47]

Other factors to be considered are:

---

[43]IC 24-5-11.5-13.

[44]IC 24-5-11.5-14.

[45]Cox by Zick v. Nichols, 690 N.E.2d 750 (Ind. Ct. App. 1998), reh'g denied, (Apr. 1, 1998); Hartford Acc. & Indem. Co. v. Dana Corp., 690 N.E.2d 285 (Ind. Ct. App. 1997), transfer denied, 698 N.E.2d 1191 (Ind. 1998) (citing Restatement (Second) of Conflicts, §§ 188, 193); Schaffert by Schaffert v. Jackson Nat. Life Ins. Co., 687 N.E.2d 230 (Ind. Ct. App. 1997), transfer denied, 698 N.E.2d 1188 (Ind. 1998).

[46]Hartford Acc. & Indem. Co. v. Dana Corp., 690 N.E.2d 285 (Ind. Ct. App. 1997), transfer denied, 698 N.E.2d 1191 (Ind. 1998).

Annotation References: Conflict of laws as to validity, enforceability, and effect of ancillary restrictive covenant not to compete, on contract of employment or for sale of business, 70 ALR2d 1292.

What law governs as to proper party plaintiff in contract action, 62 ALR2d 486.

What law governs in determining whether facts and circumstances operate to terminate, breach, rescind, or repudiate a contract, 50 ALR2d 254.

What law governs validity, effect, and construction of separation or property settlement agreements, 18 ALR2d 760.

[47]Hartford Acc. & Indem. Co. v. Dana Corp., 690 N.E.2d 285 (Ind. Ct. App. 1997), transfer denied, 698 N.E.2d 1191 (Ind. 1998); Schaffert by Schaffert v. Jackson Nat. Life Ins. Co., 687 N.E.2d 230 (Ind. Ct. App. 1997), transfer denied, 698 N.E.2d 1188 (Ind. 1998).

Annotation References: Construction and application of state statutes or rules of court predicating in personam jurisdiction over

- the place of contracting
- the place the contract was negotiated
- the place the contract is to be performed
- the location of the subject matter of the contract
- the parties' domiciles, residences, nationalities, places of incorporation, and places of business[48]

The place of contracting, standing alone, is relatively insignificant in this analysis.[49] The place where the contract was negotiated is of less importance when there is no one single place of negotiation, as where the parties conduct their negotiations from separate states by mail or telephone, rather than by meeting in person.[50]

◆ **Practice Guide:** A contract entered into in an airplane over Indiana is considered to have been entered into in Indiana.[51]

The place where the contract is to be performed bears little weight when it is uncertain or unknown at the time the parties form the contract.[52]

◆ **Illustration:** The law of Indiana, rather than that of New York, applied in an action for breach of a contractual indemnity provision where the final act of acceptance of the contract occurred in New York, the seller's home office was in New York, negotiations and agreements by the purchaser occurred in Oklahoma, the purchaser's principal office was in Oklahoma, and the machine purchased was actually shipped from the seller's subsidiary's office in Missouri, but the machine was located in Indiana, both parties' substantial performance of the contract requirements was to occur in Indiana, and the facts giving rise to

---

nonresidents or foreign corporations on making or performing a contract within the state, 23 ALR3d 551.

[48]Schaffert by Schaffert v. Jackson Nat. Life Ins. Co., 687 N.E.2d 230 (Ind. Ct. App. 1997), transfer denied, 698 N.E.2d 1188 (Ind. 1998).

[49]Hartford Acc. & Indem. Co. v. Dana Corp., 690 N.E.2d 285 (Ind. Ct. App. 1997), transfer denied, 698 N.E.2d 1191 (Ind. 1998).

[50]Hartford Acc. & Indem. Co. v. Dana Corp., 690 N.E.2d 285 (Ind. Ct. App. 1997), transfer denied, 698 N.E.2d 1191 (Ind. 1998).

[51]IC 8-21-4-7.

[52]Hartford Acc. & Indem. Co. v. Dana Corp., 690 N.E.2d 285 (Ind. Ct. App. 1997), transfer denied, 698 N.E.2d 1191 (Ind. 1998).

the indemnity claim related to the condition or operation of the machine in Indiana.[53]

◆ **Caution:** Recall that forum selection clauses are generally enforceable in Indiana.[54] The most-intimate contacts test applies only when the parties have not otherwise agreed as to the applicable law.[55]

§ 121 Conditions precedent to suit

Unless the contract provides otherwise, a party is not required to provide notice of defects or an opportunity to cure before bringing suit for breach of contract.

West's Digest, Contracts ☞327(1)-327(4).

Generally, a party may bring a breach-of-contract action upon the slightest breach of the contract by the other party.[56] The parties may, however, include in their contract a provision requiring some other action before suit may be brought. Typically, these provisions require that the performing party be given notice of any defects in his or her performance and an opportunity to cure the defect.[57]

Unless such a provision appears in the contract, a party need not be afforded an opportunity to cure as a condition precedent to his or her opponent's initiation of an action in most cases;[58] however, even in the absence of such a provision, before an action for breach of the implied warranty of habitability may be maintained, the homeowner must provide notice of the defect and an opportunity to cure

---

[53]Dohm & Nelke, a div. of Cashin Systems Corp. v. Wilson Foods Corp., 531 N.E.2d 512 (Ind. Ct. App. 3d Dist. 1988).

[54]For discussion of the enforceability of forum selection clauses, see § 49.

[55]Kolentus v. Avco Corp., 798 F.2d 949 (7th Cir. 1986) (applying Indiana law).

[56]Miller Brewing Co. v. Best Beers of Bloomington, Inc., 608 N.E.2d 975 (Ind. 1993), reh'g denied, (June 23, 1993).

[57]Brown v. Russell, 105 Ind. 46, 4 N.E. 428 (1886) (written notice of breach); Burras v. Canal Const. and Design Co., 470 N.E.2d 1362 (Ind. Ct. App. 1st Dist. 1984) (notice and opportunity to cure); J.F. Seiberling & Co. v. Rodman, (1896) 14 Ind. App. 460, 43 N.E. 38 (notice of defects and reasonable time to remedy them).

Annotation References: Provision in employment contract requiring written notice before instituting action, 4 ALR3d 439.

[58]Aamco Transmission v. Air Systems, Inc., 459 N.E.2d 1215, 44 A.L.R.4th 1163 (Ind. Ct. App. 2d Dist. 1984).

it.[59] Although there is no particular form for giving notice of defect constituting breach of implied warranty of fitness for habitation, the owner must at least inform the builder of the problem and give him or her a reasonable opportunity to cure it.[60]

A party need not necessarily perform all of its obligations under the contract before bringing an action for breach of contract.[61]

§ 122 Defenses

A defense to a breach-of-contract action must present a legal reason why the plaintiff should not recover.

West's Digest, Contracts ⚖328(1)-328(5).

To constitute a good defense to an action based on a contract, the matter alleged must be germane to the cause of action pleaded and present a legal reason why the plaintiff should not recover on the agreement.[62]

Any matter tending to render the contract void or voidable may also provide a defense.[63] Defenses to breach-of-contract actions include:

- the plaintiff's failure to comply with a condition precedent[64]

- the requirement by the statute of frauds that an oral contract was to be in writing[65]

---

[59]Nelson v. Marchand, 691 N.E.2d 1264 (Ind. Ct. App. 1998).

[60]Jordan v. Talaga, 532 N.E.2d 1174 (Ind. Ct. App. 4th Dist. 1989), reh'g denied, (Mar. 13, 1989) and transfer denied, (Oct. 3, 1989).

[61]§ 115.

[62]Colton v. Vandervolgen, 87 Ind. 361, 1882 WL 6541 (1882); Berry v. Bates, 2 Blackf. 118, 1828 WL 1045 (Ind. 1828).

[63]For discussion of matters affecting the validity of assent to a contract, see §§ 31 et seq.

For discussion of illegal contracts, see §§ 56 et seq.

[64]Indiana & Michigan Elec. Co. v. Terre Haute Industries, Inc., 507 N.E.2d 588 (Ind. Ct. App. 1st Dist. 1987), reh'g denied, (June 12, 1987) and transfer denied, 525 N.E.2d 1247 (Ind. 1988); United Farm Bureau Mut. Ins. Co. v. Wolfe, 178 Ind. App. 435, 382 N.E.2d 1018 (1st Dist. 1978).

For discussion of pleading performance of conditions precedent, see §§ 105, 129.

[65]Moridge Mfg. Co. v. Butler, 451 N.E.2d 677, 36 U.C.C. Rep. Serv.

- waiver of a contract requirement[66]
- rescission of the agreement[67]
- accord and satisfaction[68]
- failure to bring the action within the time specified by the statute of limitations[69]
- lack of consideration[70]

◆ **Caution:** Failure of consideration is not a defense against a holder in due course.[71]

An insured's failure to cooperate in his or her defense is a defense against a claim that the insurance company breached its contractual duty to defend the insured.[72]

Defenses are generally to be presented in the defendant's responsive pleading.[73] Certain defenses, however, such as lack of jurisdiction, incorrect venue, insufficiency of process or service, failure to state a claim upon which relief may be granted, failure to join a necessary or indispensable party, and the pendency of the action in another Indiana court, may be made by motion[74] and will be waived if they are not included in a motion or responsive pleading.[75]

The performance of a contract, or the offer of performance, after a suit for breach of the contract has been brought, will

---

(CBC) 1548 (Ind. Ct. App. 3d Dist. 1983); Lawshe v. Glen Park Lumber Co., Inc., 176 Ind. App. 344, 375 N.E.2d 275 (3d Dist. 1978).

As to the statute of frauds, see I.L.E., Statute of Frauds.

[66]Nelson v. Gurley, 673 N.E.2d 497 (Ind. Ct. App. 1996).

[67]Mabin v. Webster, 129 Ind. 430, 28 N.E. 863 (1891).

[68]Collins v. Stanfield, 139 Ind. 184, 38 N.E. 1091 (1894).

[69]For discussion of the statutes of limitations applicable in contract actions, see § 123.

[70]Trial R. 9.1(C).

[71]IC 26-1-3-408.

Firth v. Farmers-Citizens Bank, 460 N.E.2d 191, 38 U.C.C. Rep. Serv. (CBC) 212 (Ind. Ct. App. 1st Dist. 1984); Parrish v. Terre Haute Sav. Bank, 431 N.E.2d 132 (Ind. Ct. App. 4th Dist. 1982), reh'g denied, 438 N.E.2d 1 (Ind. Ct. App. 4th Dist. 1982) and transfer denied, (Feb. 4, 1985).

For discussion of holders in due course, see I.L.E., Negotiable Instruments.

[72]Potomac Ins. Co. v. Stanley, 281 F.2d 775 (7th Cir. 1960) (applying Indiana law).

[73]Trial R. 12(B).

[74]Trial R. 12(B).

[75]Trial R. 12(H).

not act as a bar to prosecution of the pending suit[76] unless the performance is with the express or implied consent of the plaintiff or unless he or she has accepted what was done as partial or complete discharge of the agreement.[77] One unexecuted contract can never be set up in bar of an action based upon another independent unexecuted contract.[78]

§ 123   Time to sue and limitations

Actions on written contracts must generally be brought within 10 years after the cause of action accrues; actions on contracts not in writing must be brought within six years.

West's Digest, Contracts ☞329.

An action on a contract in writing, other than an action for the payment of money and including most mortgages, must be commenced within 10 years after the cause of action accrues, unless the contract was entered into before September 1, 1982, in which case the action must be commenced within 20 years after the cause of action accrues.[79] However, if the action is brought on a promissory note, bill of exchange, or other written contract for the payment of money executed after August 31, 1982, the action must be commenced within six years after the cause of action accrues, unless the contract was executed before September 1, 1982, in which case the action must be brought within 10 years after the cause of action accrues.[80] The mere existence of any written document associated with a contract cause of action does not allow the plaintiff to avoid the shorter statute of limitations for unwritten contracts; the written document must in fact be the basis for the claim being pressed.[81]

◆ **Illustration:** The six-year period applied to an action to set aside a corporation's transfer of stock to its

---

[76]Potomac Ins. Co. v. Stanley, 281 F.2d 775 (7th Cir. 1960) (applying Indiana law).

[77]Indiana, B. & W. Ry. Co. v. Adams, 112 Ind. 302, 14 N.E. 80 (1887).

[78]Welshbillig v. Dienhart, 65 Ind. 94, 1878 WL 6258 (1878).

[79]IC 34-11-2-11.

[80]IC 34-11-2-9.

[81]McMahan v. Snap on Tool Corp., 478 N.E.2d 116 (Ind. Ct. App. 4th Dist. 1985).

president, even though the transfer was recorded in the corporate minutes.[82]

An action on an account or a contract not in writing must be brought within six years after the cause of action accrues.[83] This provision applies to both implied and express contracts.[84] A claim for a breach of the implied warranty of habitability is also subject to a six-year statute of limitations.[85]

The applicable statute of limitations is to be ascertained according to the nature of the harm alleged, rather than according to the form of the pleadings.[86] For instance, an action seeking rescission of a contract on the grounds of fraud is governed by the six-year statute of limitations for fraud.[87]

Generally, a cause of action for breach of contract or breach of warranty accrues at the time the plaintiff discovers or should have discovered, in the exercise of ordinary diligence, the breach or the damage caused by it.[88] This may, however, be altered by statute. For instance, in an action brought to recover a balance due upon a mutual, open, and current ac-

---

[82]INB Nat. Bank v. Moran Elec. Service, Inc., 608 N.E.2d 702 (Ind. Ct. App. 1st Dist. 1993), transfer denied, (Apr. 14, 1993).

[83]IC 34-11-2-7(1).

Movement for Opportunity and Equality v. General Motors Corp., 622 F.2d 1235 (7th Cir. 1980) (applying Indiana law) (shorter period provided for actions which must rely on parol evidence, including memories).

[84]Amermac, Inc. v. Gordon, 182 Ind. App. 116, 394 N.E.2d 946, 27 U.C.C. Rep. Serv. (CBC) 447 (2d Dist. 1979).

[85]Lechner v. Reutepohler, 545 N.E.2d 1144 (Ind. Ct. App. 1st Dist. 1989).

[86]Whitehouse v. Quinn, 477 N.E.2d 270 (Ind. 1985); French v. Hickman Moving and Storage, 400 N.E.2d 1384 (Ind. Ct. App. 3d Dist. 1980); O.K. Sand and Gravel, Inc. v. Martin Marietta Corp., 786 F. Supp. 1442 (S.D. Ind. 1992) (applying Indiana law) (two-year limitations period for injury to personal property, rather than 10-year period for breach of written contract, applied where nature of claim indicated that it was for breach of fiduciary duty rather than breach of contract).

[87]INB Nat. Bank v. Moran Elec. Service, Inc., 608 N.E.2d 702 (Ind. Ct. App. 1st Dist. 1993), transfer denied, (Apr. 14, 1993).

[88]Habig v. Bruning, 613 N.E.2d 61 (Ind. Ct. App. 2d Dist. 1993), transfer denied, (July 7, 1993) (claim accrued when homeowners could have discovered that their property had been damaged when roof leaked, rather than when job was completed); Lift-A-Loft Corp. v. Rodes-Roper-Love Ins. Agency, Inc., 975 F.2d 1305 (7th Cir. 1992), reh'g denied, (Nov. 9, 1992) (applying Indiana law) (contract claim against insurance agency for failing to obtain liability insurance from insurer accrued no later than time that insured learned of insurer's pending liquidation).

count between the parties, the cause of action accrues on the date of the last item proved in the account on either side.[89] The statute of limitations for an action based upon the breach of an enforceable contract to make a will generally does not commence until the decedent's death.[90]

A contract action may also be subject to a statute of repose, which sets a cap on the time within which an action may be brought regardless of the time the cause of action accrues.[91] For instance, a contract action based on professional medical services which were rendered or which should have been rendered must be brought within two years from the date of the complained-of act, omission, or neglect.[92] Contract actions based on any deficiency, or alleged deficiency, in the design, planning, supervision, construction, or observation of construction of an improvement to real property, or on any injury to the person or to real or personal property arising out of such a deficiency, must be brought within 10 years from the date of substantial completion of the improvement or, if the action is for deficiency in design, within 12 years after the completion and submission of plans and specifications to the owner, whichever is shorter.[93] A statute of repose does not expand the applicable statute of limitations.[94]

The parties may provide in their contract that some limitations period other than the one provided by Indiana statute will apply to actions brought on the contract.[95]

---

[89]IC 34-11-3-1.

[90]Matter of Carroll's Estate, 436 N.E.2d 864 (Ind. Ct. App. 2d Dist. 1982).

[91]Jordan v. Talaga, 532 N.E.2d 1174 (Ind. Ct. App. 4th Dist. 1989), reh'g denied, (Mar. 13, 1989) and transfer denied, (Oct. 3, 1989).

[92]IC 34-11-2-3.

[93]IC 35-15-1-2.

[94]Jordan v. Talaga, 532 N.E.2d 1174 (Ind. Ct. App. 4th Dist. 1989), reh'g denied, (Mar. 13, 1989) and transfer denied, (Oct. 3, 1989).

[95]Lumpkins v. Grange Mut. Companies, 553 N.E.2d 871 (Ind. Ct. App. 2d Dist. 1990) (two years).

Annotation References: Choice of law as to applicable statute of limitations in contract actions, 78 ALR3d 639.

A party's renunciation of an executory contract before or after the time of performance entitles the other party to sue immediately.[96]

§ 124 Parties

A party in a breach-of-contract action must be a party to the contract or in privity with a party and must be the real party in interest.

West's Digest, Contracts ⊛330(1)-330(4330(1)-330(4).

An action based on contract may be brought only against a party to the contract or against those in privity with the party.[97] An assignee of a contract, or a person in a similar position, may sue to enforce the contract. For instance, an employee welfare benefit fund which is contractually entitled to receive contributions from employers on behalf of its members is entitled to sue the employers if they fail to make such payments to the fund.[98] In fact, where there has been an assignment of a contract right or cause of action, the action must ordinarily be prosecuted by the assignee.[99]

Only the real party in interest may bring suit to recover damages allegedly resulting from breach of contract.[1] To acquire real party in interest status, the person must have a

---

[96]Indiana Life Endowment Co. v. Reed, 54 Ind. App. 450, 103 N.E. 77 (Div. 1 1913).

[97]Broadhurst v. Moenning, 633 N.E.2d 326 (Ind. Ct. App. 5th Dist. 1994); Gonzales v. Kil Nam Chun, 465 N.E.2d 727 (Ind. Ct. App. 4th Dist. 1984) (employee of person who borrowed scaffold could not bring action for breach of contract after scaffold collapsed against person employer borrowed it from, as employee was not party to contract); Implement Service, Inc. v. Tecumseh Products Co., 726 F. Supp. 1171 (S.D. Ind. 1989) (third party retained to provide approval of work as condition precedent to acceptance of work was not party to contract and could not be sued on it).

[98]Indiana Carpenters Cent. and Western Indiana Pension Fund v. Seaboard Sur. Co., 601 N.E.2d 352 (Ind. Ct. App. 2d Dist. 1992), reh'g denied, (Mar. 9, 1993) and transfer denied, 615 N.E.2d 892 (Ind. 1993).

[99]Hardy v. Blazer, 29 Ind. 226, 1867 WL 3098 (1867).

As to assignments of contract rights, see I.L.E. Assignments.

[1]Trial R. 17(A).

Rollins Burdick Hunter of Utah, Inc. v. Board of Trustees of Ball State University, 665 N.E.2d 914, 110 Ed. Law Rep. 373 (Ind. Ct. App. 1996) (university was real party in interest where payments were made through university foundation and alumni association, but were made with university funds); Cook v. City of Evansville, 178 Ind. App. 20, 381 N.E.2d 493 (1st Dist. 1978).

present and substantial interest in the relief which is sought.[2]

A person has standing to bring an action if he or she has suffered sufficient injury to confer jurisdiction on a court.[3] Even if a person is a party to a disputed contract, he or she is not a proper plaintiff in a breach-of-contract action unless he or she suffered injury from the breach.[4]

A third-party beneficiary to a contract may sue to enforce the contract.[5] He or she may not, however, be sued on the contract.[6] A party to a third-party beneficiary contract may sue to enforce the contract without joining the third-party beneficiary, although he or she must identify the third-party beneficiary and his or her relationship to the third-party beneficiary.[7]

If a partnership which was a party to a contract has been dissolved, the partner who is entitled to wind up the partnership's affairs is the real party in interest in an action on the contract.[8]

Homeowners to whom the implied warranty of habitability

---

[2]Knapp v. National Building & Loan Ass'n of Hammond, 212 Ind. 217, 7 N.E.2d 938 (1937); Cook v. City of Evansville, 178 Ind. App. 20, 381 N.E.2d 493 (1st Dist. 1978); A—. B—. v. C—. D—., 150 Ind. App. 535, 277 N.E.2d 599 (Div. 2 1971).

[3]City of Indianapolis, for and on Behalf of City-County Council of City of Indianapolis and Marion County v. Indiana State Bd. of Tax Com'rs, 261 Ind. 635, 308 N.E.2d 868 (1974); Cook v. City of Evansville, 178 Ind. App. 20, 381 N.E.2d 493 (1st Dist. 1978).

Annotation References: What law governs as to proper party plaintiff in contract action, 62 ALR2d 486.

[4]Aikens v. Alexander, 397 N.E.2d 319 (Ind. Ct. App. 4th Dist. 1979) (active members of public employees retirement fund who had not yet retired lacked standing to seek order enjoining transfer of funds to retirement fund); Cook v. City of Evansville, 178 Ind. App. 20, 381 N.E.2d 493 (1st Dist. 1978) (city which acted as conduit to collect service charges from union members, which were then to be paid to union, was not real party in interest, as it had no demonstrable pecuniary interest or other substantial interest in recovery and disbursement of funds).

[5]Implement Service, Inc. v. Tecumseh Products Co., 726 F. Supp. 1171 (S.D. Ind. 1989); Copeland v. Summers, 138 Ind. 219, 35 N.E. 514 (1893), reh'g denied, 138 Ind. 219, 37 N.E. 971 (1894).

[6]Implement Service, Inc. v. Tecumseh Products Co., 726 F. Supp. 1171 (S.D. Ind. 1989).

[7]Trial R. 17(A)(1).

[8]Marksill Specialties, Inc. v. Barger, 428 N.E.2d 65 (Ind. Ct. App. 3d Dist. 1981).

runs may bring an action for breach of the warranty against not only the builder, but also the developer of a residential area who has approved for construction land with a latent defect, such as its location in a flood plain.[9] Furthermore, not only the original owners of the home, but also a subsequent purchaser, may seek damages for a breach of the implied warranty.[10]

All persons having an interest in obtaining the relief demanded in an action should be joined as plaintiffs;[11] thus, if two or more parties to a contract have a common interest in the damages to be recovered for its breach and their respective separate interests in the damages to be recovered are not conclusively established by the contract, the parties must all join as plaintiffs.[12]

The mere naming of a person in a contract as the agent of one of the parties to perform his or her agreement does not make such person a necessary or proper party in an action to enforce performance of such a contract against his or her principal.[13]

Surviving obligees may bring an action on a joint contract without joining the heirs of a deceased obligee, because the law vests the entire right to benefit from the obligation in the survivors.[14]

A plaintiff may file an action to recover from a single party to the contract, even if others are severally liable on the contract, without joining the others.[15]

§ 125   Complaint, generally

The complaint in a breach-of-contract case must contain a short and plain statement showing that the pleader is entitled to relief and a demand for relief.

West's Digest, Contracts ☞332(1)-337(5).

A complaint, counterclaim, cross-claim, or third-party

---

[9]Jordan v. Talaga, 532 N.E.2d 1174 (Ind. Ct. App. 4th Dist. 1989), reh'g denied, (Mar. 13, 1989) and transfer denied, (Oct. 3, 1989).

[10]Deckard v. Ratcliff, 553 N.E.2d 523 (Ind. Ct. App. 1st Dist. 1990).

[11]Trial R. 19.

[12]Spencer v. McGuffin, 190 Ind. 308, 130 N.E. 407, 14 A.L.R. 385 (1921).

[13]Dahoney v. Hall, 20 Ind. 264, 1863 WL 1959 (1863).

[14]Indiana, Bloomington & Western Ry. Co. v. Adamson, 114 Ind. 282, 15 N.E. 5 (1888).

[15]Carmichael v. Arms, 51 Ind. App. 689, 100 N.E. 302 (Div. 1 1912).

claim must contain a short and plain statement of the claim showing that the pleader is entitled to relief and a demand for the relief to which the pleader deems him- or herself entitled;[16] thus, to make a prima facie case of breach of contract, the plaintiff must establish the defendant's contractual obligations and show how the defendant violated those obligations.[17] Each averment of the complaint is to be simple, concise, and direct. No technical forms of pleading or motions are required.[18] Complaints, like other pleadings, are to be construed so as to do substantial justice, lead to disposition on the merits, and avoid litigation of procedural points.[19]

The complaint in a breach-of-contract action need not state all elements of the cause of action, as long as it states facts upon which the plaintiff may be granted relief.[20] Time and place need be stated only with sufficient specificity to enable the opposing party to prepare his or her defense.[21] The facts alleged in the complaint are taken as true, and dismissal is appropriate only where it appears that the plaintiff could not be granted any relief on the facts as pleaded.[22]

The plaintiff need not aver his or her capacity to sue, the defendant's capacity to be sued, the authority of a party to

---

[16]Trial R. 8(A).

Forms References: Complaint, petition, or declaration. 7A Am Jur Pleading and Practice Forms, Annotated (rev. ed.), Contracts §§ 10-13.

Complaint, petition, or declaration for breach of written contract. 7A Am Jur Pleading and Practice Forms, Annotated (rev. ed.), Contracts §§ 69, 70.

Complaint, petition, or declaration for breach of oral contract. 7A Am Jur Pleading and Practice Forms, Annotated (rev. ed.), Contracts § 71.

[17]Pepsi-Cola Co. v. Steak 'N Shake, Inc., 981 F. Supp. 1149, 35 U.C.C. Rep. Serv. 2d (CBC) 423 (S.D. Ind. 1997) (applying Indiana law).

[18]Trial R. 8(E).

[19]Trial R. 8(F).

[20]Indiana Carpenters Cent. and Western Indiana Pension Fund v. Seaboard Sur. Co., 601 N.E.2d 352 (Ind. Ct. App. 2d Dist. 1992), reh'g denied, (Mar. 9, 1993) and transfer denied, 615 N.E.2d 892 (Ind. 1993); Rasp v. Hidden Valley Lake, Inc., 487 N.E.2d 1338 (Ind. Ct. App. 1st Dist. 1986), appeal after remand, 519 N.E.2d 153 (Ind. Ct. App. 4th Dist. 1988), reh'g denied, (Mar. 8, 1988).

For discussion of the elements of a cause of action for breach of contract, see § 119.

[21]Trial R. 10(F).

[22]Trial R. 12(B)(6).

sue or be sued in a representative capacity, or the legal existence of an organization that has been made a party. If the
defendant wishes to assert that a party lacks capacity,
authority, or legal existence, the matter must be pleaded as
an affirmative defense.[23]

In pleading the performance or occurrence of conditions
precedent in a contract, it is sufficient to aver generally that
all conditions precedent have been performed, have occurred,
or have been excused.[24]

As a general proposition, the complaint in a contract action must proceed on some definite theory, which must be
adhered to throughout the trial and on appeal.[25]

§ 126 —Inclusion of written contract

**In an action on a written contract, a copy of the contract
must be filed with the complaint.**

West's Digest, Contracts ☞333(2).

In an action on a written contract, the plaintiff must attach the contract to the complaint.[26] Where a plaintiff brings
an action on a verbal agreement which was later reduced to
writing, the writing, or a copy of it, must be attached to the
complaint.[27]

If the party suing on the contract fails to attach a copy to
the complaint, the opposing party may raise the matter in
his or her first responsive pleading, or in a motion filed before
the first responsive pleading. The court may, in its sound
discretion, order that the plaintiff comply with the rule and
that the plaintiff add to the pleadings his or her reason for

---

Indiana Carpenters Cent. and Western Indiana Pension Fund v.
Seaboard Sur. Co., 601 N.E.2d 352 (Ind. Ct. App. 2d Dist. 1992), reh'g
denied, (Mar. 9, 1993) and transfer denied, 615 N.E.2d 892 (Ind. 1993).

[23]Trial R. 9(A).

For discussion of affirmative defenses, see § 129.

[24]Trial R. 9(C).

For discussion of conditions precedent, see §§ 87 et seq.

Forms References: Complaint, petition, or declaration—Allegation—Performance of condition precedent. 7A Am Jur Pleading and
Practice Forms, Annotated (rev. ed.), Contracts § 50.

[25]Indianapolis Real Estate Board v. Willson, 98 Ind. App. 72, 187 N.E.
400 (1933).

[26]Trial R. 9.2(A).

[27]Ice v. Ball, 102 Ind. 42, 1 N.E. 66 (1885).

failing to comply, or the court may allow the action to continue without further pleading.[28] If the plaintiff fails to amend the complaint as ordered by the court within a reasonable time, the complaint may be dismissed after a hearing.[29] Dismissal in such a case is not for failure to state a claim for relief but for failure to comply with the rules and court orders.[30]

Generally, when a pleading is based upon a written instrument filed with the pleading, execution of that instrument is deemed to be established without proof of the authenticity of the signature, unless execution is denied under oath in the responsive pleading or in an affidavit.[31] However, when the party who executed the instrument is deceased, is an infant, is incompetent, or is in insolvency proceedings at the time proof is required, or if he or she becomes so, proper execution may not be presumed and is deemed to have been denied even if it has not been specifically denied in a responsive pleading.[32]

Only the instrument on which the action is founded must be filed with the complaint. The rule does not require that every document pertaining to the contract or growing out of the transaction between the parties be attached.[33]

§ 127 —Damages

A complaint must specifically request any items of special damages.

West's Digest, Contracts ☜337(3).

Items of special damage must be specifically stated in the

---

[28]Trial R. 9.2(F).

[29]Trial R. 41(E).

Wilson v. Palmer, 452 N.E.2d 426 (Ind. Ct. App. 4th Dist. 1983).

[30]Wilson v. Palmer, 452 N.E.2d 426 (Ind. Ct. App. 4th Dist. 1983).

[31]Trial R. 9.2(B).

[32]Trial R. 9.2(G).

Miller v. NBD Bank, N.A., 701 N.E.2d 282 (Ind. Ct. App. 1998).

[33]Emmons v. Kiger, 23 Ind. 483, 1864 WL 2033 (1864) (deed not be attached to complaint for breach of contract for sale of land); Wysor Land Co. v. Jones, 24 Ind. App. 451, 56 N.E. 46 (1900) (plaintiff in action for breach of street construction contract not required to attach engineer's plans and specifications); Webster v. Smith, 4 Ind. App. 44, 30 N.E. 139 (1892) (where complaint alleged breach of contract by failure to sign note as surety, it was not necessary to attach note).

complaint.[34] Special damages are the actual, but not necessary, result of the breach complained of,[35] and they include such items as consequential damages, interest, and attorney fees.[36]

If no answer is filed in an action, the plaintiff will be limited to the relief demanded in the complaint.[37] If, however, the case is contested, the plaintiff may recover all damages which are justified by the evidence.[38]

§ 128   Answer

Averments in the complaint are admitted if they are not denied, but a general denial is sufficient.

West's Digest, Contracts ☞338(1)-344.

The averments in the complaint, except those pertaining to the amount of damages, are admitted if they are not denied.[39]

An answer or other responsive pleading must state in short and plain terms the defenses to each claim asserted by the plaintiff and must admit or deny the statements set forth in the complaint.[40] If the defendant lacks knowledge or information sufficient to form a belief as to the truth of an averment in the complaint, his or her statement that he or she lacks such knowledge will be considered a denial. If the defendant intends in good faith to deny only a part or a qualification of an averment, the defendant is to specify what part is true and deny the remainder. All denials are to be fairly responsive to the substance of the claims denied.[41] The answer may either specifically deny designated averments or

---

[34]Trial R. 9(G).

[35]Black's Law Dictionary.

[36]Indiana & Michigan Elec. Co. v. Terre Haute Industries, Inc., 507 N.E.2d 588 (Ind. Ct. App. 1st Dist. 1987), reh'g denied, (June 12, 1987) and transfer denied, 525 N.E.2d 1247 (Ind. 1988).

[37]Trial R. 9(G).

[38]Indiana & Michigan Elec. Co. v. Terre Haute Industries, Inc., 507 N.E.2d 588 (Ind. Ct. App. 1st Dist. 1987), reh'g denied, (June 12, 1987) and transfer denied, 525 N.E.2d 1247 (Ind. 1988).

[39]Trial R. 8(D).

[40]Trial R. 8(B).

Forms References: Answer. 7A Am Jur Pleading and Practice Forms, Annotated (rev. ed.), Contracts §§ 14-26.

[41]Trial R. 8(B).

paragraphs in the complaint, or generally deny all of the averments except those expressly admitted.[42]

If in good faith the defendant intends to deny all the averments in the complaint, he or she may do so by general denial.[43]

> ◆ **Caution:** This provision is expressly made subject to the provisions of Rule 11, which provides sanctions for filing a groundless pleading.[44]

Note, however, that a general denial does not raise affirmative defenses.[45]

§ 129 —Affirmative defenses

Affirmative defenses must be pleaded in the answer.

West's Digest, Contracts ☞328(1)-328(5),

An answer must set forth any affirmative defenses the defendant may have, including:

- accord and satisfaction
- arbitration and award
- discharge in bankruptcy
- duress
- estoppel
- failure of consideration
- fraud
- illegality
- improper venue
- injury by fellow servant
- insufficiency of process or service of process
- laches
- lack of jurisdiction over the person
- lack of jurisdiction over the subject-matter
- license
- payment

---

[42]Trial R. 8(B).

[43]Trial R. 8(B).

[44]Trial R. 8(B), 11.

[45]Thompson v. City of Aurora, 263 Ind. 187, 325 N.E.2d 839 (1975); United Farm Bureau Mut. Ins. Co. v. Wolfe, 178 Ind. App. 435, 382 N.E.2d 1018 (1st Dist. 1978).

- release
- res judicata
- statute of frauds
- statute of limitations
- waiver
- the same action pending in another state court of Indiana
- any other matter constituting an avoidance, matter of abatement, or affirmative defense[46]

In contract cases, lack of consideration[47] and failure of a condition precedent[48] are also affirmative defenses and must be pleaded in the answer. An affirmative defense not specifically pleaded in the answer or raised at trial is waived.[49] A suit on a contract does not automatically raise all contractual defenses.[50]

The circumstances of two affirmative defenses, fraud[51] and failure of a condition precedent,[52] must be pleaded with particularity; however, malice, intent, knowledge, and other conditions of mind which may be relevant to a claim of

---

[46]Trial R. 8(C).

Forms References: Answers setting forth various affirmative defenses. 7A Am Jur Pleading and Practice Forms, Annotated (rev. ed.), Contracts §§ 17-26.

[47]Trial R. 9.1(C).

[48]Indiana & Michigan Elec. Co. v. Terre Haute Industries, Inc., 507 N.E.2d 588 (Ind. Ct. App. 1st Dist. 1987), reh'g denied, (June 12, 1987) and transfer denied, 525 N.E.2d 1247 (Ind. 1988).

[49]Nelson v. Gurley, 673 N.E.2d 497 (Ind. Ct. App. 1996); Indiana & Michigan Elec. Co. v. Terre Haute Industries, Inc., 507 N.E.2d 588 (Ind. Ct. App. 1st Dist. 1987), reh'g denied, (June 12, 1987) and transfer denied, 525 N.E.2d 1247 (Ind. 1988); United Farm Bureau Mut. Ins. Co. v. Wolfe, 178 Ind. App. 435, 382 N.E.2d 1018 (1st Dist. 1978).

For discussion of trial of unpleaded issues by consent, see § 131.

[50]United Farm Bureau Mut. Ins. Co. v. Wolfe, 178 Ind. App. 435, 382 N.E.2d 1018 (1st Dist. 1978).

[51]Trial R. 9(B).

For discussion of fraud as a reason for avoiding a contract, see § 35.

[52]Trial R. 9(C).

United Farm Bureau Mut. Ins. Co. v. Wolfe, 178 Ind. App. 435, 382 N.E.2d 1018 (1st Dist. 1978).

For discussion of conditions precedent, see §§ 87 et seq.

fraud,[53] and a denial of excuse, such as impossibility,[54] may be made generally.

If the answer mistakenly designates a defense as a counterclaim or a counterclaim as a defense, it will be treated as if it had been properly designated.[55]

§ 130 Reply

A reply is to be filed to a counterclaim, but not to an affirmative defense unless the court so orders.

West's Digest, Contracts 🔑345.

The plaintiff must reply to a counterclaim against him or her,[56] or the averments in the counterclaim will be taken as admitted.[57] A reply to a counterclaim should not include denials or allegations relating to other matters in the answer without a court order.[58]

Although generally no reply to an answer is permitted, the court may, in its discretion, order that a reply to an answer be filed.[59] No reply is to be filed to an affirmative defense unless the court so orders.[60]

§ 131 Issues, proof, and variance

An issue which is not raised in the pleadings or tried by consent is waived.

West's Digest, Contracts 🔑346(1)-346(16).

The pleadings, contentions of the parties, and pretrial orders set out a preliminary guide to the conduct of trial. Ei-

---

[53]Trial R. 9(B).

[54]Trial R. 9(C).

For discussion of impossibility and other excuses for nonperformance, see § 111.

[55]Trial R. 8(C).

[56]Trial R. 7(A)(2).

[57]Trial R. 8(D).

Commercial Credit Corp. v. Miller, 151 Ind. App. 580, 280 N.E.2d 856 (3d Dist. 1972).

[58]Adams v. Luros, 406 N.E.2d 1199 (Ind. Ct. App. 1st Dist. 1980).

[59]Trial R. 7(A).

[60]Adams v. Luros, 406 N.E.2d 1199 (Ind. Ct. App. 1st Dist. 1980); Schafer v. Buckeye Union Ins. Co., 178 Ind. App. 70, 381 N.E.2d 519 (3d Dist. 1978).

ther party may, at any time, demand strict adherence to those issues raised prior to the commencement of trial.[61] An issue which is not raised in a pleading or litigated is waived.[62] For instance, if the parties have raised only the issue of the existence of an oral contract before trial, the plaintiff may not raise the issue of the existence of an implied contract during trial.[63]

If the trial court permits the introduction at trial of an issue not raised prior to trial, an objecting party is entitled to a reasonable continuance in order to prepare to meet the newly raised issue; however, where the trial has ended without objection, the evidence actually presented controls, and the jury may be instructed on any theory of recovery the evidence supports.[64]

New issues cannot be interjected under the pretense that the evidence is relevant to an issue which has already been pleaded.[65] A party will not be deemed to have consented by implication to the trial of an unpleaded issue unless he or she has been given some notice of the existence of that issue.[66] This rule allows the opposing party to object to the introduction of evidence pertaining to the unpleaded issue or to seek a continuance to meet the new issue.[67]

◆ **Illustration:** In an action for wrongful discharge

---

[61]Terre Haute Regional Hosp., Inc. v. El-Issa, 470 N.E.2d 1371 (Ind. Ct. App. 1st Dist. 1984), reh'g denied, (Jan. 4, 1985) and transfer denied, (Mar. 28, 1985).

[62]United Farm Bureau Mut. Ins. Co. v. Wolfe, 178 Ind. App. 435, 382 N.E.2d 1018 (1st Dist. 1978).

[63]Decatur-Kocher Lumber, Inc. v. Ehrsam, 136 Ind. App. 397, 201 N.E.2d 568 (Div. 2 1964).

[64]Terre Haute Regional Hosp., Inc. v. El-Issa, 470 N.E.2d 1371 (Ind. Ct. App. 1st Dist. 1984), reh'g denied, (Jan. 4, 1985) and transfer denied, (Mar. 28, 1985); Urbanational Developers, Inc. v. Shamrock Engineering, Inc., 175 Ind. App. 416, 372 N.E.2d 742 (3d Dist. 1978).

[65]Terre Haute Regional Hosp., Inc. v. El-Issa, 470 N.E.2d 1371 (Ind. Ct. App. 1st Dist. 1984), reh'g denied, (Jan. 4, 1985) and transfer denied, (Mar. 28, 1985); Svetich v. Svetich, 425 N.E.2d 191 (Ind. Ct. App. 3d Dist. 1981).

[66]Terre Haute Regional Hosp., Inc. v. El-Issa, 470 N.E.2d 1371 (Ind. Ct. App. 1st Dist. 1984), reh'g denied, (Jan. 4, 1985) and transfer denied, (Mar. 28, 1985); Svetich v. Svetich, 425 N.E.2d 191 (Ind. Ct. App. 3d Dist. 1981); Elkhart County Farm Bureau Co-op. Ass'n, Inc. v. Hochstetler, 418 N.E.2d 280 (Ind. Ct. App. 3d Dist. 1981).

[67]Terre Haute Regional Hosp., Inc. v. El-Issa, 470 N.E.2d 1371 (Ind. Ct.

brought by a doctor against the hospital which had employed him, a breach-of-contract claim based on the hospital's alleged violation of its bylaws was tried by consent where (1) the trial court's preliminary instructions, given to the parties two days before they were read to the jury, stated that the doctor was contending that the violations of the bylaws constituted a breach of, or interference with, his contract with the hospital; (2) potential jurors were questioned during voir dire about the possibility of the bylaws constituting a contract; and (3) during the hearing on the hospital's motion for judgment on the evidence, made at the close of the doctor's case in chief, the doctor contended that breach of contract was a theory in the case, and the hospital, although stating that it did not consent to trial of the contract theory, did not object or seek a continuance.[68]

Some issues have been held to be fairly raised by other issues. For instance, a defendant who has raised a defense of the entire failure of consideration may prove a partial want or failure of consideration.[69]

§ 132 Presumptions and burden of proof

The party required to plead any matter has the burden of proving that matter.

West's Digest, Contracts ☞348.

A party required to affirmatively plead any matter has the burden of proving that matter.[70] The burden of proving waiver, for instance, is on the party claiming it.[71]

App. 1st Dist. 1984), reh'g denied, (Jan. 4, 1985) and transfer denied, (Mar. 28, 1985).

[68]Terre Haute Regional Hosp., Inc. v. El-Issa, 470 N.E.2d 1371 (Ind. Ct. App. 1st Dist. 1984), reh'g denied, (Jan. 4, 1985) and transfer denied, (Mar. 28, 1985).

[69]Sinex v. Toledo, L. & B.R. Co., 27 Ind. 365, 1866 WL 2569 (1866); Landry's Adm'r v. Durham, 21 Ind. 232, 1863 WL 2151 (1863).

[70]Trial R. 8(C).

[71]van de Leuv v. Methodist Hosp. of Indiana, Inc., 642 N.E.2d 531 (Ind. Ct. App. 3d Dist. 1994), reh'g denied, (Feb. 23, 1995); Ogle v. Wright, 172 Ind. App. 309, 360 N.E.2d 240 (1st Dist. 1977); Hidden Valley Lake, Inc. v. Kersey, 169 Ind. App. 339, 348 N.E.2d 674 (1st Dist. 1976).

A plaintiff seeking to recover in an action on a contract has the burden of establishing the existence of the contract,[72] the defendant's breach of it,[73] and the resulting damage to the plaintiff.[74] The defendant has the burden of proof on any matters of avoidance,[75] including affirmative defenses.[76]

Although formerly the law required a person in a position of mental or physical advantage over another person to demonstrate that a transaction between the two was fair,[77] this is generally no longer the case, and a person claiming that he or she entered into a transaction because of duress or undue influence has the burden of proof on that matter.[78] This is not the case, however, where a confidential relationship between the two exists; if the dominant party in such a relationship receives an advantage from a transaction, the dominant party must prove that the transaction was conducted at arms' length and is valid.[79] Confidential relationships for this purpose include attorney/client,

---

[72]Pauley v. Ford Electronics and Refrigeration Corp., 941 F. Supp. 794 (S.D. Ind. 1996) (applying Indiana law); Daniels v. Indiana Trust Co., 222 Ind. 36, 51 N.E.2d 838 (1943); Ochoa v. Ford, 641 N.E.2d 1042 (Ind. Ct. App. 1994).

[73]Pauley v. Ford Electronics and Refrigeration Corp., 941 F. Supp. 794 (S.D. Ind. 1996) (applying Indiana law); Indiana-American Water Co., Inc. v. Town of Seelyville, 698 N.E.2d 1255, 38 U.C.C. Rep. Serv. 2d (CBC) 1133 (Ind. Ct. App. 1998).

[74]Roder v. Niles, 61 Ind. App. 4, 111 N.E. 340 (Div. 2 1916).

[75]Sutton v. Roth, Wehrly, Heiny, Inc., 418 N.E.2d 229 (Ind. Ct. App. 3d Dist. 1981).

[76]Trial R. 8(C), 9.1(C) (lack of consideration).

Godfrey v. Crisler, 121 Ind. 203, 22 N.E. 999 (1889) (payment); Achey v. Stephens, 8 Ind. 411, 1856 WL 3705 (1856) (lack of mental capacity to consent); Rogers v. Worth, 4 Blackf. 186, 1836 WL 2225 (Ind. 1836) (fraud); Indiana & Michigan Elec. Co. v. Terre Haute Industries, Inc., 507 N.E.2d 588 (Ind. Ct. App. 1st Dist. 1987), reh'g denied, (June 12, 1987) and transfer denied, 525 N.E.2d 1247 (Ind. 1988) (failure of condition precedent).

[77]Goodbar v. Lidikay (State Report Title: Goodbar v. Lidikey), 136 Ind. 1, 35 N.E. 691 (1893).

[78]Matter of Estate of Neu, 588 N.E.2d 567 (Ind. Ct. App. 3d Dist. 1992).

[79]Reiss v. Reiss, 516 N.E.2d 7 (Ind. 1987).

principal/agent, and parent/child,[80] but do not include siblings[81] and no longer include husband and wife.[82]

The defendant has the burden of proving matters mitigating his or her liability for damages.[83]

It is presumed that a contract on which an action is brought is legal, and the defendant has the burden of proving illegality.[84] If it is a contract governed by foreign law, it is presumably legal under that law[85] and if shown to be illegal under foreign law, may be presumed to have been governed by and legal under Indiana law.[86]

Presumptions of law need not be stated in a pleading.[87]

§ 133   Questions of law and fact

Questions of the existence of a contract and the interpretation of an unambiguous contract are for the court; the construction of an ambiguous contract is for the jury, where extrinsic evidence is necessary.

West's Digest, Contracts ☞352(1)-352(6).

When the existence, rather than the validity, of a contract is at issue and the evidence is conflicting or admits of more than one inference, the existence of a contract is a factual determination;[88] however, the existence of a contract when

---

[80]Matter of Smith, 572 N.E.2d 1280 (Ind. 1991) (attorney and client); Reiss v. Reiss, 516 N.E.2d 7 (Ind. 1987).

[81]Matter of Estate of Neu, 588 N.E.2d 567 (Ind. Ct. App. 3d Dist. 1992).

[82]Womack v. Womack, 622 N.E.2d 481 (Ind. 1993); Matter of Estate of Goins, 615 N.E.2d 897 (Ind. Ct. App. 5th Dist. 1993), reh'g denied, (Aug. 19, 1993) and transfer denied, (Dec. 29, 1993).

[83]Cincinnati, I., St. L. & C. Ry. Co. v. Lutes, 112 Ind. 276, 11 N.E. 784 (1887), reh'g denied, 112 Ind. 276, 14 N.E. 706 (1887).

[84]Hogston v. Bell, 185 Ind. 536, 112 N.E. 883 (1916); Kosiba v. Gary Wholesale Grocery Co., 91 Ind. App. 71, 170 N.E. 105 (1930) (defendant in suit had burden to prove note was given in compromise of criminal prosecution).

[85]Crake v. Crake, 18 Ind. 156, 1862 WL 1968 (1862).

[86]Cable Co. v. McElhoe, 58 Ind. App. 637, 108 N.E. 790 (Div. 2 1915).

[87]Trial R. 9.1(E).

[88]City of Indianapolis v. Twin Lakes Enterprises, Inc., 568 N.E.2d 1073 (Ind. Ct. App. 1st Dist. 1991), reh'g denied, (May 16, 1991) and transfer denied, (Dec. 12, 1991).

the facts are undisputed is generally a question of law for the court.[89]

The construction of an unambiguous written contract is generally a question of law for the court.[90] If, however, a contract is ambiguous or uncertain and its meaning is to be determined by extrinsic evidence, its construction is a matter for the factfinder.[91] If the ambiguity arises because of the language used in the contract and not because of extrinsic facts, its construction is purely a question of law to be determined by the trial court.[92] It is only where a contract is ambiguous and its interpretation requires extrinsic evidence that the fact-finder must determine the facts upon which the contract rests;[93] thus, when a trial court has entered summary judgment in a contract dispute, it has determined either that the contract is not ambiguous or uncertain as a matter of law, and the trial court need only apply the terms of the contract; or that the contract is ambiguous, but the ambiguity may be resolved without the aid of factual deter-

---

[89]Orr v. Westminster Village North, Inc., 689 N.E.2d 712 (Ind. 1997); Keating v. Burton, 617 N.E.2d 588 (Ind. Ct. App. 4th Dist. 1993), reh'g denied, (Sept. 14, 1993) and transfer denied, (Dec. 29, 1993); City of Indianapolis v. Twin Lakes Enterprises, Inc., 568 N.E.2d 1073 (Ind. Ct. App. 1st Dist. 1991), reh'g denied, (May 16, 1991) and transfer denied, (Dec. 12, 1991).

[90]Peoples Bank & Trust Co. v. Price, 714 N.E.2d 712 (Ind. Ct. App. 1999), transfer denied, (Nov. 19, 1999); Ancich v. Mobil Oil Corp., 422 N.E.2d 1320 (Ind. Ct. App. 4th Dist. 1981).

[91]First Federal Sav. Bank of Indiana v. Key Markets, Inc., 559 N.E.2d 600 (Ind. 1990); Peoples Bank & Trust Co. v. Price, 714 N.E.2d 712 (Ind. Ct. App. 1999), transfer denied, (Nov. 19, 1999); Bicknell Minerals, Inc. v. Tilly, 570 N.E.2d 1307 (Ind. Ct. App. 4th Dist. 1991), reh'g denied, (July 10, 1991) and transfer denied, (Feb. 26, 1992).

For discussion of the admissibility of extrinsic evidence, see § 137.

[92]First Federal Sav. Bank of Indiana v. Key Markets, Inc., 559 N.E.2d 600 (Ind. 1990); McEnroy v. St. Meinrad School of Theology, 713 N.E.2d 334, 136 Ed. Law Rep. 541 (Ind. Ct. App. 1999), transfer denied, (Nov. 19, 1999); Bicknell Minerals, Inc. v. Tilly, 570 N.E.2d 1307 (Ind. Ct. App. 4th Dist. 1991), reh'g denied, (July 10, 1991) and transfer denied, (Feb. 26, 1992); R. R. Donnelley & Sons, Co. v. Henry-Williams, Inc., 422 N.E.2d 353 (Ind. Ct. App. 3d Dist. 1981).

[93]Grain Dealers Mut. Ins. Co. v. Wuethrich, 716 N.E.2d 596 (Ind. Ct. App. 1999).

minations.[94] Whether a contract is ambiguous to begin with is a question of law for the court.[95]

The question of whether facts have occurred which constitute a breach of contract is a question of fact to be determined by the jury.[96] For example, it is a question of fact whether the terms of the contract have been complied with[97] or whether the work has been done properly[98] and adequately.[99] The question of whether the plaintiff's damages were the proximate result of the breach is also for the jury.[1]

If there is no statute or rule prohibiting the agreement,[2] whether a contract is against public policy is a question of law dependent on the circumstances of the particular case.[3]

---

[94]Bicknell Minerals, Inc. v. Tilly, 570 N.E.2d 1307 (Ind. Ct. App. 4th Dist. 1991), reh'g denied, (July 10, 1991) and transfer denied, (Feb. 26, 1992), Midwestern Indem. Co. v. Lettler Const. Co., Inc., 463 N.E.2d 1130 (Ind. Ct. App. 2d Dist. 1984); Ancich v. Mobil Oil Corp., 422 N.E.2d 1320 (Ind. Ct. App. 4th Dist. 1981).

[95]Western Ohio Pizza, Inc. v. Clark Oil & Refining Corp., 704 N.E.2d 1086 (Ind. Ct. App. 1999), transfer denied, 714 N.E.2d 176 (Ind. 1999).

[96]Hanging Rock Iron Co. v. P.H. & F.M. Roots Co., 10 F.2d 154 (C.C.A. 7th Cir. 1925).

[97]Gewartowski v. Tomal, 125 Ind. App. 481, 123 N.E.2d 580 (1955); Polus v. Conner, 92 Ind. App. 465, 176 N.E. 234 (1931).

[98]Morris v. Fox, 79 Ind. App. 389, 135 N.E. 663 (Div. 1 1922).

[99]Charles M. Oberlin Co. v. Woolverton, 86 Ind. App. 331, 157 N.E. 445 (1927).

[1]Strong v. Commercial Carpet Co., Inc., 163 Ind. App. 145, 322 N.E.2d 387 (1st Dist. 1975), reh'g denied, 163 Ind. App. 145, 324 N.E.2d 834 (1st Dist. 1975) and transfer denied, (Nov. 25, 1975).

[2]Straub v. B.M.T. by Todd, 645 N.E.2d 597 (Ind. 1994), reh'g denied, (Apr. 12, 1995); Mutual Sec. Life Ins. Co. by Bennett v. Fidelity and Deposit Co. of Maryland, 659 N.E.2d 1096 (Ind. Ct. App. 1995), transfer denied (Ind. May 17, 1996).

[3]Trotter v. Nelson, 684 N.E.2d 1150 (Ind. 1997); DeKalb Chiropractic Center, Inc. v. Bio-Testing Innovation, Inc., 678 N.E.2d 412 (Ind. Ct. App. 1997), reh'g denied, (June 17, 1997); Parker v. Camp, 656 N.E.2d 882 (Ind. Ct. App. 1995); Ross Clinic, Inc. v. Tabion, 419 N.E.2d 219 (Ind. Ct. App. 3d Dist. 1981).

For discussion of contracts in violation of public policy, see §§ 43 et seq.

The intention of the parties to a contract is a factual matter to be determined by the jury from all the surrounding circumstances.[4]

Whether there has been a waiver of a contract provision is ordinarily a question of fact,[5] in the sense that whether the facts necessary to constitute a waiver exist;[6] however, the question of what facts are necessary to establish a waiver is one of law.[7] Similarly, whether a party seeking rescission of a contract is acting within a reasonable time is ordinarily question of fact, but where the facts have been ascertained, it becomes a question of law.[8]

Questions regarding the modification of a contract are ones of fact and are to be determined by the trier of fact upon the evidence in each case.[9]

The question of whether a covenant not to compete is reasonable, as it must be to be valid, is a question of law for the court.[10]

Issues of whether a party to a contract made misrepresentations to induce the other to enter into the contract, and

---

[4]Ochoa v. Ford, 641 N.E.2d 1042 (Ind. Ct. App. 1994); Dickison v. Hargitt, 611 N.E.2d 691 (Ind. Ct. App. 1st Dist. 1993).

For discussion of the importance of the parties' intent and how it is determined, see §§ 59 et seq.

[5]van de Leuv v. Methodist Hosp. of Indiana, Inc., 642 N.E.2d 531 (Ind. Ct. App. 3d Dist. 1994), reh'g denied, (Feb. 23, 1995).

[6]Jackson v. DeFabis, 553 N.E.2d 1212 (Ind. Ct. App. 1st Dist. 1990).

For discussion of waiver of contract provisions, see § 114.

[7]Jackson v. DeFabis, 553 N.E.2d 1212 (Ind. Ct. App. 1st Dist. 1990).

[8]INB Nat. Bank v. Moran Elec. Service, Inc., 608 N.E.2d 702 (Ind. Ct. App. 1st Dist. 1993), transfer denied, (Apr. 14, 1993).

For discussion of rescission, see §§ 98 et seq.

[9]Gilliana v. Paniaguas, 708 N.E.2d 895 (Ind. Ct. App. 1999), reh'g denied, (June 8, 1999) and transfer denied, (Oct. 13, 1999); Zemco Mfg., Inc. v. Pecoraro, 703 N.E.2d 1064 (Ind. Ct. App. 1998), transfer denied, 714 N.E.2d 172 (Ind. 1999).

For discussion of the modification of a contract, see §§ 93 et seq.

[10]Raymundo v. Hammond Clinic Ass'n, 449 N.E.2d 276 (Ind. 1983); Wagler Excavating Corp. v. McKibben Const., Inc., 679 N.E.2d 155 (Ind. Ct. App. 1997), transfer denied, 690 N.E.2d 1181 (Ind. 1997); Medical Specialists, Inc. v. Sleweon, 652 N.E.2d 517 (Ind. Ct. App. 1995), transfer denied, (Sept. 28, 1995); Brunner v. Hand Industries, Inc., 603 N.E.2d 157 (Ind. Ct. App. 3d Dist. 1992).

Covenants not to compete, generally, are discussed in I.L.E., Employment.

whether the latter relied upon the alleged misrepresentations, are questions of fact which should be submitted to the jury where the evidence is conflicting.[11]

Questions of a party's capacity to contract are questions of fact for the jury when the evidence on the matter is conflicting.[12]

Although the ultimate burden of proving that a written contract was executed is on the party claiming the contract's validity, execution is presumed, so that the trier of fact must find that the contract was executed unless evidence is introduced which would support a contrary finding.[13]

§ 134 Findings and judgment

The judgment must conform to the findings of fact and the conclusions on the findings.

West's Digest, Contracts ☞354.

A judgment is clearly erroneous, and will be reversed, when it is unsupported by findings of fact and conclusions on the findings,[14] and findings of fact are clearly erroneous when the record is without facts or reasonable inferences to support them.[15] Where no findings are made, the general judgment entered by the court is presumed to be based upon findings supported by the evidence.[16]

When a party has requested specific findings of fact, a

---

[11]Campbell v. Criterion Group, 621 N.E.2d 342 (Ind. Ct. App. 1st Dist. 1993), appeal after remand, 701 N.E.2d 616 (Ind. Ct. App. 1998).

For discussion of the inducement of a contract by fraud, see §§ 35 et seq.

[12]Cummings v. Henry, 10 Ind. 109, 1858 WL 4246 (1858) (intoxication).

For discussion of a party's mental condition as affecting his or her ability to contract, see § 31.

[13]Trial R. 9.2(D).

[14]Real Estate Support Services, Inc. v. Nauman, 644 N.E.2d 907 (Ind. Ct. App. 1st Dist. 1994), reh'g denied, (Mar. 6, 1995) and transfer denied, (July 17, 1995); Boswell Grain and Elevator, Inc. v. Kentland Elevator and Supply, Inc., 593 N.E.2d 1224 (Ind. Ct. App. 3d Dist. 1992).

[15]Ahuja v. Lynco Ltd. Medical Research, 675 N.E.2d 704 (Ind. Ct. App. 1996), transfer denied, 683 N.E.2d 590 (Ind. 1997); Real Estate Support Services, Inc. v. Nauman, 644 N.E.2d 907 (Ind. Ct. App. 1st Dist. 1994), reh'g denied, (Mar. 6, 1995) and transfer denied, (July 17, 1995).

[16]Ray v. Goldsmith, 400 N.E.2d 176 (Ind. Ct. App. 2d Dist. 1980); Rieth-Riley Const. Co., Inc. v. Auto-Owners Mut. Ins. Co., 408 N.E.2d 640 (Ind. Ct. App. 3d Dist. 1980).

reviewing court cannot affirm the judgment on any legal basis, but must determine whether the trial court's findings are sufficient to support the judgment.[17] If the trial court enters specific findings of fact and conclusions of law sua sponte, the specific findings control only as to the issues they cover, while the standard of review for a general judgment applies to any issue upon which the court has not made findings.[18]

§ 135 Instructions

The court should instruct the jury on contract principles, including consideration; validity and legality; and, where appropriate, rescission and construction.

West's Digest, Contracts ⚏353(1)-353(11).

Instructions, in a contract action, should clearly and correctly state the law applicable to the issues raised.[19] A trial court should reject misleading and confusing instructions tendered by the parties.[20] The trial court must examine the requested instructions and determine if they apply to the issues of the case and are supported by the evidence.[21]

---

[17]Trial R. 52(A), discussed in I.L.E., Trial.

Ahuja v. Lynco Ltd. Medical Research, 675 N.E.2d 704 (Ind. Ct. App. 1996), transfer denied, 683 N.E.2d 590 (Ind. 1997); Boswell Grain and Elevator, Inc. v. Kentland Elevator and Supply, Inc., 593 N.E.2d 1224 (Ind. Ct. App. 3d Dist. 1992).

[18]Real Estate Support Services, Inc. v. Nauman, 644 N.E.2d 907 (Ind. Ct. App. 1st Dist. 1994), reh'g denied, (Mar. 6, 1995) and transfer denied, (July 17, 1995); Boswell Grain and Elevator, Inc. v. Kentland Elevator and Supply, Inc., 593 N.E.2d 1224 (Ind. Ct. App. 3d Dist. 1992).

[19]Olds v. Lochner, 57 Ind. App. 269, 106 N.E. 889 (Div. 1 1914); Gastlin v. Weeks, 2 Ind. App. 222, 28 N.E. 331 (1891).

Forms References: Instructions to jury. 7A Am Jur Pleading and Practice Forms, Annotated (rev. ed.), Contracts §§ 110-114.

[20]Foster v. United Home Imp. Co., Inc., 428 N.E.2d 1351 (Ind. Ct. App. 4th Dist. 1981) (where competent, probative evidence pertaining to quantum meruit was introduced, court properly rejected tendered instruction which tended to suggest that plaintiff could recover only if contract were proven).

[21]Coleman v. Chapman, 139 Ind. App. 385, 220 N.E.2d 285 (Div. 2 1966).

The court should instruct the jury on consideration,[22] validity or legality of the contract,[23] and, where appropriate, abandonment or rescission.[24] Where a contract is ambiguous, so that interpretation is a question for the jury, the court should instruct the jury on the principles of contract construction.[25]

Where there is a dispute as to the terms of an oral contract, the court must submit issues on what the contract contained, together with appropriate instructions governing the law on each issue, and the court may not properly merely instruct that the jury is to determine what the contract is and how it shall be construed, because the legal effect of a contract is for the court.[26] If abandonment or rescission of the contract is an issue, it must likewise be covered by the instructions.[27]

As is the case in other civil actions, it is error to give instructions which operate so as to invade the province of the jury.[28]

B. EVIDENCE

Research References

17A Am Jur 2d, Contracts § 746.
17B C.J.S., Contracts §§ 718-769.
West's Digest, Contracts ☞347-350.
ALR Digest: Contracts § 546
ALR Index: Adhesion Contracts; Anticipatory Breach; Anticipatory Renunciation or Repudiation; Bids and Bidding; Cancellation of Rescission; Consideration; Contracts; Covenants; Covenants Not to Compete; Estoppel and Waiver; Executory Contracts; Implied Contracts; Offer and Acceptance; Parol Contracts and Agreements; Parol Evidence; Third-Party Beneficiaries; Unconscionability

---

[22]Mader v. Cool, 14 Ind. App. 299, 42 N.E. 945 (1896).

[23]Louthain v. Miller, 85 Ind. 161, 1882 WL 6374 (1882).

[24]Brown v. Langner, 25 Ind. App. 538, 58 N.E. 743 (1900).

[25]Southern, School Bldgs., Inc. v. Loew Elec., Inc., 407 N.E.2d 240 (Ind. Ct. App. 3d Dist. 1980).

For discussion of the interpretation of an ambiguous contract as a question for the court or for the jury, see § 78.

[26]Bump v. McGrannahan, 61 Ind. App. 136, 111 N.E. 640 (Div. 1 1916).

[27]Brown v. Langner, 25 Ind. App. 538, 58 N.E. 743 (1900).

[28]Week v. Rawie, 48 Ind. App. 599, 96 N.E. 206 (Div. 1 1911).

§ 136   Admissibility of evidence, generally

Evidence admitted in a breach-of-contract trial must be relevant.

West's Digest, Contracts ☜349(1)-349(7).

As in other civil actions, competent evidence with regard to matters put in issue by the pleadings is admissible in contract actions.[29] Evidence not relevant to the agreement forming the basis of the action or to the parties' rights thereunder may not be admitted;[30] thus, where a written instrument is offered in evidence, which, of itself, shows nothing making it relevant or material, and is accompanied by no offer of other evidence to show its relevance, it is properly excluded.[31] Facts authorizing a plaintiff's recovery from the detendant on a basis independent of the agreement may not be presented.[32]

> ◆ **Illustration:** In an action for breach of contract, where the evidence established that the contract sued on had been replaced by a new contract under which the parties had acted for more than seven years, the trial court erred in admitting into evidence unsigned carbon copies of letters relevant to the old contract written more than six years after the old contract was replaced.[33]

Other agreements concerning different transactions between the parties to the lawsuit have no evidentiary value; thus, they are inadmissible.[34]

---

[29]State ex rel. Croy v. Gregory, 132 Ind. 387, 31 N.E. 952 (1892).

[30]Sax v. Zanger, 184 Ind. 262, 111 N.E. 1 (1916); Herlihy Mid-Continent Co. v. Northern Indiana Public Service Co., 245 F.2d 440 (7th Cir. 1957) (applying Indiana law) (in action by building contractor against owner to recover amounts allegedly due under construction contracts, evidence of previous contracts in which contractor was paid by owners amount of a certain state tax was improperly received in evidence in view of fact that it had no probative value in interpreting whether owner was liable to contractor for such tax under the terms of the parties' contracts).

[31]Grover & Baker Sewing Mach. Co. v. Newby, 58 Ind. 570, 1877 WL 6579 (1877).

[32]Carter v. Gordon, 121 Ind. 383, 23 N.E. 268 (1890).

[33]Armour & Co. v. Anderson, 114 Ind. App. 485, 51 N.E.2d 496 (1943).

[34]Harrisburgh Car Mfg. Co. v. Sloan, 120 Ind. 156, 21 N.E. 1088 (1889).

Evidence of one party's subjective understanding of a contract is not admissible;[35] however, a written memorandum of an admittedly parol agreement, signed only by one of the parties, may be competent evidence to establish the terms of the agreement if it is accompanied by other evidence or proof of the circumstances tending to show that the signer's adversary assented to the memorandum.[36]

Where the parties' communications made during negotiations of the contract are merged into the final written document, the earlier communications are inadmissible in an action on the written document.[37] Evidence of the course of dealings between the parties is, however, admissible to prove that a contract between them came into being.[38]

In a breach-of-contract suit, absent a prayer for punitive damages[39] or a claim of fraud,[40] the defendant's state of mind is not relevant, and evidence on the matter cannot be introduced.

§ 137   —Parol evidence

If a written instrument is ambiguous, the court may resort to extrinsic evidence to determine the parties' intention.

West's Digest, Contracts ☞349(1)-349(7).

Where a written contract is not introduced into evidence, evidence of an oral contract may be introduced.[41]

Normally, the intentions of the parties to a contract are to

---

[35]Aetna Freight Lines, Inc. v. Adamson, 139 Ind. App. 335, 204 N.E.2d 372 (Div. 1 1965).

[36]Cook v. Anderson, 20 Ind. 15, 1863 WL 1917 (1863).

[37]Ralya v. Atkins, 157 Ind. 331, 61 N.E. 726 (1901).

[38]Freeman v. Mayer, 95 F.3d 569 (7th Cir. 1996), reh'g and suggestion for reh'g en banc denied, (Oct. 2, 1996) (applying Indiana law); Indiana Farm Bureau Co-op. Ass'n, Inc. v. Ennis, 574 N.E.2d 322 (Ind. Ct. App. 1st Dist. 1991); Moridge Mfg. Co. v. Butler, 451 N.E.2d 677, 36 U.C.C. Rep. Serv. (CBC) 1548 (Ind. Ct. App. 3d Dist. 1983).

[39]Peterson v. Culver Educational Foundation, 402 N.E.2d 448 (Ind. Ct. App. 1st Dist. 1980).

[40]As to fraud in the inducement of a contract, see §§ 35 et seq.

[41]Swanson-Nunn Realty Co. v. Gentry, 134 Ind. App. 580, 186 N.E.2d 574 (Div. 2 1962).

Annotation References: Admissibility of evidence to establish oral antenuptial agreement, 81 ALR3d 453.

be determined from the four corners of the document;[42] thus, when a written contract is introduced into evidence, a court interpreting it will first attempt to determine the intent of the parties at the time the contract was made as disclosed by the language used in the contract to express their rights and duties.[43] Where the paper trail left by the contracting parties is not clear, however, the court must look to other sources to determine the parties' intent and understanding.[44] If the contract is ambiguous or uncertain in its terms, the rules of contract construction and extrinsic evidence may be employed in giving effect to the parties' reasonable expectations.[45]

The written instrument must be ambiguous before extrinsic evidence will be admitted.[46] Where the terms of a contract are clear, the meaning of the contract is determined as a matter of law from the language of the contract.[47] Where the terms of the instrument are susceptible of a clear and unambiguous construction, evidence of the intent of the par-

---

[42]Boswell Grain and Elevator, Inc. v. Kentland Elevator and Supply, Inc., 593 N.E.2d 1224 (Ind. Ct. App. 3d Dist. 1992); Keithley's Auction Service v. Children of Jesse Wright, 579 N.E.2d 657 (Ind. Ct. App. 4th Dist. 1991).

[43]R. R. Donnelley & Sons, Co. v. Henry-Williams, Inc., 422 N.E.2d 353 (Ind. Ct. App. 3d Dist. 1981); Rieth-Riley Const. Co., Inc. v. Auto-Owners Mut. Ins. Co., 408 N.E.2d 640 (Ind. Ct. App. 3d Dist. 1980); Shahan v. Brinegar, 181 Ind. App. 39, 390 N.E.2d 1036 (1st Dist. 1979).

[44]JWP Zack, Inc. v. Hoosier Energy Rural Elec. Co-op., Inc., 709 N.E.2d 336 (Ind. Ct. App. 1999).

[45]Chicago Southshore & South Bend R.R. v. Itel Rail Corp., 658 N.E.2d 624 (Ind. Ct. App. 1995); Anderson v. Horizon Homes, Inc., 644 N.E.2d 1281 (Ind. Ct. App. 5th Dist. 1995), transfer denied, (Apr. 21, 1995); Boswell Grain and Elevator, Inc. v. Kentland Elevator and Supply, Inc., 593 N.E.2d 1224 (Ind. Ct. App. 3d Dist. 1992); Keithley's Auction Service v. Children of Jesse Wright, 579 N.E.2d 657 (Ind. Ct. App. 4th Dist. 1991); R. R. Donnelley & Sons, Co. v. Henry-Williams, Inc., 422 N.E.2d 353 (Ind. Ct. App. 3d Dist. 1981).

Annotation References: Comment note.—The parol evidence rule and admissibility of extrinsic evidence to establish and clarify ambiguity in written contract, 40 ALR3d 1384.

[46]Sprague v. State, 203 Ind. 581, 181 N.E. 507 (1932); Wills v. Gaff, 136 Ind. App. 21, 191 N.E.2d 41 (1963).

[47]Chicago Southshore & South Bend R.R. v. Itel Rail Corp., 658 N.E.2d 624 (Ind. Ct. App. 1995); Piskorowski v. Shell Oil Co., 403 N.E.2d 838 (Ind. Ct. App. 3d Dist. 1980).

ties extrinsic to the contract is inadmissible.[48] A court will resort to the application of the rules of contract construction and the receipt of extrinsic evidence only after a careful study of the entire contract itself has failed to make clear its meaning.[49] Moreover, if the ambiguity arises because of the language used in the contract and not because of extrinsic facts, then its construction is purely a question of law to be determined by the trial court, and extrinsic evidence is not admissible.[50]

To interpret ambiguous or uncertain language in the contract, both the circumstances surrounding the execution of the contract and the parties' conduct in connection with the contract may be considered.[51] In determining the intention of parties to a contract, it is the trial court's duty to consider their intention in light of the surrounding circumstances which existed at the time the contract was made. The trial court should consider the nature of the agreement, together with all facts and circumstances leading up to the execution of contract; the relation of the parties; the nature and situation of the subject matter; and the apparent purpose of making the contract.[52]

The parol evidence rule does not bar evidence beyond the writing to show the nature of the consideration supporting a

---

[48]City of Evansville v. Old State Utility Corp., 550 N.E.2d 1339 (Ind. Ct. App. 1st Dist. 1990), appeal after remand, 576 N.E.2d 1311 (Ind. Ct. App. 1st Dist. 1991), reh'g denied, (Sept. 18, 1991); Vandalia Coal Co. v. Underwood, 55 Ind. App. 91, 101 N.E. 1047 (Div. 1 1913).

[49]Evansville-Vanderburgh School Corp. v. Moll, 264 Ind. 356, 344 N.E.2d 831 (1976).

[50]I.C.C. Protective Coatings, Inc. v. A.E. Staley Mfg. Co., 695 N.E.2d 1030 (Ind. Ct. App. 1998), transfer denied, 706 N.E.2d 174 (Ind. 1998); R. R. Donnelley & Sons, Co. v. Henry-Williams, Inc., 422 N.E.2d 353 (Ind. Ct. App. 3d Dist. 1981); Huntington Mut. Ins. Co. v. Walker, 181 Ind. App. 618, 392 N.E.2d 1182 (1st Dist. 1979); Clyde E. Williams & Associates, Inc. v. Boatman, 176 Ind. App. 430, 375 N.E.2d 1138 (1st Dist. 1978).

[51]Haxton v. McClure Oil Corp., 697 N.E.2d 1277 (Ind. Ct. App. 1998); Ahuja v. Lynco Ltd. Medical Research, 675 N.E.2d 704 (Ind. Ct. App. 1996), transfer denied, 683 N.E.2d 590 (Ind. 1997); Real Estate Support Services, Inc. v. Nauman, 644 N.E.2d 907 (Ind. Ct. App. 1st Dist. 1994), reh'g denied, (Mar. 6, 1995) and transfer denied, (July 17, 1995); DeHaan v. DeHaan, 572 N.E.2d 1315 (Ind. Ct. App. 1st Dist. 1991), reh'g denied, (July 31, 1991) and transfer denied, (Feb. 14, 1992).

[52]Ruff v. Charter Behavioral Health System of Northwest Indiana, Inc., 699 N.E.2d 1171 (Ind. Ct. App. 1998), reh'g denied, (Nov. 6, 1998) and

contract[53] or that the consideration specified was given,[54] to apply the terms of a contract to its subject matter,[55] or to shed light on the circumstances under which the parties entered into the written contract.[56]

> ◆ **Illustration:** Parol evidence showing which party had developed specifications for concrete walls to be poured was admissible where the specifications were not written into the contract and the testimony did not vary any term of the contract.[57]

Parol statements are also admissible to show the abandonment of a written contract and entry into a subsequent verbal one.[58]

A point not covered by an express contract may be implied by the court in carrying out the intention of the parties.[59] Terms so implied have the same effect as if they were expressly included in the contract by the parties.[60] A term may not be implied if the contract includes an express term on the same matter.[61]

Generally, where the parties to an agreement have reduced the agreement to a written document and have stated in an integration clause that the written document embodies the complete agreement between the parties, the parol evidence rule prohibits courts from considering parol

---

transfer denied, 714 N.E.2d 170 (Ind. 1999); Stahl v. Illinois Oil Co., 45 Ind. App. 211, 90 N.E. 632 (Div. 1 1910).

[53]Kentucky & Indiana Bridge Co. v. Hall, 125 Ind. 220, 25 N.E. 219 (1890).

[54]Kintner v. Jones, 122 Ind. 148, 23 N.E. 701 (1890).

[55]Stockwell v. Whitehead, 47 Ind. App. 423, 94 N.E. 736 (Div. 2 1911); Ames v. Ames, 46 Ind. App. 597, 91 N.E. 509 (Div. 1 1910).

[56]Ransdel v. Moore, 153 Ind. 393, 53 N.E. 767 (1899); Kentucky & Indiana Bridge Co. v. Hall, 125 Ind. 220, 25 N.E. 219 (1890).

[57]Millner v. Mumby, 599 N.E.2d 627 (Ind. Ct. App. 5th Dist. 1992).

[58]Toledo, St. L. & K. C. R. Co. v. Levy, 127 Ind. 168, 26 N.E. 773 (1891).

[59]Rieth-Riley Const. Co., Inc. v. Auto-Owners Mut. Ins. Co., 408 N.E.2d 640 (Ind. Ct. App. 3d Dist. 1980).

[60]Wills v. Gaff, 136 Ind. App. 21, 191 N.E.2d 41 (1963).

[61]Wills v. Gaff, 136 Ind. App. 21, 191 N.E.2d 41 (1963) (employer's written statement of personnel policy stating goal of encouraging reasonable length of service and employer's policy of giving yearly contracts directly following April board meeting could not be implied into employment contract specifically stating that it was for one-year period commencing on September 1, to preclude its termination following August 31).

or extrinsic evidence for the purpose of varying or adding to the terms of the written contract,[62] unless there has been a showing of fraud, mistake, ambiguity, illegality, duress, or undue influence.[63] However, parol evidence may be considered as long as it has not been offered to vary the terms of the written contract;[64] thus, parol evidence may be considered to show that fraud, unintentional misrepresentation, or mistake entered into the formation of a contract.[65]

§ 138 Weight and sufficiency of evidence

The plaintiff in a breach-of-contract action must prove his or her case by a preponderance of the evidence.

West's Digest, Contracts ☞350(1)-350(3).

The plaintiff in a breach-of-contract action must prove his or her case by a preponderance of the evidence.[66] Rescission[67] and abandonment[68] must also be established by a preponderance of the evidence in order to be of any advantage to one seeking to benefit from their claimed existence.

---

[62]Franklin v. White, 493 N.E.2d 161 (Ind. 1986); Millner v. Mumby, 599 N.E.2d 627 (Ind. Ct. App. 5th Dist. 1992); Kruse Classic Auction Co., Inc. v. Aetna Cas. & Sur. Co., 511 N.E.2d 326 (Ind. Ct. App. 3d Dist. 1987), reh'g denied, (Oct. 28, 1987) and transfer denied, (May 31, 1988).

[63]Kruse Classic Auction Co., Inc. v. Aetna Cas. & Sur. Co., 511 N.E.2d 326 (Ind. Ct. App. 3d Dist. 1987), reh'g denied, (Oct. 28, 1987) and transfer denied, (May 31, 1988) (evidence that defendants did not intend to sign contract unless third parties also signed it was not admissible); Turnpaugh v. Wolf, 482 N.E.2d 506 (Ind. Ct. App. 4th Dist. 1985), reh'g denied, (Oct. 25, 1985); Orme v. Estate of Kruwell, 453 N.E.2d 355 (Ind. Ct. App. 4th Dist. 1983).

[64]Millner v. Mumby, 599 N.E.2d 627 (Ind. Ct. App. 5th Dist. 1992).

[65]Franklin v. White, 493 N.E.2d 161 (Ind. 1986); Ruff v. Charter Behavioral Health System of Northwest Indiana, Inc., 699 N.E.2d 1171 (Ind. Ct. App. 1998), reh'g denied, (Nov. 6, 1998) and transfer denied, 714 N.E.2d 170 (Ind. 1999) (fraud); Millner v. Mumby, 599 N.E.2d 627 (Ind. Ct. App. 5th Dist. 1992); Brames v. Crates, 399 N.E.2d 437, 28 U.C.C. Rep. Serv. (CBC) 419 (Ind. Ct. App. 3d Dist. 1980) (mistake); Vernon Fire & Cas. Ins. Co. v. Thatcher, 152 Ind. App. 692, 285 N.E.2d 660 (2d Dist. 1972), reh'g denied, 152 Ind. App. 692, 287 N.E.2d 776 (2d Dist. 1972), transfer denied, 260 Ind. 55, 292 N.E.2d 606 (1973) (misrepresentation).

[66]Rollins Burdick Hunter of Utah, Inc. v. Board of Trustees of Ball State University, 665 N.E.2d 914, 110 Ed. Law Rep. 373 (Ind. Ct. App. 1996).

[67]Baughan v. Brown, 122 Ind. 115, 23 N.E. 695 (1890).

[68]Kearns v. Burling, 14 Ind. App. 143, 42 N.E. 646 (1896).

The plaintiff's right to recover on a contract which is in evidence may be sufficiently established by his or her testimony alone,[69] particularly where the defendant subsequently testifies with the full knowledge of the plaintiff's evidence and fails to state or produce contrary facts.[70]

Where the plaintiff's action is for the reasonable value of goods sold pursuant to a contract, the contract price is itself prima facie evidence of the value.[71]

Where a copy of a written instrument is filed with the complaint and is uncontested, the instrument may be admitted into evidence without proof of its existence.[72]

---

[69]Lindenborg v. M & L Builders & Brokers, Inc., 158 Ind. App. 311, 302 N.E.2d 816 (3d Dist. 1973) (testimony of homeowners concerning variations from specifications and poor workmanship constituted sufficient evidence of substantial breach of contract for construction of home to support rescission of contract).

[70]Illinois Surety Co. v. State, 69 Ind. App. 450, 122 N.E. 30 (Div. 2 1919).

[71]Cullen-Friestedt Co. v. Turley, 50 Ind. App. 468, 97 N.E. 946 (1912).

[72]Mechanics Laundry & Supply, Inc. v. Wilder Oil Co., Inc., 596 N.E.2d 248 (Ind. Ct. App. 5th Dist. 1992), reh'g denied, (Aug. 27, 1992) and transfer denied, (Dec. 17, 1992).

As to the necessity of attaching a written contract to the complaint, see § 126.

CONTRIBUTION

Rosemary E. Williams, J.D.

Scope of Topic

This article discusses the general principles governing the right of one of several persons who share a common burden, obligation, or liability to be reimbursed by his or her co-obligors, where the person pays or satisfies the common obligation, or pays more than his or her fair or pro rata share.

Treated Elsewhere

Adjoining landowners, contribution among, see I.L.E., Adjoining Landowners

Coguarantors, contribution among, see I.L.E., Guaranty

Comparative fault, generally, see I.L.E., Negligence

Corporate promoters, stockholders, officers, and directors, contribution among, see I.L.E., Corporations

Cosureties, contribution among, see I.L.E., Suretyship

Cotenants, contribution among, see I.L.E., Tenancy in Common

Devisees, legatees, and heirs, contribution among, see I.L.E., Descent and Distribution; Wills

Indemnity, generally, see I.L.E., Indemnity

Insurance, generally, see I.L.E., Insurance

Joint and several liability of tortfeasors, generally, see I.L.E., Torts

Partners, contribution among, see I.L.E., Partnership

Subrogation, generally, see I.L.E., Subrogation

Research References

Text References

18 Am Jur 2d, Contribution §§ 1-136.
18 C.J.S., Contribution §§ 1-31.

Annotation References

ALR Digest: Contribution §§ 1-14
ALR Index: Contribution; Indemnity; Joint Tortfeasors; Subrogation; Uniform Contribution Among Tortfeasors Act

Forms References

5A Am Jur Legal Forms 2d, Contribution §§ 69:1-69:43.

7A Am Jur Pleading and Practice Forms, Annotated (rev. ed.),
Contribution §§ 1-60.

Trial Strategy References

Validity and Applicability of Contractual Allocations of Environmental Risk, 34 Am Jur POF3d 465; Proof of Excess Insurer's
Cause of Action Against Primary Insurer, 28 Am Jur POF3d
5067.

Hidden and Multiple Defendant Tort Litigation, 68 Am Jur Trials
503.

Miscellaneous References

Indiana Practice, Procedural Forms with Practice Commentary
§ 43.04.

Statutory References

IC 13-23-13-8; IC 23-2-1-19; IC 23-4-1-15; IC 23-4-1-34; IC 26-1-
3.1-116; IC 26-1-3.1-419; IC 29-1-14-4; IC 29-1-14-5; IC 32-1-6-
22; IC 34-11-9-4; IC 34-22-1-5; IC 34-22-1-6; IC 34-24-4-9; IC 34-
51-2-12

KeyCite®: Cases and other legal materials listed in KeyCite Scope
can be researched through West Group's KeyCite service on
Westlaw®. Use KeyCite to check citations for form, parallel
references, prior and later history, and comprehensive citator
information, including citations to other decisions and secondary
materials.

Table of Parallel References:

To convert General Index references to section references in this volume,
or to ascertain the disposition (or current equivalent) of articles in the
prior edition of this publication, see the Table of Parallel References
at the beginning of this volume.

§ 1   Generally
§ 2   Common liability
§ 3   —Joint wrongdoers
§ 4   —Payment or discharge
§ 5   Actions

§ 1   Generally

**Contribution applies where equity between two or more
parties requires equality of burden and one party has
discharged more of that burden than its pro rata share.**

West's Digest, Contribution ⚷1.

The concept of contribution arises in equity and is based
upon theories of natural justice. It applies to any relationship where equity between the parties requires equality of

burden or obligation and one of the parties concerned has discharged more than its fair share of the common burden.[1]

Contribution and indemnity are analogous; however, contribution is distinguished from indemnity in that contribution involves partial reimbursement of one party who has discharged or paid more than his or her share of a common liability, while indemnity requires reimbursement of the entire amount of a liability.[2] A right of indemnity is created from a contract, express or implied, while the right of contribution is implied by the relationship of the parties and the existence of a common burden.[3]

Contribution is distinguished from subrogation in that subrogation is recognized and enforced in actions at law, while contribution exists as an equitable remedy. In equity, however, subrogation may confer a broader right than contribution.[4]

§ 2 Common liability

Contribution applies only between those bound by a common liability, and as between obligors, each ordinarily is liable in contribution for one half of the common liability.

West's Digest, Contribution ☞2-4.

The doctrine of contribution applies only between those bound by a common liability.[5] The right of contribution oper-

---

[1]Cook v. Cook, 92 Ind. 398, 1884 WL 10314 (1884); Loudermilk v. Citizens Bank of Mooresville, 505 N.E.2d 107 (Ind. Ct. App. 1st Dist. 1987); Estate of Leinbach v. Leinbach, 486 N.E.2d 2 (Ind. Ct. App. 3d Dist. 1985); McLochlin v. Miller, 139 Ind. App. 443, 217 N.E.2d 50, 3 U.C.C. Rep. Serv. (CBC) 526 (Div. 1 1966).

[2]Mullen v. Cogdell, 643 N.E.2d 390 (Ind. Ct. App. 5th Dist. 1994), reh'g denied, (Jan. 25, 1995) and transfer denied, (May 16, 1995); Estate of Leinbach v. Leinbach, 486 N.E.2d 2 (Ind. Ct. App. 3d Dist. 1985).

As to indemnity, generally, see I.L.E., Indemnity.

[3]Mullen v. Cogdell, 643 N.E.2d 390 (Ind. Ct. App. 5th Dist. 1994), reh'g denied, (Jan. 25, 1995) and transfer denied, (May 16, 1995) (contribution); Morris v. McDonald's Corp., 650 N.E.2d 1219 (Ind. Ct. App. 1995) (indemnity).

[4]Erie Ins. Co. v. George, 681 N.E.2d 183 (Ind. 1997).

As to subrogation, generally, see I.L.E., Subrogation.

[5]Warring v. Hill, 89 Ind. 497, 1883 WL 5570 (1883); In re Amburgey, 68 B.R. 768 (Bankr. S.D. Ind. 1987) (applying Indiana law).

ates to make those who assume or are assessed a common liability bear it in equal proportions.[6]

Contribution has been applied as between sureties[7] and to liability on a bond.[8]

The right of contribution may also apply to liability on a note or other financial instrument, but depends upon the sequence and nature of the liability of the parties claiming or resisting contribution. Where two or more persons have the same liability on a note or other financial instrument as makes, drawers, acceptors, endorsers acting jointly, or anomalous endorsers, any party who pays the obligation embodied in the note or instrument, or an amount totaling more than his or her share of the principal obligation, is entitled to receive from any other party having the same joint and several liability contribution in accordance with applicable law.[9] If more than one accommodation party endorses a note as an accommodation to the maker, then the endorsers have joint and several liability to the holder of the note, and the right of contribution applies.[10] This right of contribution may be modified or waived through the agreement of the parties to

---

[6]Estate of Leinbach v. Leinbach, 486 N.E.2d 2 (Ind. Ct. App. 3d Dist. 1985); McLochlin v. Miller, 139 Ind. App. 443, 217 N.E.2d 50, 3 U.C.C. Rep. Serv. (CBC) 526 (Div. 1 1966).

[7]First Nat. Bank of South Bend v. Mayr, 189 Ind. 299, 127 N.E. 7 (1920); Alexander v. Blackburn, 178 Ind. 66, 98 N.E. 711 (1912).

Remedies of sureties against their principals, codefendants, and cosureties are provided by statute.—IC 34-22-1-5 (retaining judgment for benefit of surety); IC 34-22-1-6 (codefendants and co-sureties).

As to suretyship, generally, see I.L.E., Suretyship.

Forms References:　Cosureties. 7A Am Jur Pleading and Practice Forms, Annotated (rev. ed.), Contribution §§ 15-22.

[8]Stevens v. Tucker, 87 Ind. 109, 1882 WL 6814 (1882) (co-sureties); Salyers v. Ross, 15 Ind. 130, 1860 WL 4203 (1860) (finding no liability).

[9]IC 26-1-3.1-116 (contribution by joint payees).

Fleck v. Ragan, 514 N.E.2d 1287, 5 U.C.C. Rep. Serv. 2d (CBC) 644 (Ind. Ct. App. 3d Dist. 1987); Matter of Smith's Estate, 180 Ind. App. 198, 388 N.E.2d 287 (3d Dist. 1979); Hartung v. Architects Hartung/Odle/Burke, Inc., 157 Ind. App. 546, 301 N.E.2d 240, 13 U.C.C. Rep. Serv. (CBC) 308 (1st Dist. 1973).

Forms References:　Commercial Paper. 7A Am Jur Pleading and Practice Forms, Annotated (rev. ed.), Contribution §§ 11-14.

[10]IC 26-1-3.1-116(b).

the note or instrument,[11] but the discharge of a party having joint and several liability will not be heard as a defense to a suit for contribution.[12]

♦ **Observation:** The right of contribution where one obligor is an accommodation party is limited by statute. If one of the parties with joint and several liability is an "accommodation party" and the other is the "accommodated" party,[13] a statute[14] applies to bar contribution by the accommodated party from the accommodation party;[15] however, the accommodation party is entitled to seek reimbursement from the accommodated party.[16]

The doctrine of contribution is equally applicable where a claim against or a lien upon land is discharged by one of those jointly liable, unless that grantee had prior notice of the encumbrance.[17]

♦ **Observation:** Where one or more persons owns realty with improvements consisting of unoccupied condominium units, the co-owners are bound to contribute pro rata in the percentages of their ownership toward the expenses of administration, maintenance, and repair of the general common areas and facilities, and in some cases of the limited common areas and facilities of the building, as well as toward any other expense agreed upon lawfully by the co-owners.[18]

Indiana accords with the common and statutory law of

---

[11]IC 26-1-3.1-116(b).

[12]IC 26-1-3.1-116(c).

[13]IC 26-1-3.1-116(a), defining an "accommodation" party and an "accommodated" party.

[14]IC 26-1-1.3-419(e).

[15]Buchta v. Seng, 444 N.E.2d 1250 (Ind. Ct. App. 1st Dist. 1983).

[16]IC 26-1-3.1-419(e).

[17]Kaufman v. Elder, 154 Ind. 157, 56 N.E. 215 (1900); Windell v. Miller, 687 N.E.2d 585 (Ind. Ct. App. 1997) (cotenants not liable due to "words of severance"); Hancock v. Wiggins, 28 Ind. App. 449, 63 N.E. 242 (Div. 1 1902) (inter-spousal transfer); Springer v. Foster, 27 Ind. App. 15, 60 N.E. 720 (1901) (partial grantee with notice of mortgage cannot claim contribution); Jenkins v. Craig, 22 Ind. App. 192, 53 N.E. 427 (1899) (grantee of land subject to judgment lien).

Forms References: Cotenants. 7A Am Jur Pleading and Practice Forms, Annotated (rev. ed.), Contribution §§ 27, 28.

[18]IC 32-1-6-22(a) (expenses and pro rata contributions among owners of unoccupied condominium units).

most states in making partners to a general partnership jointly and severally liable for the debts of the partnership;[19] however, where one or more of the partners pays or discharges more than his or her proportionate share of the partnership obligations upon dissolution of the partnership, a right of contribution from the other partners exists and has been codified.[20] In the event that the dissolution is caused by the death or bankruptcy of any partner, however, and the partner incurring the obligation on behalf of the partnership knew of the dissolution or had knowledge or notice of the death or bankruptcy of the partner before incurring the partnership debt, the right of contribution is extinguished.[21]

§ 3   —Joint wrongdoers

One joint wrongdoer cannot claim contribution from the others, absent express statutory authority permitting such recovery.

West's Digest, Contribution ☞5.

The general rule in Indiana is that there is no right to contribution between joint wrongdoers, unless (1) a statute expressly authorizes such recovery,[22] or (2) the parties have

---

[19]IC 23-4-1-15.

Forms References: Partners. 7A Am Jur Pleading and Practice Forms, Annotated (rev. ed.), Contribution §§ 23-26.

[20]IC 23-4-1-34.

[21]IC 23-4-1-34(a)-(c).

[22]Mullen v. Cogdell, 643 N.E.2d 390 (Ind. Ct. App. 5th Dist. 1994), reh'g denied, (Jan. 25, 1995) and transfer denied, (May 16, 1995); Sanders v. Cole Mun. Finance, 489 N.E.2d 117 (Ind. Ct. App. 3d Dist. 1986), reh'g denied, (Apr. 18, 1986) and transfer denied, (Sept. 15, 1986); Elcona Homes Corp. v. McMillan Bloedell, Ltd., 475 N.E.2d 713 (Ind. Ct. App. 3d Dist. 1985), reh'g denied, (May 9, 1985) and transfer denied, (July 9, 1985); Gomez v. Adams, 462 N.E.2d 212 (Ind. Ct. App. 2d Dist. 1984); Justice v. CSX Transp., Inc., 908 F.2d 119 (7th Cir. 1990), reh'g denied, (Aug. 21, 1990) (applying Indiana law).

As to joint and several liability of tortfeasors, generally, see I.L.E., Torts.

Annotation References: Right of tortfeasor to contribution from joint tortfeasor who is spouse or otherwise in close familial relationship to injured party, 25 ALR4th 1120.

When statute of limitations commences to run against claim for contribution or indemnity based on tort, 57 ALR3d 867.

expressly contracted for such contribution.[23] For this purpose, "joint tortfeasors" have been defined as those who act together in committing a wrong, or whose acts, if independent of each other, unite in causing a single injury to the plaintiff.[24] There is no implied obligation to contribute, and if any such liability is created by express promise, the promise must rest upon some consideration other than the fact of the tort and the relation of the parties in the tortious transaction.[25]

♦ **Observation:** The common-law rule against contribution among joint tortfeasors is codified in the Comparative Fault Act, which provides that in any civil action for recovery of compensatory damages where issues of comparative fault arise, there is no right of contribution among tortfeasors;[26] however, nothing in the Comparative Fault Act affects or expands any contractual rights of indemnity.[27]

The common-law rule barring recovery for contribution among joint tortfeasors has been modified by several statutes. Under the Indiana statutes governing securities regulation, all persons liable for deceptive practices are provided by statute with a right of contribution to the same extent as would be applicable to contribution under contract.[28] Indiana environmental laws governing liability of owners or operators for costs or corrective actions regarding

---

Propriety and effect of jury's apportionment of damages as between tortfeasors jointly and severally liable, 46 ALR3d 801.

Forms References: Joint Tortfeasors. 7A Am Jur Pleading and Practice Forms, Annotated (rev. ed.), Contribution §§ 29-41.

[23]Avery v. Mapco Gas Products, Inc., 18 F.3d 448 (7th Cir. 1994) (applying Indiana law).

[24]United Farm Bureau Mut. Ins. Co. v. Blossom Chevrolet, 668 N.E.2d 1289 (Ind. Ct. App. 1996), transfer denied, 679 N.E.2d 1327 (Ind. 1997) and transfer denied, (May 14, 1997) and (disapproved of on other grounds by, Pelo v. Franklin College of Indiana, 715 N.E.2d 365 (Ind. 1999)).

[25]Indianapolis Power & Light Co. v. Brad Snodgrass, Inc., 578 N.E.2d 669 (Ind. 1991) (indemnification unchanged by Comparative Fault Act); Nichols v. Nowling, 82 Ind. 488, 1882 WL 6900 (1882).

[26]IC 34-51-2-12.

As to comparative fault, generally, see I.L.E., Negligence.

[27]IC 34-51-2-12.

As to indemnity, generally, see I.L.E., Indemnity.

[28]IC 23-2-1-19(d).

discharge or leakage from underground storage tanks provide that any person who pays to the state the costs arising from a release from an underground storage tank, or who undertakes corrective action resulting from such a release, is entitled to receive contribution from any person who owned or operated the tank in question at the time the release occurred.[29] Moreover, persons found liable in civil damages for knowingly participating in illegal drug marketing, or for injuries arising from an individual's drug use, may assert a right of contribution as against another person subjected to the same liability.[30]

§ 4 —Payment or discharge

Contribution depends on actual discharge of the common liability.

West's Digest, Contribution ☞6.

Actual payment or discharge of a joint liability by the person claiming contribution is a necessary condition to exercise of the right.[31] While payment of the common obligation must be made under legal compulsion to entitle the payor to demand contribution, the existence of the legal obligation to pay is sufficient; the payor need not wait until suit is brought to enforce the common obligation to claim the right of contribution.[32]

◆ **Caution:** A joint debtor or a surety who pays the debt, or part of it, after it has been barred by limitations may not enforce contribution.[33]

§ 5 Actions

An action for contribution may be maintained at law.

---

[29]IC 13-23-13-8(b).

[30]IC 34-24-4-9(a).

[31]Harter v. Songer, 138 Ind. 161, 37 N.E. 595 (1894); Estate of Leinbach v. Leinbach, 486 N.E.2d 2 (Ind. Ct. App. 3d Dist. 1985); McLochlin v. Miller, 139 Ind. App. 443, 217 N.E.2d 50, 3 U.C.C. Rep. Serv. (CBC) 526 (Div. 1 1966); In re Amburgey, 68 B.R. 768 (Bankr. S.D. Ind. 1987) (applying Indiana law).

[32]McLochlin v. Miller, 139 Ind. App. 443, 217 N.E.2d 50, 3 U.C.C. Rep. Serv. (CBC) 526 (Div. 1 1966).

As to actions for contribution, generally, see § 5.

[33]IC 34-11-9-4.

West's Digest, Contribution ⟳8, 9.

An action for contribution may be maintained at law, and tried by a jury, even though the right of contribution rests on equitable principles.[34]

Where there are multiple obligors who are severally and jointly liable on an obligation, the entirety of the obligation may be enforced by the holder against one or another of the obligors, against all of them, or against any combination of them; however, as between the obligors, each is ordinarily liable to discharge or pay on his or her portion of the obligation pari passu.[35] Evidence may be introduced to show who is liable on a note or other obligation, the payment of which is the basis of a claim for contribution.[36]

In an action for contribution, the complaint must show every element necessary to make liable the particular defendant or defendants sued. The elements pleaded and shown include a statement of the plaintiff's interest or payment sufficient to establish the claimed right of contribution.[37] Payment by a joint or joint and several obligor, upon a judgment entered on the primary obligation, will not necessarily bar contribution as long as the relationship of the parties giving rise to the right of contribution was not determined in the judgment action.[38] On the other hand, it has been held that if the complaint claiming contribution for a tort does not show the nature of the wrong for which judgment was obtained, the general rule of no contribution among wrongdoers will prevail.[39]

◆ **Practice Guide:** There is one statutory exception to the pleading rules regarding joinder of co-obligors,

---

[34]Michael v. Albright, 126 Ind. 172, 25 N.E. 902 (1890).

[35]Thompson v. Wayne Smith Const. Co., Inc., 640 N.E.2d 408 (Ind. Ct. App. 2d Dist. 1994) (distinguishing "joint" liability from "joint and several" liability); George v. Massey Harris Co., 109 Ind. App. 305, 34 N.E.2d 956 (1941).

[36]First Nat. Bank of Goodland v. Pothuisje, 217 Ind. 1, 25 N.E.2d 436, 130 A.L.R. 1238 (1940); Voss v. Lewis, 126 Ind. 155, 25 N.E. 892 (1890).

[37]Keesler v. Loy, 220 Ind. 332, 43 N.E.2d 615 (1942); Keesler v. Loy, 220 Ind. 332, 43 N.E.2d 615 (1942); Kimmel v. Captain, 107 Ind. App. 621, 24 N.E.2d 435 (1940).

[38]Voss v. Lewis, 126 Ind. 155, 25 N.E. 892 (1890).

[39]Hunt v. Lane, 9 Ind. 248, 1857 WL 3598 (1857).

As to the rule against contribution among joint wrongdoers, see § 3.

sureties, and parties jointly and severally liable on a common obligation. Where the co-obligor on a joint contract or joint judgment is deceased, no action may be brought by complaint and summons against the probate estate's representative and any other person or persons, or his or their legal representatives. The claimant may only enforce collection against the estate of the decedent by filing a claim in the court having jurisdiction over the estate.[40] This rule brings within the scope of the probate proceeding every contract executed jointly by the decedent with any other person or persons, and every joint judgment founded on such a contract, as by statute each of these obligations is deemed to be joint and several for the purpose of determining whether a claim must be filed in the probate proceeding.[41]

---

[40]IC 29-1-14-4.
[41]IC 29-1-14-5.

CONVERSION

Lisa D. Horowitz, J.D.

Scope of Topic

This article discusses the equitable doctrine of conversion; that is, constructive alteration in the nature of property whereby real estate is considered for certain purposes as personalty, or vice versa. This article also discusses the tort of conversion; that is, the act of wrongfully exercising dominion over another's personal property in denial of, or inconsistent with, the owner's rights. The discussion of tortious conversion includes civil causes of action for violation of Indiana's criminal conversion statute.

Treated Elsewhere

Carriers, deviation of property, delay, nondelivery of goods, and other acts of as conversion, see I.L.E., Carriers

Criminal conversion, criminal penalties for, see I.L.E., Theft and Related Offenses

Minerals, wrongful taking of, see I.L.E., Mining

Partners, conversion by, see I.L.E., Partnerships

Sales of goods, conversion and repossession of property in, see I.L.E., Sales of Personal Property

Tax avoidance, conversion of property for, see I.L.E., Taxation

Tenants in common, liabilities and remedies of for conversion, see I.L.E., Tenancy in Common

Trespass to personal property, see I.L.E., Trespass

Research References

Text References

18 Am Jur 2d, Conversion.
27A Am Jur 2d, Equitable Conversion.
18 C.J.S., Conversion.
89 C.J.S., Trover and Conversion.

West's Digest References

West's Digest, Conversion.
West's Digest, Trover and Conversion.

Annotation References

ALR Digest: Conversion; Equitable Conversion; Equity; Personal Property; Property; Replevin; Sale and Transfer of Property
ALR Index: Conversion

Forms References

20A Am Jur Legal Forms 2d, Wills § 266:521. (equitable conversion—failure of testator's purpose)

7A Am Jur Pleading and Practice Forms, Annotated (rev. ed.), Conversion.

9A Am Jur Pleading and Practice Forms, Annotated (rev. ed.), Equitable Conversion.

Trial Strategy References

Bailee's Liability for Damage, Loss, or Theft of Bailed Property, 46 Am Jur POF3d 361; Liability of Creditor and Repossession Agent for Wrongful Repossession and Tortious Acts Committed During Repossession, 42 Am Jur POF3d 355; Proof of Theft Within Property Insurance Coverage, 37 Am Jur POF3d 91; Damages for Loss of Personal Property With Little or No Market Value, 3 Am Jur POF3d 171.

Constructive Bailment, 39 Am Jur POF2d 501; Justifiable Destruction of Animal, 37 Am Jur POF2d 711; Sufficiency of Notice of Secured Party's Proposed Disposition of Collateral, 35 Am Jur POF2d 517; Landlord's Conversion of Tenant's Property, 32 Am Jur POF2d 659; Abandonment of Tangible Personal Property, 25 Am Jur POF2d 685.

Commonsense Principles of Civil Litigation, 52 Am Jur Trials 1; Solving Statutes of Limitation Problems, 4 Am Jur Trials 441; Tactics and Strategy of Pleading, 3 Am Jur Trials 681; Selecting the Remedy, 3 Am Jur Trials 637; Investigating the Civil Case, 1 Am Jur Trials 357.

Miscellaneous References

Indiana Practice, Procedural Forms with Practice Commentary §§ 15.01 et seq., 28.04, 40.34, 65.22, 65.23.

Statutory References

IC 26-1-3.1-420; IC 26-1-8.1-302; IC 26-1-8.1-303; IC 26-1-9-501; IC 26-1-9-507; IC 29-1-13-6; IC 29-1-13-9; IC 29-1-15-1; IC 32-4-5-5; IC 34-1-2-2; IC 34-24-3-1; IC 34-24-3-3; IC 34-51-3-2; IC 35-41-2-2; IC 35-41-1-23; IC 35-43-4-1; IC 35-43-4-3

Court Rules

Trial R. 8

KeyCite®: Cases and other legal materials listed in KeyCite Scope can be researched through West Group's KeyCite service on Westlaw®. Use KeyCite to check citations for form, parallel references, prior and later history, and comprehensive citator information, including citations to other decisions and secondary materials.

Table of Parallel References:
To convert General Index references to section references in this volume, or to ascertain the disposition (or current equivalent) of articles in the prior edition of this publication, see the Table of Parallel References at the beginning of this volume.

I. EQUITABLE CONVERSION (§§ 1 TO 9)

A. IN GENERAL (§§ 1 TO 3)

B. APPLICATION TO WILLS (§§ 4 TO 7)

C. OTHER BASES FOR EQUITABLE CONVERSION (§§ 8 TO 9)

II. WRONGFUL CONVERSION OF PERSONAL PROPERTY (§§ 10 TO 36)

A. IN GENERAL (§§ 10 TO 22)

B. DAMAGES AND OTHER AMOUNTS RECOVERABLE (§§ 23 TO 28)

C. ACTIONS (§§ 29 TO 36)

I. EQUITABLE CONVERSION

A. IN GENERAL

§ 1 Definition and application, generally

§ 2 Treatment of property

§ 3 —Under Probate Code

B. APPLICATION TO WILLS

§ 4 Generally

§ 5 Intent and directions of testator

§ 6 Time of conversion

§ 7 What law governs

C. OTHER BASES FOR EQUITABLE CONVERSION

§ 8 Executory contract for sale of realty

§ 9 Sale of realty under statute or court order

II. WRONGFUL CONVERSION OF PERSONAL PROPERTY

A. IN GENERAL

§ 10 Tortious conversion, generally
§ 11 Demand for return of property
§ 12 Civil recovery for criminal conversion
§ 13 Property subject to conversion
§ 14 —Money
§ 15 Acts constituting conversion, generally
§ 16 Acts constituting criminal conversion
§ 17 Conduct and liability of particular persons, or with respect to particular property
§ 18 —Bailees
§ 19 —Landowners and landlords
§ 20 —Lienholders and secured parties
§ 21 —Negotiable instruments and persons dealing therewith
§ 22 Rights of third persons

B. DAMAGES AND OTHER AMOUNTS RECOVERABLE

§ 23 Generally
§ 24 Measures of compensatory damages
§ 25 —Household goods
§ 26 Special and punitive damages; attorney fees
§ 27 Mitigation or reduction of damages
§ 28 Damages and other amounts recoverable for criminal conversion

C. ACTIONS

§ 29 Generally
§ 30 Limitation of actions
§ 31 Choice of law
§ 32 Defenses
§ 33 Pleading
§ 34 Burden of proof; evidence
§ 35 Questions of law and fact
§ 36 Instructions; findings and judgment

I. EQUITABLE CONVERSION

A. IN GENERAL

Research References
IC 29-1-13-6; IC 29-1-15-1

27A Am Jur 2d, Equitable Conversion §§ 1-4.
18 C.J.S., Conversion §§ 1-4.
West's Digest, Conversion ⊕1, 3, 20.
ALR Digest: Equitable Conversion § 1
ALR Index: Conversion; Equitable Conversion; Equity; Personal
 Property; Property; Replevin; Sale and Transfer of Property

§ 1 Definition and application, generally

Equitable conversion is a legal fiction through which real property is deemed personalty, and vice versa.

West's Digest, Conversion ⊕1, 3, 20.

In equity, conversion is the exchange of property from real to personal, or from personal to real, which takes place under some circumstances in the consideration of the law, such as to give effect to directions in a will or settlement, or to stipulations in a contract, although no such change has actually taken place.[1] In Indiana, equitable conversion may apply to property passing by will or statute at death,[2] including executory contracts for the sale of real property,[3] and to property sold under statute or court order.[4]

§ 2 Treatment of property

Under the equitable conversion doctrine, the form into which the property changes is not material, for equity will follow the property into whatever form it may assume in order to secure it for the person entitled to it.

West's Digest, Conversion ⊕3, 20.

Under the doctrine of equitable conversion, the form into which property changes is not material, for equity will follow the property into whatever form it may assume in order to

---

[1] 18 C.J.S., Conversion § 1.
[2] Regarding equitable conversion as applied to wills, see §§ 4 et seq.
 As to treatment of property under the Probate Code, see § 3.
[3] § 8.
[4] § 9.

secure it for the person entitled to it.[5] From the time of its
equitable conversion, property is treated as of the kind and
form into which it is converted. The rights of the parties
thereto are determined with relation to the character into
which it is changed.[6] The property will continue to be treated
as being in its original form until the person entitled to it
elects to accept it in its converted form.[7] After an equitable
conversion of realty has taken place, the beneficiaries may
all agree to take the realty in its original condition rather
than the proceeds from the impending sale, but one of the
beneficiaries may not elect to take his or her share in the
land without the consent of the others.[8]

> ◆ **Practice Pointer:** Real estate owned by a partnership
> is treated as personal property, even if the title is taken
> in the name of one of the partners.[9]

§ 3   —Under Probate Code

> **Indiana's Probate Code specifies when real estate or an
> interest therein subject to the Code will be treated as
> personalty, and when certain personalty must be treated
> as realty.**

West's Digest, Conversion ☞3, 20.

Indiana's Probate Code provides that unless foreclosure
has been completed and the redemption period has expired
prior to a decedent's death, the following property interests
are to be deemed personal assets in the hands of the
decedent's personal representative and must be distributed
and accounted for as such:

- real property mortgages
- the interest in the mortgaged premises conveyed by a
  mortgage

---

[5]McGuffey v. McClain, 130 Ind. 327, 30 N.E. 296 (1892); Funk v. Funk,
563 N.E.2d 127 (Ind. Ct. App. 1st Dist. 1990), transfer denied, (July 19,
1991).

[6]Duckwall v. Lease, 106 Ind. App. 664, 20 N.E.2d 204 (1939).

As to the treatment of real property as personalty and vice versa,
under the Probate Code, see § 3.

[7]Staser v. Gaar, Scott & Co., 168 Ind. 131, 79 N.E. 404 (1906).

[8]Duckwall v. Lease, 106 Ind. App. 664, 20 N.E.2d 204 (1939); Walling
v. Scott, 50 Ind. App. 23, 96 N.E. 481 (Div. 2 1911), reh'g denied, 50 Ind.
App. 23, 97 N.E. 388 (Div. 2 1912).

[9]Dickey v. Shirk, 128 Ind. 278, 27 N.E. 733 (1891).

- the debt secured by a mortgage
- any real estate acquired by the personal representative in settlement of a debt or liability
- property sold by the decedent on a written contract, the purchase price of which shall not have been paid in full prior to decedent's death[10]

Any sale, mortgage, lease, or exchange of any such real property after the decedent's death must be made pursuant to the statutes governing such transactions by a personal representative, unless the decedent's will provides otherwise.[11]

> ◆ **Observation:** The Official Comments to the statute observe that because real and personal property are generally treated alike in the Probate Code, this provision is unnecessary for most purposes and will be infrequently applied, but that it may nevertheless be helpful in cases where a will distinguishing between real and personal property must be construed in connection with the administration of an estate.[12]

When a personal representative sells real property, upon court order any surplus of the proceeds of such sale which remains after the final settlement of the account shall be considered real property, and shall be disposed of among the persons and in the same proportions as the real property would have been had it not been sold.[13]

B. APPLICATION TO WILLS

Research References

IC 32-4-5-5

27A Am Jur 2d, Equitable Conversion §§ 5-8, 12, 16.
18 C.J.S., Conversion §§ 10-20.
West's Digest, Conversion ☜2, 15-19, 21.
ALR Digest: Equitable Conversion §§ 4-10
ALR Index: Conversion; Equitable Conversion; Equity; Personal Property; Property; Replevin; Sale and Transfer of Property

---

[10]IC 29-1-13-6(a).

Regarding equitable conversion as applied to executory contracts for the sale of real property, generally, see § 8.

[11]IC 29-1-13-6(a), referring to IC 29-1-15-1 et seq.

Regarding equitable conversion as applied to wills, see §§ 4 et seq.

[12]IC 29-1-13-6, Commission Comments.

[13]IC 29-1-13-6(b).

20A Am Jur Legal Forms 2d, Wills § 266:521.

9A Am Jur Pleading and Practice Forms, Annotated (rev. ed.), Equitable Conversion §§ 12, 13.

§ 4   Generally

When land is directed to be sold and turned into money, courts of equity in dealing with the subject will consider it as personalty, unless so to consider the realty will clearly defeat the intention of the testator.

West's Digest, Conversion ☞15-18.

It is a well-settled rule in equity in the construction of wills that when land is directed to be sold and turned into money, courts of equity in dealing with the subject will consider it as personalty, unless so to consider the realty will clearly defeat the intention of the testator.[14] As between a testator and specific beneficiaries, the rule of conversion attaches so long as no other rights intervene; however, the rights of third parties may change this rule.[15]

If property has been devised to an executor with absolute power of sale, an heir has no interest in the realty entitling him or her to recover rents from the executor.[16] Where a will directs the executor to convert all realty into personalty, he or she is entitled to immediate possession of the realty at the testator's death, and may bring an action in trespass for damages.[17]

◆ **Observation:** Rents and profits from realty collected after the testator's death, even though ordinarily part of the reversion, may be devised by a testator to his or her executor to be used in discharging the testator's indebted-

---

[14]18 C.J.S., Conversion § 10.

As to the testator's intent, generally, see § 5.

Forms References: Complaint, petition, or declaration—To construe will—As to clause directing sale of real property—By residuary legatee claiming proceeds of sale. 9A Am Jur Pleading and Practice Forms, Annotated (rev. ed.), Equitable Conversion § 12.

Answer—Defense—Property passes under terms of will—Testator's subsequent contract to sell ineffective to defeat will. 9A Am Jur Pleading and Practice Forms, Annotated (rev. ed.), Equitable Conversion § 13.

[15]Comer v. Light, 175 Ind. 367, 94 N.E. 325 (1911).

[16]Life v. Stricler, 87 Ind. App. 281, 156 N.E. 575 (1927).

[17]Pittsburgh, Ft. W. & C. Ry. Co. v. Swinney, 97 Ind. 586, 1884 WL 5731 (1884).

ness without the realty being changed into personalty under the equitable conversion doctrine.[18]

§ 5 Intent and directions of testator

To work a conversion of a testator's land into money, there must be an adequate expression in the will of an absolute intention that the land shall be sold and turned into money. A direction in a will to distribute proceeds, coupled with an absolute power to sell, is a sufficient statement of intent, and will work a conversion.

West's Digest, Conversion ⊛16(1)-16(3), 21(2).

In the context of wills, equitable conversion applies to carry out the testator's intent,[19] and the doctrine should never be used to defeat such intent.[20]

To work a conversion of a testator's land into money, there must be an adequate expression in the will of an absolute intention that the land shall be sold and turned into money.[21] A mere declaration of intention to work a conversion is not sufficient.[22]

A direction in a will to distribute proceeds, coupled with an absolute power to sell, is a sufficient statement of intent, and will work a conversion.[23] Without the direction to distribute proceeds, a power of sale will not work a conversion,

---

[18]Lockridge v. Citizens Trust Co. of Greencastle, 110 Ind. App. 253, 37 N.E.2d 728 (1941).

[19]Funk v. Funk, 563 N.E.2d 127 (Ind. Ct. App. 1st Dist. 1990), transfer denied, (July 19, 1991); In re Richard's Estate, 419 N.E.2d 1012 (Ind. Ct. App. 4th Dist. 1981).

Forms References: Equitable conversion—Failure of testator's purpose. 20A Am Jur Legal Forms 2d, Wills § 266:521.

[20]Duckwall v. Lease, 106 Ind. App. 664, 20 N.E.2d 204 (1939).

A court may not allow partition of any real estate contrary to the expressed intention of the testator.—IC 32-4-5-5.

Annotation References: Rights of surviving spouse taking under or against will as affected by provision in will directing conversion, 33 ALR3d 1280.

[21]Moore v. Livingston, 148 Ind. App. 275, 265 N.E.2d 251 (Div. 1 1970); Walling v. Scott, 50 Ind. App. 23, 96 N.E. 481 (Div. 2 1911), reh'g denied, 50 Ind. App. 23, 97 N.E. 388 (Div. 2 1912); Funk v. Funk, 563 N.E.2d 127 (Ind. Ct. App. 1st Dist. 1990), transfer denied, (July 19, 1991).

[22]Comer v. Light, 175 Ind. 367, 93 N.E. 660 (1911), reh'g denied, 175 Ind. 367, 94 N.E. 325 (1911); Moore v. Livingston, 148 Ind. App. 275, 265 N.E.2d 251 (Div. 1 1970).

[23]Rumsey v. Durham, 5 Ind. 71, 1854 WL 3155 (1854); Moore v.

even though a sale and reinvestment would have the same effect.[24] Failure to designate by whom a sale should be made does not impair the power of sale.[25]

§ 6 Time of conversion

Generally, where no time is stated in the will, conversion takes place as of the testator's death. The time is dependent on intent, however, and conversion may take place at a different time designated by the testator.

West's Digest, Conversion ☞19

The time of conversion will depend on the testator's intent and may be immediately upon the testator's death.[26] Where a will contains a direction to convert property, with no time specified, conversion is generally deemed to take place as of the testator's death.[27]

Conversion may also be fixed to take place immediately upon the death of a life tenant,[28] or upon the exercise of a power to sell.[29] The time of conversion also may be made contingent upon the vesting of a contingent remainder.[30]

§ 7 What law governs

The law of the place where realty is situated determines whether a devise thereof effects an equitable conversion into personalty.

West's Digest, Conversion ☞2.

The law of the place where realty is situated determines whether a devise thereof effects an equitable conversion into personalty.[31] If that law works an equitable conversion, the

---

Livingston, 148 Ind. App. 275, 265 N.E.2d 251 (Div. 1 1970); Life v. Stricler, 87 Ind. App. 281, 156 N.E. 575 (1927).

[24]Porter v. Union Trust Co. of Indianapolis, 182 Ind. 637, 108 N.E. 117 (1915).

[25]Duckwall v. Lease, 106 Ind. App. 664, 20 N.E.2d 204 (1939).

[26]Nelson v. Nelson, 36 Ind. App. 331, 75 N.E. 679 (Div. 1 1905).

[27]Moore v. Livingston, 148 Ind. App. 275, 265 N.E.2d 251 (Div. 1 1970).

[28]Lantz v. Caraway, 180 Ind. 484, 103 N.E. 335 (1913).

[29]Dillman v. Fulwider, 57 Ind. App. 632, 105 N.E. 124 (Div. 2 1914).

[30]Dickey v. Citizens' State Bank of Fairmount, 98 Ind. App. 58, 180 N.E. 36 (1932).

[31]Duckwall v. Lease, 106 Ind. App. 664, 20 N.E.2d 204 (1939).

law of the testator's domicile will control how the personalty is distributed.[32]

C.   OTHER BASES FOR EQUITABLE CONVERSION

Research References

IC 29-1-13-6

27A Am Jur 2d, Equitable Conversion §§ 9, 10, 13-15, 17, 18.
18 C.J.S., Conversion §§ 5-9, 21-28.
West's Digest, Conversion ☞5-13.
ALR Digest: Equitable Conversion §§ 2, 3, 8-10
ALR Index: Conversion; Equitable Conversion; Equity; Personal
   Property; Property; Replevin; Sale and Transfer of Property
9A Am Jur Pleading and Practice Forms, Annotated (rev. ed.), Eq-
   uitable Conversion § 11.

§ 8   Executory contract for sale of realty

An executory contract for the sale of land ordinarily works a conversion, the seller's interest thereunder being deemed personalty, and the buyer's interest treated as realty. If the seller under an executory land sale contract dies intestate, the interest secured by the retained title is deemed personalty and is distributed as such.

West's Digest, Conversion ☞10-13.

A contract for the sale of real property ordinarily works a conversion, equity treating the vendor as holding the land in trust for the purchaser, and the purchaser as a trustee of the purchase price for the vendor.[33] From the time the contract is executed, the seller's interest thereunder is deemed personalty, and the buyer's interest is realty.[34]

◆ **Observation:** The buyer under an executory land sale

---

[32]Moore v. Livingston, 148 Ind. App. 275, 265 N.E.2d 251 (Div. 1 1970); Duckwall v. Lease, 106 Ind. App. 664, 20 N.E.2d 204 (1939).

[33]Bucher v. Young, 94 Ind. App. 586, 158 N.E. 581 (1927); Matter of Jones, 768 F.2d 923 (7th Cir. 1985) (applying Indiana law).

Forms References: Complaint, petition, or declaration—By vendee of executory contract—For declaratory judgment on right of vendee to proceeds of fire insurance policy held by vendor. 9A Am Jur Pleading and Practice Forms, Annotated (rev. ed.), Equitable Conversion § 11.

[34]Board of Com'rs of Madison County v. Midwest Associates, Inc., 144 Ind. App. 264, 245 N.E.2d 853 (Div. 1 1969), transfer denied, 253 Ind. 551, 255 N.E.2d 807 (1970).

contract, as equitable owner, is responsible for taxes.[35] A purchaser who does not take title may still be liable for taxes on real property and the property is subject to government foreclosure and sale to satisfy a tax lien.[36]

The Probate Code provides that property sold by a decedent on a written contract, the purchase price of which shall not have been paid in full prior to the decedent's death, is deemed a personal asset in the hands of the decedent's personal representative and must be distributed and accounted for as such.[37] This provision does not apply to sales by persons other than the decedent, such as those made under the authority of a power of attorney, or by a guardian for an incompetent testator.

◆ **Illustrations:** Equitable conversion did not apply to cause the unpaid balance of a land contractor on a testator's farm to pass to the testator's wife as personal property, thereby disinheriting the heirs of the proceeds, where the farm was not sold by the testator himself, but by his attorney under authority of a power of attorney at a time when the testator was in a coma.[38] The conversion statute also did not apply where co-guardians sold an incompetent person's real property on contract.[39]

Equitable conversion does not apply in deciding whether a transfer takes place where a contract for sale of realty held by the entireties is incomplete at the time of the spouse's death.[40]

If the devisees of a life estate and of the remainder join in a sale and conveyance of the land, equity will regard the proceeds as real estate.[41]

§ 9 Sale of realty under statute or court order

Generally, where land is sold under statute or by court

---

[35]Stark v. Kreyling, 207 Ind. 128, 188 N.E. 680 (1934).

[36]Matter of Jones, 768 F.2d 923 (7th Cir. 1985) (applying Indiana law).

[37]IC 29-1-13-6(a).

As to the treatment of property under the Probate Code, generally, see § 3.

[38]Funk v. Funk, 563 N.E.2d 127 (Ind. Ct. App. 1st Dist. 1990), transfer denied, (July 19, 1991).

[39]In re Richard's Estate, 419 N.E.2d 1012 (Ind. Ct. App. 4th Dist. 1981).

[40]State v. Weinstein's Estate, 141 Ind. App. 395, 228 N.E.2d 23 (Div. 2 1967), reh'g denied, 141 Ind. App. 399, 229 N.E.2d 741 (Div. 2 1967).

[41]Clifford v. Farmer, 79 Ind. 529, 1881 WL 6844 (1881).

order for a particular purpose, the land is deemed converted into personalty in so far as necessary to accomplish the sale's purpose.

West's Digest, Conversion ⊜5-9.

As a general rule, where land is sold under statute or by court order for a specific purpose, the land is deemed converted into personalty in so far as is necessary to accomplish the purpose of the sale. Where the court orders realty sold to pay debts, the conversion into money is complete only to the extent and for the purposes for which the sale was authorized, and any surplus continues in its original character of realty. Therefore, any surplus must be applied to the payment of a judgment obtained against the heir and duly docketed after the death of the ancestor and before the sale.[42]

Where real property is sold under court order, it is not converted to personalty until the sale is completed.[43]

II. WRONGFUL CONVERSION OF PERSONAL PROPERTY

A. IN GENERAL

Research References

IC 26-1-3.1-420; IC 26-1-8.1-302; IC 26-1-8.1-303; IC 26-1-9-501; IC 26-1-9-507; IC 29-1-13-9; IC 34-24-3-1; IC 35-41-2-2; IC 35-41-1-23; IC 35-43-4-1; IC 35-43-4-3

18 Am Jur 2d, Conversion §§ 1-6.
89 C.J.S., Trover and Conversion §§ 1 et seq.
West's Digest, Trover and Conversion ⊜1-12, 18, 25.
ALR Digest: Conversion §§ 1 et seq.
ALR Index: Conversion; Equitable Conversion; Equity; Personal Property; Property; Replevin; Sale and Transfer of Property
7A Am Jur Pleading and Practice Forms, Annotated (rev. ed.), Conversion §§ 51-146.
Bailee's Liability for Damage, Loss, or Theft of Bailed Property, 46 Am Jur POF3d 361; Liability of Creditor and Repossession Agent for Wrongful Repossession and Tortious Acts Committed During Repossession, 42 Am Jur POF3d 355.
Justifiable Destruction of Animal, 37 Am Jur POF2d 711.

---

[42]18 C.J.S., Conversion §§ 22, 23.
[43]Shaffner v. Briggs, 36 Ind. 55, 1871 WL 5167 (1871).

§ 10 Tortious conversion, generally

Conversion is a tort in which one appropriates the personal property of another to the tortfeasor's own use and benefit, in derogation of the owner's rights, or wrongfully destroys or withholds another's personalty. Recovery on a conversion claim requires that the plaintiff have an immediate, unqualified right to possession based on a superior claim of title.

West's Digest, Trover and Conversion ⊂1, 3, 4, 18.

The tort of conversion consists either in the appropriation of the personal property of another to the party's own use and benefit, or in its destruction, or in exercising dominion over it, in exclusion and defiance of the rights of the owner or lawful possessor, or in withholding it from his or her possession, under a claim and title inconsistent with the owner's.[44]

Recovery on a claim of conversion requires of the plaintiff an immediate, unqualified right to possession based on a superior claim of title.[45] The plaintiff must establish that he or she owned the property, and that the defendant's possession was unauthorized or without consent.[46] Because ownership is necessary, there is no liability for conversion where property has been abandoned.[47]

It has long been recognized that the essence of conversion is the wrongful invasion of another's property rights, not the

---

[44]Shourek v. Stirling, 621 N.E.2d 1107 (Ind. 1993), appeal after remand, 652 N.E.2d 865 (Ind. Ct. App. 1995); Computers Unlimited, Inc. v. Midwest Data Systems, Inc., 657 N.E.2d 165 (Ind. Ct. App. 1995); Howard Dodge & Sons, Inc. v. Finn, 181 Ind. App. 209, 391 N.E.2d 638, 26 U.C.C. Rep. Serv. (CBC) 886 (3d Dist. 1979).

As to the definition, elements, and requirements of civil recovery for criminal conversion, generally, see § 12.

[45]Shourek v. Stirling, 621 N.E.2d 1107 (Ind. 1993), appeal after remand, 652 N.E.2d 865 (Ind. Ct. App. 1995); Howard Dodge & Sons, Inc. v. Finn, 181 Ind. App. 209, 391 N.E.2d 638, 26 U.C.C. Rep. Serv. (CBC) 886 (3d Dist. 1979); Noble v. Moistner, 180 Ind. App. 414, 388 N.E.2d 620 (4th Dist. 1979); Schwartz v. Oberweis, 826 F. Supp. 280 (N.D. Ind. 1993) (applying Indiana law).

[46]Yoder Feed Service v. Allied Pullets, Inc., 171 Ind. App. 692, 359 N.E.2d 602 (3d Dist. 1977).

[47]Right Reason Publications v. Silva, 691 N.E.2d 1347 (Ind. Ct. App. 1998); McDonald v. McDonald, 631 N.E.2d 522 (Ind. Ct. App. 3d Dist. 1994), reh'g denied, (Aug. 8, 1994).

intent with which the invasion is carried out.[48] Conversion is a strict liability tort in which the actor's intent and knowledge are irrelevant to liability.[49] Therefore, wrongful intent is not required for ordinary tortious conversion,[50] and the plaintiff need show only that the defendant intended to perform the acts which deprived the plaintiff of his or her rights to the property.[51]

◆ **Caution:** Proof of knowing or intentional conduct on the defendant's part is necessary to civil recovery for criminal conversion.[52]

The fact of conversion is not dependent upon the subsequent application of the converted property.[53]

Conversion is a single wrongful act; the victim is not required to justify the rightness of his or her position by keeping open a tender to repay money owed, when the tender did not work to prevent the conversion in the first place. Also, no tender is necessary in a conversion case where a repossessing party fails to give notice of its intent to dispose of the property.[54]

§ 11 Demand for return of property

A demand for return of the converted goods is necessary

---

[48]Seip v. Gray, 227 Ind. 52, 83 N.E.2d 790 (1949); Chesterton State Bank v. Coffey, 454 N.E.2d 1233 (Ind. Ct. App. 4th Dist. 1983).

[49]U. S. v. Topeka Livestock Auction, Inc., 392 F. Supp. 944, 17 U.C.C. Rep. Serv. (CBC) 517 (N.D. Ind. 1975) (applying Indiana law).

[50]Catellier v. Depco, Inc., 696 N.E.2d 75 (Ind. Ct. App. 1998); Computers Unlimited, Inc. v. Midwest Data Systems, Inc., 657 N.E.2d 165 (Ind. Ct. App. 1995).

Mens rea is not an essential element in the tort of conversion, and the defendant's good faith in assuming dominion over the plaintiff's goods is immaterial.—Sikora v. Barney, 138 Ind. App. 686, 207 N.E.2d 846 (Div. 2 1965).

[51]Kozma v. Medtronic, Inc., 925 F. Supp. 602 (N.D. Ind. 1996) (applying Indiana law).

[52]As to the definition, elements, and requirements of civil recovery for criminal conversion, generally, see § 12.

[53]Peoples State Bank v. Kelly, 78 Ind. App. 418, 136 N.E. 30 (1922).

[54]Chesterton State Bank v. Coffey, 454 N.E.2d 1233 (Ind. Ct. App. 4th Dist. 1983).

Trial Strategy References: Liability of Creditor and Repossession Agent for Wrongful Repossession and Tortious Acts Committed During Repossession, 42 Am Jur POF3d 355.

**where the defendant's possession of the property was
initially lawful, unless the circumstances show that the
demand would have been unavailing; however, no demand
is necessary when the defendant's possession of the property was initially unlawful.**

West's Digest, Trover and Conversion ☞9.

Demand for return of the converted goods is sometimes a
requirement of recovery for tortious conversion. A demand is
necessary where the defendant's possession of the property
was initially lawful, unless the circumstances show that the
demand would have been unavailing.[55] Where a demand is
required, it need not be in formal words.[56]

> ◆ **Illustration:** Where owner of pullets had arranged for
> truckers to drive 200 miles to retrieve pullets from grower,
> and had so advised grower, but on the date that trucks
> were scheduled to arrive, grower made telephone call to
> owner refusing to allow removal of pullets, owner's
> demand was sufficient and the grower's telephone call was
> a sufficient tortious act to sustain complaint of conver-
> sion.[57]

No demand is necessary when the defendant's possession
of the property was initially unlawful,[58] or where the property was criminally converted.[59] If the converter has disposed
of the property to some third person, the owner is not
required to make a demand to the third person for its return,
but may bring an immediate action against the converter.[60]
If the owner elects to seek his or her remedy against the
third person, the owner must first demand return of the

---

[55]THQ Venture v. SW, Inc., 444 N.E.2d 335 (Ind. Ct. App. 1st Dist.
1983); Tucker v. Capital City Riggers, 437 N.E.2d 1048 (Ind. Ct. App. 1st
Dist. 1982).

[56]Yoder Feed Service v. Allied Pullets, Inc., 171 Ind. App. 692, 359
N.E.2d 602 (3d Dist. 1977).

[57]Yoder Feed Service v. Allied Pullets, Inc., 171 Ind. App. 692, 359
N.E.2d 602 (3d Dist. 1977).

[58]French v. Hickman Moving and Storage, 400 N.E.2d 1384 (Ind. Ct.
App. 3d Dist. 1980).

[59]Lambert v. Yellowbird, Inc., 496 N.E.2d 406 (Ind. Ct. App. 4th Dist.
1986), decision clarified on denial of reh'g, 498 N.E.2d 80 (Ind. Ct. App.
4th Dist. 1986), transfer denied, (Jan. 21, 1987).

As to civil recovery for criminal conversion, generally, see § 12.

[60]Miller v. Long, 126 Ind. App. 482, 131 N.E.2d 348 (1956), reh'g
denied, 126 Ind. App. 482, 132 N.E.2d 272 (1956).

property and have the demand refused. The mere purchase of goods from one who does not own them, and does not have the right to sell them, does not constitute conversion unless the purchaser refuses to return the goods on demand or has converted them to his or her own use so the purchaser cannot return them when requested to do so.[61]

§ 12   Civil recovery for criminal conversion

A person who knowingly or intentionally exerts unauthorized control over the property of another commits criminal conversion, and may be liable for up to three times the loss in damages, plus costs and attorney fees.

West's Digest, Trover and Conversion ⚷1, 3, 4, 9(3), 18.

Under an Indiana statute, treble damages and other amounts may be recovered in a civil action for the criminal conversion of property.[62] An action for criminal conversion is distinct from an action for ordinary tortious conversion.[63] A criminal conviction is not necessary for the plaintiff to recover civil damages under the criminal conversion statute.[64] Nevertheless, all elements of the alleged criminal act must be proved by the claimant[65] by a preponderance of the evi-

---

[61]Sherry v. Picken, 10 Ind. 375, 1858 WL 4035 (1858); Wood v. Cohen, 6 Ind. 455, 1855 WL 3603 (1855); Valentine v. Duff, 7 Ind. App. 196, 34 N.E. 453 (1893).

[62]IC 34-24-3-1.

As to the damages and amounts recoverable for criminal conversion, generally, see §§ 28 et seq.

As to criminal liability for conversion, see I.L.E., Theft and Related Offenses.

[63]Lambert v. Yellowbird, Inc., 496 N.E.2d 406 (Ind. Ct. App. 4th Dist. 1986), decision clarified on denial of reh'g, 498 N.E.2d 80 (Ind. Ct. App. 4th Dist. 1986), transfer denied, (Jan. 21, 1987) (criminal conversion).

As to recovery for tortious conversion, generally, see § 10.

[64]White v. Indiana Realty Associates II, 555 N.E.2d 454 (Ind. 1990); Gilliana v. Paniaguas, 708 N.E.2d 895 (Ind. Ct. App. 1999), reh'g denied, (June 8, 1999) and transfer denied, (Oct. 13, 1999); Huff v. Biomet, Inc., 654 N.E.2d 830 (Ind. Ct. App. 1995).

[65]Gilliana v. Paniaguas, 708 N.E.2d 895 (Ind. Ct. App. 1999), reh'g denied, (June 8, 1999) and transfer denied, (Oct. 13, 1999).

dence.[66] The statute.is a penal measure and should be strictly construed.[67]

In a civil action brought pursuant to the criminal conversion statute, the elements necessary to establish such conversion are those set forth in the statute.[68] As stated therein, a person who knowingly[69] or intentionally[70] exerts unauthorized control[71] over the property of another person commits criminal conversion.[72] Thus, unlike ordinary tortious conversion,[73] criminal conversion requires proof that the defendant intended to deprive the plaintiff of his or her rights in the property.[74] The intent requirement further distinguishes criminal conversion from cases of mere breach of contract or failure to pay debt that the statute was not intended to reach.[75]

Recovery for criminal and ordinary tortious conversion

---

[66]White v. Indiana Realty Associates II, 555 N.E.2d 454 (Ind. 1990); Excel Industries, Inc. v. Signal Capital Corp., 574 N.E.2d 946 (Ind. Ct. App. 3d Dist. 1991), transfer denied, (Jan. 23, 1992); Roake v. Christensen, 528 N.E.2d 789 (Ind. Ct. App. 2d Dist. 1988).

[67]NationsCredit Commercial Corp. v. Grauel Enterprises, Inc., 703 N.E.2d 1072 (Ind. Ct. App. 1998), reh'g denied, (Mar. 15, 1999) and transfer denied, (Aug. 12, 1999).

[68]Anderson v. Indianapolis Indiana AAMCO Dealers Advertising Pool, 678 N.E.2d 832 (Ind. Ct. App. 1997), transfer denied, 690 N.E.2d 1183 (Ind. 1997); DBC Capital Fund, Inc. v. Snodgrass, 551 N.E.2d 475, 11 U.C.C. Rep. Serv. 2d (CBC) 696 (Ind. Ct. App. 1st Dist. 1990).

[69]For purposes of the statute, a person engages in conduct "knowingly" if, at the time of the conduct, the person is aware of a high probability that he or she is doing so.—IC 35-41-2-2(b).

[70]For purposes of the statute, a person engages in conduct "intentionally" if, when he or she engages in the conduct, it is the person's conscious objective to do so.—IC 35-41-2-2(a).

[71]As to what constitutes unauthorized control for purposes of criminal conversion, see § 16.

[72]IC 35-43-4-3.

[73]§ 10.

[74]NationsCredit Commercial Corp. v. Grauel Enterprises, Inc., 703 N.E.2d 1072 (Ind. Ct. App. 1998), reh'g denied, (Mar. 15, 1999) and transfer denied, (Aug. 12, 1999); Baker v. R & R Const., Inc., 662 N.E.2d 661 (Ind. Ct. App. 1996), reh'g denied, (June 3, 1996) and transfer denied, (Nov. 19, 1996).

[75]NationsCredit Commercial Corp. v. Grauel Enterprises, Inc., 703 N.E.2d 1072 (Ind. Ct. App. 1998), reh'g denied, (Mar. 15, 1999) and transfer denied, (Aug. 12, 1999); Midland-Guardian Co. v. United Consumers Club, Inc., 499 N.E.2d 792 (Ind. Ct. App. 3d Dist. 1986), reh'g

also differ as to the necessity for a demand by the plaintiff that the defendant return the property. No demand for return of criminally converted property is necessary,[76] while for tortious conversion, a demand is necessary if the defendant's possession of the property was initially lawful, unless such demand would have been unavailing.[77]

Yet another distinction between tortious and criminal conversion is the amount recoverable. For tortious conversion, the measure of damages is generally the market value of the item at the time of conversion, plus interest,[78] and the plaintiff may also recover punitive damages where appropriate.[79] In contrast, recovery for criminal conversion may be up to three times the amount of the actual loss, plus specified costs and attorney fees.[80]

§ 13   Property subject to conversion

An action for tortious conversion generally lies only with respect to tangible personal property, or tangible evidence of title to intangible or real property.

West's Digest, Trover and Conversion ☞2.

An action for tortious conversion may only be brought with respect to tangible personal property, or tangible evidence of title to intangible or real property.[81] Among the types of property that have been recognized as the proper subject of a claim for conversion are: unattached houses[82] and fixtures,[83]

---

denied, 502 N.E.2d 1354 (Ind. Ct. App. 3d Dist. 1987), transfer denied, (Oct. 15, 1987).

[76]Lambert v. Yellowbird, Inc., 496 N.E.2d 406 (Ind. Ct. App. 4th Dist. 1986), decision clarified on denial of reh'g, 498 N.E.2d 80 (Ind. Ct. App. 4th Dist. 1986), transfer denied, (Jan. 21, 1987).

[77]§ 11.

[78]§ 24.

[79]§ 26.

[80]§ 28.

[81]89 C.J.S., Trover and Conversion § 11.

Forms References: Property Subject to Conversion—Motor Vehicles. 7A Am Jur Pleading and Practice Forms, Annotated (rev. ed.), Conversion §§ 127-138.

[82]Sikora v. Barney, 138 Ind. App. 686, 207 N.E.2d 846 (Div. 2 1965).

[83]Lau v. Indiana Nat. Bank, 506 N.E.2d 70 (Ind. Ct. App. 4th Dist.

household goods,[84] animals,[85] sand and gravel,[86] growing crops,[87] natural gas,[88] and money.[89]

Indiana's version of the Uniform Commercial Code states that the law of conversion of personal property applies to negotiable instruments.[90]

For purposes of civil recovery under the criminal conversion statute,[91] "property" means anything of value, and includes:[92]

- a gain or advantage or anything that might reasonably be regarded as such by the beneficiary

---

1987); Trust & Savings Bank of Rensselaer v. Brushahan, 88 Ind. App. 257, 148 N.E. 427 (Div. 2 1925).

Forms References: Property Subject to Conversion—Fixtures and Property Severed From Realty. 7A Am Jur Pleading and Practice Forms, Annotated (rev. ed.), Conversion §§ 139-146.

[84]Mitchell v. Mitchell, 685 N.E.2d 1083 (Ind. Ct. App. 1997), reh'g denied, (Sept. 17, 1997) and transfer granted, opinion vacated on other grounds, 698 N.E.2d 1194 (Ind. 1998) and opinion aff'd in part, vacated in part on other grounds, 695 N.E.2d 920 (Ind. 1998).

[85]Yoder Feed Service v. Allied Pullets, Inc., 171 Ind. App. 692, 359 N.E.2d 602 (3d Dist. 1977).

Forms References: Property Subject to Conversion—Animals. 7A Am Jur Pleading and Practice Forms, Annotated (rev. ed.), Conversion §§ 120-126.

Trial Strategy References: Justifiable Destruction of Animal, 37 Am Jur POF2d 711.

[86]O.K. Sand & Gravel, Inc. v. Martin Marietta Technologies, Inc., 36 F.3d 565, 30 Fed. R. Serv. 3d (LCP) 20 (7th Cir. 1994) (applying Indiana law).

[87]Richardson v. Scroggham, 159 Ind. App. 400, 307 N.E.2d 80 (1st Dist. 1974).

[88]Crystal Ice & Cold Storage Co. v. Marion Gas Co., 35 Ind. App. 295, 74 N.E. 15 (Div. 1 1905); Plymouth Fertilizer Co., Inc. v. Balmer, 488 N.E.2d 1129 (Ind. Ct. App. 3d Dist. 1986), reh'g denied, (Apr. 4, 1986) and transfer denied, (July 14, 1986).

[89]§ 14.

[90]IC 26-1-3.1-420(a).

Annotation References: Payee's right of recovery, in conversion under UCC S3-419(1) (c), for money paid on unauthorized indorsement, 23 ALR4th 855.

Forms References: Property Subject to Conversion—Written Instruments. 7A Am Jur Pleading and Practice Forms, Annotated (rev. ed.), Conversion §§ 103-119.

[91]As to civil recovery for criminal conversion, generally, see § 12.

[92]IC 35-41-1-23(a).

- real property, personal property, money, labor, and services
- intangibles
- commercial instruments
- written instruments concerning labor, services, or property
- written instruments otherwise of value to the owner, such as a public record, deed, will, credit card, or letter of credit
- a signature to a written instrument
- extension of credit
- trade secrets
- contract rights, choses in action, and other interests in or claims to wealth
- electricity, gas, oil, and water
- captured or domestic animals, birds, and fish
- food and drink
- human remains

§ 14 —Money

Money may be the subject of an action for conversion, but it must be a separately identifiable chattel or a separate account over which the plaintiff retains ownership.

West's Digest, Trover and Conversion ⬤⬤2.

Money may be the subject of an action for conversion; however, it must be a separately identifiable chattel or a separate account over which the plaintiff retains ownership.[93] For there to be conversion, the money must be a determinate sum which the defendant was entrusted to apply to a certain purpose, such as insurance premiums.[94] Where funds are

---

[93]Summit Account and Computer Service, Inc. v. RJH of Florida, Inc., 690 N.E.2d 723 (Ind. Ct. App. 1998), reh'g denied, (Mar. 9, 1998) and transfer denied, 706 N.E.2d 169 (Ind. 1998); Huff v. Biomet, Inc., 654 N.E.2d 830 (Ind. Ct. App. 1995); Midland-Guardian Co. v. United Consumers Club, Inc., 499 N.E.2d 792 (Ind. Ct. App. 3d Dist. 1986), reh'g denied, 502 N.E.2d 1354 (Ind. Ct. App. 3d Dist. 1987), transfer denied, (Oct. 15, 1987).

[94]Huff v. Biomet, Inc., 654 N.E.2d 830 (Ind. Ct. App. 1995); Stevens v. Butler, 639 N.E.2d 662 (Ind. Ct. App. 3d Dist. 1994), transfer denied, (Dec. 20, 1994); Nehi Beverage Co., Inc. of Indianapolis v. Sims, 509

properly intermingled or were not meant to be segregated, no action for conversion will lie.[95]

♦ **Illustration:** A vendor of real property who retained an earnest-money deposit after the purchaser demanded its return when the land purchase agreement fell through was not liable to the purchaser on a conversion theory, in that the vendor was not under any obligation to return the specific money which the purchaser had given him, the parties did not set up an escrow account or deliver money to any third party for safekeeping, and nothing in the conduct of the parties or in the wording of the receipt for the earnest money indicated that the parties intended for the purchaser to retain any ownership or possessory rights in that specific fund.[96]

§ 15 Acts constituting conversion, generally

Any unauthorized act that deprives an owner of property permanently or indefinitely, or any unauthorized and wrongful exercise of dominion and control over another's property rights inconsistently with the owner's rights, is a conversion.

West's Digest, Trover and Conversion ⬦4-8, 10-12.

Any unauthorized act which deprives an owner of property permanently, or for an indefinite time, or any unauthorized and wrongful exercise of dominion and control over another's property rights to the exclusion of, or inconsistently with, the owner's rights, is a conversion.[97] Acts of conversion include a taking from the owner without the owner's consent,[98] a wrongful invasion of an owner's absolute right to

---

N.E.2d 1125 (Ind. Ct. App. 2d Dist. 1987), reh'g denied, (Dec. 22, 1987) and transfer denied, (Oct. 26, 1988).

[95]Huff v. Biomet, Inc., 654 N.E.2d 830 (Ind. Ct. App. 1995); Excel Industries, Inc. v. Signal Capital Corp., 574 N.E.2d 946 (Ind. Ct. App. 3d Dist. 1991), transfer denied, (Jan. 23, 1992); Kopis v. Savage, 498 N.E.2d 1266 (Ind. Ct. App. 4th Dist. 1986).

[96]Kopis v. Savage, 498 N.E.2d 1266 (Ind. Ct. App. 4th Dist. 1986).

[97]Matter of Burdick, 65 B.R. 105 (Bankr. N.D. Ind. 1986) (applying Indiana law).

Forms References: Acts Constitution Conversion. 7A Am Jur Pleading and Practice Forms, Annotated (rev. ed.), Conversion §§ 14-39.

[98]Rinker v. Rinker, 20 Ind. 185, 1863 WL 2105 (1863); National Fleet Supply, Inc. v. Fairchild, 450 N.E.2d 1015, 36 U.C.C. Rep. Serv. (CBC)

and dominion over property,[99] an unwarranted assumption of ownership,[1] an illegal use or abuse of a chattel,[2] and a wrongful detention after demand.[3] Perpetrators of a fraud may be held liable for conversion of the property obtained by the fraud.[4] Where two or more persons participate in the acts constituting the conversion, they will be jointly liable.[5]

Conversion may occur where a principal refuses to deliver goods for which an agent has received payment.[6] A person who is not the owner, but who sells and delivers goods without authorization, is also liable for conversion.[7] Conversely, a sale with authority does not constitute conversion.[8]

When a third person gains possession of personal property from a person having no authority to dispose of it, and he or she subsequently exercises dominion over it, the third person thereby becomes liable to the owner for conversion.[9]

It is unlawful to seize property of another without legal process, lien, or agreement and to hold it until a debt is

---

480 (Ind. Ct. App. 3d Dist. 1983) (abrogated on other grounds by, Mitchell v. Mitchell, 695 N.E.2d 920 (Ind. 1998)).

[99]Foley v. Colby, 148 Ind. App. 391, 266 N.E.2d 619 (Div. 2 1971).

[1]Bishplinghoff v. Bauer, 52 Ind. 519, 1876 WL 6442 (1876).

[2]Block v. Talge, 221 Ind. 658, 51 N.E.2d 81 (1943).

[3]Yoder Feed Service v. Allied Pullets, Inc., 171 Ind. App. 692, 359 N.E.2d 602 (3d Dist. 1977).

[4]Eppert v. Lowish, 91 Ind. App. 231, 168 N.E. 616 (1929), reh'g denied, 91 Ind. App. 231, 169 N.E. 884 (1930).

[5]Terrell v. Butterfield, 92 Ind. 1, 1883 WL 5725 (1883); Stephenson v. Feezer, 55 Ind. 416, 1876 WL 6868 (1876); Kavanaugh v. Taylor, 2 Ind. App. 502, 28 N.E. 553 (1891).

[6]Tippecanoe Beverages, Inc. v. S.A. El Aguila Brewing Co., 833 F.2d 633, 24 Fed. R. Evid. Serv. (LCP) 336 (7th Cir. 1987) (applying Indiana law) (Spanish brewer liable where brewer's American agent vanished after receiving a payment from the distributor for beer which was never shipped by the brewer).

[7]Sikora v. Barney, 138 Ind. App. 686, 207 N.E.2d 846 (Div. 2 1965).

[8]Beaver Products Co. v. Voorhees, 81 Ind. App. 181, 142 N.E. 717 (Div. 2 1924).

[9]Alexander v. Swackhamer, 105 Ind. 81, 4 N.E. 433 (1886), reh'g denied, 105 Ind. 81, 5 N.E. 908 (1886); Harlan v. Brown, 4 Ind. App. 319, 30 N.E. 928 (1892).

paid.[10] Conversion may also result from a wrongful seizure under legal process or proceedings, or from a wrongful confiscation of private property by public authorities;[11] however, where property was taken under proper legal process, the original owner generally may not recover from either the officer or the ultimate holder.[12]

An action for conversion is not a substitute for a breach of contract claim. A simple refusal to pay a debt does not constitute conversion.[13] Mere nonfeasance or failure to perform a duty imposed by contract or implied by law does not constitute a conversion.[14] Failing to hire honest employees has also been held not to constitute conversion.[15]

§ 16 Acts constituting criminal conversion

Criminal conversion is defined by statute as the knowing or intentional exertion of unauthorized control over the property of another person. The statute specifies the acts that may constitute unauthorized control.

West's Digest, Trover and Conversion ⚖4-8, 10-12.

Criminal conversion, for which civil recovery is authorized,[16] is defined by statute as the knowing[17] or intentional[18] exertion of unauthorized control over the property of

---

[10]Tucker v. Capital City Riggers, 437 N.E.2d 1048 (Ind. Ct. App. 1st Dist. 1982).

[11]89 C.J.S., Trover and Conversion § 40.

Forms References: Who May Bring Action; Parties Liable—Persons Seizing, or Having Property Seized, Under Process of Law. 7A Am Jur Pleading and Practice Forms, Annotated (rev. ed.), Conversion §§ 95-102.

[12]Dawson v. Sparks, 77 Ind. 88, 1881 WL 7263 (1881); Moore v. Winstead, 24 Ind. App. 56, 55 N.E. 777 (1899).

[13]Kopis v. Savage, 498 N.E.2d 1266 (Ind. Ct. App. 4th Dist. 1986).

[14]National Fleet Supply, Inc. v. Fairchild, 450 N.E.2d 1015, 36 U.C.C. Rep. Serv. (CBC) 480 (Ind. Ct. App. 3d Dist. 1983) (abrogated on other grounds by, Mitchell v. Mitchell, 695 N.E.2d 920 (Ind. 1998)).

[15]Eagle Mach. Co. v. American Dist. Tel. Co., 127 Ind. App. 403, 140 N.E.2d 756 (1957).

[16]As to civil recovery for criminal conversion, generally, see § 10.

[17]For purposes of the statute, a person engages in conduct "knowingly" if, at the time of the conduct, the person is aware of a high probability that he or she is doing so.—IC 35-41-2-2(b).

[18]For purposes of the statute, a person engages in conduct "intention-

another person.[19] For purposes of the statute, exerting control over property means obtaining, taking, carrying, driving, leading away, concealing, abandoning, selling, conveying, encumbering, or possessing property, or securing, transferring, or extending a right to property.[20]

A person's control over the property of another person is "unauthorized," for purposes of the criminal conversion statute, if it is exerted:[21]

- without the other person's consent
- in a manner or to an extent other than that to which the other person has consented
- by transferring or encumbering other property while failing to disclose a lien, adverse claim, or other legal impediment to the enjoyment of such other property
- by creating or confirming a false impression in the other person
- by failing to correct a false impression that the accused knows is influencing the other person, if the accused stands in a relationship of special trust to the other person
- by promising performance that the person knows will not be performed
- by expressing an intention to damage the property or impair the rights of any other person

§ 17 Conduct and liability of particular persons, or with respect to particular property

The identity of the persons, or the type of property, involved in a particular transaction may have a bearing on whether there has been a conversion.

West's Digest, Trover and Conversion ⚖4-8, 10-12.

An agent's refusal to deliver goods purchased on behalf of

---

ally" if, when he or she engages in the conduct, it is the person's conscious objective to do so.—IC 35-41-2-2(a).

[19] IC 35-43-4-3.

As to what constitutes unauthorized control of property for purposes of criminal liability for theft, generally, see I.L.E., Theft and Related Offenses.

[20] IC 35-43-4-1(a).

[21] IC 35-43-4-1(b).

the agent's principal constitutes conversion of the goods.[22] An agent cannot escape personal liability for conversion simply because he or she acted on behalf of a principal,[23] and a principal cannot escape liability for conversions committed by its agent.[24]

An auctioneer who sells stolen property or property as to which there is a valid lien is liable for conversion, even where the auctioneer did not have knowledge of the principal's lack of authority to sell.[25]

If a member of a partnership converts funds to the use of the partnership, the firm, and each member of the firm, is liable for the conversion.[26] On the other hand, although a corporate officer may be held liable for treble damages for criminal conversion, the corporate officer and the corporation would not each be liable for such damages.[27]

An employer's continued acceptance of employee health premiums, after the employee's insurance coverage has terminated, constitutes conversion.[28] A bank is liable for

---

[22]Nading v. Howe, 23 Ind. App. 690, 55 N.E. 1032 (1900).

Forms References: Who May Bring Action; Parties Liable—In General. 7A Am Jur Pleading and Practice Forms, Annotated (rev. ed.), Conversion §§ 51-74.

[23]Howard Dodge & Sons, Inc. v. Finn, 181 Ind. App. 209, 391 N.E.2d 638, 26 U.C.C. Rep. Serv. (CBC) 886 (3d Dist. 1979).

[24]Tippecanoe Beverages, Inc. v. S.A. El Aguila Brewing Co., 833 F.2d 633, 24 Fed. R. Evid. Serv. (LCP) 336 (7th Cir. 1987) (applying Indiana law) (Spanish brewer liable where brewer's American agent vanished after receiving a payment from the distributor for beer which brewer never shipped).

[25]Bottema v. Producers Livestock Ass'n, 174 Ind. App. 206, 366 N.E.2d 1189 (1st Dist. 1977).

[26]Comer v. Hayworth, 30 Ind. App. 144, 65 N.E. 595 (Div. 1 1902).

Annotation References: Liability of corporate directors or officers for negligence in permitting conversion of property of third persons by corporation, 29 ALR3d 660.

[27]Roake v. Christensen, 528 N.E.2d 789 (Ind. Ct. App. 2d Dist. 1988).

As to civil recovery for criminal conversion, generally, see § 12.

As to damages and other amounts recoverable for criminal conversion, see § 28.

[28]Roake v. Christensen, 528 N.E.2d 789 (Ind. Ct. App. 2d Dist. 1988).

conversion when it wrongfully pays out a savings account without authority to do so.[29]

If a person converts to the person's own use the personal property of a decedent before the appointment of a personal representative, the person is liable to the estate for the value of the property converted.[30] A fiduciary engaged in a pattern of taking funds from a decedent's estate without legal authority commits criminal conversion.[31]

Criminal conversion is committed where one knowingly or intentionally transfers or reproduces recorded sounds or a live performance without consent of the owner of the master recording or the live performance, with intent to distribute the reproductions for a profit.[32]

§ 18 —Bailees

A bailee may be liable for conversion where he or she refuses to deliver the goods pursuant to the terms of the bailment contract, or misdelivers or misappropriates the goods.

West's Digest, Trover and Conversion ⚭4-8, 10-12.

Where a bailee refuses to deliver the goods pursuant to the terms of the bailment contract, the bailee loses the lien on the goods and is liable for conversion.[33] The bailee is also liable for conversion if he or she voluntarily delivers the

---

[29]Indianapolis Saenger Chor, Inc. v. American Fletcher Nat. Bank & Trust Co., 149 Ind. App. 665, 274 N.E.2d 728 (Div. 1 1971).

[30]IC 29-1-13-9.

Forms References: Who May Bring Action; Parties Liable—Administrators, Executors, and Guardians. 7A Am Jur Pleading and Practice Forms, Annotated (rev. ed.), Conversion §§ 75-80.

[31]Matter of Woolbert, 672 N.E.2d 412 (Ind. 1996); Matter of Clanin, 619 N.E.2d 269 (Ind. 1993).

[32]IC 35-43-4-1(b)(8).

[33]Mockford v. Iles, 217 Ind. 137, 26 N.E.2d 42 (1940).

Annotation References: Elements and measure of damages recoverable from bailee for loss, destruction, or conversion of personal papers, photographs, or paintings, 9 ALR4th 1245.

Forms References: Who May Bring Action; Parties Liable—Bailors and Bailees. 7A Am Jur Pleading and Practice Forms, Annotated (rev. ed.), Conversion §§ 81-94.

Trial Strategy References: Bailee's Liability for Damage, Loss, or Theft of Bailed Property, 46 Am Jur POF3d 361.

goods to the wrong person[34] or misappropriates the bailed item.[35]

A conversion by a bailee implies some wrongful act, and mere nonfeasance or failure to perform a duty imposed by contract or implied by law does not constitute a conversion.[36] If a bailee handles the goods of the bailor in the manner customary in the trade of the bailee, the bailee will not be liable for conversion.[37]

§ 19 —Landowners and landlords

A landowner's refusal to admit a stranger to the premises to retrieve goods claimed by the stranger does not constitute conversion, but the landowner is liable if he or she refuses to give up previously converted goods that are stored on the property. A landlord may be liable for conversion by refusing to permit a tenant to return to the rented property to recover his or her possessions.

West's Digest, Trover and Conversion ☞4-8, 10-12.

A landowner's refusal to admit a stranger to his or her premises for the purpose of retrieving goods assertedly belonging to the stranger does not constitute conversion;[38] however, the property the stranger attempts to claim must have gotten onto the landowner's premises without any action of the landowner, and the landowner will be liable if he or she refuses to give up previously converted goods that are stored on the property.[39]

A landlord may be a bailee where he or she has charge of a tenant's possessions, and may be liable for conversion by refusing to permit a tenant to return to the rented property to recover such possessions.[40] A landlord may also be guilty of conversion by breaking the lock on an apartment building's

---

[34]Cleveland, C., C. & St. L. R. Co. v. Wright, 25 Ind. App. 525, 58 N.E. 559 (1900).

[35]Monarch Buick Co. v. Kennedy, 138 Ind. App. 1, 209 N.E.2d 922 (Div. 2 1965).

[36]Vandalia R. Co. v. Upson Nut Co., 55 Ind. App. 252, 101 N.E. 114 (1913).

[37]Morningstar v. Cunningham, 110 Ind. 328, 11 N.E. 593 (1887).

[38]Chicago, I. & L. Ry. Co. v. Pope, 99 Ind. App. 280, 188 N.E. 594 (1934).

[39]Valentine v. Duff, 7 Ind. App. 196, 33 N.E. 529 (1893), reh'g denied, 7 Ind. App. 196, 34 N.E. 453 (1893).

[40]Campbell v. Criterion Group, 621 N.E.2d 342 (Ind. Ct. App. 1st Dist. 1993), appeal after remand, 701 N.E.2d 616 (Ind. Ct. App. 1998).

storage locker and disposing of a tenant's property stored therein.[41]

§ 20 —Lienholders and secured parties

Lienholders and secured parties may be liable for conversion if they fail to return goods or dispose of them improperly.

West's Digest, Trover and Conversion ☞4-8, 10-12.

A refusal to release goods held under a lien does not constitute conversion by the lienor,[42] unless the lienee has tendered the amount due on the lien, and the lienor has refused to accept the tender.[43]

Indiana statutes govern the disposal of property subject to a security interest.[44] A secured party is subject to liability to a debtor or to any person entitled to receive notice of a disposition of collateral if the secured party does not comply with statutory requirements for disposition of the collateral.[45] Where a party has a security interest in an item which gives a possessory right, taking possession of that item will not constitute conversion.[46]

§ 21 —Negotiable instruments and persons dealing therewith

A negotiable instrument is converted if it is taken by transfer, other than a negotiation, from a person not entitled to enforce the instrument, or if a bank makes or obtains payment with respect to the instrument for a person not entitled to enforce the instrument or receive payment.

West's Digest, Trover and Conversion ☞4-8, 10-12.

Indiana's version of the Uniform Commercial Code provides that a negotiable instrument is converted if it is

---

As to the liability for conversion of bailees, generally, see § 18.

[41]Foley v. Colby, 148 Ind. App. 391, 266 N.E.2d 619 (Div. 2 1971).

[42]Welker v. Appleman, 44 Ind. App. 699, 90 N.E. 35 (Div. 1 1909).

[43]Yoder Feed Service v. Allied Pullets, Inc., 171 Ind. App. 692, 359 N.E.2d 602 (3d Dist. 1977).

[44]IC 26-1-9-501 et seq.

[45]IC 26-1-9-507.

[46]Matter of Vitreous Steel Products Co., 911 F.2d 1223, 12 U.C.C. Rep. Serv. 2d (CBC) 549 (7th Cir. 1990), reh'g denied, (Oct. 5, 1990).

taken by transfer, other than a negotiation, from a person not entitled to enforce the instrument, or if a bank makes or obtains payment with respect to the instrument for a person not entitled to enforce the instrument or receive payment.[47]

> ◆ **Observation:** While the Commercial Code lists ways in which a negotiable instrument may be converted, it does not set forth the elements constituting the tort of conversion, which are found in the principles of law and equity which supplement the Code.[48]

A representative, other than a depositary bank, who has in good faith dealt with a negotiable instrument or its proceeds on behalf of one who was not the person entitled to enforce the instrument is not liable in conversion to that person beyond the amount of any proceeds that it has not paid out.[49]

An action for conversion of an instrument may not be brought by: (1) the issuer or acceptor of the instrument, or (2) a payee or endorsee who did not receive delivery of the instrument either directly or through delivery to an agent or a copayee.[50]

§ 22 Rights of third persons

> **Third persons who purchase converted property from the original converter generally do not obtain title to the property, even when the purchase was made in good faith for value, except in cases of strong societal interest, such as corporate stock. Generally, one who receives money in good faith for valuable consideration prevails over the victim of conversion.**

West's Digest, Trover and Conversion ☞25.

Third persons coming into possession of converted goods seldom are favored by the courts.[51] If the original conversion was a theft, a purchaser from the thief can generally acquire

---

[47]IC 26-1-3.1-420(a).

Annotation References: Payee's right of recovery, in conversion under UCC § 3-419(1) (c), for money paid on unauthorized indorsement, 23 ALR4th 855.

[48]Yeager & Sullivan, Inc. v. Farmers Bank, 162 Ind. App. 15, 317 N.E.2d 792, 15 U.C.C. Rep. Serv. (CBC) 892 (2d Dist. 1974).

[49]IC 26-1-3.1-420(c).

[50]IC 26-1-3.1-420(a).

[51]Marshall v. Beeber, 53 Ind. 83, 1876 WL 6464 (1876).

no title, regardless of his or her innocence or good faith in making the purchase.[52] An exception exists where there is a strong societal interest in promoting the free flow of an item, such as corporate stock.[53]

◆ **Observation:** Indiana statutes set forth the rights acquired by a stock purchaser and identify the class of individuals who are "protected purchasers."[54]

If a bailee executes a chattel mortgage on the goods entrusted to his or her care, and the mortgagee forecloses on the mortgage, the mortgagee obtains no title to the goods, but is liable in damages to the bailor.[55] Where a bailor clothes the bailee with apparent ownership of the goods by allowing the goods to be put in a common mass, the bailor is estopped to assert title to the goods against an innocent purchaser for value.[56]

As a general rule, one who receives money in good faith for valuable consideration prevails over the victim of conversion. Therefore, a defendant was not liable for conversion, where the defendant, without knowledge, received from an embezzler money from time to time in sales transactions.[57] On the other hand, one who receives money feloniously converted by another as payment for a pre-existing debt acquires no title to the money.[58]

B.   DAMAGES AND OTHER AMOUNTS
RECOVERABLE

Research References
IC 26-1-3.1-420; IC 34-24-3-1; IC 34-24-3-3; IC 34-51-3-2

18 Am Jur 2d, Conversion §§ 105-142.
89 C.J.S., Trover and Conversion §§ 161-201.
West's Digest, Trover and Conversion ⊜41, 43-60.

---

[52]Shearer v. Evans, 89 Ind. 400, 1883 WL 5858 (1883).

[53]Citizens' Street Ry. Co. v. Robbins, 128 Ind. 449, 26 N.E. 116 (1891).

[54]IC 26-1-8.1-302; IC 26-1-8.1-303.

[55]Schindler v. Westover, 99 Ind. 395, 1884 WL 5892 (1884).

As to the liability of a bailee for conversion, generally, see § 18.

[56]Preston v. Witherspoon, 109 Ind. 457, 9 N.E. 585 (1886).

[57]Ohio Cas. Ins. Co. v. Smith, 297 F.2d 265 (7th Cir. 1962) (applying Indiana law).

[58]Porter v. Roseman, 165 Ind. 255, 74 N.E. 1105 (1905).

ALR Digest: Conversion § 50
ALR Index: Conversion; Equitable Conversion; Equity; Personal
    Property; Property; Replevin; Sale and Transfer of Property
7A Am Jur Pleading and Practice Forms, Annotated (rev. ed.),
    Conversion §§ 40-50.
Damages for Loss of Personal Property With Little or No Market
    Value, 3 Am Jur POF3d 171.

§ 23   Generally

**As a general rule, damages for conversion are the
amount necessary to compensate plaintiff or all actual
losses or injuries sustained as a natural result of the
defendant's wrong.**

West's Digest, Trover and Conversion ☞41.

As a general rule, the plaintiff's damages in an action for
tortious conversion are measured by the sum necessary to
compensate the plaintiff for all actual losses or injuries
sustained as a natural and proximate result of the defendant's wrong.[59] Such damages are generally measured by
fair market value at time of conversion, plus interest,[60] and
the plaintiff may also recover punitive damages where appropriate.[61] In a civil action for criminal conversion, the
plaintiff may recover up to three times the amount of the
loss, plus specified costs and attorney fees.[62] If there has been
a technical conversion, the defendant is liable for at least
nominal damages, even if the property has been returned to
the plaintiff.[63]

------

[59]Johnson v. Culver, 116 Ind. 278, 19 N.E. 129 (1888); Yoder Feed Service v. Allied Pullets, Inc., 171 Ind. App. 692, 359 N.E.2d 602 (3d Dist.
1977).
    Annotation References: Comment note.—measure of damages for
conversion of corporate stock or certificate, 31 ALR3d 1286.
    Forms References: Damages. 7A Am Jur Pleading and Practice
Forms, Annotated (rev. ed.), Conversion §§ 40-50.
    [60]§ 24.
    Trial Strategy References: Damages for Loss of Personal Property
With Little or No Market Value, 3 Am Jur POF3d 171.
    [61]§ 26.
    [62]§ 28.
    [63]Coffel v. Perry, 452 N.E.2d 1066 (Ind. Ct. App. 2d Dist. 1983).

Damages for conversion are largely within the discretion of the trier of facts, and will seldom be disturbed on appeal unless there exists obvious prejudice.[64]

A plaintiff having only a special or qualified right or interest may recover the full value of the converted property, as against a stranger; but as against one having an interest or right in the property, recovery is limited to the value of the plaintiff's interest or right.[65]

§ 24   Measures of compensatory damages

Generally, compensatory damages for tortious conversion are measured by the fair market value at the time of conversion, plus interest.

West's Digest, Trover and Conversion ☞41, 43-54.

The measure of damages for tortious conversion is generally the fair market value of the goods at the time and place of conversion, plus interest.[66] A failure to award interest may be reversible error.[67]

Fair market value has been defined as the price at which a willing buyer and seller will trade,[68] or the value at which a prudent owner would sell if he or she could choose the time and terms.[69] In this connection, conversion has been described as a "forced sale" of the item converted.[70] An award of any damages beyond the value of the converted property at the time of the conversion should not be speculative and

---

[64]Sikora v. Barney, 138 Ind. App. 686, 207 N.E.2d 846 (Div. 2 1965).

[65]Carson v. Hanawalt, 50 Ind. App. 409, 98 N.E. 448 (Div. 1 1912).

[66]Chaiken v. Eldon Emmor & Co., Inc., 597 N.E.2d 337 (Ind. Ct. App. 3d Dist. 1992), transfer denied, (Jan. 26, 1993); THQ Venture v. SW, Inc., 444 N.E.2d 335 (Ind. Ct. App. 1st Dist. 1983).

[67]Fort Wayne Nat. Bank v. Scher, 419 N.E.2d 1308 (Ind. Ct. App. 3d Dist. 1981).

[68]Sikora v. Barney, 138 Ind. App. 686, 207 N.E.2d 846 (Div. 2 1965).

[69]Bottema v. Producers Livestock Ass'n, 174 Ind. App. 206, 366 N.E.2d 1189 (1st Dist. 1977).

[70]Plymouth Fertilizer Co., Inc. v. Balmer, 488 N.E.2d 1129 (Ind. Ct. App. 3d Dist. 1986), reh'g denied, (Apr. 4, 1986) and transfer denied, (July 14, 1986).

should compensate the plaintiff only for actual damage or loss.[71]

The amount retained by the converter is not necessarily a proper measure of damages as, for example, in the case of a private sale by the converter.[72] Evidence of sales prices of property similar to the converted property may be received,[73] but evidence of a private sale, where the converters did not represent the owner's best interests, was not proper.[74]

Where property fluctuates in value, a different measure of damages may be applied. For corporate stock, the measure of damages is the highest intermediate value of the stock between the time of conversion and a reasonable time after the owner has received notice of the conversion.[75]

Lost profits may be a proper measure of value when converted property is destroyed.[76] Where the converted property is returned, a proper measure of damages is the fair rental value for the period of the conversion.[77]

Notwithstanding any statute providing a measure of damages for conversion,[78] in an action for conversion of a negotiable instrument, the measure of liability is presumed to be the amount payable on the instrument, but recovery may not exceed the amount of the plaintiff's interest in the instrument.[79]

The value of converted growing crops may include estimates of the value of the crop when it is harvested, and is not limited to the value of the crop at the time of conversion.

---

[71]Universal C. I. T. Credit Corp. v. Shepler, 164 Ind. App. 516, 329 N.E.2d 620, 17 U.C.C. Rep. Serv. (CBC) 602 (1st Dist. 1975).

[72]Bottema v. Producers Livestock Ass'n, 174 Ind. App. 206, 366 N.E.2d 1189 (1st Dist. 1977).

[73]Sikora v. Barney, 138 Ind. App. 686, 207 N.E.2d 846 (Div. 2 1965).

[74]Bottema v. Producers Livestock Ass'n, 174 Ind. App. 206, 366 N.E.2d 1189 (1st Dist. 1977).

[75]Chaiken v. Eldon Emmor & Co., Inc., 597 N.E.2d 337 (Ind. Ct. App. 3d Dist. 1992), transfer denied, (Jan. 26, 1993).

[76]Jerry Alderman Ford Sales, Inc. v. Bailey, 154 Ind. App. 632, 291 N.E.2d 92, 12 U.C.C. Rep. Serv. (CBC) 47 (2d Dist. 1972), reh'g denied and opinion modified on other grounds, 154 Ind. App. 632, 294 N.E.2d 617, 12 U.C.C. Rep. Serv. (CBC) 442 (2d Dist. 1973).

[77]Coffel v. Perry, 452 N.E.2d 1066 (Ind. Ct. App. 2d Dist. 1983).

[78]See, for example, IC 34-24-3-1 (criminal conversion), discussed in § 28.

[79]IC 26-1-3.1-420(b).

The estimate is to be arrived at from all material facts that would affect it, including quality of the land, its fertility and productivity, and the probability or improbability that a particular crop would mature on a particular tract.[80]

§ 25 —Household goods

When household goods are converted, the measure of damages is not fair market value, but rather the value to the owner.

West's Digest, Trover and Conversion ☞47.

When the items converted are used household goods, fair market value is not the measure of damages.[81] Courts attempt to determine the value of the goods to the owner, based on the actual money loss resulting from being deprived of the property, or the difference in actual value caused by the injury.[82] The court should consider any fact which goes to show the true value of the items, including cost, condition, and age, as well as any damage through use, decay, or otherwise.[83] If the property has little or no market value, and is of a special or higher value to the plaintiff, the value to be taken as the measure of recovery is the actual and fair value to the plaintiff, provided it is not merely fanciful or sentimental.[84]

§ 26 Special and punitive damages; attorney fees

If special damages are pleaded and proved, they may be

---

[80]Richardson v. Scroggham, 159 Ind. App. 400, 307 N.E.2d 80 (1st Dist. 1974).

[81]Cannon v. Northside Transfer Co., Inc., 427 N.E.2d 712 (Ind. Ct. App. 2d Dist. 1981).

Annotation References: Valuation of wearing apparel or household goods kept by owner for personal use, in action for loss or conversion of, or injury to, such property, 34 ALR3d 816.

[82]Cannon v. Northside Transfer Co., Inc., 427 N.E.2d 712 (Ind. Ct. App. 2d Dist. 1981).

[83]Cannon v. Northside Transfer Co., Inc., 427 N.E.2d 712 (Ind. Ct. App. 2d Dist. 1981); Anchor Stove & Furniture Co. v. Blackwood, 109 Ind. App. 357, 35 N.E.2d 117 (1941)

[84]Anchor Stove & Furniture Co. v. Blackwood, 109 Ind. App. 357, 35 N.E.2d 117 (1941); Mitchell v. Mitchell, 685 N.E.2d 1083 (Ind. Ct. App. 1997), reh'g denied, (Sept. 17, 1997) and transfer granted, opinion vacated on other grounds, 698 N.E.2d 1194 (Ind. 1998) and opinion aff'd in part, vacated in part on other grounds, 695 N.E.2d 920 (Ind. 1998).

> recovered by the plaintiff in an action for tortious conversion, and where a conversion has been malicious, wanton, or reckless, punitive damages may also be awarded.

West's Digest, Trover and Conversion ☞54, 60.

If special damages are pleaded and proved, the plaintiff may recover for all injuries or losses sustained as a direct and proximate result of a tortious conversion.[85] Under Indiana law, mental anguish is not recoverable as damages for such a wrong.[86]

Where a conversion has been malicious, wanton, or reckless, it is proper to submit to the jury the question of exemplary or punitive damages.[87] Actual damages are necessary before a court will award punitive damages for conversion.[88] The facts relied upon to support the recovery of punitive damages must be proved by clear and convincing evidence.[89] An award of punitive damages for conversion will be upheld on appeal unless it is so excessive as to shock the conscience.[90]

Plaintiff may not recover both punitive damages for tortious conversion and the amounts provided for under Indiana's criminal conversion statute.[91] It is not a defense in an action seeking punitive damages for tortious conversion that the defendant is subject to criminal prosecution for the act or omission that gave rise to the civil action.[92]

---

[85]Miller v. Long, 126 Ind. App. 482, 131 N.E.2d 348 (1956), reh'g denied, 126 Ind. App. 482, 132 N.E.2d 272 (1956).

[86]Jeffersonville Silgas, Inc. v. Wilson, 154 Ind. App. 398, 290 N.E.2d 113 (1st Dist. 1972).

[87]Monarch Buick Co. v. Kennedy, 138 Ind. App. 1, 209 N.E.2d 922 (Div. 2 1965).

[88]Indiana & Michigan Elec. Co. v. Terre Haute Industries, Inc., 507 N.E.2d 588 (Ind. Ct. App. 1st Dist. 1987), reh'g denied, (June 12, 1987) and transfer denied, 525 N.E.2d 1247 (Ind. 1988).

[89]IC 34-51-3-2.

[90]Richardson v. Scroggham, 159 Ind. App. 400, 307 N.E.2d 80 (1st Dist. 1974).

[91]IC 34-24-3-3.

As to damages and other amounts recoverable for criminal conversion, generally, see § 28.

[92]IC 34-24-3-3.

For tortious conversion, absent statutory or contractual agreement, attorney fees are not available.[93]

§ 27 Mitigation or reduction of damages

The defendant in an action for conversion may mitigate the plaintiff's damages by showing that proceeds of the converted property were applied to discharge a debt of the plaintiff, by the discharge of a lien on the converted property, or by return of the converted property to its owner.

West's Digest, Trover and Conversion ☜56-59.

A converter may mitigate damages otherwise due for the conversion by showing that the proceeds of the converted property were applied to discharge a debt owed by the injured party.[94] Mitigation may also be shown by the discharge of a lien to which the converted property was subject,[95] or by return of the converted property to its owner.[96] The burden is on the defendant to prove any facts in favor of mitigation.[97]

Where a defendant repudiates the possession of goods under a contract with the plaintiff and converts them to his or her own use, the defendant may not claim the benefit of the contract in mitigation of damages, because to do so would be to claim under inconsistent rights.[98]

If the converter increases the value of the converted item, the amount of the plaintiff's recovery depends on the nature of the act constituting conversion. If the converter acted through a mistake, damages will be reduced by the amount by which the converter's labor increased the value.[99]

---

[93]Yates-Cobb v. Hays, 681 N.E.2d 729 (Ind. Ct. App. 1997).

[94]Yeager & Sullivan, Inc. v. Farmers Bank, 162 Ind. App. 15, 317 N.E.2d 792, 15 U.C.C. Rep. Serv. (CBC) 892 (2d Dist. 1974).

[95]Yeager & Sullivan, Inc. v. Farmers Bank, 162 Ind. App. 15, 317 N.E.2d 792, 15 U.C.C. Rep. Serv. (CBC) 892 (2d Dist. 1974).

[96]Smith v. Downing, 6 Ind. 374, 1855 WL 3581 (1855); Coffel v. Perry, 452 N.E.2d 1066 (Ind. Ct. App. 2d Dist. 1983).

[97]Yeager & Sullivan, Inc. v. Farmers Bank, 162 Ind. App. 15, 317 N.E.2d 792, 15 U.C.C. Rep. Serv. (CBC) 892 (2d Dist. 1974).

[98]Yoder Feed Service v. Allied Pullets, Inc., 171 Ind. App. 692, 359 N.E.2d 602 (3d Dist. 1977).

[99]Plymouth Fertilizer Co., Inc. v. Balmer, 488 N.E.2d 1129 (Ind. Ct.

§ 28 Damages and other amounts recoverable for criminal conversion

For criminal conversion, a plaintiff may recover up to three times the actual damages suffered, as well as costs, attorney fees, and other expenses.

West's Digest, Trover and Conversion ☞41, 54, 55, 60.

By statute, if a person suffers a pecuniary loss as the result of a criminal conversion, the victim may bring a civil action against the person who caused the loss for the following items:[1]

- an amount not to exceed three times the actual damages
- the costs of the action
- a reasonable attorney fee
- actual travel expenses that are not otherwise reimbursed and are incurred to file papers and attend court proceedings related to the recovery of a civil judgment, or to provide witnesses to testify in court proceedings
- a reasonable amount to compensate the person suffering loss for time used to file papers and attend court proceedings, or to travel to and from the place where papers are filed and court proceedings are held
- actual and direct and indirect expenses incurred by the person suffering loss to compensate employees and agents for the time used to file papers and attend court proceedings, or to travel to and from the place where papers are filed and court proceedings are held
- all other reasonable costs of collection

Where prejudgment interest is a proper element of actual damages for conversion, an award of such interest may be trebled under the statute, along with other actual damages.[2] For purposes of the statute, a "reasonable attorney's fee" includes appellate fees.[3]

App. 3d Dist. 1986), reh'g denied, (Apr. 4, 1986) and transfer denied, (July 14, 1986).

[1]IC 34-24-3-1.

[2]Midland-Guardian Co. v. United Consumers Club, Inc., 499 N.E.2d 792 (Ind. Ct. App. 3d Dist. 1986), reh'g denied, 502 N.E.2d 1354 (Ind. Ct. App. 3d Dist. 1987), transfer denied, (Oct. 15, 1987).

[3]Rakes v. Wright, 498 N.E.2d 101 (Ind. Ct. App. 4th Dist. 1986),

The right to collect treble damages for criminal conversion is a personal right which is not assignable.[4]

C. ACTIONS

Research References

IC 34-1-2-2
Trial R. 8

18 Am Jur 2d, Conversion §§ 57-180.
89 C.J.S., Trover and Conversion §§ 63-201.
West's Digest, Trover and Conversion ☞ 13-18, 22, 28, 32, 33, 35-40, 64, 66-70.
ALR Digest: Conversion §§ 37.5-52
ALR Index: Conversion; Equitable Conversion; Equity; Personal Property; Property; Replevin; Sale and Transfer of Property
7A Am Jur Pleading and Practice Forms, Annotated (rev. ed.), Conversion §§ 9-13.

§ 29 Generally

An action for conversion is a tort remedy to recover the value of the property, not the property itself.

West's Digest, Trover and Conversion ☞13-18.

An action for conversion is a tort action. It is a remedy to recover the value of the property wrongfully converted, and not the specific property itself. The action will lie even though it is not an exclusive remedy and other remedies are available.[5]

The action will not lie unless, at the time of the conversion, the plaintiff had a general or special right of property and a right of possession, or actual possession.[6] The plaintiff must prove the right to possession on the strength of his or her own title, not merely the weakness of the defendant's title or

---

opinion amended on other grounds, 500 N.E.2d 234 (Ind. Ct. App. 4th Dist. 1986); Lambert v. Yellowbird, Inc., 496 N.E.2d 406 (Ind. Ct. App. 4th Dist. 1986), decision clarified on denial of reh'g, 498 N.E.2d 80 (Ind. Ct. App. 4th Dist. 1986), transfer denied, (Jan. 21, 1987).

[4]Hart Conversions, Inc. v. Pyramid Seating Co., Inc., 658 N.E.2d 129 (Ind. Ct. App. 1995).

[5]Lambert v. Yellowbird, Inc., 496 N.E.2d 406 (Ind. Ct. App. 4th Dist. 1986), decision clarified on denial of reh'g, 498 N.E.2d 80 (Ind. Ct. App. 4th Dist. 1986), transfer denied, (Jan. 21, 1987).

[6]Bricker v. Hughes, 4 Ind. 146, 1853 WL 3294 (1853); Grady v. Newby, 6 Blackf. 442, 1843 WL 2981 (Ind. 1843); Ax v. Schloot, 118 Ind. App. 458,

right of possession.[7] An executor or administrator having title or right of immediate possession may maintain an action for conversion of the decedent's goods.[8]

Joint owners of a chattel may unite in an action for a conversion of it, without showing the exact interest in it of each, and a part owner may maintain an action for the conversion of his or her interest.[9]

§ 30 Limitation of actions

The limitations period for commencing a conversion action is prescribed by statute, and begins to run only when the tortfeasor manifests an intent to permanently deprive the owner of the personal property.

West's Digest, Trover and Conversion ⊙⇒28.

An action for conversion is governed by a two-year statute of limitations.[10] The limitations period begins to run only when the tortfeasor manifests an intent to deprive the owner of the personal property permanently.[11] The statute begins to run even if the plaintiff does not have notice, unless the defendant has actively concealed the conversion.[12]

No demand is necessary to commence running the statute of limitations for conversion.[13]

---

81 N.E.2d 379 (1948); Blumberg v. Coleman, 75 Ind. App. 293, 129 N.E. 489 (Div. 2 1921).

[7]Tucker v. Capital City Riggers, 437 N.E.2d 1048 (Ind. Ct. App. 1st Dist. 1982).

[8]Clegg v. Bamberger, 110 Ind. 536, 9 N.E. 700 (1887).

[9]Scott v. Ramsey, 82 Ind. 330, 1882 WL 6184 (1882); Carson v. Hanawalt, 50 Ind. App. 409, 98 N.E. 448 (Div. 1 1912).

[10]IC 34-1-2-2.

Browning v. Walters, 616 N.E.2d 1040 (Ind. Ct. App. 1st Dist. 1993), opinion adhered to on reh'g, 620 N.E.2d 28 (Ind. Ct. App. 1st Dist. 1993) (criminal conversion); Buchonok v. Emerick, 558 N.E.2d 1092 (Ind. 1990) (tortious conversion).

[11]Buchonok v. Emerick, 558 N.E.2d 1092 (Ind. 1990).

Annotation References: When statute of limitations begins to run against action for conversion of property by theft, 79 ALR3d 847.

[12]French v. Hickman Moving and Storage, 400 N.E.2d 1384 (Ind. Ct. App. 3d Dist. 1980).

[13]French v. Hickman Moving and Storage, 400 N.E.2d 1384 (Ind. Ct. App. 3d Dist. 1980).

§ 31 Choice of law

The law of the place where the conversion occurred governs an action for conversion.

West's Digest, Trover and Conversion ⚬⟶13.

An action for conversion is governed by the law of the place where the conversion occurred.[14]

◆ **Illustration:** Indiana law applied where the removal of parts from a New Mexico corporation's helicopter transmission and the placement of those parts on an Indiana corporation's helicopter—and, therefore, the unauthorized control over the transmission, took place in Indiana.[15]

Under Indiana's choice-of-law rules, Indiana law would apply to the question of exemplary damages on a conversion claim, where the action giving rise to liability occurred in Indiana.[16]

§ 32 Defenses

In general, the defendant in a conversion action may raise any defense which disproves the plaintiff's right of recovery or disproves the defendant's liability.

West's Digest, Trover and Conversion, ⚬⟶22.

In general, any defense may be set up which disproves the right of recovery in the plaintiff or negates liability on the part of the defendant. For example, if the goods were handled according to the common usage of the defendant's trade and were converted through no fault of the defendant, he or she may assert these facts as a valid defense.[17] The defendant may also raise as a defense the defendant's own title or

---

As the necessity of a demand for the return of converted property, generally, see § 11.

[14]Lambert v. Yellowbird, Inc., 496 N.E.2d 406 (Ind. Ct. App. 4th Dist. 1986), decision clarified on denial of reh'g, 498 N.E.2d 80 (Ind. Ct. App. 4th Dist. 1986), transfer denied, (Jan. 21, 1987).

[15]Lambert v. Yellowbird, Inc., 496 N.E.2d 406 (Ind. Ct. App. 4th Dist. 1986), decision clarified on denial of reh'g, 498 N.E.2d 80 (Ind. Ct. App. 4th Dist. 1986), transfer denied, (Jan. 21, 1987) (criminal conversion).

[16]Western Smelting & Metals, Inc. v. Slater Steel, Inc., 621 F. Supp. 578 (N.D. Ind. 1985) (applying Indiana law).

[17]Bottenberg v. Nixon, 97 Ind. 106, 1884 WL 5709 (1884).

rights to possession, or the rights of a third person to the property.[18]

The right to bring an action for conversion may be defeated by any act or conduct which amounts to an estoppel, such as ratification of the tortious act.[19] A release, signed in consideration of the return of part of the property, will not bar an action to recover the value of the rest of the property.[20] A return of the converted property will not bar an action, but operates only in mitigation of damages.[21]

Good faith is not a defense to a claim for tortious conversion.[22]

§ 33   Pleading

At a minimum, the complaint in a conversion action must allege that plaintiff owned the property in question at the time of its conversion, that the defendant converted such property to his or her own use, and that the plaintiff has been damaged as a result.

West's Digest, Trover and Conversion ☜32, 33.

A complaint alleging that the plaintiff owns and is entitled to possession of the property therein described, that the defendant converted such property to his or her own use, and that the plaintiff has been damaged, is sufficient to state a cause of action conversion.[23]

◆ **Practice Guide:** As with any claim for relief, the complaint should contain a short and plain statement of the claim showing that the pleader is entitled to relief, and a

---

[18]Noble v. Moistner, 180 Ind. App. 414, 388 N.E.2d 620 (4th Dist. 1979).

[19]Cooper v. Smith, 119 Ind. 313, 21 N.E. 887 (1889); Leary v. Moran, 106 Ind. 560, 7 N.E. 236 (1886).

[20]Fitzgerald v. Smith, 1 Ind. 310, 1848 WL 4186 (1848).

[21]Smith v. Downing, 6 Ind. 374, 1855 WL 3581 (1855).

As to mitigation of damages, generally, see § 27.

[22]Computers Unlimited, Inc. v. Midwest Data Systems, Inc., 657 N.E.2d 165 (Ind. Ct. App. 1995); Indiana & Michigan Elec. Co. v. Terre Haute Industries, Inc., 507 N.E.2d 588 (Ind. Ct. App. 1st Dist. 1987), reh'g denied, (June 12, 1987) and transfer denied, 525 N.E.2d 1247 (Ind. 1988); Sikora v. Barney, 138 Ind. App. 686, 207 N.E.2d 846 (Div. 2 1965).

[23]Seip v. Gray, 227 Ind. 52, 83 N.E.2d 790 (1949); Page v. Johnson, 97 Ind. App. 40, 184 N.E. 419 (1933); Schwartz v. Oberweis, 826 F. Supp. 280 (N.D. Ind. 1993) (applying Indiana law).

demand for relief to which the pleader deems him- or herself entitled.[24]

The complaint must describe the converted property; a general description is usually sufficient.[25] The complaint should also state the value of the property converted, or at least that the property is of some value,[26] and should set forth the time of conversion.[27]

The plaintiff in a conversion action must show in the complaint, by direct allegation or necessary inference from facts well pleaded, that at the time of conversion he or she had title, either general or specific, to the property, coupled with the right of immediate possession, and that the property had been wrongfully converted by the defendant to his or her own use.[28] It is not necessary to negates title in the defendant.[29] Where the complaint states that the plaintiff is the owner of the converted goods, it is unnecessary to allege that he or she was in possession of the goods[30] or was entitled to possession.[31]

Where conversion is alleged in terms, it is not necessary that the complaint also allege that a demand was made on the defendant for the property before instituting the action, and that the defendant refused to deliver the goods.[32]

---

[24]Trial R. 8.

[25]First Nat. Bank v. Ransford, 55 Ind. App. 663, 104 N.E. 604 (Div. 1 1914).

[26]Recht v. Glickstein, 162 Ind. 32, 69 N.E. 667 (1904); Jerry Alderman Ford Sales, Inc. v. Bailey, 154 Ind. App. 632, 291 N.E.2d 92, 12 U.C.C. Rep. Serv. (CBC) 47 (2d Dist. 1972), reh'g denied and opinion modified, 154 Ind. App. 632, 294 N.E.2d 617, 12 U.C.C. Rep. Serv. (CBC) 442 (2d Dist. 1973).

[27]89 C.J.S., Trover and Conversion § 101.

[28]Waters v. Delagrange, 183 Ind. 497, 109 N.E. 758 (1915); Noble v. Moistner, 180 Ind. App. 414, 388 N.E.2d 620 (4th Dist. 1979).

[29]First Nat. Bank v. Gibbins, 7 Ind. App. 629, 35 N.E. 31 (1893).

[30]Crystal Ice & Cold Storage Co. v. Marion Gas Co., 35 Ind. App. 295, 74 N.E. 15 (Div. 1 1905); Lafara v. Teal, 27 Ind. App. 580, 61 N.E. 794 (Div. 1 1901).

[31]Baals v. Stewart, 109 Ind. 371, 9 N.E. 403 (1886).

[32]Collins v. State, 192 Ind. 86, 131 N.E. 390 (1921); Knowlton v. School City of Logansport, 75 Ind. 103, 1881 WL 6487 (1881); Bunger v. Roddy, 70 Ind. 26, 1880 WL 6505 (1880).

As the necessity of a demand for the return of converted property, generally, see § 11.

§ 34 Burden of proof; evidence

The plaintiff in a conversion action bears the burden of establishing the material allegations of the complaint and of every fact essential to recovery.

West's Digest, Trover and Conversion ☞35-40.

In an action for conversion, the plaintiff has the burden of establishing the material allegations of the complaint, and the burden is on the plaintiff to prove every fact essential to his or her right to recover,[33] as well as the amount of loss.[34]

Under Indiana law, for intentional torts such as conversion, the burden of proof and the right to prevail must be shown by a fair preponderance of the evidence.[35] The same character of evidence which will suffice in other actions to establish title to, or possession or right to possession of, chattels will suffice to prove these facts in an action for conversion.[36] Possession is prima facie evidence of ownership, which may be rebutted. The burden of proof does not shift to defendant.[37]

The defendant's refusal to surrender another's personalty, when called on to do so, affords presumption that the defendant has converted it, at least until the contrary appears.[38] A claim by the defendant that he or she did not know of plaintiff's ownership or claim of ownership is an affirmative claim, and the defendant must bear the burden of proving it.[39]

The plaintiff has the burden of proving the damages sustained by him or her, and for this purpose he or she must show the value of the property; the burden is on the defendant to prove facts which will authorize a reduction or mitigation of the damages claimed.[40]

---

[33]Noble v. Moistner, 180 Ind. App. 414, 388 N.E.2d 620 (4th Dist. 1979).

[34]Yeager & Sullivan, Inc. v. Farmers Bank, 162 Ind. App. 15, 317 N.E.2d 792, 15 U.C.C. Rep. Serv. (CBC) 892 (2d Dist. 1974).

[35]In re Tomsic, 104 B.R. 22 (Bankr. N.D. Ind. 1987) (applying Indiana law).

[36]Sikora v. Barney, 138 Ind. App. 686, 207 N.E.2d 846 (Div. 2 1965).

[37]Noble v. Moistner, 180 Ind. App. 414, 388 N.E.2d 620 (4th Dist. 1979).

[38]Chicago, I. & L. Ry. Co. v. Pope, 99 Ind. App. 280, 188 N.E. 594 (1934).

[39]Cathcart v. Dalton, 71 Ind. App. 650, 125 N.E. 519 (Div. 2 1919).

[40]89 C.J.S., Trover and Conversion § 121.

§ 35 Questions of law and fact

In actions for conversion, questions of law are for the court and questions of fact are for the jury.

West's Digest, Trover and Conversion ☞64, 66.

In actions for conversion, questions of law are for the court and questions of fact are for the jury.[41] For example, the question of whether a party has title or the right to possession of the item claimed to have been converted is one of fact for the jury,[42] as is the question of whether one to whom possession of the property has been given was authorized to sell the property.[43] Whether the evidence establishes a conversion, as well as the identification and value of the property and the motive of the defendant, are also jury questions.[44] Whether a demand has been made for the property is a jury question,[45] as is the question of whether exemplary damages are appropriate where the defendant's conduct has been malicious or reckless.[46]

The court should withdraw the case from the jury where the evidence does not make out a prima facie case, or the defendant fails to establish an indispensable part of his or her evidence. The judge also may direct the jury to return a particular verdict in a proper case.[47]

§ 36 Instructions; findings and judgment

Instructions given in a conversion action must state correctly the law applicable to the case. Where trial is by the court, factual findings must be supported by the evidence and be responsive to all material issues, and the judgment must conform to, and be supported by, the pleadings and evidence.

West's Digest, Trover and Conversion ☞64, 67-70.

Instructions given in an action for conversion must state

---

[41]Sikora v. Barney, 138 Ind. App. 686, 207 N.E.2d 846 (Div. 2 1965); Ederer v. Wilbur Lumber Co., 122 Ind. App. 308, 104 N.E.2d 581 (1952).

[42]Ax v. Schloot, 116 Ind. App. 366, 64 N.E.2d 668 (1946).

[43]Sikora v. Barney, 138 Ind. App. 686, 207 N.E.2d 846 (Div. 2 1965).

[44]89 C.J.S., Trover and Conversion § 143.

[45]89 C.J.S., Trover and Conversion § 146.

[46]Monarch Buick Co. v. Kennedy, 138 Ind. App. 1, 209 N.E.2d 922 (Div. 2 1965).

[47]89 C.J.S., Trover and Conversion § 149.

correctly the law applicable to the case. The defendant is entitled to an instruction on the burden of proof. Requested instructions, which are correct as to the law, should be given.[48]

Where trial is by the court, the findings of fact must be supported by the evidence and be responsive to and cover all material issues. The findings in turn must support the conclusions of law.[49] The judgment must conform to, and be supported by, the pleadings and evidence; otherwise it will be erroneous.[50]

CORAM NOBIS

The title Coram Nobis has been omitted from this volume. See now the discussion of post-conviction remedies in I.L.E., CRIMINAL LAW.

---

[48]Craig v. Citizens Trust Co., 217 Ind. 434, 26 N.E.2d 1006 (1940); Hendrickson & Sons Motor Co. v. Osha, 165 Ind. App. 185, 331 N.E.2d 743 (1st Dist. 1975).

Forms References: Instructions to Jury. 7A Am Jur Pleading and Practice Forms, Annotated (rev. ed.), Conversion §§ 9-13.

[49]Lesh v. Davison, 181 Ind. 429, 104 N.E. 642 (1914).

[50]Bricker v. Whisler, 65 Ind. App. 492, 117 N.E. 550 (Div. 1 1917).

CORONERS

David J. Rynkowski, J.D.

Scope of Topic

This article discusses the law governing elected county public officials who are vested with medical-legal duties, the most important of which is investigating the causes and circumstances of sudden and violent death. The discussion includes the nature of the office of coroner; the tenure, duties, and liabilities of persons holding that office; and procedure relating to the formal presentation of evidence concerning a death, that is, the inquest.

Treated Elsewhere

Autopsies and dead bodies in general, see I.L.E., Dead Bodies

Cemeteries, removal of remains from, see I.L.E. Cemeteries

County, coroner as officer of, see I.L.E., Counties

Death and dead bodies, generally, see I.L.E., Death; Dead Bodies

Evidence or verdict in coroner's inquest, use of in other criminal or civil proceedings, see I.L.E., Criminal Law; Evidence; Homicide; Insurance

Homicide prosecutions, effect of inquests and findings therein, see I.L.E., Homicide

Insurance cases, effect of inquests and findings therein, see I.L.E., Insurance

Sheriff, performance by coroners of the duties of a sheriff, see I.L.E., Sheriffs and Constables

Witness, impeachment of by prior inconsistent statements made at coroner's inquest, see I.L.E., Witnesses

Research References

Text References

18 Am Jur 2d, Coroners or Medical Examiners.
18 C.J.S., Coroners and Medical Examiners.

West's Digest References

West's Digest, Coroners.

Annotation References

ALR Digest: Coroner
ALR Index: Coroners and Medical Examiners

Forms References

5B Am Jur Legal Forms 2d, Coroners or Medical Examiners.

7A Am Jur Pleading and Practice Forms, Annotated (rev. ed.), Coroners or Medical Examiners.

Trial Strategy References

Presumption or Inference of Death From Unexplained Disappearance, 45 Am Jur POF3d 307; Damages for Loss of Chance of Cure, 12 Am Jur POF3d 621.

Physician's Failure to Disclose Diagnosis or Test Result, 42 Am Jur POF2d 405; Cause of Death as Determined from Autopsy, 39 Am Jur POF2d 1; Adequacy of Consent to Autopsy, 34 Am Jur POF2d 557; Qualification of Medical Expert Witness, 33 Am Jur POF2d 179; Time of Death—Medicolegal Considerations, 16 Am Jur POF2d 87; Accidental Death—Food Asphyxiation, 2 Am Jur POF2d 49.

Wrongful Death of Minor in Police Custody, 69 Am Jur Trials 1; Forensic Pathology in Homicide Cases, 40 Am Jur Trials 501; Crib Death Litigation, 37 Am Jur Trials 1; Pathologist as Expert Witness; Malpractice Considerations, 33 Am Jur Trials 467; Wrongful Death Actions, 12 Am Jur Trials 317; Homicide, 7 Am Jur Trials 477; Basis of Medical Testimony, 6 Am Jur Trials 109; Locating Scientific and Technical Experts, 2 Am Jur Trials 293; Locating and Preserving Evidence in Criminal Cases, 1 Am Jur Trials 555; Investigating the Criminal Case; General Principles, 1 Am Jur Trials 481.

Miscellaneous References

Indiana Practice, Criminal Procedure—Pretrial §§ 1.3, 2.2.

Indiana Practice, Evidence §§ 403.108, 501.531, 703.107, 803.109.

Statutory References

Ind Const Art 4, §§ 2, 6

IC 4-23-6.5-7; IC 4-23-6.5-8; IC 5-14-3-1 et seq.; IC 36-2-16-7; IC 36-2-14-1 et seq.

KeyCite®: Cases and other legal materials listed in KeyCite Scope can be researched through West Group's KeyCite service on Westlaw®. Use KeyCite to check citations for form, parallel references, prior and later history, and comprehensive citator information, including citations to other decisions and secondary materials.

Table of Parallel References:

To convert General Index references to section references in this volume, or to ascertain the disposition (or current equivalent) of articles in the prior edition of this publication, see the Table of Parallel References at the beginning of this volume.

I. IN GENERAL (§§ 1 TO 3)

II. INVESTIGATION OF DEATH (§§ 4 TO 10)

I. IN GENERAL

§ 1   Nature and duties of office, generally

§ 2   Election, qualification, training, and compensation

§ 3   Appointment and compensation of deputies and other staff

II. INVESTIGATION OF DEATH

§ 4   Generally; disturbance of body or scene of death

§ 5   Certificate of death

§ 6   Autopsy

§ 7   Summoning and examination of witnesses

§ 8   Verdict and report; arrest warrant

§ 9   Disclosure of information

§ 10   Disposition of body or property

I. IN GENERAL

Research References

Ind Const Art 4, §§ 2, 6

IC 4-23-6.5-7; IC 4-23-6.5-8; IC 36-2-14-2; IC 36-2-14-4; IC 36-2-14-5; IC 36-2-14-7; IC 36-2-16-7; IC 36-2-14-14; IC 36-2-14-15

18 Am Jur 2d, Coroners or Medical Examiners §§ 1-6.
18 C.J.S., Coroners §§ 1-9, 27-33.
West's Digest, Coroners ⊯1-8, 22-25.
ALR Digest: Coroner § 1
ALR Index: Coroners and Medical Examiners

§ 1 Nature and duties of office, generally

A coroner is a public officer with largely medical-legal duties, chief among which is the investigation of deaths by violence or casualty, or which are suspicious, unnatural, or unexplained.

West's Digest, Coroners ⊯1, 8.

A coroner is a public officer with largely medical-legal duties, chief among which is the investigation of deaths by violence or casualty, or which are suspicious, unnatural, or unexplained.[1] The office of coroner is not a judicial one, and its activities are subject to judicial review.[2]

In addition to his or her medical-legal duties, the coroner may perform law-enforcement duties under certain circumstances; thus, the coroner performs the duties of the county sheriff when the sheriff is interested or incapacitated from serving[3] and has no chief deputy who may perform the duties.[4] A sheriff is "incapacitated" for this purpose when he or she has a mental or physical disability of such an extreme nature that the sheriff is unable to discharge the duties of the office, and he or she is "interested" when his or her personal interest or involvement in official duties would render performance of those duties a conflict of interest or a breach of the public trust.[5]

If there is a warrant issued commanding the arrest of the sheriff, or if the sheriff has to be committed to the county jail, the coroner or other legally authorized person may serve the warrant. During the imprisonment of the sheriff, the coroner shall have custody of the jail in which the sheriff is imprisoned and shall discharge the duties of the sheriff until the sheriff is legally discharged from custody.[6] This is true even when there is a chief deputy, who shall perform all other duties.[7]

The coroner or a representative of the office shall, when invited, attend meetings of the Commission of Forensic Science for consultation on matters concerning the interests of the Commission, the office of coroner, or both. The county fiscal body shall pay the expenses of the coroner attending such meetings.[8]

---

[1] 18 Am Jur 2d, Coroners or Medical Examiners §§ 1, 7.

As to investigations of death by the coroner, see §§ 4 et seq.

[2] Sandy v. Board of Com'rs of Morgan County, 171 Ind. 674, 87 N.E. 131 (1909).

[3] IC 36-2-14-4(1).

[4] IC 36-2-14-4(2).

[5] 1978 Op.Atty.Gen. 22.

[6] IC 36-2-14-5.

[7] 1985 Op.Atty.Gen. 15.

[8] IC 36-2-14-14.

§2 Election, qualification, training, and compensation

Coroners are elected county residents with a four-year term of office.

West's Digest, Coroners ☞2, 3, 6.

Coroners are elected in each county at general elections, along with other county officers.[9] The term of office of the county coroner is four years[10] and continues until a successor is elected and qualified.[11] If elected to replace an elected coroner who left office before his or her term expired, the new coroner's term of office is four years and not the unexpired part of the predecessor's term.[12] No one is eligible to hold the office of coroner more than eight years in any period of 12 years.[13]

A county coroner must reside within the county in which he or she was elected and forfeits office upon ceasing to be a resident of the county.[14] A coroner may not simultaneously serve as the county health officer.[15]

Coroners and deputy coroners must receive continuing education training as established by the Coroner's Training Board.[16] The board makes rules as to how coroners and deputy coroners are to be trained, and a fund is established to pay for the expenses of providing this training.[17]

By statute, compensation for a coroner who is a licensed physician must be 50% higher than compensation for a coroner who is not a licensed physician It is up to the county to determine if someone is a licensed physician for this purpose.[18] The Attorney General has opined that a chiropractor[19] and a veterinarian[20] are both licensed physicians within the statute's purview.

---

[9]Ind Const Art 4 § 2.

[10]Ind Const Art 4 § 2; IC 36-2-14-2.

[11]IC 36-2-14-2(b).

[12]1966 Op.Atty.Gen. 55.

[13]Ind Const Art 4 § 2.

[14]Ind Const Art 4 § 6; IC 36-2-14-2(a).

[15]1988 Op.Atty.Gen. 12.

[16]IC 4-23-6.5-7.

[17]IC 4-23-6.5-8.

[18]IC 36-2-14-15.

[19]1965 Op.Atty.Gen. 30.

§ 3 Appointment and compensation of deputies and other staff

A county coroner may appoint deputies and clerical employees as authorized by the county fiscal body. The coroner also has authority to select physicians to make postmortem examinations, and the county must pay for the physicians whom he or she selects.

West's Digest, Coroners ☞4.

A county coroner may appoint the number of deputies and clerical employees authorized by the county fiscal body.[21] Such deputies are public officers.[22]

A statute provides that if a physician is required to attend an investigation and make a postmortem examination, the coroner shall certify this service to the county executive, who shall order payment for the physician from the county treasury.[23] Under this statute, a coroner has authority to select physicians to make postmortem examinations, and the county must pay for the physicians whom he or she selects.[24] A chemist, as well as a physician or surgeon, may recover for services rendered at the request of the coroner on a postmortem examination.[25]

II. INVESTIGATION OF DEATH

Research References

IC 5-14-3-1; IC 5-14-3-4; IC 36-2-14-16 to IC 36-2-14-18; IC 36-2-14-6 to IC 36-2-14-13

18 Am Jur 2d, Coroners or Medical Examiners §§ 7-17.
18 C.J.S., Coroners and Medical Examiners §§ 10-26.
West's Digest, Coroners ☞8-21.
ALR Digest: Coroner §§ 2, 3
ALR Index: Coroners and Medical Examiners
5B Am Jur Legal Forms 2d, Coroners or Medical Examiners §§ 73:1-73:19.

---

[20]1968 Op.Atty.Gen. 36.

[21]IC 36-2-16-7.

[22]1937 Op.Atty.Gen. 163.

[23]IC 36-2-14-7.

As to postmortem examinations, generally, see § 6.

[24]Board of Com'rs of Dearborn County v. Bond, 88 Ind. 102, 1882 WL 7048 (1882).

[25]Board of Com'rs of Bartholomew County v. Jameson, 86 Ind. 154, 1882 WL 6446 (1882).

7A Am Jur Pleading and Practice Forms, Annotated (rev. ed.),
  Coroners or Medical Examiners §§ 1-39.
Cause of Death as Determined from Autopsy, 39 Am Jur POF2d 1;
  Adequacy of Consent to Autopsy, 34 Am Jur POF2d 557.

§ 4 Generally; disturbance of body or scene of death

**The coroner is required to investigate the manner and
cause of a person's death whenever he or she is notified
that the person has died from violence or by casualty; has
died in apparently good health or in a suspicious, unusual,
or unnatural manner; or has been found dead. The body at
the scene of death may not be disturbed until after the coroner has had a chance to investigate and collect evidence
as to the cause of death.**

West's Digest, Coroners ☞8-11.

The county coroner is required to investigate the manner
and cause of a person's death in the county whenever the
coroner is notified that the person has died from violence or
by casualty; has died in apparently good health or in a
suspicious, unusual, or unnatural manner; or has been found
dead. In such cases, the coroner shall, before the scene of
death is disturbed, notify the law-enforcement agency having jurisdiction in the area. That agency shall assist the coroner in conducting an investigation of how the person died
and a medical investigation of the cause of death.[26]

◆ **Observation:** It is a criminal offense to knowingly or
intentionally fail to immediately notify the coroner or a
law-enforcement agency of the discovery of the body of a
person who has died from violence or in an apparently
suspicious, unusual, or unnatural manner.[27]

The body and scene of death may not be disturbed until
the coroner has photographed them in a manner that most
fully discloses how the person died. The coroner or law-
enforcement officer may order a body to be moved before
photographs are taken if the position or location of the body
unduly interferes with activities carried on where the body
is found; however, the body may not be moved from the im-

[26]IC 36-2-14-6(a).
[27]IC 36-2-14-17(a).

mediate area and must be moved without substantially destroying or altering the evidence present.[28]

◆ **Observation:** It is a felony for a person, without the permission of the coroner or a law-enforcement officer, to knowingly or intentionally move or transport from the scene of death the body of a person who has died from violence or in an apparently suspicious, unusual, or unnatural manner.[29]

§ 5 Certificate of death

The coroner must file a certificate of death within 72 hours of being notified of the death.

West's Digest, Coroners ☞8.

The coroner shall file a coroner's certificate of death with the person in charge of internment within 72 hours of being notified of the death.[30]

If the cause of death cannot be established within 72 hours, the coroner shall file a certificate of death with the cause of death being designated as "deferred pending further action." As soon as the actual cause of death is determined, the coroner shall file a supplemental report indicating the exact findings with the local health officer having jurisdiction, who shall make it a part of the official records.[31]

◆ **Observation:** The coroner is free to reopen an investigation if his or her original reports on the death are not correct or are in doubt, and he or she may conduct an inquest if a certificate is filed providing that the cause of

---

[28]IC 36-2-14-6(c)

Although funeral arrangements, such as the ordering of the embalming of a body, are without the power of the coroners, where there is an automobile fatality on the highway, the coroner may cause the body to be removed from the highway to some funeral director's establishment, if for no other reason than to remove the body from the highway and to afford him or her a better opportunity to make the examination and determination required by the statutes.—1955 Op.Atty.Gen. 24.

[29]IC 36-2-14-17.

[30]IC 36-2-14-6(b).

As to public disclosure of the coroner's reports and records, generally, see § 9.

Forms References: Certificate of Death. 5B Am Jur Legal Forms 2d, Coroners or Medical Examiners § 73:19.

[31]IC 36-2-14-6.

death is deferred pending further action, even though a grand jury has met and not returned an indictment.[32]

§ 6 Autopsy

The coroner may perform an autopsy to aid in determining the cause of death, regardless of whether there is evidence of a crime. The coroner may also decide not to perform an autopsy if the deceased's family so requests, two or more witnesses corroborate the circumstances surrounding the death, and two physicians sign an affidavit stating the cause of death.

West's Digest, Coroners ☞14, 16.

The general purpose of an autopsy is to determine, where there has been a death from an unknown cause, by what means the person met his or her death.[33] Such a postmortem is intended to be a scientific investigation concerning the cause of death as determined from the corpse itself, and the decision whether to perform an autopsy as part of an inquiry into the circumstances of death is based on the professional expertise and discretion of the coroner.[34] The coroner's authority in this respect must be reasonably, and not arbitrarily, exercised.[35]

It is not necessary that there be some evidence of a crime before a coroner assumes jurisdiction and decides to perform an autopsy.[36] An autopsy should not be ordered unless it will materially assist the coroner in his or her investigation.[37] Once the coroner takes jurisdiction, the coroner has unlimited prerogative to order an autopsy if it is done to further

---

[32]1987 Op.Atty.Gen. 10.

Forms References: Inquests. 7A Am Jur Pleading and Practice Forms, Annotated (rev. ed.), Coroners or Medical Examiners §§ 11-27.

[33]18 Am Jur 2d, Coroners or Medical Examiners § 10.

Forms References: Autopsies and Medical Examinations. 5B Am Jur Legal Forms 2d, Coroners or Medical Examiners §§ 73:11-73:19.

Autopsies. 7A Am Jur Pleading and Practice Forms, Annotated (rev. ed.), Coroners or Medical Examiners §§ 4-10.

Trial Strategy References: Cause of Death as Determined from Autopsy, 39 Am Jur POF2d 1.

[34]Stath v. Williams, 174 Ind. App. 369, 367 N.E.2d 1120 (3d Dist. 1977).

[35]18 Am Jur 2d, Coroners or Medical Examiners § 10.

[36]Stath v. Williams, 174 Ind. App. 369, 367 N.E.2d 1120 (3d Dist. 1977).

[37]1955 Op.Atty.Gen. 24.

the inquiry into the cause of death.[38] An autopsy can only be performed when the coroner deems it necessary, and if a coroner can form an opinion as to the cause of death based solely on the appearance of the body without doing an autopsy, the coroner may testify to such an opinion without the benefits of the autopsy.[39]

A statute provides that whenever a coroner deems it necessary in the discharge of his or her duties to have an autopsy performed, or is requested to do so by the prosecuting attorney, the coroner shall employ a physician certified by the American Board of Pathology, or one who has an unlimited license to practice medicine in the state of Indiana and is acting under the direction of a physician certified by the American Board of Pathology, to perform the autopsy. This physician shall be paid a fee of at least $50 from the county treasury.[40]

> ◆ **Observation:** A person who in good faith orders or performs a medical examination or autopsy under statutory authority is immune from civil liability for damages for ordering or performing the examination or autopsy.[41]

A county coroner has the option not to perform an autopsy if three conditions are met:

> (1) the deceased's family[42] requests that an autopsy not be performed;
>
> (2) two or more witnesses who corroborate the circumstances surrounding the death are present; and
>
> (3) two licensed physicians who have made two separate examinations of the decedent certify the same cause

---

[38]Lee v. Weston, 402 N.E.2d 23 (Ind. Ct. App. 4th Dist. 1980).

[39]Jaudon v. State, 255 Ind. 114, 262 N.E.2d 851 (1970).

[40]IC 36-2-14-6(d).

[41]IC 36-2-14-13.

Annotation References: Liability for wrongful autopsy, 18 ALR4th 858.

Forms References: Liability of Coroner or Medical Examiner; Injunctive Relief. 7A Am Jur Pleading and Practice Forms, Annotated (rev. ed.), Coroners or Medical Examiners §§ 28-39.

[42]For this purpose, the deceased's family consists of any of the following: a spouse; a child if the deceased has no spouse; a parent if the deceased has no spouse or child; a sibling if the deceased has no spouse, child, or parent; or a grandparent if the deceased has no spouse, parent, child, or sibling.—IC 36-2-14-6(e).

of death in an affidavit signed 24 hours after death and filed with the Circuit Court clerk.[43]

§ 7 Summoning and examination of witnesses

Coroners can subpoena witnesses, compel them to answer questions and produce documents, and record their testimony.

West's Digest, Coroners ☞13.

As part of his or her investigation of a death, the coroner may cause witnesses to be summoned by subpoena and require them to produce documents relevant to the investigation.[44] The coroner shall examine persons wanting to testify and may examine persons he or she has summoned by subpoena.[45] Witnesses are required to answer under oath all questions concerning the death under investigation.[46]

◆ **Observation:** A witness testifying before a county coroner is entitled to the same fees as a witness testifying in the Circuit Court for the county.[47]

The testimony of every witness at a coroner's investigation shall be reduced to writing and signed by the witness. The coroner shall, by either recognizance or reasonable sum, bind any witness whose testimony relates to a trial of a person convened in the death to give evidence in court and shall send the written evidence and recognizance of the witness to the court. The coroner shall commit to the county jail a witness who refuses to enter into the recognizance required by this section.[48]

§ 8 Verdict and report; arrest warrant

After his or her investigation is completed, the coroner must draw up a verdict and a report and may issue a warrant commanding a law-enforcement officer to arrest and take before a court any person whom the coroner has charged with a felony.

---

[43]IC 36-2-14-6(e).

Trial Strategy References: Adequacy of Consent to Autopsy, 34 Am Jur POF2d 557.

[44]1979 Op.Atty.Gen. 27.

[45]IC 36-2-14-7(a).

[46]IC 36-2-14-7(a).

[47]IC 36-2-14-8.

[48]IC 36-2-14-9.

West's Digest, Coroners ☞18, 19.

After viewing the body, hearing the evidence, and making all necessary inquiries, the coroner shall draw up and sign his or her verdict on the death under consideration.[49]

♦ **Observation:** Although a coroner's verdict is not admissible in a criminal prosecution as to the cause of death,[50] a coroner's verdict is admissible to prove the time of death.[51]

In addition to his or her verdict, the coroner is required to make a written report giving an accurate description of the deceased person, the name of the deceased person, and the amount of money and property found with the body.[52]

After conducting an investigation of the death of a person by felony, the coroner may issue a warrant commanding a law-enforcement officer to arrest and take before a court the person whom the coroner has charged with a felony. The court shall proceed with the case as if the person had been arrested on a complaint filed with the court.[53]

§ 9 Disclosure of information

While the coroner's office is required by statute to make available for public inspection and copying a number of particular facts and documents relating to the investigation of a death, certain investigatory materials can be withheld from the public.

West's Digest, Coroners ☞15.

The statute governing coroners provides that when a coroner investigates a death, his or her office is required to make available for public inspection and copying the name, age,

---

[49]IC 36-2-14-10.

[50]Indiana Steel Products Co. v. Leonard, 126 Ind. App. 669, 131 N.E.2d 162 (1956); Craiger v. Modern Woodmen of America, 40 Ind. App. 279, 80 N.E. 429 (1907).

Annotation References: Admissibility of testimony of coroner or mortician as to cause of death in homicide prosecution, 71 ALR3d 1265.

[51]Indiana Steel Products Co. v. Leonard, 126 Ind. App. 669, 131 N.E.2d 162 (1956).

[52]IC 36-2-14-10.

As to disclosure of the coroner's reports and records, see § 9.

As disposition of the body and property, see § 10.

[53]IC 36-2-14-12.

address, sex, and race of the deceased; the address where the body was found; the location where the death occurred; the agency to which the death was reported and the name of the person reporting the death; the name of the public official or government employee present at the scene of the death; and the name of the person pronouncing the death. The report must further set forth the date of the autopsy, the name of the person who performed it, and where it was performed, and it must state a conclusion as to the probable cause, manner, and mechanism of death. In addition, the coroner must report the location to which the body was removed, the person who determined the location to which the body was to be removed, and the authority under which it was removed. Finally, the coroner's office must make available for public inspection and copying the coroner's certificate of death, as well as his or her investigatory report and verdict.[54]

Upon written request from the next of kin of the decedent or of an insurance company investigating a claim arising from the death of an individual upon which the autopsy was performed, a coroner shall make available a full copy of the autopsy report; however, the insurance company is prohibited from publicly disclosing any information contained in the report beyond that which may legally be disclosed by the coroner, unless it is used to investigate, settle, or pay a claim.[55]

Because county coroners are elected government officials, the general rule is that a coroner's official records are subject to public disclosure pursuant to Indiana's Sunshine Law.[56] A coroner, however, is also a law-enforcement agency within the meaning of the Sunshine Law exception for "investiga-

---

[54]IC 36-2-14-18(a).

As to the coroner's certificate of death, generally, see § 5.

As to the coroner's investigatory report and verdict, generally, see § 8.

[55]IC 36-2-14-18(c).

As to insurance, generally, see I.L.E., Insurance.

[56]Althaus v. Evansville Courier Co., 615 N.E.2d 441 (Ind. Ct. App. 1st Dist. 1993), reh'g denied, (Oct. 28, 1993), referring to IC 5-14-3-1 et seq.

As to disclosure of public records generally, see I.L.E., Records.

tory records."[57] Thus, apart from those items of information discussed above which the coroner is required to disclose by the general coroner's statute, it is within the coroner's discretion to release or withhold investigatory records compiled pursuant to an autopsy involving a death from violence or casualty; or which occurs in a suspicious, unusual, or unnatural manner; or of someone in apparently good health or who has been found dead.[58]

A county coroner or coroner's deputy who receives an investigatory record from a law-enforcement agency must treat the investigatory record with the same confidentiality as the law-enforcement agency would treat that record.[59]

§ 10 Disposition of body or property

> **Statutes provide for the disposition of bodies left with the coroner and of money or other personal property which is owned by a deceased person, or which is found on a body or at the scene of death, where the death is subject to a coroner's investigation.**

West's Digest, Coroners ☞20.

A statute provides that, if no one can be located to take custody of a dead body left with the coroner, or if there is a person to take custody of the body, but that person cannot or will not assume financial responsibility for disposition of the body, then the coroner may order the burial or cremation of the body, if the county's population is greater than 400,000. If the deceased died without leaving money or other means necessary to defray funeral expenses, the coroner may contract with a licensed funeral director to dispose of the body, and the necessary and reasonable expenses for disposing of the body shall be paid by the county auditor upon the order of the coroner.[60]

Where no one entitled thereto claims money or other

---

[57]Heltzel v. Thomas, 516 N.E.2d 103 (Ind. Ct. App. 3d Dist. 1987), reh'g denied, (Jan. 20, 1988) and transfer denied, 529 N.E.2d 345 (Ind. 1988), referring to IC 5-14-3-4(b)(1).

[58]Althaus v. Evansville Courier Co., 615 N.E.2d 441 (Ind. Ct. App. 1st Dist. 1993), reh'g denied, (Oct. 28, 1993), referring to IC 36-2-14-6 as discussed in § 4.

[59]IC 36-2-14-18(b).

[60]IC 36-2-14-16 (applicable to counties with a population greater than 400,000).

personal property owned by a deceased person whose death is subject to a coroner's investigation, or to money or property which is found on a body or at the scene of death, the coroner is required by statute to take possession of the property, publish a description of the deceased and the name of the deceased, if known, and make a reasonable search to find a person who is entitled to the money or other personal property. If no person entitled to the money comes forward after the coroner's compliance with such procedures, the coroner must deliver the money to the county treasurer for deposit in the county general fund. As to unclaimed personal property other than money that has an intrinsic value, the coroner must deliver such property to the sheriff for sale at any auction that the sheriff conducts under law, and the sheriff must deposit the receipts from the auction in the county general fund.[61]

---

[61]IC 36-2-14-11.

CORPORATIONS

Elizabeth Williams, J.D. and Thomas Muskus, J.D.

Scope of Topic

This article discusses the law of corporations as applied in general to all corporations, regardless of their character and the particular businesses in which they may be engaged, including business, not-for-profit, and professional corporations. Included are existence and organization of corporations; corporate name, seal, domicile, bylaws, and records; shares; transfer of shares; dividends; status, rights, duties, and liabilities of shareholders and members, including shareholders' and members' meetings and voting; directors, officers, and agents, including their selection and removal and their rights, duties, and liabilities; powers, functions, and liabilities of corporations, including tort and criminal liability and actions by and against corporations; insolvency and receivers of corporations; dissolution; consolidation; and foreign corporations.

Treated Elsewhere

Associations and unincorporated companies generally, see I.L.E., Associations, Clubs and Societies

Municipal and other public corporations, see I.L.E., Municipal Corporations

Particular businesses or purposes, companies formed for, see I.L.E., Banks and Banking; Beneficial Associations; Building and Loan Associations; Insurance; and other specific titles

Public utility companies, see I.L.E., Carriers; Electricity; Public Service Commission; Railroads; Telecommunications

Research References

Text References

18, 18A, 18B, 19 Am Jur 2d, Corporations.
18, 19 C.J.S., Corporations.

Annotation References

ALR Digest: Corporations
ALR Index: Articles of Incorporation; Assets; Bylaws; Charter; Close Corporation; Consolidation or Merger; Corporate Bonds and Bondholders; Corporate Officers, Directors, and Agents; Corporate Opportunity; Corporate Responsibility Doctrine;

Corporate Stock and Stockholders; Corporations; Dissolution or Liquidation; Dividends; Domicile and Residence; Foreign Corporations; Forfeitures; Liquidation or Dissolution; Minority Stockholders; Names; Nonprofit Institutions or Organizations; Professional Corporations and Associations; Promoters; Prospectus; Proxies; Reports; Seal; Stock-Option Plans; Subsidiary

Forms References

6, 6A, 6B Am Jur Legal Forms 2d, Corporations.

7A, 7B Am Jur Pleading and Practice Forms, Annotated (rev. ed.), Corporations.

Trial Strategy References

Invalidity of Judgment of Court of Foreign Country, 9 Am Jur POF3d 687; Corporate Director's Breach of Fiduciary Duty to Creditors, 16 Am Jur POF3d 583; Tortious Interference by Parent Corporation With Subsidiary's Contract With Third Party, 17 Am Jur POF3d 685; Liability of a Director to a Corporation for Mismanagement, 29 Am Jur POF3d 133; CERCLA Liability of Parent, Subsidiary, and Successor Corporations, 34 Am Jur POF3d 387; Grounds for Disregarding the Corporate Entity and Piercing the Corporate Veil, 45 Am Jur POF3d 1; Liability of Nonprofit Corporation for Engaging in For-Profit Business Activities, 46 Am Jur POF3d 431; Liability of Shareholder for Wrongfully Transferring or Assigning Corporate Common Stock Shares to Third Party, 47 Am Jur POF3d 138.

Valuation of Stock of Closely Held Corporation, 2 Am Jur POF2d 1; Waiver of Right to Enforce "First Option" Stock Purchase Agreement, 3 Am Jur POF2d 379; Reasonableness of Corporate Officer's Compensation, 4 Am Jur POF2d 425; Oppressive Conduct by Majority Shareholders, Directors, or Those in Control of Corporation, 5 Am Jur POF2d 645; Dissension or Deadlock of Corporate Directors or Shareholder, 6 Am Jur POF2d 387; Personal Liability of Corporate Officers on Promissory Note, 8 Am Jur POF2d 193; Controlling Stockholder's Beach of Duty to Investigate Motive and Intent of Purchaser Before Selling Stock, 9 Am Jur POF2d 261; Participation by Corporate Officer in Illegal Issuance of Securities, 9 Am Jur POF2d 577; Failure to Disclose Material Facts to Stock Purchaser, 11 Am Jur POF2d 271; Improper Issuance of Corporate Stock to Directors or Officers, 15 Am Jur POF2d 417; Book Value, 16 Am Jur POF2d 253; Liability of Parent Corporation for Acts of Subsidiary, 16 Am Jur POF2d 679; De Facto Merger of Two Corporations, 20 Am Jur POF2d 609; Wrongful Failure of Corporate Directors to Declare Dividend, 22 Am Jur POF2d 593; Proper Purpose for Shareholder's Inspection of Corporate Books and Records, 24 Am Jur POF2d 71; Corporate Opportunity Doctrine—Fairness of

CORPORATIONS

Corporate Official's Acquisition of Business Opportunity, 30 Am Jur POF2d 291; Gift of Corporate Stock, 39 Am Jur POF2d 373; Establishment of Person's Domicile, 39 Am Jur POF2d 587.

Income Tax Litigation—Validity of Professional Corporation Organized to Practice Law, 28 Am Jur Proof of Facts 65.

Locating Public Record, 2 Am Jur Trials 409; Selecting the Forum—Plaintiff's Position, 3 Am Jur Trials 553; Franchise Litigation, 21 Am Jur Trials 453; Age Discrimination in Employment Action Under ADEA, 29 Am Jur Trials 2; Wrongful Discharge of At-Will Employee, 31 Am Jur Trials 317; Bad Faith Tort Remedy for Breach of Contract, 34 Am Jur Trials 343; Private Cost Recovery Actions Under CERCLA, 57 Am Jur Trials 1; U.S. EPA Action Under the Comprehensive Environmental Response, Compensation, and Liability Act (Superfund), 68 Am Jur Trials 1.

Miscellaneous References

5 Indiana Practice, Legal Business Forms §§ 441-514.
17-20 Indiana Practice, Business Organizations §§ 8.1 et seq.

Statutory References

Ind Const Art 11, §§ 13, 14

IC 8-1-2-1; IC 8-4-1-1; IC 15-7-1-1; IC 23-1-2-6; IC 23-1-17-1 to IC 23-1-17-4; IC 23-1-18-1 to IC 23-1-18-10; IC 23-1-20-3; IC 23-1-20-5; IC 23-1-20-7; IC 23-1-20-11; IC 23-1-20-21; IC 23-1-20-23; IC 23-1-20-24; IC 23-1-20-26; IC 23-1-20-28; IC 23-1-20-29; IC 23-1-20-30; IC 23-1-21-1 to IC 23-1-21-7; IC 23-1-22-1 to IC 23-1-22-3; IC 23-1-22-5; IC 23-1-23-1 to IC 23-1-23-3; IC 23-1-24-1 to IC 23-1-24-3; IC 23-1-25-1 to IC 23-1-25-4; IC 23-1-26-1 to IC 23-1-26-9; IC 23-1-27-1; IC 23-1-27-2; IC 23-1-28-1 to IC 23-1-28-5; IC 23-1-29-1 to IC 23-1-29-7; IC 23-1-30-1 to IC 23-1-30-9; IC 23-1-31-1; IC 23-1-31-2; IC 23-1-32-1 to IC 23-1-32-5; IC 23-1-33-1 to IC 23-1-33-10; IC 23-1-34-1 to IC 23-1-34-6; IC 23-1-35-1; IC 23-1-35-2; IC 23-1-35-4; IC 23-1-36-1 to IC 23-1-36-4; IC 23-1-37-2; IC 23-1-37-7 to IC 23-1-37-15; IC 23-1-38-1 to IC 23-1-38-9; IC 23-1-39-1 to IC 23-1-39-3; IC 23-1-40-1; IC 23-1-40-3 to IC 23-1-40-7; IC 23-1-42-1; IC 23-1-44-1 to IC 23-1-44-20; IC 23-1-45-1 to IC 23-1-45-7; IC 23-1-47-1; IC 23-1-49-1; IC 23-1-49-3; IC 23-1-49-5 to IC 23-1-49-7; IC 23-1-49-9; IC 23-1-50-2; IC 23-1-50-3; IC 23-1-51-1; IC 23-1-52-1 to IC 23-1-52-5; IC 23-1-53-1 to IC 23-1-53-4; IC 23-1-54-2; IC 23-1.5-1-1; IC 23-1.5-1-8; IC 23-1.5-2-1; IC 23-1.5-2-3; IC 23-1.5-2-6; IC 23-1.5-2-8; IC 23-1.5-2-9; IC 23-1.5-2-11.1; IC 23-1.5-3-1 to IC 23-1.5-3-3; IC 23-1.5-3-6; IC 23-6-4-1; IC 23-15-1-1; IC 23-17-1-1; IC 23-17-2-7; IC 23-17-2-8; IC 23-17-2-17 to IC 23-17-2-19; IC 23-17-2-23; IC 23-17-2-25; IC 23-17-3-2; IC 23-17-3-7 to IC 23-17-3-9; IC 23-17-4-2; IC 23-17-4-4; IC 23-17-5-1 to IC 23-17-5-3; IC 23-17-6-1 to IC 23-17-6-3; IC 23-

17-7-1 to IC 23-17-7-9; IC 23-17-8-1 to IC 23-17-8-3; IC 23-17-9-1; IC 23-17-9-2; IC 23-17-10-1; IC 23-17-10-2; IC 23-17-10-4 to IC 23-17-10-8; IC 23-17-11-1 to IC 23-17-11-9; IC 23-17-12-1 to IC 23-17-12-15; IC 23-17-13-1; IC 23-17-13-2; IC 23-17-13-4; IC 23-17-14-1 to IC 23-17-14-4; IC 23-17-15-1 to IC 23-17-15-6; IC 23-17-16-2; IC 23-17-16-7 to IC 23-17-16-15; IC 23-17-17-1 to IC 23-17-17-10; IC 23-17-18-1; IC 23-17-18-2; IC 23-17-19-1; IC 23-17-19-3 to IC 23-17-19-5; IC 23-17-21-1; IC 23-17-21-2; IC 23-17-22-1 to IC 23-17-22-7; IC 23-17-24-1; IC 23-17-26-9; IC 23-17-27-1 to IC 23-17-27-8; IC 23-17-28-1 to IC 23-17-28-3; IC 23-17-28-6 to IC 23-17-28-8; IC 23-17-29-1 to IC 23-17-29-10; IC 26-1-3.1-202; IC 26-1-8.1-101; IC 26-1-8.1-102; IC 26-1-8.1-108; IC 26-1-8.1-112; IC 26-1-8.1-113; IC 26-1-8.1-204 to IC 26-1-8.1-207; IC 26-1-8.1-210; IC 26-1-8.1-301 to IC 26-1-8.1-304; IC 26-1-8.1-306; IC 26-1-8.1-307; IC 26-1-8.1-401 to IC 26-1-8.1-406; IC 26-1-9-101; IC 26-1-9-115; IC 27-1-7-1; IC 27-17-10-3; IC 28-1-1-1; IC 28-7-1-1; IC 28-12-1-1; IC 32-1-2-4; IC 32-4-1.5-15; IC 32-4-1.6-10; IC 32-4-1.6-11; IC 32-8-15-1; IC 32-12-1-1; IC 34-1-32-1; IC 34-9-1-1; IC 34-48-1-1; IC 34-48-1-2; IC 34-48-1-7 to IC 34-48-1-9; IC 34-48-2-1; IC 34-48-3-2; IC 34-52-1-1; IC 35-33-10-7; IC 35-41-2-3; IC 36-7-4-1003

U.S. Const., Art. I, § 10

15 U.S.C.A. § 78a

Court Rules

Trial R. 4.6, 23.1, 75

KeyCite®: Cases and other legal materials listed in KeyCite Scope can be researched through West Group's KeyCite service on Westlaw®. Use KeyCite to check citations for form, parallel references, prior and later history, and comprehensive citator information, including citations to other decisions and secondary materials.

Table of Parallel References:

To convert General Index references to section references in this volume, or to ascertain the disposition (or current equivalent) of articles in the prior edition of this publication, see the Table of Parallel References at the beginning of this volume.

I. IN GENERAL (§§ 1 TO 7)

II. FORMATION AND EXISTENCE OF CORPORATION (§§ 8 TO 35)

A. IN GENERAL (§§ 8 TO 11)

B. FORMATION OF CORPORATION (§§ 12 TO 27)

C. RECORDS, REPORTS, AND FILING OF DOCUMENTS (§§ 28 TO 35)

III. SHARES (§§ 36 TO 45)

IV. TRANSFER OF SHARES (§§ 46 TO 57)

V. DIVIDENDS AND ADDITIONAL SHARES (§§ 58 TO 64)

VI. SHAREHOLDERS AND MEMBERS (§§ 65 TO 95)
A. IN GENERAL (§§ 65 TO 79)
B. MEETINGS (§§ 80 TO 86)
C. VOTING (§§ 87 TO 95)

VII. DIRECTORS, OFFICERS, AND AGENTS (§§ 96 TO 121)
A. IN GENERAL (§§ 96 TO 107)
B. AUTHORITY AND FUNCTIONS (§§ 108 TO 114)
C. RIGHTS, DUTIES, AND LIABILITIES (§§ 115 TO 121)

I. IN GENERAL

§ 1 Nature of corporation
§ 2 Governing law; types of corporations
§ 3 —Role of contract law
§ 4 Purposes
§ 5 Powers of state
§ 6 Statutory changes in corporation laws
§ 7 Disregarding the corporate entity; "piercing the corporate veil"

II. FORMATION AND EXISTENCE OF CORPORATION

A. IN GENERAL

§ 8 Generally

§ 9 Effect of defective incorporation or organization
§ 10 Attacks on corporate existence
§ 11 Estoppel to deny corporate existence

B. FORMATION OF CORPORATION

§ 12 Articles of incorporation
§ 13 Amendment of articles of incorporation
§ 14 —Filing requirements
§ 15 Restatement of articles of incorporation
§ 16 Professional corporations; certificate of registration
§ 17 Incorporators
§ 18 Name of corporation
§ 19 —Professional corporations
§ 20 —Foreign corporations
§ 21 —Assumed name
§ 22 —Change of name
§ 23 Seal
§ 24 Registered office and agent
§ 25 Organizational meeting
§ 26 Bylaws
§ 27 —Amendment of bylaws

C. RECORDS, REPORTS, AND FILING OF DOCUMENTS

§ 28 Records
§ 29 Annual and biennial reports
§ 30 Annual financial statements
§ 31 Filing of documents
§ 32 Forms
§ 33 Execution of documents submitted for filing
§ 34 Method of submission; copies of documents submitted
§ 35 Secretary of State's refusal to file document

III. SHARES

§ 36 Generally
§ 37 Classes and series of shares
§ 38 Subscriptions
§ 39 —Conditional subscriptions
§ 40 Issuance of shares
§ 41 —Preemptive rights
§ 42 Stock options

§ 43   Consideration
§ 44   Certificates
§ 45   Reacquisition by corporation

IV.   TRANSFER OF SHARES

§ 46   Generally
§ 47   Restrictions on right to transfer
§ 48   Valuation of shares of closely held corporation
§ 49   Delivery; effect
§ 50   Endorsement
§ 51   Registration of transfer
§ 52   —Demand that corporation not register transfer
§ 53   Guarantees to purchaser
§ 54   Assurances to corporation
§ 55   Warranties to purchaser and corporation
§ 56   Transfer of securities on death of owner
§ 57   Rights of creditors and pledgees in shares

V.   DIVIDENDS AND ADDITIONAL SHARES

§ 58   Generally
§ 59   Record date
§ 60   Prohibited distributions
§ 61   Share dividends
§ 62   Rights of preferred stockholders generally
§ 63   Directors' discretion to declare dividends
§ 64   Right to compel declaration of dividend, or to collect
         declared dividend

VI.   SHAREHOLDERS AND MEMBERS

A.   IN GENERAL

§ 65   Shareholders generally
§ 66   Members of not-for-profit corporations
§ 67   —Termination of membership
§ 68   —Delegates
§ 69   Management of corporate affairs
§ 70   Right to information
§ 71   —Voting list
§ 72   Dealings between stockholders in same corporation
§ 73   Dealings with corporation
§ 74   Action by shareholders on behalf of corporation
§ 75   —Demand on corporation

§ 76   —Committee of disinterested directors or persons
§ 77   Actions by stockholders on their own behalf
§ 78   Liability for corporate acts and debts generally
§ 79   Enforcement of nonprofit corporation's liability against
       members

B. MEETINGS

§ 80   Generally
§ 81   Annual and regular meetings
§ 82   Special meetings
§ 83   Court-ordered meetings
§ 84   Action taken without meeting
§ 85   Notice of meeting
§ 86   Record date

C. VOTING

§ 87   Voting list
§ 88   Business corporations, generally
§ 89   Not-for-profit corporations, generally
§ 90   Quorum; votes required
§ 91   —Voting groups
§ 92   —Special voting rights
§ 93   Proxy voting
§ 94   Acceptance of signature
§ 95   Voting trusts and voting agreements

VII. DIRECTORS, OFFICERS, AND AGENTS

A. IN GENERAL

§ 96   Generally
§ 97   Election of directors
§ 98   —Cumulative voting
§ 99   —Election by classes or units
§ 100   Directors' term of office
§ 101   —Staggered terms
§ 102   Election or appointment of officers
§ 103   Resignation of director
§ 104   Removal of director
§ 105   —Court order
§ 106   Vacancies on board of directors
§ 107   Removal and resignation of officers

B. AUTHORITY AND FUNCTIONS

§ 108 Generally
§ 109 Emergency powers
§ 110 Directors' meetings
§ 111 —Action taken without meeting
§ 112 —Notice of meetings
§ 113 —Quorum
§ 114 —Committees

C. RIGHTS, DUTIES, AND LIABILITIES

§ 115 Generally
§ 116 Compensation
§ 117 Standard of conduct; business judgment rule
§ 118 Conflicts of interest
§ 119 Liability for unlawful distributions
§ 120 Liability for corporate debts and acts
§ 121 Indemnification

I. IN GENERAL

Research References

U.S. Const., Art. I, § 10
Ind Const Art 11, §§ 13, 14
IC 8-1-2-1; IC 8-4-1-1; IC 15-7-1-1; IC 23-1-17-1 to IC 23-1-17-4; IC
    23-1-20-5; IC 23-1-20-11; IC 23-1-22-1; IC 23-1.5-1-1; IC 23-1.5-
    1-8; IC 23-1.5-2-1; IC 23-1.5-2-3; IC 23-6-4-1; IC 23-17-1-1; IC
    23-17-2-7; IC 23-17-2-19; IC 23-17-2-23; IC 23-17-2-25; IC 27-1-
    7-1; IC 28-1-1-1; IC 28-7-1-1; IC 28-12-1-1

18 Am Jur 2d, Corporations §§ 1-27, 42-97.
18 C.J.S., Corporations §§ 1-66.
West's Digest, Corporations ☞1-41.
ALR Digest: Corporations §§ 1-4, 29, 29.5
ALR Index: Articles of Incorporation; Assets; Bylaws; Charter;
    Close Corporation; Consolidation or Merger; Corporate Bonds
    and Bondholders; Corporate Officers, Directors, and Agents;
    Corporate Opportunity; Corporate Responsibility Doctrine;
    Corporate Stock and Stockholders; Corporations; Dissolution or
    Liquidation; Dividends; Domicile and Residence; Foreign
    Corporations; Forfeitures; Liquidation or Dissolution; Minority
    Stockholders; Names; Nonprofit Institutions or Organizations;
    Professional Corporations and Associations; Promoters; Prospec-
    tus; Proxies; Reports; Seal; Stock-Option Plans; Subsidiary
Grounds for Disregarding the Corporate Entity and Piercing the
    Corporate Veil, 45 Am Jur POF3d 1.

§ 1 Nature of corporation

A corporation is a distinct artificial legal entity.

West's Digest, Corporations ⊙1-1.3.

A corporation is an artificial and independent legal entity which derives its existence from statutory authority.[1]

A corporation is by definition not a natural person,[2] and so has no capacity to act as a natural person, for instance as an incorporator,[3] an attorney,[4] or even a crime victim, where some human attribute is necessary for such status.[5]

Although it can act only through its shareholders, officers, and other agents,[6] a corporation is separate and distinct from its shareholders and officers,[7] even if one shareholder owns a majority of the stock in the corporation.[8] Similarly, a corporation's status as an entity distinct from its stockholders is unaffected by the fact that the majority of its stock may be controlled by the same interests that control the stock of another corporation,[9] and generally, the status of

---

[1]Winkler v. V.G. Reed & Sons, Inc., 638 N.E.2d 1228 (Ind. 1994); Benevolent and Protective Order of Elks Local 291 v. Mooney, 666 N.E.2d 970 (Ind. Ct. App. 1996), transfer denied, 673 N.E.2d 766 (Ind. 1996).

1953 Op.Atty.Gen. 440 (corporation is legal fiction and artificial entity created by legislation and formed by procedures prescribed by statute).

[2]1953 Op.Atty.Gen. 440.

[3]1953 Op.Atty.Gen. 440; 1941 Op.Atty.Gen. 353 (only natural persons can act as incorporators).

[4]Indiana Dept. of Public Welfare v. Chair Lance Service, Inc., 523 N.E.2d 1373 (Ind. 1988) (corporation is creature of statute and can neither practice law nor act in person).

[5]Doyle v. State, 468 N.E.2d 528 (Ind. Ct. App. 4th Dist. 1984), reh'g denied, (Oct. 18, 1984) and transfer denied, (Mar. 21, 1985) (charge of theft by deception could not be grounded on alleged creation of false impression in "mind" of corporation, where no human director or shareholder of corporation was deceived).

[6]Indiana Dept. of Public Welfare v. Chair Lance Service, Inc., 523 N.E.2d 1373 (Ind. 1988).

[7]State, Civil Rights Com'n v. County Line Park, Inc., 718 N.E.2d 768 (Ind. Ct. App. 1999), reh'g denied, (Dec. 15, 1999); Mullis v. Brennan, 716 N.E.2d 58 (Ind. Ct. App. 1999); McQuade v. Draw Tite, Inc., 659 N.E.2d 1016 (Ind. 1995); Winkler v. V.G. Reed & Sons, Inc., 638 N.E.2d 1228 (Ind. 1994).

[8]Benson v. Warble, 146 Ind. App. 307, 255 N.E.2d 230 (Div. 2 1970).

[9]Hart, Schaffner & Marx v. Campbell, 110 Ind. App. 312, 38 N.E.2d 895 (1942).

corporations as separate and distinct legal entities is not affected by the fact that they have common officers and stockholders.[10]

> ◆ **Observation:** In some cases it is necessary to disregard the fiction of distinct corporate existence and to hold as a matter of equity that a separate and distinct legal entity does not exist; this doctrine is generally limited in application to the prevention of fraud and injustice in cases involving the rights of third persons.[11]

An unincorporated association does not become a corporation merely by virtue of its affiliation with a corporation.[12]

§ 2 Governing law; types of corporations

Indiana corporations are governed primarily by the Indiana Business Corporation Law and the Indiana Nonprofit Corporation Act.

West's Digest, Corporations ☞3, 12.1-13.

A corporation is governed by the law under which it was created, by applicable legislative enactments, and by the corporate charter or articles of incorporation.[13] When a corporation is created, the state's constitutional and statutory law become part of a corporation's articles of incorporation.[14]

---

[10]Benner-Coryell Lumber Co. v. Indiana Unemployment Compensation Bd., 218 Ind. 20, 29 N.E.2d 776 (1940); Clarke Auto Co. v. Fyffe, 124 Ind. App. 222, 116 N.E.2d 532 (1954); Hart, Schaffner & Marx v. Campbell, 110 Ind. App. 312, 38 N.E.2d 895 (1942).

[11]§§ 78, 120.

[12]Benevolent and Protective Order of Elks Local 291 v. Mooney, 666 N.E.2d 970 (Ind. Ct. App. 1996), transfer denied, 673 N.E.2d 766 (Ind. 1996) (local chapter of incorporated national benevolent society was not corporation).

[13]Scott v. Anderson Newspapers, Inc., 477 N.E.2d 553 (Ind. Ct. App. 4th Dist. 1985), reh'g denied, (June 19, 1985) and transfer denied, (Nov. 4, 1985); Indiana Dept. of State Revenue v. Frank Purcell Walnut Lumber Co., 152 Ind. App. 122, 282 N.E.2d 336 (2d Dist. 1972) (as resident of state under whose laws it was formed, corporation is governed by law of jurisdiction where it was created, and is subject to that jurisdiction's power of taxation).

For discussion of the corporate charter, see § 12.

[14]Brenner v. Powers, 584 N.E.2d 569 (Ind. Ct. App. 3d Dist. 1992), reh'g denied, (Apr. 21, 1992) and transfer denied, (Dec. 18, 1992); Scott v.

The Indiana Business Corporations Law[15] governs the formation, operation, and termination of all Indiana domestic for-profit corporations, whether incorporated before the statute's effective date of July 31, 1987,[16] and to all for-profit corporations incorporated under a law other than that of Indiana that want to transact business in Indiana,[17] although foreign corporations that were authorized to transact business in Indiana on July 31, 1987, are not required to obtain new certificates of authority under the Business Corporations Law to transact business.[18] This includes close, or closely held, corporations,[19] which are typically corporations with relatively few shareholders whose shares are not traded in the securities market,[20] and public corporations,[21] which are founded by the government for public purposes.[22] Private corporations may render public service and yet retain their

---

Anderson Newspapers, Inc., 477 N.E.2d 553 (Ind. Ct. App. 4th Dist. 1985), reh'g denied, (June 19, 1985) and transfer denied, (Nov. 4, 1985).

[15]IC 23-1-17-1 et seq.

[16]IC 23-1-17-3(a).

As to definition of "corporation" or "domestic corporation" under the statute, see IC 23-1-20-5.

Legal Periodicals: Indiana experiment in corporate law: A critique. 24 Val.U.L.Rev. 185 (1990).

Millon, Redefining Corporate Law. 24 Ind. L. Rev. 223 (1991).

Smith, Recent Developments in Corporation Law. 26 Ind. L. Rev. 780 (1993).

[17]IC 23-1-17-4.

As to definition of "foreign corporation" under the statute, see IC 23-1-20-11.

[18]IC 23-1-17-4.

For discussion of requirements pertaining to foreign corporations, see §§ 209 et seq.

[19]Melrose v. Capitol City Motor Lodge, Inc., 705 N.E.2d 985 (Ind. 1998).

[20]Melrose v. Capitol City Motor Lodge, Inc., 705 N.E.2d 985 (Ind. 1998); Barth v. Barth, 659 N.E.2d 559 (Ind. 1995), appeal after remand, 693 N.E.2d 954 (Ind. Ct. App. 1998), transfer denied, 706 N.E.2d 169 (Ind. 1998); Maul v. Van Keppel, 714 N.E.2d 707 (Ind. Ct. App. 1999).

[21]Melrose v. Capitol City Motor Lodge, Inc., 705 N.E.2d 985 (Ind. 1998).

[22]Board of Trustees of Vincennes University v. State of Indiana, 55 U.S. 268, 14 How. 268, 14 L. Ed. 416 (1852), on remand to, 5 Ind. 77, 1854 WL 109 (1854), on reh'g, (Nov. 6, 1854); Todd v. Citizens' Gas Co. of Indianapolis, 46 F.2d 855 (C.C.A. 7th Cir. 1931) (applying Indiana law).

As to municipal and other public corporations, see I.L.E., Municipal Corporations.

character as private,[23] the distinguishing feature being that they do not possess political power.[24]

Business corporations may also be holding companies. A holding company is a type of super-corporation which owns or controls such a dominant interest in one or more other corporations that it can dictate their policies through voting power, or which is in position to control or materially influence the management of one or more companies by virtue of its ownership of securities in another company or other companies.[25]

Not-for-profit corporations are governed by the Indiana Nonprofit Corporation Act.[26] A not-for-profit corporation governed by this statute may be a public benefit, mutual benefit, or religious corporation.[27]

Professional corporations are governed both by their own statute[28] and by the Business Corporation Law, although the professional corporations statute applies if there is a conflict between the two.[29]

Other types of corporations are governed by special statutes. These include:

- financial institutions in general[30]
- banks[31]

---

[23]Bullock v. Billheimer, 175 Ind. 428, 94 N.E. 763 (1911).

[24]Board of Trustees of Vincennes University v. State of Indiana, 55 U.S. 268, 14 How. 268, 14 L. Ed. 416 (1852), on remand to, 5 Ind. 77, 1854 WL 109 (1854), on reh'g, (Nov. 6, 1854) (land-grant university is not public corporation).

[25]Kelley, Glover & Vale v. Heitman, 220 Ind. 625, 44 N.E.2d 981 (1942).

[26]IC 23-17-1-1 et seq.

[27]IC 23-17-2-7.

For discussion of the purposes for which not-for-profit corporations may be formed, see § 4.

[28]IC 23-1.5-1-1 et seq.

Annotation References: Practice by attorneys and physicians as corporate entities or associations under professional service corporation statutes, 4 ALR3d 383.

[29]IC 23-1.5-2-1.

[30]IC 28-1-1-1 et seq.

[31]IC 28-12-1-1 et seq.

As to banks, see I.L.E., Banks and Banking.

- credit unions[32]
- business development credit corporations[33]
- insurance companies[34]
- agricultural cooperatives[35]
- public service corporations or public utilities[36]
- railroads[37]
- trust companies[38]

§ 3   —Role of contract law

Contract law plays a large part in the regulation of corporations.

West's Digest, Corporations ☞12.1-13.

Contract law plays a large part in the regulation of corporations, as a corporation's articles of incorporation and bylaws are considered to constitute a contract between the state and the corporation, between the corporation and its members, and among the members.[39] This is true of both business and not-for-profit corporations.[40] Thus, in determining what rights are created by corporate organizational

---

[32]IC 28-7-1-1 et seq.

[33]IC 23-6-4-1 et seq.

As to public corporations in general, including business development credit corporations, see I.L.E., Municipal Corporations.

[34]IC 27-1-7-1 et seq.

As to insurance companies generally, see I.L.E., Insurance.

[35]IC 15-7-1-1 et seq.

[36]IC 8-1-2-1 et seq.

As to public utility companies, see I.L.E., Carriers; Electricity; Public Service Commission; Telecommunication.

[37]IC 8-4-1-1 et seq.

Applicability of Business Corporation Law to a railroad incorporated before July 1, 1990, see IC 23-1-17-3.1.

As to railroads generally, see I.L.E., Railroads.

[38]IC 28-1-1-1 et seq.

As to trusts and trustees, see I.L.E., Trusts.

[39]Brenner v. Powers, 584 N.E.2d 569 (Ind. Ct. App. 3d Dist. 1992), reh'g denied, (Apr. 21, 1992) and transfer denied, (Dec. 18, 1992); Scott v. Anderson Newspapers, Inc., 477 N.E.2d 553 (Ind. Ct. App. 4th Dist. 1985), reh'g denied, (June 19, 1985) and transfer denied, (Nov. 4, 1985); Orchard Ridge Country Club, Inc. v. Schrey, 470 N.E.2d 780 (Ind. Ct. App. 3d Dist. 1984).

[40]National Bd. of Examiners for Osteopathic Physicians and Surgeons,

documents, Indiana courts have routinely applied the general rules governing contract interpretation and enforcement.[41] Share subscriptions and transfers also involve questions of contract law.[42]

◆ **Practice Guide:** In construing the government's grant of power to a corporation, the words of the grant are to be taken most strongly against the corporation.[43]

§ 4 Purposes

Corporations may generally engage in any lawful business.

West's Digest, Corporations ☞14(1)-14(5).

A corporation incorporated under the Business Corporation Law may engage in any lawful business unless a limited purpose is set forth in its articles of incorporation.[44] However, if the corporation engages in a business that is subject to regulation under another Indiana statute, and that statute contains provisions for incorporation, the corporation may not incorporate under the Business Corporation Law.[45]

Not-for-profit corporations may be public-benefit corporations, religious corporations, or mutual-benefit corporations.[46] Public-benefit corporations are formed for charitable or public purposes, and are exempt from federal taxation.[47] Religious corporations are organized primarily or exclusively for religious purposes.[48] Mutual-benefit corpora-

---

Inc. v. American Osteopathic Ass'n, 645 N.E.2d 608 (Ind. Ct. App. 4th Dist. 1994).

[41]National Bd. of Examiners for Osteopathic Physicians and Surgeons, Inc. v. American Osteopathic Ass'n, 645 N.E.2d 608 (Ind. Ct. App. 4th Dist. 1994); Scott v. Anderson Newspapers, Inc., 477 N.E.2d 553 (Ind. Ct. App. 4th Dist. 1985), reh'g denied, (June 19, 1985) and transfer denied, (Nov. 4, 1985).

[42]§ 38 (subscriptions), §§ 46 et seq. (transfer of shares).

[43]Schisler v. Merchants Trust Co. of Muncie, 228 Ind. 594, 94 N.E.2d 665 (1950).

[44]IC 23-1-22-1(a).

[45]IC 23-1-22-1(b).

For a list of statutes governing special types of corporations, see § 2.

[46]§ 2.

[47]IC 23-17-2-23.

[48]IC 23-17-2-25.

tions are those not-for-profit corporations that are not public-benefit corporations or religious corporations.[49]

A professional corporation may be formed to render certain types of professional services which may legally be performed only by a licensed or certified professional. These services are:[50]

- accounting services
- architectural or engineering services
- legal services
- health care services
- veterinary services
- real estate sales or brokering

§ 5 Powers of state

A corporation can exist only by virtue of statutory authority.

West's Digest, Corporations ☞4.

The power to create corporations is one of the attributes of sovereignty. No corporation can exist without the consent of the sovereign, and a corporation can exist only by virtue of statutory authority,[51] and as creatures of the Legislature, corporations possess only such powers as are expressly or by necessary implication given by their charters or general laws.[52]

---

[49]IC 23-17-2-19.

[50]IC 23-1.5-2-3(a).

Health care professionals in this context are licensed chiropractors, dentists, nurses, optometrists, pharmacists, physical therapists, physicians, podiatrists, psychologists, speech-language pathologists, and audiologists. IC 23-1.5-1-8.

Annotation References: Practice by attorneys and physicians as corporate entities or associations under professional service corporation statutes, 4 ALR3d 383.

[51]Scott v. Anderson Newspapers, Inc., 477 N.E.2d 553 (Ind. Ct. App. 4th Dist. 1985), reh'g denied, (June 19, 1985) and transfer denied, (Nov. 4, 1985); Hall v. Essner, 208 Ind. 99, 193 N.E. 86 (1934) (only legislature can create corporation).

[52]1933 Op.Atty.Gen. 8.

The Indiana Constitution gives the state Legislature the power to create corporations,[53] and imposes no limit on the powers that may be conferred on a corporation.[54] However, except for banking corporations, the state constitution forbids the Legislature to create a corporation by special act.[55] This prohibition is confined to private corporations; the Legislature may create a public corporation by special act.[56] The Legislature may also regulate the exercise of power already possessed by a corporation without violating the constitutional prohibition against the creation of corporations by special act.[57]

The Legislature is also constitutionally empowered to fix the individual liability of stockholders.[58]

§ 6   Statutory changes in corporation laws

Corporation statutes may be amended only where the Legislature has reserved the power to do so.

West's Digest, Corporations ⊸12.2, 13, 38-41.

The United States Supreme Court has held that the legislature of any state has the right to modify the charter of a public corporation or abolish it at its discretion.[59] Generally, however, the legislature may amend an act under which a company is incorporated without violating any constitutional

---

[53]Ind Const Art 11, § 13.

[54]City of Aurora v. West, 9 Ind. 74, 1857 WL 3692 (1857).

[55]Ind Const Art 11, § 13.

Union Ins. Co. v. State ex rel. Indiana Dept. of Ins., 401 N.E.2d 1372 (Ind. Ct. App. 2d Dist. 1980).

[56]Orbison v. Welsh, 242 Ind. 385, 179 N.E.2d 727 (1962) (section does not apply to Indiana Port Commission); In re Train Collision at Gary, Ind. on Jan. 18, 1993, 654 N.E.2d 1137 (Ind. Ct. App. 1995), reh'g denied, (Jan. 5, 1996) and transfer denied, (Dec. 13, 1996) (Legislature properly created Northern Indiana Commuter Transportation District pursuant to statute, as entity was not private corporation, but was created for public purpose).

[57]In re Train Collision at Gary, Ind. on Jan. 18, 1993, 654 N.E.2d 1137 (Ind. Ct. App. 1995), reh'g denied, (Jan. 5, 1996) and transfer denied, (Dec. 13, 1996) (amendment to statute making any transportation district created under statute a municipal corporation did not violate prohibition against creation of corporations by special act).

[58]Ind Const Art 11, § 14.

For discussion of stockholder liability for a corporation's acts and debts, see § 78.

[59]Board of Trustees of Vincennes University v. State of Indiana, 55 U.S.

417

rights, only if that power has been reserved by the legislature.[60] The Business Corporation Law reserves to the General Assembly the power to amend or repeal all or part of the statute at any time, and all corporations subject to the statute will be governed by the amendment or repeal.[61] Any corporation incorporated under a law containing a reservation of powers clause is deemed to have consented, ab initio, to future amendments or repeals.[62]

Where the state has reserved no such power in the statute, it must do so in the corporation's charter, or the corporation must expressly or implicitly accept the amendment, before it may be subject to the amendment.[63] This is so because the United States Constitution forbids the states to make any law impairing the obligation of contracts.[64] The amendment must be within the scope of the power reserved.[65]

> ◆ **Observation:** The reservation of powers clause in the 1949 version of the General Corporation Act was accidentally listed as having been repealed in the 1978 amendments. The clause was restored in 1986 with the General Assembly noting that the inclusion of the reservation of powers clause in the list of repealed sections had been a clerical error, and declaring that its reinstatement of the clause was to be retroactive to July 1, 1978. A corporation incorporated between 1978 and 1986 is therefore subject to the 1987 Business Corporation Law.[66]

268, 14 How. 268, 14 L. Ed. 416 (1852), on remand to, 5 Ind. 77, 1854 WL 109 (1854), on reh'g, (Nov. 6, 1854).

[60]Denny v. Brady, 201 Ind. 59, 163 N.E. 489 (1928).

[61]IC 23-1-17-2.

[62]In re Pennsylvania College Cases, 80 U.S. 190, 20 L.Ed. 550, 13 Wall. 190 (1871); FGS Enterprises, Inc. v. Shimala, 625 N.E.2d 1226 (Ind. 1993), reh'g denied, (Aug. 16, 1994).

[63]Mowrey v. Indianapolis & C.R. Co., 17 F. Cas. 930, No. 9891 (C.C.D. Ind. 1866).

[64]U.S. Const., Art. I, § 10.

For discussion of a corporation's charter as a contract, see § 2.

[65]Martin v. Junction R. Co., 12 Ind. 605, 1859 WL 4725 (1859); Booe v. Junction R. Co., 10 Ind. 93, 1857 WL 5765 (1857) (provision in charter that Legislature may amend it if corporation so desires does not permit amendments not asked for by shareholders of corporation).

[66]FGS Enterprises, Inc. v. Shimala, 625 N.E.2d 1226 (Ind. 1993), reh'g denied, (Aug. 16, 1994).

§ 7 Disregarding the corporate entity; "piercing the corporate veil"

Indiana courts are reluctant to disregard a corporate entity, but will do so to prevent fraud or injustice to a third party.

West's Digest, Corporations ⚷1.4.

Indiana courts are reluctant to disregard a corporate entity,[67] but will do so to prevent fraud or injustice to a third party.[68] The burden is on the party seeking to pierce the corporate veil to prove that the corporate form was so ignored, controlled, or manipulated that it was merely an instrumentality of another, and that misuse of the corporate form would constitute a fraud or promote injustice.[69]

In determining whether a party seeking to pierce the corporate veil has met its burden of showing that corporate form was abused, a court considers whether the party has presented evidence showing:[70]

- undercapitalization
- absence of corporate records
- fraudulent representations by corporate shareholders or directors

---

[67]Winkler v. V.G. Reed & Sons, Inc., 638 N.E.2d 1228 (Ind. 1994); State, Civil Rights Com'n v. County Line Park, Inc., 718 N.E.2d 768 (Ind. Ct. App. 1999), reh'g denied, (Dec. 15, 1999); Gurnik v. Lee, 587 N.E.2d 706 (Ind. Ct. App. 2d Dist. 1992).

[68]Aronson v. Price, 644 N.E.2d 864 (Ind. 1994), reh'g denied, (May 18, 1995); Winkler v. V.G. Reed & Sons, Inc., 638 N.E.2d 1228 (Ind. 1994); State, Civil Rights Com'n v. County Line Park, Inc., 718 N.E.2d 768 (Ind. Ct. App. 1999), reh'g denied, (Dec. 15, 1999); Hart v. Steel Products, Inc., 666 N.E.2d 1270 (Ind. Ct. App. 1996), reh'g denied, (Aug. 22, 1996) and transfer denied, 683 N.E.2d 582 (Ind. 1997).

Trial Strategy References: Grounds for Disregarding the Corporate Entity and Piercing the Corporate Veil, 45 Am Jur POF3d 1.

[69]Winkler v. V.G. Reed & Sons, Inc., 638 N.E.2d 1228 (Ind. 1994); Aronson v. Price, 644 N.E.2d 864 (Ind. 1994), reh'g denied, (May 18, 1995); Wabash Grain, Inc. v. Smith, 700 N.E.2d 234 (Ind. Ct. App. 1998), reh'g denied, (Dec. 7, 1998) and transfer denied, 714 N.E.2d 173 (Ind. 1999); Hart v. Steel Products, Inc., 666 N.E.2d 1270 (Ind. Ct. App. 1996), reh'g denied, (Aug. 22, 1996) and transfer denied, 683 N.E.2d 582 (Ind. 1997).

[70]Hart v. Steel Products, Inc., 666 N.E.2d 1270 (Ind. Ct. App. 1996), reh'g denied, (Aug. 22, 1996) and transfer denied, 683 N.E.2d 582 (Ind. 1997); National Soffit & Escutcheons, Inc. v. Superior Systems, Inc., 98 F.3d 262 (7th Cir. 1996) (applying Indiana law).

- use of corporation to promote fraud, injustice, or illegal activities
- payment by corporation of individual obligations
- commingling of assets and affairs
- failure to observe required corporate formalities
- other shareholder acts or conduct ignoring, controlling, or manipulating corporate form

Other factors include whether the corporate form has been adhered to, whether corporate assets are treated as such or as personal assets, and whether there has been an attempt to deceive third parties.[71]

The legal fiction of a separate corporate identity will be disregarded to the extent the distinction between the corporation and the individual no longer exists,[72] but only where the corporate form is unfairly used to prevent a party from recovering from the corporate shareholders personally.[73]

◆ **Illustrations:** Piercing the corporate veil was warranted where the principal of a corporation advertised himself as the corporation's owner, the contractor's licenses that he advertised were held in his name alone, and the corporation had never issued stock.[74] Furthermore, a corporation was a debtor's alter ego, and corporate identity would be disregarded, where testimony showed that the plaintiff bank had dealt with the debtor for several years before the execution of the promissory note at issue; the debtor submitted an individual financial statement in which he included both personal and corporate assets and stated that he owned all the stock in the corporation; the bank's vice-president testified that at the time of the loan he believed the debtor owned all of the corporate stock, although the debtor testified that he had transferred the stock to his children; and minutes of shareholder meetings and other documentation supported the conclusion

---

[71]Winkler v. V.G. Reed & Sons, Inc., 638 N.E.2d 1228 (Ind. 1994).

[72]County Line Towing, Inc. v. Cincinnati Ins. Co., 714 N.E.2d 285 (Ind. Ct. App. 1999), transfer denied, (Jan. 7, 2000); Merchants Nat. Bank & Trust Co. of Indianapolis v. H.L.C. Enterprises, Inc., 441 N.E.2d 509 (Ind. Ct. App. 1st Dist. 1982) (where corporation is shareholder's alter ego).

[73]County Line Towing, Inc. v. Cincinnati Ins. Co., 714 N.E.2d 285 (Ind. Ct. App. 1999), transfer denied, (Jan. 7, 2000).

[74]A.B.C. Home & Real Estate Inspection, Inc. v. Plummer, 500 N.E.2d 1257 (Ind. Ct. App. 3d Dist. 1986), reh'g denied, (Jan. 21, 1987).

that the president was the sole stockholder at the time of the loan.[75]

Similarly, in the case of a corporate shareholder, in order to prevent fraud or injustice, the fiction of corporate entity may be disregarded where one corporation is so organized and controlled and its affairs are so conducted that it is a mere instrumentality or conduit of another corporation.[76] Justification for piercing the corporate veil may exist where innocent third parties have no way of knowing with which entity they are dealing.[77] Identity of corporate officers and the filing of consolidated tax returns are considerations favoring piercing the corporate veil where the shareholder sought to be held liable is another corporation.[78]

◆ **Practice Guide:** An attempt to pierce the corporate veil is equitable by nature, and the plaintiff in such a case is not entitled to a jury trial.[79]

---

[75]Lambert v. Farmers Bank, Frankfort, Ind., 519 N.E.2d 745 (Ind. Ct. App. 1st Dist. 1988).

[76]Stacey-Rand, Inc. v. J.J. Holman, Inc., 527 N.E.2d 726 (Ind. Ct. App. 1st Dist. 1988), reh'g denied, (Oct. 17, 1988); Extra Energy Coal Co. v. Diamond Energy and Resources, Inc., 467 N.E.2d 439 (Ind. Ct. App. 3d Dist. 1984); Urbanational Developers, Inc. v. Shamrock Engineering, Inc., 175 Ind. App. 416, 372 N.E.2d 742 (3d Dist. 1978).

[77]Detrick v. Midwest Pipe & Steel, Inc., 598 N.E.2d 1074 (Ind. Ct. App. 3d Dist. 1992) (although two corporations owned no interest in each other, there was no identity of shareholders, directors, or officers between corporations, and corporate funds were not commingled, fact question as to whether one corporate was conduit for another existed where plaintiff claimed that second corporation was created for sole purpose of hauling product of first corporation); Stacey-Rand, Inc. v. J.J. Holman, Inc., 527 N.E.2d 726 (Ind. Ct. App. 1st Dist. 1988), reh'g denied, (Oct. 17, 1988).

[78]Archem, Inc. v. Simo, 549 N.E.2d 1054 (Ind. Ct. App. 1st Dist. 1990), reh'g denied, (Mar. 27, 1990) and transfer denied, (Aug. 31, 1990) and cert. dismissed, 498 U.S. 1076, 111 S. Ct. 944, 112 L. Ed. 2d 1032 (1991); Stacey-Rand, Inc. v. J.J. Holman, Inc., 527 N.E.2d 726 (Ind. Ct. App. 1st Dist. 1988), reh'g denied, (Oct. 17, 1988); Extra Energy Coal Co. v. Diamond Energy and Resources, Inc., 467 N.E.2d 439 (Ind. Ct. App. 3d Dist. 1984).

[79]Stacey-Rand, Inc. v. J.J. Holman, Inc., 527 N.E.2d 726 (Ind. Ct. App. 1st Dist. 1988), reh'g denied, (Oct. 17, 1988).

II. FORMATION AND EXISTENCE OF CORPORATION

A. IN GENERAL

Research References

IC 23-1-18-9; IC 23-1-18-10; IC 23-1-21-1; IC 23-1-21-3; IC 23-1-22-2; IC 23-17-29-9; IC 23-17-29-10

18, 18A Am Jur 2d, Corporations §§ 98-332.
18 C.J.S., Corporations §§ 67-121.
West's Digest, Corporations ☞28(.5)-35.
ALR Digest: Corporations §§ 5-28
ALR Index: Articles of Incorporation; Assets; Bylaws; Charter; Close Corporation; Consolidation or Merger; Corporate Bonds and Bondholders; Corporate Officers, Directors, and Agents; Corporate Opportunity; Corporate Responsibility Doctrine; Corporate Stock and Stockholders; Corporations; Dissolution or Liquidation; Dividends; Domicile and Residence; Foreign Corporations; Forfeitures; Liquidation or Dissolution; Minority Stockholders; Names; Nonprofit Institutions or Organizations; Professional Corporations and Associations; Promoters; Prospectus; Proxies; Reports; Seal; Stock-Option Plans; Subsidiary

§ 8   Generally

A corporation is formed upon the delivery of signed articles of incorporation to the Secretary of State for filing.

West's Digest, Corporations ☞35.

A corporation is formed when the incorporators sign the articles of incorporation and cause them to be delivered to the Secretary of State for filing.[80] Unless a delayed effective date is specified, a corporation's existence begins when the articles of incorporation are filed.[81] A corporation's existence continues for the period specified in its articles of incorporation, or perpetually if no limitation is specified.[82]

◆ **Caution:** It is a Class A misdemeanor to sign a document the signer knows is false in any material respect

---

[80]IC 23-1-21-1.

    As to the contents of articles of incorporation, see § 12.

[81]IC 23-1-21-3(a).

[82]IC 23-1-22-2.

with intent that the document be delivered to the Secretary of State for filing.[83]

After the articles of incorporation have been filed, the incorporators or directors are to hold an organizational meeting,[84] and are to adopt bylaws governing the corporation.[85]

§ 9   Effect of defective incorporation or organization

A de facto corporation is one which exists for all practical purposes, but is not strictly speaking a legal corporation because of a failure to comply with some legal formality in organization.

West's Digest, Corporations ☞28(.5)-28(3), 32(3).

Even if a corporation has not been properly organized or incorporated, and so lacks the status of a de jure corporation,[86] defective incorporation or organization does not necessarily render corporate acts or transactions void. The organization may still be a de facto corporation and thus, for all practical purposes, a corporate body with appropriate powers.[87] A de facto corporation is an association which actually exists for all practical purposes as a corporate body, but which, because of failure to comply with some provision of the law,[88] has no legal right to corporate existence as against a direct attack by the state. As such, it is distinguishable from a corporation de jure, a corporation which is in all respects legal.[89] Thus, where an organization has operated for a number of years as a corporation and rights have been acquired and established, at least a de facto corporate existence is strongly implied.[90]

The conditions for the existence of a de facto corporation

---

[83]IC 23-1-18-10; IC 23-17-29-10.

[84]§ 25.

[85]§ 26.

[86]Burk v. Mead, 159 Ind. 252, 64 N.E. 880 (1902).

[87]Sunman-Dearborn Community School Corp. v. Kral-Zepf-Freitag and Associates, 167 Ind. App. 339, 338 N.E.2d 707 (1st Dist. 1975).

[88]Aetna Life Ins. Co. of Hartford, Conn. v. Weatherhogg, 103 Ind. App. 506, 4 N.E.2d 679 (1936) (failure to properly file articles of incorporation).

[89]Marion Bond Co. v. Mexican Coffee & Rubber Co., 160 Ind. 558, 65 N.E. 748 (1902); Cruse v. Axtell, 50 Ind. 49, 1875 WL 5770 (1875).

[90]Anderson v. Kinser, 241 Ind. 555, 173 N.E.2d 914 (1961); Western

are well-settled and indisputable.[91] De facto corporate existence requires a valid law under which the corporation might have been organized;[92] a bona fide attempt to incorporate under that law, and colorable or apparent compliance with the law; and[93] an actual exercise of corporate powers[94]

The contracts of de facto corporations may generally be enforced by and against them in the same way and to the same extent as if they were de jure corporations.[95]

Generally, an organization cannot be a de facto corporation if the statute under which it was purportedly incorporated is unconstitutional,[96] because there cannot be a de facto corporation unless a de jure corporation is possible.[97]

§ 10 Attacks on corporate existence

Any attack on an organization's status as a de jure corporation must be made by the state in a direct action.

West's Digest, Corporations ☞29(.5)-29(2).

Although the existence of a corporation may be collaterally attacked when the corporation could not legally become a

---

Mach. Works v. Edwards Mach. & Tool Corp., 223 Ind. 655, 63 N.E.2d 535 (1945).

[91]Dowdle v. Central Brick Co., 206 Ind. 242, 189 N.E. 145 (1934); Clark v. American Cannel Coal Co., 165 Ind. 213, 73 N.E. 1083 (1905).

[92]Jennings v. Dark, 175 Ind. 332, 92 N.E. 778 (1910); Sunman-Dearborn Community School Corp. v. Kral-Zepf-Freitag and Associates, 167 Ind. App. 339, 338 N.E.2d 707 (1st Dist. 1975).

[93]Sterne v. Fletcher American Co., 204 Ind. 35, 181 N.E. 37 (1932); Clark v. American Cannel Coal Co., 165 Ind. 213, 73 N.E. 1083 (1905); Sunman-Dearborn Community School Corp. v. Kral-Zepf-Freitag and Associates, 167 Ind. App. 339, 338 N.E.2d 707 (1st Dist. 1975).

[94]Sunman-Dearborn Community School Corp. v. Kral-Zepf-Freitag and Associates, 167 Ind. App. 339, 338 N.E.2d 707 (1st Dist. 1975); Malone v. State, 547 N.E.2d 1101 (Ind. Ct. App. 1st Dist. 1989), transfer denied, (Mar. 23, 1990); John Mohr and Sons v. Apex Terminal Warehouses, Inc., 422 F.2d 638 (7th Cir. 1970) (applying Indiana law).

[95]Doty v. Patterson, 155 Ind. 60, 56 N.E. 668 (1900); Sunman-Dearborn Community School Corp. v. Kral-Zepf-Freitag and Associates, 167 Ind. App. 339, 338 N.E.2d 707 (1st Dist. 1975) (de facto corporation has power to contract).

[96]Clark v. American Cannel Coal Co., 165 Ind. 213, 73 N.E. 1083 (1905).

[97]Indiana Bond Co. v. Ogle, 22 Ind. App. 593, 54 N.E. 407 (1899).

corporation de jure,[98] the validity of a de facto corporate existence can generally be questioned only directly by the state,[99] in a quo warranto action.[1] The Secretary of State's filing of a corporation's articles of incorporation is conclusive proof that the incorporators satisfied all conditions precedent to incorporation except in a proceeding by the state to cancel or revoke the incorporation or involuntarily dissolve the corporation.[2]

Thus, a ruling as to the valid existence of a corporation cannot be made in a collateral proceeding,[3] unless the right to make such a collateral attack is conferred by an express statutory declaration,[4] and any person other than the state dealing with a de facto corporation must assume it to be a de jure corporation.[5] This rule has been applied to cases involving contracts between purported corporations and third parties,[6] but its application is not limited to such cases.[7] Not even the state may challenge the existence of a de jure

---

[98]Clark v. American Cannel Coal Co., 165 Ind. 213, 73 N.E. 1083 (1905) (after expiration of period fixed by law for its existence, corporation is not even de facto, and its existence is subject to collateral attack).

[99]Anderson v. Kinser, 241 Ind. 555, 173 N.E.2d 914 (1961); Western Mach. Works v. Edwards Mach. & Tool Corp., 223 Ind. 655, 63 N.E.2d 535 (1945); Doty v. Patterson, 155 Ind. 60, 56 N.E. 668 (1900) (stockholders in de facto corporation cannot be held liable as partners).

[1]Anderson v. Kinser, 241 Ind. 555, 173 N.E.2d 914 (1961); Western Mach. Works v. Edwards Mach. & Tool Corp., 223 Ind. 655, 63 N.E.2d 535 (1945).

[2]IC 23-1-21-3(b).

[3]Joliff v. Muncie Electric Light Co., 181 Ind. 650, 105 N.E. 234 (1914); Smith v. Cleveland, C., C. & St. L. Ry. Co., 170 Ind. 382, 81 N.E. 501 (1907); Marion Bond Co. v. Mexican Coffee & Rubber Co., 160 Ind. 558, 65 N.E. 748 (1902); Cleveland, C., C. & St. L. Ry. Co. v. Feight, 41 Ind. App. 416, 84 N.E. 15 (Div. 1 1908).

[4]Western Mach. Works v. Edwards Mach. & Tool Corp., 223 Ind. 655, 63 N.E.2d 535 (1945).

[5]Crowder v. Town of Sullivan, 128 Ind. 486, 28 N.E. 94 (1891).

[6]Marion Bond Co. v. Mexican Coffee & Rubber Co., 160 Ind. 558, 65 N.E. 748 (1902); Baker v. Neff, 73 Ind. 68, 1880 WL 6569 (1880).

[7]Joint County Park Bd. of Ripley, Dearborn and Decatur Counties v. Stegemoller, 228 Ind. 103, 88 N.E.2d 686 (1949), reh'g denied, 228 Ind. 103, 89 N.E.2d 720 (1950) (eminent domain); Doty v. Patterson, 155 Ind. 60, 56 N.E. 668 (1900).

corporation collaterally, but must do so in direct proceedings.[8]

> ◆ **Practice Guide:** A certificate of existence or, in the case of a foreign corporation, of authority to do business in Indiana, may be relied upon as conclusive evidence that the corporation exists or is entitled to do business in Indiana, subject to any qualification stated in the certificate.[9] Such certificates may be furnished by the Secretary of State at the request of any person,[10] and are to set forth various information as required by statute.[11] Courts predating the Business Corporation Law and the Nonprofit Corporations Act have also ruled that corporate existence may be proved by the production of the corporation's articles of incorporation[12] or its records,[13] or by parol testimony,[14] and that parties may also stipulate to a corporation's existence.[15]

§ 11 Estoppel to deny corporate existence

A person who has dealt with an organization as a corporation is estopped to deny the organization's corporate existence.

West's Digest, Corporations ☞34(1)-34(8).

A person who has contracted with, or otherwise dealt with, a company as a corporation is estopped to deny its corporate existence.[16] Thus, in the absence of fraud, even if an organization cannot show that it is a de facto corporation, a creditor who deals with the organization as a corporation, believes

---

[8]Jennings v. Dark, 175 Ind. 332, 92 N.E. 778 (1910); Clark v. American Cannel Coal Co., 165 Ind. 213, 73 N.E. 1083 (1905).

[9]IC 23-1-18-9(c); IC 23-17-29-9(c).

[10]IC 23-1-18-9(a); IC 23-17-29-9(a).

[11]IC 23-1-18-9(b); IC 23-17-29-9(b).

[12]Porter v. State ex rel. Dunkleberg, 141 Ind. 488, 40 N.E. 1061 (1895).

[13]Whitesides v. Franklin College, 53 Ind. 93, 1876 WL 8457 (1876); Vawter v. Franklin College, 53 Ind. 88, 1876 WL 6798 (1876).

[14]Norton v. State, 74 Ind. 337, 1881 WL 6444 (1881); Von Hauger v. State, 252 Ind. 619, 251 N.E.2d 116 (1969).

[15]Rikhoff v. Brown's Rotary Shuttle Sewing Mach. Co., 68 Ind. 388, 1879 WL 5677 (1879).

[16]Doty v. Patterson, 155 Ind. 60, 56 N.E. 668 (1900); Sunman-Dearborn Community School Corp. v. Kral-Zepf-Freitag and Associates, 167 Ind. App. 339, 338 N.E.2d 707 (1st Dist. 1975); Aetna Life Ins. Co. of Hartford, Conn. v. Weatherhogg, 103 Ind. App. 506, 4 N.E.2d 679 (1936).

the corporation to be in existence, and relies on the credit of the supposed corporation is estopped from holding the organization's shareholders liable as partners.[17]

◆ **Illustration:** An appellant who has treated an organization as a corporation by suing it, securing a receiver for it, and obtaining a judgment against it as such, is estopped to assert that the organization is not a corporation.[18]

The mere fact that a person contracting with a corporation is estopped to deny that it existed as a corporation on the date of the contract does not preclude him or her, or his or her successors, from asserting a subsequent cessation of its existence.[19]

The corporation itself may also be estopped to deny its corporate existence where it has contracted a debt or incurred a liability in its corporate capacity.[20] A corporation's promoters and incorporators,[21] and stockholders such as those who are sued by the corporation to recover improperly received dividends,[22] may also be estopped to deny the existence of a corporation.

B. FORMATION OF CORPORATION

Research References

IC 23-1-21-1; IC 23-1-21-2; IC 23-1-21-5 to IC 23-1-21-7; IC 23-1-22-2; IC 23-1-23-1 to IC 23-1-23-3; IC 23-1-24-1 to IC 23-1-24-3; IC 23-1-38-1 to IC 23-1-38-3; IC 23-1-38-5 to IC 23-1-38-9; IC 23-1-39-1 to IC 23-1-39-3; IC 23-1-49-6; IC 23-1.5-2-8; IC 23-1.5-2-9; IC 23-15-1-1; IC 23-17-3-2; IC 23-17-3-7 to IC 23-17-3-9; IC 23-

---

[17]Jennings v. Dark, 175 Ind. 332, 92 N.E. 778 (1910); Sunman-Dearborn Community School Corp. v. Kral-Zepf-Freitag and Associates, 167 Ind. App. 339, 338 N.E.2d 707 (1st Dist. 1975); Edward Shoes, Inc. v. Orenstein, 333 F. Supp. 39 (N.D. Ind. 1971) (applying Indiana law).

[18]First Nat. Bank v. Dovetail Body & Gear Co., 143 Ind. 534, 42 N.E. 924 (1896).

[19]Clark v. American Cannel Coal Co., 165 Ind. 213, 73 N.E. 1083 (1905).

[20]Sunman-Dearborn Community School Corp. v. Kral-Zepf-Freitag and Associates, 167 Ind. App. 339, 338 N.E.2d 707 (1st Dist. 1975); Pilliod v. Angola Ry. & Power Co., 46 Ind. App. 719, 91 N.E. 829 (1910).

[21]Shafer v. Moriarty, 46 Ind. 9, 1874 WL 6083 (1874); Harwood v. Masquelette, 95 Ind. App. 338, 181 N.E. 380 (1932).

For discussion of incorporators, see § 17.

[22]Shiffer v. Akenbrook, 75 Ind. App. 149, 130 N.E. 241 (Div. 2 1921).

For discussion of dividends, see §§ 58 et seq.

17-5-1 to IC 23-17-5-3; IC 23-17-6-1 to IC 23-17-6-3; IC 23-17-
17-1; IC 23-17-17-3 to IC 23-17-17-10; IC 23-17-18-1; IC 23-17-
19-3

18, 18A Am Jur 2d, Corporations §§ 98-332.
18 C.J.S., Corporations §§ 67-121.
West's Digest, Corporations ☞18, 30(1)-30(5), 43-47, 51-58, 298(1).
ALR Digest: Corporations §§ 5-28, 41-44, 166-173
ALR Index: Articles of Incorporation; Assets; Bylaws; Charter;
    Close Corporation; Consolidation or Merger; Corporate Bonds
    and Bondholders; Corporate Officers, Directors, and Agents;
    Corporate Opportunity; Corporate Responsibility Doctrine;
    Corporate Stock and Stockholders; Corporations; Dissolution or
    Liquidation; Dividends; Domicile and Residence; Foreign
    Corporations; Forfeitures; Liquidation or Dissolution; Minority
    Stockholders; Names; Nonprofit Institutions or Organizations;
    Professional Corporations and Associations; Promoters; Prospec-
    tus; Proxies; Reports; Seal; Stock-Option Plans; Subsidiary
6 Am Jur Legal Forms 2d, Corporations §§ 74:101, 74:125, 74:134,
    74:137, 74:148, 74:150, 74:177, 74:844, 74:845, 74:902, 74:903,
    74:935, 74:940, 74:991, 74:993.
6A Am Jur Legal Forms 2d, Corporations § 74:1351.
7A Am Jur Pleading and Practice Forms, Annotated (rev. ed.),
    Corporations §§ 10, 11.

§ 12   Articles of incorporation

**Statutes require that specified information be contained
in the articles of incorporation for business and not-for-
profit corporations.**

West's Digest, Corporations ☞18.

The articles of incorporation for a business corporation
must set forth:[23]

- the corporation's name
- the number of shares the corporation is authorized to
  issue

------

[23]IC 23-1-21-2(a).

As to requirements for corporate names, see §§ 18 et seq.

Forms References: Corporations organized for profit—Articles or
certificates of incorporation—General form. 6 Am Jur Legal Forms 2d,
Corporations § 74:148.

Corporations organized for profit—Articles of incorporation, with option for subchapter S election. 6 Am Jur Legal Forms 2d, Corporations
§ 74:150.

Corporations organized for profit—Articles of incorporation—Indiana.
6 Am Jur Legal Forms 2d, Corporations § 74:177.

- the street address of the corporation's initial registered office in Indiana and the name of its initial registered agent at that office
- the name and address of each incorporator

The articles of incorporation for a not-for-profit corporation must contain:[24]

- the corporation's name
- one of the following statements: "This corporation is a public benefit corporation;" "This corporation is a mutual benefit corporation;" "This corporation is a religious corporation"
- the street address of the corporation's initial registered office in Indiana and the name of the corporation's initial registered agent at that office
- the name and address of each incorporator
- whether the corporation will have members
- provisions that are not inconsistent with any law regarding the distribution of assets on dissolution

In addition to the matters noted above, the articles of incorporation of a business corporation may set forth any of the following:[25]

- the names and addresses of the individuals who are to serve as the initial directors
- provisions not inconsistent with law regarding: (1) the purpose or purposes for which the corporation is organized; (2) managing the business and regulating the affairs of the corporation; (3) defining, limiting, and regulating the powers of the corporation, its board of directors, and shareholders; (4) a par value for authorized shares or classes of shares; (5) the imposition of personal liability on shareholders for the debts of the corporation to a specified extent and upon specified conditions

---

[24]IC 23-17-3-2.

As to requirements for names for not-for-profit corporations, see §§ 18 et seq.

Forms References: Articles of incorporation—Nonprofit corporation—Stock corporation. 6 Am Jur Legal Forms 2d, Corporations § 74:844.

Articles of incorporation—nonprofit corporation—Nonstock corporation. 6 Am Jur Legal Forms 2d, Corporations § 74:845.

[25]IC 23-1-21-2(b).

For discussion of matters to be set forth in a corporation's bylaws, see § 26.

- any provision that under the statute is required or permitted to be set forth in the bylaws

The articles of incorporation for a business corporation need not set forth any of the corporate powers enumerated in the Business Corporation Law.[26]

When a corporation is formed under Indiana law, the state's constitutional and statutory law become part of its articles of incorporation.[27]

§ 13 Amendment of articles of incorporation

A corporation's articles of incorporation may be amended by vote of the shareholders or, in some cases, of the board of directors.

West's Digest, Corporations ⚖18.

Shareholders have no vested property rights arising from any provision in the articles of incorporation.[28] Therefore, a corporation may amend its articles of incorporation at any time to add or change a provision that is required or permitted to be in the articles of incorporation, or to delete a provision that is not required, according to the law in effect on the effective date of the amendment.[29] For instance, an amendment may be adopted to extinguish the preemptive rights of a group of shareholders.[30] The amendment of articles of incorporation does not create a new corporation,[31] nor does it affect a cause of action existing against or in favor of the corporation, a proceeding to which the corporation is a

---

[26]IC 23-1-21-2(c).

The powers of a corporation as enumerated in IC 23-1-22-2, are discussed in §§ 122 et seq.

[27]Westport Stone Co. v. Thomas, 175 Ind. 319, 94 N.E. 406 (1911); Scott v. Anderson Newspapers, Inc., 477 N.E.2d 553 (Ind. Ct. App. 4th Dist. 1985), reh'g denied, (June 19, 1985) and transfer denied, (Nov. 4, 1985); Bajdek v. Board of Trustees of Am. Legion Pulaski Post No. 357 Trust for Veterans of World War I, 132 Ind. App. 116, 173 N.E.2d 61 (1961); Mercantile Commercial Bank v. Southwestern Indiana Coal Corporation, 93 Ind. App. 313, 169 N.E. 91 (1929), reh'g denied, 93 Ind. App. 313, 171 N.E. 310 (1930).

[28]IC 23-1-38-1(b).

[29]IC 23-1-38-1(a); IC 23-17-17-3.

[30]Scott v. Anderson Newspapers, Inc., 477 N.E.2d 553 (Ind. Ct. App. 4th Dist. 1985), reh'g denied, (June 19, 1985) and transfer denied, (Nov. 4, 1985).

[31]1902 Op.Atty.Gen. 111.

party, or the pre-existing rights of persons other than shareholders of the corporation.[32]

Unless the articles of incorporation provide otherwise, the corporation's board of directors may make amendments without shareholder or member action to:[33]

- extend the duration of the corporation, if it was incorporated at a time when limited duration was required by law
- delete the names and addresses of the initial directors
- delete the name and address of the initial registered agent or registered office, if a statement of change is on file with the Secretary of State
- change each issued and unissued authorized share of an outstanding class into a greater number of whole shares or a lesser number of whole shares and fractional shares if the corporation has only shares of that class outstanding
- change the corporate name by substituting the word "corporation," "incorporated," "company," "limited," or an abbreviation for one of those words, for a similar word or abbreviation in the name, or by adding, deleting, or changing a geographical attribution for the name
- reduce the number of authorized shares solely as the result of a cancellation of treasury shares
- include a statement identifying the corporation as a public benefit, mutual benefit, or religious corporation.
- make any other change expressly permitted by the Business Corporation Law to be made without shareholder action

These limitations on the types of amendments the board may adopt without shareholder action do not apply if the corporation has not yet issued shares, in which case the directors or,

---

[32]IC 23-1-38-9.

[33]IC 23-1-38-2.

As to similar requirements under Indiana Nonprofit Corporation Act see, IC 23-17-17-4(a).

Forms References: Directors' resolution amending articles or certificate—General form—No shareholder action required. 6 Am Jur Legal Forms 2d, Corporations § 74:902.

if the directors have not been selected, the incorporators, may adopt any permissible amendment.[34]

The board of directors may also submit proposals for amendments to the shareholders.[35] Generally, the board of directors must recommend the amendment to the shareholders before it may be adopted. However, board recommendation is not necessary if the board determines that it should make no recommendation because of some special circumstances such as a conflict of interest, and communicates the basis for that determination to the shareholders.[36] The board of directors may condition its submission of the proposed amendment on any basis.[37]

Before the meeting at which the shareholders or members are to vote on the proposed amendment, the corporation is to notify each shareholder or member, whether he or she is entitled to vote,[38] of the meeting, and must state that a purpose of the meeting is to consider the proposed amendment. The notice must contain a copy or a summary of the proposed amendment.[39] Generally, the shareholders or members entitled to vote must approve the amendment by a majority of the votes entitled to be cast on the amendment before it may be adopted.[40]

§ 14   —Filing requirements

Amended articles of incorporation are required to be filed with the Secretary of State pursuant to statute.

West's Digest, Corporations ⊸18.

---

[34]IC 23-1-38-5.

As to similar requirements under Indiana Nonprofit Corporation Act see, IC 23-17-17-4(b).

[35]IC 23-1-38-3(a).

Forms References: Directors' resolution amending articles or certificate—General form—Submittal to vote of shareholders. 6 Am Jur Legal Forms 2d, Corporations § 74:903.

[36]IC 23-1-38-3(b)(1).

[37]IC 23-1-38-3(c).

[38]As to the voting list, see §§ 87 et seq.

[39]IC 23-1-38-3(d); IC 23-17-17-5(c).

For discussion of notice of shareholders' and members' meetings, see § 85.

[40]IC 23-1-38-3(b)(3); IC 23-17-17-6(e).

For discussion of shareholder and member voting, see §§ 87 et seq.

Amended articles of incorporation must be filed with the Secretary of State. The amendments must set forth:[41]

- the name of the corporation
- the text of each amendment adopted
- if an amendment provides for an exchange, reclassification, or cancellation of issued shares, provisions for implementing the amendment, if not contained in the amendment itself
- the date of each amendment's adoption
- if an amendment was adopted by the incorporators or board of directors without shareholder action, a statement to that effect and that shareholder action was not required
- if an amendment was approved by the shareholders: (1) the designation, number of outstanding shares, number of votes entitled to be cast by each voting group entitled to vote separately on the amendment, and number of votes of each voting group represented at the meeting; and (2) either the total number of votes cast for and against the amendment by each voting group entitled to vote separately on the amendment, or the total number of votes cast for the amendment by each voting group and a statement that the number cast for the amendment by each voting group was sufficient for approval by that voting group

Somewhat different requirements apply when the articles of incorporation are amended to carry out a plan of reorganization ordered by a court under federal statute.[42]

§ 15 Restatement of articles of incorporation

Articles of incorporation may be restated and filed with

---

[41]IC 23-1-38-6(a).

As to similar requirements under Indiana Nonprofit Corporation Act see, IC 23-17-17-7(a).

For discussion of voting and voting groups, see §§ 87 et seq.

Forms References: Articles of amendment—Prior to issuance of stock—by directors' resolution. 6 Am Jur Legal Forms 2d, Corporations § 74:935.

Articles of amendment—After issuance of shares—By vote of the shareholders. 6 Am Jur Legal Forms 2d, Corporations § 74:940.

[42]IC 23-1-38-8; IC 23-17-17-10.

For discussion of a corporation's insolvency, see §§ 168 et seq.

**the Secretary of State with or without amendments to the
original articles.**

West's Digest, Corporations ☞18.

Articles of incorporation may be restated and filed with
the Secretary of State with or without amendments to the
original articles.[43] Properly adopted restated articles of
incorporation supersede the original articles of incorporation
and all amendments to them.[44] A substantive change in the
articles of incorporation, however, may be accomplished only
by amendment, not by restatement.[45]

§ 16 Professional corporations; certificate of registration

**A professional corporation must receive a certificate of
registration before it may apply for a certificate of incorporation.**

West's Digest, Corporations ☞30(1)-30(5).

The Secretary of State may issue a certificate of incorporation for a professional corporation only if a certificate of
registration has first been obtained.[46] Application for a certificate of registration is to be made to the authority which
regulates the professionals forming the corporation, and
must contain the name and address of the proposed corporation and any other information required by the authority.[47]
Upon a determination that the professionals involved in the
corporation are properly licensed, and that the corporation
will be properly organized, and upon receipt of the proper
fee, the regulating authority is to issue a certificate of
registration for the corporation.[48] The incorporators must
present the certificate of registration to the Secretary of
State at the time the articles of incorporation are presented

---

[43]IC 23-1-38-7; IC 23-17-17-8.

[44]IC 23-1-38-7(e); IC 23-17-17-9(c).

[45]National Bd. of Examiners for Osteopathic Physicians and Surgeons,
Inc. v. American Osteopathic Ass'n, 645 N.E.2d 608 (Ind. Ct. App. 4th
Dist. 1994).

[46]IC 23-1.5-2-9(a).

[47]IC 23-1.5-2-9(b).

[48]IC 23-1.5-2-9(c).

for filing,[49] and the Secretary of State, within 60 days after filing the articles of incorporation, must issue a certificate of incorporation if the articles of incorporation conform to law.[50]

§ 17 Incorporators

An incorporator may enter into contracts with the corporation to be formed, and the corporation may adopt contracts entered into between the incorporator and third parties.

West's Digest, Corporations ⚯30(1)-30(5).

The incorporator of a corporation is the person who signs the articles of incorporation and causes them to be delivered to the Secretary of State for filing. There may be more than one incorporator.[51] A corporation has the right to make contracts with its incorporators, also referred to as promoters, to pay them for their services and to purchase property from them.[52] However, a promoter who brings about the organization of a corporation and aids in securing subscriptions has been held to occupy a fiduciary relationship toward the corporation and its stockholders and those expected to buy stock. Thus, if the incorporator expects to be paid for his or her services, it should be made clear to all of them.[53] Despite the fact that the promoter has a right to sell property to a corporation, because his or her relation is fiduciary, he or she may sell property to it only when there is an independent board of officers representing the corporation.[54]

A corporation may also adopt or ratify a promoter's contract with a third party, thereby binding itself to the contract, unless some provision in the corporation's charter

---

[49]IC 23-1.5-2-9(d).

[50]IC 23-1.5-2-9(e).

Forms References: Articles or certificate of incorporation for professional corporation—General form. 6A Am Jur Legal Forms 2d, Corporations § 74:1351.

[51]IC 23-1-21-1.

[52]Kiess v. Eason, 442 F.2d 712 (7th Cir. 1971) (applying Indiana law); Bruner v. Brown, 139 Ind. 600, 38 N.E. 318 (1894).

[53]Cushion Heel Shoe Co. v. Hartt, 181 Ind. 167, 103 N.E. 1063 (1914) (disapproved of on other grounds by, Indianapolis Blue Print & Mfg. Co. v. Kennedy, 215 Ind. 409, 19 N.E.2d 554 (1939)).

[54]Parker v. Boyle, 178 Ind. 560, 99 N.E. 986 (1912).

or an applicable statute provides otherwise.[55] Ratification of
a promoter's contract may be implied.[56] However, if some
requirement for incorporation is not met, the purported
corporation will be treated as a partnership or sole
proprietorship, and the promoter will be personally liable for
obligations created by any contract entered into in his or her
own name.[57] Generally, where an individual or sole trader or
partnership organizes a corporation to take over his or her
business and transfers assets used in the business to the
corporation, it becomes in effect merely the alter ego of the
incorporator, and the corporation is liable for the incorporator's pre-existing debts and liabilities.[58]

If the corporation does not adopt a contract after the
corporation comes into existence, the contract is not binding
on the corporation.[59] Even if the corporation adopts the
contract after the corporation is formed, the promoter is not
discharged from personal liability on the contract,[60] unless
the promoter and the third party have agreed that the promoter will not be personally liable.[61] The promoter may also
sue and recover on a contract he or she personally made with
a third party, even if the contract was made on behalf of the
corporation.[62]

If a de jure corporation is ultimately not formed because of
a procedural defect, the business may nonetheless be a de
facto corporation, in which case contracts entered into by the
promoter on behalf of the purported corporation will be bind-

---

[55]Indianapolis Blue Print & Mfg. Co. v. Kennedy, 215 Ind. 409, 19
N.E.2d 554 (1939).

[56]Indianapolis Blue Print & Mfg. Co. v. Kennedy, 215 Ind. 409, 19
N.E.2d 554 (1939).

[57]Sterne v. Fletcher American Co., 204 Ind. 35, 181 N.E. 37 (1932);
A.B.C. Home & Real Estate Inspection, Inc. v. Plummer, 500 N.E.2d 1257
(Ind. Ct. App. 3d Dist. 1986), reh'g denied, (Jan. 21, 1987).

[58]Dudlo Mfg. Co. v. Varley Duplex Magnet Co., 253 F. 745 (C.C.A. 7th
Cir. 1918) (applying Indiana law) (corporation organized to take over business of partnership was estopped to deny that it had infringed patent,
where partnership had acknowledged infringement and agreed to cease,
and corporation continued infringing manufacturing method).

[59]Mt. Pleasant Coal Co. v. Watts, 91 Ind. App. 501, 151 N.E. 7 (1926).

[60]Mt. Pleasant Coal Co. v. Watts, 91 Ind. App. 501, 151 N.E. 7 (1926);
Hilgemeier v. Bower Mfg. Co., 81 Ind. App. 191, 139 N.E. 691 (Div. 2 1923).

[61]Kincaid v. Lazar, 405 N.E.2d 615 (Ind. Ct. App. 1st Dist. 1980).

[62]Sterne v. Fletcher American Co., 204 Ind. 35, 181 N.E. 37 (1932); Kincaid v. Lazar, 405 N.E.2d 615 (Ind. Ct. App. 1st Dist. 1980).

ing on the de facto corporation.[63] The promoter of a corporation which is ultimately not formed is not liable for profits which buyers of stock might have made by the resale of the stock, although any liability incurred by the buyers in connection with the execution of the contract to buy preferred stock of the corporation to be organized is enforceable against the promoter who executed the contract on the projected corporation's behalf.[64]

§ 18 Name of corporation

A corporation's name must contain some word or abbreviation indicating its corporate status, and must be distinguishable from other corporate names in use or reserved.

West's Digest, Corporations ☞43-46.

A corporation's name must contain the word "corporation," "incorporated," "company," or "limited," or the abbreviation "corp.," "inc.," "co.," or "ltd.," or one of those words or abbreviations in another language.[65] This provision, however, does not require an Indiana corporation to use words designating its corporate form in its signage, business forms, invoices, or business cards, as long as it uses such words for purposes of the issuance of its corporate charter. A corporation is not required by statute to do business under the name in which it was incorporated.[66]

A corporation's name may not contain language stating or implying that the corporation is organized for a purpose other than one permitted under the statute under which the corporation is organized and the corporation's articles of incorporation.[67]

Generally, a corporation's name must be distinguishable, on the records of the Secretary of State, from that of any

---

[63]Aetna Life Ins. Co. of Hartford, Conn. v. Weatherhogg, 103 Ind. App. 506, 4 N.E.2d 679 (1936).

For discussion of de facto corporations, see § 9.

[64]Sterne v. Fletcher American Co., 204 Ind. 35, 181 N.E. 37 (1932).

[65]IC 23-1-23-1(a)(1); IC 23-17-5-1(a)(1) (nonprofit corporations).

[66]Aronson v. Price, 644 N.E.2d 864 (Ind. 1994), reh'g denied, (May 18, 1995).

For discussion of the registration of a corporation's assumed name, see § 21.

[67]IC 23-1-23-1(a)(2); IC 23-17-5-1(a)(2) (nonprofit corporations).

other business or not-for-profit corporation incorporated or
authorized to do business in Indiana, from a reserved
corporate name, and from the name of a foreign corporation
registered with the Secretary of State.[68] The name of a not-
for-profit corporation must also be distinguishable from the
fictitious name of any foreign business or nonprofit corporation authorized to transact business in Indiana under that
name because a real name is unavailable.[69] If the corporation has chosen a name that is not distinguishable from another name already in use or reserved, it may nonetheless
apply to the Secretary of State for authorization to use the
name. The Secretary of State must authorize the corporation's use of the name if the corporation that is using or has
reserved the name files its written consent, signed by one of
its current officers, to the applicant's use of the name, or if
the applicant delivers to the Secretary of State a certified
copy of a final judgment establishing the applicant's right to
use the name in Indiana.[70] In addition, a corporation may
use a name already in use in Indiana by a corporation that
is incorporated or authorized to do business in Indiana if the
corporation seeking to use the name has merged with the
other corporation, has been formed by reorganization of the
other corporation, or has acquired all or substantially all of
the assets, including the corporate name, of the other corporation.[71]

A person may reserve the exclusive use of a corporate
name, including a fictitious name to be used by a foreign
corporation whose real name is not available in Indiana, by
filing with the Secretary of State an application stating the
applicant's name and address and the name the applicant
seeks to reserve. If the Secretary of State finds that the name
is available, he or she must reserve the name for the applicant's exclusive use for a period of 120 days, which may

---

[68]IC 23-1-23-1(b); IC 23-17-5-1(b)(1), (2).

Forms References: Complaint, petition, or declaration—Injunction
sought against use of corporate name. 7A Am Jur Pleading and Practice
Forms, Annotated (rev. ed.), Corporations §§ 10, 11.

[69]IC 23-17-5-1(b)(3).

[70]IC 23-1-23-1(c); IC 23-17-5-1(c) (nonprofit corporations).

Forms References: Directors' resolution—Consent to use of similar
corporate name. 6 Am Jur Legal Forms 2d, Corporations § 74:134.

[71]IC 23-1-23-1(d); IC 23-17-5-1(d) (nonprofit corporations).

be renewed.[72] The person who has reserved the name may transfer the reservation to another person by delivering to the Secretary of State a signed notice of the transfer stating the name and address of the person to whom the transfer is made.[73]

♦ **Observation:** Indiana Attorney General opinions pronounced under predecessor statutes to the Business Corporation Law stated that the Secretary of State is not prohibited from filing articles of incorporation in the corporation's name contains a copyrighted word;[74] that incorporators cannot legally be given the right to use the name of the State of Indiana as part of their corporate name;[75] that a personal name cannot be appropriated exclusively as part of a corporate name so as to prevent another person of the same name from using it in the name of a corporation he or she forms;[76] that a corporation may not preempt a particular word for its sole corporate use;[77] and that the Secretary of State may file amended articles of incorporation extending the existence of a private corporation utilizing a family name, over the protest against the use of the name by the original incorporator, who had since severed his connection with the company.[78]

§ 19 —Professional corporations

Professional corporations are subject to statutory restrictions as to their names, and a licensing authority may impose others.

West's Digest, Corporations ☞43-46.

The name of a professional corporation:[79]

(1) must include the words "Professional Services

---

[72]IC 23-1-23-2(a); IC 23-17-5-2(a) (nonprofit corporations).

Forms References: Application for reservation of corporate name. 6 Am Jur Legal Forms 2d, Corporations § 74:125.

[73]IC 23-1-23-2(b); IC 23-17-5-2(b) (nonprofit corporations).

[74]1923-1924 Op.Atty.Gen. 683.

[75]1953 Op.Atty.Gen. 1.

[76]1933 Op.Atty.Gen. 96; 1931-1932 Op.Atty.Gen. 93.

[77]1931-1932 Op.Atty.Gen. 93 (Secretary of State could not reject articles of corporation using name of Indiana Automobile Club, even though nonprofit corporation named Indiana Automobile Association already existed).

[78]1927-1928 Op.Atty.Gen. 88.

[79]IC 23-1.5-2-8(a).

Corporation" or "Professional Corporation" or an abbreviation of these words;

(2) may not contain any word or phrase that indicates or implies any purpose or power not possessed by corporations organizable as professional corporations; and

(3) may not contain any word or phrase that indicates that it is organized for any purpose other than that listed in the articles of incorporation.

Only a professional corporation in which all shareholders are licensed physicians may use the term "medical" in its corporate name.[80]

The authority that licenses or certificates the professionals involved in the corporation may impose additional requirements as to the names of professional corporations.[81]

§ 20   —Foreign corporations

Names of foreign corporations are subject to requirements similar to those imposed on domestic corporations; if a foreign corporation's name does not satisfy these requirements, the corporation may add words indicating corporate status to its name, or may operate under an assumed name.

West's Digest, Corporations ⊶43-46.

If a foreign corporation's name does not satisfy the requirements for corporate names under the Business Corporation Law, it may add to its name, for use in Indiana, one of the required words or abbreviations indicating its status as a corporation,[82] or, if its name is unavailable in Indiana, it may use a fictitious name to transact business in the state if it files with the Secretary of State a copy of a resolution, made by its board of directors and certified by its secretary, adopting the fictitious name.[83]

Generally, a foreign corporation's name must be distinguishable, upon the Secretary of State's records, from

---

[80]IC 23-1.5-2-8(a).

[81]IC 23-1.5-2-8(b).

[82]IC 23-1-49-6(a)(1).

For discussion of requirements for names of domestic corporations, see §§ 18 et seq.

[83]IC 23-1-49-6(a)(2).

the names of corporations, including not-for-profit corporations, incorporated or authorized to do business in Indiana, reserved corporate names, registered corporate names of other foreign corporations, and fictitious names of other foreign corporations authorized to do business in Indiana.[84] Like a domestic corporation, however, a foreign corporation may apply to the Secretary of State for authorization to use in Indiana the name of a corporation incorporated or authorized to transact business in Indiana, and the Secretary of State must authorize the foreign corporation's use of the name if the other corporation consents to the use in writing and properly changes its name, or if the foreign corporation delivers to the Secretary of State a certified copy of a final judgment establishing its right to use the name in Indiana.[85] A foreign corporation may also use a corporate name already used in Indiana by a corporation incorporated or authorized to transact business in Indiana if the foreign corporation has merged with the other corporation, has been formed by reorganization of the other corporation, or has acquired substantially all of the other corporation's assets, including its name.[86]

If a foreign corporation's name is distinguishable from those of other corporations in the Secretary of State's records, the foreign corporation may register its name by filing with the Secretary of State an application setting forth the corporate name, the state or country and date of its incorporation, and a brief description of the nature of the business in which it is engaged. The application must be accompanied by a certificate of existence, or a similar document, from the state or country in which the applicant is incorporated.[87] The name is registered for the applicant's exclusive use upon the effective date of the application.[88] The applicant may renew the registration each year by filing a renewal application meeting the requirements of the original application. If a proper renewal application is filed between

---

[84]IC 23-1-49-6(b).

[85]IC 23-1-49-6(c).

For discussion of changes of corporate names, see § 22.

[86]IC 23-1-49-6(d).

[87]IC 23-1-23-3(a), (b); IC 23-17-5-3(a), (b) (foreign nonprofit corporations).

[88]IC 23-1-23-3(c); IC 23-17-5-3(c) (foreign nonprofit corporation).

October 1 and December 31, the registration will be renewed
for the following year.[89] A foreign corporation whose name is
registered in Indiana may qualify under that name to do
business in Indiana,[90] or it may consent to the use of the
name by a domestic organization subsequently incorporated
under the Business Corporation Law, or another foreign
corporation subsequently authorized to do business in Indiana.[91]

If a foreign corporation authorized to transact business in
Indiana changes its corporate name to one that does not
satisfy the requirements for corporate names, it may not
transact business in Indiana under the new name until it
adopts a name satisfying the statutory requirements and
obtains an amended certificate of authority to do business in
the state.[92]

§ 21 —Assumed name

> **A corporation doing business under a name other than
> the one in which it is incorporated must file an assumed
> name certificate in each county where it does business or
> has an office.**

West's Digest, Corporations ☞46.

The Business Corporation Law[93] and Nonprofit Corporation Act[94] do not control the use of fictitious names.

A corporation that conducts business in Indiana under a
name, designation, or title other than the one shown by its
articles of incorporation must file an assumed name certificate in the office of the county recorder of each county in
which an office or place of business of the corporation. The
certificate must show the assumed name, the corporation's
full name, and the address of the corporation's principal

---

[89]IC 23-1-23-3(d); IC 23-17-5-3(d) (foreign nonprofit corporation).

[90]IC 23-1-23-3(e); IC 23-17-5-3(e) (foreign nonprofit corporation)

For discussion of foreign corporations doing business in Indiana, see
§§ 20 et seq.

[91]IC 23-1-23-3(e); IC 23-17-5-3(e) (foreign nonprofit corporation).

[92]IC 23-1-49-6(e).

For discussion of the requirements for corporate names, see § 18.

[93]IC 23-1-23-1(f).

[94]IC 23-17-5-1(e).

place of business in Indiana.[95] If the corporation does not have an office or place of business in Indiana, the certificate is to be filed in the county where the corporation's registered office is located, and must state the assumed name, the name of the registered agent, and the address of the registered office.[96] The filing required by this section is intended to provide information to litigants and others as to the true party in interest when a corporation makes a contract or conducts business under an assumed name. The requirement protects the public from fraud by preventing business entities from concealing their identities.[97] A corporation's failure to comply with the assumed name registration requirement does not expose its shareholders to personal liability[98] or invalidate contracts entered into by the corporation.[99]

§ 22   —Change of name

A corporation may change its name through an amendment to its articles of incorporation.

West's Digest, Corporations ☞47.

A corporation may change its name by amending its articles of incorporation.[1] After an amendment changing a corporation's name has become effective, the corporation may file a copy of the articles of amendment with the county recorder of each county in Indiana in which the corporation has real property at the time the amendment becomes effective. The validity of a change in name is not, however, affected by a corporation's failure to do so.[2]

An amendment changing a corporation's name does not abate a proceeding brought by or against the corporation in

---

[95]IC 23-15-1-1(a).

[96]IC 23-15-1-1(g).

[97]Aronson v. Price, 644 N.E.2d 864 (Ind. 1994), reh'g denied, (May 18, 1995); Parker v. Rod Johnson Farm Service, Inc., 179 Ind. App. 190, 384 N.E.2d 1129, 25 U.C.C. Rep. Serv. (CBC) 1263 (3d Dist. 1979) (under predecessor statute).

[98]Aronson v. Price, 644 N.E.2d 864 (Ind. 1994), reh'g denied, (May 18, 1995).

[99]Parker v. Rod Johnson Farm Service, Inc., 179 Ind. App. 190, 384 N.E.2d 1129, 25 U.C.C. Rep. Serv. (CBC) 1263 (3d Dist. 1979) (under predecessor statute).

[1]As to amendment of articles of incorporation, see § 13.

[2]IC 23-1-38-6(b).

its former name,[3] or otherwise affect the liability of the corporation.[4]

§ 23   Seal

A corporation may, but is not required to, have and use a corporate seal.

West's Digest, Corporations ☜51.

A corporation may have a corporate seal, which it may alter at will, and may use it or a facsimile of it by impressing it, affixing it, or reproducing it in any other manner.[5] The use of a corporate seal is not necessary, however, and does not affect the validity of any instrument, notwithstanding any other statutes.[6]

§ 24   Registered office and agent

Every corporation incorporated or doing business in Indiana must maintain a registered office and agent.

West's Digest, Corporations ☜52.

A corporation that is incorporated or authorized to do business in Indiana must continuously maintain a registered office and registered agent in Indiana.[7] The registered agent must be an individual who resides in Indiana and whose business office is identical with the registered office; a domestic corporation or not-for-profit domestic corporation whose business office is identical with the registered office; or a foreign corporation or not-for-profit foreign corporation authorized to transact business in Indiana whose business office is identical with the registered office.[8]

---

[3]IC 23-1-38-9.

[4]Lindenborg v. M & L Builders & Brokers, Inc., 158 Ind. App. 311, 302 N.E.2d 816 (3d Dist. 1973).

[5]IC 23-1-22-2(2).

Forms References: Resolution—Adoption of corporate seal. 6 Am Jur Legal Forms 2d, Corporations § 74:137.

[6]IC 23-1-22-2(2).

[7]IC 23-1-24-1; IC 23-17-6-1 (nonprofit corporations).

[8]IC 23-1-24-1(2); IC 23-17-6-1(2) (nonprofit corporations).

A corporation may change its registered office or agent by delivering a statement of change to the Secretary of State.[9] The statement must set forth:[10]

- the name of the corporation
- the street address of its current registered office
- if the current registered office is to be changed, the street address of the new registered office
- the name of its current registered agent
- if the current registered agent is to be changed, the name of the new registered agent and the new agent's written consent or a representation that the new registered agent has consented (either on the statement or attached to it) to the appointment

A change of registered office or agent for a business corporation must also contain a statement that, after the change is made, the street addresses of its registered office and the business office of its registered agent will be identical.[11] The Nonprofit Corporations Act requires that the two offices have the same address, but does not require that a statement to that effect be included in the statement of change.[12] If a registered agent changes the street address of his or her business office, he or she may change the street address of the registered office of any corporation that he or she serves by notifying the corporation in writing of the change and signing and filing with the Secretary of State a proper statement of the change which recites that the corporation has been notified of the change.[13]

A corporation's registered agent may resign as agent by signing and filing with the Secretary of State a statement of resignation, which may include a statement that the registered office is also terminated.[14] The Secretary of State, after filing the statement, is to mail one copy of it to the corporation at its principal office, if its address is known, and one copy to the corporation's registered office, if it has

---

[9]IC 23-1-24-2(a); IC 23-17-6-2(a) (nonprofit corporations).

[10]IC 23-1-24-2(a); IC 23-17-6-2(a) (nonprofit corporations).

[11]IC 23-1-24-2(a)(6).

[12]IC 23-17-6-2(b).

[13]IC 23-1-24-2(b); IC 23-17-6-2(c) (nonprofit corporations).

[14]IC 23-1-24-3(a); IC 23-17-6-3(a) (nonprofit corporations).

not been discontinued.[15] The agency appointment terminates
on the 31st day after the date on which the statement was
filed. If the registered office is discontinued, the discontinuance is also effective on that date.[16]

> ◆ **Caution:** The location of a corporation's registered of-
> fice does not necessarily indicate the corporation's domi-
> cile or residence. Generally, even though a corporation
> may have offices or places of business elsewhere,[17] a
> corporation's domicile or residence is the county and city
> in which its principal office or place of business is located,
> as designated in its charter or certificate of incorporation.[18]
> A corporation's citizenship may be only in the state where
> it was created.[19]

§ 25 Organizational meeting

**The organization of a new corporation is to be completed
at an organizational meeting of the directors,
incorporators, or subscribers.**

West's Digest, Corporations ☜298(1).

After an organization is incorporated, an organizational
meeting is to be held to complete the organization of the
corporation by electing or appointing officers, adopting
bylaws, and carrying on any other business brought before
the meeting. If the corporation's initial directors are named
in the articles of incorporation, the initial directors are to
hold the meeting, at the call of a majority of the directors.[20]
If the initial directors are not named in the articles of
incorporation, the incorporators are to hold a meeting to elect
a board of directors, who will then complete the organization

---

[15]IC 23-1-24-3(b); IC 23-17-6-3(b) (nonprofit corporations).

[16]IC 23-1-24-3(c); IC 23-17-6-3(c) (nonprofit corporations).

[17]Paul Heuring Motors, Inc. v. State Bd. of Tax Com'rs, 620 N.E.2d 39
(Ind. Tax Ct. 1993); Indiana Dept. of State Revenue v. Frank Purcell
Walnut Lumber Co., 152 Ind. App. 122, 282 N.E.2d 336 (2d Dist. 1972).

[18]Paul Heuring Motors, Inc. v. State Bd. of Tax Com'rs, 620 N.E.2d 39
(Ind. Tax Ct. 1993).

[19]Vandevoir v. Southeastern Greyhound Lines, 152 F.2d 150 (C.C.A.
7th Cir. 1945) (applying Indiana law); Indiana Dept. of State Revenue v.
Frank Purcell Walnut Lumber Co., 152 Ind. App. 122, 282 N.E.2d 336 (2d
Dist. 1972).

[20]IC 23-1-21-5(a)(1); IC 23-17-3-7(a)(1) (nonprofit corporation).

Forms References: Call and notice of organizational meeting of
incorporators. 6 Am Jur Legal Forms 2d, Corporations § 74:101.

of the corporation.[21] If the corporation will not have a board of directors,[22] the corporation's subscribers will hold the meeting and complete the organization of the corporation.[23] The organizational meeting is not required to be held in Indiana.[24]

A corporation's incorporators or subscribers may take any action required or permitted at an organizational meeting without a meeting, if the action taken is evidenced by one or more written consents that describe the action taken and are signed by each incorporator or subscriber.[25]

§ 26 Bylaws

Courts will generally not interfere with a corporation's bylaws governing the corporation's business and regulating its affairs.

West's Digest, Corporations ☞53-58.

Every corporation has a continuous power to enact bylaws, which is inherent as an incident of its existence.[26] A corporation's incorporators or directors are to adopt initial bylaws for the corporation.[27] The bylaws may contain any provision for managing the corporation's business and regulating its affairs that it not inconsistent with any law or the corporation's articles of incorporation.[28] A corporation's bylaws govern matters of internal discipline, policy, and

---

[21]IC 23-1-21-5(a)(2); IC 23-17-3-7(a)(2) (nonprofit corporation; in a nonprofit corporation, the incorporators may also complete the organization themselves).

[22]As to election of directors, see § 97.

[23]IC 23-1-21-5(a)(3).

[24]IC 23-1-21-5(c); IC 23-17-3-7(c) (nonprofit corporation).

[25]IC 23-1-21-5(b); IC 23-17-3-7(b) (nonprofit corporation; action may be taken by incorporators).

[26]Orchard Ridge Country Club, Inc. v. Schrey, 470 N.E.2d 780 (Ind. Ct. App. 3d Dist. 1984).

[27]IC 23-1-21-6(a); IC 23-17-3-8(a) (nonprofit corporations).

[28]IC 23-1-21-6(b); IC 23-17-3-8(b) (nonprofit corporations).

Forms References: Bylaws—Business Corporation. 6 Am Jur Legal Forms 2d, Corporations § 74:991.

Bylaws—Nonprofit corporation. 6 Am Jur Legal Forms 2d, Corporations § 74:993.

management.[29] In addition, if a business corporation's articles of incorporation expressly authorize such action, the corporation's shareholders, but not its board of directors, may adopt a bylaw fixing a greater quorum or voting requirement for shareholders than is required by the Business Corporation Law.[30]

A corporation's bylaws, along with its articles of incorporation, are generally considered to be a contract between the corporation and its members and among the members themselves.[31] Indiana courts will not interfere with questions of a corporation's policy, doctrine, or discipline,[32] or otherwise with the internal affairs of a private organization, unless a personal liberty or property right is jeopardized.[33] The courts will do no more than compel adherence to the corporation's charter and to the purpose for which the corporation was organized.[34]

> ◆ **Illustration:** Although the bylaws of a private not-for-profit hospital required that proposed amendments to the bylaws be referred to a special committee, they did not require that the special committee report favorably on the proposed amendments. Thus, the hospital complied sufficiently with its bylaws in adopting an amendment requiring its physicians to obtain professional liability insurance, even though the committee had recommended that each

---

[29]Orchard Ridge Country Club, Inc. v. Schrey, 470 N.E.2d 780 (Ind. Ct. App. 3d Dist. 1984).

[30]IC 23-1-39-2.

For discussion of quorums and voting, see §§ 87 et seq.

[31]National Bd. of Examiners for Osteopathic Physicians and Surgeons, Inc. v. American Osteopathic Ass'n, 645 N.E.2d 608 (Ind. Ct. App. 4th Dist. 1994) (both for-profit and not-for-profit corporations); Brenner v. Powers, 584 N.E.2d 569 (Ind. Ct. App. 3d Dist. 1992), reh'g denied, (Apr. 21, 1992) and transfer denied, (Dec. 18, 1992) (not-for-profit corporations).

[32]Orchard Ridge Country Club, Inc. v. Schrey, 470 N.E.2d 780 (Ind. Ct. App. 3d Dist. 1984).

[33]Brenner v. Powers, 584 N.E.2d 569 (Ind. Ct. App. 3d Dist. 1992), reh'g denied, (Apr. 21, 1992) and transfer denied, (Dec. 18, 1992); Lozanoski v. Sarafin, 485 N.E.2d 669 (Ind. Ct. App. 3d Dist. 1985), reh'g denied, (Mar. 14, 1986) and transfer denied, (June 26, 1986); Orchard Ridge Country Club, Inc. v. Schrey, 470 N.E.2d 780 (Ind. Ct. App. 3d Dist. 1984); STP Corp. v. U. S. Auto Club, Inc., 286 F. Supp. 146 (S.D. Ind. 1968) (applying Indiana law).

[34]Orchard Ridge Country Club, Inc. v. Schrey, 470 N.E.2d 780 (Ind. Ct. App. 3d Dist. 1984).

physician be left to make his or her own decision as to whether to acquire insurance.[35]

A bylaw which is inconsistent with an applicable statute, or with the articles of incorporation governing a corporation, is void.[36]

A corporation's directors may also adopt bylaws to be effective only in an emergency, unless the articles of incorporation provide otherwise.[37] An emergency exists for purposes of this provision if an extraordinary event prevents a quorum of the corporation's directors from assembling in time to deal with the business for which the meeting has been or is to be called.[38] Emergency bylaws may make all provisions necessary for managing the corporation during the emergency, including procedures for calling a board meeting, quorum requirements for the meeting, and the designation of additional or substitute directors.[39] Emergency bylaws are effective only as long as the emergency lasts,[40] A corporation is bound by corporate action taken in good faith in accordance with the emergency bylaws, and such action may not be used to impose liability on a corporate director, officer, employee, or agent.[41]

§ 27 —Amendment of bylaws

Generally, a corporation's directors may amend or repeal the bylaws.

West's Digest, Corporations ⊕56.

Only the corporation's board of directors may amend or repeal a business corporation's bylaws, unless the articles of incorporation provide otherwise.[42]

In a nonprofit corporation, the board of directors or, until the directors have been chosen, the incorporators may amend or repeal the bylaws unless the articles of incorporation, the

---

[35]Renforth v. Fayette Memorial Hospital Ass'n, Inc., 178 Ind. App. 475, 383 N.E.2d 368 (1978).

[36]Presbyterian Assur. Fund v. Allen, 106 Ind. 593, 7 N.E. 317 (1886).

[37]IC 23-1-21-7(a); IC 23-17-3-9(a) (nonprofit corporations).

[38]IC 23-1-21-7(d); IC 23-17-3-9(d) (nonprofit corporations).

[39]IC 23-1-21-7(a); IC 23-17-3-9(a) (nonprofit corporations).

[40]IC 23-1-21-7(b); IC 23-17-3-9(b) (nonprofit corporations).

[41]IC 23-1-21-7(c); IC 23-17-3-9(c) (nonprofit corporations).

[42]IC 23-1-39-1.

bylaws, or the Nonprofit Corporations Act provide otherwise.[43] The articles of incorporation may also require that an amendment to a nonprofit corporation's bylaws be approved by a specified person other than the board of directors, and this requirement may be amended only with the written approval of that person.[44]

A nonprofit corporation must provide notice, including a statement that the purpose of the meeting is to consider a proposed amendment to the bylaws and a copy or summary of the amendment, of any meeting of directors at which an amendment is to be approved.[45] The notice must also comply with the statute's provisions for membership approval of mergers.[46]

If a bylaw adopted by a business corporation's shareholders fixes a greater quorum or voting requirement for shareholders than is required by the Business Corporation Law, the bylaw may not be amended or repealed by the board of directors.[47] A business corporation's bylaw requiring more than a majority of the directors to constitute a quorum or fulfill a voting requirement may be amended or repealed only by the shareholders, if it was originally adopted by the shareholders, and only by the board of directors, if it was originally adopted by the board of directors.[48]

C. RECORDS, REPORTS, AND FILING OF DOCUMENTS

Research References

IC 23-1-18-1 to IC 23-1-18-8; IC 23-1-24-3; IC 23-1-49-9; IC 23-1-52-1; IC 23-1-53-3; IC 23-1-53-4; IC 23-1.5-2-11.1; IC 23-17-6-3; IC 23-17-26-9; IC 23-17-27-1; IC 23-17-27-6; IC 23-17-27-8; IC 23-17-29-1 to IC 23-17-29-8

---

[43]IC 23-17-18-1(a) (subject to class voting rules).

The members of a class in a nonprofit corporation may vote as a separate voting group on proposed amendments to the corporation's bylaws under certain circumstances. For discussion of class voting in nonprofit corporations, see § 89.

[44]IC 23-17-17-1.

[45]IC 23-17-18-1(b).

[46]IC 23-17-18-1(b), referring to IC 23-17-19-3(d).

For discussion of approval of mergers, see §§ 203 et seq.

[47]IC 23-1-39-2(b).

[48]IC 23-1-39-3(a).

18A Am Jur 2d, Corporations §§ 333-347.
18 C.J.S., Corporations § 110.
West's Digest, Corporations ☞22, 59, 311.
ALR Digest: Corporations § 28
ALR Index: Articles of Incorporation; Assets; Bylaws; Charter; Close Corporation; Consolidation or Merger; Corporate Bonds and Bondholders; Corporate Officers, Directors, and Agents; Corporate Opportunity; Corporate Responsibility Doctrine; Corporate Stock and Stockholders; Corporations; Dissolution or Liquidation; Dividends; Domicile and Residence; Foreign Corporations; Forfeitures; Liquidation or Dissolution; Minority Stockholders; Names; Nonprofit Institutions or Organizations; Professional Corporations and Associations; Promoters; Prospectus; Proxies; Reports; Seal; Stock-Option Plans; Subsidiary
6A Am Jur Legal Forms 2d, Corporations § 74:1843.

§ 28 Records

Corporations are required by statute to maintain certain records.

West's Digest, Corporations ☞59, 311.

A corporation may speak or act officially only through minutes and records made at properly organized meetings.[49]

A corporation must keep as permanent records minutes of all meetings of its shareholders or members and board of directors, a record of all actions taken by the shareholders or members or board of directors without a meeting, and a record of all actions taken by a committee of the board of directors in place of the board of directors on behalf of the corporation.[50] The corporation must also maintain appropriate accounting records.[51]

A business corporation must maintain a record of its

---

[49]Jones v. State ex rel. Indiana Livestock Sanitary Bd., 240 Ind. 230, 163 N.E.2d 605 (1960).

[50]IC 23-1-52-1(a).

As to similar provisions under the Nonprofit Corporation Act, see IC 23-17-27-1(a).

Annotation References: Persons liable, under statutes, imposing, upon directors, officers, or trustees of a corporation, personal liability for its debts on accounts of their failure to file or publish reports required by law as to corporate matters, 39 ALR3d 428.

Forms References: Minutes of annual stockholders' meeting. 6A Am Jur Legal Forms 2d, Corporations § 74:1843.

[51]IC 23-1-52-1(b); IC 23-17-27-1(b) (nonprofit corporations).

shareholders in a form that permits preparation of a list of the names and addresses of all shareholders, in alphabetical order by class of shares showing the number and class of shares held by each;[52] a nonprofit corporation must maintain a record of its members in like form, in alphabetical order by class, showing the number of votes each member is entitled to cast.[53] The records are to be maintained in written form, or in another form which may be converted into written form within a reasonable time.[54]

A corporation is required to keep the following records at its principal office:[55]

- its articles or restated articles of incorporation and all amendments to them currently in effect
- its bylaws or restated bylaws and all amendments to them currently in effect
- all written communications to shareholders generally within the past three years, including financial statements
- the most recent annual report delivered to the Secretary of State

A business corporation must also maintain the following records at its principal place of business:[56]

- resolutions adopted by its board of directors fixing the relative rights, preferences, and limitations of classes or series of outstanding shares
- the minutes of all shareholders' meetings, and records of all action taken by shareholders without a meeting, for the past three years
- a list of the names and business addresses of current directors and officers

---

[52]IC 23-1-52-1(c).

[53]IC 23-17-27-1(c).

[54]IC 23-1-52-1(d); IC 23-17-27-1(d) (nonprofit corporations).

[55]IC 23-1-52-1(e)(1), (2), (5), (7); IC 23-17-27-1(e)(1), (2), (5), (7).

For discussion of financial statements furnished to shareholders, see § 30.

Although the statute calls for the corporation to maintain a copy of its most recent annual report, reports are now required only biennially of business corporations. For discussion of biennial reports to the Secretary of State, see § 29.

[56]IC 23-1-52-1(e)(3), (4), (6).

For discussion of classes and series of shares, see § 37.

A nonprofit corporation must maintain the following records at its principal place of business:[57]

- resolutions adopted by the corporation's board of directors relating to the characteristics, qualifications,
  rights, limitations, and obligations of members or a
  class or category of members
- the minutes of all meetings of members and records of
  all actions approved by the members for the past three
  years
- a list of the names and business or home addresses of
  the corporation's current directors and officers

§ 29 Annual and biennial reports

**Business corporations must file biennial reports, and
nonprofit corporations annual reports, with the Secretary
of State's office.**

West's Digest, Corporations ⇒59.

Corporations governed by the Business Corporation Law
or the Professional Corporations Act are to file with the Secretary of State biennial reports.[58] A biennial report is to be
made on a form prescribed and furnished by the department
of revenue and the Secretary of State's office.[59] Not-for-profit
corporations are to file annual reports on a form prescribed
and furnished by the Secretary of State;[60] the Secretary of
State may mail the annual report form to an address shown
for the corporation on its last annual report, and the
corporation's failure to receive the form does not relieve the
corporation of its duty to deliver a report.[61]

Reports for both business and nonprofit corporations must
set forth each of the following:[62]

- the name of the corporation and the state or country
  under whose law it is incorporated
- the address of its registered office and the name of its
  registered agent at that office in Indiana

---

[57]IC 23-17-27-1(e)(3), (4), (6).

[58]IC 23-1-53-3(a); IC 23-1.5-2-11.1.

[59]IC 23-1-53-3(a); IC 23-1-53-4(e).

For discussion of forms prescribed and furnished by the Secretary of
State's office, see § 32.

[60]IC 23-17-27-8(a), (b).

[61]IC 23-17-27-8(f).

[62]IC 23-1-53-3(a); IC 23-17-27-8(b).

- the address of its principal office
- the names and business addresses of its directors, its secretary, and the highest executive officer of the corporation

The information in the report must be current as of the date the report is executed on behalf of the corporation.[63] A non-profit corporation may file an amendment to its annual report if the information set forth in the report changes after the report is delivered to the Secretary of State's office and before the next due date, as long as the change is not required to be made by an amendment to the articles of incorporation. An amendment to an annual report must set forth the name of the corporation as shown on the Secretary of State's records and the information as changed.[64]

If a report does not contain the required information, the Secretary of State must promptly notify the reporting corporation in writing and return the report to it for correction. If the report is corrected to contain the required information and delivered to the Secretary of State within 30 days after the effective date of notice, it is deemed to be timely filed.[65]

A business corporation's first biennial report must be delivered to the Secretary of State in the second year following the calendar year in which a domestic corporation was incorporated or a foreign corporation was authorized to transact business.[66] Generally, the report is due during the same month as the month in which the corporation was incorporated or authorized to transact business,[67] although the Secretary of State may accept a report during the two months before the month it is due.[68] However, the Secretary of State, in cooperation with the state department of revenue, may provide for a domestic corporation's filing of its biennial report at the same time the corporation files its state income tax return,[69] in which case the report is due when the

---

[63]IC 23-1-53-3(b); IC 23-17-27-8(c).

[64]IC 23-17-27-8(g).

[65]IC 23-1-53-3(f); IC 23-17-27-8(e).

[66]IC 23-1-53-3(c).

[67]IC 23-1-53-3(c).

[68]IC 23-1-53-3(e).

[69]IC 23-1-53-4(a).

corporation's adjusted gross income tax return is due.[70] The corporation may file the report either with the department of revenue, which will then forward the report to the Secretary of State's office,[71] or directly with the Secretary of State.[72]

A nonprofit corporation's first annual report must be delivered to the Secretary of State in the year following the year in which the corporation was incorporated or authorized to transact business. The report is due during the same month as the month in which the corporation was incorporated or authorized to transact business. Subsequent annual reports must be delivered to the Secretary of State during that same month in the following years. although the Secretary of State may accept annual reports during the two months before that month.[73]

§ 30 Annual financial statements

Corporations must prepare annual financial statements upon the request of a shareholder or member.

West's Digest, Corporations ☞59.

A corporation must prepare, on the written request of any shareholder or member, annual financial statements, including a balance sheet as of the end of the most recently completed fiscal year; in the case of a business corporation, an income statement for that year, and a statement of changes in shareholders' equity for that year; and in the case of a not-for-profit corporation, a statement of operations for that year.[74] If the annual financial statements are reported upon by a public accountant, the public accountant's report must accompany them. If not, the statements must be accompanied by a statement of the president or the person responsible for the corporation's accounting records stating the person's reasonable belief that the statements were or were not prepared on the basis of generally accepted accounting principles and, if not, describing the basis of preparation, and describing any respects in which the statements were

---

[70]IC 23-1-53-3(d).

[71]IC 23-1-53-4(d).

[72]IC 23-1-53-4(b).

[73]IC 23-17-27-8(d).

[74]IC 23-1-53-1(a); IC 23-17-27-6(a).

not prepared on a basis of accounting consistent with the statements prepared for the preceding year.[75]

§ 31 Filing of documents

Corporate documents filed with the Secretary of State must meet certain requirements as to form and content.

West's Digest, Corporations ⬤➾22.

Under the statute governing business corporations, documents to be filed with the Secretary of State, including articles of incorporation,[76] bylaws[77] and biennial reports[78] must meet the following requirements to be entitled to filing:[79]

- the statute must require or permit that the document be filed in the Secretary of State's office
- the document must contain the information required by the statute, and may contain other information
- the document must be typewritten or printed, legible, and otherwise suitable for processing
- the document must be in English; however, a corporate name need not be in English if it is written in English letters or Arabic or Roman numerals, and the certificate of existence required of foreign corporations need not be in English if it is accompanied by a reasonably authenticated English translation
- the document must be properly executed
- tf the Secretary of State has prescribed a mandatory form for the document, the document must be in or on the prescribed form
- the document must be properly delivered and the correct filing fee paid

Substantially the same requirements apply to nonprofit corporations.[80]

---

[75]IC 23-1-53-1(b); IC 23-17-27-6(b).

[76]As to articles of incorporations, see § 12.

[77]As to bylaws, see § 26.

[78]As to annual and biennial reports, see § 29.

[79]IC 23-1-18-1.

For discussion of execution of documents submitted to the Secretary of State for filing, see § 33.

[80]IC 23-17-29-1.

The required filing fee may be paid by credit card, debit card, charge card, or similar method.[81] Fee schedules for business[82] and nonprofit[83] corporations are set forth in the corporation statutes.

The Secretary of State's certification stamp on, or a certification attached to, a document is conclusive evidence that the original document is on file with the Secretary of State.[84] Generally, a document accepted for filing is effective at the time and on the date of filing, as evidenced by the Secretary of State's endorsement on the original document, or at such later time on the date the document is filed as is specified in the document.[85] A document may also specify a delayed effective date, which is not to be later than the 90th day after the document was actually filed. If no time is specified for tho dolayod offootivo dato, tho documcnt io considcrcd to have been filed at 12:01 a.m. on that date.[86]

A corporation may correct a filed document which contains an incorrect statement or was defectively executed, attested, sealed, verified, or acknowledged.[87]

§ 32   Forms

The Secretary of State may prescribe forms for documents filed with him or her.

West's Digest, Corporations ⊙⊸22.

The Secretary of State may prescribe and, on request, furnish forms for documents permitted or required to be filed under the statutes pertaining to business and nonprofit corporations. The use of these forms is generally not mandatory; however, the use of forms for a foreign corporation's application for a certificate of authority to transact business in Indiana, a foreign corporation's application for a certificate of withdrawal, and annual and biennial reports, is manda-

---

[81]IC 23-1-18-1(j); IC 23-17-29-1(e).

[82]IC 23-1-18-3.

[83]IC 23-17-29-3.

[84]IC 23-1-18-8; IC 23-17-29-8.

[85]IC 23-1-18-4(a); IC 23-17-29-4(a).

[86]IC 23-1-18-4(b); IC 23-17-29-4(b).

[87]IC 23-1-18-5; IC 23-17-29-5.

tory if the Secretary of State so requires and if the form so states.[88]

§ 33 Execution of documents submitted for filing

A corporate document to be filed with the Secretary of State must be signed by a director, incorporator, or fiduciary.

West's Digest, Corporations ☞22.

A document submitted for filing with the Secretary of State under the Business Corporation Law must be signed by at least one of the following:[89]

- the chairman of the board of directors of the corporation or by any of its officers
- an incorporator, if directors have not been selected or the corporation has not been formed
- if the corporation is in the hands of a receiver, trustee, or other court-appointed fiduciary, by that fiduciary.

The person executing the document must sign it and state beneath or opposite the signature his or her name and the capacity in which he or she is signing.[90]

A signature on a document filed under the Business Corporation Law may be a facsimile. As part of the execution of a document, the document may, but is not required to, contain the corporate seal, an attestation by the secretary or an assistant secretary, and an acknowledgment, verification, or proof.[91]

Substantially the same requirements apply to nonprofit corporations.[92]

§ 34 Method of submission; copies of documents submitted

Generally, documents may be submitted for filing by electronic means.

---

[88]IC 23-1-18-2; IC 23-17-29-2.

[89]IC 23-1-18-1(g).

For discussion of corporate officers and directors, see §§ 99 et seq.

For discussion of incorporators, see § 17.

For discussion of corporations in receivership, see §§ 168 et seq.

[90]IC 23-1-18-1(g).

[91]IC 23-1-18-1(g).

[92]IC 23-17-29-1(a)(6), (7); IC 23-17-29-1(b).

West's Digest, Corporations ☞22.

Except for biennial reports,[93] a document may be delivered to the Secretary of State for filing by hand, mail, telecopy, facsimile, or other form of electronic transmission meeting the requirements established by the Secretary of State.[94] If the document is delivered for filing by hand or by mail, it must be accompanied by one copy,[95] unless the document to be filed is the resignation of the corporation's registered agent,[96] in which case two copies must be filed with the original.[97] The Secretary of State's office is to make any necessary copies of documents delivered by some form of electronic transmission.[98]

§ 35 Secretary of State's refusal to file document

The Secretary of State must file a proper document submitted to him of her for filing; a corporation may appeal the secretary's refusal to file a document.

West's Digest, Corporations ☞22.

If a document submitted to the Secretary of State for filing satisfies the statutory requirements, the Secretary of State must file the document[99] and deliver a file-stamped copy of the document and a receipt for the filing fee, or an acknowledgment of receipt if no fee is required, to the corporation or its representative.[1]

If the Secretary of State refuses to file a document, the Secretary of State shall return it to the domestic or foreign corporation or its representative within 10 days after the document was delivered, together with a brief, written

---

[93]§ 29.

[94]IC 23-1-18-1.1(a); IC 23-17-29-1.1(a).

[95]IC 23-1-18-1.1(b)(2); IC 23-17-29-1.1(b)(2).

[96]IC 23-1-24-3 (resignation of agent of domestic business corporation); IC 23-1-49-9 (resignation of agent of foreign business corporation); IC 23-17-6-3 (resignation of agent of domestic nonprofit corporation); IC 23-17-26-9 (resignation of agent of foreign nonprofit corporation).

[97]IC 23-1-18-1.1(b)(1); IC 23-17-29-1.1(b)(1).

[98]IC 23-1-18-1.1(c); IC 23-17-29-1.1(c).

[99]IC 23-1-18-6(a); IC 23-17-29-6(a).

[1]IC 23-1-18-6(b); IC 23-17-29-6(b).

explanation of the reason for the refusal.[2] The Secretary of State's duty to file corporate documents is ministerial, and his or her filing of or refusal to file a document does not affect the validity or invalidity of the document in whole or part; relate to the correctness or incorrectness of information contained in the document; or create a presumption that the document is valid or invalid or that information contained in the document is correct or incorrect.[3]

The corporation may appeal the Secretary of State's refusal to file a document delivered for filing to the circuit or superior court of the county where the corporation's principal office, or registered office if it has no principal office in Indiana, is or will be located. The appeal is commenced by petitioning the court to compel filing the document and by attaching to the petition the document and the Secretary of State's explanation of the refusal to file.[4] The court may summarily order the Secretary of State to file the document or take other action the court considers appropriate.[5] The court's final decision may be appealed as in other civil proceedings.[6]

III. SHARES

Research References

IC 23-1-2-6; IC 23-1-20-3; IC 23-1-20-23; IC 23-1-20-26; IC 23-1-25-1 to IC 23-1-25-4; IC 23-1-26-1; IC 23-1-26-2; IC 23-1-26-5 to IC 23-1-26-7; IC 23-1-26-9; IC 23-1-27-1; IC 23-1-27-2; IC 23-1-53-2; IC 23-1-54-2; IC 23-1.5-3-1 to IC 23-1.5-3-3; IC 26-1-8.1-102; IC 26-1-8.1-205; IC 26-1-8.1-206; IC 26-1-8.1-210; IC 26-1-8.1-303; IC 26-1-8.1-405; IC 26-1-8.1-406
15 U.S.C.A. § 78a

18A Am Jur 2d, Corporations §§ 423-680.
18 C.J.S., Corporations §§ 122-216.
West's Digest, Corporations ☞60-110.
ALR Digest: Corporations §§ 174-243
ALR Index: Articles of Incorporation; Assets; Bylaws; Charter; Close Corporation; Consolidation or Merger; Corporate Bonds and Bondholders; Corporate Officers, Directors, and Agents;

---

[2]IC 23-1-18-6(c); IC 23-17-29-6(c).
[3]IC 23-1-18-6(d); IC 23-17-29-6(d).
[4]IC 23-1-18-7(a); IC 23-17-29-7(a).
[5]IC 23-1-18-7(b); IC 23-17-29-7(b).
[6]IC 23-1-18-7(c); IC 23-17-29-7(c).

Corporate Opportunity; Corporate Responsibility Doctrine;
Corporate Stock and Stockholders; Corporations; Dissolution or
Liquidation; Dividends; Domicile and Residence; Foreign
Corporations; Forfeitures; Liquidation or Dissolution; Minority
Stockholders; Names; Nonprofit Institutions or Organizations;
Professional Corporations and Associations; Promoters; Prospec-
tus; Proxies; Reports; Seal; Stock-Option Plans; Subsidiary

6 Am Jur Legal Forms 2d, Corporations §§ 74:83-74:85.

6B Am Jur Legal Forms 2d, Corporations §§ 74:2161, 74:2163,
74:2171, 74:2272, 74:2321, 74:2326.

7A Am Jur Pleading and Practice Forms, Annotated (rev. ed.),
Corporations § 62.

Liability of Shareholder for Wrongfully Transferring or Assigning
Corporate Common Stock Shares to Third Party, 47 Am Jur
POF3d 138.

Failure to Disclose Material Facts to Stock Purchaser, 11 Am Jur
POF2d 271.; Waiver of Right to Enforce "First Option" Stock
Purchase Agreement, 3 Am Jur POF2d 379.

§ 36   Generally

A share is a unit of a corporation's proprietary interests.

West's Digest, Corporations ⟺60-68.

Under the Business Corporation Law, "shares" are the
units into which a business corporation's proprietary
interests are divided.[7] A "share of stock" has also been
defined as a proportional part of certain rights in the
management and profits of a corporation during its existence,
and in the assets upon dissolution, and is evidence of the
stockholder's ratable share in the distribution of the assets
on the winding up of the corporation's business.[8] Corporate
stock is a type of personal property.[9]

---

[7]IC 23-1-20-23.

[8]Department of Treasury of Indiana v. Crowder, 214 Ind. 252, 15
N.E.2d 89 (1938) (overruled in part on other grounds by, Department of
Treasury of Indiana v. Muessel, 218 Ind. 250, 32 N.E.2d 596 (1941)) and
(overruling on other grounds recognized by, Sherwin-Williams Co. v. Indiana Dept. of State Revenue, 673 N.E.2d 849 (Ind. Tax Ct. 1996)); Markle
v. Burgess, 176 Ind. 25, 95 N.E. 308 (1911); DRW Builders, Inc. v.
Richardson, 679 N.E.2d 902 (Ind. Ct. App. 1997), reh'g denied, (June 20,
1997).

[9]Root's Estate v. Blackwood, 120 Ind. App. 545, 94 N.E.2d 489 (1950).

A person who owns shares of stock in a corporation does not own the capital, which belongs to the corporation, considered as a legal person.[10]

Not-for-profit corporations have no stock, as they have members instead of shareholders.[11]

§ 37 Classes and series of shares

A corporation's shares may be divided into classes, and the classes into series.

West's Digest, Corporations ⊙60-68.

A corporation's articles of incorporation are required to prescribe the number of shares the corporation is authorized to issue.[12] "Authorized shares" are the shares a corporation is authorized to issue.[13] The articles of incorporation need not authorize more than one class of shares;[14] however, if more than one class is authorized, the articles must prescribe the number of shares in each class and a distinguishing designation for each class. Before the shares in a class may be issued, the articles of incorporation must describe the preferences, limitations, and relative rights of that class.[15] The authorized classes of shares must include one or more classes of shares that together have unlimited voting rights, and one or more classes of shares that together are entitled to receive the corporation's net assets upon dissolution.[16] These classes are generally known respectively as

---

[10]Department of Treasury of Indiana v. Crowder, 214 Ind. 252, 15 N.E.2d 89 (1938) (overruled in part on other grounds by, Department of Treasury of Indiana v. Muessel, 218 Ind. 250, 32 N.E.2d 596 (1941)) and (overruling on other grounds recognized by, Sherwin-Williams Co. v. Indiana Dept. of State Revenue, 673 N.E.2d 849 (Ind. Tax Ct. 1996)); SFN Shareholders Grantor Trust v. Indiana Dept. of State Revenue, 603 N.E.2d 194 (Ind. Tax Ct. 1992) (shareholders do not own assets of corporation).

[11]As to members of not-for-profit corporations, see § 66.

For discussion of shareholders, see §§ 66 et seq.

[12]IC 23-1-25-1(a).

[13]IC 23-1-20-3.

[14]IC 23-1-25-1, Official Comment.

[15]IC 23-1-25-1(a).

[16]IC 23-1-25-1(b).

common stock and preferred stock.[17] In addition, the articles of incorporation may authorize one or more classes of shares that:[18]

- have special, conditional, or limited voting rights, or no right to vote, except to the extent prohibited by the Business Corporation Law
- are redeemable or convertible, as specified in the articles of incorporation
- entitle the holders to distributions calculated in any manner, including dividends that may be cumulative, noncumulative, or partially cumulative
- have preference over any other class of shares with respect to distributions, including dividends and distributions upon the dissolution of the corporation

Generally, the preferences, limitations, and relative rights of all of the shares of each class must be identical.[19] However, if the articles of incorporation so provide, the corporation's board of directors may create one or more series of shares within a class,[20] each of which is to be given a distinguishing designation,[21] and may determine, in whole or in part, the preferences, limitations, and relative voting and other rights of any class or series of shares, before the shares of that class or within the series have been issued.[22] All shares of the same series must have identical preferences, limitations, and relative rights. Moreover, except to the extent the description of the series provides otherwise, the shares of each series must have preferences, limitations, and relative rights identical to those of shares in other series of the same class.[23]

---

[17]For discussion of the dissolution of a corporation, see §§ 194 et seq.

Forms References: Common stock certificate. 6B Am Jur Legal Forms 2d, Corporations § 74:2161.

Preferred stock certificate. 6B Am Jur Legal Forms 2d, Corporations § 74:2171.

[18]IC 23-1-25-1(c), (d).

For discussion of shareholder voting, see §§ 71 et seq.

For discussion of distributions to shareholders, see §§ 58 et seq.

[19]IC 23-1-25-1(a).

[20]IC 23-1-25-2(a).

[21]IC 23-1-25-2(b).

[22]IC 23-1-25-2(a).

[23]IC 23-1-25-2(c).

§ 38 Subscriptions

Subscriptions for the sale of shares are governed by the rules governing contracts generally.

West's Digest, Corporations ☞75-78, 80(1)-80(12), 115-121.

A subscriber is a person who subscribes for, or agrees in writing to purchase, shares in a corporation, whether before or after incorporation.[24] A subscription for the purchase of shares is a contract, and is governed by the same legal principles as apply in the case of contracts generally. As with other contracts, consideration is necessary to render a subscription agreement enforceable by either the corporation or the subscriber,[25] and the existence of an express share purchase agreement precludes the implication of such an agreement.[26] A subscription agreement obtained by fraud is subject to rescission.[27]

A subscription for shares entered into before incorporation is irrevocable for six months, unless the subscription agreement provides a longer or shorter period or all the subscribers agree to revocation.[28] The board of directors may determine the terms for payment of subscriptions entered into before incorporation, unless the terms are specified in the subscription agreement.[29] Shares issued pursuant to subscriptions entered into before incorporation are fully paid and nonassessable when the corporation receives the consideration specified in the subscription agreement.[30] So far as practicable, a call for payment of subscriptions by the board of directors must be uniform as to all shares of the

---

[24]IC 23-1-20-26

Forms References: Preincorporation stock subscription. 6 Am Jur Legal Forms 2d, Corporations §§ 74:83-74:85.

[25]Marion Trust Co. v. Bennett, 169 Ind. 346, 82 N.E. 782 (1907).

As to contracts in general, see I.L.E., Contracts.

[26]Brown v. Mid-American Waste Systems, Inc., 924 F. Supp. 92 (S.D. Ind. 1996).

[27]Orbison v. Lesh, 205 Ind. 340, 184 N.E. 771 (1933); Dorsey Mach. Co. v. McCaffrey, 139 Ind. 545, 38 N.E. 208 (1894); William B. Joyce & Co. v. Eiffert, 56 Ind. App. 190, 105 N.E. 59 (Div. 2 1914).

[28]IC 23-1-26-1(a).

[29]IC 23-1-26-1(b).

[30]IC 23-1-26-1(c).

same class or series, unless the subscription agreement specifies otherwise.[31]

If a subscriber defaults in payment under a subscription agreement entered into before incorporation, the corporation may collect the amount owed as any other debt, or, unless the subscription agreement provides otherwise, may rescind the agreement and sell the shares if the debt remains unpaid more than 20 days after the corporation has sent the subscriber written demand for payment.[32]

A subscription agreement entered into after incorporation is a contract between the subscriber and the corporation subject to the provisions of the Business Corporation Law pertaining to consideration.[33]

§ 39 —Conditional subscriptions

A subscription agreement may be subject to a condition precedent.

West's Digest, Corporations ☞81.

Subscription agreements may also, like other contracts, be subject to conditions precedent. Thus, corporations may take subscriptions to stock on the condition that they shall be binding on the subscribers only in case a certain aggregate amount is subscribed.[34] In such a case, the subscription becomes absolute when the corporation obtains the required amount.[35]

§ 40 Issuance of shares

A corporation may issue the number of shares of each class or series authorized by the articles of incorporation, as amended if necessary.

West's Digest, Corporations ☞94-98.

A corporation may issue the number of shares of each class

---

[31]IC 23-1-26-1(b).

[32]IC 23-1-26-1(d).

[33]IC 23-1-26-1(e).

For discussion of consideration for shares, see § 43.

[34]Shick v. Citizens' Enterprise Co., 15 Ind. App. 329, 44 N.E. 48 (1896).

As to conditions precedent to contracts, see I.L.E., Contracts.

[35]Cravens v. Eagle Cotton Mills Co., 120 Ind. 6, 21 N.E. 981 (1889).

or series authorized by the articles of incorporation.[36] Thus, if the board of directors determines the preferences, limitations, and rights of a class or series of shares, it may not issue any shares of that series or class until it files with the Secretary of State articles of amendment setting forth:[37]

    (1) the name of the corporation;

    (2) the text of the amendment determining the preferences, limitations, and rights of the class or series;

    (3) the date the amendment was adopted; and

    (4) a statement that the amendment was duly adopted by the board of directors.

Shareholder action is not necessary for such an amendment.[38]

After they have been issued, shares are outstanding until they are reacquired, redeemed, converted, or canceled.[39] At all times shares of a corporation are outstanding, one or more shares that together have unlimited voting rights and one or more shares that together are entitled to receive the net assets of the corporation upon dissolution must be outstanding.[40]

A person who is entitled to the issue or validation of a share, but who has not received a valid share because the corporation has issued shares in excess of its power to do so, may compel the corporation to purchase and deliver to him or her, or register in his or her name, a share identical to the one to which the person is entitled, if such a share is reasonably available for purchase.[41] If no identical share is available for purchase, the person may recover from the issuer the price he or she, or the last purchaser for value, paid for the share, with interest from the date of demand.[42]

A corporation need not issue only full shares. It may issue

---

[36]IC 23-1-25-3(a).

[37]IC 23-1-25-2(d).

For discussion of amendment of the articles of incorporation, see § 13.

[38]IC 23-1-25-2(d).

[39]IC 23-1-25-3(a).

For discussion of a corporation's reacquisition of shares, see § 45.

[40]IC 23-1-25-3(c).

[41]IC 26-1-8.1-210(a), (c).

[42]IC 26-1-8.1-210(d).

fractions of a share or pay in money the value of fractions of a share; arrange for disposition of fractional shares by the shareholders; and/or issue scrip in registered or bearer form entitling the holder to receive a full share upon surrendering enough scrip to equal a full share.[43]

> ◆ **Observation:** Under this section and a provision permitting a corporation's directors to amend the articles of incorporation to change each authorized share into a lesser number of whole and fractional shares, a corporation may implement a reverse stock split, in which the corporation's shares are reduced by a certain proportion, with the shareholders retaining their proportional interests.[44]

The holder of a fractional share is entitled to vote, receive dividends, participate in the assets of the corporation upon dissolution, and exercise other rights of a shareholder. The holder of scrip is not entitled to any of these rights unless the scrip provides for them.[45] Scrip may also be subject to conditions authorized by the board of directors. For instance, the directors may provide that the scrip will become void if it is not exchanged for full shares before a specified date, or that the shares for which the scrip is exchangeable may be sold and the proceeds paid to the scripholders.[46]

A professional corporation may issue shares, fractional shares, and rights or options to purchase shares only to individuals, general partnerships, and other professional corporations who are, or whose partners are, authorized to render professional services of the type rendered by the corporation, or to the trustee of a qualified trust.[47] The profession's licensing authority may further restrict the issuance of shares to prevent violations of the profession's ethi-

---

[43]IC 23-1-25-4(a).

Forms References: Certificate—Fractional share of common stock. 6B Am Jur Legal Forms 2d, Corporations § 74:2163.

[44]FGS Enterprises, Inc. v. Shimala, 625 N.E.2d 1226 (Ind. 1993), reh'g denied, (Aug. 16, 1994).

[45]IC 23-1-25-4(c).

[46]IC 23-1-25-4(d).

[47]IC 23-1.5-3-1(a).

Annotation References: Propriety, under state statutes or bar association or court rules, of formation of multistate law partnership or professional service corporation, 6 ALR4th 1251.

cal standards.[48] Shares of a professional corporation may be transferred only to persons to whom they are permitted to be issued,[49] and the restrictions on transfer must be stated conspicuously on the face of each share certificate.[50]

§ 41 —Preemptive rights

Shareholders may be granted preemptive rights to acquire shares issued by the corporation.

West's Digest, Corporations ☞96.

Generally, a corporation's shareholders have no preemptive right to acquire the corporation's unissued shares, except to the extent provided in the articles of incorporation.[51] However, where the articles of incorporation include a statement that the corporation elects to have preemptive rights, several principles apply to the corporation's shares, and to securities convertible into or carrying a right to subscribe for or acquire shares.[52] These principles may be limited by an express provision in the articles of incorporation.[53]

First, the corporation's shareholders will have a preemptive right to acquire proportional amounts of the corporation's unissued shares when the board decides to issue them. The board is to prescribe uniform terms and conditions to provide the shareholders a fair and reasonable opportunity to exercise the right.[54]

Second, a shareholder may waive the preemptive right. If

---

[48]IC 23-1.5-3-1(b).

[49]IC 23-1.5-3-1(c).

[50]IC 23-1.5-3-1(d).

Trial Strategy References: Failure to Disclose Material Facts to Stock Purchaser, 11 Am Jur POF2d 271.

[51]IC 23-1-27-1(a).

Forms References: Reciprocal first refusal options. 6B Am Jur Legal Forms 2d, Corporations § 74:2272.

Complaint, petition, or declaration to set aside issuance of shares in excess of preemptive right—By stockholder. 7A Am Jur Pleading and Practice Forms, Annotated (rev. ed.), Corporations § 62.

[52]IC 23-1-27-1(b), (c).

[53]IC 23-1-27-1(b).

[54]IC 23-1-27-1(b)(1).

Annotation References: Dominant shareholder's accountability to minority for profit, bonus, or the like, received on sale of stock to outsiders, 38 ALR3d 1385.

the waiver is written, it is irrevocable, even if it is not supported by consideration.[55]

Third, a corporation's adoption of preemptive rights does not give shareholders a preemptive right with respect to:[56]

- shares issued as compensation to directors, officers, agents, or employees of the corporation, its subsidiaries, or its affiliates
- shares issued to satisfy conversion or option rights created to provide compensation to directors, officers, agents, or employees of the corporation, its subsidiaries, or its affiliates
- shares authorized in the articles of incorporation that are issued within six months from the effective date of incorporation
- shares sold otherwise than for money

Fourth, a corporation's adoption of preemptive rights does not give preemptive rights with respect to shares of any class to holders of shares of any class without general voting rights but with preferential rights to distributions or assets.[57]

Fifth, holders of shares of any class of common stock have no preemptive rights with respect to shares of preferred stock unless the shares of preferred stock are convertible into or carry a right to subscribe for or acquire shares without preferential rights.[58]

Finally, after shares subject to preemptive rights have been offered to, but not acquired by, shareholders, the shares may be issued to any person for the next year at a consideration set by the board of directors that is not lower than the consideration set for the exercise of preemptive rights. After the expiration of one year, the shares may be offered at lower

---

Trial Strategy References: Liability of Shareholder for Wrongfully Transferring or Assigning Corporate Common Stock Shares to Third Party, 47 Am Jur POF3d 138.

[55]IC 23-1-27-1(b)(2).

Trial Strategy References: Waiver of Right to Enforce "First Option" Stock Purchase Agreement, 3 Am Jur POF2d 379.

[56]IC 23-1-27-1(b)(3).

[57]IC 23-1-27-1(b)(4).

[58]IC 23-1-27-1(b)(5).

consideration, but this offer is subject to the shareholders' preemptive rights.[59]

A shareholder's preemptive rights under the law in existence before August 1, 1987, the effective date of the Business Corporation Law, generally continue in effect as under prior law.[60] However, if the corporation's articles of incorporation are subsequently amended with respect to preemptive rights, the Business Corporation Law's preemptive rights provisions become applicable to all shareholders' preemptive rights on the effective date of the amendment.[61] Thus, a corporation subject to the Business Corporation Law that had preemptive rights before August 1, 1987, is not subject to the Business Corporation Law's preemptive rights provisions unless and until it amends the provisions of its articles of incorporation concerning such rights. Amendment of any aspect of the provisions on preemptive rights will be sufficient, however, to make the Business Corporation Law provisions applicable.[62]

◆ **Caution:** A shareholder who is aware of the corporation's issuance of shares but fails to object to the proposal to offer the shares to the public is precluded from later asserting a claim to preemptive rights regarding the shares.[63]

§ 42 Stock options

A corporation may create or issue options for the purchase of its shares.

West's Digest, Corporations ☜98.

A corporation acting through its board of directors may create or issue rights, options, or warrants for the purchase of the corporation's shares or other securities, or those of any successor in interest of the corporation. The board of directors is to determine the terms upon which the rights, options, or warrants are issued, their form and content, and the consideration for which the shares or other securities are

---

[59]IC 23-1-27-1(b)(6).

[60]IC 23-1-54-2.

[61]IC 23-1-54-2.

[62]IC 23-1-27-1, Official Comment.

[63]Cressy v. Shannon Continental Corp., 177 Ind. App. 224, 378 N.E.2d 941 (3d Dist. 1978).

to be issued. The rights, options, or warrants may be issued with or without consideration, and may, but need not, be issued pro rata.[64] Options to purchase shares of the corporation's stock are frequently given employees as part of a compensation package, or as an inducement to stay with the corporation. Some stock option plans also require that the employee sell his or her stock acquired through an option plan back to the corporation if his or her employment terminates for any reason other than death or retirement.[65] Others require that the employee be employed by the corporation for a certain length of time before he or she may exercise a stock option.[66]

An optionee whose employer breaches a stock option agreement by failing to permit the optionee to purchase stock as agreed is entitled to damages based on the difference between the option price and the highest intermediate market price between the date of breach and a reasonable time thereafter.[67]

◆ **Comment:** Through the provision for the issuance of rights to purchase shares of "any successor in interest of the corporation,"[68] a corporation's board of directors has statutory authority to adopt "flip-over pills" or "poison pills," arrangements under which an acquiring party's acquisition of a certain percentage of shares of the corporation can trigger rights of other shareholders of the corporation to acquire shares or other securities of the acquiring party at specified prices. Although not all such arrangements are permissible, they can be a legitimate means for protecting minority shareholders in takeover situations, both by granting specific rights to such shareholders and

---

[64]IC 23-1-26-5.

Forms References: Option to purchase stock. 6B Am Jur Legal Forms 2d, Corporations § 74:2321.

[65]Biberstine v. New York Blower Co., 625 N.E.2d 1308 (Ind. Ct. App. 5th Dist. 1993), reh'g denied, (Jan. 24, 1994) and transfer dismissed, (Apr. 12, 1994).

Forms References: Employee stock option agreement. 6B Am Jur Legal Forms 2d, Corporations § 74:2326.

[66]Rauser v. LTV Electrosystems, Inc., 437 F.2d 800 (7th Cir. 1971) (applying Indiana law); Haag v. International Tel. & Tel. Corp., 342 F.2d 566 (7th Cir. 1965) (applying Indiana law).

[67]Rauser v. LTV Electrosystems, Inc., 437 F.2d 800 (7th Cir. 1971) (applying Indiana law).

[68]IC 23-1-26-5.

by giving the board of directors additional leverage in negotiating, on behalf of the shareholders, with potential acquirers.[69]

§ 43 Consideration

The board of directors may determine what consideration is adequate for shares.

West's Digest, Corporations 99(1)-99(3).

A corporation's board of directors,[70] or the shareholders, if the articles of incorporation reserve such power to them,[71] may authorize the issuance of shares for consideration consisting of any tangible or intangible property or benefit to the corporation, including cash, promissory notes, services performed, contracts for services to be performed, or other securities of the corporation.[72]

> ◆ **Illustration:** An inventor's assignment to a corporation of a patent application and his services in organizing the corporation were consideration for the shares issued to him.[73]

The corporation may issue shares for consideration the directors or, if appropriate, the shareholders determine to be adequate. This determination is conclusive as the adequacy of consideration for the issuance of shares relates to whether the shares are validly issued, fully paid, and nonassessable.[74] The directors need not necessarily affirmatively agree as to what constitutes adequate consideration, as long as they acquiesce in the issuance of shares for consideration.[75] When the corporation receives the consideration for which shares are authorized to be issued, the shares issued in exchange are fully paid and nonassessable.[76] A corporation may pay the expenses of selling or underwriting its shares, and of

---

[69]IC 23-1-26-5, Official Comment.

For discussion of corporate takeovers, see §§ 202 et seq.

[70]IC 23-1-26-2(b).

[71]IC 23-1-26-2(a).

[72]IC 23-1-26-2(b).

[73]Kiess v. Eason, 442 F.2d 712 (7th Cir. 1971) (applying Indiana law).

[74]IC 23-1-26-2(c).

[75]Garbe v. Excel Mold, Inc., 397 N.E.2d 296 (Ind. Ct. App. 1st Dist. 1979) (under former IC 23-1-2-6(e)).

[76]IC 23-1-26-2(d).

organizing or reorganizing the corporation, from the consideration received for shares.[77]

If shares are authorized to be issued for promissory notes or for promises to render services in the future, a corporation must generally report in writing to the shareholders the number of shares authorized to be so issued.[78] This is not required of corporations subject to the Securities Exchange Act of 1934 which have complied with that act's proxy disclosure provisions.[79] Moreover, if shares are issued for a promissory note, or for a contract for future services or benefits, the corporation may, but is not required to, place the shares in escrow or otherwise restrict their transfer. It may also credit distributions in respect of the shares against their purchase price, until the services are performed, the note is paid, or the benefits received. If the services are not performed, the note is not paid, or the benefits are not received, the shares escrowed or restricted and the distributions credited may be cancelled in whole or in part.[80]

§ 44   Certificates

A share may, but need not, be represented by a certificate.

West's Digest, Corporations ☞95, 96, 109.

A certificate of stock is a written acknowledgment by the corporation of the interest of the shareholder in corporate property,[81] and is documentary evidence of title to shares of stock.[82] Shares may, but need not be, represented by certificates,[83] unless the articles of incorporation or bylaws

---

[77]IC 23-1-26-9.

[78]IC 23-1-26-2(b); IC 23-1-53-2(b).

[79]IC 23-1-53-2(b), referring to 15 U.S.C.A. §§ 78a et seq.

[80]IC 23-1-26-2(e).

[81]Markle v. Burgess, 176 Ind. 25, 95 N.E. 308 (1911).

[82]Markle v. Burgess, 176 Ind. 25, 95 N.E. 308 (1911); DRW Builders, Inc. v. Richardson, 679 N.E.2d 902 (Ind. Ct. App. 1997), reh'g denied, (June 20, 1997).

Forms References: Common stock certificate. 6B Am Jur Legal Forms 2d, Corporations § 74:2161.

Preferred stock certificate. 6B Am Jur Legal Forms 2d, Corporations § 74:2171.

[83]IC 23-1-26-6(a).

provide otherwise.[84] Thus, possession of a share certificate is not essential to ownership of shares or to the exercise of shareholder's rights.[85] Unless the Business Corporation Law or another statute expressly provides otherwise, the rights and obligations of shareholders of the same class or series of shares are identical regardless of whether their shares are represented by certificates.[86]

A share certificate may be in bearer form, in which case it is payable to the bearer according to its terms, and no endorsement is necessary,[87] or in registered form, in which case the certificate specifies the person entitled to the share or shares it represents, and the transfer of the shares may be registered on the corporation's books.[88]

If share certificates are issued, each must, at a minimum, state on its face:[89]

(1) the name of the issuing corporation and that it is organized under the law of Indiana;

(2) the name of the person to whom the certificate is issued; and

(3) the number and class of shares and the designation of the series, if any, the certificate represents.

In addition, certificates representing scrip must be conspicuously labeled "scrip."[90] If the certificate does not bear all of this information, any person may complete it by filling in the blanks as authorized. Even if the blanks are incorrectly filled in, the certificate will be enforceable by a purchaser who took it for value without notice of the incorrectness.[91] If a certificate was originally completed, but has been improperly or even fraudulently altered, the certificate is enforceable only according to its original terms.[92]

---

[84]IC 23-1-26-7(a).

[85]DRW Builders, Inc. v. Richardson, 679 N.E.2d 902 (Ind. Ct. App. 1997), reh'g denied, (June 20, 1997).

[86]IC 23-1-26-6(a).

[87]IC 26-1-8.1-102(2).

[88]IC 26-1-8.1-102(13).

[89]IC 23-1-26-6(b).

[90]IC 23-1-25-4(b).

For discussion of scrip and fractional shares, see § 40.

[91]IC 26-1-8.1-206(a).

[92]IC 26-1-8.1-206(b).

◆ **Comment:** A corporation may protect itself against liability for incorrectly completed certificates by making sure the certificate is complete before the authorized officer signs it.[93]

If the issuing corporation is authorized to issue different classes of shares or different series within a class, the designations, relative rights, preferences, and limitations applicable to each class, the variations in those matters determined for each series, and the board's authority to determine variations for future series, must be summarized on the front or back of each certificate. In the alternative, each certificate may state conspicuously on its front or back that the corporation will furnish the shareholder this information on request in writing and without charge.[94] Each certificate must also be signed by at least two officers designated in the bylaws or by the board of directors, or, if the corporation has only one officer, by that officer.[95] The signature may be manual or in facsimile.[96] The certificate is valid even if the person who signed it no longer holds office when the certificate is issued.[97] In addition, a certificate may also bear the corporate seal, or a facsimile of the seal.[98]

A forged or otherwise unauthorized signature on a share certificate is generally ineffective. It is, however, effective in favor of a purchaser of the share for value who is without notice of the lack of authority, and the signature was made by a person entrusted by the corporation with signing the certificate, or an employee of the corporation entrusted with responsible handling of the certificate.[99]

Within a reasonable time after shares without certificates have been issued or transferred, the corporation must send the shareholder a written statement of the information required to appear on share certificates, including the infor-

---

[93]IC 26-1-8.1-206, Official Comment.

[94]IC 23-1-26-6(c).

[95]IC 23-1-26-6(d)(1).

For discussion of what officers a corporation must have, see § 102.

[96]IC 23-1-26-6(d)(1).

[97]IC 23-1-26-6(e).

[98]IC 23-1-26-6(d)(2).

[99]IC 26-1-8.1-205.

mation noted above and information regarding restrictions on transfer of the shares.[1]

A corporation must replace a share certificate that has been lost, destroyed, or stolen if the owner of the certificate so requests before the corporation is notified that the certificate has been acquired by a protected purchaser, and if the owner files with the corporation a sufficient indemnity bond and satisfies other reasonable requests made by the corporation.[2] If the owner fails to notify the corporation within a reasonable time that a share certificate has been lost, destroyed, or stolen, the owner may not claim a replacement or assert a claim for wrongful registration of the transfer of the share.[3] If, after the corporation issues a new certificate, a protected purchaser of the original certificate presents the original certificate for registration of transfer, the corporation is to register the transfer, unless an overissue would result. In addition to any rights on the indemnity bond, an issuer may recover the new certificate from a person to whom it was issued or any person taking under that person, except a protected purchaser.[4]

A protected purchaser is a purchaser of a certificated or uncertificated share who gives value, has no notice of any adverse claim to the security, and obtains control of the security.[5] A protected purchaser acquires the rights of a purchaser and an interest in the security free of any adverse claim.[6]

§ 45 Reacquisition by corporation

A corporation may acquire its own shares, and may be prohibited from reissuing them.

West's Digest, Corporations ⚯110.

A corporation may acquire its own shares, which are then

---

[1]IC 23-1-26-7(b).

For discussion of restrictions on transfer of shares, see § 47.

[2]IC 26-1-8.1-405(a).

[3]IC 26-1-8.1-406.

For discussion of registration of transfers of shares, see § 51.

[4]IC 26-1-8.1-405(b).

For discussion of registration of transfers of shares, see § 51.

[5]IC 26-1-8.1-303(a).

[6]IC 26-1-8.1-303(b).

considered authorized but unissued unless the articles of incorporation or a resolution of the board provide otherwise.[7] For instance, a corporation may contract for the sale of its shares, with a clause providing that the corporation will buy back the shares at a fixed price if the purchaser later sells them.[8] Fixed price stock buy-back arrangements are generally upheld by courts so long as they are not tainted with fraud.[9]

If the articles of incorporation prohibit the corporation's reissue of shares it has acquired, the number of authorized shares is reduced by the number of shares acquired by the corporation, effective upon amendment of the articles of incorporation.[10] Such an amendment may be adopted without shareholder action. The articles of amendment are to be delivered to the Secretary of State and are required to set forth: the name of the corporation; the reduction in the number of authorized shares, itemized by class and series; and the total number of authorized shares, itemized by class and series, remaining after reduction of the shares.[11]

A corporation has authority to use, hold, acquire, cancel, and dispose of treasury shares as defined in prior law. Treasury shares were defined in prior law as the corporation's own outstanding shares which it has acquired, and which it has not canceled but holds to be used or disposed of in the furtherance of some corporate purpose.[12] If the corporation cancels treasury shares, they are to be treated as authorized but unissued shares unless the board adopts an amendment to the articles of incorporation to reduce the number of authorized shares.[13]

A professional corporation may purchase its own shares

---

[7]IC 23-1-27-2(a).

[8]Anacomp, Inc. v. Wright, 449 N.E.2d 610 (Ind. Ct. App. 1st Dist. 1983) (where corporation and prospective employee entered into sale and buy-back agreement in contemplation of subsequent negotiation of definitive employment contract, fact that employment contract was never reached did not warrant rescission of stock agreement, which was separate, independent, and fully-executed agreement).

[9]Anacomp, Inc. v. Wright, 449 N.E.2d 610 (Ind. Ct. App. 1st Dist. 1983).

[10]IC 23-1-27-2(b).

[11]IC 23-1-27-2(c).

[12]IC 23-1-27-2(d) (referring to prior statute IC 23-1-1-1 which was repealed effective August 1, 1987).

[13]IC 23-1-27-2(e).

from a person who is disqualified to render services of the type for which the corporation was created, unless the corporation is insolvent or the purchase would make it insolvent.[14] Shares of a deceased shareholder or disqualified person may also be transferred to a qualified person.[15]

IV. TRANSFER OF SHARES

Research References

IC 23-1-26-8; IC 23-1.5-3-6; IC 26-1-8.1-101; IC 26-1-8.1-102; IC 26-1-8.1-108; IC 26-1-8.1-112; IC 26-1-8.1-113; IC 26-1-8.1-204; IC 26-1-8.1-207; IC 26-1-8.1-301; IC 26-1-8.1-302; IC 26-1-8.1-304; IC 26-1-8.1-306; IC 26-1-8.1-307; IC 26-1-8.1-401 to IC 26-1-8.1-404; IC 26-1-9-101; IC 26-1-9-115; IC 32-4-1.5-15; IC 32-4-1.6-10; IC 32-4-1.6-11

18A Am Jur 2d, Corporations §§ 681-727.
18 C.J.S., Corporations §§ 217-292.
West's Digest, Corporations ☞111-149.
ALR Digest: Corporations §§ 203-220
ALR Index: Articles of Incorporation; Assets; Bylaws; Charter; Close Corporation; Consolidation or Merger; Corporate Bonds and Bondholders; Corporate Officers, Directors, and Agents; Corporate Opportunity; Corporate Responsibility Doctrine; Corporate Stock and Stockholders; Corporations; Dissolution or Liquidation; Dividends; Domicile and Residence; Foreign Corporations; Forfeitures; Liquidation or Dissolution; Minority Stockholders; Names; Nonprofit Institutions or Organizations; Professional Corporations and Associations; Promoters; Prospectus; Proxies; Reports; Seal; Stock-Option Plans; Subsidiary
6B Am Jur Legal Forms 2d, Corporations §§ 74:2245, 74:2246, 74:2262-74:2267, 74:2291, 74:2292, 74:2301, 74:2341-74:2348, 74:2355, 74:2385, 74:2405, 74:2406.
Failure to Disclose Material Facts to Stock Purchaser, 11 Am Jur POF2d 271.

§ 46 Generally

Shareholders may transfer their shares to other shareholders or to strangers.

West's Digest, Corporations ☞111, 111.5, 115-121(7).

---

[14]IC 23-1.5-3-2.
[15]IC 23-1.5-3-3.

Sales and other transfers of securities, including shares of corporate stock, are governed by the Indiana version of Article 8 of the Uniform Commercial Code.[16]

As a rule, a contract for the sale of shares is governed by the same principles as govern contracts generally.[17] Thus, there must be an offer of a purchase or sale on the one part and an acceptance thereof on the other, in which the minds of the parties meet as to their mutual obligations.[18] The court is to give effect to clear and unambiguous language in a contract for the sale of shares, while ambiguities in such contracts are to be resolved through trial.[19] Moreover, a subscription agreement or other contract for the sale of shares must be construed, if possible, so as to effectuate the intention of the parties, and such intention must be ascertained from a consideration of the language of the contract interpreted as a whole.[20] A contract for the transfer of stock may be for the benefit of a third party.[21]

A contract for the sale of shares may be unenforceable due to unconscionability.[22] Such a contract may be rescinded for fraud[23] or failure to perform,[24] whereupon the party rescinding the sale must offer to return the stock or other consider-

---

[16]IC 26-1-8.1-101 et seq.

[17]Stech v. Panel Mart, Inc., 434 N.E.2d 97 (Ind. Ct. App. 3d Dist. 1982).

As to contracts generally, see I.L.E., Contracts.

Forms References: Offers to purchase stock. 6B Am Jur Legal Forms 2d, Corporations §§ 74:2291, 74:2292.

Offer to sell stock. 6B Am Jur Legal Forms 2d, Corporations § 74:2301.

Stock purchase agreements. Am Jur Legal Forms 2d, Corporations §§ 74:2341-74:2348.

[18]Neu v. Woods, 103 Ind. App. 342, 7 N.E.2d 531 (1937); Fast v. Baker, 76 Ind. App. 677, 131 N.E. 57 (Div. 2 1921); Atkins v. Kattman, 50 Ind. App. 233, 97 N.E. 174 (Div. 2 1912).

[19]Shortridge v. Platis, 458 N.E.2d 301 (Ind. Ct. App. 3d Dist. 1984); Stech v. Panel Mart, Inc., 434 N.E.2d 97 (Ind. Ct. App. 3d Dist. 1982).

[20]Rauh v. Fletcher Savings & Trust Co., 207 Ind. 638, 194 N.E. 334 (1935); Anacomp, Inc. v Wright, 449 N.E.2d 610 (Ind. App. 1983).

[21]Krull v. Pierce, 117 Ind. App. 638, 71 N.E.2d 617 (1947).

[22]Stech v. Panel Mart, Inc., 434 N.E.2d 97 (Ind. Ct. App. 3d Dist. 1982).

[23]Groub v. Blish, 88 Ind. App. 309, 153 N.E. 895 (1926); Barnard v. First Nat. Bank of Newpoint, 61 Ind. App. 634, 111 N.E. 451 (Div. 2 1916).

[24]Yost v. McCarty, 123 Ind. App. 288, 108 N.E.2d 718 (1952).

ation which he or she has received under the contract.[25] Where a complaint rests solely on the alleged breach of an express contract for the sale of stock, no recovery can be had on an implied contract theory.[26]

The statute of frauds does not apply to contracts for the sale of securities.[27]

§ 47   Restrictions on right to transfer

Restrictions may be imposed through the articles of incorporation, the bylaws, or an agreement, and the holder of shares subject to a restriction must have at least constructive notice of the restriction.

West's Digest, Corporations ☞113.

A corporation may impose restrictions on the transfer, or on the registration of the transfer, of any class or series of the corporation's shares, or of a security convertible into or carrying a right to subscribe for or acquire shares,[28] through a provision in the articles of incorporation or bylaws, through an agreement among shareholders, or through an agreement between the corporation and the shareholders.[29] The repeal or amendment of a bylaw of a corporation restricting the transfer of stock does not alter or relax restrictions upon the sale of stock embodied in an agreement between stockholders.[30] A restriction on transfer does not affect shares issued before the restriction was adopted, unless the holders of the shares are parties to the restriction agreement, or unless they voted in favor of the restriction.[31] Restrictions may be imposed to maintain the corporation's status when it is de-

---

[25]Brumbaugh v. Mellinger, 68 Ind. App. 410, 120 N.E. 676 (1918); Barnard v. First Nat. Bank of Newpoint, 61 Ind. App. 634, 111 N.E. 451 (Div. 2 1916).

[26]Neu v. Woods, 103 Ind. App. 342, 7 N.E.2d 531 (1937).

[27]IC 26-1-8.1-113.

[28]IC 23-1-26-8(e).

[29]IC 23-1-26-8(a).

As to registration of transfers, see § 51.

Forms References: Petition of application to enforce restriction on transfer of shares as authorized by articles of incorporation or bylaws—By stockholder. 7A Am Jur Pleading and Practice Forms, Annotated (rev. ed.), Corporations § 99.

[30]Doss v. Yingling, 204 Ind. 571, 185 N.E. 281 (1933).

[31]IC 23-1-26-8(a).

pendent on the number or identity of its shareholders, to preserve exemptions under federal or state securities law, or for any other reasonable purpose.[32]

A restriction on transfer or the registration of transfer may, among other things:[33]

(1) obligate the shareholder first to offer the corporation or other persons (separately, consecutively, or simultaneously) an opportunity to acquire the restricted shares;

(2) obligate the corporation or other persons (separately, consecutively, or simultaneously) to acquire the restricted shares;

(3) require the corporation, the holders of any class of its shares, or another person to approve the transfer of the restricted shares, if the requirement is not manifestly unreasonable, or

(4) prohibit the transfer of the restricted shares to designated persons or classes of persons, if the prohibition is not manifestly unreasonable.

Restrictions are not read broadly.[34]

◆ **Illustration:** A stock purchase agreement requiring shares in a closely held corporation to be first offered to "another shareholder" before being sold to a nonshareholder did not require the selling shareholder to provide written notice of his offer to sell the stock to all of the corporation's other shareholders, or to offer to sell the stock to all of the other shareholders, where he had made the offer to one other shareholder.[35]

A statutorily authorized restriction on transfer or the registration of transfer is valid and enforceable against the holder of a share, or against his or her transferee, if the restriction's existence is noted conspicuously on the front or

---

[32]IC 23-1-26-8(c).

[33]IC 23-1-26-8(d).

For discussion of preemptive rights to acquire shares, see § 41.

[34]Hardy v. South Bend Sash & Door Co., Inc., 603 N.E.2d 895 (Ind. Ct. App. 3d Dist. 1992), reh'g denied, (Jan. 13, 1993) and transfer denied, (Mar. 24, 1993).

[35]Hardy v. South Bend Sash & Door Co., Inc., 603 N.E.2d 895 (Ind. Ct. App. 3d Dist. 1992), reh'g denied, (Jan. 13, 1993) and transfer denied, (Mar. 24, 1993).

back of the certificate[36] or is contained in the information statement required for uncertificated shares,[37] or if the registered owner has otherwise been notified of the restriction.[38] If the restriction is not so noted, or the registered owner so notified, the restriction is not enforceable against a person without knowledge of it.[39]

> ◆ **Caution:** Even if a right of first refusal for the purchase of shares is not expressly granted, the shareholders of a closely held corporation may be obligated by their fiduciary duty toward each other to disclose to the corporation's other shareholders the availability of outstanding shares for sale and to afford them the opportunity to purchase the shares.[40]

A professional corporation must notify the authority which regulates members of the profession of a change in the ownership of any of the corporation's shares within 30 days after the date of the change. Notice of change in ownership must contain the names and post office addresses of the transferor shareholder and the transferee shareholder.[41]

§ 48   Valuation of shares of closely held corporation

Because there is generally no market for the shares of a closely held corporation, shareholders of such corporations may agree as to the price of the shares, or as to a method for determining the price.

West's Digest, Corporations ☞114.

Closely held corporations generally find no market for their shares, as the only people interested in the business are the

---

[36]IC 23-1-26-8(b); IC 26-1-8.1-204(1).

Forms References: Statement on stock certificate—Notice of restrictions on negotiability. 6B Am Jur Legal Forms 2d, Corporations §§ 74:2262-74:2267.

[37]IC 23-1-26-8(b).

[38]IC 26-1-8.1-204(2).

[39]IC 23-1-26-8(b).

Trial Strategy References: Failure to Disclose Material Facts to Stock Purchaser, 11 Am Jur POF2d 27.

[40]Cressy v. Shannon Continental Corp., 177 Ind. App. 224, 378 N.E.2d 941 (3d Dist. 1978).

For discussion of fiduciary duty among the shareholders of close corporations, see § 72.

[41]IC 23-1.5-3-6(b).

shareholders, sometimes referred to as "incorporated partners," who are intimately involved with the corporation. Because there is no market, it is difficult and speculative to value a close corporation's shares.[42] As a result of this difficulty, Indiana permits the shareholders in closely held corporations to enter into fixed price stock agreements, in which the shareholders or directors of the corporation determine the price of the corporation's shares, or a method of determining the price.[43]

Such agreements often call for sale of the shares at book value. To determine stock's book value per share, the corporation's net worth as shown on the corporate books is divided by the number of its outstanding shares.[44] However, the parties to such agreements are also free to use methods of valuation other than book value.[45] Agreements frequently provide that the price of the stock is to be determined periodically by the shareholders.[46] The method of valuation is a matter for the parties rather than the court.[47]

◆ **Practice Guide:** The shareholders of a close corpora-

---

[42]Krukemeier v. Krukemeier Mach. & Tool Co., Inc., 551 N.E.2d 885 (Ind. Ct. App. 1st Dist. 1990).

Legal Periodicals: Evolution of Effective Remedies for Minority Shareholders and its Impact Upon Valuation of Minority Shares. 65 Notre Dame L. Rev. 425 (1990).

[43]Hardy v. South Bend Sash & Door Co., Inc., 603 N.E.2d 895 (Ind. Ct. App. 3d Dist. 1992), reh'g denied, (Jan. 13, 1993) and transfer denied, (Mar. 24, 1993); Krukemeier v. Krukemeier Mach. & Tool Co., Inc., 551 N.E.2d 885 (Ind. Ct. App. 1st Dist. 1990).

Forms References: Stock purchase (buy-sell) agreement between corporation and sole shareholders—Purchase option during shareholder's lifetime—Provision for determination of purchase price. 6B Am Jur Legal Forms 2d, Corporations § 74:2355.

[44]Krukemeier v. Krukemeier Mach. & Tool Co., Inc., 551 N.E.2d 885 (Ind. Ct. App. 1st Dist. 1990).

[45]Hardy v. South Bend Sash & Door Co., Inc., 603 N.E.2d 895 (Ind. Ct. App. 3d Dist. 1992), reh'g denied, (Jan. 13, 1993) and transfer denied, (Mar. 24, 1993); Krukemeier v. Krukemeier Mach. & Tool Co., Inc., 551 N.E.2d 885 (Ind. Ct. App. 1st Dist. 1990).

[46]See, for instance, Hardy v. South Bend Sash & Door Co., Inc., 603 N.E.2d 895 (Ind. Ct. App. 3d Dist. 1992), reh'g denied, (Jan. 13, 1993) and transfer denied, (Mar. 24, 1993) (value to be determined periodically by mutual agreement of stockholders); Stech v. Panel Mart, Inc., 434 N.E.2d 97 (Ind. Ct. App. 3d Dist. 1982) (value to be established by stockholders at each annual meeting).

[47]Hardy v. South Bend Sash & Door Co., Inc., 603 N.E.2d 895 (Ind. Ct.

tion may agree to maintain insurance policies on their lives in order to ensure that cash will be available to the other shareholders to purchase a deceased shareholder's shares.[48]

§ 49 Delivery; effect

Upon delivery of a security, the purchaser acquires all of the transferor's rights in it.

West's Digest, Corporations ⊕114.

Generally, upon delivery of a certificated or uncertificated security to a purchaser, the purchaser acquires all rights in the security the transferor had or had power to transfer.[49] However, the purchaser of a limited interest acquires rights only to the extent of the interest purchased,[50] and the purchaser of a certificated security who, as a previous holder of the security, had notice of an adverse claim, does not improve its position by taking from a protected purchaser.[51]

A certificated security is delivered when any of the following occur:[52]

- the purchaser acquires possession of the security certificate
- another person, other than a securities intermediary, either acquires possession of the security certificate on behalf of the purchaser or, having previously acquired possession of the certificate, acknowledges that it holds the certificate for the purchaser

---

App. 3d Dist. 1992), reh'g denied, (Jan. 13, 1993) and transfer denied, (Mar. 24, 1993); Krukemeier v. Krukemeier Mach. & Tool Co., Inc., 551 N.E.2d 885 (Ind. Ct. App. 1st Dist. 1990).

[48]Melrose v. Capitol City Motor Lodge, Inc., 705 N.E.2d 985 (Ind. 1998); Krukemeier v. Krukemeier Mach. & Tool Co., Inc., 551 N.E.2d 885 (Ind. Ct. App. 1st Dist. 1990).

[49]IC 26-1-8.1-302(a). Curtis v. Beckett, 114 Ind. App. 221, 50 N.E.2d 920 (1943) (transfer of stock in insolvent corporation carried with it to transferee rights and liabilities of transferor).

[50]IC 26-1-8.1-302(b).

[51]IC 26-1-8.1-302(c).

For discussion of protected purchasers, see § 44.

[52]IC 26-1-8.1-301(a).

A securities intermediary is a clearing corporation or a person, such as a broker, who in the ordinary course of business maintains securities accounts for others.—IC 26-1-8.1-102(14).

- a securities intermediary acting on behalf of the purchaser acquires possession of the security certificate, but only if the certificate is in registered form and has been specially endorsed to the purchaser by an effective endorsement

Thus, registration of the transfer of a certificated security is not necessary to vest the purchaser with title to the security.[53]

An uncertificated security is delivered when: the corporation which issued the shares registers the purchaser as the registered owner, whether upon original issue of the shares or registration of their transfer; or another person, other than a securities intermediary, either becomes the registered owner of the uncertificated security on behalf of the purchaser or, having previously become the registered owner, acknowledges that it holds the security for the purchaser.[54]

§ 50 Endorsement

A certificated security is transferred by endorsement and delivery of the certificate.

West's Digest, Corporations ☞124-126.

A certificated security must be endorsed upon transfer. Endorsement may be special or in blank.[55] An endorsement in blank includes an endorsement to bearer. A special endorsement specifies to whom a security is to be transferred or who has power to transfer it. A holder may convert a blank endorsement to a special endorsement.[56] An endorsement intended to transfer only some of the units represented by a security certificate is effective to the extent of the endorse-

---

[53]In re Krause, 114 B.R. 582 (Bankr. N.D. Ind. 1988) (under former statute).

[54]IC 26-1-8.1-301(b).

For discussion of registration of certificated and uncertificated securities, see § 51.

[55]IC 26-1-8.1-304(a).

Forms References: Assignment on reverse side of stock certificate. 6B Am Jur Legal Forms 2d, Corporations § 74:2245.

Assignment by separate instrument. 6B Am Jur Legal Forms 2d, Corporations § 74:2246.

[56]IC 26-1-8.1-304(a).

ment.[57] Transfer of a certificated security is complete upon delivery of the endorsed certificate, or, if the endorsement is on a separate document, delivery of both the document and the certificate.[58]

If a registered certificated security has been delivered to a purchaser without a necessary endorsement, the purchaser is not a protected purchaser until the certificate is properly supplied. As against the transferor, however, a transfer of the shares represented by the certificate is complete upon delivery, and the purchaser has a specifically enforceable right to have the endorsement supplied.[59]

An endorsement of a security certificate in bearer form may give notice of an adverse claim to the certificate, but it does not otherwise affect a right to registration that the holder possesses.[60]

§ 51 Registration of transfer

The purchaser of a registered security is entitled to transfer of the registration upon proper request.

West's Digest, Corporations ⚎124-126.

Unless otherwise agreed, the transferor of a security must, on due demand, supply the purchaser with proof of his or her authority to transfer the security, or with any other requisite necessary to obtain registration of the transfer. If the transfer is not for value, the transferor need not comply with the demand unless the purchaser pays the necessary expenses for obtaining transfer. The purchaser may reject or rescind the transfer if the transferor fails to comply with the demand within a reasonable time.[61]

If a certificated security in registered form is presented to the issuing corporation with a request to register its transfer, or an instruction is presented to the issuing corporation with a request to register transfer of an uncertificated security,

---

[57] IC 26-1-8.1-304(b).

[58] IC 26-1-8.1-304(c).

[59] IC 26-1-8.1-304(d).

For the definition of "protected purchaser," see § 44.

[60] IC 26-1-8.1-304(e).

[61] IC 26-1-8.1-307.

the corporation shall register the transfer as requested if all of the following requirements are satisfied:[62]

    (1) under the terms of the security, the person seeking registration of transfer is eligible to have the security registered in his or her name;

    (2) the endorsement or instruction is made by the appropriate person or by an agent who has actual authority to act on behalf of the appropriate person;

    (3) reasonable assurance is given that the endorsement or instruction is genuine and authorized;

    (4) any applicable law relating to the collection of taxes has been complied with;

    (5) the transfer does not violate any restriction on transfer properly imposed by the issuing corporation;

    (6) a demand that the issuer not register transfer has not become effective, or such a demand has been properly made but no legal process or indemnity bond has been obtained; and

    (7) the transfer is in fact rightful, or is to a protected purchaser.

Until the proper presentment of a certificated security for registration of its transfer, or of an instruction requesting registration of the transfer of an uncertificated security, the issuing corporation may treat the registered owner as the person entitled to exercise the rights and powers of a shareholder.[63]

A corporation which is under a duty to register the transfer of a security is liable to a person properly requesting registration, or to that person's principal, for loss resulting from failure or refusal to register the transfer, or for unreasonable delay in registration.[64]

---

[62]IC 26-1-8.1-401(a).

    For discussion of restrictions on transfer, see § 47.

    For discussion of demands not to register transfer, see § 52.

    For discussion of protected purchasers, see § 44.

[63]IC 26-1-8.1-207(a).

[64]IC 26-1-8.1-401(b).

A corporation is also liable if it has registered the transfer of a security to a person who is not entitled to it, and the transfer was registered:[65]

(1) under an ineffective endorsement or instruction, such as a forged endorsement;

(2) after an effective demand, with which the corporation failed to comply, that the issuer not register transfer;

(3) after the issuer had been served with an injunction, restraining order, or other legal process enjoining it from registering the transfer, issued by a court of competent jurisdiction, and the issuer had a reasonable opportunity to act on the injunction, restraining order, or other legal process; or

(4) by an issuing corporation acting in collusion with the wrongdoer.

Otherwise, a corporation is not liable to a shareholder or other person who suffers loss as a result of the transfer of shares made under an effective endorsement or instruction to register a transfer.[66]

An issuing corporation that is liable for wrongful registration of transfer shall, on demand, provide the person entitled to the security with a like security, and any payments or distributions that the person did not receive as a result of the wrongful registration, unless such action would result in an overissue.[67]

§ 52 —Demand that corporation not register transfer

A shareholder whose certificates have been lost, destroyed, or stolen may demand that the issuing corporation not register transfer of the shares.

West's Digest, Corporations ☞128-136.

A person who may appropriately make an endorsement or originate an instruction may demand that the corporation not register transfer of a share by notifying the corporation,

---

[65]IC 26-1-8.1-404(a).

For discussion of demand that transfer not be registered, see § 52.

[66]IC 26-1-8.1-404(c).

[67]IC 26-1-8.1-404(b).

For discussion of the corporation's duties if an overissue would result, see § 40.

identifying the registered owner of the certificate and the issue of which the share it represents is a part, and providing an address for the person making the demand.[68] This provision is designed for the use of shareholders whose share certificates have been lost or stolen.[69] The demand is effective only if the corporation receives it at a time and in a manner giving it reasonable opportunity to act on the demand.[70] The shareholder's notification to the corporation that the certificates have been lost will constitute a demand that the corporation not register transfer.[71]

If, after receiving such a demand, another person requests that the corporation register the transfer of the shares, the corporation must notify both the person demanding registration and the person who demanded that the transfer not be registered that registration has been requested, that a previous demand that no transfer be registered had been made, and that the corporation will withhold registration for up to thirty days to permit the person who initiated the demand to obtain legal process or an indemnity bond.[72] To be able to hold the corporation liable for registration of transfer, the person who demanded that the transfer not be registered must, within the time stated in the corporation's communication, either obtain an appropriate injunction prohibiting the corporation from registering the transfer, or file with the corporation an indemnity bond the corporation considers sufficient to protect the corporation and its agents from any loss they may suffer by refusing to register the transfer.[73]

The provisions relating to demand that the corporation

---

[68]IC 26-1-8.1-403(a).

Forms References: Notice to corporate issuer of loss, destruction, or theft of stock certificate—Request for issuance of duplicate certificate. 6B Am Jur Legal Forms 2d, Corporations § 74:2405.

Notice to corporate issuer of loss, destruction, or theft of stock certificate—To stop transfer of lost or stolen certificate. 6B Am Jur Legal Forms 2d, Corporations § 74:2406.

[69]IC 26-1-8.1-403(a), Official Comment.

[70]IC 26-1-8.1-403(a).

For discussion of the replacement of lost, stolen, or destroyed certificates, see § 44.

[71]IC 26-1-8.1-403(a), Official Comment.

[72]IC 26-1-8.1-403(b), (c).

[73]IC 26-1-8.1-403(d).

not register transfer do not relieve an issuer from liability for registering transfer under an endorsement or instruction that was not effective.[74]

§ 53 Guarantees to purchaser

A signature, endorsement, or instruction to register the transfer of a share may be guaranteed.

West's Digest, Corporations ⊕128-136.

The signature of an endorser may be guaranteed, in which case the guarantor warrants that at the time of signing:[75]

   (1) the signature was genuine;

   (2) the signer was an appropriate person to make the endorsement, or if the signature is by an agent, the agent had actual authority to act on behalf of the appropriate person; and

   (3) the signer had legal capacity to sign.

A person who guarantees an endorsement of a security certificate makes the preceding warranties, and also warrants the rightfulness of the transfer in all respects.[76]

The signature of the originator of an instruction directing that the corporation register the transfer of an uncertificated security may also be guaranteed. A person who guarantees such a signature warrants that at the time of signing:[77]

   (1) the signature was genuine;

   (2) the signer was an appropriate person to originate the instruction, or if the signature is by an agent, the agent had actual authority to act on behalf of the appropriate person; and

   (3) the signer had legal capacity to sign.

In addition, a person who specially guarantees the signature of the originator of an instruction to register transfer warrants not only the three points noted above, but also that the person specified in the instruction as the registered owner of the uncertificated security will be the registered owner, and that the transfer of the uncertificated

---

[74]IC 26-1-8.1-403(e).

   For discussion of such liability, see § 51.

[75]IC 26-1-8.1-306(a).

[76]IC 26-1-8.1-306(e).

[77]IC 26-1-8.1-306(b).

security requested in the instruction will be registered by the issuer free from all liens, security interests, restrictions, and claims other than those specified in the instruction.[78] A person who guarantees an instruction requesting the transfer of an uncertificated security makes the warranties of a special signature guarantor, and also warrants the rightfulness of the transfer in all respects.[79]

A corporation may not require any of the guarantees discussed in this section as a condition to registration of the transfer of shares.[80] The warranties made by these guarantees are made to a person taking or dealing with the security in reliance on the guaranty, and the guarantor is liable to that person for loss resulting from breach of the warranties. An endorser or originator of an instruction whose signature, endorsement, or instruction has been guaranteed is liable to a guarantor for any loss suffered by the guarantor as a result of breach of the warranties of the guarantor.[81]

§ 54 Assurances to corporation

A corporation may demand certain assurances that an endorsement or an instruction to register transfer is genuine and authorized.

West's Digest, Corporations ☞128-136.

A corporation whose shares are transferred may require any of the following assurances that each endorsement or instruction to register transfer is genuine and authorized:[82]

- in all cases, a guaranty of the signature of the person making an endorsement or originating an instruction including, in the case of an instruction, reasonable assurance of identity
- if the endorsement is made or the instruction is originated by an agent, appropriate assurance of actual authority to sign
- if the endorsement is made or the instruction is originated by a fiduciary, appropriate evidence of the fiduciary's appointment or incumbency

---

[78]IC 26-1-8.1-306(c).
[79]IC 26-1-8.1-306(f).
[80]IC 26-1-8.1-306(g).
[81]IC 26-1-8.1-306(h).
[82]IC 26-1-8.1-402(a).

- if there is more than one fiduciary, reasonable assurance that all who are required to sign have done so
- if the endorsement is made or the instruction is originated by a person who is not included in one of the categories listed above, assurance appropriate to the case corresponding as nearly as may be to the above provisions

A corporation may elect to require other reasonable assurances as well.[83]

A signature guaranty to a corporation is one signed by or on behalf of a person the corporation reasonably believes to be responsible. The corporation may adopt standards for responsibility of guarantors if the standards are not manifestly unreasonable.[84]

In the case of a fiduciary appointed or qualified by a court, appropriate evidence of the fiduciary's appointment or incumbency is a certificate issued by the court not more than 60 days before the transfer of shares is sought.[85] In any other case, a copy of a document showing the appointment, a certificate issued by a responsible person, or, in the absence of such a document or certificate, any other evidence the corporation reasonably considers appropriate may serve as the required evidence of a fiduciary's appointment or incumbency.[86]

§ 55 Warranties to purchaser and corporation

Persons who take various actions in connection with the transfer of shares make certain warranties to the purchaser and issuer of the shares.

West's Digest, Corporations ⟳120.

A person who transfers a certificated security to a purchaser for value warrants to the purchaser that:[87]

(1) the certificate is genuine and has not been materially altered;

---

[83]IC 26-1-8.1-402(b).

[84]IC 26-1-8.1-402(c)(1).

[85]IC 26-1-8.1-402(c)(2)(i).

[86]IC 26-1-8.1-402(c)(2)(ii).

[87]IC 26-1-8.1-108(a).

Forms References: Seller's warranties. 6B Am Jur Legal Forms 2d, Corporations § 74:2385.

(2) the transferor or endorser does not know of any fact that might impair the validity of the security;

(3) there is no adverse claim to the security;

(4) the transfer does not violate any restriction on transfer;

(5) if the transfer is by endorsement, that the endorsement is made by an appropriate person, or if the endorsement is by an agent, the agent has actual authority to act on behalf of the appropriate person; and

(6) the transfer is otherwise effective and rightful.

An endorser, if the transfer is by endorsement, makes the same warranties to any subsequent purchaser.[88]

A person who originates an instruction that the registration of an uncertificated security be transferred to a purchaser for value warrants to the purchaser that: the instruction is made by an appropriate person, or if the instruction is by an agent, the agent has actual authority to act on behalf of the appropriate person; the security is valid; and there is no adverse claim to the security.[89] Such person also warrants to the purchaser that at the time the instruction is presented to the issuer that the purchaser will be entitled to the registration of transfer; the transfer will be registered by the issuer free from all liens, security interests, restrictions, and claims other than those specified in the instruction; the transfer will not violate any restriction on transfer; and the requested transfer will otherwise be effective and rightful.[90]

A broker that delivers a security certificate to its customer, or causes its customer to be registered as the owner of an uncertificated security, makes to the customer the warranties provided in the two preceding paragraphs, and also has the rights and privileges of a purchaser as set forth above.[91] The warranties of and in favor of the broker acting as an agent are in addition to applicable warranties given by and in favor of the customer.[92]

---

[88]IC 26-1-8.1-108(a).

[89]IC 26-1-8.1-108(b).

[90]IC 26-1-8.1-108(b).

[91]IC 26-1-8.1-108(i).

[92]IC 26-1-8.1-108(i).

A person who transfers an uncertificated security to a purchaser for value and does not instruct the corporation to register the transfer warrants that:[93]

(1) the uncertificated security is valid;

(2) there is no adverse claim to the security;

(3) the transfer does not violate any restriction on transfer; and

(4) the transfer is otherwise effective and rightful.

A person who endorses a security certificate warrants to the corporation that issued the shares represented by the certificate that there is no adverse claim to the security, and that the endorsement is effective.[94] Unless otherwise agreed, a person does not assume an obligation that the security will be honored by the issuer.[95]

A person who originates an instruction for registration of transfer of an uncertificated security warrants to the issuing corporation that the instruction is effective, and that at the time the instruction is presented to the corporation, the purchaser will be entitled to the registration of transfer.[96] Furthermore, a person who presents a certificated security for registration of transfer, or for payment or exchange, warrants to the corporation which issued it that the presenter is entitled to the registration, payment, or exchange. However, a purchaser for value and without notice of adverse claims to whom transfer is registered warrants only that he or she has no knowledge of any unauthorized signature in a necessary endorsement.[97]

Except as otherwise provided in the following paragraph, a broker acting for a customer makes to the corporation and a purchaser of shares the warranties provided in all of the preceding paragraphs in the section.[98]

If a person acts as agent of another in delivering a certificated security to a purchaser, the identity of the principal was known to the person to whom the certificate was delivered, and the certificate delivered by the agent was

---

[93]IC 26-1-8.1-108(c).

[94]IC 26-1-8.1-108(d).

[95]IC 26-1-8.1-304(f).

[96]IC 26-1-8.1-108(e).

[97]IC 26-1-8.1-108(f).

[98]IC 26-1-8.1-108(i).

received by the agent from the principal or from another person at the direction of the principal, the person delivering the security certificate warrants only that he or she has authority to act for the principal and does not know of any adverse claim to the certificated security.[99] The same warranties, and only those warranties, are made by a secured party who redelivers a security certificate received, or after payment and on order of the debtor delivers the security certificate to another person.[1]

§ 56   Transfer of securities on death of owner

Shares may be transferred to a designated beneficiary upon the owner's death.

West's Digest, Corporations ☞113, 114

Under the Uniform Act on Transfer on Death Securities, a security may be registered to designate a beneficiary to whom the security is to be transferred on the owner's death. The designation of the beneficiary may be canceled or changed by the owner at any time without the beneficiary's consent.[2] On the death of the sole owner of a security, or the last to die of all multiple owners, the ownership of registered securities for which a beneficiary is designated passes to the beneficiary or beneficiaries who survive all of the owners. If there are multiple beneficiaries, they hold the security as tenants in common after the death of the last owner until the security is divided. If no beneficiary survives the death of all owners, the security belongs to the estate of the deceased sole owner or the estate of the last to die of all multiple owners.[3]

Personal property in the possession and name of both a husband and wife is to become the sole property of the surviving spouse upon the death of the other, unless a contrary intention is clearly expressed in writing.[4] This provision did not prohibit a wife from entering into a stock

---

[99]IC 26-1-8.1-108(g).

[1]IC 26-1-8.1-108(h).

[2]IC 32-4-1.6-10.

[3]IC 32-4-1.6-11.

[4]IC 32-4-1.5-15.

purchase agreement by which she was obligated to sell her husband's interest in stock upon his death.[5]

§ 57   Rights of creditors and pledgees in shares

Shares of stock may be attached by a creditor, or pledged as security for a loan.

West's Digest, Corporations ☞123(1)-123(24), 136.

In general, a creditor may reach a debtor's interest in a certificated security only by actual seizure of the certificate. However, if the certificate has been surrendered to the corporation, the security may be reached by legal process upon the issuer,[6] and if the certificate is in the possession of, or an uncertificated security registered in the name of, a secured party, the security may be reached by legal process on the secured party.[7] Otherwise, a debtor's interest in an uncertificated security may be reached only by legal process upon the corporation that issued the security.[8]

It is well-settled that shares in the capital stock of a corporation can be pledged to secure the payment of an obligation.[9] Where there is an express contract by the owner of record of corporation stock creating a pledge to secure a debt, the other party to the contract becomes a pledgee with a lien upon the stock which may be converted into ownership by foreclosure. A pledge of stock does not divest the pledgor of his or her ownership; the general property in the stock remains in the pledgor subject to the pledgee's lien and until the stock is sold under foreclosure by the pledgee.[10]

A pledgee who has at least a potential right to sell the pledged shares to satisfy a debt is authorized to maintain an action against the officers of the corporation to prevent them from dissipating its assets, and to set aside a fraudulent transfer of the assets, particularly where the rights of in-

---

[5]Stech v. Panel Mart, Inc., 434 N.E.2d 97 (Ind. Ct. App. 3d Dist. 1982).

[6]IC 26-1-8.1-112(a).

[7]IC 26-1-8.1-112(d).

[8]IC 26-1-8.1-112(b).

[9]18 C.J.S., Corporations § 253.

[10]Fardy v. Mayerstein, 221 Ind. 339, 47 N.E.2d 315 (1943), reh'g denied, 221 Ind. 339, 47 N.E.2d 966 (1943).

nocent parties have not intervened.[11] However, a pledgee's property interest in pledged shares of stock does not give the pledgee the right to speak either for or instead of the pledgor, or for any other owner of stock, in a class action brought for the benefit of stockholders.[12]

The sale of pledged stock under a contract authorizing the pledgee to sell to him- or herself without notice and without restriction as to price may be voidable if the pledgee has not acted in good faith and has violated the terms of the pledge to the damage of the pledgor. However, if the pledgee has acted in good faith and caused no damage to the pledgor, the sale is not voidable.[13]

◆ **Practice Guide:** Pledges of shares of stock as security are subject to the rules applicable to secured transactions.[14]

V. DIVIDENDS AND ADDITIONAL SHARES

Research References

IC 23-1-20-7; IC 23-1-20-21; IC 23-1-26-4; IC 23-1-28-1 to IC 23-1-28-5; IC 23-17-21-1; IC 23-17-21-2

18B Am Jur 2d, Corporations §§ 1168-1340.
18 C.J.S., Corporations §§ 293-304.
West's Digest, Corporations ☞150-157.
ALR Digest: Corporation §§ 247-257.5
ALR Index: Articles of Incorporation; Assets; Bylaws; Charter; Close Corporation; Consolidation or Merger; Corporate Bonds and Bondholders; Corporate Officers, Directors, and Agents; Corporate Opportunity; Corporate Responsibility Doctrine; Corporate Stock and Stockholders; Corporations; Dissolution or Liquidation; Dividends; Domicile and Residence; Foreign Corporations; Forfeitures; Liquidation or Dissolution; Minority Stockholders; Names; Nonprofit Institutions or Organizations;

---

[11]General Ice & Coal Co. v. George, 214 Ind. 518, 14 N.E.2d 1002 (1938).

[12]Fardy v. Mayerstein, 221 Ind. 339, 47 N.E.2d 315 (1943), reh'g denied, 221 Ind. 339, 47 N.E.2d 966 (1943).

[13]National Mill Supply Co. v. State ex rel. Morton, 211 Ind. 243, 6 N.E.2d 543, 109 A.L.R. 1101 (1937).

[14]IC 26-1-9-101 et seq.

As to perfection of security interest in investment property see, IC 26-1-9-115(4).

As to secured transactions generally, see I.L.E., Secured Transactions.

Professional Corporations and Associations; Promoters; Prospectus; Proxies; Reports; Seal; Stock-Option Plans; Subsidiary
6B Am Jur Legal Forms 2d, Corporations §§ 74:2455, 74:2456, 74:2465.
7B Am Jur Pleading and Practice Forms, Corporations § 316.
Wrongful Failure of Corporate Directors to Declare Dividend, 22 Am Jur POF2d 593.

§ 58 Generally

A corporation may issue a distribution in money or other property, or a dividend in shares, at the discretion of the directors.

West's Digest, Corporations ☞152, 155(1), 155(2).

A distribution is a corporation's direct or indirect transfer of money or other property, except the corporation's own shares, or its incurrence or transfer of indebtedness to or for the benefit of its shareholders. A distribution may be in the form of a declaration of payment of a dividend; a purchase, redemption, or other acquisition of shares; a distribution of indebtedness; or otherwise.[15] A board of directors may authorize, and the corporation may make, distributions to its shareholders subject to restrictions imposed by the articles of incorporation and the Business Corporation Law.[16]

The right to receive dividends, or distributions, is an incident of stock ownership which applies equally to stock and cash dividends. Whoever owns the stock in a corporation at the time a dividend is declared also owns the dividend.[17]

Dividends are generally to be paid from unreserved and unrestricted earned surplus.[18] They may be paid only out of

---

[15]IC 23-1-20-7.

For discussion of share dividends, see § 61.

Forms References: Resolution of directors—Dividend declaration. 6B Am Jur Legal Forms 2d, Corporations §§ 74:2455, 74:2456.

[16]IC 23-1-28-1.

For discussion of statutory limitations on distributions, see § 60.

[17]Anacomp, Inc. v. Wright, 449 N.E.2d 610 (Ind. Ct. App. 1st Dist. 1983) (even though corporation was entitled to return of stock after employment negotiations fell through, prospective employee was entitled to retain dividends paid on shares he owned during negotiations).

[18]Cole Real Estate Corp. v. Peoples Bank & Trust Co., 160 Ind. App. 88, 310 N.E.2d 275 (3d Dist. 1974).

profits earned by the corporation,[19] and a corporation may not pay dividends out of capital except in the process of dissolution.[20] The profits out of which dividends may be paid are what remains after defraying the corporation's expenses of operation, including loans falling due and interest on the loans.[21]

Corporate earnings and profits remain the property of the corporation until they are severed from the corporation's assets and distributed as dividends. It is the declaration of a dividend which creates both the dividend itself and the right of the stockholder to demand and receive it.[22] In other words, a dividend is not a debt to the stockholders until it is legally declared.[23]

> ◆ **Practice Guide:** Generally, a not-for-profit corporation may not make distributions.[24] However, a mutual benefit corporation may purchase the corporation's memberships if, after the purchase is completed, the corporation will be able to pay its debts as they come due, and the corporation's total assets will at least equal the sum of its total liabilities.[25] Not-for-profit corporations may also make certain distributions upon dissolution,[26] and may make distributions to members or governmental entities in conformity with the corporation's purposes, if after any distribution is completed the corporation would be able to pay the corporation's debts as the debts become due, and the corporation's total assets would at least equal the corporation's total liabilities.[27]

§ 59 Record date

The board may set the date to determine the identity of

---

[19]Cring v. Sheller Wood Rim Mfg. Co., 98 Ind. App. 310, 183 N.E. 674 (1932).

[20]Krull v. Pierce, 117 Ind. App. 638, 71 N.E.2d 617 (1947).

For discussion of the dissolution of a corporation, see §§ 194 et seq.

[21]Fricke v. Angemeier, 53 Ind. App. 140, 101 N.E. 329 (Div. 1 1913).

[22]Rubens v. Marion-Washington Realty Corp., 116 Ind. App. 55, 59 N.E.2d 907 (1945).

[23]Fricke v. Angemeier, 53 Ind. App. 140, 101 N.E. 329 (Div. 1 1913).

[24]IC 23-17-21-1.

[25]IC 23-17-21-2(a).

[26]IC 23-17-21-2(b).

For discussion of the dissolution of a corporation, see §§ 194 et seq.

[27]IC 23-17-21-2(c).

the corporation's shareholders for purposes of making a distribution.

West's Digest, Corporations ☞152.

The board of directors may fix a record date, declaration date, and payment date with respect to any share dividend or distribution to a corporation's shareholders.[28] The record date is the date as of which the identity of the corporation's shareholders is to be determined.[29] If the board does not fix the record date to determine shareholders entitled to a distribution, other than a distribution involving the repurchase or reacquisition of shares, the date is that on which the board authorizes the distribution.[30]

§ 60 Prohibited distributions

A corporation may not make a distribution if doing so will leave it unable to pay its debts or to satisfy the rights of preferred stockholders upon dissolution.

West's Digest, Corporations ☞153.

A corporation may not make a distribution if, after giving it effect, the corporation would not be able to pay its debts as they become due in the usual course of business.[31] A distribution is also prohibited if, after it is given effect, the corporation's total assets would be less than the sum of its total liabilities plus, unless the articles of incorporation permit otherwise, the amount that would be needed to satisfy the preferential rights upon dissolution of shareholders whose preferential rights are superior to those receiving the distribution, if the corporation were to be dissolved at the time of the distribution.[32] Thus, corporate property must be appropriated to the corporation's debts before any distribution of it is made to its shareholders.[33]

The board of directors may base a determination that a distribution is not prohibited either on financial statements

---

[28]IC 23-1-28-2.

[29]IC 23-1-20-21.

[30]IC 23-1-28-2; IC 23-1-26-4(c).

[31]IC 23-1-28-3(1).

[32]IC 23-1-28-3(2).

For discussion of the dissolution of a corporation, see §§ 194 et seq.

[33]Ross v. Tavel, 418 N.E.2d 297 (Ind. Ct. App. 1st Dist. 1981).

prepared on the basis of accounting practices and principles that are reasonable in the circumstances, or on a fair valuation or other method that is reasonable in the circumstances.[34]

The date on which the effect of a distribution is to be measured to determine whether the distribution is prohibited is calculated according to the type of distribution to be made. If the distribution is made by the corporation's purchase, redemption, or other acquisition of its shares, the date is that on which money or other property is transferred, or debt incurred, by the corporation, or the date the shareholder to whom the distribution is to be made ceases to be a shareholder with respect to the acquired shares, whichever is earlier.[35] If the distribution is of any other indebtedness, the date is that on which the indebtedness is distributed.[36] In all other cases, the date is the date on which the distribution is authorized, if the payment occurs within 120 days after the date of authorization, or the date payment is made, if it is made more than 120 days after the date of authorization.[37]

§ 61   Share dividends

Share dividends are distributions of shares added through assets turned into capital.

West's Digest, Corporations ☞157.

Unless the articles of incorporation provide otherwise, a corporation may issue shares pro rata and without consideration to its shareholders, or to the shareholders of one or more classes or series.[38] Such an issuance of shares may be in the form of a share dividend or a share split, but will be considered a share dividend for purposes of the Business Corporation Law.[39]

Share dividends are similar to share splits in that both

---

[34]IC 23-1-28-4.

[35]IC 23-1-28-5(1).

[36]IC 23-1-28-5(2).

[37]IC 23-1-28-5(3).

[38]IC 23-1-26-4(a).

For discussion of classes and series of shares, see § 37.

Forms References: Resolution of directors—stock dividend. 6B Am Jur Legal Forms 2d, Corporations § 74:2465.

[39]IC 23-1-26-4(a).

result in an increased number of shares owned by each shareholder affected. Stock dividends, however, involve the distribution of shares added through assets transformed into capital, whereas stock splits involve a mere increase in the number of shares without altering the amount of capital, surplus, or segregated earnings. A stock split, therefore, is essentially a matter of form and not of substance, as it does not change the stockholder's proportionate ownership or participating interest in the corporation.[40] For instance, if an amendment to a corporation's articles of incorporation authorizes a 20-for-1 stock split, a shareholder who owned 1,500 shares before the split will own 30,000 afterwards, but his or her proportionate interest in the corporation will not be affected.[41] While the corporation's denomination of an issue of stock to shareholders as a stock dividend or a stock split may be useful and definitive for certain purposes, courts will, where necessary, look beyond that denomination to determine whether the additional shares were issued as a result of a transfer of accumulated earnings into capital or as a mere increase in the number of shares of stock.[42]

Shares of one class or series may not be issued as a share dividend in respect of shares of another class or series unless:[43]

   (1) the articles of incorporation so authorize;

   (2) a majority of the votes entitled to be cast by the class or series to be issued approve the issue; or

   (3) there are no outstanding shares of the class or series to be issued.

§ 62 Rights of preferred stockholders generally

Preferred stock's preference as to dividends is a matter of contract between the preferred stockholder and the corporation.

West's Digest, Corporations ⟜156.

---

[40]Anacomp, Inc. v. Wright, 449 N.E.2d 610 (Ind. Ct. App. 1st Dist. 1983).

[41]Kiess v. Eason, 442 F.2d 712 (7th Cir. 1971) (applying Indiana law).

[42]Anacomp, Inc. v. Wright, 449 N.E.2d 610 (Ind. Ct. App. 1st Dist. 1983) (where corporation, upon declaration of dividend, transferred surplus into its common stock account and issued it to shareholders so that they maintained same proportion of stock equity in corporate assets, transfer of additional shares to shareholders was stock dividend, not stock split).

[43]IC 23-1-26-4(b).

The preference which preferred stock enjoys over common stock as to dividends is entirely a matter of contract, and the contract is generally set forth in the articles of incorporation, bylaws, or stock certificates.[44] The sale and delivery by a corporation to a stockholder of a certificate for preferred stock, which certificate sets forth a formula for the payment of dividends, creates a contract between the corporation and the stockholder under which the corporation covenants to declare and pay dividends according to the formula.[45]

A preferred stockholder is not entitled to a lien on the assets of the corporation to secure the payment of the face value of his or her preferred stock plus unpaid dividends.[46]

§ 63 Directors' discretion to declare dividends

The declaration of a dividend is in the directors' sound discretion.

West's Digest, Corporations ☞155(2), 155(5).

Subject to statutory restrictions, the power to declare dividends is within the discretion of the board of directors.[47] As a general rule, the directors are the sole judges as to the propriety of declaring dividends and the courts will not interfere with the proper exercise of that discretion; however, directors are not allowed to use their power illegally, wantonly, or oppressively.[48] A corporation's directors may, in their discretion, choose to retain its surplus earnings rather than making a distribution, to insure financial stability and for internal policies and programs, as long as they do not do so in bad faith. A corporation may not, in bad faith or

---

[44]Shaffer v. McCulloch, 192 F. 801 (C.C.A. 7th Cir. 1911) (applying Indiana law).

[45]Rubens v. Marion-Washington Realty Corp., 116 Ind. App. 55, 59 N.E.2d 907 (1945).

[46]Cring v. Sheller Wood Rim Mfg. Co., 98 Ind. App. 310, 183 N.E. 674 (1932).

[47]Cole Real Estate Corp. v. Peoples Bank & Trust Co., 160 Ind. App. 88, 310 N.E.2d 275 (3d Dist. 1974).

For discussion of statutorily prohibited distributions, see § 60.

[48]W.Q. O'Neall Co. v. O'Neall, 108 Ind. App. 116, 25 N.E.2d 656 (1940).

through oppressive action, refrain from declaring a dividend clearly warranted by its profit position.[49]

§ 64 Right to compel declaration of dividend, or to collect declared dividend

A shareholder may bring an action to compel the declaration of a dividend, where the directors have acted in bad faith in failing to declare one, or to collect a declared dividend which has not been paid.

West's Digest, Corporations ⊕155(2), 155(4), 155(5).

A shareholder may bring an action in equity against the corporation to recover his or her share of the accumulated profits if the directors have acted in bad faith in failing to declare a dividend.[50]

◆ **Practice Guide:** The directors are not necessarily indispensable parties in such a suit,[51] and a shareholder need not make a demand for corporate action before bringing such a suit.[52]

Preferred stockholders may also maintain an action to compel the directors of a corporation to declare and pay a dividend on preferred stock, and a court may order dividends paid out of earnings when the board of directors has acted in bad faith in failing and refusing to declare such dividends. A court may not, however, order the corporation to declare and pay dividends in the future so long as it possesses surplus or earnings from which to pay such dividends, since the matter

---

[49]Cole Real Estate Corp. v. Peoples Bank & Trust Co., 160 Ind. App. 88, 310 N.E.2d 275 (3d Dist. 1974).

Forms References: Complaint, petition, or declaration by minority shareholder to require declaration and payment of dividend. 7B Am Jur Pleading and Practice Forms, Annotated (rev. ed.), Corporations § 316.

Trial Strategy References: Wrongful Failure of Corporate Directors to Declare Dividend, 22 Am Jur POF2d 593.

[50]Rubens v. Marion-Washington Realty Corp., 116 Ind. App. 55, 59 N.E.2d 907 (1945).

Trial Strategy References: Wrongful Failure of Corporate Directors to Declare Dividend, 22 Am Jur POF2d 593.

[51]W.Q. O'Neall Co. v. O'Neall, 108 Ind. App. 116, 25 N.E.2d 656 (1940).

[52]Cole Real Estate Corp. v. Peoples Bank & Trust Co., 160 Ind. App. 88, 310 N.E.2d 275 (3d Dist. 1974).

of declaring dividends rests in the sound discretion of the directors.[53]

When a dividend has been properly declared, and has become payable, a stockholder to whom the corporation, on demand, has refused to pay his or her share may maintain an action at law against the corporation for the amount due.[54]

VI. SHAREHOLDERS AND MEMBERS

A. IN GENERAL

Research References

IC 23-1-20-24; IC 23-1-20-30; IC 23-1-22-5; IC 23-1-26-3; IC 23-1-30-1; IC 23-1-30-4; IC 23-1-32-1 to IC 23-1-32-5; IC 23-1-52-2 to IC 23-1-52-5; IC 23-1-53-2; IC 23-1.5-2-6; IC 23-17-2-8; IC 23-17-2-17; IC 23-17-2-18; IC 23-17-7-1 to IC 23-17-7-9; IC 23-17-8-1 to IC 23-17-8-3; IC 23-17-9-1; IC 23-17-9-2; IC 23-17-11-1; IC 23-17-11-2; IC 23-17-17-2; IC 23-17-27-2 to IC 23-17-27-5; IC 23-17-27-7; IC 34-1-32-1; IC 34-52-1-1

15 U.S.C.A § 78a

Trial R. 23.1

18A Am Jur 2d, Corporations §§ 728-947.

18 C.J.S., Corporations §§ 305-361, 397-432.

West's Digest, Corporations ⊖170-280.

ALR Digest: Corporations §§ 224-302

ALR Index: Articles of Incorporation; Assets; Bylaws; Charter; Close Corporation; Consolidation or Merger; Corporate Bonds and Bondholders; Corporate Officers, Directors, and Agents; Corporate Opportunity; Corporate Responsibility Doctrine; Corporate Stock and Stockholders; Corporations; Dissolution or Liquidation; Dividends; Domicile and Residence; Foreign Corporations; Forfeitures; Liquidation or Dissolution; Minority Stockholders; Names; Nonprofit Institutions or Organizations; Professional Corporations and Associations; Promoters; Prospectus; Proxies; Reports; Seal; Stock-Option Plans; Subsidiary

7A Am Jur Pleading and Practice Forms, Annotated (rev. ed.), Corporations §§ 45, 48, 51, 52, 158, 159, 161-164, 190, 214, 215.

Proper Purpose for Shareholder's Inspection of Corporate Books and Records, 24 Am Jur POF2d 71; Liability of Parent Corporation for Acts of Subsidiary, 20 Am Jur POF2d 679.

---

[53]W.Q. O'Neall Co. v. O'Neall, 108 Ind. App. 116, 25 N.E.2d 656 (1940).

[54]Rubens v. Marion-Washington Realty Corp., 116 Ind. App. 55, 59 N.E.2d 907 (1945); Fricke v. Angemeier, 53 Ind. App. 140, 101 N.E. 329 (Div. 1 1913).

§ 65 Shareholders generally

A shareholder, as the owner of shares of the corporation's stock, owns an interest in the corporation.

West's Digest, Corporations ☞170, 174.

A shareholder of a business corporation is a person in whose name shares of the corporation's stock are registered in the corporation's records, or the beneficial owner of shares to the extent of the rights he or she holds in the shares.[55] If shares are registered in substantially similar names, the persons in whose names they are registered will constitute one shareholder if it is reasonable to believe that the names represent the same person.[56]

Three or fewer co-owners of shares constitute one shareholder. If there are four or more co-owners of shares, each co-owner counts as a separate shareholder.[57] An entity, such as a corporation, limited liability company, partnership, trust, or estate may be a shareholder,[58] as may the fiduciaries of a trust, estate, or account.[59]

A shareholder owns an interest in the corporation.[60] By contrast, a creditor of a corporation generally does not own an interest in the corporation arising from the indebtedness, although he or she may also be a stockholder of the corporation.[61] Thus, a stockholder is not a creditor, and a person cannot be both a creditor and a stockholder by virtue of the same instrument in respect to the same fund.[62]

The relation between a corporation and its stockholders is one of contract, and the rights, interests, and obligations of a corporation's shareholders arise out of a contract embodied in the articles of incorporation, bylaws, provisions of the stock certificate, and pertinent statutes.[63]

A person claiming to be a stockholder has the burden of

---

[55]IC 23-1-20-24.

[56]IC 23-1-20-30(b).

[57]IC 23-1-20-30(a)(1).

[58]IC 23-1-20-30(a)(2).

[59]IC 23-1-20-30(a)(3).

[60]Grover v. Cavanaugh, 40 Ind. App. 340, 82 N.E. 104 (Div. 1 1907).

[61]Major v. Major, 106 Ind. App. 90, 15 N.E.2d 754 (1938).

[62]Federal Deposit Ins. Corp. v. Department of Financial Institutions, 113 Ind. App. 14, 44 N.E.2d 992 (1942).

[63]Scott v. Anderson Newspapers, Inc., 477 N.E.2d 553 (Ind. Ct. App.

proving it.[64] The name shown on a stock certificate is evidence of ownership, but is not conclusive as to who holds legal title to the shares.[65]

Shares may be held in the name of a nominee. A corporation may adopt procedures for recognizing as a shareholder the beneficial owner of shares registered in the name of a nominee,[66] and requiring the disclosure of the names of beneficial owners. It may also adopt reasonable sanctions to ensure compliance with the disclosure procedure, including prohibiting the voting of shares whose beneficial owner is not properly disclosed, providing for the reacquisition of such shares, or withholding or paying into escrow dividends owed in respect to such shares.[67]

§ 66 Members of not-for-profit corporations

Members of a not-for-profit corporation have no ownership rights in the corporation.

West's Digest, Corporations ☞170, 174.

Not-for-profit corporations have members rather than shareholders. Members of a not-for-profit corporation do not receive ownership rights in the corporation's assets, but the right to enjoy the benefits of membership as long as they comply with membership rules and regulations.[68]

A member of a not-for-profit corporation is a person who, on more than one occasion, has the right to vote for the election of a director under the corporation's articles of incorpo-

---

4th Dist. 1985), reh'g denied, (June 19, 1985) and transfer denied, (Nov. 4, 1985).

[64]Denker v. Lloyd, 118 Ind. App. 509, 79 N.E.2d 658 (1948) (burden was on administrator claiming that his decedent was preferred stockholder to prove legal existence of such stock and ownership by decedent, or facts creating estoppel in corporation to deny such existence and ownership).

[65]Matter of Carl F. Bettner Trust, 495 N.E.2d 194, 77 A.L.R.4th 1187 (Ind. Ct. App. 1st Dist. 1986).

For discussion of stock certificates, see § 44.

[66]IC 23-1-30-4(a).

[67]IC 23-1-30-4(b).

For discussion of voting of shares, see § 87.

For discussion of dividends, see §§ 58 et seq.

[68]Orchard Ridge Country Club, Inc. v. Schrey, 470 N.E.2d 780 (Ind. Ct. App. 3d Dist. 1984).

ration or bylaws.[69] A corporation is not required to have
members.[70] A person's rights as a delegate or a director, or
the right to designate a director, do not make him or her a
member.[71]

A not-for-profit corporation may, through its articles of
incorporation or bylaws, establish criteria or procedures for
the admission of members.[72] A person may not be admitted
as a member without his or her consent.[73] Unless the articles
of incorporation or bylaws provide otherwise, members may
be admitted for no consideration or for consideration
determined by the board of directors.[74]

Unless the articles of incorporation or bylaws establish
classes of membership with different rights or obligations,
members are to have the same rights and obligations with
respect to voting, dissolution, redemption, transfer, and any
other matters.[75]

A member may transfer his or her membership, or any
right arising from his or her membership, only as provided
in the articles of incorporation or bylaws.[76] Any restriction
on transfer rights adopted after a membership is issued is
binding on the member holding that membership only if the
restriction is approved by the members and by the affected
member.[77]

§ 67 —Termination of membership

**Members of not-for-profit corporations may resign, and
their memberships may be terminated or suspended.**

West's Digest, Corporations ☞172, 173.

A member of a not-for-profit corporation may resign at any
time,[78] but resignation does not relieve him or her of any
obligations he or she may have incurred, or commitments he

---

[69]IC 23-17-2-17(a).
[70]IC 23-17-7-3.
[71]IC 23-17-2-17(b).
[72]IC 23-17-7-1(a).
[73]IC 23-17-7-1(b).
[74]IC 23-17-7-2.
[75]IC 23-17-7-4.
[76]IC 23-17-7-5(a).
[77]IC 23-17-7-5(b).
[78]IC 23-17-8-1(a).

or she may have made, before resigning.[79] Thus, specific performance of a nonprofit corporation's member's obligation may be ordered, if otherwise proper, even after the member has resigned.[80]

Unless the corporation terminates all of its members,[81] a member of a public benefit or mutual benefit corporation may not be expelled or suspended.[82]

Memberships in a public benefit or mutual benefit corporation, or the rights and benefits to which members are entitled,[83] may be terminated or suspended only if the procedure for doing so is fair and reasonable and carried out in good faith.[84] A procedure is fair and reasonable if the procedure set forth in the articles of incorporation or the bylaws requires at least 15 days written notice, which notice includes the reasons for the proposed action, and an opportunity for the member against whom the action is proposed to be taken to be heard, orally or in writing, at least five days before the effective date of the proposed action, by a person authorized to decide that the proposed action should not be taken,[85] and if the procedure is fair and reasonable under all of the relevant facts and circumstances.[86]

A member may challenge his or her expulsion or suspension, or the suspension or termination of his or her membership, through a proceeding commenced within one year after the challenged action.[87]

A member who has been expelled or suspended, or whose membership has been terminated, may be liable to the corporation for dues, assessments, or fees as a result of obligations incurred or commitments made before the

---

[79]IC 23-17-8-1(b).

[80]Jay County Rural Elec. Membership Corp. v. Wabash Valley Power Ass'n, Inc., 692 N.E.2d 905 (Ind. Ct. App. 1998), transfer denied, 706 N.E.2d 167 (Ind. 1998).

[81]IC 23-17-17-2(e).

[82]IC 23-17-8-2.

[83]IC 23-17-2-18.

[84]IC 23-17-8-2(a).

[85]IC 23-17-8-2(b)(1).

[86]IC 23-17-8-2(b)(2).

[87]IC 23-17-8-2(d).

expulsion, suspension, or termination.[88] Nonpayment of dues, assessments, or fees constitutes grounds for expelling or suspending a member or terminating or suspending his or her membership.[89] If a membership is properly transferred and the transferee has notice at the time of the transfer of the transferor's unpaid dues, assessments, or fees, the transferee is liable for the unpaid consideration, except that a transferee who is an executor, administrators, guardian, trustee, receiver, or pledgee is not personally liable, and an heir or legatee to whom a membership is properly transferred does not incur liability for any unpaid consideration is he or she surrenders the membership to the corporation.[90]

A mutual benefit corporation may purchase the membership of a member who resigns, or whose membership is terminated, for the amount and under the conditions provided in the corporation's articles of incorporation or bylaws.[91] A public benefit or religious corporation may not purchase any of its memberships, or any right arising from a membership.[92]

A public benefit or mutual benefit corporation may, by an amendment to its articles of incorporation or bylaws, terminate all of its members, or a class of its members, or redeem or cancel all memberships or a class of memberships.[93] Before it may adopt a resolution proposing such an amendment, the board of directors of a mutual benefit corporation must give notice of the general nature of the amendment to the members.[94] After the board has adopted a resolution proposing the amendment, the notice to members proposing the amendment must include a statement of 500 words or less opposing the amendment, if such a statement is submitted by five members or members with at least 3% of the corporation's voting power, whichever is less, within

---

[88]IC 23-17-8-2(e).

[89]IC 23-17-7-7(a).

[90]IC 23-17-7-7(b).

[91]IC 23-17-8-3(b).

[92]IC 23-17-8-3(a).

[93]IC 23-17-17-2(a).

For discussion of amendments to a corporation's articles of incorporation, see § 13.

For discussion of amendments to bylaws, see § 27.

[94]IC 23-17-17-2(b).

20 days after the board has voted to submit the amendment to the members for approval.[95] The amendment must be approved by the members by a majority of the votes cast by each class.[96]

§ 68 —Delegates

Delegates may be elected or appointed to have some or all of the authority of members of a not-for-profit corporation.

West's Digest, Corporations ⇐174.

If the articles of incorporation so provide, delegates may be elected or appointed to have some or all of the authority of members.[97] The articles or incorporation may provide for:[98]

- the characteristics, qualifications, rights, limitations, and obligations of delegates, including selection and removal
- calling, noticing, holding, and conducting meetings of delegates
- carrying on corporate activities during and between meetings of delegates

§ 69 Management of corporate affairs

Stockholders cannot act for the corporation, and have no authority over its operations except through their votes.

West's Digest, Corporations ⇐180.

A corporation's stockholders cannot act for the corporation either individually or collectively.[99] The business of every corporation must be managed by a board of directors.[1]

---

[95]IC 23-17-17-2(c).

[96]IC 23-17-17-2(d).

[97]IC 23-17-2-8; IC 23-17-9-1.

[98]IC 23-17-9-2.

[99]Clearwater v. Meredith, 68 U.S. 25, 17 L. Ed. 604 (1863).

[1]§§ 96 et seq., § 108.

◆ **Caution:** A corporation is estopped to deny a settlement made by its only shareholders as not being the action of the corporation itself.[2]

Whatever rights the stockholders may have to control the affairs or management of the corporation or to dictate its policies may be exercised by the holders of a majority of the shares of stock having voting power.[3] Thus, a stockholder has no legal control over the operations of the corporation other than his or her vote, and one who buys stock in a corporation takes subject to the right of the majority to elect officers and control the company and its property.[4]

§ 70 Right to information

Shareholders have a right to inspect various records created by the corporation.

West's Digest, Corporations ⚬=181(1)-181(8).

A shareholder or member has the right to inspect and copy, during regular business hours at the corporation's principal office, or, if reasonable, may receive copies of[5] any of the permanent records the corporation is required to keep. The shareholder or member must give the corporation written notice of his or her demand at least five business days before the date on which he or she wishes to inspect and copy the records.[6]

A shareholder or member may inspect and copy certain other records during regular business hours and at a reasonable location specified by the corporation, upon five days written notice, or, if reasonable, may receive copies,[7] if the shareholder or member's demand is made in good faith and

---

[2]Epperly v. E. & P. Brake Bonding, Inc., 169 Ind. App. 224, 348 N.E.2d 75 (2d Dist. 1976).

[3]Lafayette Realty Corp. v. Moller, 247 Ind. 433, 215 N.E.2d 859 (1966); Benner-Coryell Lumber Co. v. Indiana Unemployment Compensation Bd., 218 Ind. 20, 29 N.E.2d 776 (1940); Enterprise Printing & Publishing Co. v. Craig, 195 Ind. 302, 144 N.E. 542 (1924), reh'g denied, 195 Ind. 302, 145 N.E. 309 (1924).

[4]Indianapolis Dairymen's Co-op. v. Bottema, 226 Ind. 237, 79 N.E.2d 399 (1948).

[5]IC 23-1-52-3(b); IC 23-17-27-2.

[6]IC 23-1-52-2(a); IC 23-17-27-2.

For discussion of required records, see § 28.

[7]IC 23-1-52-3(b); IC 23-17-27-2.

for a proper purpose, the shareholder or member describes with reasonable particularity his or her purpose and the records he or she desires to inspect, and the records are directly connected with the shareholder or member's purpose.[8] A shareholder or member may not obtain corporate information if his or her purpose is adverse to the bests interests of the corporation.[9] The corporation may comply with a shareholder or member's demand to inspect the record of shareholders or members by providing the shareholder or member with a list of its shareholders or members that was compiled no earlier than the date of the shareholder or member's demand.[10]

Information acquired from corporate records inspected or copied under the provisions discussed above is to be used or distributed solely for proper purposes, and the shareholder, his or her agent or attorney, and any other person who obtains the information is required to use reasonable care to see that the information is not used otherwise.[11] A not-for-profit corporation's membership list may not be obtained or used for a purpose unrelated to the member's interest as a member without the consent of the board of directors. Such consent is required before a member may use all or part of the list to solicit money or property, unless the money or property will be used solely to solicit members' votes; use all or part of the list for a commercial purpose; or sell all or part of the list.[12]

The rights of inspection pertaining to shareholders of business corporations may not be abolished or limited by a

---

[8]IC 23-1-52-2(b), (c); IC 23-17-27-2(b), (c).

As to the particular records a shareholder or member may inspect and copy under these conditions, see IC 23-1-52-3(b)(1)-(3); IC 23-17-27-2(b)(1)-(3).

Forms References: Petition or application for order enforcing stockholder's right of inspection. 7A Am Jur Pleading and Practice Forms, Annotated (rev. ed.), Corporations §§ 214, 215.

Trial Strategy References: Proper Purpose for Shareholder's Inspection of Corporate Books and Records, 24 Am Jur POF2d 71.

[9]Dynamics Corp. of America v. CTS Corp., 479 N.E.2d 1352 (Ind. Ct. App. 3d Dist. 1985).

[10]IC 23-1-52-3(d); IC 23-17-27-3(d).

[11]IC 23-1-52-5.

[12]IC 23-17-27-5.

corporation's articles of incorporation or bylaws.[13] The articles of incorporation or bylaws of a religious corporation, however, may limit or abolish the right of a member to inspect and copy a corporate record.[14] The articles of incorporation of a not-for-profit corporation may limit or abolish a member's right to obtain from the corporation information as to the identity of corporation's contributors, or the right of a member or his or her agent or attorney to inspect or copy the membership list of a not-for-profit corporation if the corporation provides a reasonable means to mail communications to other members through the corporation at the expense of the member making the request.[15]

The rights of a shareholder or member to inspect the list of shareholders or members prepared in anticipation of a shareholders' or members' meeting, the rights of a shareholder or member who is in litigation with the corporation to inspect the corporation's records, and the power of a court to compel the production of corporation records for examination, are not governed by the provisions discussed above.[16] Moreover, a former shareholder has no statutory right to view the corporation's records after his or her name has been removed from the list of shareholders.[17]

The corporation may impose a reasonable charge for copies provided to the shareholder or member, not to exceed the estimated cost of production or reproduction of the records.[18] Furthermore, if a corporation improperly refuses to allow a shareholder or member to inspect and copy records, the shareholder or member may apply to the proper court for an

---

[13]IC 23-1-52-5(d).

[14]IC 23-17-27-2(e).

[15]IC 23-17-27-2(f).

[16]IC 23-1-52-2(e); IC 23-17-27-2(d).

For discussion of the right to inspect voting lists, see § 71.

[17]Biberstine v. New York Blower Co., 625 N.E.2d 1308 (Ind. Ct. App. 5th Dist. 1993), reh'g denied, (Jan. 24, 1994) and transfer dismissed, (Apr. 12, 1994) (former shareholder who claimed he had been wrongfully denied right to view shareholder list while he still owned shares forfeited any remedy that may have been available to him for that denial by failing to timely pursue remedy); Anacomp, Inc. v. Wright, 449 N.E.2d 610 (Ind. Ct. App. 1st Dist. 1983).

[18]IC 23-1-52-3(c); IC 23-17-27-3(c).

order permitting the inspection and copying of the records.[19] If the court grants the order, it must also order the corporation to pay the shareholder or member's costs, including reasonable attorneys' fees, unless the corporation proves that it refused inspection in good faith because it had a reasonable basis for doubt about the right of the shareholder or member to inspect the records demanded.[20] The court must order that the use of the records be for permitted purposes, in the case of a business corporation,[21] and may impose reasonable restrictions on the use of the records, in the case of a not-for-profit corporation.[22]

A corporation must report in writing to the shareholders or members any indemnification or advance of expenses made to a director in connection with a proceeding by or in the right of the corporation,[23] and the number of shares authorized to be issued for promissory notes of promises to render services in the future, unless a corporation subject to the federal Securities Exchange Act has complied with that statute's proxy disclosure provisions.[24]

§ 71   —Voting list

With certain limitations, shareholders have a right to inspect the corporation's list of shareholders prepared in anticipation of a shareholders' meeting.

West's Digest, Corporations ⚖181(1)-181(8).

The list of shareholders or members prepared by a corporation in anticipation of a shareholders' or members' meeting must be available for inspection by any shareholder entitled to vote at the meeting, or by any member for the purpose of communicating with other members, beginning five days before the meeting and continuing through the meeting. The list is to be available at the corporation's principal office or

[19]IC 23-1-52-4(a), (b); IC 23-17-27-4(a), (b).

[20]IC 23-1-52-4(c); IC 23-17-27-4(c).

[21]IC 23-1-52-4(d).

[22]IC 23-17-27-4(d).

[23]IC 23-1-53-2; IC 23-17-27-7.

For discussion of indemnification of directors for litigation involving the corporation, see § 121.

[24]IC 23-1-53-2.

As to the federal Securities Exchange Act, see 15 U.S.C.A §§ 78a et seq.

at a place identified in the notice of the meeting in the city where the meeting will be held. A shareholder or member, or his or her attorney or other agent authorized in writing, may, on written demand, inspect and copy the list during regular business hours and at the shareholder or member's expense.[25] The corporation must also make the list available at the meeting, and any shareholder or member, or his or her agent or attorney authorized in writing, may inspect the list at any time during the meeting or during any adjournment of the meeting.[26] If the corporation improperly refuses to allow a shareholder or member, or his or her agent, to inspect the list, the circuit or superior court of the county where the corporation's principal office or, if it has no principal office in Indiana, its registered office, is located, may order the inspection or copying on the shareholder or member's application.[27] A corporation's refusal or failure to make available the list of members does not affect the validity of an action taken at the meeting.[28]

A religious corporation's articles of incorporation or bylaws may limit or abolish a member's rights to inspect and copy the list,[29] and a public benefit corporation's articles of incorporation may do so if the corporation provides a reasonable means to mail communications concerning the corporation to other members through the corporation at the expense of the member making the request.[30]

A not-for-profit corporation may refuse to provide names or identifying information relating to contributors.[31]

§ 72 Dealings between stockholders in same corporation

Stockholders of the same corporation may deal and contract with each other; stockholders in closely held corporations owe each other a fiduciary duty.

West's Digest, Corporations ☞187.

Generally, the stockholders of a corporation may lawfully

---

[25]IC 23-1-30-1(b); IC 23-17-11-1(b).

[26]IC 23-1-30-1(c); IC 23-17-11-1(c).

[27]IC 23-1-30-1(d); IC 23-17-11-1(d).

[28]IC 23-1-30-1(d); IC 23-17-11-1(e).

[29]IC 23-17-11-1(g).

[30]IC 23-17-11-1(g).

[31]IC 23-17-11-2.

deal and contract with one another in matters affecting the corporation or its shares.[32]

Shareholders in a close corporation stand in a fiduciary relationship to each other, and must deal fairly, honestly, and openly with the corporation and with their fellow shareholders,[33] independent of their status as officers or directors.[34] A shareholder in a close corporation cannot compete for business or clients which in equity and fairness belong to the corporation,[35] must act for the benefit of the corporation,[36] and may not allow him- or herself to be distracted from the performance of his or her official duties by personal interest.[37]

◆ **Illustration:** A stockholder in a closed corporation delayed selling his stock to the corporation's other stockholder because he knew that the corporation's book value, on which the stock price would be based, would increase enormously within the next year. The selling stockholder breached his fiduciary duty to the purchasing stockholder by not telling him of his plan or explaining how his accountant came up with the proposed selling price range, where the seller's demand was at the high end of the range.[38]

Although shareholders in a close corporation who have agreed to maintain equal ownership of the stock have the duty to disclose to each other the availability of the corporation's stock for sale and to afford each other the opportunity

---

[32]18 C.J.S., Corporations § 322.

[33]Melrose v. Capitol City Motor Lodge, Inc., 705 N.E.2d 985 (Ind. 1998); Barth v. Barth, 659 N.E.2d 559 (Ind. 1995), appeal after remand, 693 N.E.2d 954 (Ind. Ct. App. 1998), transfer denied, 706 N.E.2d 169 (Ind. 1998); G & N Aircraft, Inc. v. Boehm, 703 N.E.2d 665 (Ind. Ct. App. 1998), reh'g denied, (Feb. 9, 1999); Krukemeier v. Krukemeier Mach. & Tool Co., Inc., 551 N.E.2d 885 (Ind. Ct. App. 1st Dist. 1990).

[34]Cressy v. Shannon Continental Corp., 177 Ind. App. 224, 378 N.E.2d 941 (3d Dist. 1978).

[35]Swanson v. Futures Unlimited, Inc., 457 N.E.2d 241 (Ind. Ct. App. 3d Dist. 1983).

[36]G & N Aircraft, Inc. v. Boehm, 703 N.E.2d 665 (Ind. Ct. App. 1998), reh'g denied, (Feb. 9, 1999).

[37]Motor Dispatch, Inc. v. Buggie, 177 Ind. App. 347, 379 N.E.2d 543 (3d Dist. 1978).

[38]W & W Equipment Co., Inc. v. Mink, 568 N.E.2d 564 (Ind. Ct. App. 1st Dist. 1991), reh'g denied, (May 10, 1991) and transfer denied, (Dec. 12, 1991).

to share in the purchase of the stock,[39] close corporation
shareholders are not subject to the duty to maintain equal
ownership, give each other first refusal rights, or otherwise
treat each other as partners if they have not agreed to do
so.[40]

§ 73 Dealings with corporation

**A stockholder may deal with the corporation in the same
manner as any other individual.**

West's Digest, Corporations ☞186.

In general, when acting in good faith, a stockholder may
deal with the corporation in the same manner as any other
individual; however, such transactions will be carefully
scrutinized in the interests of creditors.[41]

A member of a not-for-profit corporation may advance or
lend money to the corporation, with the money to be returned
or repaid to the member at a time and under conditions to
which the corporation and the member agree. The member
may not receive in return or repayment more than the
principal amount of the advance or loan and reasonable
interest at a rate not in excess of the market rate otherwise
available to the corporation under the same circumstances
at the time the advance or loan was made.[42]

§ 74 Action by shareholders on behalf of corporation

**In an appropriate case, a stockholder may bring a deriv-
ative action to enforce a right belonging to the corporation.**

West's Digest, Corporations ☞202-214.

A shareholder who appears to fairly and adequately represent the interests of the corporation's other shareholders
may commence a proceeding to enforce a right belonging to

---

[39]Cressy v. Shannon Continental Corp., 177 Ind. App. 224, 378 N.E.2d
941 (3d Dist. 1978).

Annotation References: Dominant shareholder's accountability to
minority for profit, bonus, or the like, received on sale of stock to outsiders,
38 ALR3d 738.

[40]Maul v. Van Keppel, 714 N.E.2d 707 (Ind. Ct. App. 1999).

[41]18 C.J.S., Corporations § 319.

[42]IC 23-17-7-9.

the corporation. For instance, shareholders may bring an action to compel the corporation's directors to perform their
legal obligations in the supervision of the corporation,[43] or to
remedy a controlling shareholder's improper manipulation of
corporate funds or wrongful diversion of corporate assets.[44]
The plaintiff must either have been a shareholder at the time
of the transaction complained of, or have become a shareholder through transfer of shares by operation of law from
one who was a shareholder at that time.[45] Such proceedings
are known as derivative proceedings.[46]

Generally, a shareholder complaining of injury to the
corporation may not maintain an action in his or her own
name, but must bring a derivative action,[47] even if he or she
has been injured as a result of the injury to the corporation.[48]
This rule is designed to prevent a multiplicity of actions
based on the same incident or transaction,[49] to protect
corporate creditors by giving the proceeds of recovery to the
corporation, to protect the interests of all shareholders rather
than allowing one shareholder to prejudice the others'
interests, and to compensate the injured shareholder by

---

[43]Matter of Strutz, 652 N.E.2d 41 (Ind. 1995).

[44]Ross v. Tavel, 418 N.E.2d 297 (Ind. Ct. App. 1st Dist. 1981).

[45]IC 23-1-32-1; Trial R. 23.1.

[46]IC 23-1-32-1 et seq.

Forms References: Complaint, petition, or declaration against officer and directors. 7A Am Jur Pleading and Practice Forms, Annotated
(rev. ed.), Corporations §§ 158, 159, 161-164.

[47]Pfaffenberger v. Brooks, 652 N.E.2d 884 (Ind. Ct. App. 1995).

[48]Barth v. Barth, 659 N.E.2d 559 (Ind. 1995), appeal after remand, 693
N.E.2d 954 (Ind. Ct. App. 1998), transfer denied, 706 N.E.2d 169 (Ind.
1998); Knauf Fiber Glass, GMBh v. Stein, 622 N.E.2d 163 (Ind. 1993),
reh'g denied, (Aug. 16, 1994) (damage suffered by shareholder who
guaranteed loans necessary to expansion of corporation's operations
induced by major customer was derivative of damages suffered by
corporation, which sustained heavy economic losses as result of expansion);
Moll v. South Central Solar Systems, Inc., 419 N.E.2d 154 (Ind. Ct. App.
1st Dist. 1981) (disapproved of on other grounds by, Enservco, Inc. v. Indiana Securities Div., 623 N.E.2d 416 (Ind. 1993)).

[49]Moll v. South Central Solar Systems, Inc., 419 N.E.2d 154 (Ind. Ct.
App. 1st Dist. 1981) (disapproved of on other grounds by, Enservco, Inc. v.
Indiana Securities Div., 623 N.E.2d 416 (Ind. 1993)).

increasing the value of his or her shares when the corporation receives the recovery.[50]

The requirement of shareholder status to commence and maintain an action on behalf of a corporation insures that the party bringing suit will have at least an indirect interest in the outcome of the litigation.[51] A director may bring a derivative action, as long as he or she is also a shareholder.[52] A beneficial owner whose shares are held by a nominee on the owner's behalf, or by a trustee in a voting trust, is a shareholder who may bring a derivative action.[53] A pledgee of stock in the corporation is also a shareholder under Indiana law, and therefore may have standing to bring a derivative action.[54] The shareholder's interest need not be represented by share certificates.[55] Despite the requirement that the complainant be a shareholder of the corporation, and the lack of express statutory authorization for a derivative action in the Nonprofit Corporation Act, a member of a not-for-profit corporation may also maintain a derivative action on behalf of the corporation.[56] A stockholder is not an adequate representative if he or she has participated in the wrong of which he or she complains.[57]

A corporation is a necessary party in a derivative suit. If the corporation is in the hands of a receiver at time of the

---

[50]W & W Equipment Co., Inc. v. Mink, 568 N.E.2d 564 (Ind. Ct. App. 1st Dist. 1991), reh'g denied, (May 10, 1991) and transfer denied, (Dec. 12, 1991).

[51]DRW Builders, Inc. v. Richardson, 679 N.E.2d 902 (Ind. Ct. App. 1997), reh'g denied, (June 20, 1997).

[52]Dotlich v. Dotlich, 475 N.E.2d 331 (Ind. Ct. App. 1st Dist. 1985), reh'g denied, (Apr. 23, 1985) and transfer denied, (July 3, 1985).

[53]IC 23-1-32-5.

[54]In re Krause, 114 B.R. 582 (Bankr. N.D. Ind. 1988) (applying Indiana law) (pledgee had standing to bring derivative action under federal derivative action rule).

[55]DRW Builders, Inc. v. Richardson, 679 N.E.2d 902 (Ind. Ct. App. 1997), reh'g denied, (June 20, 1997).

[56]Kirtley v. McClelland, 562 N.E.2d 27 (Ind. Ct. App. 1st Dist. 1990), reh'g denied, (Feb. 12, 1991) and transfer denied, (Aug. 16, 1991); Brenner v. Powers, 584 N.E.2d 569 (Ind. Ct. App. 3d Dist. 1992), reh'g denied, (Apr. 21, 1992) and transfer denied, (Dec. 18, 1992).

[57]Dotlich v. Dotlich, 475 N.E.2d 331 (Ind. Ct. App. 1st Dist. 1985), reh'g denied, (Apr. 23, 1985) and transfer denied, (July 3, 1985).

derivative suit, the receiver is also a necessary party.[58] The corporation is nominally the plaintiff in a derivative action,[59] and, because stockholders or directors of a corporation cannot recover upon causes of action belonging to the corporation,[60] all relief obtained in a derivative action belongs to the corporation.[61]

◆ **Practice Guide:** An award of punitive damages may be appropriate in a derivative action.[62]

Court approval is required for the settlement or discontinuation of a derivative action. If the court determines that a proposed discontinuance or settlement will substantially affect the interest of the corporation's shareholders or a class of shareholders, the court shall direct that notice be given the shareholders affected.[63] If the court finds that the proceeding was commenced without probable cause, it may require the plaintiff to pay any defendant's reasonable expenses, including counsel fees, incurred in defending the proceeding.[64] Attorneys' fees awarded a complaining shareholder in a derivative action should be assessed against the corporation, rather than against any defendant shareholders, because the corporation is the beneficiary of the derivative action.[65]

◆ **Practice Guide:** An attorney representing a corporation involved in a derivative action is responsible for advising the board of director on alternatives to litigation,

---

[58]Sacks v. American Fletcher Nat. Bank & Trust Co., 258 Ind. 189, 279 N.E.2d 807 (1972).

[59]Matter of Strutz, 652 N.E.2d 41 (Ind. 1995).

[60]Smith v. Kinney, 167 Ind. App. 202, 338 N.E.2d 507 (3d Dist. 1975).

[61]DRW Builders, Inc. v. Richardson, 679 N.E.2d 902 (Ind. Ct. App. 1997), reh'g denied, (June 20, 1997).

[62]Dotlich v. Dotlich, 475 N.E.2d 331 (Ind. Ct. App. 1st Dist. 1985), reh'g denied, (Apr. 23, 1985) and transfer denied, (July 3, 1985).

[63]IC 23-1-32-3(a); Trial R. 23.1.

[64]IC 23-1-32-3(b).

Annotation References: Attorneys' fees and other expenses incident to controversy respecting internal affairs of corporation as charge against the corporation, 39 ALR2d 580.

[65]DRW Builders, Inc. v. Richardson, 679 N.E.2d 902 (Ind. Ct. App. 1997), reh'g denied, (June 20, 1997); Dotlich v. Dotlich, 475 N.E.2d 331 (Ind. Ct. App. 1st Dist. 1985), reh'g denied, (Apr. 23, 1985) and transfer denied, (July 3, 1985).

including the appointing of an investigative committee of disinterested persons.[66]

§ 75 —Demand on corporation

As a general rule, before a shareholder may bring a derivative action on behalf of the corporation, he or she must demand that the corporation bring the action on its own behalf.

West's Digest, Corporations ⊕202-214.

Generally, before a shareholder may bring a derivative action on behalf of the corporation, he or she must demand that the corporation bring the action on its own behalf.[67] The complaint in a derivative action must be verified, and must allege with particularity the demand made, if any, to obtain action by the board of directors, and either that the demand was refused or ignored or why the shareholder did not make the demand. Regardless of whether a demand for action was made, if the corporation commences an investigation of the charges made in the demand or complaint, the court may stay any proceeding until the investigation is completed.[68] Requiring that the shareholder demand that the corporation bring an action on its own behalf serves to screen potential lawsuits, both by allowing corporations to attempt to resolve shareholder complaints before litigation and by giving courts more information on which to decide the merits of those suits that remain after demand.[69]

The shareholder need not make demand on the board of directors where the directors are acting in their own interests, if such a demand would be futile.[70] Demand would be futile, for instance, where the directors are charged with

---

[66]Matter of Strutz, 652 N.E.2d 41 (Ind. 1995).

As to committee of disinterested persons or directors, see § 76.

[67]Cole Real Estate Corp. v. Peoples Bank & Trust Co., 160 Ind. App. 88, 310 N.E.2d 275 (3d Dist. 1974); Boland v. Engle, 113 F.3d 706 (7th Cir. 1997) (applying Indiana law).

Forms References: Notice—Demand by stockholder for action by corporation against directors. 7A Am Jur Pleading and Practice Forms, Annotated (rev. ed.), Corporations § 190.

[68]IC 23-1-32-2; Trial R. 23.1.

[69]Boland v. Engle, 113 F.3d 706 (7th Cir. 1997) (applying Indiana law).

[70]Cole Real Estate Corp. v. Peoples Bank & Trust Co., 160 Ind. App. 88, 310 N.E.2d 275 (3d Dist. 1974).

the conversion of corporate assets, as they could not be expected to bring suit in the name of the corporation against themselves.[71] If less than a majority the directors were acting in their own interest, however, demand would not necessarily be futile.[72] Even the fact that a shareholder has asked board members to sue themselves does not automatically excuse demand, as the directors may appoint an independent committee to investigate the complaint, and as they may actually be disinterested in a potential lawsuit against themselves because the business judgment rule or directors' and officers' liability insurance will protect them from personal liability.[73]

§ 76   —Committee of disinterested directors or persons

> A corporation may establish a committee, which is not subject to the board of directors' direction or control, of three or more disinterested directors or other disinterested persons to determine whether the corporation has a legal or equitable right or remedy and whether it is in the corporation's best interests to pursue the right or remedy, if any, or to dismiss a proceeding that seeks to assert the right or remedy on the corporation's behalf.

West's Digest, Corporations ☜202-214.

A corporation may establish a committee of three or more disinterested directors or other disinterested persons to determine whether the corporation has a legal or equitable right or remedy and whether it is in the corporation's best interests to pursue the right or remedy, if any, or to dismiss a proceeding that seeks to assert the right or remedy on the corporation's behalf.[74] In making such determination, the committee is not subject to the direction or control of or termination by the board. A vacancy on the committee may be filled by the majority of the remaining members by selec-

---

[71]Wayne Pike Co. v. Hammons, 129 Ind. 368, 27 N.E. 487 (1891).

[72]Boland v. Engle, 113 F.3d 706 (7th Cir. 1997) (applying Indiana law) (where shareholder failed to show how one of corporation's two directors had personally benefited from transactions complained of, transactions had some arguable business merit, and other director was benefited only indirectly through interconnections of companies, demand was necessary).

[73]Boland v. Engle, 113 F.3d 706 (7th Cir. 1997) (applying Indiana law).

For discussion of the business judgment rule, see § 117.

[74]IC 23-1-32-4(a).

tion of another disinterested director or other disinterested person.[75]

A director or other person is disinterested if he or she:[76]

(1) has not been made a party to a derivative proceeding seeking to assert the right or remedy in question, or has been made a party but only on the basis of a frivolous or insubstantial claim or for the sole purpose of seeking to disqualify the director or other person from serving on the committee;

(2) is able under the circumstances to render a determination in the best interests of the corporation; and

(3) is not an officer, employee, or agent of the corporation or of a related corporation, unless the right or remedy under scrutiny is not assertable against a director or officer of the corporation or the related corporation.

If the committee determines that pursuit of a right or remedy through a derivative proceeding or otherwise is not in the best interests of the corporation, the merits of that determination shall be presumed to be conclusive against any shareholder making a demand or bringing a derivative proceeding with respect to such right or remedy, unless the shareholder can demonstrate that the committee was not disinterested or that its determination was not made after an investigation conducted in good faith.[77]

§ 77 Actions by stockholders on their own behalf

A stockholder may bring an action on his or her own behalf against another stockholder or the corporation.

West's Digest, Corporations ⌐189(1)-189(7), 190.

Generally, a shareholder cannot maintain an action in his or her own name to redress injury to the corporation, but must bring a derivative action instead.[78] However, a personal cause of action in favor of a stockholder arises when there is

---

[75]IC 23-1-32-4(b).

[76]IC 23-1-32-4(d).

[77]IC 23-1-32-4(c).

Annotation References: Propriety of termination of properly initiated derivative action by "independent committee" appointed by board of directors whose actions (or inaction) are under attack, 22 ALR4th 1206.

[78]W & W Equipment Co., Inc. v. Mink, 568 N.E.2d 564 (Ind. Ct. App.

a breach of a duty owed specially to the stockholder separate and distinct from any duty owed to the corporation.[79] For instance, a court of equity will provide a minority shareholder with a remedy when a majority shareholder of a close corporation, in violation of his or her fiduciary obligation, appropriates the profits of a corporation for salaries.[80] No demand for action by the corporation is necessary in such a case.[81] A shareholder is estopped to complain of actions in which he or she participated.[82]

> ◆ **Practice Guide:** A RICO claim is generally a corporate asset, rather than an individual one,[83] and an action to redress injuries caused to the corporation by RICO violations can be brought only by the corporation, or by its shareholders in a derivative suit, where the shareholder's injury resulted from the injury to the corporation.[84]

In the case of a closely held corporation, the court, in its discretion, may treat an action raising derivative claims as a direct action, exempt it from restrictions and defenses applicable only to derivative actions, and order an individual recovery, if it finds that to do so will not unfairly expose the corporation or the defendants to a multiplicity of actions, materially prejudice the interests of creditors of the corporation, or interfere with a fair distribution of the

---

1st Dist. 1991), reh'g denied, (May 10, 1991) and transfer denied, (Dec. 12, 1991).

For discussion of derivative actions, see § 74.

[79]Sacks v. American Fletcher Nat. Bank & Trust Co., 258 Ind. 189, 279 N.E.2d 807 (1972).

[80]Lowry v. Lowry, 590 N.E.2d 612 (Ind. Ct. App. 3d Dist. 1992), reh'g denied, (June 25, 1992) and transfer denied, (Sept. 10, 1992).

[81]Cole Real Estate Corp. v. Peoples Bank & Trust Co., 160 Ind. App. 88, 310 N.E.2d 275 (3d Dist. 1974).

For discussion of the demand requirement in derivative actions, see § 75.

[82]Ross v. Tavel, 418 N.E.2d 297 (Ind. Ct. App. 1st Dist. 1981) (minority shareholder who participated in allegedly improper winding up of corporate affairs was estopped to allege that such conduct was fraudulent and in breach of defendants' fiduciary duty).

[83]Sears v. Likens, 912 F.2d 889, 17 Fed. R. Serv. 3d (LCP) 873 (7th Cir. 1990) (Indiana and federal law).

[84]Gagan v. American Cablevision, Inc., 77 F.3d 951 (7th Cir. 1996), reh'g denied, (Apr. 1, 1996); Wade v. Hopper, 993 F.2d 1246, 25 Fed. R. Serv. 3d (LCP) 1278 (7th Cir. 1993), reh'g denied, (Apr. 22, 1993) (Indiana and federal law).

recovery among all interested persons.[85] Thus, a minority
shareholder in a closely held corporation may bring a lawsuit
in his or her own name to enforce a right belonging to the
corporation where the policy considerations underlying the
general derivative action requirement are not present.[86]
Because the rules applicable to derivative actions will not
apply in such a suit, a court deciding whether to permit the
action to proceed as a direct suit should consider whether
the corporation has a disinterested board that should be
permitted to consider the lawsuit's impact on the corporation. In some situations it may actually be to the benefit of
the corporation to permit the plaintiff to proceed by direct
action, as the defendant will be permitted to file a
counterclaim, which is generally prohibited in derivative
actions, and as the parties to a direct action will be responsible for their own legal fees.[87]

The measure of damages in a case against a shareholder
in a close corporation for breach of fiduciary duty is the entire
loss sustained. Punitive damages may also be available
where there is clear and convincing evidence that the defendant acted with malice, fraud, gross negligence or oppres-
siveness which was not the result of a mistake of fact or law,
honest error of judgment, overzealousness, mere negligence,

---

[85]G & N Aircraft, Inc. v. Boehm, 703 N.E.2d 665 (Ind. Ct. App. 1998),
reh'g denied, (Feb. 9, 1999); DRW Builders, Inc. v. Richardson, 679 N.E.2d
902 (Ind. Ct. App. 1997), reh'g denied, (June 20, 1997); Moll v. South
Central Solar Systems, Inc., 419 N.E.2d 154 (Ind. Ct. App. 1st Dist. 1981)
(disapproved of on other grounds by, Enservco, Inc. v. Indiana Securities
Div., 623 N.E.2d 416 (Ind. 1993)).

[86]Pfaffenberger v. Brooks, 652 N.E.2d 884 (Ind. Ct. App. 1995).

[87]Barth v. Barth, 693 N.E.2d 954 (Ind. Ct. App. 1998), transfer denied,
706 N.E.2d 169 (Ind. 1998) (minority shareholder could not bring direct
action against corporation where third shareholder had not been joined
and had not intervened in minority shareholder's suit against majority
shareholder, and direct action could unfairly expose majority shareholder
and corporation to multiplicity of actions arising from same matters alleged in minority shareholder's complaint, creditors would be prejudiced if
minority shareholder was allowed to pursue direct claim, and direct action
would interfere with fair distribution of recovery among shareholders);
Moll v. South Central Solar Systems, Inc., 419 N.E.2d 154 (Ind. Ct. App.
1st Dist. 1981) (disapproved of on other grounds by, Enservco, Inc. v. Indiana Securities Div., 623 N.E.2d 416 (Ind. 1993)).

or other human failing.[88] Generally, attorney fees are not re-coverable as damages in the absence of a statute, rule, or a contract stipulating the recovery of such fees. Thus, in a direct shareholder action, each side will normally be responsible for its own legal expenses.[89] In a direct action brought by a shareholder, a defendant may, however, re-cover attorneys' fees if the shareholder's claim is frivolous.[90] A claim is frivolous if it is established that the claim was brought for the purpose of an improper motive such as harassment or if legal counsel is unable to make a good faith, rational argument on the merits of the case.[91]

A shareholder may also bring an action against the corporation, rather than against a director or officer or an-other shareholder. For instance, a shareholder may bring an action for an injunction against a corporation based on a claim that the corporation committed an act which it had no power to commit.[92] In a shareholder's proceeding to enjoin an unauthorized corporate act, the court may enjoin or set aside the act, if equitable and if all affected persons are parties to the proceeding, and may award damages for loss, other than anticipated profits, suffered by the corporation or another party because of enjoining the unauthorized act.[93]

---

[88]G & N Aircraft, Inc. v. Boehm, 703 N.E.2d 665 (Ind. Ct. App. 1998), reh'g denied, (Feb. 9, 1999).

[89]G & N Aircraft, Inc. v. Boehm, 703 N.E.2d 665 (Ind. Ct. App. 1998), reh'g denied, (Feb. 9, 1999); DRW Builders, Inc. v. Richardson, 679 N.E.2d 902 (Ind. Ct. App. 1997), reh'g denied, (June 20, 1997).

[90]IC 34-52-1-1.

[91]G & N Aircraft, Inc. v. Boehm, 703 N.E.2d 665 (Ind. Ct. App. 1998), reh'g denied, (Feb. 9, 1999) (under former IC 34-1-32-1; minority shareholder's breach of fiduciary duty claim alleging that corporation and majority shareholder took actions reducing value of his stock was not frivolous, where trial court granted minority shareholder's motion for pre-liminary injunction, enjoining corporation from taking any action that would redirect corporation's operations or management).

[92]IC 23-1-22-5(b).

[93]IC 23-1-22-5(c).

Annotation References: Right of corporation to discharge employee who asserts right as stockholder, 84 ALR3d 1107.

A controversy over individuals' status as members of a not-for-profit corporation may be brought as a declaratory action.[94]

§ 78 Liability for corporate acts and debts generally

Generally, shareholders are not personally liable for the acts or debts of the corporation.

West's Digest, Corporations ☞215-240.

The personal liability of shareholders is determined by common law rules of agency.[95] Where an agent acted within the scope of his or her authority in signing a contract on behalf of the principal, the remedy of one seeking to enforce the contract is against the principal and not the agent. As a result, corporate officers and shareholders are generally not personally liable for the contractual obligations of the corporation.[96]

Although a corporation acts only through its agents, officers, shareholders, and employees, it is the corporate entity that is legally responsible for those acts.[97] A corporate officer or shareholder may not be held liable for the corporation's acts merely because he or she is a shareholder.[98]

Generally, shareholders' personal liability to the corporation and its creditors is limited to payment of consideration for their shares or subscriptions.[99] Unless otherwise provided in the articles of incorporation, a shareholder of a corporation is generally not personally liable for the acts or debts of

---

[94]Brenner v. Powers, 584 N.E.2d 569 (Ind. Ct. App. 3d Dist. 1992), reh'g denied, (Apr. 21, 1992) and transfer denied, (Dec. 18, 1992).

[95]Indiana Dept. of Public Welfare v. Chair Lance Service, Inc., 523 N.E.2d 1373 (Ind. 1988).

[96]Winkler v. V.G. Reed & Sons, Inc., 638 N.E.2d 1228 (Ind. 1994) (majority shareholder and president of corporation, who personally received the few assets not transferred to another corporation upon sale of first corporation, was not personally liable on employment contract, where no evidence showed that he treated corporation as his alter ego or that employee was deceived about identity of his employer).

[97]Winkler v. V.G. Reed & Sons, Inc., 638 N.E.2d 1228 (Ind. 1994).

As to disregarding the corporate entity see, § 7.

[98]American Independent Management Systems, Inc. v. McDaniel, 443 N.E.2d 98 (Ind. Ct. App. 3d Dist. 1982).

[99]IC 23-1-26-3(a).

the corporation.[1] Thus, shareholders, even sole shareholders,[2] are generally personally liable for corporate acts only to extent of their investments.[3] However, a shareholder or member may become personally liable for the acts and debts of the corporation by reason of the shareholder or member's own acts or conduct.[4]

A corporation's failure to observe corporate formalities not designed to protect the public does not expose its shareholders to personal liability.[5] However, a corporation's lack of observance of formalities can provide circumstantial evidence of shareholder abuse and shareholder use of the corporation as a conduit for personal affairs, which may be a reason for imposing personal liability.[6]

Generally, a parent corporation is not liable for the debts of its subsidiary.[7] An action by an employee against his or her employer's parent corporation for negligence must be based on the parent's alleged breach of its duty of care, separate and distinct from any vicarious liability attributable to the parent for acts of its subsidiary under the principles of agency law.[8]

◆ **Practice Guide:** An employee of a professional

---

[1]IC 23-1-26-3(b).

[2]Mishawaka Brass Mfg. Inc. v. Milwaukee Valve Co., Inc., 444 N.E.2d 855 (Ind. Ct. App. 3d Dist. 1983) (sole shareholder of predecessor corporation, who purchased equipment of predecessor corporation and leased it back for business purpose, not subject of individual liability because there was no intent to defraud).

[3]McQuade v. Draw Tite, Inc., 659 N.E.2d 1016 (Ind. 1995).

[4]IC 23-1-26-3(b); IC 23-17-7-6.

Forms References: Complaint, petition, or declaration to disregard corporate entity. 7A Am Jur Pleading and Practice Forms, Annotated (rev. ed.), Corporations §§ 45, 48, 51, 52.

[5]Aronson v. Price, 644 N.E.2d 864 (Ind. 1994), reh'g denied, (May 18, 1995) (failure to include abbreviation "Inc." on corporation's business cards or file assumed name certificate did not subject corporation's sole stockholder to personal liability).

[6]Aronson v. Price, 644 N.E.2d 864 (Ind. 1994), reh'g denied, (May 18, 1995).

[7]McQuade v. Draw Tite, Inc., 659 N.E.2d 1016 (Ind. 1995); Tolliver v. Mathas, 538 N.E.2d 971 (Ind. Ct. App. 4th Dist. 1989), reh'g denied, (July 10, 1989) and transfer denied, (Jan. 10, 1990).

[8]McQuade v. Draw Tite, Inc., 659 N.E.2d 1016 (Ind. 1995).

Annotation References: Liability of corporation for contracts of subsidiary, 38 ALR3d 1102.

corporation is liable for any negligent or wrongful act or omission in which he or she participates personally, and for the conduct of other corporation employees under his or her direction or control, to the same extent as a solo practitioner would be liable.[9] However, except as otherwise provided by statute or by rule of the licensing authority with control over the professionals in the corporation, the personal liability of a shareholder of a professional corporation is no greater in any respect than that of a shareholder of a business corporation.[10]

§ 79 Enforcement of nonprofit corporation's liability against members

A creditor of a not-for-profit corporation may reach members' liability to the corporation.

West's Digest, Corporations ☞253-279.

A creditor of a not-for-profit corporation may bring a proceeding to reach or apply a member's liability to the corporation under any of the following circumstances:[11]

- final judgment has been rendered in favor of the creditor against the corporation and execution has been returned unsatisfied in whole or in part
- the corporation has been adjudged bankrupt or a receiver has been appointed with the power to collect debts that a receiver on demand of a creditor to bring a proceeding has refused to do
- the corporation has been dissolved leaving debts unpaid

A proceeding may not be brought more than three years after the occurrence of any of the events described above.[12]

Creditors of the corporation, with or without reducing their claims to judgment, may intervene in any other creditor's proceeding brought to reach and apply unpaid amounts due

---

Trial Strategy References: Liability of Parent Corporation for Acts of Subsidiary, 20 Am Jur POF2d 679.

[9]IC 23-1.5-2-6(a), (b).

Annotation References: Professional corporation stockholders' nonmalpractice liability, 50 ALR4th 1276.

[10]IC 23-1.5-2-6(d).

[11]IC 23-17-7-8(a).

[12]IC 23-17-7-8(a).

the corporation. Members who owe amounts to the corporation may be joined in the proceeding.[13]

B. MEETINGS

Research References

IC 23-1-20-21; IC 23-1-20-29; IC 23-1-29-1 to IC 23-1-29-7; IC 23-17-10-1; IC 23-17-10-2; IC 23-17-10-4 to IC 23-17-10-8; IC 23-17-11-4; IC 23-17-28-1 to IC 23-17-28-3; IC 23-17-28-6; IC 23-17-28-7; IC 23-17-28-8; IC 27-17-10-3

18A Am Jur 2d, Corporations §§ 948-1014.
18 C.J.S., Corporations §§ 362-374.
West's Digest, Corporations ☞191-196.
ALR Digest: Corporations §§ 303-308
ALR Index: Articles of Incorporation; Assets; Bylaws; Charter; Close Corporation; Consolidation or Merger; Corporate Bonds and Bondholders; Corporate Officers, Directors, and Agents; Corporate Opportunity; Corporate Responsibility Doctrine; Corporate Stock and Stockholders; Corporations; Dissolution or Liquidation; Dividends; Domicile and Residence; Foreign Corporations; Forfeitures; Liquidation or Dissolution; Minority Stockholders; Names; Nonprofit Institutions or Organizations; Professional Corporations and Associations; Promoters; Prospectus; Proxies; Reports; Seal; Stock-Option Plans; Subsidiary
6A Am Jur Legal Forms 2d, Corporations §§ 74:1803-74:1805, 74:1813, 74:1814, 74:1833.

§ 80 Generally

Shareholders and members may hold meeting at times and places specified in the bylaws.

West's Digest, Corporations ☞191-194.

Annual, regular, and special meetings of shareholders or members may be held in or outside of Indiana, at a place stated in, or fixed in accordance with, the corporation's bylaws. If the bylaws do not establish the place for the meeting, it is to be held at the corporation's principal office.[14]

In the case of either a business or not-for-profit corporation, if the corporation's articles of incorporation or bylaws so provide, any or all of the shareholders may participate in a meeting by any means of communication by which all

---

[13]IC 23-17-7-8(b).

[14]IC 23-1-29-1(b); IC 23-1-29-2(c); IC 23-17-10-1(c); IC 23-17-10-2(d).

shareholders participating may simultaneously hear each other during the meeting, such as a conference call. A shareholder participating in a meeting by this means is deemed to be present in person at the meeting.[15]

§ 81   Annual and regular meetings

Corporations must hold annual shareholders' or members' meetings.

West's Digest, Corporations ☞191-194.

A business corporation must hold a meeting of its shareholders annually at a time stated in or fixed in accordance with its bylaws,[16] although failure to hold such a meeting does not affect the validity of any corporate action.[17]

A not-for-profit corporation with members must hold an annual membership meeting at a time stated in or fixed in accordance with the bylaws,[18] and may hold regular membership meetings at such a time.[19] However, the failure to hold an annual or regular meeting at a proper time does not affect the validity of any corporate action or work any forfeiture or dissolution of the corporation.[20] At the annual meeting, the president and chief financial officer, or their designees, shall report on the activities and financial condition of the corporation.[21] At both the annual and regular meetings, the members shall consider and act upon other matters of which they have been given proper notice.[22]

§ 82   Special meetings

The board of directors may call a special shareholders' or members' meeting.

West's Digest, Corporations ☞191-194.

A business corporation with more than 50 shareholders

---

[15]IC 23-1-29-2(d); IC 23-1-29-2(e); IC 23-17-10-2(f); IC 23-17-11-4(g).

[16]IC 23-1-29-1(a).

Annotation References: Remedies to restrain or compel holding of stockholders' meetings, 48 ALR2d 615.

[17]IC 23-1-29-1(c).

[18]IC 23-17-10-1(a).

[19]IC 23-17-10-1(b).

[20]IC 23-17-10-1(f).

[21]IC 23-17-10-1(d)(1).

[22]IC 23-17-10-1(d)(2).

must hold a special meeting of shareholders on call of its board of directors or a person or persons, such as shareholders or officers, specifically authorized to do so by the articles of incorporation or bylaws. The percentage of votes necessary to demand a special meeting may be specified in the articles of incorporation or the bylaws; if no such provision exists, the demand for a special meeting must be made by the holders of all of the votes entitled to be cast on an issue.[23]

A business corporation with 50 or fewer shareholders must hold a special meeting of its shareholders on call of its board of directors or a person or persons specifically authorized to do so by the articles of incorporation or bylaws; or on written demand for the meeting, signed by the holders of at least 25% of all the votes entitled to be cast on any issue proposed to be considered at the proposed special meeting. The demand must describe the purpose for which the meeting it to be held, and must be dated and delivered to the corporation's secretary.[24]

Only business of which the shareholders have been given proper notice may be conducted at a special shareholders' meeting.[25]

A not-for-profit corporation with members must hold a special meeting of members either on call of the corporation's president of board of directors, or other person, such as a member or officer, specifically authorized to do so by the articles of incorporation or bylaws;[26] or, except as provided in the articles of incorporation or bylaws of a religious corporation, if the holders of at least 10% of all the votes entitled to be cast on an issue proposed to be considered at the proposed special meeting sign, date, and deliver to the corporation's secretary at least one written demand for the meeting describing the purpose for which the meeting is to be held.[27] If the members demand a special meeting, but notice for such a meeting is not given within 30 days after the

---

[23]IC 23-1-29-2(a).

Forms References: Call of special stockholders' meeting. 6A Am Jur Legal Forms 2d, Corporations §§ 74:1803-74:1805.

[24]IC 23-1-29-2(b).

[25]IC 23-1-29-2(d).

[26]IC 23-17-10-2(a)(1).

[27]IC 23-17-10-2(a)(2).

written demand is delivered to the corporation's secretary, a person signing the demand may set the time and place for, and give notice of, the meeting.[28] Only those matters that are within the purposes described in the meeting notice may be conducted at a special meeting of members.[29]

§ 83 Court-ordered meetings

The appropriate court may order that a shareholders' or members' meeting be held.

West's Digest, Corporations ☞191-194.

The circuit or superior court of the county where a corporation's principal office (or, if none in Indiana, its registered office) is located may order that a meeting be held, and may fix the time and place of the meeting, on application of any of the following:[30]

- any shareholder or member of the corporation, or other person, entitled to participate in an annual meeting, if an annual meeting was not held within the earlier of six months after the end of the corporation's fiscal year or 15 months after its last annual meeting
- a shareholder or member who signed a demand for a special meeting, if notice of the special meeting was not given within 60 days after the date the demand was delivered to the corporation's secretary, or the special meeting was not held in accordance with the notice
- a member or other person entitled to participate in a regular meeting of a not-for-profit corporation if a regular meeting is not held within 40 days after the date it was required to be held

A court-ordered meeting is to be conducted in accordance with the corporation's articles of incorporation and bylaws.[31]

§ 84 Action taken without meeting

Shareholders and members may take certain actions without a meeting.

West's Digest, Corporations ☞191-194.

---

[28]IC 23-17-10-2(c).
[29]IC 23-17-10-2(e).
[30]IC 23-1-29-3; IC 27-17-10-3(a).
[31]IC 23-1-29-3; IC 27-17-10-3(a).

Action required or permitted to be taken at a business corporation's shareholders' meeting may be taken without a meeting if it is taken by all shareholders entitled to vote on the action. The action must be evidenced by written consent describing the action taken, signed by all the shareholders entitled to vote on the action, and delivered to the corporation for inclusion in the minutes or filing with the corporate records.[32] If notice to the nonvoting shareholders of a proposed action is required by the Business Corporation Law, and the action is to be taken by unanimous consent of the voting shareholders, the corporation must give the nonvoting shareholders written notice of the proposed action at least 10 days before the action is taken. The notice must contain or be accompanied by the same material that, under this article, would have been required to be sent to nonvoting shareholders in a notice of meeting at which the proposed action would have been submitted to the shareholders for action.[33]

In the case of a not-for-profit corporation, unless the articles of incorporation or bylaws limit or prohibit such action, action required or permitted to be approved by the members may be taken without a meeting of members if the action is approved by members holding at least 80% of the votes entitled to be cast on the action. The action must be evidenced by at least one written consent describing the action taken that is signed by the holders of 80% of the votes entitled to be cast on the issue, and is delivered to the corporation for inclusion in the minutes or filing with the corporation's records. Requests for written consents must be delivered to all members.[34]

If action is to be taken without a meeting of the members of a not-for-profit corporation, the corporation must deliver a written ballot to every member entitled to vote on the matter.[35] A written ballot must set forth each proposed action and provide an opportunity to vote for or against each.[36] Approval by written ballot is valid only when the number of votes cast by ballot equals or exceeds the quorum required

---

[32]IC 23-1-29-4(a).
[33]IC 23-1-29-4(e).
[34]IC 23-17-10-4(a).
[35]IC 23-17-10-8(a).
[36]IC 23-17-10-8(b).

to be present at a meeting authorizing the action, and the number of approvals equals or exceeds the number of votes that would be required to approve the matter at a meeting at which the total number of votes cast was the same as the number of votes cast by ballot.[37] A solicitation for votes by written ballot must indicate the number of responses needed to meet the quorum requirements, state the percentage of approvals necessary to approve each matter other than the election of directors, and specify the time by which a ballot must be received by the corporation to be counted.[38] Except as otherwise provided in articles of incorporation or bylaws, a written ballot may not be revoked.[39]

Consents signed to permit action without a meeting have the effect of votes cast at a meeting, and may be so described in any document.[40]

Action properly taken without a meeting is effective when the last necessary shareholder or member signs the consent, unless the consent specifies a different prior or subsequent effective date.[41]

§ 85 Notice of meeting

Corporations must provide their shareholders or members with notice of a meeting.

West's Digest, Corporations ☞194.

A business corporation is to notify shareholders of the date, time, and place of each annual and special shareholders' meeting no fewer than 10 nor more than 60 days before the meeting date.[42] The notice period is to be counted backwards from the date of the meeting, rather than forwards from the

---

[37]IC 23-17-10-8(c).

[38]IC 23-17-10-8(d).

[39]IC 23-17-10-8(e).

[40]IC 23-1-29-4(d); IC 23-17-10-4(c).

[41]IC 23-1-29-4(c); IC 23-17-10-4(d).

[42]IC 23-1-29-5(a).

Forms References: Notice—Regular or special meeting. 6A Am Jur Legal Forms 2d, Corporations § 74:1813.

Notice—Annual meeting. 6A Am Jur Legal Forms 2d, Corporations § 74:1814.

date notice is provided.[43] Unless the Business Corporation Law or the articles of incorporation require otherwise, the corporation is required to give notice only to shareholders entitled to vote at the meeting,[44] and notice of an annual meeting need not include a description of the purpose or purposes for which the meeting is called.[45] Notice of a special meeting, however, must include a description of the purpose or purposes for which the meeting is called.[46]

A not-for-profit corporation shall give notice consistent with the corporation's bylaws of meetings of members in a fair and reasonable manner.[47] Notice is fair and reasonable if the following occur:[48]

- the corporation notifies the corporation's members of the place, date, and time of each annual, regular, and special meeting of members not less than 10 days, or, if notice is mailed by other than first class or registered mail, 30 days to 60 days, before the meeting date

- notice of an annual or a regular meeting includes a description of any matter or matters to be considered at the meeting that must be approved by the members

- notice of a special meeting includes a description of the purpose for which the meeting is called

- for a corporation, other than a veteran's organization, having more than 1,000 members, notice of the place, date, and time of an annual, regular, or special meeting, and in the case of a special meeting, the purpose of the special meeting, may be given by one publication in a newspaper of general circulation, printed in English, in the county in which the corporation has the corporation's principal office if the publication is made no fewer than 10 days and no more than 30 days before the meeting date

---

[43]Hilligoss v. Associated Companies, Inc., 589 N.E.2d 1202 (Ind. Ct. App. 1st Dist. 1992), transfer denied, (July 8, 1992).

[44]IC 23-1-29-5(a).

[45]IC 23-1-29-5(b).

[46]IC 23-1-29-5(c).

[47]IC 23-17-10-5(a).

[48]IC 23-17-10-5(c).

Other means of giving notice may also be fair and reasonable when all the circumstances are considered if proper notice of matters to be considered at the meeting is given.[49]

Unless the bylaws require otherwise, if an annual, regular, or special shareholders' or members' meeting is adjourned to a different date, time, or place, notice need not be given of the new date, time, or place if the new date, time, or place is announced at the meeting before adjournment, unless a new record date is fixed, in which case notice of the adjourned meeting must be given to persons who are shareholders as of the new record date.[50]

A shareholder or member may waive any notice required by the applicable statute, articles of incorporation, or bylaws before or after the date and time stated in the notice. The waiver must be in writing and be delivered to the corporation for inclusion in the minutes or filing with the corporate records.[51] The provision applicable to not-for-profit corporations adds the specific requirement that the waiver be signed by the member entitled to the notice.[52] A member or shareholder's attendance at a meeting waives objection to lack of notice or defective notice of the meeting, unless the member or shareholder objects at the beginning of the meeting to holding the meeting or transacting business at the meeting, and waives objection to the consideration of a particular matter at the meeting that is not within the purpose or purposes described in the meeting notice, unless the member or shareholder objects to considering the matter when it is presented.[53]

Generally, notice given under the Business Corporation Law or the Nonprofit Corporations Act must be in writing unless oral notice is authorized by the corporation's articles of incorporation or bylaws.[54] Notice may be communicated in person, by telephone, telegraph, teletype, or other form of

---

[49]IC 23-17-10-5(b).

[50]IC 23-1-29-5(e); IC 23-17-10-5(d).

For discussion of record date, see § 59.

[51]IC 23-1-29-6(a); IC 23-17-10-6(a)(1), (3).

Forms References: Waiver of notice. 6A Am Jur Legal Forms 2d, Corporations § 74:1833.

[52]IC 23-17-10-6(a)(2).

[53]IC 23-1-29-6(b); IC 23-17-10-6(b).

[54]IC 23-1-20-29(a); IC 23-17-28-1.

wire or wireless communicated, by mail, or in a newspaper of general circulation in the area where published or by radio, television, or other form of public broadcast communication, if it is otherwise in proper form.[55] In the case of a business corporation, notice may be given by publication only if personal notice is impracticable.[56] In the case of a not-for-profit corporation, a written notice or report delivered as part of a newsletter, magazine, or other publication regularly sent to members constitutes written notice if the publication is addressed or delivered to the member's address shown in the corporation's current list of members, or if members are residents of the same household and have the same address in the corporation's current list of members, if addressed or delivered to one of the members at the address appearing on the current list of members.[57]

Written notice by a corporation to a shareholder or member is effective when mailed, if it is correctly addressed to the shareholder or member's address shown in the corporation's current records.[58] Oral notice is effective when it is communicated.[59]

If the applicable statute prescribes notice requirements for particular circumstances, those requirements govern. If the corporation's articles of incorporation of bylaws prescribe notice requirements not inconsistent with the applicable statute, those requirements govern.[60]

§ 86 Record date

The record date, or date as of which the shareholders' or members' identities are determined, may be determined according to the bylaws.

West's Digest, Corporations ⊶194.

The record date is the date as of which the identities of shareholders entitled to notice of a meeting are determined.[61]

A corporation's bylaws may fix or provide the manner of

---

[55]IC 23-1-20-29(b); IC 23-17-28-2.

[56]IC 23-1-20-29(b).

[57]IC 23-17-28-6.

[58]IC 23-1-20-29(c); IC 23-17-28-3.

[59]IC 23-1-20-29(f); IC 23-17-28-7.

[60]IC 23-1-20-29(g); IC 23-17-28-8.

[61]IC 23-1-20-21.

fixing the record date in order to determine the shareholders or members entitled to notice of a meeting, to demand a special meeting, to vote, or to take any other action. If the bylaws do not fix or provide a method for fixing the record date, the board of directors may fix a future date as the record date.[62] In the case of a not-for-profit corporation, if a record date is not fixed, the record date is determined as follows:[63]

- if members are entitled to notice of a members' meeting, the record date is the business day preceding the date on which notice is given, or if notice is waived, at the close of business on the business day preceding the day on which the meeting is held
- if members are entitled to vote at a members' meeting, the record date is the date of the meeting
- if members are entitled to exercise any rights in respect of any other lawful action, the record date is the day on which the board of directors adopts the resolution relating the action or the 60th day before the date of other action, whichever is later

A record date may not be more than 70 days before the meeting or action requiring a determination of shareholders or members.[64]

A determination of shareholders or members entitled to notice of or to vote at a shareholders' or membership meeting is effective for any adjournment of the meeting unless the board of directors fixes a new record date.[65] The board of directors of a business corporation must fix a new record date if the meeting is adjourned to a date more than 120 days after the date fixed for the original meeting,[66] and the board of a not-for-profit corporation must fix a new record date if the meeting is adjourned to a date more than 70 days after the record date for determining members entitled to notice of the original meeting.[67] If a court orders a meeting adjourned to a date more than 120 days after the date fixed for the original meeting, the court may provide that the orig-

---

[62]IC 23-1-29-7(a); IC 23-17-10-7(a).

[63]IC 23-17-10-7(a).

[64]IC 23-1-29-7(b); IC 23-17-10-7(b).

[65]IC 23-1-29-7(c); IC 23-17-10-7(c).

[66]IC 23-1-29-7(c).

[67]IC 23-17-10-7(c).

inal record date continues in effect, or it may fix a new record date.[68]

C. VOTING

Research References

IC 23-1-20-28; IC 23-1-30-1 to IC 23-1-30-3; IC 23-1-30-5 to IC 23-1-30-8; IC 23-1-31-1; IC 23-1-31-2; IC 23-1-38-3; IC 23-1-38-4; IC 23-17-11-1; IC 23-17-11-3 to IC 23-17-11-6; IC 23-17-11-9; IC 23-17-18-2

18A Am Jur 2d, Corporations §§ 1015-1167.
18 C.J.S., Corporations §§ 375-396.
West's Digest, Corporations ☞197-201.
ALR Digest: Corporations §§ 310-322.5
ALR Index: Articles of Incorporation; Assets; Bylaws; Charter; Close Corporation; Consolidation or Merger; Corporate Bonds and Bondholders; Corporate Officers, Directors, and Agents, Corporate Opportunity; Corporate Responsibility Doctrine; Corporate Stock and Stockholders; Corporations; Dissolution or Liquidation; Dividends; Domicile and Residence; Foreign Corporations; Forfeitures; Liquidation or Dissolution; Minority Stockholders; Names; Nonprofit Institutions or Organizations; Professional Corporations and Associations; Promoters; Prospectus; Proxies; Reports; Seal; Stock-Option Plans; Subsidiary
6A Am Jur Legal Forms 2d, Corporations §§ 74:1855-74:1862, 74:1864, 74:1865, 74:1883-74:1885.

§ 87 Voting list

Before a meeting, a corporation must prepare a list of all shareholders or members who are entitled to notice of the meeting.

West's Digest, Corporations ☞194.

After fixing a record date for a meeting, a corporation shall prepare an alphabetical list of the names of all of its shareholders or members who are entitled to notice of the meeting.[69] Business corporations are to arrange the list by voting group, and within each voting group by class or series of shares.[70] A business corporation must show the address of and number of shares owned by each shareholder on the

---

[68]IC 23-1-29-7(d); IC 23-17-10-7(d).

[69]IC 23-1-30-1(a); IC 23-17-11-1(a).

[70]IC 23-1-30-1(a).

For discussion of classes and series of shares, see § 37.

list,[71] and a not-for-profit corporation must show the address of each member and the number of votes he or she is entitled to cast at the meeting.[72] A not-for-profit corporation must also prepare a list of its members if any, who are entitled to vote at the meeting, but not entitled to notice of the meeting. This list is to be prepared on the same basis as, and be part of, the main list of members.[73]

§ 88 Business corporations, generally

Each share in a business corporation is entitled to one vote.

West's Digest, Corporations ☞197.

In a business corporation, each outstanding share is generally entitled to one vote, unless the articles of incorporation provide otherwise.[74] Shares are not entitled to vote, however, if they are owned, directly or indirectly, by a second corporation, and the first corporation owns, directly or indirectly, a majority of the shares entitled to vote for directors of the second corporation;[75] thus, a subsidiary may not vote shares of its parent corporation, if the parent owns a majority of the subsidiary's shares.[76] A corporation may vote any shares, including its own, it holds in or for an employee benefit plan or in any other fiduciary capacity.[77] Shares redeemable by the corporation are not entitled to vote after the corporation has mailed notice of redemption to the holders and irrevocably obligated itself, through the deposit in a financial institution of a sum sufficient to redeem the shares, to pay the redemption price on surrender of the shares.[78]

§ 89 Not-for-profit corporations, generally

Each member of a not-for-profit corporation is entitled to one vote.

For discussion of voting groups, see § 91.

[71] IC 23-1-30-1(a).
[72] IC 23-17-11-1(a).
[73] IC 23-17-11-1(a).
[74] IC 23-1-30-2(a).
[75] IC 23-1-30-2(b).
[76] IC 23-1-30-2, Official Comment.
[77] IC 23-1-30-2(c).
[78] IC 23-1-30-2(d).

West's Digest, Corporations ☞197.

Unless the articles of incorporation provide otherwise, each member of a not-for-profit corporation is entitled to one vote on each matter voted on by the members.[79] If a membership is recorded in the names of two or more persons, the vote of one person binds all of them. The votes are divided on a pro rata basis if more than one of them votes.[80]

Unless at least one-third of the corporation's voting power is present in person or by proxy, the only matters that may be voted upon at an annual or a regular meeting of members are those matters that are described in the meeting notice.[81]

§ 90   Quorum; votes required

A quorum must be present before shareholders or members may act on a matter.

West's Digest, Corporations ☞195.

In a business corporation, shares entitled to vote as a separate voting group may take action on a matter at a meeting only if a quorum of those shares exists with respect to that matter. Unless the articles of incorporation or the Business Corporation Law provide otherwise, a majority of the votes entitled to be cast on the matter by the voting group constitutes a quorum of that voting group for action on that matter.[82] The articles of incorporation may provide for a greater quorum or voting requirement for shareholders or voting groups of shareholders than is provided for by the statute.[83]

In a not-for-profit corporation, 10% of the votes entitled to be cast on a matter constitutes a quorum for action on the matter.[84] A not-for-profit corporation's articles of incorporation or bylaws may be amended to decrease the quorum by approval of the members or, unless prohibited by the articles of incorporation or the bylaws, the board of directors;[85] an

---

[79]IC 23-17-11-3(a).
[80]IC 23-17-11-3(b).
[81]IC 23-17-11-4(d).
[82]IC 23-1-30-6(a).
[83]IC 23-1-30-8.
[84]IC 23-17-11-4(a).
[85]IC 23-17-11-4(b).

amendment to increase the quorum must be approved by the members.[86]

Once a share or vote is represented for any purpose at a shareholders' or members' meeting, it is deemed present for quorum purposes for the remainder of the meeting and for any adjournment of that meeting unless a new record date is or must be set for that adjourned meeting.[87]

If a quorum exists, action on a matter other than the election of directors by a voting group is approved if the votes cast within the voting group favoring the action exceed the votes cast opposing the action, unless the articles of incorporation or the applicable statute require a greater number of affirmative votes.[88]

§ 91 —Voting groups

A voting group is all shares of a class or series entitled to vote and be counted together.

West's Digest, Corporations ⇒197.

A voting group consists of all shares of one or more classes or series entitled to vote and be counted together collectively on a matter brought up at a shareholders' meeting.[89]

If the articles of incorporation or the Business Corporation Law provide for voting by a single voting group on a matter, action on that matter is taken when voted upon by that voting group.[90] If two or more voting groups are to vote on a matter, action on that matter is taken only when voted upon by each of those voting groups counted separately. A matter may be voted on by one voting group even though no vote is taken by another voting group entitled to vote on the matter.[91]

---

[86]IC 23-17-11-4(c).

[87]IC 23-1-30-6(b); IC 23-17-11-4(e).

[88]IC 23-1-30-6(c); IC 23-17-11-5(a).

For discussion of the election of directors, see § 97.

Annotation References: Validity, construction, and effect of provision in charter or bylaw requiring supermajority vote, 80 ALR4th 667.

[89]IC 23-1-20-28.

[90]IC 23-1-30-7(a).

[91]IC 23-1-30-7(b).

§ 92 —Special voting rights

Shareholders of a class or series of shares may vote on certain matters, even if they are nonvoting shares.

West's Digest, Corporations ⊕197.

The holders of the outstanding shares of a class or series of shares in a business corporation are entitled to vote as a separate voting group on a proposed amendment to the articles of incorporation, even if the shares are nonvoting shares, if the amendment would:[92]

(1) increase or decrease the aggregate number of authorized shares of the class; effect an exchange or reclassification of all or part of the shares of the class into shares of another class;

(2) effect an exchange or reclassification, or create the right of exchange, of all or part of the shares of another class into shares of the class;

(3) change the designation, rights, preferences, or limitations of all or part of the shares of the class;

(4) change the shares of all or part of the class into a different number of shares of the same class;

(5) create a new class of shares having rights or preferences with respect to distributions or to dissolution that are prior, superior, or substantially equal to the shares of the class;

(6) increase the rights, preferences, or number of authorized shares of any class that, after giving effect to the amendment, will have rights or preferences with respect to distributions or to dissolution that are prior, superior, or substantially equal to the shares of the class;

(7) limit or deny an existing preemptive right of all or part of the shares of the class; or

(8) cancel or otherwise affect rights to distributions or dividends that have accumulated but not yet been declared on all or part of the shares of the class.

If a proposed amendment that entitles two or more series of shares to vote as separate voting groups would affect those series in the same or a substantially similar way, the shares

---

[92]IC 23-1-38-4(a), (b), (d).

of all the series so affected must vote together as a single voting group on the proposed amendment.[93]

Unless a greater vote or a vote by voting groups is required by statute, the articles of incorporation, or the board of directors, an amendment to a business corporation's articles of incorporation must be approved by a majority of the votes entitled to be cast on the amendment by any voting group with respect to which the amendment would create dissenters' voting rights, and by the necessary votes of every other voting group entitled to vote on the amendment.[94]

The members of a class in a public benefit corporation may vote as a separate voting group on a proposed amendment to the bylaws, even if the articles of incorporation or bylaws provide that the class may not vote on the proposed amendment, if the amendment would change the rights of that class as to voting in a manner different from its effect on another class or members of another class.[95]

The members of a class in a mutual benefit corporation may vote as a separate voting group on a proposed amendment to the bylaws, even if the articles of incorporation or bylaws provide that the class may not vote on the proposed amendment, if the amendment would any of the following:[96]

- affect the rights, privileges, preferences, restrictions, or conditions of the class as to voting, dissolution, redemption, or transfer of memberships in a manner different than the amendment would affect another class
- change the rights, privileges, preferences, restrictions, or conditions of the class as to voting, privileges, preferences, restrictions, or conditions of another class
- increase or decrease the number of memberships authorized for the class
- increase the number of memberships authorized for another class
- effect an exchange, reclassification, or termination of all or part of the memberships of the class
- authorize a new class of memberships

---

[93] IC 23-1-38-4(c).
[94] IC 23-1-38-3(e).
[95] IC 23-17-18-2(a), (e).
[96] IC 23-17-18-2(b), (e).

The members of a class of a religious corporation may vote as a separate voting group on a proposed amendment to the bylaws only if a class vote is provided for in articles of incorporation or bylaws.[97]

§ 93 Proxy voting

Shareholders and members may vote by proxy.

West's Digest, Corporations ☞198(1)-198(6).

A shareholder or member may vote his or her shares or membership in person or by proxy.[98] Subject to the validity of the signature on the appointment of the proxy, and to express limitations in the appointment, a corporation is entitled to accept the proxy's vote or other action as that of the shareholder making the appointment.[99]

A shareholder or member may authorize a person or persons to act as his or her proxy by signing an appointment form, either personally or through his or her agent.[1] A business corporation shareholder may also appoint a proxy through a facsimile signature,[2] or through the transmission of an electronic submission, such as a voice mail or e-mail message or fax,[3] or by any other method allowed by law.[4]

A proxy appointment is effective when it is received by the corporation's secretary or other officer or agent authorized to tabulate votes; it is valid for 11 months, unless the appointment expressly provides a shorter or longer period.[5]

The appointment of a proxy in a not-for-profit corporation

---

[97]IC 23-17-18-2(c).

[98]IC 23-1-30-3(a); IC 23-17-11-6(a).

[99]IC 23-1-30-3(i); IC 23-17-11-6(f).

Annotation References: Misrepresentation in proxy solicitation—state cases, 20 ALR4th 1287.

Corporations: Power of inspectors of election relating to irregular or conflicting proxies, 44 ALR3d 1443.

[1]IC 23-1-30-3(b)(1)(A); IC 23-17-11-6(b).

Forms References: Proxies. 6A Am Jur Legal Forms 2d, Corporations §§ 74:1855-74:1862.

[2]IC 23-1-30-3(b)(1)(B).

[3]IC 23-1-30-3(b)(2); IC 23-1-30-3(c).

[4]IC 23-1-30-3(b)(3).

[5]IC 23-1-30-3(d); IC 23-17-11-6(c).

is revocable by the member.[6] In a business corporation, a shareholder may revoke a proxy unless the appointment conspicuously states that it is irrevocable and the appointment is coupled with an interest, such as a pledge, an agreement to purchase shares, an extension of credit, a clause in the proxy's contract of employment with the corporation requiring the appointment, or a voting agreement.[7] Such an appointment is revoked when the interest with which it is coupled is extinguished.[8] A purchaser of shares subject to an irrevocable appointment may revoke the appointment if he or she did not know of its existence when he or she acquired the shares, and the existence of the irrevocable appointment was not noted conspicuously on the certificate representing the shares or on the information statement for shares without certificates.[9]

The death or incapacity of the shareholder or member appointing a proxy does not affect the right of the corporation to accept the proxy's authority unless notice of the death or incapacity is received by the secretary or other officer or agent authorized to tabulate votes before the proxy exercises the proxy's authority under the appointment.[10]

§ 94   Acceptance of signature

A corporation may accept a signature on a vote or other document if the signature corresponds to the name of a shareholder or member.

West's Digest, Corporations ☞197.

A corporation acting in good faith is entitled to accept and give effect to a vote, consent, waiver, or proxy appointment if the signature on the document corresponds to the name of a shareholder or member.[11] If the signature does not correspond to the name of a shareholder or member, a corpora-

---

[6]IC 23-17-11-6(d).

[7]IC 23-1-30-3(e).

For discussion of voting agreements, see § 95.

Forms References: Revocation of proxy. 6A Am Jur Legal Forms 2d, Corporations §§ 74:1864, 74:1865.

[8]IC 23-1-30-3(g).

[9]IC 23-1-30-3(h).

[10]IC 23-1-30-3(f); IC 23-17-11-6(e).

[11]IC 23-1-30-5(a); IC 23-17-11-9(a).

tion acting in good faith may nonetheless accept and give effect to the document if any of the following apply:[12]

- the shareholder or member is an entity and the name purports to be that of an officer or agent of the entity
- the name purports to be that of an administrator, executor, guardian, or conservator representing a shareholder of a business corporation, or a member of a mutual benefit corporation, and, if the corporation requests, evidence of fiduciary status acceptable to the corporation has been presented with respect to the vote, consent, waiver, or proxy appointment
- the name purports to be that of a receiver or trustee in bankruptcy of a shareholder of a business corporation, or a member of a mutual benefit corporation, and, if the corporation requests, evidence of this status acceptable to the corporation has been presented with respect to the vote, consent, waiver, or proxy appointment
- the name purports to be that of a pledgee, beneficial owner, or attorney-in-fact of a shareholder, or an attorney-in-fact of a member, and, if the corporation requests, evidence acceptable to the corporation of the person's authority to act for the shareholder or member has been presented with respect to the vote, consent, waiver, or proxy appointment
- a shareholder or member consists of two or more persons as cotenants or fiduciaries and the name purports to be the name of at least one of the co-owners, and the person acting appears to be acting on behalf of all the co-owners

The inspectors or the persons making a determination of the validity of proxies submitted in a business corporation shall specify the information upon which they rely in determining the validity of a proxy.[13] A business or not-for-profit corporation is entitled to reject a vote, consent, waiver, or proxy appointment if the secretary or other officer or agent authorized to tabulate votes, acting in good faith, has reasonable basis for doubt about the validity of the signature on a writing or about the signatory's authority to sign for the

---

[12]IC 23-1-30-5(b); IC 23-17-11-9(b).

[13]IC 23-1-30-5(c).

shareholder or member.[14] A business corporation may also
reject such a document if the officer, acting in good faith, has
reasonable basis to doubt the validity of an electronic
submission or the submitter's authority to make the electronic transmission.[15] Neither a corporation nor an officer
who properly accepts or rejects a vote, consent, waiver, or
proxy appointment may be held liable in damages to the
shareholder or member for the consequences of the acceptance or rejection.[16] Corporate action based on the acceptance or rejection of a vote, consent, waiver, or proxy appointment is valid unless a court of competent jurisdiction
determines otherwise.[17]

§ 95 Voting trusts and voting agreements

**Shareholders may transfer their votes to a trustee, or
may agree as to how their votes will be cast.**

West's Digest, Corporations ⊶198.1(1)-199.

A voting trust confers on the trustee the right to vote or
otherwise act for one or more shareholders. A shareholder or
shareholders may create a voting trust by signing an agreement setting out the provisions of the trust and transferring
their shares to the trustee. The trustee is then to prepare a
list showing the names and addresses of the owners of beneficial interests in the trust and the number and classes of
shares each owner has transferred to the trust, and deliver
copies of the list and agreement to the corporation's principal
office.[18] A voting trust cannot be created by will.[19]

A voting trust becomes effective on the date the first shares
subject to the trust are registered in the trustee's name, and
generally may not be made irrevocable for a period of more
than 10 years after its effective date unless the rights
granted by the trust are coupled with an interest in the

---

[14]IC 23-1-30-5(c)(1); IC 23-17-11-9(c).

[15]IC 23-1-30-5(c)(2).

[16]IC 23-1-30-5(d); IC 23-17-11-9(d).

[17]IC 23-1-30-5(e); IC 23-17-11-9(e).

[18]IC 23-1-31-1(a).

Forms References: Voting trust agreements. 6A Am Jur Legal
Forms 2d, Corporations §§ 74:1883-74:1885.

[19]Matter of Carl F. Bettner Trust, 495 N.E.2d 194, 77 A.L.R.4th 1187
(Ind. Ct. App. 1st Dist. 1986).

shares to which the rights relate. The rights are considered to be coupled with an interest in the shares if they are reserved or given in connection with:[20]

    (1) an option, authority, or contract to buy or sell the shares or part of the shares, a pledge of the shares or part of the shares to secure the performance or nonperformance of any act;

    (2) the performance or nonperformance of any act, or an agreement therefor, by the corporation issuing the shares; or

    (3) any other act or thing constituting an interest sufficient in law to support a power coupled with it.

A voting trust agreement may provide for extension of the trustee's rights for additional periods of not more than 10 years each if the beneficial owners of the shares assent in writing to the extension.[21] If an irrevocable voting trust is extended, the voting trustee must deliver copies of the extension agreement and list of beneficial owners to the corporation's principal office. An extension agreement binds only those parties signing it.[22]

Two or more shareholders may also sign an agreement as to the manner in which they will vote their shares. Such an agreement is not subject to the rules governing voting trusts, and is specifically enforceable.[23]

VII. DIRECTORS, OFFICERS, AND AGENTS

A. IN GENERAL

Research References

IC 23-1-30-9; IC 23-1-33-1 to IC 23-1-33-9; IC 23-1-36-1; IC 23-1-36-3; IC 23-1-36-4; IC 23-17-11-7; IC 23-17-11-8; IC 23-17-12-1 to IC 23-17-12-14; IC 23-17-14-1; IC 23-17-14-3; IC 23-17-14-4

18B Am Jur 2d, Corporations §§ 1341-1683.
19 C.J.S., Corporations §§ 433-459.
West's Digest, Corporations ☞281-295.
ALR Digest: Corporations §§ 114-117, 159-164

---

[20] IC 23-1-31-1(b).

[21] IC 23-1-31-1(b).

[22] IC 23-1-31-1(c).

[23] IC 23-1-31-2.

Forms References: Voting agreements. 6A Am Jur Legal Forms 2d, Corporations §§ 74:1881, 74:1825.

ALR Index: Articles of Incorporation; Assets; Bylaws; Charter;
    Close Corporation; Consolidation or Merger; Corporate Bonds
    and Bondholders; Corporate Officers, Directors, and Agents;
    Corporate Opportunity; Corporate Responsibility Doctrine;
    Corporate Stock and Stockholders; Corporations; Dissolution or
    Liquidation; Dividends; Domicile and Residence; Foreign
    Corporations; Forfeitures; Liquidation or Dissolution; Minority
    Stockholders; Names; Nonprofit Institutions or Organizations;
    Professional Corporations and Associations; Promoters; Prospec-
    tus; Proxies; Reports; Seal; Stock-Option Plans; Subsidiary
6A Am Jur Legal Forms 2d, Corporations §§ 74:1582, 74:1583,
    74:1603, 74:1614, 74:1615.

§ 96   Generally

**A corporation must have a board of directors or some
person to perform the board's duties.**

West's Digest, Corporations ☜281, 282.

A not-for-profit corporation, or a business corporation with
more than fifty shareholders, must have a board of directors.[24] A business corporation with 50 or fewer shareholders
may dispense with the board of directors or limit the authority of the board by describing in its articles of incorporation
who will perform some or all of the duties of the board of
directors.[25]

A business corporation's board of directors must consist of
one or more individuals, with the number specified in, or
fixed in accordance with, the articles of incorporation or
bylaws.[26] The articles of incorporation may establish a range
for the number of directors by fixing a minimum and
maximum number. If such a range is established, the
number of directors may be fixed or changed from time to
time within that range by the board of directors.[27]

A not-for-profit corporation's board of directors must have
at least three members, with the number specified in, or fixed
in accordance with, the articles of incorporation or bylaws.[28]
This number may be increased or decreased by an amendment to, or in a manner prescribed by, the articles of

---

[24]IC 23-1-33-1(a), (c); IC 23-17-12-1(a).

[25]IC 23-1-33-1(c).

[26]IC 23-1-33-3(a).

[27]IC 23-1-33-3(b).

[28]IC 23-17-12-3(a).

incorporation or bylaws, but the number may not be less than three.[29]

A corporation's articles of incorporation or bylaws may prescribe qualifications for the corporation's directors.[30] A director of a not-for-profit corporation must be an individual.[31] Unless the articles of incorporation or the bylaws so require, a director of a business corporation need not be an Indiana resident.[32]

§ 97   Election of directors

Directors are usually elected at the shareholders' or members' annual meeting.

West's Digest, Corporations ☞283(1), 283(2).

Directors of a business corporation are elected at the first annual shareholders' meeting and at each annual meeting thereafter unless their terms are staggered.[33] Unless the articles of incorporation provide otherwise, directors are elected by a plurality of the votes cast by the shares or members entitled to vote in the election at a meeting at which a quorum is present.[34]

If a not-for-profit corporation has members, all of its directors except the initial directors are to be elected at the first annual members' meeting, and at each annual meeting thereafter, unless the articles of incorporation or bylaws provide another time or method of election, or provide for the appointment or designation of directors by another person.[35] If the corporation does not have members, all the directors except the initial directors are to be elected, designated,

---

[29]IC 23-17-12-3(b).

Forms References: Shareholders' resolution—Increase in number of directors. 6A Am Jur Legal Forms 2d, Corporations § 74:1582.

Shareholders' resolution—Reduction in number of directors. 6A Am Jur Legal Forms 2d, Corporations § 74:1583.

[30]IC 23-1-33-2; IC 23-17-12-2(b).

[31]IC 23-17-12-2(a).

[32]IC 23-1-33-2.

[33]IC 23-1-33-3(c).

For discussion of annual meetings, see § 81.

For discussion of directors' terms of office, see § 100.

[34]IC 23-1-30-9(a); IC 23-17-11-7(a).

[35]IC 23-17-12-4(a).

or appointed as provided in the articles of incorporation or bylaws. If a method of election, designation, or appointment is not set forth in articles of incorporation or bylaws, the directors other than the initial directors shall be elected by the board of directors.[36]

§ 98 —Cumulative voting

If the articles of incorporation so provide, shareholders or members may cumulate their votes for directors.

West's Digest, Corporations ☞283(2).

Votes may not be cumulated unless the articles of incorporation provide otherwise.[37] If, however, the articles of incorporation provide that the members or shareholders, or a designated group or class of members or shareholders, are entitled to cumulate their votes for directors, the designated shareholders or members may multiply the number of votes they are entitled to cast by the number of directors for whom they are entitled to vote, and cast that number of votes for a single candidate, or distribute the votes among two or more candidates.[38] Cumulative voting is not permitted at a particular meeting unless the meeting notice or proxy statement accompanying the notice of the meeting states conspicuously that cumulative voting is authorized, or a member or shareholder who has the right to cumulate votes gives at least 48-hours notice to the corporation of his or her intent to cumulate his or her votes during the meeting. If one shareholder or member gives this notice, all other shareholders in the same voting group or members in the same class participating in the election are entitled to cumulate their votes without giving further notice.[39]

Members of a not-for-profit corporation may not vote cumulatively if the directors and members are identical.[40]

§ 99 —Election by classes or units

Directors may be elected by specified classes of shares, or by members on the basis of an organizational or geographic unit.

[36]IC 23-17-12-4(b).
[37]IC 23-1-30-9(b); IC 23-17-11-7(b).
[38]IC 23-1-30-9(c); IC 23-17-11-7(c).
[39]IC 23-1-30-9(d); IC 23-17-11-7(d).
[40]IC 23-17-11-7(f).

West's Digest, Corporations ☞283(2).

A business corporation's articles of incorporation may authorize the election of all or a specified number of directors by the holders of one or more classes of shares. Each class entitled to elect one or more directors is a separate voting group for purposes of electing directors.[41]

A not-for-profit corporation's articles of incorporation may provide that directors are to be elected:[42]

(1) on the basis of a chapter or other organizational unit;

(2) by region or other geographic unit;

(3) by preferential voting; or

(4) by any other reasonable method.

§ 100 Directors' term of office

Generally, directors of business corporations are elected for one year; directors of not-for-profit corporations may serve for up to five years.

West's Digest, Corporations ☞291.

The terms of the initial directors of a business corporation expire at the first shareholders meeting at which directors are elected.[43] The terms of all other directors of a business corporation expire at the next annual shareholders meeting following their election unless their terms are staggered.[44] A decrease in the number of directors does not shorten an incumbent director's term.[45] The term of a director elected to fill a vacancy expires at the end of the term for which the director's predecessor was elected.[46]

In a not-for-profit corporation, the articles of incorporation or bylaws must specify the directors' terms of office, which are not to exceed five years unless the director is designated or appointed. If no term is specified, the term is one year. Directors may be elected for successive terms.[47] Subject to the provisions for removal of a director, a decrease in the

---

[41]IC 23-1-33-4.

[42]IC 23-17-11-8.

[43]IC 23-1-33-5(a).

[44]IC 23-1-33-5(b).

[45]IC 23-1-33-5(c).

[46]IC 23-1-33-5(d).

[47]IC 23-17-12-5(a).

number of directors or term of office does not shorten an incumbent director's term.[48] Unless the articles of incorporation or bylaws provide otherwise, the term of a director filling a vacancy in the office of a director elected by members expires at the next election of directors by members, and the term of a director filling any other vacancy expires at the end of the unexpired term that the director is filling.[49]

Despite the expiration of his or her term, a director in either a business or a not-for-profit corporation continues to serve until a successor is elected and qualifies or until there is a decrease in the number of directors.[50]

§ 101   —Staggered terms

The articles of incorporation or bylaws of a corporation may provide for staggered directors' terms.

West's Digest, Corporations ☞291.

The articles of incorporation of a business corporation, or the bylaws, if they are authorized to do so, may provide for staggered directors' terms by dividing the directors into two roughly equal groups, or three if there are more than two directors.[51] The terms of directors in the first group expire at the first annual shareholders meeting after their election, the terms of the second group expire at the second annual shareholders meeting after their election, and the terms of the third group, if any, expire at the third annual shareholders meeting after their election. At each annual shareholders meeting held thereafter, directors shall be chosen for a term of two or three years to succeed those whose terms expire.[52]

In a not-for-profit corporation, the directors' terms may be staggered by dividing the directors into an unspecified number of groups. The terms of office of each group of directors need not be uniform.[53]

§ 102   Election or appointment of officers

A business corporation must have at least one officer, while a not-for-profit corporation must have at least three.

---

[48]IC 23-17-12-5(b).

[49]IC 23-17-12-5(c).

[50]IC 23-1-33-5(e); IC 23-17-12-5(d).

[51]IC 23-1-33-6(a).

[52]IC 23-1-33-6(b).

[53]IC 23-17-12-6.

West's Digest, Corporations ☞284.

A business corporation's officers are as described in the bylaws, or as elected or appointed by the directors or an officer in accordance with the bylaws.[54] When the election of officers is by the directors, strict observance of all formalities is not required.[55] Each business corporation must have at least one officer.[56] A not-for-profit corporation, unless its articles of incorporation or bylaws provide otherwise, must have a president, a secretary, a treasurer, and other officers as appointed by the board of directors.[57] One of the officers, to be considered the secretary, is to be responsible for preparing minutes of the directors' and shareholders' or members' meetings and for authenticating the corporation's records.[58] The same individual may hold more than one office in a corporation.[59]

The election or appointment of an officer does not create contract rights.[60]

§ 103 Resignation of director

A director may resign by delivering written notice to the board or a corporate officer.

West's Digest, Corporations ☞292.

A director of a business corporation may resign at any time by delivering written notice to the board of directors, the chairman of the board of directors, the secretary of the corporation, or another designated officer, if the articles of incorporation or bylaws so provide.[61]

In a not-for-profit corporation, the written notice of resignation must be delivered to the board of directors, the presid-

---

[54]IC 23-1-36-1(a), (b).

[55]Shaw v. Bankers' Nat. Life Ins. Co., 61 Ind. App. 346, 112 N.E. 16 (Div. 2 1916).

[56]IC 23-1-36-1(a).

[57]IC 23-17-14-1(a).

[58]IC 23-1-36-1(c); IC 23-17-14-1(b).

[59]IC 23-1-36-1(d); IC 23-17-14-1(c).

[60]IC 23-1-36-4(a); IC 23-17-14-4(a)

[61]IC 23-1-33-7(a).

Forms References: Resignation of director. 6A Am Jur Legal Forms 2d, Corporations §§ 74:1614, 74:1615.

ing officer of the board of directors, or the president or secretary of the corporation.[62]

The resignation is effective when the notice is delivered unless the notice specifies a later date.[63] If the resignation of a director of a not-for-profit corporation is made effective at a later date, the board of directors may fill the pending vacancy before the effective date if the board provides that the successor will not take office until the effective date of the resignation.[64]

§ 104 Removal of director

A director may be removed by the shareholders, members, or directors of a corporation.

West's Digest, Corporations ☞294.

A director of a business corporation may be removed in any manner provided in the articles of incorporation.[65] The shareholders, members, or directors of either a business corporation or a not-for-profit corporation may remove a director without cause unless the articles of incorporation provide otherwise.[66] The members may remove the entire board of a not-for-profit corporation.[67] If a director was elected by a voting group of shareholders, or an organizational or geographic group of members, only that group may participate in a vote to remove the director.[68]

A director may be removed by the shareholders or members only at a meeting called for the purpose of removing the director. The meeting notice must state that the purpose, or one of the purposes, of the meeting is removal of the director.[69]

In a business corporation, if cumulative voting is authorized, a director may not be removed if the number of

---

[62]IC 23-17-12-7(a).

[63]IC 23-1-33-7(b); IC 23-17-12-7(b).

[64]IC 23-17-12-7(b).

[65]IC 23-1-33-8(a).

[66]IC 23-1-33-8(a); IC 23-17-12-8(a).

Forms References: Shareholders' resolution removing director. 6A Am Jur Legal Forms 2d, Corporations § 74:1603.

[67]IC 23-17-12-8(g).

[68]IC 23-1-33-8(b); IC 23-17-12-8(b).

[69]IC 23-1-33-8(d); IC 23-17-12-8(e).

votes sufficient to elect the director under cumulative voting is voted against the director's removal. If cumulative voting is not authorized, a director may be removed only if the number of votes cast to remove the director exceeds the number of votes cast not to remove the director.[70]

Generally, a director of a not-for-profit corporation may be removed by its members only if the number of votes cast to remove the director would be sufficient to elect the director at a meeting to elect directors.[71] If cumulative voting is authorized, a director may not be removed if the number of votes, or of votes of a group which elected the director, sufficient to elect the director under cumulative voting is voted against the director's removal,[72] or if the entire number of directors authorized at the time of the director's most recent election were then being elected.[73] In determining if a director is protected from removal under these provisions, it is assumed that the votes against removal are cast in an election for the number of directors of the class to which the director to be removed belonged on the date of the director's election.[74]

In a not-for-profit corporation, a director elected by the board of directors may be removed with or without cause by the vote of a majority of the directors then in office, unless a greater number is set forth in articles of incorporation or bylaws. However, a director elected by the board of directors to fill the vacancy of a director elected by the members may be removed without cause by the members but not by the board of directors.[75] A majority of the directors in office may remove a director for reasons set forth in the articles of incorporation or bylaws, if at the beginning of the director's term of office the articles of incorporation or bylaws provided that the director may be removed for such reasons.[76]

A religious corporation's articles of incorporation or bylaws may limit the application of the provisions pertaining to re-

---

[70]IC 23-1-33-8(c).

For discussion of cumulative voting, see § 98.

[71]IC 23-17-12-8(c).

[72]IC 23-17-11-7(e); IC 23-17-12-8(d).

[73]IC 23-17-11-7(e).

[74]IC 23-17-12-8(f).

[75]IC 23-17-12-9.

[76]IC 23-17-12-10.

moval of directors, or set forth the vote and procedures by which the board of directors or a person may remove, with or without cause, a director elected by the members or the board of directors.[77]

A designated director of a not-for-profit corporation may be removed by an amendment to articles of incorporation or bylaws deleting or changing the designation.[78] Except as provided in articles of incorporation or bylaws, an appointed director may be removed with or without cause by the person appointing the director. The person removing the director must do so by giving written notice of the removal to the director, and to the presiding officer of the board of directors or the corporation's president or secretary. The removal is effective upon notice, unless the notice specifies a future effective date.[79]

§ 105   —Court order

A director of a not-for-profit corporation may be removed by court order.

West's Digest, Corporations ☞294.

A director of a not-for-profit corporation may be removed by court order in a proceeding commenced in the circuit or superior court of the county in which the corporation's principal office located by the corporation, or by at least 10% of the members of a class entitled to vote for directors, if the court finds that:[80]

(1) the director engaged in fraudulent or dishonest conduct, or gross abuse of his or her authority or discretion, with respect to the corporation;

(2) a final judgment has been entered finding that the director has violated a statutory standard of conduct; or

(3) removal is in the best interests of the corporation.

A court that removes a director may bar the director from serving on the board of directors for a period prescribed by

---

[77]IC 23-17-12-11.

[78]IC 23-17-12-12(a).

[79]IC 23-17-12-12(b).

[80]IC 23-17-12-13(a).

the court.[81] The corporation must be made a party defendant to a proceeding for such a court order.[82] The articles of incorporation or bylaws of a religious corporation may limit or prohibit the application of the provisions pertaining to removal of a director by court order.[83]

§ 106   Vacancies on board of directors

> **A vacancy on the board of directors may be filled by the directors, shareholders, or members.**

West's Digest, Corporations ⊶295.

Unless the articles of incorporation or bylaws provide otherwise, if a vacancy on the board of directors, including one resulting from an increase in the number of directors, occurs, the board of directors or the shareholders or members may fill the vacancy. If the directors remaining in office constitute fewer than a quorum of the board, they may fill the vacancy by the affirmative vote of a majority of all the directors remaining in office.[84] If the vacant office was held by a director elected by a voting group of shareholders, or a group of members, only the holders of shares of that voting group or the members of that group are entitled to vote to fill the vacancy if it is filled by the shareholders or members.[85]

Unless the articles of incorporation or bylaws of a not-for-profit corporation provide otherwise, if a vacant office was held by an appointed director, only the person who appointed the director may fill the vacancy.[86] If a vacant office was held by a designated director, the vacancy must be filled as provided in articles of incorporation or bylaws. In the absence of an applicable article of incorporation or bylaw, the vacancy may not be filled by the board of directors.[87]

A vacancy that will occur at a specific later date because of a resignation effective at a later date may be filled before the

---

[81]IC 23-17-12-13(b).

[82]IC 23-17-12-13(c).

[83]IC 23-17-12-13(d).

[84]IC 23-1-33-9(a); IC 23-17-12-14(a).

[85]IC 23-1-33-9(b); IC 23-17-12-14(a)(1).

[86]IC 23-17-12-14(b).

[87]IC 23-17-12-14(c).

vacancy occurs. However, the new director may not take office until the vacancy occurs.[88]

§ 107 Removal and resignation of officers

Officers may resign at any time, and may be removed by the board of directors.

West's Digest, Corporations ☞292, 294.

A corporate officer may resign at any time by delivering notice to the board of directors, the chairperson of the board, or the secretary of the corporation, or to another officer designated in the articles of incorporation or bylaws.[89] A resignation is effective when the notice is delivered unless the notice specifies a later effective date. If a resignation is made effective at a later date and the corporation accepts the future effective date, the board of directors may fill the pending vacancy before the effective date if the board of directors provides that the successor does not take office until the effective date of the resignation.[90]

A corporation's board of directors may remove any officer at any time with or without cause.[91] Similarly, an officer who appoints another officer or assistant officer may remove the appointed officer or assistant officer at any time with or without cause.[92]

An officer's removal or resignation does not affect his or her contract rights, if any, with the corporation, or the corporation's contract rights, if any, with the officer.[93]

A claimant of a corporate office may be enjoined by one occupying such office under claim of right from purporting or assuming to act as holder of the office until he or she establishes his or her title thereto in an action at law,

---

[88]IC 23-1-33-9(c); IC 23-17-12-14(d).

[89]IC 23-1-36-3(a); IC 23-17-14-3(a).

Forms References: Resignation of officer. 6A Am Jur Legal Forms 2d, Corporations §§ 74:1612, 74:1613.

[90]IC 23-1-36-3(b); IC 23-17-14-3(b).

[91]IC 23-1-36-3(c); IC 23-17-14-3(c).

Forms References: Directors' resolution removing officer. 6A Am Jur Legal Forms 2d, Corporations § 74:1604.

[92]IC 23-1-36-3(d); IC 23-17-14-3(d).

[93]IC 23-1-36-4(b); IC 23-17-14-4(b).

thereby protecting the incumbent's possession from any unlawful intrusion.[94]

B.   AUTHORITY AND FUNCTIONS

Research References

IC 23-1-22-3; IC 23-1-33-1; IC 23-1-34-1; IC 23-1-34-2; IC 23-1-34-4 to IC 23-1-34-6; IC 23-1-36-2; IC 23-17-12-1; IC 23-17-14-2; IC 23-17-15-1 to IC 23-17-15-6

18B Am Jur 2d, Corporations §§ 1483-1634.
19 C.J.S., Corporations §§ 460-474.
West's Digest, Corporations ⇔296-306.
ALR Digest: Corporations §§ 118-129, 159-164
ALR Index: Articles of Incorporation; Assets; Bylaws; Charter; Close Corporation; Consolidation or Merger; Corporate Bonds and Bondholders; Corporate Officers, Directors, and Agents; Corporate Opportunity; Corporate Responsibility Doctrine; Corporate Stock and Stockholders; Corporations; Dissolution or Liquidation; Dividends; Domicile and Residence; Foreign Corporations; Forfeitures; Liquidation or Dissolution; Minority Stockholders; Names; Nonprofit Institutions or Organizations; Professional Corporations and Associations; Promoters; Prospectus; Proxies; Reports; Seal; Stock-Option Plans; Subsidiary
6A Am Jur Legal Forms 2d, Corporations §§ 74:1694, 74:1696.

§ 108   Generally

The board of directors exercises the corporation's powers and directs the management of its affairs.

West's Digest, Corporations ⇔296.

All of a corporation's powers are to be exercised by or under the authority of, and the corporation's business and affairs managed under the direction of, its board of directors, subject to any limitations in the articles of incorporation.[95]

Each officer of a corporation has the authority and must perform the duties set forth in the bylaws and, to the extent consistent with the bylaws, the duties prescribed by the board of directors or by an officer authorized by the board of

---

[94]Grothe v. Herschbach, 153 Ind. App. 224, 286 N.E.2d 868 (3d Dist. 1972).

[95]IC 23-1-33-1(b); IC 23-17-12-1(b).

Cole Real Estate Corp. v. Peoples Bank & Trust Co., 160 Ind. App. 88, 310 N.E.2d 275 (3d Dist. 1974) (law invests board of directors with broad discretion in management of corporation and operation of its business).

directors to prescribe the duties of other officers.[96] An agent, including a corporate officer, has no authority to act contrary to the known wishes and instructions of his or her principal, the corporation.[97]

§ 109   Emergency powers

The directors of business corporations are also granted emergency powers.

West's Digest, Corporations ☞297.

The directors of business corporations are also granted emergency powers, which they may exercise when an extraordinary event prevents a quorum of the corporation's directors from assembling in time to deal with the business for which a meeting has been or is to be called.[98] During or in anticipation of such an emergency, the directors may modify the corporation's lines of succession to accommodate the incapacity of any director, officer, employee, or agent, and relocate the corporation's principal office, designate alternative principal offices or regional officer, or authorize the officers to do so.[99]

During an emergency, notice of a board meeting need be given only to those directors whom it is practicable to reach, and may be given in any practicable manner, including by publication and radio broadcast.[1] One or more of the corporation's officers present at a board meeting during an emergency may be deemed to be directors for the meeting, in order of rank and within the same rank in order of seniority, as necessary to achieve a quorum.[2]

Corporate action taken in good faith, in accordance with the statute, to further the ordinary business affairs of the corporation is binding on the corporation, and may not be used to impose liability on a corporate director, officer, employee, or agent.[3]

---

[96] IC 23-1-36-2; IC 23-17-14-2.

[97] Menard, Inc. v. Dage-MTI, Inc., 698 N.E.2d 1227 (Ind. Ct. App. 1998).

[98] IC 23-1-22-3(a), (d).

[99] IC 23-1-22-3(a).

[1] IC 23-1-22-3(b)(1).

[2] IC 23-1-22-3(b)(2).

[3] IC 23-1-22-3(c).

§ 110 Directors' meetings

Directors may hold regular or special meetings.

West's Digest, Corporations ☞298(.5)-298(7).

A corporate board of directors may hold regular or special meetings inside or outside of Indiana.[4] A regular meeting is one whose time and place is fixed by the bylaws or the board of directors. All other meetings are special meetings.[5] Unless the articles of incorporation or bylaws provide otherwise, the board may permit any or all of the directors to participate in a meeting by, or conduct a meeting through the use of, any means of communication by which all directors participating may simultaneously hear each other during the meeting. A director participating in a meeting by such means is considered to be present in person at the meeting.[6]

A director cannot vote by proxy.[7]

§ 111 —Action taken without meeting

Directors may act without a meeting if the action is taken by all directors.

West's Digest, Corporations ☞297.

Unless the articles of incorporation or bylaws provide otherwise, action required or permitted to be taken at a board of directors' meeting may be taken without a meeting if the action is taken by all members of the board. The action must be evidenced by at least one written consent describing the action taken, signed by each director, and included in the minutes or filed with the corporate records reflecting the action taken.[8] Action taken without a meeting, in the manner allowed by this provision is effective when the last director signs the consent, unless the consent specifies a different effective date.[9] A consent signed by a director has the effect

---

[4]IC 23-1-34-1(a); IC 23-17-15-1(b).

[5]IC 23-17-15-1(a).

[6]IC 23-1-34-1(b); IC 23-17-15-1(c).

[7]Dowdle v. Central Brick Co., 206 Ind. 242, 189 N.E. 145 (1934).

[8]IC 23-1-34-2(a); IC 23-17-15-2(a).

[9]IC 23-1-34-2(b); IC 23-17-15-2(b).

of a vote cast at a meeting, and may be described as such in any document.[10]

§ 112 —Notice of meetings

Directors must be given at least two days notice of special meetings, but may waive any required notice.

West's Digest, Corporations ⇔298(3).

Regular board meetings may be held without notice of the date, time, place, or purpose of the meeting, unless the articles of incorporation or bylaws provide otherwise.[11] A special meeting of the board must be preceded by at two days notice of the date, time, and place of the meeting, but the notice need not describe the purpose of the meeting, unless the articles of incorporation or bylaws provide otherwise.[12]

Unless the articles of incorporation or bylaws of a not-for-profit corporation provide otherwise, the presiding officer of a board of directors, the corporation's president, or 20% of the directors in office may call and give notice of a meeting of the board of directors.[13]

A director may waive any required notice of a meeting. Generally, the waiver must be in writing, signed by the director entitled to notice, and filed with the minutes or corporate records.[14] A director's attendance at or participation in a meeting also waives any required notice to the director, unless the director at the beginning of the meeting, or promptly upon his or her arrival at the meeting, objects to holding the meeting or transacting business at the meeting and does not thereafter vote for or assent to action taken at the meeting.[15]

§ 113 —Quorum

A quorum is generally a majority of the directors, and an

---

[10]IC 23-1-34-2(c); IC 23-17-15-2(c).

[11]IC 23-1-34-3(a); IC 23-17-15-3(a).

[12]IC 23-1-34-3(b); IC 23-17-15-3(b).

Forms References: Notice of special meeting. 6A Am Jur Legal Forms 2d, Corporations § 74:1694.

[13]IC 23-17-15-3(c).

[14]IC 23-1-34-4(a); IC 23-17-15-4(a).

Forms References: Waiver of notice and consent to meeting. 6A Am Jur Legal Forms 2d, Corporations § 74:1696.

[15]IC 23-1-34-4(b); IC 23-17-15-4(b).

act taken by the directors when a quorum is present is an act of the corporation.

West's Digest, Corporations ☞298(5).

In a business corporation, a quorum of the board of directors consists of a majority of the number of directors, if the board has a fixed size.[16] If the board has a variable size, a quorum is a majority of the number prescribed, or, if no number is prescribed, a majority of the number of directors in office immediately before the meeting begins.[17] The articles of incorporation or bylaws may require a greater number for a quorum,[18] and may authorize a quorum to consist of no fewer than one-third of the fixed, actual, or prescribed number of directors as determined under the preceding sentences.[19]

In the case of a not-for-profit corporation, except as provided in the Nonprofit Corporation Act, articles of incorporation, or bylaws, a quorum of a board of director consists of a majority of the directors in office immediately before a meeting begins. The articles of incorporation or bylaws may not authorize a quorum of fewer then one-third of the directors in office or two directors, whichever is greater.[20]

Unless the articles of incorporation or bylaws provide otherwise, the affirmative vote of a majority of directors present is an act of the board of directors, either of a business or a not-for-profit corporation, as long as a quorum is present.[21] In a business corporation, a director who is present at a board or committee meeting when corporate action is taken is deemed to have assented to the action unless any of the following occur:[22]

- the director objects at the beginning of the meeting, or promptly upon his or her arrival, to holding the meeting or transacting business at it
- the director's dissent or abstention from the action taken is entered in the minutes of the meeting

---

[16] IC 23-1-34-5(a)(1).

[17] IC 23-1-34-5(a)(2).

[18] IC 23-1-34-5(a).

[19] IC 23-1-34-5(b).

[20] IC 23-17-15-5(a).

[21] IC 23-1-34-5(c); IC 23-17-15-5(b).

[22] IC 23-1-34-5(d).

- the director delivers written notice of his or her dissent or abstention to the presiding officer of the meeting before the meeting's adjournment, or to the secretary of the corporation immediately after adjournment

The right of dissent or abstention is not available to a director who votes in favor of the action taken.[23]

§ 114 —Committees

**A board of directors may appoint committees to exercise
the board's authority, within certain limitations.**

West's Digest, Corporations ☞299.

Unless the articles of incorporation or bylaws provide
otherwise, a board of directors may create one or more committees and appoint at least two members of the board to
serve on them.[24] A committee created by a business corporation may have one or more members who serve at the pleasure of the board of directors.[25] The creation of a committee
and appointment of its members must be approved by the
greater of a majority of all the directors in office when the
action is taken, or a majority of directors present as long as
a quorum is present.[26] Committees are governed by the rules
discussed above pertaining to board meetings, action without
meetings, notice, and quorum and voting requirements.[27]

To the extent specified by the board of directors, or in the
articles of incorporation or bylaws, a committee may exercise
the authority of the board of directors.[28] However, a business
corporation's committee may not do any of the following:[29]

- authorize distributions, except that a committee, or
  an executive officer of the corporation designated by
  the board of directors, may authorize or approve a
  reacquisition of shares or other distribution if done according to a formula or method, or within a range,
  prescribed by the board of directors

---

[23]IC 23-1-34-5(d).

[24]IC 23-1-34-6(a); IC 23-17-15-6(a).

[25]IC 23-1-34-6(a).

[26]IC 23-1-34-6(b); IC 23-17-15-6(b).

[27]IC 23-1-34-6(c); IC 23-17-15-6(c).

[28]IC 23-1-34-6(d); IC 23-17-15-6(d).

For discussion of the board's authority and functions, see §§ 108 et
seq.

[29]IC 23-1-34-6(e).

- approve or propose to the shareholders action that must be approved by the shareholders
- fill vacancies on the board of directors or on any of its committees
- adopt, amend, or repeal bylaws
- approve a plan of merger not requiring shareholder approval
- authorize or approve the issuance or sale or a contract for sale of shares, or determine the designation and relative rights, preferences, and limitations of a class or series of shares, except within limits prescribed by the board of directors
- adopt, amend, or repeal the articles of incorporation

A committee of a not-for-profit corporation may not do any of the following:[30]

- authorize distributions
- approve or recommend to members the corporation's dissolution or merger, or the sale, pledge, or transfer of all or substantially all of the corporation's assets
- elect, appoint, or remove directors or fill vacancies on the board of directors or on a committee
- adopt, amend, or repeal articles of incorporation or bylaws

A not-for-profit corporation's articles of incorporation may authorize a person or a group of persons, or prescribe the manner of designating a person or a group of persons, to exercise some or all of the powers that would otherwise be exercised by a board of directors. To the extent authorized, the person or group of persons has the duties and responsibilities of the directors, and the directors are relieved to that extent from their duties and responsibilities. Persons appointed under this provision are considered directors for purposes of the statutory provisions pertaining to standards of conduct and indemnification for directors.[31]

---

[30]IC 23-17-15-6(e).

[31]IC 23-17-12-1(c).

For discussion of directors' standards of conduct, see § 117.

For discussion of indemnification of officers and directors, see § 121.

C. RIGHTS, DUTIES, AND LIABILITIES

Research References

IC 23-1-21-4; IC 23-1-33-10; IC 23-1-34-6; IC 23-1-35-1; IC 23-1-35-2; IC 23-1-35-4; IC 23-1-37-2; IC 23-1-37-7 to IC 23-1-37-15; IC 23-17-12-15; IC 23-17-13-1; IC 23-17-13-2; IC 23-17-13-4; IC 23-17-15-6; IC 23-17-16-2; IC 23-17-16-7 to IC 23-17-16-15

18B Am Jur 2d, Corporations §§ 1684-1989.
19 C.J.S., Corporations §§ 475-553.
West's Digest, Corporations ☜307-369.
ALR Digest: Corporations §§ 118-158
ALR Index: Articles of Incorporation; Assets; Bylaws; Charter; Close Corporation; Consolidation or Merger; Corporate Bonds and Bondholders; Corporate Officers, Directors, and Agents; Corporate Opportunity; Corporate Responsibility Doctrine; Corporate Stock and Stockholders; Corporations; Dissolution or Liquidation; Dividends; Domicile and Residence; Foreign Corporations; Forfeitures; Liquidation or Dissolution; Minority Stockholders; Names; Nonprofit Institutions or Organizations; Professional Corporations and Associations; Promoters; Prospectus; Proxies; Reports; Seal; Stock-Option Plans; Subsidiary
6A Am Jur Legal Forms 2d, Corporations § 74:1731.
Grounds for Disregarding the Corporate Entity and Piercing the Corporate Veil, 45 Am Jur POF3d 1; Liability of a Director to a Corporation for Mismanagement, 29 Am Jur POF3d 133.
Corporate Opportunity Doctrine—Fairness of Corporate Official's Acquisition of Business Opportunity, 30 Am Jur POF2d 291; Personal Liability of Corporate Officers on Promissory Note, 8 Am Jur POF2d 193; Oppressive Conduct by Majority Shareholders, Directors, or Those in Control of Corporation, 5 Am Jur POF2d 645; Reasonableness of Corporate Officer's Compensation, 4 Am Jur POF2d 425.

§ 115 Generally

Directors and officers owe a fiduciary duty to the corporation and the shareholders.

West's Digest, Corporations ☜307.

As a general rule, officers and directors owe a fiduciary duty to the corporation as well as corporate stockholders regarding matters that affect the general well-being of the corporation.[32] For instance, a corporate director acting for the corporation in the purchase of its own stock owes a fidu-

---

[32]Biberstine v. New York Blower Co., 625 N.E.2d 1308 (Ind. Ct. App.

ciary duty to the shareholder from whom the stock is purchased, and must disclose to the shareholder facts affecting the value of the stock.[33] This duty applies to not-for-profit corporations as well as business corporations.[34]

However, the fiduciary duty is imposed on directors and officers only regarding matters that affect the general well-being of the corporation. Where the actions of a director affect individual rights, rather than the interests of the corporation or stockholders generally, no fiduciary duty exists.[35] Thus, a corporate director who sells his or her personal shares or buys shares from other shareholders for his or her personal ownership owes no fiduciary duty to disclose information he or she possesses regarding the value of the stock to the other shareholders, provided that such a sale does not affect the general well-being of the corporation.[36]

Breach of a fiduciary duty may form the basis of a claim for constructive fraud. Constructive fraud consists of a duty existing by virtue of the parties' relationship, a representation or omission which violates that duty, and detrimental reliance on the representation or admission by the individ-

5th Dist. 1993), reh'g denied, (Jan. 24, 1994) and transfer dismissed, (Apr. 12, 1994); Yerke v. Batman, 176 Ind. App. 672, 376 N.E.2d 1211 (1st Dist. 1978).

[33]Hardy v. South Bend Sash & Door Co., Inc., 603 N.E.2d 895 (Ind. Ct. App. 3d Dist. 1992), reh'g denied, (Jan. 13, 1993) and transfer denied, (Mar. 24, 1993); Fleetwood Corp. v. Mirich, 404 N.E.2d 38 (Ind. Ct. App. 3d Dist. 1980) (disclosure of information from appraisal required where stock was acquired by director of corporation and value of stock depended on appraisal).

[34]Matter of Wabash Valley Power Ass'n, Inc., 72 F.3d 1305 (7th Cir. 1995) (applying Indiana law).

[35]Biberstine v. New York Blower Co., 625 N.E.2d 1308 (Ind. Ct. App. 5th Dist. 1993), reh'g denied, (Jan. 24, 1994) and transfer dismissed, (Apr. 12, 1994) (directors' termination of plaintiff's employment as vice-president, denial of access to corporate records, and exclusion from stock redemption offer was not breach of fiduciary duty, as actions bore no relation to management of corporate property and did not affect rights of shareholders generally); Yerke v. Batman, 176 Ind. App. 672, 376 N.E.2d 1211 (1st Dist. 1978).

[36]Hardy v. South Bend Sash & Door Co., Inc., 603 N.E.2d 895 (Ind. Ct. App. 3d Dist. 1992), reh'g denied, (Jan. 13, 1993) and transfer denied, (Mar. 24, 1993); Fleetwood Corp. v. Mirich, 404 N.E.2d 38 (Ind. Ct. App. 3d Dist. 1980).

ual to whom the duty is owed.[37] However, expressions of value used to arrive at a mutually agreed upon price are opinions and do not constitute misrepresentations of past or existing facts, and therefore cannot form the basis of a fraud claim.[38]

A director may owe a fiduciary duty to the corporation and shareholders in more than one capacity.[39]

A director charged with a breach of fiduciary duty has the burden of proving that he or she acted in good faith.[40]

> ◆ **Practice Guide:** Directors' actions in their official capacity, such as acquiring property or making loans to the corporation, are governed by the business judgment rule.[41] Directors acting as individuals may engage in distinct enterprises of the same general class of business as the corporation is engaged in, but may not wrongfully use the corporation's resources in such an enterprise or enter into a competing business of such a nature as to cripple or injure the corporation.[42] Likewise, a corporation

---

[37]Hardy v. South Bend Sash & Door Co., Inc., 603 N.E.2d 895 (Ind. Ct. App. 3d Dist. 1992), reh'g denied, (Jan. 13, 1993) and transfer denied, (Mar. 24, 1993); Medtech Corp. v. Indiana Ins. Co., 555 N.E.2d 844 (Ind. Ct. App. 1st Dist. 1990), transfer denied, (Oct. 18, 1990).

[38]Hardy v. South Bend Sash & Door Co., Inc., 603 N.E.2d 895 (Ind. Ct. App. 3d Dist. 1992), reh'g denied, (Jan. 13, 1993) and transfer denied, (Mar. 24, 1993).

[39]Hartung v. Architects Hartung/Odle/Burke, Inc., 157 Ind. App. 546, 301 N.E.2d 240, 13 U.C.C. Rep. Serv. (CBC) 308 (1st Dist. 1973)) (individual owed fiduciary duty as director and officer, and as shareholder of close corporation).

For discussion of the fiduciary duty among shareholders of close corporations, see § 72.

[40]Dotlich v. Dotlich, 475 N.E.2d 331 (Ind. Ct. App. 1st Dist. 1985), reh'g denied, (Apr. 23, 1985) and transfer denied, (July 3, 1985) (where director of close corporation retained title to real property ultimately belonging to corporation, director was required to show his actions were honest and in good faith); Zaring v. Kelly, 74 Ind. App. 581, 128 N.E. 657 (Div. 2 1920).

[41]§ 117.

[42]Central Ry. Signal Co. v. Longden, 194 F.2d 310 (7th Cir. 1952).

Trial Strategy References: Corporate Opportunity Doctrine— Fairness of Corporate Official's Acquisition of Business Opportunity, 30 Am Jur POF2d 291.

generally has no interest in its officers' and directors' private dealings in their stock holdings.[43]

§ 116 Compensation

The board of directors may fix the directors' compensation and determine what is fair and reasonable compensation for corporate officers.

West's Digest, Corporations ☞308.

The board of directors may fix the director's compensation unless the articles of incorporation or bylaws provide otherwise.[44] A director may be entitled to compensation under an implied contract, if he or she performs services clearly outside his or her ordinary duties as a director or officer under circumstances showing that it all of the parties understood that the services were to be paid for.[45]

The board of directors is to determine what is fair and reasonable compensation for corporate officers, and a court may not substitute its judgment for the director's decision.[46] If a shareholder challenges the officer's compensation, the shareholder has the burden of establishing that the compensation is unreasonable.[47]

◆ **Illustration:** Where expert evidence at the trial of an overcompensation claim showed that a corporation's officers had been undercompensated before 1986, and that in 1987, when they received increased compensation, total dividends paid were more than three times greater than in the preceding year, the minority shareholder plaintiff failed to show that the officers' increased compensation was unjust or oppressive, and it was not fraudulent where

---

[43]Pippenger v. McQuik's Oilube, Inc., 854 F. Supp. 1411 (S.D. Ind. 1994) (applying Indiana law).

[44]IC 23-1-33-10; IC 23-17-12-15.

[45]Kenner v. Whitelock, 152 Ind. 635, 53 N.E. 232 (1899); Huntington Fuel Co. v. McIlwaine, 41 Ind. App. 328, 82 N.E. 1001 (Div. 2 1907).

[46]Lowry v. Lowry, 590 N.E.2d 612 (Ind. Ct. App. 3d Dist. 1992), reh'g denied, (June 25, 1992) and transfer denied, (Sept. 10, 1992).

[47]Lowry v. Lowry, 590 N.E.2d 612 (Ind. Ct. App. 3d Dist. 1992), reh'g denied, (June 25, 1992) and transfer denied, (Sept. 10, 1992); Krukemeier v. Krukemeier Mach. & Tool Co., Inc., 551 N.E.2d 885 (Ind. Ct. App. 1st Dist. 1990).

the increase was granted in a board meeting with minutes available for the minority shareholder's inspection.[48]

An officer may be entitled to compensation under an implied contract, if he or she performs services clearly outside his or her ordinary duties as a director or officer under circumstances showing that it all of the parties understood that the services were to be paid for.[49] The remuneration of a manager or other officer may be designated as a certain share of, or commission on, the net profit of the company.[50]

> ◆ **Practice Guide:** Corporate officers often enter into "golden parachute" agreements to provide them a certain amount of security, such as continued employment or the payment of a lump sum, in the event of a change of corporate ownership.[51]

§ 117   Standard of conduct; business judgment rule

Directors must discharge their duties in good faith, with the care an ordinarily prudent person would exercise under similar circumstances, and in a manner the director reasonably believes to be in the corporation's best interests.

West's Digest, Corporations ☞312-317.

A corporate director must discharge his or her duties, including his or her duties as a committee member, in good faith, with the care an ordinarily prudent person would exercise under similar circumstances, and in a manner the director reasonably believes to be in the best interests of the

---

[48]Krukemeier v. Krukemeier Mach. & Tool Co., Inc., 551 N.E.2d 885 (Ind. Ct. App. 1st Dist. 1990).

[49]Kenner v. Whitelock, 152 Ind. 635, 53 N.E. 232 (1899); Greensboro & New Castle Junction Turnpike Co. v. Stratton, 120 Ind. 294, 22 N.E. 247 (1889); Huntington Fuel Co. v. McIlwaine, 41 Ind. App. 328, 82 N.E. 1001 (Div. 2 1907).

Trial Strategy References: Reasonableness of Corporate Officer's Compensation, 4 Am Jur POF2d 425.

[50]Indiana Veneer & Lumber Co. v. Hageman, 57 Ind. App. 668, 105 N.E. 253 (Div. 1 1914).

[51]Matter of Forum Group, Inc., 82 F.3d 159 (7th Cir. 1996) (applying Indiana law).

corporation, based on facts known to the director.[52] A director is not liable for any action taken as a director, or any failure to take an action, unless he or she has breached or failed to perform the duties of his or her office in accordance with the statutory standards of conduct, and the breach or failure to perform constitutes willful misconduct or recklessness.[53]

> ◆ **Observation:** Before 1987, when the Business Corporations Act became effective, directors were subject to the same standard of conduct as they are under the Business Corporation Law; however, a plaintiff was not required to show that the directors committed willful misconduct or acted recklessly before the directors could be held liable for a breach of the standards. The added clause did not operate retroactively.[54]

This standard, known as the business judgment rule, protects directors from liability only if their decisions were informed ones.[55] In discharging his or her duties, a director is entitled to rely on information, opinions, reports, or statements, including financial statements and other data, if they were prepared or presented by:[56]

- one or more officers or employees of the corporation whom the director reasonably believes to be reliable and competent in the matters presented

---

[52]IC 23-1-35-1(a); IC 23-17-13-1(a).

[53]IC 23-1-35-1(e); IC 23-17-13-1(d).

Trial Strategy References: Liability of a Director to a Corporation for Mismanagement, 29 Am Jur POF3d 133.

Oppressive Conduct by Majority Shareholders, Directors, or Those in Control of Corporation, 5 Am Jur POF2d 645.

Legal Periodicals: A Call for More Lenient Director Liability Standards for Small, Charitable Nonprofit Corporations. 71 Ind. L. J. 967 (1996).

The Proper Standard for Directors' Negligence Liability. 66 Notre Dame L. Rev. 37 (1990).

[54]Brane v. Roth, 590 N.E.2d 587 (Ind. Ct. App. 1st Dist. 1992), reh'g denied, (June 1, 1992) and transfer denied, (Oct. 6, 1992).

[55]Brane v. Roth, 590 N.E.2d 587 (Ind. Ct. App. 1st Dist. 1992), reh'g denied, (June 1, 1992) and transfer denied, (Oct. 6, 1992) (where evidence showed that directors made no meaningful attempts to be informed of hedging activities and their effects on corporation's financial position, they were not protected from liability by business judgment rule).

[56]IC 23-1-35-1(b); IC 23-17-13-1(b)(1)-(3).

- legal counsel, public accountants, or other persons as to matters the director reasonably believes are within the person's professional or expert competence
- a committee of the board of directors of which the director is not a member if the director reasonably believes the committee merits confidence

A director of a religious corporation may also rely on religious authorities and ministers, priests, rabbis, or other persons whose position or duties in the religious organization the director believes justify reliance and confidence and whom the director believes to be reliable and competent in the matters presented.[57] A director is not acting in good faith if he or she has knowledge concerning the matter in question that makes reliance on the documents unwarranted.[58]

◆ **Caution:** The creation of, delegation of authority to, or action by a committee does not alone constitute compliance by a director with these standards of conduct.[59]

In considering the best interests of the corporation, a director of a business corporation may consider the effects of any action on shareholders, employees, suppliers, and customers of the corporation, and communities in which offices or other facilities of the corporation are located, and any other factors the director considers pertinent.[60] None of these groups or interests is necessarily dominant or controlling in the directors' decision making. The statute states expressly that judicial decisions of other jurisdictions which impose a different or higher degree of scrutiny on directors, especially in relation to a potential change of control of the corporation, are inconsistent with the proper application of the business judgment rule, and that the general assembly, in enacting the standards, intended to reaffirm that directors have full discretion to weigh as they deem appropriate the factors to be considered in determining the corporation's best interests, and to protect directors and their actions taken in the good faith exercise of their business judgment after reasonable

---

[57]IC 23-17-13-1(b)(4).

[58]IC 23-1-35-1(c); IC 23-17-13-1(c).

[59]IC 23-1-34-6(f); IC 23-17-15-6(f).

For discussion of committees, see § 114.

[60]IC 23-1-35-1(d).

investigation.[61] The directors may consider both the short-term and long-term best interests of the corporation, considering the effects of their actions on the corporation's shareholders and other groups or interests they are permitted to consider, as well as any other factors the directors deem pertinent.[62]

If the directors of a business corporation make a determination as to an action in accordance with the statutory standards, with the approval of a majority of the disinterested directors, that determination shall conclusively be presumed to be valid unless it can be demonstrated that the determination was not made in good faith after reasonable investigation.[63]

In a not-for-profit corporation, a director is not considered to be a trustee with respect to a corporation or with respect to any property held or administered by the corporation, including property that may be subject to restrictions imposed by the donor or transferor of the property.[64]

§ 118 Conflicts of interest

A director's conflict of interest in a transaction does not necessarily make the transaction void or voidable.

West's Digest, Corporations ☞318.

For business corporations, a conflict of interest transaction is a transaction with the corporation in which a director of the corporation has a direct or indirect interest.[65] A director has an indirect interest in a transaction if another entity in which the director has a material financial interest, or in which the director is a general partner, is a party to the transaction; or if another entity of which the director is a director, officer, of trustee is a party to the transaction and

---

[61]IC 23-1-35-1(f).

Legal Periodicals: Fort, The Corporation as Mediating Institution: An Efficacious Synthesis of Stakeholder Theory and Corporate Constituency Statutes. 73 Notre Dame L.Rev. 173 (November 1997).

[62]IC 23-1-35-1(g).

[63]IC 23-1-35-1(g).

As to factors for determining whether director is disinterested, see IC 23-1-35-1(h).

[64]IC 23-17-13-1(e).

[65]IC 23-1-35-2(a).

the transaction is, or is required to be, considered by the board of directors.[66]

A conflict of interest transaction, however, is not automatically void or voidable merely because of a director's interest.[67] Such a transaction is not voidable by the corporation solely on the basis of the director's interest in the transaction if:[68]

  (1) the material facts of the transaction and the director's interest were disclosed or known to the board of directors or a committee of the board of directors, and the board of directors or committee authorized, approved, or ratified the transaction;

  (2) the material facts of the transaction and the director's interest were disclosed or known to the shareholders entitled to vote and they authorized, approved, or ratified the transaction; or the transaction was fair to the corporation.

A conflict of interest transaction is authorized, approved, or ratified by the board of directors or a committee, and a quorum is considered present for that purpose, if the transaction receives the affirmative vote of a majority of the directors or committee members who have no direct or indirect interest in the transaction. A transaction may not be authorized, approved, or ratified under this section by a single director. The presence of, or a vote cast by, a director with a direct or indirect interest in the transaction does not affect the validity of the board's vote if the authorization, approval, or ratification is otherwise proper.[69]

Shares owned by or voted under the control of a director who has a direct or indirect interest in the transaction, and shares owned by or voted under the control of another entity in which a director is a director, officer, or trustee, may be counted in a vote of shareholders to determine whether to authorize, approve, or ratify a conflict of interest transaction.[70]

---

[66]IC 23-1-35-2(b).

[67]Melrose v. Capitol City Motor Lodge, Inc., 705 N.E.2d 985 (Ind. 1998).

[68]IC 23-1-35-2(a).

[69]IC 23-1-35-2(c).

[70]IC 23-1-35-2(d).

Substantially similar provisions apply to not-for-profit corporations.[71]

§ 119 Liability for unlawful distributions

A director may be personally liable to the corporation for unlawful distributions.

West's Digest, Corporations ☞316(1).

A director who commits willful misconduct or acts recklessly in voting for or assenting to a distribution made in violation of the applicable statute or the articles of incorporation is personally liable to the corporation for the amount of the distribution that exceeds the amount that could have been properly distributed.[72] A director who is held liable for an unlawful distribution is entitled to contribution from every other director who committed willful misconduct or acted recklessly in voting for or assenting to the distribution.[73] In addition, a business corporation director held liable for an unlawful distribution is entitled to contribution from each shareholder in the amount the shareholder received,[74] and a not-for-profit corporation is entitled to contribution from each person who received an unlawful distribution in the amount of the distribution accepted, regardless of whether the person knew the distribution was improper.[75]

§ 120 Liability for corporate debts and acts

Corporate officers and directors are not personally liable for debts and acts of the corporation based solely on their status as directors and officers.

West's Digest, Corporations ☞325-369.

As with shareholders, the personal liability of corporate officers is determined by common law rules of agency. Where an agent such as a corporate officer acted within the scope of his or her authority in signing a contract on behalf of the principal, the remedy of one seeking to enforce the contract

---

[71]IC 23-17-13-2.

[72]IC 23-1-35-4(a); IC 23-17-13-4(a).

For discussion of distributions, see §§ 58 et seq.

[73]IC 23-1-35-4(b)(1); IC 23-17-13-4(b)(1).

[74]IC 23-1-35-4(b)(2).

[75]IC 23-17-13-4(b)(2).

is against the principal and not the agent.[76] As a result, a corporate officer acting on behalf of the corporation is generally not liable for the corporation's obligations, whether based on contract,[77] tort,[78] or the violation of a statute.[79]

However, although Indiana courts are reluctant to pierce the corporate veil, they will do so in order to prevent fraud or unfairness to a third party.[80] An officer or director of a corporation may be held individually liable for the corporation's debts and contracts only where he or she has personally guaranteed the corporation's obligation, or where he or she has treated the corporation as a conduit for personal business affairs, and the imposition of personal liability is necessary to avoid injustice.[81]

> ◆ **Illustration:** The president of a corporation was properly held personally liable, and another corporation of which he was also president was properly held liable, for

---

[76]Winkler v. V.G. Reed & Sons, Inc., 638 N.E.2d 1228 (Ind. 1994).

[77]Winkler v. V.G. Reed & Sons, Inc., 638 N.E.2d 1228 (Ind. 1994) (corporation president who signed employment contract with employee in his capacity as president was not personally liable for alleged breach of contract, as there was no evidence president treated corporation as his alter ego or that employee was deceived about identity of employer); Hart v. Steel Products, Inc., 666 N.E.2d 1270 (Ind. Ct. App. 1996), reh'g denied, (Aug. 22, 1996) and transfer denied, 683 N.E.2d 582 (Ind. 1997).

[78]Roake v. Christensen, 528 N.E.2d 789 (Ind. Ct. App. 2d Dist. 1988); Wauchop v. Domino's Pizza, Inc., 832 F. Supp. 1572 (N.D. Ind. 1993) (applying Indiana law).

[79]State, Civil Rights Com'n v. County Line Park, Inc., 718 N.E.2d 768 (Ind. Ct. App. 1999), reh'g denied, (Dec. 15, 1999) (officers of incorporated mobile home park not personally liable for alleged violation of Fair Housing Act in policy excluding residents with more than four children).

[80]State, Civil Rights Com'n v. County Line Park, Inc., 718 N.E.2d 768 (Ind. Ct. App. 1999), reh'g denied, (Dec. 15, 1999); Wauchop v. Domino's Pizza, Inc., 832 F. Supp. 1572 (N.D. Ind. 1993) (applying Indiana law).

For discussion of the burden of proof, and of factors courts consider in determining whether to pierce the corporate veil, see § 7.

Trial Strategy References: Grounds for Disregarding the Corporate Entity and Piercing the Corporate Veil, 45 Am Jur POF3d 1.

[81]Weeks v. Kerr, 486 N.E.2d 10 (Ind. Ct. App. 4th Dist. 1985), reh'g denied, (Jan. 14, 1986) and transfer denied, (May 7, 1986); Wauchop v. Domino's Pizza, Inc., 832 F. Supp. 1572 (N.D. Ind. 1993) (applying Indiana law); Puller Mortg. Associates, Inc. v. Keegan, 829 F. Supp. 1507 (S.D. Ind. 1993) (applying Indiana law).

Trial Strategy References: Personal Liability of Corporate Officers on Promissory Note, 8 Am Jur POF2d 193.

the balance due on a promissory note of the corporation, where evidence showed that the individual was the president and sole director of both corporations, both corporations designated their principal place of business at the same address and were engaged in the same business, the president told the lender at the time he signed the promissory note as president of the first corporation that he could simply form another corporation if he encountered financial difficulties with the first corporation, and the second corporation had been incorporated shortly after the note was signed, paying the first corporation $250,000 for its property and equipment.[82]

Directors or officers may, of course, so contract as to create personal obligation on their part. An officer who executes an obligation for the payment of money which on its face does not show that he or she signed as an officer is personally bound thereby.[83]

A corporate officer cannot escape liability for fraud or other wrongdoing by claiming that he or she acted on behalf of the corporation when he or she personally participated in the wrongdoing.[84] If a corporate officer undertakes action in his or her own interest and in a manner destructive of the corporation or the rights of other stockholders, he or she may be held accountable in the name of the corporation.[85] Although an officer or director may be held personally liable if he or she actually engaged in tortious or unlawful activity, a corporate official may not be personally liable for others' acts taken in response to the official's implementation of a

---

[82]Henderson v. Sneath Oil Co., Inc., 638 N.E.2d 798 (Ind. Ct. App. 4th Dist. 1994).

[83]Fishers Grain Co. v. Sparks, 223 Ind. 133, 58 N.E.2d 932 (1945).

[84]Gable v. Curtis, 673 N.E.2d 805 (Ind. Ct. App. 1996); Stepp v. Duffy, 654 N.E.2d 767 (Ind. Ct. App. 1995), reh'g denied, (Oct. 24, 1995) and transfer denied, (Apr. 23, 1996) and appeal after remand, 686 N.E.2d 148 (Ind. Ct. App. 1997), reh'g denied, (Nov. 4, 1997) and transfer denied, 698 N.E.2d 1188 (Ind. 1998); Roake v. Christensen, 528 N.E.2d 789 (Ind. Ct. App. 2d Dist. 1988) (officer was liable for corporation's conversion of amounts paid by employee for health insurance where officer was only corporate officer or employee involved and continued to accept payments from employee even after insurance policy was canceled); American Independent Management Systems, Inc. v. McDaniel, 443 N.E.2d 98 (Ind. Ct. App. 3d Dist. 1982).

[85]G & N Aircraft, Inc. v. Boehm, 703 N.E.2d 665 (Ind. Ct. App. 1998), reh'g denied, (Feb. 9, 1999).

corporate policy, even if the official controlled the decision to adopt the policy.[86]

An outside director who functions as a figurehead for a corporation may also be personally liable as a director, despite his or her ignorance of the corporation's business.[87]

◆ **Caution:** Persons purporting to act as or on behalf of a corporation, knowing there was no incorporation under the applicable statute, are jointly and severally liable for all liabilities created while they were so acting.[88]

§ 121 Indemnification

A corporation may, and in some cases must, indemnify its officers and directors for liability and expenses incurred in defending actions against them.

West's Digest, Corporations ☞345.

Both the Business Corporation Law and the Nonprofit Corporation Act contain provisions for the indemnification of their officers and directors against certain liabilities sought to be imposed by third persons. "Director," in this context, includes a current or past director of the corporation and an individual who, while a director of a corporation, is or was serving at the corporation's request as a director, officer, partner, member, manager, trustee, employee, or agent of another corporation or other entity, whether for profit or not. Unless the context requires otherwise, the term also includes a director's estate or personal representative.[89]

If an individual has been made a party to a legal proceeding, whether threatened, pending, or completed, and whether criminal or civil,[90] because he or she is or was a

---

[86]Wauchop v. Domino's Pizza, Inc., 832 F. Supp. 1572 (N.D. Ind. 1993) (applying Indiana law) (corporate officer of pizza company could not be held liable for automobile accident allegedly caused by company's policy of delivery of pizza within half an hour).

[87]F.D.I.C. v. Bierman, 2 F.3d 1424, 127 A.L.R. Fed. 703 (7th Cir. 1993) (abrogation recognized on other grounds by, F.D.I.C. v. Gladstone, 44 F. Supp. 2d 81 (D. Mass. 1999)) (applying Indiana law).

[88]IC 23-1-21-4.

[89]IC 23-1-37-2; IC 23-17-16-2.

Forms References: Directors' indemnification agreement. 6A Am Jur Legal Forms 2d, Corporations § 74:1731.

[90]IC 23-1-37-7; IC 23-17-16-7.

director, the corporation may indemnify the individual against liability incurred in the proceeding if:[91]

    (1) the individual's conduct was in good faith;

    (2) in the case of conduct in the individual's official capacity with the corporation, the individual reasonably believed that his or her conduct was in the corporation's best interests;

    (3) and in all other cases, the individual reasonably believed that his or her conduct was not opposed to the corporation's best interest; and

    (4) in the case of a criminal proceeding, the individual either had reasonable cause to believe that his or her conduct was lawful, or had no reasonable cause to believe that his or her conduct was unlawful.

If the conduct was taken with respect to an employee benefit plan for a purpose the director reasonably believed to be in the interests of the participants in and beneficiaries of the plan, the director need only have reasonably believed that his or her conduct was not opposed to the corporation's best interest.[92] The termination of a proceeding by judgment, order, settlement, conviction, or upon a plea of nolo contendere or its equivalent is not, of itself, determinative that the director did not meet the required standard of conduct.[93]

Indemnification against reasonable expenses incurred by the director in connection with the proceeding is mandatory if the director was wholly successful, on the merits or otherwise, in defending a proceeding to which he or she was made a party because of his or her position as a director.[94] Furthermore, a corporation may pay for or reimburse the director's reasonable expenses before the proceeding is finally disposed of, unless its articles of incorporation provide otherwise, if the director affirms in writing his or her good faith belief that he or she has met the standard of conduct for indemnification of liability and undertakes in writing to repay the advance if it is ultimately determined that he or she did not meet the required standard of conduct, and if the facts known at the time to those making the determination

---

[91]IC 23-1-37-8(a); IC 23-17-16-8(a).

[92]IC 23-1-37-8(b); IC 23-17-16-8(b).

[93]IC 23-1-37-8(c); IC 23-17-16-8(c).

[94]IC 23-1-37-9; IC 23-17-16-9.

would not preclude indemnification.[95] The required undertaking must be an unlimited general obligation of the director, but need not be secured and may be accepted without reference to the director's financial ability to make repayment.[96]

Unless the corporation's articles of incorporation provide otherwise, a director may apply for a court order requiring that the corporation indemnify him or her. The court may order indemnification if it finds that the director is entitled to mandatory indemnification or that, regardless of whether the director has met the standard of conduct for indemnification of liability, he or she is fairly and reasonably entitled to indemnification in view of all the relevant circumstances.[97] If the court finds that the director is entitled to mandatory indemnification, it must order the corporation to may the director's expenses incurred in obtaining the court order.[98]

If the determination that indemnification is permissible is made by the directors, a committee, or the shareholders or members, authorization of indemnification and evaluation of the reasonableness of expenses is to be made in the same manner. If permissibility is determined by special legal counsel, authorization of indemnification and evaluation of the reasonableness of expenses is to be made by those entitled to select counsel.[99]

Unless the articles of incorporation provide otherwise, corporate officers are also entitled to mandatory indemnification of expenses and to apply for court-ordered indemnification as discussed above,[1] and the corporation may indemnify and advance expenses to an officer, employee, or agent of the corporation, regardless of whether he or she is also a director, as authorized by the applicable statute or by the corporation's articles of incorporation or bylaws, general or

---

[95]IC 23-1-37-10(a); IC 23-17-16-10(a).

As to factors determining whether director may be indemnified for liability or for expenses before final disposition of the case, see IC 23-1-37-10(c); IC 23-17-16-10(c).

[96]IC 23-1-37-10(b); IC 23-17-16-10(b).

[97]IC 23-1-37-11; IC 23-17-16-11.

[98]IC 23-1-37-11(1); IC 23-17-16-11(1).

[99]IC 23-1-37-12(c); IC 23-17-16-12(c).

As to procedures for determination of authorization of indemnity, see IC 23-1-37-12 (b); IC 23-17-16-12(b).

[1]IC 23-1-37-13(1); IC 23-17-16-13(1).

specific action of its board of directors, or contract.[2] Indemnity provisions may, for instance, be included in an agreement for the acquisition of a corporation, and may be enforced by the purchaser or a successor to the purchaser.[3]

Aside from the indemnification and advance rights granted by statute, a person may have other indemnification or advance rights under the corporation's articles of incorporation or bylaws, a resolution of the board of directors, shareholders, or members, or any other authorization adopted at any time, after notice, by a majority vote of all the voting shares or members.[4] The statutes do not limit a corporation's power to pay or reimburse expenses incurred by a director, officer, employee, or agent in connection with his or her appearance as a witness in a proceeding when the person has not been made a defendant or respondent to the proceeding.[5]

A corporation may insure its directors, officers, employees, and agents against liability asserted against or incurred by such persons in those capacities or arising from their status as directors, officers, employees, and agents, regardless of whether the corporation would have power to indemnify the individual against that liability.[6] In the case of a business corporation, the insurer may be owned or otherwise affiliated with the corporation, regardless of whether the insurer does business with other persons.[7]

---

[2]IC 23-1-37-13(2), (3); IC 23-17-16-13(2), (3).

[3]Markham v. Prutsman Mirror Co., 565 N.E.2d 385 (Ind. Ct. App. 4th Dist. 1991).

[4]IC 23-1-37-15(a); IC 23-17-16-15(a).

[5]IC 23-1-37-15(c); IC 23-17-16-15(c).

[6]IC 23-1-37-14; IC 23-17-16-14.

[7]IC 23-1-37-14.

Table of Statutes, Rules and Regulations

INDIANA CONSTITUTION

Article 1	Section No.	Article 4	Section No.
22	CONTEMPT:8	15	CONTEMPT:2

Article 4	Section No.	Article 11	Section No.
2	CORONERS:2	13	CORPORATNS:5
6	CORONERS:2	14	CORPORATNS:5

INDIANA STATUTES & REGULATIONS

Indiana Code

IC §	Section No.	IC §	Section No.
2-3-5-1	CONTIN:6, 8	23-1-2-6(e)	CORPORATNS:43
2-7-1-1	CONTRACTS:53	23-1-17-1	CORPORATNS:2
2.2-4-1(b)	CONTRACTS:15	23-1-17-2	CORPORATNS:6
4-13.6-5-11	CONTRACTS:45	23-1-17-3(a)	CORPORATNS:2
4-23-6.5-7	CORONERS:2	23-1-17-3.1	CORPORATNS:2
4-23-6.5-8	CORONERS:2	23-1-17-4	CORPORATNS:2
5-14-3-1	CORONERS:9	23-1-18-1	CORPORATNS:31
5-14-3-4(b)(1)	CORONERS:9	23-1-18-1(g)	CORPORATNS:33
8-1-2-1	CORPORATNS:2	23-1-18-1(j)	CORPORATNS:31
8-1-2-106	CONTRACTS:51	23-1-18-1.1(a)	CORPORATNS:34
8-3-1-13	CONTRACTS:51	23-1-18-1.1(b)(1)	CORPORATNS:34
8-4-1-1	CORPORATNS:2	23-1-18-1.1(b)(2)	CORPORATNS:34
8-21-4-7	CONTRACTS:120	23-1-18-1.1(c)	CORPORATNS:34
10-5-10-1	CONTRACTS:31	23-1-18-2	CORPORATNS:32
13-23-13-8(b)	CONTRIB:3	23-1-18-3	CORPORATNS:31
14-27-3-1	CONTEMPT:2	23-1-18-4(a)	CORPORATNS:31
15-2.1-24-24	CONTEMPT:2	23-1-18-4(b)	CORPORATNS:31
15-7-1-1	CORPORATNS:2	23-1-18-5	CORPORATNS:31
20-1-19-19	CONTRACTS:45		
22-1-1-17	CONTEMPT:2		

IC §	Section No.	IC §	Section No.
23-1-18-6(a)	CORPORATNS:35	23-1-21-6(a)	CORPORATNS:26
23-1-18-6(b)	CORPORATNS:35	23-1-21-6(b)	CORPORATNS:26
23-1-18-6(c)	CORPORATNS:35	23-1-21-7(a)	CORPORATNS:26
23-1-18-6(d)	CORPORATNS:35	23-1-21-7(b)	CORPORATNS:26
23-1-18-7(a)	CORPORATNS:35	23-1-21-7(c)	CORPORATNS:26
23-1-18-7(b)	CORPORATNS:35	23-1-21-7(d)	CORPORATNS:26
23-1-18-7(c)	CORPORATNS:35	23-1-22-1(a)	CORPORATNS:4
23-1-18-8	CORPORATNS:31	23-1-22-1(b)	CORPORATNS:4
23-1-18-9(a)	CORPORATNS:10	23-1-22-2	CORPORATNS:8, 12
23-1-18-9(b)	CORPORATNS:10	23-1-22-2(2)	CORPORATNS:23
23-1-18-9(c)	CORPORATNS:10	23-1-22-3(a)	CORPORATNS:109
23-1-18-10	CORPORATNS:8	23-1-22-3(b)(1)	CORPORATNS:109
23-1-20-3	CORPORATNS:37	23-1-22-3(b)(2)	CORPORATNS:109
23-1-20-5	CORPORATNS:2	23-1-22-3(c)	CORPORATNS:109
23-1-20-7	CORPORATNS:58	23-1-22-3(d)	CORPORATNS:109
23-1-20-11	CORPORATNS:2	23-1-22-5(b)	CORPORATNS:77
23-1-20-21	CORPORATNS:59, 86	23-1-22-5(c)	CORPORATNS:77
23-1-20-23	CORPORATNS:36	23-1-23-1(a)(1)	CORPORATNS:18
23-1-20-24	CORPORATNS:65	23-1-23-1(a)(2)	CORPORATNS:18
23-1-20-26	CORPORATNS:38	23-1-23-1(b)	CORPORATNS:18
23-1-20-28	CORPORATNS:91	23-1-23-1(c)	CORPORATNS:18
23-1-20-29(a)	CORPORATNS:85	23-1-23-1(d)	CORPORATNS:18
23-1-20-29(b)	CORPORATNS:85	23-1-23-1(f)	CORPORATNS:21
23-1-20-29(c)	CORPORATNS:85	23-1-23-2(a)	CORPORATNS:18
23-1-20-29(f)	CORPORATNS:85	23-1-23-2(b)	CORPORATNS:18
23-1-20-29(g)	CORPORATNS:85	23-1-23-3(a)	CORPORATNS:20
23-1-20-30(a)(1)	CORPORATNS:65	23-1-23-3(b)	CORPORATNS:20
23-1-20-30(a)(2)	CORPORATNS:65	23-1-23-3(c)	CORPORATNS:20
23-1-20-30(a)(3)	CORPORATNS:65	23-1-23-3(d)	CORPORATNS:20
23-1-20-30(b)	CORPORATNS:65	23-1-23-3(e)	CORPORATNS:20
23-1-21-1	CORPORATNS:8, 17	23-1-24-1	CORPORATNS:24
23-1-21-2(a)	CORPORATNS:12	23-1-24-1(2)	CORPORATNS:24
23-1-21-2(b)	CORPORATNS:12	23-1-24-2(a)	CORPORATNS:24
23-1-21-2(c)	CORPORATNS:12	23-1-24-2(a)(6)	CORPORATNS:24
23-1-21-3(a)	CORPORATNS:8	23-1-24-2(b)	CORPORATNS:24
23-1-21-3(b)	CORPORATNS:10	23-1-24-3	CORPORATNS:34
23-1-21-4	CORPORATNS:120	23-1-24-3(a)	CORPORATNS:24
23-1-21-5(a)(1)	CORPORATNS:25	23-1-24-3(b)	CORPORATNS:24
23-1-21-5(a)(2)	CORPORATNS:25	23-1-24-3(c)	CORPORATNS:24
23-1-21-5(a)(3)	CORPORATNS:25	23-1-25-1	CORPORATNS:37
23-1-21-5(b)	CORPORATNS:25	23-1-25-1(a)	CORPORATNS:37
23-1-21-5(c)	CORPORATNS:25	23-1-25-1(b)	CORPORATNS:37

IC §	Section No.	IC §	Section No.
23-1-25-1(c)	CORPORATNS:37	23-1-27-1	CORPORATNS:41
23-1-25-1(d)	CORPORATNS:37	23-1-27-1(a)	CORPORATNS:41
23-1-25-2(a)	CORPORATNS:37	23-1-27-1(b)	CORPORATNS:41
23-1-25-2(b)	CORPORATNS:37	23-1-27-1(b)(1)	CORPORATNS:41
23-1-25-2(c)	CORPORATNS:37	23-1-27-1(b)(2)	CORPORATNS:41
23-1-25-2(d)	CORPORATNS:40	23-1-27-1(b)(3)	CORPORATNS:41
23-1-25-3(a)	CORPORATNS:40	23-1-27-1(b)(4)	CORPORATNS:41
23-1-25-3(c)	CORPORATNS:40	23-1-27-1(b)(5)	CORPORATNS:41
23-1-25-4(a)	CORPORATNS:40	23-1-27-1(b)(6)	CORPORATNS:41
23-1-25-4(b)	CORPORATNS:44	23-1-27-1(c)	CORPORATNS:41
23-1-25-4(c)	CORPORATNS:40	23-1-27-2(a)	CORPORATNS:45
23-1-25-4(d)	CORPORATNS:40	23-1-27-2(b)	CORPORATNS:45
23-1-26-1(a)	CORPORATNS:38	23-1-27-2(c)	CORPORATNS:45
23-1-26-1(b)	CORPORATNS:38	23-1-27-2(d)	CORPORATNS:45
23-1-26-1(c)	CORPORATNS:38	23-1-27-2(e)	CORPORATNS:45
23-1-26-1(d)	CORPORATNS:38	23-1-28-1	CORPORATNS:58
23-1-26-1(e)	CORPORATNS:38	23-1-28-2	CORPORATNS:59
23-1-26-2(a)	CORPORATNS:43	23-1-28-3(1)	CORPORATNS:60
23-1-26-2(b)	CORPORATNS:43	23-1-28-3(2)	CORPORATNS:60
23-1-26-2(c)	CORPORATNS:43	23-1-28-4	CORPORATNS:60
23-1-26-2(d)	CORPORATNS:43	23-1-28-5(1)	CORPORATNS:60
23-1-26-2(e)	CORPORATNS:43	23-1-28-5(2)	CORPORATNS:60
23-1-26-3(a)	CORPORATNS:78	23-1-28-5(3)	CORPORATNS:60
23-1-26-3(b)	CORPORATNS:78	23-1-29-1(a)	CORPORATNS:81
23-1-26-4(a)	CORPORATNS:61	23-1-29-1(b)	CORPORATNS:80
23-1-26-4(b)	CORPORATNS:61	23-1-29-1(c)	CORPORATNS:81
23-1-26-4(c)	CORPORATNS:59	23-1-29-2(a)	CORPORATNS:82
23-1-26-5	CORPORATNS:42	23-1-29-2(b)	CORPORATNS:82
23-1-26-6(a)	CORPORATNS:44	23-1-29-2(c)	CORPORATNS:80
23-1-26-6(b)	CORPORATNS:44	23-1-29-2(d)	CORPORATNS:80, 82
23-1-26-6(c)	CORPORATNS:44	23-1-29-2(e)	CORPORATNS:80
23-1-26-6(d)(1)	CORPORATNS:44	23-1-29-3	CORPORATNS:83
23-1-26-6(d)(2)	CORPORATNS:44	23-1-29-4(a)	CORPORATNS:84
23-1-26-6(e)	CORPORATNS:44	23-1-29-4(c)	CORPORATNS:84
23-1-26-7(a)	CORPORATNS:44	23-1-29-4(d)	CORPORATNS:84
23-1-26-7(b)	CORPORATNS:44	23-1-29-4(e)	CORPORATNS:84
23-1-26-8(a)	CORPORATNS:47	23-1-29-5(a)	CORPORATNS:85
23-1-26-8(b)	CORPORATNS:47	23-1-29-5(b)	CORPORATNS:85
23-1-26-8(c)	CORPORATNS:47	23-1-29-5(c)	CORPORATNS:85
23-1-26-8(d)	CORPORATNS:47	23-1-29-5(e)	CORPORATNS:85
23-1-26-8(e)	CORPORATNS:47	23-1-29-6(a)	CORPORATNS:85
23-1-26-9	CORPORATNS:43	23-1-29-6(b)	CORPORATNS:85

IC §	Section No.	IC §	Section No.
23-1-29-7(a)	CORPORATNS:86	23-1-30-9(b)	CORPORATNS:98
23-1-29-7(b)	CORPORATNS:86	23-1-30-9(c)	CORPORATNS:98
23-1-29-7(c)	CORPORATNS:86	23-1-30-9(d)	CORPORATNS:98
23-1-29-7(d)	CORPORATNS:86	23-1-31-1(a)	CORPORATNS:95
23-1-30-1(a)	CORPORATNS:87	23-1-31-1(b)	CORPORATNS:95
23-1-30-1(b)	CORPORATNS:71	23-1-31-1(c)	CORPORATNS:95
23-1-30-1(c)	CORPORATNS:71	23-1-31-2	CORPORATNS:95
23-1-30-1(d)	CORPORATNS:71	23-1-32-1	CORPORATNS:74
23-1-30-2	CORPORATNS:88	23-1-32-2	CORPORATNS:75
23-1-30-2(a)	CORPORATNS:88	23-1-32-3(a)	CORPORATNS:74
23-1-30-2(b)	CORPORATNS:88	23-1-32-3(b)	CORPORATNS:74
23-1-30-2(c)	CORPORATNS:88	23-1-32-4(a)	CORPORATNS:76
23-1-30-2(d)	CORPORATNS:88	23-1-32-4(b)	CORPORATNS:76
23-1-30-3(a)	CORPORATNS:93	23-1-32-4(c)	CORPORATNS:76
23-1-30-3(b)(1)(A) ..	CORPORATNS:93	23-1-32-4(d)	CORPORATNS:76
23-1-30-3(b)(1)(B) ..	CORPORATNS:93	23-1-32-5	CORPORATNS:74
23-1-30-3(b)(2) ..	CORPORATNS:93	23-1-33-1(a)	CORPORATNS:96
23-1-30-3(b)(3) ..	CORPORATNS:93	23-1-33-1(b)	CORPORATNS:108
23-1-30-3(c)	CORPORATNS:93	23-1-33-1(c)	CORPORATNS:96
23-1-30-3(d)	CORPORATNS:93	23-1-33-2	CORPORATNS:96
23-1-30-3(e)	CORPORATNS:93	23-1-33-3(a)	CORPORATNS:96
23-1-30-3(f)	CORPORATNS:93	23-1-33-3(b)	CORPORATNS:96
23-1-30-3(g)	CORPORATNS:93	23-1-33-3(c)	CORPORATNS:97
23-1-30-3(h)	CORPORATNS:93	23-1-33-4	CORPORATNS:99
23-1-30-3(i)	CORPORATNS:93	23-1-33-5(a)	CORPORATNS:100
23-1-30-4(a)	CORPORATNS:65	23-1-33-5(b)	CORPORATNS:100
23-1-30-4(b)	CORPORATNS:65	23-1-33-5(c)	CORPORATNS:100
23-1-30-5(a)	CORPORATNS:94	23-1-33-5(d)	CORPORATNS:100
23-1-30-5(b)	CORPORATNS:94	23-1-33-5(e)	CORPORATNS:100
23-1-30-5(c)	CORPORATNS:94	23-1-33-6(a)	CORPORATNS:101
23-1-30-5(c)(1) ..	CORPORATNS:94	23-1-33-6(b)	CORPORATNS:101
23-1-30-5(c)(2) ..	CORPORATNS:94	23-1-33-7(a)	CORPORATNS:103
23-1-30-5(d)	CORPORATNS:94	23-1-33-7(b)	CORPORATNS:103
23-1-30-5(e)	CORPORATNS:94	23-1-33-8(a)	CORPORATNS:104
23-1-30-6(a)	CORPORATNS:90	23-1-33-8(b)	CORPORATNS:104
23-1-30-6(b)	CORPORATNS:90	23-1-33-8(c)	CORPORATNS:104
23-1-30-6(c)	CORPORATNS:90	23-1-33-8(d)	CORPORATNS:104
23-1-30-7(a)	CORPORATNS:91	23-1-33-9(a)	CORPORATNS:106
23-1-30-7(b)	CORPORATNS:91	23-1-33-9(b)	CORPORATNS:106
23-1-30-8	CORPORATNS:90	23-1-33-9(c)	CORPORATNS:106
23-1-30-9(a)	CORPORATNS:97	23-1-33-10	CORPORATNS:116
		23-1-34-1(a)	CORPORATNS:110

IC §	Section No.	IC §	Section No.
23-1-34-1(b)	CORPORATNS:110	23-1-36-3(c)	CORPORATNS:107
23-1-34-2(a)	CORPORATNS:111	23-1-36-3(d)	CORPORATNS:107
23-1-34-2(b)	CORPORATNS:111	23-1-36-4(a)	CORPORATNS:102
23-1-34-2(c)	CORPORATNS:111	23-1-36-4(b)	CORPORATNS:107
23-1-34-3(a)	CORPORATNS:112	23-1-37-2	CORPORATNS:121
23-1-34-3(b)	CORPORATNS:112	23-1-37-7	CORPORATNS:121
23-1-34-4(a)	CORPORATNS:112	23-1-37-8(a)	CORPORATNS:121
23-1-34-4(b)	CORPORATNS:112	23-1-37-8(b)	CORPORATNS:121
23-1-34-5(a)	CORPORATNS:113	23-1-37-8(c)	CORPORATNS:121
23-1-34-5(a)(1)	CORPORATNS:113	23-1-37-9	CORPORATNS:121
23-1-34-5(a)(2)	CORPORATNS:113	23-1-37-10(a)	CORPORATNS:121
23-1-34-5(b)	CORPORATNS:113	23-1-37-10(b)	CORPORATNS:121
23-1-34-5(c)	CORPORATNS:113	23-1-37-10(c)	CORPORATNS:121
23-1-34-5(d)	CORPORATNS:113	23-1-37-11	CORPORATNS:121
23-1-34-6(a)	CORPORATNS:114	23-1-37-11(1)	CORPORATNS:121
23-1-34-6(b)	CORPORATNS:114	23-1-37-12(b)	CORPORATNS:121
23-1-34-6(c)	CORPORATNS:114	23-1-37-12(c)	CORPORATNS:121
23-1-34-6(d)	CORPORATNS:114	23-1-37-13(1)	CORPORATNS:121
23-1-34-6(e)	CORPORATNS:114	23-1-37-13(2)	CORPORATNS:121
23-1-34-6(f)	CORPORATNS:117	23-1-37-13(3)	CORPORATNS:121
23-1-35-1(a)	CORPORATNS:117	23-1-37-14	CORPORATNS:121
23-1-35-1(b)	CORPORATNS:117	23-1-37-15(a)	CORPORATNS:121
23-1-35-1(c)	CORPORATNS:117	23-1-37-15(c)	CORPORATNS:121
23-1-35-1(d)	CORPORATNS:117	23-1-38-1(a)	CORPORATNS:13
23-1-35-1(e)	CORPORATNS:117	23-1-38-1(b)	CORPORATNS:13
23-1-35-1(f)	CORPORATNS:117	23-1-38-2	CORPORATNS:13
23-1-35-1(g)	CORPORATNS:117	23-1-38-3(a)	CORPORATNS:13
23-1-35-1(h)	CORPORATNS:117	23-1-38-3(b)(1)	CORPORATNS:13
23-1-35-2(a)	CORPORATNS:118	23-1-38-3(b)(3)	CORPORATNS:13
23-1-35-2(b)	CORPORATNS:118	23-1-38-3(c)	CORPORATNS:13
23-1-35-2(c)	CORPORATNS:118	23-1-38-3(d)	CORPORATNS:13
23-1-35-2(d)	CORPORATNS:118	23-1-38-3(e)	CORPORATNS:92
23-1-35-4(a)	CORPORATNS:119	23-1-38-4(a)	CORPORATNS:92
23-1-35-4(b)(1)	CORPORATNS:119	23-1-38-4(b)	CORPORATNS:92
23-1-35-4(b)(2)	CORPORATNS:119	23-1-38-4(c)	CORPORATNS:92
23-1-36-1(a)	CORPORATNS:102	23-1-38-4(d)	CORPORATNS:92
23-1-36-1(b)	CORPORATNS:102	23-1-38-5	CORPORATNS:13
23-1-36-1(c)	CORPORATNS:102	23-1-38-6(a)	CORPORATNS:14
23-1-36-1(d)	CORPORATNS:102	23-1-38-6(b)	CORPORATNS:22
23-1-36-2	CORPORATNS:108	23-1-38-7	CORPORATNS:15
23-1-36-3(a)	CORPORATNS:107	23-1-38-7(e)	CORPORATNS:15
23-1-36-3(b)	CORPORATNS:107	23-1-38-8	CORPORATNS:14

IC §	Section No.	IC §	Section No.
23-1-38-9	CORPORATNS:13, 22	23-1-53-3(a)	CORPORATNS:29
23-1-39-1	CORPORATNS:27	23-1-53-3(b)	CORPORATNS:29
23-1-39-2	CORPORATNS:26	23-1-53-3(c)	CORPORATNS:29
23-1-39-2(b)	CORPORATNS:27	23-1-53-3(d)	CORPORATNS:29
23-1-39-3(a)	CORPORATNS:27	23-1-53-3(e)	CORPORATNS:29
23-1-49-6(a)(1)	CORPORATNS:20	23-1-53-3(f)	CORPORATNS:29
23-1-49-6(a)(2)	CORPORATNS:20	23-1-53-4(a)	CORPORATNS:29
23-1-49-6(b)	CORPORATNS:20	23-1-53-4(b)	CORPORATNS:29
23-1-49-6(c)	CORPORATNS:20	23-1-53-4(d)	CORPORATNS:29
23-1-49-6(d)	CORPORATNS:20	23-1-53-4(e)	CORPORATNS:29
23-1-49-6(e)	CORPORATNS:20	23-1-54-2	CORPORATNS:41
23-1-49-9	CORPORATNS:34	23-1.5-1-1	CORPORATNS:2
23-1-52-1(a)	CORPORATNS:28	23-1.5-1-8	CORPORATNS:4
23-1-52-1(b)	CORPORATNS:28	23-1.5-2-1	CORPORATNS:2
23-1-52-1(c)	CORPORATNS:28	23-1.5-2-3(a)	CORPORATNS:4
23-1-52-1(d)	CORPORATNS:28	23-1.5-2-6(a)	CORPORATNS:78
23-1-52-1(e)(1)	CORPORATNS:28	23-1.5-2-6(b)	CORPORATNS:78
23-1-52-1(e)(2)	CORPORATNS:28	23-1.5-2-6(d)	CORPORATNS:78
23-1-52-1(e)(3)	CORPORATNS:28	23-1.5-2-8(a)	CORPORATNS:19
23-1-52-1(e)(4)	CORPORATNS:28	23-1.5-2-8(b)	CORPORATNS:19
23-1-52-1(e)(5)	CORPORATNS:28	23-1.5-2-9(a)	CORPORATNS:16
23-1-52-1(e)(6)	CORPORATNS:28	23-1.5-2-9(b)	CORPORATNS:16
23-1-52-1(e)(7)	CORPORATNS:28	23-1.5-2-9(c)	CORPORATNS:16
23-1-52-2(a)	CORPORATNS:70	23-1.5-2-9(d)	CORPORATNS:16
23-1-52-2(b)	CORPORATNS:70	23-1.5-2-9(e)	CORPORATNS:16
23-1-52-2(c)	CORPORATNS:70	23-1.5-2-11.1	CORPORATNS:29
23-1-52-2(e)	CORPORATNS:70	23-1.5-3-1(a)	CORPORATNS:40
23-1-52-3(b)	CORPORATNS:70	23-1.5-3-1(b)	CORPORATNS:40
23-1-52-3(b)(1)-(3)	CORPORATNS:70	23-1.5-3-1(c)	CORPORATNS:40
23-1-52-3(c)	CORPORATNS:70	23-1.5-3-1(d)	CORPORATNS:40
23-1-52-3(d)	CORPORATNS:70	23-1.5-3-2	CORPORATNS:45
23-1-52-4(a)	CORPORATNS:70	23-1.5-3-3	CORPORATNS:45
23-1-52-4(b)	CORPORATNS:70	23-1.5-3-6(b)	CORPORATNS:47
23-1-52-4(c)	CORPORATNS:70	23-2-1-19(d)	CONTRIB:3
23-1-52-4(d)	CORPORATNS:70	23-4-1-15	CONTRIB:2
23-1-52-5	CORPORATNS:70	23-4-1-34	CONTRIB:2
23-1-52-5(d)	CORPORATNS:70	23-4-1-34(a)-(c)	CONTRIB:2
23-1-53-1(a)	CORPORATNS:30	23-6-4-1	CORPORATNS:2
23-1-53-1(b)	CORPORATNS:30	23-15-1-1(a)	CORPORATNS:21
23-1-53-2	CORPORATNS:70	23-15-1-1(g)	CORPORATNS:21
23-1-53-2(b)	CORPORATNS:43	23-17-1-1	CORPORATNS:2
		23-17-2-7	CORPORATNS:2

IC §	Section No.	IC §	Section No.
23-17-2-8	CORPORATNS:68	23-17-7-1(a)	CORPORATNS:66
23-17-2-17(a)	CORPORATNS:66	23-17-7-1(b)	CORPORATNS:66
23-17-2-17(b)	CORPORATNS:66	23-17-7-2	CORPORATNS:66
23-17-2-18	CORPORATNS:67	23-17-7-3	CORPORATNS:66
23-17-2-19	CORPORATNS:4	23-17-7-4	CORPORATNS:66
23-17-2-23	CORPORATNS:4	23-17-7-5(a)	CORPORATNS:66
23-17-2-25	CORPORATNS:4	23-17-7-5(b)	CORPORATNS:66
23-17-3-2	CORPORATNS:12	23-17-7-6	CORPORATNS:78
23-17-3-7(a)(1)	CORPORATNS:25	23-17-7-7(a)	CORPORATNS:67
23-17-3-7(a)(2)	CORPORATNS:25	23-17-7-7(b)	CORPORATNS:67
23-17-3-7(b)	CORPORATNS:25	23-17-7-8(a)	CORPORATNS:79
23-17-3-7(c)	CORPORATNS:25	23-17-7-8(b)	CORPORATNS:79
23-17-3-8(a)	CORPORATNS:26	23-17-7-9	CORPORATNS:73
23-17-3-8(b)	CORPORATNS:26	23-17-8-1(a)	CORPORATNS:67
23-17-3-9(a)	CORPORATNS:26	23-17-8-1(b)	CORPORATNS:67
23-17-3-9(b)	CORPORATNS:26	23-17-8-2	CORPORATNS:67
23-17-3-9(c)	CORPORATNS:26	23-17-8-2(a)	CORPORATNS:67
23-17-3-9(d)	CORPORATNS:26	23-17-8-2(b)(1)	CORPORATNS:67
23-17-5-1(a)(1)	CORPORATNS:18	23-17-8-2(b)(2)	CORPORATNS:67
23-17-5-1(a)(2)	CORPORATNS:18	23-17-8-2(d)	CORPORATNS:67
23-17-5-1(b)(1)	CORPORATNS:18	23-17-8-2(e)	CORPORATNS:67
23-17-5-1(b)(2)	CORPORATNS:18	23-17-8-3(a)	CORPORATNS:67
23-17-5-1(b)(3)	CORPORATNS:18	23-17-8-3(b)	CORPORATNS:67
23-17-5-1(c)	CORPORATNS:18	23-17-9-1	CORPORATNS:68
23-17-5-1(d)	CORPORATNS:18	23-17-9-2	CORPORATNS:68
23-17-5-1(e)	CORPORATNS:21	23-17-10-1(a)	CORPORATNS:81
23-17-5-2(a)	CORPORATNS:18	23-17-10-1(b)	CORPORATNS:81
23-17-5-2(b)	CORPORATNS:18	23-17-10-1(c)	CORPORATNS:80
23-17-5-3(a)	CORPORATNS:20	23-17-10-1(d)(1)	CORPORATNS:81
23-17-5-3(b)	CORPORATNS:20	23-17-10-1(d)(2)	CORPORATNS:81
23-17-5-3(c)	CORPORATNS:20	23-17-10-1(f)	CORPORATNS:81
23-17-5-3(d)	CORPORATNS:20	23-17-10-2(a)(1)	CORPORATNS:82
23-17-5-3(e)	CORPORATNS:20	23-17-10-2(a)(2)	CORPORATNS:82
23-17-6-1	CORPORATNS:24	23-17-10-2(c)	CORPORATNS:82
23-17-6-1(2)	CORPORATNS:24	23-17-10-2(d)	CORPORATNS:80
23-17-6-2(a)	CORPORATNS:24	23-17-10-2(e)	CORPORATNS:82
23-17-6-2(b)	CORPORATNS:24	23-17-10-2(f)	CORPORATNS:80
23-17-6-2(c)	CORPORATNS:24	23-17-10-4(a)	CORPORATNS:84
23-17-6-3	CORPORATNS:34	23-17-10-4(c)	CORPORATNS:84
23-17-6-3(a)	CORPORATNS:24	23-17-10-4(d)	CORPORATNS:84
23-17-6-3(b)	CORPORATNS:24	23-17-10-5(a)	CORPORATNS:85
23-17-6-3(c)	CORPORATNS:24	23-17-10-5(b)	CORPORATNS:85

IC §	Section No.	IC §	Section No.
23-17-10-5(c)	CORPORATNS:85	23-17-11-7(f)	CORPORATNS:98
23-17-10-5(d)	CORPORATNS:85	23-17-11-8	CORPORATNS:99
23-17-10-6(a)(1)	CORPORATNS:85	23-17-11-9(a)	CORPORATNS:94
23-17-10-6(a)(2)	CORPORATNS:85	23-17-11-9(b)	CORPORATNS:94
23-17-10-6(a)(3)	CORPORATNS:85	23-17-11-9(c)	CORPORATNS:94
23-17-10-6(b)	CORPORATNS:85	23-17-11-9(d)	CORPORATNS:94
23-17-10-7(a)	CORPORATNS:86	23-17-11-9(e)	CORPORATNS:94
23-17-10-7(b)	CORPORATNS:86	23-17-12-1(a)	CORPORATNS:96
23-17-10-7(c)	CORPORATNS:86	23-17-12-1(b)	CORPORATNS:108
23-17-10-7(d)	CORPORATNS:86	23-17-12-1(c)	CORPORATNS:114
23-17-10-8(a)	CORPORATNS:84	23-17-12-2(a)	CORPORATNS:96
23-17-10-8(b)	CORPORATNS:84	23-17-12-2(b)	CORPORATNS:96
23-17-10-8(c)	CORPORATNS:84	23-17-12-3(a)	CORPORATNS:96
23-17-10-8(d)	CORPORATNS:84	23-17-12-3(b)	CORPORATNS:96
23-17-10-8(e)	CORPORATNS:84	23-17-12-4(a)	CORPORATNS:97
23-17-11-1(a)	CORPORATNS:87	23-17-12-4(b)	CORPORATNS:97
23-17-11-1(b)	CORPORATNS:71	23-17-12-5(a)	CORPORATNS:100
23-17-11-1(c)	CORPORATNS:71	23-17-12-5(b)	CORPORATNS:100
23-17-11-1(d)	CORPORATNS:71	23-17-12-5(c)	CORPORATNS:100
23-17-11-1(e)	CORPORATNS:71	23-17-12-5(d)	CORPORATNS:100
23-17-11-1(g)	CORPORATNS:71	23-17-12-6	CORPORATNS:101
23-17-11-2	CORPORATNS:71	23-17-12-7(a)	CORPORATNS:103
23-17-11-3(a)	CORPORATNS:89	23-17-12-7(b)	CORPORATNS:103
23-17-11-3(b)	CORPORATNS:89	23-17-12-8(a)	CORPORATNS:104
23-17-11-4(a)	CORPORATNS:90	23-17-12-8(b)	CORPORATNS:104
23-17-11-4(b)	CORPORATNS:90	23-17-12-8(c)	CORPORATNS:104
23-17-11-4(c)	CORPORATNS:90	23-17-12-8(d)	CORPORATNS:104
23-17-11-4(d)	CORPORATNS:89	23-17-12-8(e)	CORPORATNS:104
23-17-11-4(e)	CORPORATNS:90	23-17-12-8(f)	CORPORATNS:104
23-17-11-4(g)	CORPORATNS:80	23-17-12-8(g)	CORPORATNS:104
23-17-11-5(a)	CORPORATNS:90	23-17-12-9	CORPORATNS:104
23-17-11-6(a)	CORPORATNS:93	23-17-12-10	CORPORATNS:104
23-17-11-6(b)	CORPORATNS:93	23-17-12-11	CORPORATNS:104
23-17-11-6(c)	CORPORATNS:93	23-17-12-12(a)	CORPORATNS:104
23-17-11-6(d)	CORPORATNS:93	23-17-12-12(b)	CORPORATNS:104
23-17-11-6(e)	CORPORATNS:93	23-17-12-13(a)	CORPORATNS:105
23-17-11-6(f)	CORPORATNS:93	23-17-12-13(b)	CORPORATNS:105
23-17-11-7(a)	CORPORATNS:97	23-17-12-13(c)	CORPORATNS:105
23-17-11-7(b)	CORPORATNS:98	23-17-12-13(d)	CORPORATNS:105
23-17-11-7(c)	CORPORATNS:98	23-17-12-14(a)	CORPORATNS:106
23-17-11-7(d)	CORPORATNS:98	23-17-12-14(a)(1)	CORPORATNS:106
23-17-11-7(e)	CORPORATNS:104		

IC §	Section No.
23-17-12-14(b)	CORPORATNS:106
23-17-12-14(c)	CORPORATNS:106
23-17-12-14(d)	CORPORATNS:106
23-17-12-15	CORPORATNS:116
23-17-13-1(a)	CORPORATNS:117
23-17-13-1(b)(1)-(3)	CORPORATNS:117
23-17-13-1(b)(4)	CORPORATNS:117
23-17-13-1(c)	CORPORATNS:117
23-17-13-1(d)	CORPORATNS:117
23-17-13-1(e)	CORPORATNS:117
23-17-13-2	CORPORATNS:118
23-17-13-4(a)	CORPORATNS:119
23-17-13-4(b)(1)	CORPORATNS:119
23-17-13-4(b)(2)	CORPORATNS:119
23-17-14-1(a)	CORPORATNS:102
23-17-14-1(b)	CORPORATNS:102
23-17-14-1(c)	CORPORATNS:102
23-17-14-2	CORPORATNS:108
23-17-14-3(a)	CORPORATNS:107
23-17-14-3(b)	CORPORATNS:107
23-17-14-3(c)	CORPORATNS:107
23-17-14-3(d)	CORPORATNS:107
23-17-14-4(a)	CORPORATNS:102
23-17-14-4(b)	CORPORATNS:107
23-17-15-1(a)	CORPORATNS:110
23-17-15-1(b)	CORPORATNS:110
23-17-15-1(c)	CORPORATNS:110
23-17-15-2(a)	CORPORATNS:111
23-17-15-2(b)	CORPORATNS:111
23-17-15-2(c)	CORPORATNS:111
23-17-15-3(a)	CORPORATNS:112
23-17-15-3(b)	CORPORATNS:112
23-17-15-3(c)	CORPORATNS:112
23-17-15-4(a)	CORPORATNS:112
23-17-15-4(b)	CORPORATNS:112
23-17-15-5(a)	CORPORATNS:113
23-17-15-5(b)	CORPORATNS:113
23-17-15-6(a)	CORPORATNS:114
23-17-15-6(b)	CORPORATNS:114
23-17-15-6(c)	CORPORATNS:114
23-17-15-6(d)	CORPORATNS:114
23-17-15-6(e)	CORPORATNS:114
23-17-15-6(f)	CORPORATNS:117
23-17-16-2	CORPORATNS:121
23-17-16-7	CORPORATNS:121
23-17-16-8(a)	CORPORATNS:121
23-17-16-8(b)	CORPORATNS:121
23-17-16-8(c)	CORPORATNS:121
23-17-16-9	CORPORATNS:121
23-17-16-10(a)	CORPORATNS:121
23-17-16-10(b)	CORPORATNS:121
23-17-16-10(c)	CORPORATNS:121
23-17-16-11	CORPORATNS:121
23-17-16-11(1)	CORPORATNS:121
23-17-16-12(b)	CORPORATNS:121
23-17-16-12(c)	CORPORATNS:121
23-17-16-13(1)	CORPORATNS:121
23-17-16-13(2)	CORPORATNS:121
23-17-16-13(3)	CORPORATNS:121
23-17-16-14	CORPORATNS:121
23-17-16-15(a)	CORPORATNS:121
23-17-16-15(c)	CORPORATNS:121
23-17-17-1	CORPORATNS:27
23-17-17-2(a)	CORPORATNS:67
23-17-17-2(b)	CORPORATNS:67
23-17-17-2(c)	CORPORATNS:67
23-17-17-2(d)	CORPORATNS:67
23-17-17-2(e)	CORPORATNS:67
23-17-17-3	CORPORATNS:13
23-17-17-4(a)	CORPORATNS:13
23-17-17-4(b)	CORPORATNS:13
23-17-17-5(c)	CORPORATNS:13
23-17-17-6(e)	CORPORATNS:13
23-17-17-7(a)	CORPORATNS:14
23-17-17-8	CORPORATNS:15
23-17-17-9(c)	CORPORATNS:15
23-17-17-10	CORPORATNS:14
23-17-18-1(a)	CORPORATNS:27
23-17-18-1(b)	CORPORATNS:27
23-17-18-2(a)	CORPORATNS:92
23-17-18-2(b)	CORPORATNS:92

IC §	Section No.
23-17-18-2(c)....	CORPORATNS:92
23-17-18-2(e)....	CORPORATNS:92
23-17-19-3(d)....	CORPORATNS:27
23-17-21-1	CORPORATNS:58
23-17-21-2(a)....	CORPORATNS:58
23-17-21-2(b)....	CORPORATNS:58
23-17-21-2(c)....	CORPORATNS:58
23-17-26-9	CORPORATNS:34
23-17-27-1(a)....	CORPORATNS:28
23-17-27-1(b)....	CORPORATNS:28
23-17-27-1(c)....	CORPORATNS:28
23-17-27-1(d)....	CORPORATNS:28
23-17-27-1(e)(1) .	CORPORATNS:28
23-17-27-1(e)(2) .	CORPORATNS:28
23-17-27-1(e)(3) .	CORPORATNS:28
23-17-27-1(e)(4) .	CORPORATNS:28
23-17-27-1(e)(5) .	CORPORATNS:28
23-17-27-1(e)(6) .	CORPORATNS:28
23-17-27-1(e)(7) .	CORPORATNS:28
23-17-27-2	CORPORATNS:70
23-17-27-2(b)....	CORPORATNS:70
23-17-27-2(b)(1)-(3) ..	CORPORATNS:70
23-17-27-2(c)....	CORPORATNS:70
23-17-27-2(d)....	CORPORATNS:70
23-17-27-2(e)....	CORPORATNS:70
23-17-27-2(f)	CORPORATNS:70
23-17-27-3(c)....	CORPORATNS:70
23-17-27-3(d)....	CORPORATNS:70
23-17-27-4(a)....	CORPORATNS:70
23-17-27-4(b)....	CORPORATNS:70
23-17-27-4(c)....	CORPORATNS:70
23-17-27-4(d)....	CORPORATNS:70
23-17-27-5	CORPORATNS:70
23-17-27-6(a)....	CORPORATNS:30
23-17-27-6(b)....	CORPORATNS:30
23-17-27-7	CORPORATNS:70
23-17-27-8(a)....	CORPORATNS:29
23-17-27-8(b)....	CORPORATNS:29
23-17-27-8(c)....	CORPORATNS:29
23-17-27-8(d)....	CORPORATNS:29
23-17-27-8(e)....	CORPORATNS:29

IC §	Section No.
23-17-27-8(f)	CORPORATNS:29
23-17-27-8(g)....	CORPORATNS:29
23-17-28-1	CORPORATNS:85
23-17-28-2	CORPORATNS:85
23-17-28-3	CORPORATNS:85
23-17-28-6	CORPORATNS:85
23-17-28-7	CORPORATNS:85
23-17-28-8	CORPORATNS:85
23-17-29-1	CORPORATNS:31
23-17-29-1(a)(6) .	CORPORATNS:33
23-17-29-1(a)(7) .	CORPORATNS:33
23-17-29-1(b)....	CORPORATNS:33
23-17-29-1(e)....	CORPORATNS:31
23-17-29-1.1(a)..	CORPORATNS:34
23-17-29-1.1(b)(1) ..	CORPORATNS:34
23-17-29-1.1(b)(2) ..	CORPORATNS:34
23-17-29-1.1(c)..	CORPORATNS:34
23-17-29-2	CORPORATNS:32
23-17-29-3	CORPORATNS:31
23-17-29-4(a)....	CORPORATNS:31
23-17-29-4(b)....	CORPORATNS:31
23-17-29-5	CORPORATNS:31
23-17-29-6(a)....	CORPORATNS:35
23-17-29-6(b)....	CORPORATNS:35
23-17-29-6(c)....	CORPORATNS:35
23-17-29-6(d)....	CORPORATNS:35
23-17-29-7(a)....	CORPORATNS:35
23-17-29-7(b)....	CORPORATNS:35
23-17-29-7(c)....	CORPORATNS:35
23-17-29-8	CORPORATNS:31
23-17-29-9(a)....	CORPORATNS:10
23-17-29-9(b)....	CORPORATNS:10
23-17-29-9(c)....	CORPORATNS:10
23-17-29-10	CORPORATNS:8
24-1-1-1...........	CONTRACTS:51
24-1-2-1...........	CONTRACTS:56
24-1-2-3.......	CONTRACTS:53, 56
24-1-2-7...........	CONTRACTS:53
24-4-9-19	CONTRACTS:45
24-5-7-10	CONTRACTS:115
24-5-11.5-12	CONTRACTS:119

IC §	Section No.
24-5-11.5-13 ..... CONTRACTS:119
24-5-11.5-14 ..... CONTRACTS:119
24-5-13-15 .... CONTRACTS:115
25-34.1-3-2........ CONTRACTS:55
26-1-1-1 .... CONTRACTS:111
26-1-1-101 .... CONTRACTS:15
26-1-1.3-419(e)........ CONTRIB:2
26-1-2-106(1) CONTRACTS:15
26-1-2-201 .... CONTRACTS:11
26-1-2-204 .... CONTRACTS:10
26-1-2-207 .... CONTRACTS:93
26-1-2-207(1) CONTRACTS:11
26-1-2-306(1)....... CONTRACTS:2
26-1-2-309(3) CONTRACTS:86
26-1-2-316 .... CONTRACTS:47
26-1-2-508.. CONTRACTS:111, 115
26-1-2-719 .... CONTRACTS:47
26-1-3-408 ... CONTRACTS:18, 122
26-1-3.1-116 .... CONTRIB:2
26-1-3.1-116(a) CONTRIB:2
26-1-3.1-116(b) CONTRIB:2
26-1-3.1-116(c)......... CONTRIB:2
26-1-3.1-419(e)......... CONTRIB:2
26-1-3.1-420(a) . CONVERSION:13, 21
26-1-3.1-420(b) .. CONVERSION:24
26-1-3.1-420(c) .. CONVERSION:21
26-1-8.1-101..... CORPORATNS:46
26-1-8.1-102(2).. CORPORATNS:44
26-1-8.1-102(13). CORPORATNS:44
26-1-8.1-102(14). CORPORATNS:49
26-1-8.1-108(a).. CORPORATNS:55
26-1-8.1-108(b).. CORPORATNS:55
26-1-8.1-108(c) .. CORPORATNS:55
26-1-8.1-108(d).. CORPORATNS:55
26-1-8.1-108(e).. CORPORATNS:55
26-1-8.1-108(f) .. CORPORATNS:55
26-1-8.1-108(g).. CORPORATNS:55
26-1-8.1-108(h).. CORPORATNS:55
26-1-8.1-108(i) .. CORPORATNS:55
26-1-8.1-112(a).. CORPORATNS:57
26-1-8.1-112(b).. CORPORATNS:57

IC §	Section No.
26-1-8.1-112(d).. CORPORATNS:57
26-1-8.1-113..... CORPORATNS:46
26-1-8.1-204(1).. CORPORATNS:47
26-1-8.1-204(2).. CORPORATNS:47
26-1-8.1-205..... CORPORATNS:44
26-1-8.1-206..... CORPORATNS:44
26-1-8.1-206(a).. CORPORATNS:44
26-1-8.1-206(b).. CORPORATNS:44
26-1-8.1-207(a).. CORPORATNS:51
26-1-8.1-210(a).. CORPORATNS:40
26-1-8.1-210(c).. CORPORATNS:40
26-1-8.1-210(d).. CORPORATNS:40
26-1-8.1-301(a).. CORPORATNS:49
26-1-8.1-301(b).. CORPORATNS:49
26-1-8.1-302..... CONVERSION:22
26-1-8.1-302(a).. CORPORATNS:49
26-1-8.1-302(b).. CORPORATNS:49
26-1-8.1-302(c).. CORPORATNS:49
26-1-8.1-303..... CONVERSION:22
26-1-8.1-303(a).. CORPORATNS:44
26-1-8.1-303(b).. CORPORATNS:44
26-1-8.1-304(a).. CORPORATNS:50
26-1-8.1-304(b).. CORPORATNS:50
26-1-8.1-304(c).. CORPORATNS:50
26-1-8.1-304(d).. CORPORATNS:50
26-1-8.1-304(e).. CORPORATNS:50
26-1-8.1-304(f) .. CORPORATNS:55
26-1-8.1-306(a).. CORPORATNS:53
26-1-8.1-306(b).. CORPORATNS:53
26-1-8.1-306(c) .. CORPORATNS:53
26-1-8.1-306(e).. CORPORATNS:53
26-1-8.1-306(f) .. CORPORATNS:53
26-1-8.1-306(g).. CORPORATNS:53
26-1-8.1-306(h).. CORPORATNS:53
26-1-8.1-307..... CORPORATNS:51
26-1-8.1-401(a).. CORPORATNS:51
26-1-8.1-401(b).. CORPORATNS:51
26-1-8.1-402(a).. CORPORATNS:54
26-1-8.1-402(b).. CORPORATNS:54
26-1-8.1-402(c)(1) .. CORPORATNS:54
26-1-8.1-402(c)(2)(i)

IC §	Section No.	IC §	Section No.
	.. CORPORATNS:54	29-3-8-2	CONTRACTS:31
26-1-8.1-402(c)(2)(ii)		29-3-8-5(b)	CONTRACTS:31
	.. CORPORATNS:54	29-3-8-7	CONTRACTS:31
26-1-8.1-403(a)	CORPORATNS:52	31-1-11.5-1	CONTRACTS:45
26-1-8.1-403(b)	CORPORATNS:52	31-1-11.5-12(d)	CONTRACTS:47
26-1-8.1-403(c)	CORPORATNS:52	31-11-7-1	CONTRACTS:3
26-1-8.1-403(d)	CORPORATNS:52	31-16-12-1	CONTEMPT:8
26-1-8.1-403(e)	CORPORATNS:52	31-16-12-6	CONTEMPT:8, 21
26-1-8.1-404(a)	CORPORATNS:51	31-32-14-1	CONTEMPT:2
26-1-8.1-404(b)	CORPORATNS:51	32-1-6-22(a)	CONTRIB:2
26-1-8.1-404(c)	CORPORATNS:51	32-2-1-1	CONTRACTS:28
26-1-8.1-405(a)	CORPORATNS:44	32-2-1.5-4	CONTRACTS:28
26-1-8.1-405(b)	CORPORATNS:44	32-4-1.5-15	CORPORATNS:56
26-1-8.1-406	CORPORATNS:44	32-4-1.6-10	CORPORATNS:56
26-1-9-101	CORPORATNS:57	32-4-1.6-11	CORPORATNS:56
26-1-9-115(4)	CORPORATNS:57	32-4-5-5	CONVERSION:5
26-1-9-501	CONVERSION:20	32-8-3-1(c)	CONTRACTS:25
26-1-9-507	CONVERSION:20	33-2-1-4	CONTEMPT:2, 8
26-2-5-1	CONTRACTS:45, 47	33-4-2-8	CONTEMPT:2
27-1-7-1	CORPORATNS:2	33-4-3-8(c)	CONTIN:1
27-1-12-15	CONTRACTS:31	33-4-11-24	CONTEMPT:10
27-1-20-30	CONTRACTS:51	33-5-2-5(c)	CONTIN:1
27-17-10-3(a)	CORPORATNS:83	33-10.5-2-5	CONTEMPT:2
28-1-1-1	CORPORATNS:2	33-21-1-9	CONTEMPT:8
28-7-1-1	CORPORATNS:2	34-1-2-2	CONVERSION:30
28-12-1-1	CORPORATNS:2	34-1-10-10	CONTEMPT:2
29-1-7-3	CONTEMPT:1, 8	34-1-32-1	CORPORATNS:77
29-1-11-3	CONTRACTS:81	34-11-2-3	CONTRACTS:123
29-1-13-6	CONVERSION:3	34-11-2-7(1)	CONTRACTS:123
29-1-13-6(a)	CONVERSION:3, 8	34-11-2-9	CONTRACTS:123
29-1-13-6(b)	CONVERSION:3	34-11-2-11	CONTRACTS:123
29-1-13-9	CONVERSION:17	34-11-3-1	CONTRACTS:123
29-1-14-4	CONTRIB:5	34-11-9-4	CONTRIB:4
29-1-14-5	CONTRACTS:81;	34-12-2-6	CONTEMPT:1
	CONTRIB:5	34-22-1-5	CONTRIB:2
29-1-15-1	CONVERSION:3	34-22-1-6	CONTRIB:2
29-3-1-10	CONTRACTS:31	34-24-3-1	CONVERSION:12, 24, 28
29-3-1-10(1)	CONTRACTS:31		
29-3-1-10(2)	CONTRACTS:31	34-24-3-3	CONVERSION:26
29-3-1-10(3)	CONTRACTS:31	34-24-4-9(a)	CONTRIB:3
29-3-1-13	CONTRACTS:31	34-26-1-14	CONTEMPT:1, 18
29-3-4-2	CONTRACTS:31	34-26-1-15	CONTEMPT:18

IC §	Section No.	IC §	Section No.
34-26-1-16	CONTEMPT:18	34-47-3-7(b)	CONTEMPT:19
34-33-3-6	CONTIN:1	34-47-3-7(c)	CONTEMPT:19
34-35-3-3	CONTEMPT:15	34-47-3-7(d)	CONTEMPT:19
34-37-1-1(a)	CONTRACTS:29	34-47-3-7(e)	CONTEMPT:19
34-37-1-1(b)	CONTRACTS:29	34-47-3-7(f)	CONTEMPT:19
34-37-1-2	CONTRACTS:29	34-47-3-8	CONTEMPT:2
34-47-1-1	CONTEMPT:1, 10	34-47-3-8(a)	CONTEMPT:19
34-47-1-1(b)	CONTEMPT:4	34-47-3-8(b)	CONTEMPT:19
34-47-2-1	CONTEMPT:1, 3, 4, 10	34-47-3-8(c)	CONTEMPT:19
34-47-2-1(a)	CONTEMPT:7	34-47-3-8(d)	CONTEMPT:19
34-47-2-1(b)	CONTEMPT:7	34-47-4-1(a)	CONTEMPT:18
34-47-2-2	CONTEMPT:1, 7, 11	34-47-4-1(b)	CONTEMPT:18
34-47-2-3(1)	CONTEMPT:12	34-47-4-1(c)	CONTEMPT:18
34-47-2-3(2)	CONTEMPT:12	34-47-4-2(a)	CONTEMPT:18
34-47-2-3(3)	CONTEMPT:12	34-47-4-2(b)	CONTEMPT:18
34-47-2-4(a)	CONTEMPT:16	34-47-4-2(c)	CONTEMPT:18
34-47-2-4(b)	CONTEMPT:16	34-47-4-2(d)	CONTEMPT:18
34-47-2-4(d)	CONTEMPT:16	34-47-4-2(e)	CONTEMPT:18
34-47-2-4(d)(2)	CONTEMPT:21	34-51-2-12	CONTRIB:3
34-47-2-5(a)	CONTEMPT:22	34-51-3-2	CONVERSION:26
34-47-2-5(b)	CONTEMPT:16	34-52-1-1	CORPORATNS:77
34-47-2-5(c)	CONTEMPT:16	35-15-1-2	CONTRACTS:123
34-47-2-5(d)	CONTEMPT:16	35-34-2-5(c)	CONTEMPT:10
34-47-2-5(e)	CONTEMPT:16, 22	35-34-2-5.5	CONTEMPT:7
34-47-2-5(f)	CONTEMPT:22	35-37-3-3(c)	CONTEMPT:11
34-47-2-7	CONTEMPT:2	35-37-5-2(g)	CONTEMPT:10
34-47-3-1	CONTEMPT:3, 4, 8, 10	35-41-1-23(a)	CONVERSION:13
34-47-3-2	CONTEMPT:8	35-41-2-2(a)	CONVERSION:12, 16
34-47-3-3	CONTEMPT:12	35-41-2-2(b)	CONVERSION:12, 16
34-47-3-4(a)	CONTEMPT:13	35-43-4-1(a)	CONVERSION:16
34-47-3-4(b)	CONTEMPT:13	35-43-4-1(b)	CONVERSION:16
34-47-3-5(a)	CONTEMPT:18	35-43-4-1(b)(8)	CONVERSION:17
34-47-3-5(b)	CONTEMPT:18	35-43-4-3	CONVERSION:12, 16
34-47-3-5(c)	CONTEMPT:18	35-44-1-1(a)(2)	CONTRACTS:53
34-47-3-5(d)	CONTEMPT:18	36-2-14-2	CORONERS:2
34-47-3-6	CONTEMPT:11	36-2-14-2(a)	CORONERS:2
34-47-3-6(a)	CONTEMPT:20	36-2-14-2(b)	CORONERS:2
34-47-3-6(b)	CONTEMPT:20	36-2-14-4(1)	CORONERS:1
34-47-3-6(c)	CONTEMPT:20, 21	36-2-14-4(2)	CORONERS:1
34-47-3-6(d)	CONTEMPT:22	36-2-14-5	CORONERS:1
34-47-3-7	CONTEMPT:15	36-2-14-6	CORONERS:5, 9
34-47-3-7(a)	CONTEMPT:19	36-2-14-6(a)	CORONERS:4

IC §	Section No.
36-2-14-6(b)	CORONERS:5
36-2-14-6(c)	CORONERS:4
36-2-14-6(d)	CORONERS:6
36-2-14-6(e)	CORONERS:6
36-2-14-7	CORONERS:3
36-2-14-7(a)	CORONERS:7
36-2-14-8	CORONERS:7
36-2-14-9	CORONERS:7
36-2-14-10	CORONERS:8
36-2-14-11	CORONERS:10
36-2-14-12	CORONERS:8
36-2-14-13	CORONERS:6
36-2-14-14	CORONERS:1
36-2-14-15	CORONERS:2
36-2-14-16	CORONERS:10
36-2-14-17	CORONERS:4
36-2-14-17(a)	CORONERS:4
36-2-14-18(a)	CORONERS:9
36-2-14-18(b)	CORONERS:9
36-2-14-18(c)	CORONERS:9
36-2-16-7	CORONERS:3

INDIANA RULES

Indiana Trial Rules

Rule	Section No.
7(A)	CONTRACTS:130
7(A)(2)	CONTRACTS:130
8	CONVERSION:33
8(A)	CONTRACTS:125
8(B)	CONTRACTS:128
8(C)	CONTRACTS:129, 132
8(D)	CONTRACTS:128, 130
8(E)	CONTRACTS:125
8(F)	CONTRACTS:125
9(A)	CONTRACTS:125
9(B)	CONTRACTS:128, 129
9(C)	CONTRACTS:125, 129
9(G)	CONTRACTS:127
9.1(C)	CONTRACTS:122, 129, 132
9.1(E)	CONTRACTS:132
9.2(A)	CONTRACTS:126
9.2(B)	CONTRACTS:126
9.2(D)	CONTRACTS:133
9.2(F)	CONTRACTS:126
9.2(G)	CONTRACTS:126
9.2(H)	CONTRACTS:29
10(F)	CONTRACTS:125
11	CONTRACTS:128
12(B)	CONTRACTS:122
12(B)(6)	CONTRACTS:125
12(H)	CONTRACTS:122
17(A)	CONTRACTS:124
17(A)(1)	CONTRACTS:124
19	CONTRACTS:124
23.1	CORPORATNS:74, 75
37	CONTEMPT:1, 8, 11; CONTIN:3
41(E)	CONTRACTS:126
45	CONTEMPT:10
52(A)	CONTRACTS:134
53.5	CONTIN:1, 2, 3, 4, 5, 13, 16
56	CONTEMPT:1
65	CONTEMPT:8
70	CONTEMPT:8

Indiana Rules of Professional Conduct

Rule   **Section No.**
7.3(f) CONTRACTS:55

INDIANA ADMINISTRATIVE CODE

45 IAC §   **Section No.**
2.2-4-1(b) 15

UNITED STATES CONSTITUTION, CODES, AND REGULATIONS

United States Constitution

Art I   **Section No.**
10 . . . . CORPORATNS:6

United States Code Annotated

11 USCA §	**Section No.**	**29 USCA §**	**Section No.**
1129(a)(4)	CONTRACTS:56	185	CONTRACTS:119
15 USCA §	**Section No.**		
78a et seq. . .	CORPORATNS:43, 70		

INDEX

ABSENCE OR PRESENCE
Continuance, **Contin § 3-6, 8**

ACCOMPLICES
Contempt, **Contempt § 8**

ACCRUAL OF CAUSE OF ACTION
Breach of contract, **Contracts § 123**

ADJOURNMENT
See index heading CONTINUANCE

ADMINISTRATION OF JUSTICE
Contract impeding, **Contracts § 49**

ADMISSIONS AND DECLARATIONS
Continuance, **Contin § 5**

AFFIDAVITS
Contempt, **Contempt § 17**
Continuance, **Contin § 13**

AGREEMENTS
See index heading CONTRACTS AND AGREEMENTS

AMBIGUITY
Contracts, **Contracts § 58, 76, 133, 137**

AMENDMENT OF PLEADINGS
Continuance, **Contin § 10**

AMENDMENT OR MODIFICATION
Contempt, change in conditions, **Contempt § 10**
Continuances, **Contin § 10**

AMENDMENT OR MODIFICATION—Cont'd
Contracts. See index heading CONTRACTS AND AGREEMENTS
Conversion. See index heading CONVERSION

ANSWER
Breach of contract, **Contracts § 128, 129**
Contempt, **Contempt § 15, 20**

ANTENUPTIAL AGREEMENTS
General discussion, **Contracts § 20, 50**

APPEAL AND REVIEW
Contempt, **Contempt § 22, 23**
Continuance, **Contin § 18**
Contracts, breach of, **Contracts § 134**

APPOINTMENT
Deputy coroners, **Coroners § 3**

ARRAIGNMENT
Contempt, **Contempt § 16**

ARREST
Coroners, arrest warrants, **Coroners § 8**

ASSAULT
Contempt for assault of witnesses, jurors, or court officials, **Contempt § 12**

ASSIGNMENT
Contracts, assignment of performance, **Contracts § 107**

ATTACHMENT WRITS
Contempt, **Contempt § 18**

ATTORNEYS
Contempt, **Contempt § 7, 21**
Continuance for absence of counsel,
   Contin § 6, 8
Fees. See index headingATTORNEYS'
   FEES

ATTORNEYS' FEES
Contempt, **Contempt § 21**
Contracts and agreements,
   Contracts § 55
Conversion, **Conver § 12, 26, 28;
   Conver § 26**

AUTOPSY
Coroners, **Coroners § 6**

BAIL AND RECOGNIZANCE
Contempt, **Contempt § 18**

BAILMENTS
Conversion, **Conver § 18; Conver
   § 22**

BIDS AND BIDDING
Contracts and agreements,
   Contracts § 8

BILLS AND NOTES
Contribution, **Contrib § 2**

BONDS OR SECURITY
Conversion, secured party liable for,
   Conver § 20

BREACH OF CONTRACT
See index heading CONTRACTS AND
   AGREEMENTS

**BUILDING AND
   CONSTRUCTION
   CONTRACTS**
General discussion, **Contracts § 90,
91**

BURDEN OF PROOF
See index heading PRESUMPTIONS
   AND BURDEN OF PROOF

**CERTIFICATES AND
   CERTIFICATION**
Coroners, death certificate, **Coroners
   § 5**

CHANGE OF VENUE
Contempt, **Contempt § 15, 19**

CHILDREN AND MINORS
Contracts. See index heading
   CONTRACTS AND AGREEMENTS

CIVIL CONTEMPT
General discussion, **Contempt § 5,
15**

COERCION OR DURESS
Contracts and agreements,
   Contracts § 42

COMPENSATION
See index heading WAGES, SALARIES,
   AND COMPENSATION

CONSENT AND APPROVAL
Contracts. See index heading
   CONTRACTS AND AGREEMENTS

CONSIDERATION
Contracts. See index heading
   CONTRACTS AND AGREEMENTS

**CONSTRUCTION AND
   INTERPRETATION**
Contracts. See index heading
   CONTRACTS AND AGREEMENTS

CONTEMPT
General discussion, **Contempt
   § 1-23**
Accomplices, **Contempt § 8**
Affidavits, contents of, **Contempt
   § 17**
Answer and determination,
   Contempt § 15, 20
Appeal and review, **Contempt § 22,
23**

CONTEMPT—Cont'd

Arraignments, generally, **Contempt § 16**

Assaulting witnesses, jurors, or court officials, **Contempt § 12**

Assessment of punishment, **Contempt § 21**

Attachment, **Contempt § 18**

Attorneys, **Contempt § 7**

Attorneys' fees, **Contempt § 21**

Bail, **Contempt § 18**

Change in conditions after issuance of order, **Contempt § 10**

Change of venue, **Contempt § 15, 19**

Child support orders, **Contempt § 18**

Citation, **Contempt § 18**

Civil contempt, **Contempt § 5, 15**

Compensatory judgment for civil contempt, **Contempt § 21**

Conflicting evidence, appeals, **Contempt § 23**

Conspiracy, penalties, **Contempt § 21**

Construction of orders, **Contempt § 9**

Constructive notice of court order, **Contempt § 8**

Contemptuous publications, **Contempt § 13**

Court officers, intimidation or influence of, **Contempt § 12**

Criminal contempt, **Contempt § 5**

Definitions

   general discussion, **Contempt § 1**

   civil contempt, **Contempt § 5**

   criminal contempt, **Contempt § 5**

   direct contempt, **Contempt § 4**

De novo trial motions, **Contempt § 22**

Deposition, failure to appear, **Contempt § 10**

Direct contempt, **Contempt § 4**

CONTEMPT—Cont'd

Direct criminal contempt, **Contempt § 16**

Discretion of court in citing for contempt, **Contempt § 14**

Disruptive or disrespectful conduct or remarks, **Contempt § 7**

End of court proceedings, waiting to cite contempt until, **Contempt § 2**

Erroneous orders, **Contempt § 9**

Evidence, **Contempt § 8, 11, 12, 20, 23**

Extension of time for showing cause, **Contempt § 18**

Failure to appear, **Contempt § 10**

False testimony, **Contempt § 11**

Fines and penalties

   general discussion, **Contempt § 21**

   appeal, minimum penalties for, **Contempt § 22**

   jury duty, failure to appear for, **Contempt § 10**

General Assembly, contempt powers of, **Contempt § 3**

Good faith, **Contempt § 6**

Hearing, failure to appear, **Contempt § 10**

Hindrance of process or order, **Contempt § 8**

Immunity from prosecution, failure to testify, **Contempt § 11**

Impossibility of performance, **Contempt § 9**

Indirect contempt, **Contempt § 4**

Indirect criminal contempt, **Contempt § 17**

Influencing witnesses, jurors, or court officers, **Contempt § 12**

Intent or motive, **Contempt § 6**

Intimidating, witnesses, jurors, or court officers, **Contempt § 12**

Judgments, orders, and decrees

   change in conditions after issuance of order, **Contempt § 10**

CONTEMPT—Cont'd
Judgments, orders, and decrees
—Cont'd
  compensatory judgment,
    Contempt § 21
  construction of orders,
    Contempt § 9
  constructive notice of order,
    Contempt § 8
  erroneous orders, **Contempt § 9**
Jurisdiction, **Contempt § 18**
Jurors, intimidation or influence,
    Contempt § 12
Jury service, failure to appear,
    Contempt § 10
Legislative regulation of contempt
    power, **Contempt § 3**
Limitation of punishment for direct
    contempt, **Contempt § 4**
Motive or intent, **Contempt § 6**
New trial motions, **Contempt § 22**
Notice and knowledge
  general discussion, **Contempt
    § 18**
  court order, constructive notice
    of, **Contempt § 8**
  direct criminal contempt, sum-
    mary punishment, **Contempt
    § 16**
  sheriff, notice of persons taken
    into custody, **Contempt § 18**
Orders. Judgments, orders, and
  decrees, above
Perjury, **Contempt § 11**
Personal jurisdiction over contem-
  nor, **Contempt § 18**
Power, who has, **Contempt § 2**
Presumptions and burden of proof,
    Contempt § 8, 20, 23
Proceedings, generally, **Contempt
    § 14**
Process and service of process,
    Contempt § 8, 12, 18
Profanity, **Contempt § 7**
Provocation, **Contempt § 7**

CONTEMPT—Cont'd
Publications as contemptuous,
    Contempt § 13
Punishment, **Contempt § 21**
Questions of law and fact, **Contempt
    § 13**
Refusal to be sworn or testify,
    Contempt § 11
Rules, **Contempt § 18**
Same act as civil and criminal act,
    Contempt § 5
Sanctions, **Contempt § 21**
Sarcastic remarks, **Contempt § 7**
Service of process, **Contempt § 8,
    12, 18**
Special judge, **Contempt § 19**
Specificity of order, **Contempt § 9**
Standard of review, **Contempt § 23**
Statutory sanctions, **Contempt § 7**
Summary punishment, **Contempt
    § 16, 17**
Testimony, failure to give,
    Contempt § 11
Time or date
  end of court proceedings, waiting
    to cite contempt until,
    Contempt § 2
  extension of time for showing
    cause, **Contempt § 18**
  punishment, **Contempt § 11**
Trial or hearing, failure to appear,
    Contempt § 10
Venue, change of, **Contempt § 15,
    19**
Verification of pleadings, **Contempt
    § 17**
Void orders, **Contempt § 9**
Witnesses, intimidation or influence
  of, **Contempt § 12**
Words and phrases. Definitions,
  above
Written charges, necessity of,
    Contempt § 16
Written statement of fact by judge,
    appeals, **Contempt § 23**

CONTINUANCE
General discussion, **Contin § 1-18**
Absence
    evidence or witness, **Contin § 3-5**
    party or counsel, **Contin § 6, 8**
Admissions to prevent, **Contin § 5**
Affidavits, **Contin § 13**
Amendment of pleadings, **Contin § 10**
Appeal and review, **Contin § 18**
Attorney, absence of, **Contin § 6, 8**
Costs of actions, **Contin § 16**
Counsel, absence of, **Contin § 6, 8**
Court's own motion, **Contin § 14**
Diligence in procuring evidence or witnesses, **Contin § 4**
Discretion of court, **Contin § 1**
Evidence or witnesses, **Contin § 3-5**
Good cause for, **Contin § 2**
Grounds for continuance, **Contin § 2**
Hearings, **Contin § 15**
Illness, **Contin § 7**
Motions, generally, **Contin § 13**
Parties
    absence of, **Contin § 6, 8**
    change of, **Contin § 10**
Prejudice, **Contin § 12**
Procedure, generally, **Contin § 13-18**
Public sentiment or prejudice, **Contin § 12**
Rescission of, **Contin § 17**
Stipulation of parties, **Contin § 14**
Sua sponte motions, **Contin § 14**
Surprise, generally, **Contin § 9**
Time to prepare, lack of, **Contin § 11**
Witnesses, **Contin § 3-5**

CONTRACTS AND AGREEMENTS
General discussion, **Contracts § 1-138**
Acceptance, **Contracts § 7, 10-12**

CONTRACTS AND AGREEMENTS—Cont'd
Accrual of action for breach, **Contracts § 123**
Actual fraud, generally, **Contracts § 35**
Additional compensation for extra work, **Contracts § 91**
Adhesion contracts, **Contracts § 48**
Affection and love as consideration, **Contracts § 22**
Affirmative defenses to breach action, **Contracts § 129**
Altered performance, **Contracts § 118**
Ambiguity, **Contracts § 58, 76, 133, 137**
Amendment or modification
    general discussion, **Contracts § 93**
    beach of contract for altered performance, **Contracts § 118**
    building and construction contracts, **Contracts § 90, 91**
    consideration for, **Contracts § 94**
    contracts harmful to justice, **Contracts § 49**
    impossibility of performance based on change in law, **Contracts § 112**
    operation and effect of modification, **Contracts § 96**
    oral modification of written contract, **Contracts § 95**
    questions of law and fact, **Contracts § 133**
    third persons, **Contracts § 109**
And/or, defined, **Contracts § 65**
Answer, **Contracts § 128, 129**
Antenuptial agreements, **Contracts § 20, 50**
Appeal and review, findings of fact, **Contracts § 134**
Approval. Consent and approval, below

**CONTRACTS AND
  AGREEMENTS—Cont'd**
Assent, generally, **Contracts § 31-42**
Assignment of performance,
  Contracts § 107
At any time, defined, **Contracts § 65**
Attorneys' fees, **Contracts § 55, 127**
Averments in complaint, **Contracts
  § 128**
Bids, **Contracts § 8**
Blue pencil doctrine, **Contracts § 57**
Breach of contract
  general discussion, **Contracts
    § 113-118**
  actions for, generally, **Contracts
    § 119-138**
  acts constituting, **Contracts
    § 113**
  altered performance, **Contracts
    § 118**
  deviations, **Contracts § 118**
  effect, generally, **Contracts
    § 115, 116**
  forfeiture, **Contracts § 116**
  substantial or partial perfor-
    mance, **Contracts § 117, 118**
  waiver of breach or defective
    performance, **Contracts § 114**
Building and construction contracts,
  compensation, **Contracts § 90, 91**
Burden of proof. Presumptions and
  burden of proof, below
Capacity to contract, questions of
  law and fact, **Contracts § 133**
Capacity to sue for breach,
  Contracts § 125
Charges added to price, **Contracts
  § 15**
Children
  necessaries, contract for,
    Contracts § 32
  promises to, generally,
    Contracts § 20
  voidance at option of child,
    Contracts § 31

**CONTRACTS AND
  AGREEMENTS—Cont'd**
Clerical errors affecting intent,
  Contracts § 70
Communication of acceptance,
  Contracts § 12
Compensation, generally, **Contracts
  § 89-92**
Competition, covenants against,
  Contracts § 21, 52
Complaint in breach actions, gener-
  ally, **Contracts § 125-131**
Conditions, generally, **Contracts
  § 87, 88, 105**
Conditions precedent, generally,
  Contracts § 105, 109, 121
Conduct of parties, modification
  implied from, **Contracts § 93**
Conflict of laws, **Contracts § 120**
Consent and approval
  general discussion, **Contracts
    § 31-42**
  mutual consent to modification of
    contract, **Contracts § 96**
  performance, sufficiency of,
    Contracts § 108
  refusal to accept tender,
    Contracts § 106
Consideration
  general discussion, **Contracts
    § 13-24**
  adequacy of, **Contracts § 24**
  benefit or detriment, **Contracts
    § 16**
  construing documents together,
    Contracts § 73
  employment, **Contracts § 21**
  failure of, **Contracts § 23**
  forbearance, **Contracts § 17**
  jury instructions, **Contracts
    § 135**
  modification, consideration for,
    Contracts § 94
  past consideration, **Contracts
    § 18**

CONTRACTS AND
AGREEMENTS—Cont'd
Consideration—Cont'd
  performance of legal obligation,
    Contracts § 19
  personal rights, relations and
    services, **Contracts § 20**
  promissory estoppel, **Contracts**
    § 14
  rescission, **Contracts § 99**
  sufficiency, generally, **Contracts**
    § 15
Construction and interpretation
  general discussion, **Contracts**
    § 58-78
  conflicting clauses, generally,
    Contracts § 72
  construing instruments together,
    Contracts § 73
  drafting party, construction
    against, **Contracts § 68**
  general and specific words,
    Contracts § 69
  implied terms, **Contracts § 75**
  intent of parties, **Contracts § 9;**
    Contracts § 60
  language of contract, intent
    determined by, **Contracts § 60**
  omissions or mistakes,
    Contracts § 70
  oral contracts, generally,
    Contracts § 62
  parties, construction by,
    Contracts § 76
  questions of law and fact,
    Contracts § 78
  reasonable and equitable
    construction, **Contracts § 67**
  recitals, **Contracts § 71**
  severability of contract,
    Contracts § 77
  validity of contract, construction
    favoring, **Contracts § 66**
  whole, construction as,
    Contracts § 61

CONTRACTS AND
AGREEMENTS—Cont'd
Construction and interpretation
  —Cont'd
  written contracts, generally,
    Contracts § 63
Constructive contracts, **Contracts**
  § 6
Constructive fraud, generally,
  Contracts § 35
Contracts implied at law, **Contracts**
  § 6
Contravention of public policy,
  Contracts § 43-57
Conversion, **Conver § 8, 15**
Copy of contract to accompany com-
  plaint, **Contracts § 126**
Counterclaim, reply to, **Contracts**
  § 130
Counter offers, **Contracts § 11**
Covenants not to compete,
  Contracts § 21, 52
Criminal penalties for illegal
  contracts, **Contracts § 56**
Damages, **Contracts § 127**
Date. Time or date, below
Death of party, termination of
  contract, **Contracts § 86**
Deceit as not element of fraud,
  Contracts § 35
Defective performance, waiver of,
  Contracts § 114
Defenses, **Contracts § 35, 43, 122,**
  129
Definiteness and certainty,
  Contracts § 2
Definitions
  adhesion contract, **Contracts**
    § 48
  and/or, **Contracts § 65**
  at any time, **Contracts § 65**
  consideration, **Contracts § 15**
  immediate, **Contracts § 65**
  necessaries, **Contracts § 32**
Delegation of performance,
  Contracts § 107

CONTRACTS AND
AGREEMENTS—Cont'd
Delivery, **Contracts § 29**
Demand for payment, time for,
Contracts § 84
Demand for performance, **Contracts
§ 104**
Demand for relief, **Contracts § 125**
Denial in answer, **Contracts § 128**
Deviations in performance,
Contracts § 118
Drafting party, construction against,
Contracts § 68
Duration of contract, **Contracts § 86**
Duress, **Contracts § 42**
Election of remedies for fraud,
Contracts § 40
Entirety, interpretation of contract in,
Contracts § 61
Entirety of contract affecting legality,
Contracts § 57
Equitable construction, **Contracts
§ 67**
Error. Mistake or error, below
Estoppel. Waiver and estoppel,
below
Evidence and witnesses
admissibility, generally,
Contracts § 136, 137
ambiguity in contract, **Contracts
§ 58**
breach of contract, generally,
Contracts § 119, 131
demand for performance,
Contracts § 104
modification of contract,
Contracts § 93
parol evidence, **Contracts § 137**
presumptions and burden of
proof, below
weight and sufficiency,
Contracts § 138
Exact description, **Contracts § 2**
Exculpatory clauses, **Contracts § 47,
55**

CONTRACTS AND
AGREEMENTS—Cont'd
Excuse for nonperformance,
Contracts § 111, 112
Execution, generally, **Contracts § 29**
Existing law as part of contract,
Contracts § 74
Express contracts, generally,
Contracts § 5
Extra work, compensation for,
Contracts § 91
Fact questions. Questions of law and
fact, below
Falsity of representation, **Contracts
§ 38**
Findings of fact, generally,
Contracts § 134
Fines and penalties, **Contracts § 56**
First refusal rights, **Contracts § 9**
Forbearance as consideration,
Contracts § 17
Forfeiture for breach, **Contracts
§ 116**
Formal requisites, generally,
Contracts § 25-30
Fraud, deceit, and misrepresentation
general discussion, **Contracts
§ 35-40**
effect of fraud, **Contracts § 39**
elements of fraud, generally,
Contracts § 35 et seq.
intent to deceive, **Contracts § 38**
knowledge of falsity of representation, **Contracts § 38**
mental condition, **Contracts § 31**
opinion of law, misrepresentations, **Contracts § 36**
questions of law and fact,
Contracts § 133
ratification and estoppel,
Contracts § 40
rescission, **Contracts § 102**
statute of frauds, **Contracts § 28**
Frauds, statute of, **Contracts § 28**
Frustration of purpose doctrine,
Contracts § 112

CONTRACTS AND AGREEMENTS—Cont'd

Future events, **Contracts § 36**

Governing law, **Contracts § 43**

Guardian entering into contracts, **Contracts § 31**

Household exclusion clauses, **Contracts § 55**

Illegality, generally, **Contracts § 56, 57**

Immediate, defined, **Contracts § 65**

Impeding administration of justice, **Contracts § 49**

Implied contracts, generally, **Contracts § 5**

Implied terms, **Contracts § 75**

Impossibility of performance, **Contracts § 112**

Inferences. Presumptions and burden of proof, below

Inquiries as to services, **Contracts § 7**

Instructions to jury, **Contracts § 135**

Integration clauses, **Contracts § 97**

Intentional fraud, **Contracts § 36**

Intent or motive
    construction, **Contracts § 59, 60**
    errors affecting, **Contracts § 70**
    fraud as intentional, **Contracts § 36**
    parol evidence, **Contracts § 137**
    questions of law and fact, **Contracts § 133**

Interest rate reductions, **Contracts § 19**

Issues of breach action, **Contracts § 131**

Joint and several contracts, **Contracts § 81, 124**

Judgments in breach actions, **Contracts § 134**

Jury and jury trial
    instructions, **Contracts § 135**
    questions of law and fact, below

Justice, agreements harmful to, **Contracts § 49**

CONTRACTS AND AGREEMENTS—Cont'd

Knowledge. Notice and knowledge, below

Land contracts, forfeiture for breach, **Contracts § 116**

Language of contract, intent determined by, **Contracts § 60**

Law questions. Questions of law and fact, below

Leases, **Contracts § 55, 117**

Limitation of actions, **Contracts § 123**

Limitations of performance of legal obligations, **Contracts § 19**

Love and affection as consideration, **Contracts § 22**

Marriage, antenuptial agreements, **Contracts § 20, 50**

Medium of payment, **Contracts § 92**

Mental condition of party, **Contracts § 31**

Merger, **Contracts § 97**

Mistake or error
    consent affected by, **Contracts § 33, 34**
    construction, **Contracts § 70**
    money received through mistake of fact, **Contracts § 5**
    option to purchase, exercise of, **Contracts § 9**

Modification. Amendment or modification, above

Most intimate contact rule, **Contracts § 120**

Mutual consent, rescission through, **Contracts § 102**

Mutuality of obligation, **Contracts § 4**

Mutual mistake, **Contracts § 33**

Necessaries, contracts for, **Contracts § 32**

Nonfamily member, services performed by, **Contracts § 5**

Nonperformance, excuse for, **Contracts § 111, 112**

**CONTRACTS AND
   AGREEMENTS—Cont'd**
Notice and knowledge
   nonperformance, **Contracts
      § 112**
   rescission, **Contracts § 98**
   UCC, notice of termination of
      contract, **Contracts § 86**
Number of parties necessary,
   Contracts § 3
Objection, rescission, **Contracts
   § 99**
Offer, **Contracts § 7-9**
Offer, acceptance at variance with,
   Contracts § 11
Omissions or mistakes, **Contracts
   § 70**
Opinion of law, representations of,
   Contracts § 36
Option contract, time as of the
   essence in, **Contracts § 85**
Option contracts, **Contracts § 9**
Oral contracts, generally, **Contracts
   § 62, 95, 97, 135**
Parol contracts, generally, **Contracts
   § 62, 97, 135**
Parol evidence, **Contracts § 137**
Partial illegality, **Contracts § 57**
Partial performance, breach of
   contract, **Contracts § 117, 118**
Partial performance, rescission,
   Contracts § 99
Partial rescission, **Contracts § 101**
Partial waiver, **Contracts § 114**
Parties
   general discussion, **Contracts
      § 3, 27**
   breach of contract actions,
      Contracts § 79-83
   construction by, **Contracts § 76**
   drafting party, construction
      against, **Contracts § 68**
   joint, several, or joint and several
      contracts, **Contracts § 81**
   performance, generally,
      Contracts § 103

**CONTRACTS AND
   AGREEMENTS—Cont'd**
Parties—Cont'd
   performance, sufficiency as
      determined by party,
      Contracts § 108
   privity of contract, **Contracts
      § 82**
   signature by fewer than all par-
      ties, **Contracts § 80**
   third persons, agreements for
      benefit of, **Contracts § 83**
Past consideration, **Contracts § 18**
Payment, **Contracts § 84, 92**
Performance
   general discussion, **Contracts
      § 103-112**
   assignment, **Contracts § 107**
   breach of contract, above
   conditions, performance of,
      Contracts § 105
   consideration, failure of,
      Contracts § 23
   delegation of performance,
      Contracts § 107
   demand for, **Contracts § 104**
   excuse for nonperformance,
      Contracts § 111, 112
   severability of contract,
      Contracts § 77
   substantial performance,
      Contracts § 110
   sufficiency of performance,
      Contracts § 108, 109
   tender of performance,
      Contracts § 106
   time for, **Contracts § 84-86**
Personal rights, relations and services, **Contracts § 20**
Plain meaning of words in contract,
   Contracts § 64
Pleadings in breach actions, generally, **Contracts § 125-131**
Postponing payment, **Contracts § 84**
Precedent conditions, generally,
   Contracts § 105, 109, 121

CONTRACTS AND AGREEMENTS—Cont'd

Preemption of breach action by federal law, **Contracts § 119**

Presumptions and burden of proof, **Contracts § 132**

    conflicting inferences, **Contracts § 78**

    implied contracts, **Contracts § 5**

    parol negotiations, **Contracts § 97**

    questions of law and fact, **Contracts § 133**

    unconscionable contracts, **Contracts § 7**

Prevention of performance, **Contracts § 111**

Prices, control of, **Contracts § 51**

Privity of contract, **Contracts § 82**

Promissory estoppel, consideration, **Contracts § 14**

Public offices and emoluments, **Contracts § 54**

Public policy, contravention of, generally, **Contracts § 43-57**

Public service, agreements harmful to, **Contracts § 53, 54**

Quasi-contracts, **Contracts § 6**

Questions of law and fact

    general discussion, **Contracts § 133**

    construction, **Contracts § 78**

    covenants not to compete, **Contracts § 52**

    mutual mistake, **Contracts § 33**

    parties, **Contracts § 79**

Quotation of prices as offer, **Contracts § 8**

Ratification, **Contracts § 40**

Real estate commissions, public policy, **Contracts § 55**

Reasonable and equitable construction, **Contracts § 67**

Recitals, **Contracts § 71**

Refusal to accept tender, **Contracts § 106**

CONTRACTS AND AGREEMENTS—Cont'd

Reliance on representation, **Contracts § 37**

Reply, **Contracts § 130**

Representations of opinion of law or future events, **Contracts § 36**

Rescission

    general discussion, **Contracts § 98-102**

    agreement, rescission by, **Contracts § 98**

    one party, rescission by, **Contracts § 99**

    partial rescission, **Contracts § 101**

    return to status quo, **Contracts § 100**

    time for, **Contracts § 102**

Restraint of trade, **Contracts § 51, 52**

Revocation of offer, **Contracts § 9**

Sale of public office, **Contracts § 54**

Sealing written instruments, **Contracts § 29**

Severability of contract, **Contracts § 77**

Signing and signature, generally, **Contracts § 30, 47, 80**

Silence as acceptance of offer, **Contracts § 10**

Special damages, **Contracts § 127**

Statute of frauds, **Contracts § 28**

Statute of limitations, **Contracts § 40, 123**

Statutes

    formal requisites, statutory effect, **Contracts § 28**

    fraud, statute of, **Contracts § 28**

    limitation of actions, **Contracts § 40, 123**

    public policy in absence of statute, **Contracts § 46**

    violations, **Contracts § 45**

    written contracts, **Contracts § 28**

CONTRACTS AND
  AGREEMENTS—Cont'd
Stipulations as to time, **Contracts
  § 85**
Subscription of contract, execution,
  Contracts § 29
Subsequent conditions, generally,
  Contracts § 87
Substantial performance, **Contracts
  § 110, 117, 118**
Suspension of rights to declare for-
  feiture, **Contracts § 116**
Tender of performance, **Contracts
  § 106**
Termination of contract, **Contracts
  § 86, 113**
Third persons
  benefit or detriment by,
    Contracts § 16, 83
  joint and several contracts,
    Contracts § 81
  parties to breach actions,
    Contracts § 124
  performance, sufficiency as
    determined by third party,
    Contracts § 108
  qualifying as third party to
    contract, **Contracts § 83**
Threats, **Contracts § 42**
Time or date
  actions, time for, **Contracts
    § 123**
  conditions precedent, generally,
    Contracts § 105, 109, 121
  construing instruments together,
    Contracts § 73
  demand for performance,
    Contracts § 104
  future events, **Contracts § 36**
  law existing at time of contract,
    Contracts § 74
  limitation of actions, **Contracts
    § 123**
  oral agreement, contract dating
    from making of, **Contracts
    § 27**

CONTRACTS AND
  AGREEMENTS—Cont'd
Time or date—Cont'd
  past consideration, **Contracts
    § 18**
  performance, **Contracts § 84-86**
  rescission, time for, **Contracts
    § 102**
  revocation of offer, **Contracts
    § 9**
Trade, restraint of, **Contracts § 51,
  52**
Unconscionability, **Contracts § 41**
Undue influence, **Contracts § 31, 41**
Uniform Commercial Code,
  Contracts § 2, 86
Unilateral mistake, **Contracts § 34**
Unsigned contract, **Contracts § 30**
Validity of contract, construction
  favoring, **Contracts § 66**
Variance between pleading and
  proof, **Contracts § 131**
Verbal contracts, generally,
  Contracts § 62, 95, 97, 135
Violation of statute, **Contracts § 45**
Waiver and estoppel
  assent, **Contracts § 40**
  breach of contract, waiver,
    Contracts § 114
  performance of conditions,
    **Contracts § 88; Contracts
    § 105**
  promissory estoppel,
    consideration, **Contracts § 14**
  questions of law and fact,
    Contracts § 133
Warranties, evidence as to breach of,
  Contracts § 119
Words and phrases. Definitions,
  above
Words used in construction, definitions of, **Contracts § 64, 65**
Written contracts
  general discussion, **Contracts
    § 63**

CONTRACTS AND AGREEMENTS—Cont'd

Written contracts—Cont'd
  complaint to include copy of, **Contracts § 126**
  oral contract, written instrument to replace, **Contracts § 96**
  oral modification of, **Contracts § 95**
  requirements, **Contracts § 26**
  statute of frauds, **Contracts § 28**
  statutory effect, **Contracts § 28**
Wrongful conduct affecting compensation under quasi-contract, **Contracts § 6**

CONTRIBUTION

General discussion, **Contrib § 1-5**
Accommodation parties, **Contrib § 3**
Actions, **Contrib § 5**
Common liability, **Contrib § 2**
Comparative fault act, **Contrib § 3**
Discharge, **Contrib § 4**
Exception to pleading rules, **Contrib § 5**
Improvements on property, **Contrib § 3**
Joint wrongdoers, **Contrib § 3**
Jury trial, **Contrib § 5**
Limitation of actions, **Contrib § 3**
Multiple obligors, **Contrib § 5**
Note or other financial instrument, **Contrib § 2**
Payment, **Contrib § 4**
Statute of limitations, **Contrib § 3**
Subrogation distinguished, **Contrib § 2**

CONVERSION

General discussion, **Conver § 1-36**
Acts constituting conversion, **Conver § 15, 16**
Amounts recoverable for criminal conversion, **Conver § 28**
Assets under Probate Code, **Conver § 3**

CONVERSION—Cont'd

Attorney fees, **Conver § 26**
Attorneys' fees, **Conver § 12, 26, 28**
Bailees, **Conver § 18; Conver § 22**
Breach of contract distinguished, **Conver § 15**
Burden of proof, **Conver § 34**
Choice of law, **Conver § 31**
Civil recovery from criminal conversion, **Conver § 12**
Compensatory damages, **Conver § 24**
Conduct of persons with respect to property, **Conver § 17**
Contents of complaint, **Conver § 33**
Contracts and agreements, **Conver § 8, 15**
Costs of actions, **Conver § 28**
Criminal conversion, acts constituting, **Conver § 16**
Crops, value of, **Conver § 24**
Damages
  general discussion, **Conver § 23-28**
  attorneys' fees, **Conver § 12, 26**
  civil recovery for criminal conversion, **Conver § 12**
  household goods, **Conver § 25**
  measure of compensatory damages, **Conver § 24**
  mitigation of damages, **Conver § 27**
  special and punitive damages; attorneys' fees, **Conver § 26**
  treble damages, **Conver § 28**
Death of testator as time of conversion, **Conver § 6**
Definitions, **Conver § 1**
Delivery of goods, **Conver § 15, 18**
Demand for return of property, **Conver § 11**
Directions of testator of will, **Conver § 5**
Equitable conversion, **Conver § 1-9**
Evidence
  general discussion, **Conver § 34**

CONVERSION—Cont'd
Evidence—Cont'd
  criminal conversion, **Conver
    § 10, 12**
Executors and administrators of
  wills, **Conver § 4**
Executory contract for sale of realty,
  Conver § 8
Fair market value as measure of
  damages, **Conver § 24, 25**
Fiduciary removing funds without
  authorization, **Conver § 17**
Findings and judgment, **Conver § 36**
Fluctuation of value affecting dam-
  ages, **Conver § 24**
Governing law, **Conver § 7**
Identity of persons as bearing on,
  Conver § 17
Instructions to jury, **Conver § 36**
Intent or motive, testators, **Conver
  § 5**
Joint owners bringing action,
  Conver § 29
Landlords, **Conver § 19**
Lienholders, **Conver § 20**
Life tenants, **Conver § 6**
Limitation of actions, **Conver § 30**
Lost profits as measure of damages,
  Conver § 24
Measure of compensatory damages,
  Conver § 24, 25
Mitigation of damages, **Conver § 27**
Money, **Conver § 14**
Negotiable instruments, **Conver § 21**
Partnership funds, **Conver § 17**
Personal property, wrongful conver-
  sion of, **Conver § 10-36**
Principal and agent, criminal conver-
  sion, **Conver § 17**
Probate code, **Conver § 3**
Property subject to, **Conver § 13, 14**
Punitive damages, **Conver § 26**
Questions of law and fact, **Conver
  § 35**
Reduction of damages, **Conver § 27**

CONVERSION—Cont'd
Rents and profits from realty,
  Conver § 4
Return of property, demand for,
  Conver § 11
Sale of realty, **Conver § 8, 9**
Secured parties, **Conver § 20**
Special damages, **Conver § 26**
Statute of limitations, **Conver § 30**
Stolen property, sale of, **Conver § 17**
Surplus of proceeds after sale,
  Conver § 3
Tender, **Conver § 10**
Third persons, rights of, **Conver
  § 15, 22**
Time or date
  statute of limitations, **Conver
    § 30**
  wills, conversion of property,
    Conver § 6
Tortious conversion, **Conver § 10,
  13**
Trustee removing funds without
  authorization, **Conver § 17**
Uniform Commercial Code, **Conver
  § 13, 21**
Value, measure of damages, **Conver
  § 24**
Waiver and estoppel, choice of law,
  Conver § 32
Wills, generally, **Conver § 4-7, 17**
Wrongful conversion, **Conver § 10-
  36**

COPIES AND DUPLICATES
Contract, copy to accompany complaint, **Contracts § 126**

CORONERS
General discussion, **Coroners § 1-10**
Amount of compensation, **Coroners
  § 2**
Appointment of deputies, **Coroners
  § 3**
Arrest warrant, **Coroners § 8**
Autopsy, **Coroners § 6**

CORONERS—Cont'd
Certificate of death, **Coroners § 5**
Clerical employees, **Coroners § 3**
Compensation, **Coroners § 2, 3**
Continuing education training,
   Coroners § 2
Death certificate, **Coroners § 5**
Deputies, appointment of, **Coroners
   § 3**
Disclosure of information, **Coroners
   § 9**
Disposition of body or property,
   Coroners § 10
Disturbance of body or scene of
   death, **Coroners § 4**
Duties of office, **Coroners § 1**
Election, **Coroners § 2**
Employees, appointment of,
   Coroners § 3
Examination of witnesses, **Coroners
   § 7**
Exceptions to autopsy, **Coroners § 6**
Fees for witnesses, **Coroners § 7**
Felony, disturbing body or scene of
   death, **Coroners § 4**
Forensic science meeting, attendance
   at, **Coroners § 1**
Investigation of death, generally,
   Coroners § 4-10
Law-enforcement duties performed
   by, **Coroners § 1**
Licensed physicians, **Coroners § 2**
Notice of discovery of body,
   Coroners § 4
Production of documents, **Coroners
   § 7**
Public inspection of records,
   Coroners § 9
Qualification, **Coroners § 2**
Reopening investigation, time for,
   Coroners § 5
Report, **Coroners § 8**
Residency requirements, **Coroners
   § 2**
Scene of death, disturbance of,
   Coroners § 4

CORONERS—Cont'd
Subpoenaing witnesses, **Coroners
   § 7**
Term of office, **Coroners § 2**
Time or date
   death certificate, **Coroners § 5**
   term of office, **Coroners § 2**
Training, **Coroners § 2**
Unclaimed property, **Coroners § 10**
Verdict and report, **Coroners § 8**
Witnesses, summoning and examina-
   tion of, **Coroners § 7**

COSTS AND EXPENSES
Continuance, costs of action, **Contin
   § 16**
Coroners, witness fees, **Coroners
   § 7**

COUNTERCLAIMS
Contracts and agreements, reply to
   counterclaim, **Contracts § 130**

DAMAGES
Contracts and agreements, breach,
   Contracts § 127

DEATH
Contracts, death of parties,
   Contracts § 86
Conversion, time for, **Conver § 6**

DEFENSES
Contracts and agreements,
   Contracts § 35, 43, 122, 129

DELIVERY
Contracts and agreements,
   Contracts § 29
Conversion, **Conver § 15, 18**

DEPUTIES
Coroners, **Coroners § 3**

DISCHARGE AND RELEASE
Contribution, **Contrib § 4**

DISCOVERY AND DEPOSITION
Contempt for failure to appear for
deposition, **Contempt § 10**

DURESS OR COERCION
Contracts and agreements,
Contracts § 42

ELECTION OF REMEDIES
Contracts and agreements, fraud,
Contracts § 40

ELECTIONS
Coroners, **Coroners § 2**

EQUITY
Conversion, **Conver § 1-9**

EVIDENCE AND WITNESSES
Contempt, **Contempt § 8, 11, 12, 20,
23**
Continuances, **Contin § 3-5**
Contracts. See index heading
CONTRACTS AND AGREEMENTS
Conversion. See index heading
CONVERSION
Coroners, summoning and examin-
ing witnesses, **Coroners § 7**

EXCUSE OR JUSTIFICATION
Contracts, excuse for nonperformance, **Contracts § 111, 112**

**EXECUTORS AND
ADMINISTRATORS**
Conversion, **Conver § 4**

**EXEMPTIONS AND
EXCEPTIONS**
Coroners, exceptions to autopsy,
Coroners § 6

EXPRESS CONTRACTS
General discussion, **Contracts § 5**

EXTENSION OF TIME
Contempt, extension of time to show
cause, **Contempt § 18**

FAIR MARKET VALUE
Conversion, measure of damages,
Conver § 24

FELONIES
Coroners, disturbance of body or
scene of crime, **Coroners § 4**

FIDUCIARIES
Conversion, fiduciary removing
funds without authorization,
Conver § 17

FINES AND PENALTIES
Contracts, **Contracts § 56, 116**

FORFEITURE
Contracts, **Contracts § 116**

**FRAUD, DECEIT, AND
MISREPRESENTATION**
Contracts. See index heading
CONTRACTS AND AGREEMENTS

GOOD FAITH
Contempt, **Contempt § 6**

GOVERNING LAW
Conversion, **Conver § 7**

GUARDIAN AND WARD
Contract entered into by guardian,
Contracts § 31

HEARINGS
Contempt for failure to appear,
Contempt § 10
Continuance, **Contin § 15**

**IMMUNITY FROM
PROSECUTION**
Contempt, **Contempt § 11**

IMPLIED CONTRACTS
General discussion, **Contracts § 5**

INSPECTION OF RECORDS
Coroners, **Coroners § 9**

INSTRUCTIONS TO JURY
Conversion, **Conver § 36**

INTENT OR MOTIVE
Contempt, **Contempt § 6**
Contracts. See index heading
CONTRACTS AND AGREEMENTS
Conversion, intent of testator,
Conver § 5

JOINT OWNERS
Conversion, **Conver § 29**

JUDGMENTS, ORDERS, AND DECREES
Contempt. See index heading
CONTEMPT
Contracts, judgment in breach
actions, **Contracts § 134**
Conversion, **Conver § 36**

JURISDICTION
Contempt, **Contempt § 18**

JURY AND JURY TRIAL
Contempt, **Contempt § 10, 12**
Contracts. See index heading
CONTRACTS AND AGREEMENTS
Contribution, **Contrib § 5**

LANDLORD AND TENANT
Conversion, **Conver § 19**
Leases as contracts, **Contracts § 55, 117**

LIENS AND ENCUMBRANCES
Conversion, lienholder liable for,
Conver § 20

LIMITATION OF ACTIONS
Contracts, **Contracts § 123**
Conversion, **Conver § 30**

LIMITATIONS AND RESTRICTIONS
Contempt, punishment for,
Contempt § 4

LIMITATIONS AND RESTRICTIONS—Cont'd
Contracts, performance of legal
obligations, **Contracts § 19**

LOST PROFITS
Conversion of property, **Conver § 24**

MENTAL CAPACITY
Contracts and agreements,
Contracts § 31

MISTAKE OR ERROR
Contempt, erroneous orders,
Contempt § 9
Continuance, surprise, **Contin § 9**
Contracts. See index heading
CONTRACTS AND AGREEMENTS

MONEY OR CASH
Conversion of property, **Conver § 14**

MOTIVE
See index heading INTENT OR
MOTIVE

NEGOTIABLE INSTRUMENTS
Conversion, **Conver § 21**

NEW TRIAL
Contempt, **Contempt § 22**

NOTICE AND KNOWLEDGE
Contempt. See index heading
CONTEMPT
Contracts. See index heading
CONTRACTS AND AGREEMENTS
Coroners, **Coroners § 4**
Coroners, notice of death, **Coroners § 4**

OBJECTIONS AND EXCEPTIONS
Contribution, exception to pleading
rules, **Contrib § 5**

OFFER AND TENDER
Conversion, **Conver § 4**

PAROL CONTRACTS
General discussion, **Contracts § 62, 95, 97, 135**

PARTIES
Contracts. See index heading
CONTRACTS AND AGREEMENTS

PARTNERSHIPS
Conversion of funds, **Conver § 17**

PAYMENT
Contracts and agreements,
Contracts § 84, 92
Contribution, generally, **Contrib § 4**

PERFORMANCE
Contracts. See index heading
CONTRACTS AND AGREEMENTS

PERJURY
Contempt, **Contempt § 11**

PHYSICIANS AND SURGEONS
Coroners. See index heading
CORONERS

POSTPONEMENTS
See index heading CONTINUANCE

PRESUMPTIONS AND BURDEN OF PROOF
Contempt, **Contempt § 8, 20, 23**
Contracts. See index heading
CONTRACTS AND AGREEMENTS
Conversion, **Conver § 34**

PROBATE
Conversion under Probate Code,
Conver § 3

PROFANITY
Contempt, **Contempt § 7**

PUBLICATIONS
Contempt, **Contempt § 13**

PUNITIVE DAMAGES
Conversion, **Conver § 26**

QUESTIONS OF LAW AND FACT
Contempt, **Contempt § 13**
Contracts. See index heading
CONTRACTS AND AGREEMENTS
Conversion, **Conver § 35**

RECORDS AND REPORTS
Coroners' reports, **Coroners § 8**

RENTS AND PROFITS
Conversion, **Conver § 4**

RESCISSION
Continuances, **Contin § 17**
Contracts. See index heading
CONTRACTS AND AGREEMENTS

SALARIES
See index heading WAGES, SALARIES, AND COMPENSATION

SERVICE OF PROCESS
Contempt, **Contempt § 8, 12, 18**

SICKNESS OR ILLNESS
Continuance, **Contin § 7**

SIGNING AND SIGNATURE
Contracts, **Contracts § 30, 47, 80**

STATUTE OF FRAUDS
General discussion, **Contracts § 28**
Contracts, **Contracts § 28**

STATUTE OF LIMITATIONS
Contracts and agreements,
Contracts § 40, 123

STIPULATIONS
Continuance, stipulation of parties,
Contin § 14

STIPULATIONS—Cont'd
Contracts, time stipulations,
 Contracts § 85

SUA SPONTE MOTIONS
Continuance, **Contin § 14**

SUBPOENAS
Coroners, **Coroners § 7**

SUBROGATION
Contribution distinguished from,
 Contrib § 2

SURPRISE
See index heading MISTAKE OR
 ERROR

THIRD PERSONS
Contracts. See index heading
 CONTRACTS AND AGREEMENTS
Conversion, **Conver § 15, 22;
 Conver § 22**

TIME OR DATE
Contempt. See index heading
 CONTEMPT
Contracts. See index heading
 CONTRACTS AND AGREEMENTS
Contribution, limitation of actions,
 Contrib § 3
Conversion. See index heading
 CONVERSION
Coroners. See index heading
 CORONERS

TORTS
Conversion, **Conver § 10, 13**

TRIAL OR HEARING
Contempt for failure to appear,
 Contempt § 10

TRUSTS AND TRUSTEES
Conversion, trustee removing funds
 without authorization, **Conver
 § 17**

UNDUE INFLUENCE
Contracts, **Contracts § 31, 41**

**UNIFORM COMMERCIAL
 CODE**
Contracts and agreements,
 Contracts § 2, 86
Conversion, **Conver § 13, 21**

VALUE
Conversion, measure of damages,
 Conver § 24

**VARIANCE BETWEEN
 PLEADINGS AND PROOF**
Contracts, **Contracts § 131**

VENUE
Contempt, change of venue,
 Contempt § 15, 19

VERDICT
Coroners, **Coroners § 8**

**VERIFICATION OF
 PLEADINGS**
Contempt, **Contempt § 17**

**WAGES, SALARIES, AND
 COMPENSATION**
Coroners, **Coroners § 2, 3**

WAIVER AND ESTOPPEL
Contracts. See index heading
 CONTRACTS AND AGREEMENTS
Conversion, choice of law, **Conver
 § 32**

WARRANTIES
Breach of warranty, evidence,
 Contracts § 119

WILLS
Conversion of property, **Conver
 § 4-7, 17**

**WRITING AND WRITTEN
 MATTERS**
Contempt, **Contempt § 16, 23**

WRITING AND WRITTEN MATTERS—Cont'd
Contracts. See index heading
CONTRACTS AND AGREEMENTS

WRONGFUL CONVERSION
General discussion, **Conver § 10-36**